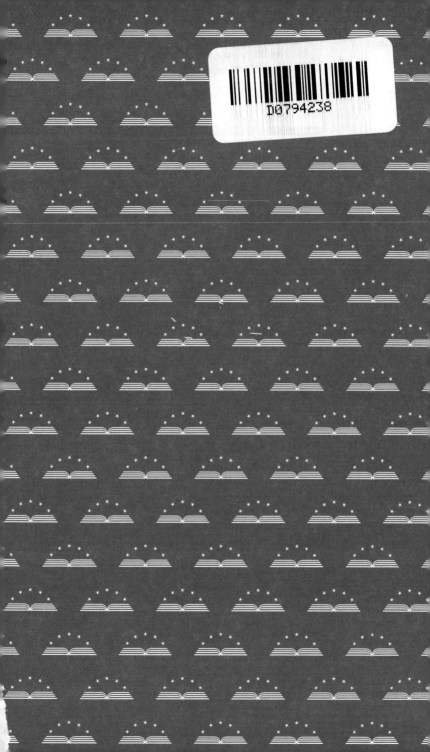

Library of America, a nonprofit organization,
champions our nation's cultural heritage
by publishing America's greatest writing in
authoritative new editions and providing resources
for readers to explore this rich, living legacy.

AMERICAN WOMEN'S SUFFRAGE

AMERICAN WOMEN'S SUFFRAGE

VOICES FROM THE LONG STRUGGLE FOR THE VOTE 1776–1965

Susan Ware, *editor*

THE LIBRARY OF AMERICA

AMERICAN WOMEN'S SUFFRAGE

Volume compilation, notes, and chronology copyright © 2020 by
Literary Classics of the United States, Inc., New York, N.Y.
All rights reserved.

No part of this book may be reproduced in any manner whatsoever without
the permission of the publisher, except in the case of brief
quotations embodied in critical articles and reviews.

Published in the United States by Library of America.
Visit our website at www.loa.org.

Some of the material in this volume is reprinted with the permission
of holders of copyright and publishing rights. See page 669.

This paper exceeds the requirements of
ANSI/NISO Z39.48–1992 (Permanence of Paper).

Distributed to the trade in the United States
by Penguin Random House Inc.
and in Canada by Penguin Random House Canada Ltd.

Library of Congress Control Number: 2019952206
ISBN 978–1–59853–664–5

First Printing
The Library of America—332

Manufactured in the United States of America

Contents

Introduction xix

PART ONE: 1776–1870

Abigail Adams and John Adams 5
Letters

New Jersey State Constitution 13
Voter Qualifications

Maria W. Stewart. 14
Lecture at the Franklin Hall

Sarah Moore Grimké. 19
from *Letters on the Equality of the Sexes*

Angelina Grimké 27
Address to the Massachusetts Legislature

Margaret Fuller 30
from "The Great Lawsuit"

**Eleanor Vincent, Lydia A. Williams, Lydia Osborn,
Susan Ormsby, Amy Ormsby, Anna Bishop** 34
Petition to the Constitutional Convention of the
State of New York

Seneca Falls Convention 36
Declaration of Sentiments and Resolutions

Sojourner Truth 43
Speech to Ohio Woman's Rights Convention

Ernestine L. Rose 45
Speech to the Second National Woman's
Rights Convention

New York Herald 59
The Woman's Rights Convention—The Last Act
of the Drama

Harriot K. Hunt 64
Tax Protest

Elizabeth Cady Stanton. 67
Address to the Legislature of New-York

Lucy Stone and Henry Browne Blackwell 84
Marriage Protest

Lucy Stone. 87
Address to the Seventh National Woman's
Rights Convention

Woman's Loyal National League. 91
Call, Resolutions, and Debate

Frances Ellen Watkins Harper. 112
Speech at the Eleventh National Woman's
Rights Convention

Sojourner Truth 116
Address to the First Annual Meeting of the
American Equal Rights Association

**Debates at the American Equal Rights Association
Meeting.** 119

Frederick Douglass 149
Woman and the Ballot

PART TWO: 1870–1900

Victoria Woodhull. 157
Address to the House Judiciary Committee

Minor v. Happersett **Ruling** 163

National Woman Suffrage Association 177
Declaration of Rights of the Women of the United States

Susan B. Anthony 185
Woman Wants Bread, Not the Ballot!

Matilda Joslyn Gage 196
Indian Citizenship

Mary Tape 199
Letter to the San Francisco Board of Education

Mormon Women of Utah 201
Protest

The New York Times 204
They Enter a Protest

George Vest 206
Remarks on the Amendment to Extend Suffrage
to Women

Alice C. Fletcher 210
The Legal Conditions of Indian Women

Anna J. Cooper 216
from *A Voice from the South, by a Black Woman
of the South*

Colorado Equal Suffrage Association 221
Suffrage Referendum Leaflet

Committee on Protest against Woman Suffrage 223
To the Constitutional Convention of New York State

Fannie Barrier Williams 228
Women in Politics

Josephine St. Pierre Ruffin 232
Address at the First National Conference of
Representatives of Black Women's Clubs

Elizabeth Cady Stanton 236
Significance and History of the Ballot

Frances E. Willard 242
The Ballot for the Home

National American Woman Suffrage Association 246
On Behalf of Hawaiian Women

Abigail Scott Duniway 249
How to Win the Ballot

PART THREE: 1900–1920

Belle Kearney 261
The South and Woman Suffrage

Annie Nathan Meyer 267
Woman's Assumption of Sex Superiority

Mary Church Terrell 275
The Progress of Colored Women

Grover Cleveland. 282
Would Woman Suffrage be Unwise?

Finley Peter Dunne 293
Mr. Dooley on Woman's Suffrage

Alice Hill Chittenden 299
The Counter Influence to Woman Suffrage

Florence H. Luscomb 307
Our Open-Air Campaign

Jane Addams 315
Why Women Should Vote

Harriot Stanton Blatch. 326
from "The Women's Political Union"

Charlotte Perkins Gilman. 332
Something to Vote For

Alice Stone Blackwell 353
Militant Methods

Leonora O'Reilly. 361
Statement before Joint Congressional Session of Congress

Max Eastman. 365
Values of the Vote

Josephine Jewell Dodge. 372
The Lesson That Came from the Sea—What it Means
to the Suffrage Cause

Marie Jenney Howe. 376
An Anti-Suffrage Monologue

Los Angeles Times. 382
Squaws Beat Militants to Right of Franchise

Alice Paul. 383
Testimony at Suffrage Parade Hearings

Helen Hamilton Gardener 391
Woman Suffrage, Which Way?

Mary Johnston 401
A Difference of Opinion

Mabel Lee 409
The Meaning of Woman Suffrage

Mary Roberts Coolidge. 416
Raising the Level of Suffrage in California,
Or What Have They Done With It?

Hazel MacKaye 419
Pageants as a Means of Suffrage Propaganda

Ida B. Wells 425
Seeking the Negro Vote

The Crisis 433
Votes for Women: A Symposium by Leading Thinkers
of Colored America

Oreola Williams Haskell 459
The Greatest Thing

Arthur Raymond Brown. 468
from *How It Feels to be the Husband of a Suffragette*

Alice Duer Miller. 473
from *Are Women People?*

Abby Scott Baker. 475
Letter to the Editor of *The Outlook*

Carrie Chapman Catt 481
The Crisis

**Boston Equal Suffrage Association for
Good Government** 508
Letter Series No. 1–10

Maud Wood Park 520
To NAWSA Congressional Chairmen

The New York Times 525
"Silent, Silly, and Offensive" and "Militants
Get 3 Days; Lack Time to Starve"

Alice Hill Chittenden 528
Woman's Service or Woman Suffrage

Lavinia Dock 531
The Young Are at the Gates

Caroline Katzenstein. 533
Prison Experiences with Emphasis on the Night of Terror

Woodrow Wilson. 543
Address to the Senate on the Nineteenth Amendment

The Suffragist 548
    Reminding the President When He Landed in Boston

Southern Women's League 553
    Declaration of Principles for the Rejection of the Proposed
    Susan B. Anthony Amendment to the Constitution of the
    United States

Maud Wood Park 555
    A Perfect Moment

PART FOUR: 1918–1965

Gertrude Foster Brown 565
    From *Your Vote and How to Use It*

***Fairchild v. Hughes* and *Leser v. Garnett* Rulings** 569

Indian Citizenship Act 575

Doris Stevens and Dr. Alice Hamilton 577
    The "Blanket" Amendment—A Debate

Ida M. Tarbell 594
    Is Woman's Suffrage a Failure?

Doris Stevens 606
    Address to the Sixth Pan American Conference,
    Havana, Cuba

Dr. Marta Robert 616
    Statement on Woman Suffrage in Porto Rico

El Congreso de Pueblo de Habla Española 621
    Resolutions Adopted by the Second Convention

Eleanor Roosevelt 632
    Women in Politics

John F. Kennedy 642
    President's Commission on the Status of Women

Fannie Lou Hamer 646
    Testimony to the Credentials Committee, Democratic
    National Convention

Constance Baker Motley 650
    Speech to the Southern Christian Leadership Conference

Chronology. 659

Note on the Texts 669

Note on the Illustrations. 679

Notes. 681

Index. 709

List of Illustrations

1. First edition of *Letters on the Equality of the Sexes* by Sarah M. Grimké (1838)

2. "Am I not a woman and a sister?" (1832)

3. James S. Baillie, "Leaders of the Woman's Rights Convention Taking an Airing" (1848)

4. *Harper's New Monthly Magazine* cartoon, "Woman's Emancipation" (1851)

5. "Woman suffrage in Wyoming Territory.—Scene at the polls in Cheyenne" (1888)

6. Photograph of Ida B. Wells (c. 1893)

7. *Woman's Journal* button with portrait of Lucy Stone

8. Photograph of Susan B. Anthony and Elizabeth Cady Stanton (c. 1891)

9. Henrietta Briggs-Wall, "American Woman and Her Political Peers" (c. 1893)

10. "The Anti-Suffrage Rose: Song" (1915)

11. Chicago Women's Suffrage Ballot Box (April 9, 1912)

12. Official program for Woman Suffrage Procession, Washington, D.C., March 3, 1913

13. Votes for women button (1914)

14. Suffrage valentine, "Since, in this progressive age" (after 1869?)

15. Rose O'Neill postcard, "Give mother the vote, we need it" (1915)

16. National American Woman Suffrage Association foreign language flyers (c. 1915)

17. W. F. Winter, "Votes for Workers" (c. 1907–18)

18. Sojourner Truth and Abraham Lincoln on the cover of *The Crisis* (August 1915)

19. Nine African American women including Nannie Burroughs at the Banner State Woman's National Baptist Convention (1915)

20. *The Crisis* cartoon, "Woman to the Rescue!" (1916)

21. Henry Mayer, "The Awakening" (1915)

22. Pin designed by Alice Paul for women arrested picketing the White House (c. 1917–19)

23. Carrie Chapman Catt after the official certification of the Nineteenth Amendment (1920)

24. Cartoon by Nina E. Allender, "Any good Suffragist the morning after" (1920)

25. Photograph of Fannie Lou Hamer at the Democratic National Convention (1964)

26. Political cartoon, "How high will she go?" (1937)

Introduction

BY SUSAN WARE

THE WOMEN'S suffrage movement had a deep sense of its own history. In many ways suffragists were our first women's historians. From 1881 to 1886, Elizabeth Cady Stanton, Susan B. Anthony, and Matilda Joslyn Gage produced the first three volumes of what they modestly called the *History of Woman Suffrage*. (A fourth volume appeared in 1902, and the fifth and sixth in 1922.) These volumes, which total more than five thousand pages, were a combination of narrative history and archive, and the material they contained has fundamentally affected how the story of the suffrage movement has been told ever since. Not surprisingly, more than a few selections in this anthology were first collected in the *History of Woman Suffrage*.

While we should acknowledge a debt to the suffragists' early efforts to preserve and document women's history, the story contained in the *History of Woman Suffrage* is at best an imperfect guide. Stanton and Anthony had an overt political agenda in compiling those volumes: they wanted to create a master narrative that privileged the Seneca Falls Convention of 1848 as the founding moment of a movement focused primarily on securing the ballot, and therefore to solidify their legacy as the main leaders of the movement. In telling their side of the story they consistently privileged sex over race, reinforcing exclusionary racial politics that marginalized the substantial contributions of African American women to the broader struggle. They also practically wrote the contributions of Lucy Stone's competing suffrage organization out of history, a slight that the final volumes repeated by focusing on the National American Woman Suffrage Association (NAWSA) at the expense of Alice Paul's National Woman's Party (NWP).

This anthology is dedicated to presenting a broader, more inclusive history of the women's suffrage movement. It does not start the story in 1848 with Seneca Falls, nor does it end with the passage of the Nineteenth Amendment in 1920. It moves beyond the East Coast–centric perspective of much suffrage history to range widely in areas like the West and the Midwest, where many of the early breakthroughs occurred and where local politics far removed from national headquarters was often messier and more complicated than the traditional top-down narrative suggests. It even ventures beyond the borders of the continental United States, putting the suffrage movement in conversation with the global movement for women's rights.

Throughout it includes the voices of a range of activists who were not just white and middle-class. The most prominent belong to African American women, whose speeches, articles, and editorials are well represented in this collection. They are joined by voices of working-class and immigrant activists who shared a more intersectional vision of women's rights that included class and race alongside gender. The centennial of the Nineteenth Amendment in 2020 demands a history that not only documents the past but also speaks to our own times.

Historians often talk of the "long nineteenth century," a period of nation-building that stretched from the American Revolution to World War I, or the "long civil rights movement," which began with Reconstruction and is still ongoing. When setting the chronological boundaries of the story of women's suffrage, why not a "long Nineteenth Amendment"? This anthology starts in 1776 with one of the most famous quotations in American history—Abigail Adams's "Remember the Ladies"—but then samples a range of lesser-known moments touching on the early history of women's rights and women's suffrage, including the fact that a few women voted in New Jersey until 1807. When Maria W. Stewart, an African American activist, spoke in Boston in 1832, she was the first American woman, black or white, to speak in public about politics and women's rights before a mixed audience that included men and women of both races. Why isn't that moment just as celebrated as the Seneca Falls Convention sixteen years later? Women's rights activism was always in conversation with other movements; it never operated in isolation. Pushing the beginning back before 1848 recognizes those interconnections.

On the other end, the "long Nineteenth Amendment" framing encourages us not to see 1920 as a hard stop to the story. This anthology extends to 1965 to chronicle women's activism in the post-suffrage era, especially that of African American women, but it could have continued straight to the present, since that activism is ongoing. Historians agree that there was no significant difference in the level or intensity of women's political engagement "across the great divide"—that is, before and after 1920. The newly formed League of Women Voters taught women how to be citizens, and commentators like Eleanor Roosevelt credited women with improving the tenor of public life. The divisions over tactics that had split the suffrage movement in the final decade before the amendment's passage continued to play out, both domestically and internationally, in the debates over the Equal Rights Amendment and protective labor legislation for women workers.

More importantly, the 1920 milestone had very little meaning for various groups of prospective female voters. American Indian women did not become fully eligible to vote until 1924, and Puerto Rican women only in 1935. African American women, most of whom still lived in the South, found their right to vote restricted by Jim Crow legislation alongside black men. For African Americans, as well as Mexican Americans and other minority voters, it was the Voting Rights Act of 1965, not the Nineteenth Amendment, that finally made the difference.

Another priority in this anthology is representing the women's suffrage movement in all its regional diversity. There are practical reasons for this focus: since so many of the early victories occurred in western states, it is impossible to tell suffrage history without foregrounding that region. But it is more than just when certain states gave women the vote—we need to look at what was happening politically in those states to understand the specific factors that led to success or defeat. Oregon, Colorado, and Utah are all western states, but they have very different suffrage stories. The West was also where the stories of American Indian women primarily unfolded.

It is also impossible to tell the history of women's suffrage without sustained attention to the South, a region that proved far less hospitable to giving women the vote than the West. Toiling in hostile territory, southern suffragists ran the gamut from outspoken racists like Belle Kearney to moderates like best-selling novelist Mary Johnston, who risked her literary reputation to write a suffrage-themed novel. Southern women's suffrage was always deeply intertwined with a commitment to maintaining white supremacy, and that connection played out at both the state and national levels, with national leaders willingly playing along with the racist arguments and practices of southern suffragists in order to keep them in the fold. That meant giving them free reign to argue that southern white women's votes could be used to outvote black men and allowing southern suffragists to exclude African American women from their organizations. Still, suffrage struggled to make headway in southern states proudly committed to states' rights and the potent cultural ideal of the southern lady.

Fully telling the history of women's suffrage means putting race at the center of the story. This cuts two ways. The first is the necessity to acknowledge the racism that plagued many of the leaders (and no doubt their followers) from the start, and not just southerners. This racism is on full display in the selections included in this anthology, but it figures more prominently at certain moments in the story, particularly during the 1860s in the immediate aftermath of the Civil War (especially in the fierce debates at the American Equal Rights Association convention in 1869), and in the 1890s, as the South imposed Jim Crow. Racist thinking is also prominent around the turn of the century, when the United States confronted questions of racial hierarchy and citizenship in relation to new territories and possessions acquired in the aftermath of the Spanish-American War. In a striking parallel to the racism of southern suffragists, elite white northern women often pushed their case by contrasting themselves with those they considered far less worthy of the vote, such as recent immigrants. These statements, cringe-worthy as they are, need to be part of the historical record.

Attention to race also leads in a different direction: to a much fuller understanding and appreciation of the contributions of African American women to the women's suffrage movement. African American women brought something that was often lacking among white suffragists: an intersectional vision that refused to separate gender from other factors such as race and class, and which made voting rights part of a larger conversation about social and political change. This vision was there from the very start, as witnessed by Maria W. Stewart's pathbreaking 1832 lecture. Sojourner Truth, Frances Ellen Watkins

Harper, Anna J. Cooper, Fannie Barrier Williams, Josephine St. Pierre Ruffin, Mary Church Terrell, Ida Wells-Barnett, and so many others followed her courageous example, all the way up to Fannie Lou Hamer and Constance Baker Motley in the 1960s. Suffrage history looks quite different when African American women insist that their voices be heard in both of the freedom movements—civil rights and women's rights—that affected their lives.

This commitment to telling a more inclusive suffrage history shaped the selections of documents in ways large and small. While no women's suffrage anthology would be complete without Abigail Adams's call to "Remember the Ladies" or the Seneca Falls Declaration of Sentiments, preference went to sources from lesser-known suffragists and lesser-known moments from across the country throughout its long history. The number of documents penned by African Americans, thirteen in all, makes this anthology stand out for giving voice to a group not always fully represented in traditional suffrage narratives. So too does its careful representation of the voices of men, American Indians, Chinese immigrants, and antisuffragists. While the majority of the documents focus on the political aspects of the women's suffrage campaign, fiction, poetry, and plays are also represented. As a rule, the documents run in their entirety; exceptions for reasons of clarity or length are clearly noted. All sources have been traced back to their original publication, rather than relying on their reproduction in texts such as the *History of Woman Suffrage* or other compilations. The result is a wide-ranging and comprehensive anthology that dramatically expands the traditional boundaries of women's suffrage historiography.

A general overview of the chronology of the women's suffrage movement provides a helpful background to understand the specific selections in this anthology. The history of the movement can be divided into four stages, drawing on the energy and talent of at least three overlapping generations of women. The initial period covers everything up to 1870. The first generation of activists had deep roots in the abolition and anti-slavery movements starting in the 1830s and 1840s. Women like Elizabeth Cady Stanton, Lucy Stone, Susan B. Anthony, Sojourner Truth, and Maria W. Stewart were the first to speak out on women's issues in the antebellum period. Their vision was often much broader than just the vote, encompassing property rights, dress reform, temperance, abolition, education, and much more. Drawn together through overlapping networks, they gathered at conventions on a yearly basis from the late 1840s through the early 1860s but eschewed a formal national organization. When the Civil War broke out in 1861, they shelved women's rights agitation for the war's duration.

Profoundly influenced by the Civil War and its aftermath, the movement entered a second stage that lasted until 1900. In some ways this period can be bounded on one end by the post–Civil War disputes that split the movement into the National Woman Suffrage Association led by Stanton and Anthony and its rival American Woman Suffrage Association led by Lucy Stone, and on the other by the eventual reuniting of the two organizations as the National American Woman Suffrage Association in 1890. But the story in this period is more complex than the overcoming of organizational rivalries. While many women involved in suffrage continued to hold broad ideas about women's rights, in these years the movement increasingly coalesced around the demand for the vote, a more narrow goal. But the ballot raised its own minefield of issues after the Civil War, none more divisive than the unfortunate pitting of the rights of newly freed African American men against those of white women in the debates over the Fourteenth and Fifteenth Amendments, the ostensible reason for the 1869 split. The ballot also raised complicated questions about the relationship between the states, which traditionally oversaw voting standards and procedures, and the federal government, offering two very different routes—state suffrage or a federal amendment—as pathways to the movement's shared goal.

In the 1870s and 1880s women's suffrage was a small movement that could point to few public successes. It was still dominated by the leaders who had come to prominence before the Civil War; some of them, like Susan B. Anthony, would hold on to power into the twentieth century. But a younger generation of leaders emerged out of the states and at the local levels, often in the Midwest and West. Women like Carrie Chapman Catt, a

graduate of Iowa State University who had been a school superintendent, and Anna Howard Shaw, an ordained minister from
Michigan, benefitted from the expanding opportunities for
higher education and careers that were available to ambitious
women in the latter half of the nineteenth century; they also
often enjoyed the financial wherewithal to devote themselves
full-time to the cause. There were some early breakthroughs in
this period, mainly in western states that enfranchised women
when they entered the Union. But in those years being a suffragist was often a lonely and discouraging proposition.

Things began to percolate in the two decades on either side
of 1900, and then exploded in the final decade leading up to
1920. The newly reunited suffrage movement provided increasingly strong and centralized national leadership. As the
selections in this anthology document, suffragists became savvy
political actors, building coalitions and making allies. The more
women voted in western states, the more politically feasible the
vote seemed. And suffragists got on board with new techniques
in public relations and publicity, embracing open-air meetings,
campaign material like buttons and posters, and public spectacles like suffrage parades, which began around 1910 and soon
were ubiquitous. All of a sudden the women's suffrage movement, which previously had conducted its meetings in church
parlors and town halls out of public view, was impossible to
ignore.

By the 1910s a third generation of suffragists was rising, best
typified by Alice Paul, a young Quaker woman who had participated in militant actions in England with British suffragettes,
including provoking arrest and then going on hunger strikes
in jail. When she returned to the United States, Paul was impatient with what she saw as the cautious approach of elders
like Shaw and Catt. Starting in 1913 with a dramatic suffrage
parade in Washington, D.C., designed to coincide with Woodrow Wilson's inauguration, Paul built her own core following,
which coalesced into the National Woman's Party. Once again
the suffrage movement was split into two rival groups—the
older, more established NAWSA, which preferred a state-by-
state approach, and the younger, brasher NWP, which focused
solely on passage of a federal amendment. NAWSA emphasized
traditional forms of political persuasion like lobbying, while the

NWP embraced militant actions such as picketing the White House. Both strategies are amply documented in the selections in this anthology. Rather than impeding the final victory, these two competing approaches actually enhanced prospects for success.

The passage of the Nineteenth Amendment in 1920 was a significant milestone, but it does not mark the end of the story. This anthology extends the chronology into a fourth stage by selectively documenting how women continued their activism in the post-suffrage era. Joining the suffragists-turned -women-citizens were rising generations of new activists, especially African American women, who labored to make American democracy meet the ideal of universal suffrage. Too young to have participated in the suffrage struggle, these activists kept up the fight in the decades after women won the vote.

⌢

For every suffragist agitating for the vote, there were many more Americans who were hostile or indifferent to the idea. Most of them were men, but their numbers included a minority of women. The persistence of the opposition helps explain why it took nearly a century to win suffrage for women. For this reason the ideology and tactics of the antisuffrage movement, which are fully documented here, are a vitally important part of suffrage history.

At first women's rights were seen as such a hysterical idea that opponents didn't even have to offer a reasoned argument against it—cartoons and editorials could simply lampoon women for stepping out of their sphere. But what had been outlandish in the 1840s was much more acceptable by the early twentieth century when women enjoyed increased access to education and the professions, more companionate marriages, and fewer children, as well as larger roles in public life through voluntary organizations, women's clubs, and even what was known as partial suffrage, which allowed women to vote in municipal elections or for school boards. Still, there is a remarkable consistency to antisuffrage ideology, which boiled down to two main ideas: women belonged in the home, not at the polls, and they did not need the vote because they had men to protect their interests.

The power of antisuffrage arguments was based in the resilience of traditional gender roles that were powerfully rooted in culture and society. This ideology reasoned that women as the weaker (if not inferior) sex belonged primarily in the domestic sphere, tending their homes and families under the watchful protection of men. Opponents of women's suffrage clung defiantly to these traditional ideals, believing that to let women join men in public life on an equal basis would be an affront to all they held sacred. In retrospect, the heat of the debate was in part a reaction to how much had already changed in women's lives, but fear of further change proved a formidable obstacle.

The suffrage movement also faced powerful organized lobbies. Liquor interests were afraid women would vote for Prohibition; machine politicians feared women voters, being outside their system of patronage, would turn them out of office; and manufacturers anticipated that newly enfranchised women would force protective legislation and child labor laws that would cut their profits. Conservative religious organizations like the Catholic Church were hostile to larger political roles for women. Perhaps surprisingly, some of the most prominent "antis" were women like Annie Nathan Meyer and Alice Hill Chittenden, who said they did not need or want the vote. That many women, especially middle-class women, were not interested in their own enfranchisement was one of the most effective weapons that opponents had in their arsenal.

To combat antisuffrage opposition as well as chip away at general indifference, the suffragists mounted a multipronged campaign dedicated to showing why women needed and deserved the vote. They alternated strategies and arguments depending on the situation and context. An appeal to justice and fairness was one of the most popular: the vote was a basic right of citizenship, and women should be treated on an equal basis with men. In a variation on this theme, suffragists updated the old revolutionary cry of "no taxation without representation" to point out that women paid taxes but had no say in the laws that governed them.

Those pro-suffrage arguments based on equality and justice coexisted with ones that stressed what women would do with their votes—the so-called expediency argument. While few suffragists ever made grandiose claims that women would end war or clean up cities, they did hope that women collectively might use their votes to address some of the urgent problems afflicting modern life. Working-class women were especially insistent about needing the vote to improve their working conditions. Suffragists' arguments from both the justice and expediency standpoints are well represented here.

With all the arguments for and against suffrage on full display, what finally pushed the movement toward victory? Certain factors stand out. The increasing numbers of women who were already voting in western states made giving all women the vote seem more inevitable; that, in turn, put antisuffrage politicians on the defensive because they feared possible retribution at the polls. At the same time, nothing terribly dramatic had happened when women started to vote: the family didn't collapse, women didn't abandon their children, and politics continued as usual. Instead of voting as a bloc, there was lots of evidence that women voted pretty much like men. Given the larger roles women were playing in modern society, enfranchising them no longer seemed like such a radical idea.

The give-and-take of partisan politics also played a role in setting up the final victory. The persistent lobbying in statehouses and in the halls of Congress finally paid off, with suffragists able to marshal a critical mass of support from male politicians who held the amendment's fate in their hands. And the militant actions of the National Woman's Party, which they kept up even during wartime, put pressure on President Woodrow Wilson and other elected officials to respond to their demands to uphold the same democratic ideals at home that the country had been fighting for abroad.

Even though the momentum seemed to be on the suffrage side, victory was never assured. The House of Representatives passed the Nineteenth Amendment on January 10, 1918, but the Senate did not follow suit until June 4, 1919, with a majority of only two votes. Then began the arduous process of winning ratification by thirty-six states. In the end, it took a tense, incredibly close vote in Tennessee to ratify the amendment. On August 26, 1920, women's right to vote was finally enshrined in the U.S. Constitution. This was an important milestone but still an incomplete victory, as the cases of African American and

American Indian women show. Still, the amendment's passage certainly was cause for celebration as women prepared to go to the polls in the 1920 presidential election.

In their 1923 survey of women's suffrage and politics, Carrie Chapman Catt and Nettie Rogers Shuler summarized the daunting organizational effort it took to win the vote for women: "During that time they were forced to conduct fifty-six campaigns of referenda to male voters; 480 campaigns to get Legislatures to submit suffrage amendments to voters; 47 campaigns to get State constitutional conventions to write woman suffrage into State constitutions; 277 campaigns to get State party conventions to include woman suffrage planks; 30 campaigns to get presidential party conventions to adopt woman suffrage planks in party platforms, and 19 campaigns with 19 successive Congresses." After that exhaustive—and exhausting—list, they stepped back to think about the struggle in more human terms: "Hundreds of women gave the accumulated possibilities of an entire lifetime, thousands gave years of their lives, hundreds of thousands gave constant interest and such aid as they could. It was a continuous, seemingly endless chain of activity. Young suffragists who helped forge the last links of that chain were not born when it began. Old suffragists who forged the first links were dead when it ended."* The century-long struggle to win the vote for women had ended, but not so the quest for women's equality. One hundred years later, the struggle continues.

～

Why does women's suffrage matter? By the early twentieth century, women had already moved far beyond the domestic sphere, yet a fundamental responsibility and privilege of citizenship was arbitrarily denied to half the population. The Nineteenth Amendment changed that increasingly untenable situation, representing a breakthrough for American women as well as a major step forward for American democracy. Three generations of women honed their political skills in the women's suffrage movement, and those skills were put to good use

---

* Carrie Chapman Catt and Nettie Rogers Shuler, *Woman Suffrage and Politics* (New York: Charles Scribner's Sons, 1923), 107–8.

after the vote was won. In their new roles as women citizens, women made a difference, which is another way of saying that women's history matters. And we have suffragists, our first women's historians, to thank for that.

Historian Anne Firor Scott provides an especially evocative image of how winning the vote was part of larger changes in women's lives and in American society more broadly: "Suffrage was a tributary flowing into the rich and turbulent river of American social development. That river is enriched by the waters of each tributary, but with the passage of time it becomes increasingly difficult to distinguish the special contributions of any one of the tributaries."* Think of the documents in this anthology—the speeches, the articles, the cartoons, the handbills and fliers, the novels and plays—as the tributaries that make up suffrage history. Each distinctive document flows into the larger stream, creating something stronger and more powerful than the individual voices. And then think of suffrage history as a powerful strand in the larger stream of U.S. history, which is richer and stronger because it heeded Elizabeth Cady Stanton's prescient statement at Seneca Falls that all men and women are created equal. The United States still lacks truly universal suffrage, but the Nineteenth Amendment represented a giant step toward that goal.

* Anne Firor Scott, "Epilogue," in Jean H. Baker, ed., *Votes for Women: The Struggle for Suffrage Revisited* (New York: Oxford University Press, 2002), 194.

AMERICAN WOMEN'S SUFFRAGE

PART ONE
1776–1870

ABIGAIL ADAMS AND JOHN ADAMS

Letters
1776

Abigail Adams (1744–1818) was an inveterate and witty correspondent who more than held her own with her husband, John Adams (1735–1826), who would later serve as the nation's second president. While John served as a delegate to the Continental Congress in Philadelphia in the spring of 1776, Abigail ran their household and farm in Braintree, Massachusetts. Her frequent and lengthy letters told her absent husband about a range of news from home while also commenting widely on the intensifying war with the British. In these excerpts Abigail raises the question of what laws the new nation might adopt, making a humorous but pointed plea to take women into account. In his next letter home, John deflects her jab, but she won't give up, returning to the point again in her reply. Two months later the colonies declared their independence from Britain but failed to grant political and legal equality either to women or to African Americans.

Abigail Adams to John Adams

Braintree March 31 1776

I wish you would ever write me a Letter half as long as I write you; and tell me if you may where your Fleet are gone? What sort of Defence Virginia can make against our common Enemy? Whether it is so situated as to make an able Defence? Are not the Gentery Lords and the common people vassals, are they not like the uncivilized Natives Brittain represents us to be? I hope their Riffel Men who have shewen themselves very savage and even Blood thirsty; are not a specimen of the Generality of the people.

I am willing to allow the Colony great merrit for having produced a Washington but they have been shamefully duped by a Dunmore.

I have sometimes been ready to think that the passion for Liberty cannot be Eaquelly Strong in the Breasts of those who have been accustomed to deprive their fellow Creatures of theirs. Of this I am certain that it is not founded upon that

5

generous and christian principal of doing to others as we would that others should do unto us.

Do not you want to see Boston; I am fearfull of the small pox, or I should have been in before this time. I got Mr. Crane to go to our House and see what state it was in. I find it has been occupied by one of the Doctors of a Regiment, very dirty, but no other damage has been done to it. The few things which were left in it are all gone. Crane has the key which he never deliverd up. I have wrote to him for it and am determined to get it cleand as soon as possible and shut it up. I look upon it a new acquisition of property, a property which one month ago I did not value at a single Shilling, and could with pleasure have seen it in flames.

The Town in General is left in a better state than we expected, more oweing to a percipitate flight than any Regard to the inhabitants, tho some individuals discoverd a sense of honour and justice and have left the rent of the Houses in which they were, for the owners and the furniture unhurt, or if damaged sufficent to make it good.

Others have committed abominable Ravages. The Mansion House of your President is safe and the furniture unhurt whilst both the House and Furniture of the Solisiter General have fallen a prey to their own merciless party. Surely the very Fiends feel a Reverential awe for Virtue and patriotism, whilst they Detest the paricide and traitor.

I feel very differently at the approach of spring to what I did a month ago. We knew not then whether we could plant or sow with safety, whether when we had toild we could reap the fruits of our own industery, whether we could rest in our own Cottages, or whether we should not be driven from the sea coasts to seek shelter in the wilderness, but now we feel as if we might sit under our own vine and eat the good of the land.

I feel a gaieti de Coar to which before I was a stranger. I think the Sun looks brighter, the Birds sing more melodiously, and Nature puts on a more chearfull countanance. We feel a temporary peace, and the poor fugitives are returning to their deserted habitations.

Tho we felicitate ourselves, we sympathize with those who are trembling least the Lot of Boston should be theirs. But they cannot be in similar circumstances unless pusilanimity and cowardise should take possession of them. They have time and warning given them to see the Evil and shun it.—I long to hear that you have declared an independancy—and by the way in the new Code of Laws which I suppose it will be necessary for you to make I desire you would Remember the Ladies, and be more generous and favourable to them than your ancestors. Do not put such unlimited power into the hands of the Husbands. Remember all Men would be tyrants if they could. If perticuliar care and attention is not paid to the Laidies we are determined to foment a Rebelion, and will not hold ourselves bound by any Laws in which we have no voice, or Representation.

That your Sex are Naturally Tyrannical is a Truth so thoroughly established as to admit of no dispute, but such of you as wish to be happy willingly give up the harsh title of Master for the more tender and endearing one of Friend. Why then, not put it out of the power of the vicious and the Lawless to use us with cruelty and indignity with impunity. Men of Sense in all Ages abhor those customs which treat us only as the vassals of your Sex. Regard us then as Beings placed by providence under your protection and in immitation of the Supreem Being make use of that power only for our happiness.

April 5

Not having an opportunity of sending this I shall add a few lines more; tho not with a heart so gay. I have been attending the sick chamber of our Neighbour Trot whose affliction I most sensibly feel but cannot discribe, striped of two lovely children in one week. Gorge the Eldest died on wedensday and Billy the youngest on fryday, with the Canker fever, a terible disorder so much like the throat distemper, that it differs but little from it. Betsy Cranch has been very bad, but upon the recovery. Becky Peck they do not expect will live out the day. Many grown persons are now sick with it, in this [   ] 5. It rages much in other Towns. The Mumps too are very frequent. Isaac is now confined with it. Our own little flock are yet well. My Heart trembles with anxiety for them. God preserve them.

I want to hear much oftener from you than I do. March 8 was the last date of any that I have yet had.—You inquire of whether I am making Salt peter. I have not yet attempted it, but after Soap making believe I shall make the experiment. I find as much as I can do to manufacture cloathing for my family which would else be Naked. I know of but one person in this part of the Town who has made any, that is Mr. Tertias Bass as he is calld who has got very near an hundred weight which has been found to be very good. I have heard of some others in the other parishes. Mr. Reed of Weymouth has been applied to, to go to Andover to the mills which are now at work, and has gone. I have lately seen a small Manuscrip describing the proportions for the various sorts of powder, fit for cannon, small arms and pistols. If it would be of any Service your way I will get it transcribed and send it to you.—Every one of your Friends send their Regards, and all the little ones. Your Brothers youngest child lies bad with convulsion fitts. Adieu. I need not say how much I am Your ever faithfull Friend.

John Adams to Abigail Adams

Ap. 14. 1776

You justly complain of my short Letters, but the critical State of Things and the Multiplicity of Avocations must plead my Excuse.—You ask where the Fleet is. The inclosed Papers will inform you. You ask what Sort of Defence Virginia can make. I believe they will make an able Defence. Their Militia and minute Men have been some time employed in training them selves, and they have Nine Battallions of regulars as they call them, maintained among them, under good Officers, at the Continental Expence. They have set up a Number of Manufactories of Fire Arms, which are busily employed. They are tolerably supplied with Powder, and are successfull and assiduous, in making Salt Petre. Their neighbouring Sister or rather Daughter Colony of North Carolina, which is a warlike Colony, and has several Battallions at the Continental Expence, as well as a pretty good Militia, are ready to assist them, and they are in very good Spirits, and seem determined to make a brave Resistance.—The Gentry are very rich, and the common People very poor. This Inequality of Property, gives an Aristocratical Turn to all their Proceedings, and occasions a strong Aversion in their Patricians, to Common Sense. But the Spirit of these Barons, is coming down, and it must submit.

It is very true, as you observe they have been duped by Dunmore. But this is a Common Case. All the Colonies are duped, more or less, at one Time and another. A more egregious Bubble was never blown up, than the Story of Commissioners coming to treat with the Congress. Yet it has gained Credit like a Charm, not only without but against the clearest Evidence. I never shall forget the Delusion, which seized our best and most sagacious Friends the dear Inhabitants of Boston, the Winter before last. Credulity and the Want of Foresight, are Imperfections in the human Character, that no Politician can sufficiently guard against.

You have given me some Pleasure, by your Account of a certain House in Queen Street. I had burned it, long ago, in Imagination. It rises now to my View like a Phœnix.—What shall I say of the Solicitor General? I pity his pretty Children, I pity his Father, and his sisters. I wish I could be clear that it is no moral Evil to pity him and his Lady. Upon Repentance they will certainly have a large Share in the Compassions of many. But let Us take Warning and give it to our Children. Whenever Vanity, and Gaiety, a Love of Pomp and Dress, Furniture, Equipage, Buildings, great Company, expensive Diversions, and elegant Entertainments get the better of the Principles and Judgments of Men or Women there is no knowing where they will stop, nor into what Evils, natural, moral, or political, they lead us.

Your Description of your own Gaiety de Coeur, charms me. Thanks be to God you have just Cause to rejoice—and may the bright Prospect be obscured by no Cloud.

As to Declarations of Independency, be patient. Read our Privateering Laws, and our Commercial Laws. What signifies a Word.

As to your extraordinary Code of Laws, I cannot but laugh. We have been told that our Struggle has loosened the bands of Government every where. That Children and Apprentices were disobedient—that schools and Colledges were grown turbulent—that Indians slighted their Guardians and Negroes grew insolent to their Masters. But your Letter was the first Intimation that another Tribe more numerous and powerfull than all the rest were grown discontented.—This is rather too coarse a Compliment but you are so saucy, I wont blot it out.

Depend upon it, We know better than to repeal our Masculine

systems. Altho they are in full Force, you know they are little more than Theory. We dare not exert our Power in its full Latitude. We are obliged to go fair, and softly, and in Practice you know We are the subjects. We have only the Name of Masters, and rather than give up this, which would compleatly subject Us to the Despotism of the Peticoat, I hope General Washington, and all our brave Heroes would fight. I am sure every good Politician would plot, as long as he would against Despotism, Empire, Monarchy, Aristocracy, Oligarchy, or Ochlocracy.—A fine Story indeed. I begin to think the Ministry as deep as they are wicked. After stirring up Tories, Landjobbers, Trimmers, Bigots, Canadians, Indians, Negroes, Hanoverians, Hessians, Russians, Irish Roman Catholicks, Scotch Renegadoes, at last they have stimulated the   to demand new Priviledges and threaten to rebell.

Abigail Adams to John Adams

Braintree May 7 1776

How many are the solitary hours I spend, ruminating upon the past, and anticipating the future, whilst you overwhelmd with the cares of State, have but few moments you can devote to any individual. All domestick pleasures and injoyments are absorbed in the great and important duty you owe your Country "for our Country is as it were a secondary God, and the First and greatest parent. It is to be preferred to Parents, Wives, Children, Friends and all things the Gods only excepted. For if our Country perishes it is as imposible to save an Individual, as to preserve one of the fingers of a Mortified Hand." Thus do I supress every wish, and silence every Murmer, acquiesceing in a painfull Seperation from the companion of my youth, and the Friend of my Heart.

I believe tis near ten days since I wrote you a line. I have not felt in a humour to entertain you. If I had taken up my pen perhaps some unbecomeing invective might have fallen from it; the Eyes of our Rulers have been closed and a Lethargy has seazd almost every Member. I fear a fatal Security has taken possession of them. Whilst the Building is on flame they tremble at the expence of water to quench it, in short two months has elapsed since the evacuation of Boston, and very little has been done in that time to secure it, or the Harbour from future invasion till the people are all in a flame; and no one among us that I have heard of even mentions expence, they think universally that there has been an amaizing neglect some where. Many have turnd out as volunteers to work upon Nodles Island, and many more would go upon Nantaskit if it was once set on foot. "Tis a Maxim of state That power and Liberty are like Heat and moisture; where they are well mixt every thing prospers, where they are single, they are destructive."

A Goverment of more Stability is much wanted in this colony, and they are ready to receive it from the Hands of the Congress, and since I have begun with Maxims of State I will add an other viz. that a people may let a king fall, yet still remain a people, but if a king let his people slip from him, he is no longer a king. And as this is most certainly our case, why not proclaim to the World in decisive terms your own importance?

Shall we not be dispiced by foreign powers for hesitateing so long at a word?

I can not say that I think you very generous to the Ladies, for whilst you are proclaiming peace and good will to Men, Emancipating all Nations, you insist upon retaining an absolute power over Wives. But you must remember that Arbitary power is like most other things which are very hard, very liable to be broken—and notwithstanding all your wise Laws and Maxims we have it in our power not only to free ourselves but to subdue our Masters, and without voilence throw both your natural and legal authority at our feet—

> "Charm by accepting, by submitting sway
> Yet have our Humour most when we obey."

I thank you for several Letters which I have received since I wrote Last. They alleviate a tedious absence, and I long earnestly for a Saturday Evening, and experience a similar pleasure to that which I used to find in the return of my Friend upon that day after a weeks absence. The Idea of a year dissolves all my Phylosophy.

Our Little ones whom you so often recommend to my care and instruction shall not be deficient in virtue or probity if the precepts of a Mother have their desired Effect, but they would

be doubly inforced could they be indulged with the example
of a Father constantly before them; I often point them to their
Sire

> "engaged in a corrupted State
> Wrestling with vice and faction."

May 9

I designd to have finished the sheet, but an opportunity offering I close only just inform you that May the 7 our privateers
took two prises in the Bay in fair sight of the Man of war, one a
Brig from Irland the other from fyall loaded with wine Brandy
and the other Beaf &c. The wind was East and a flood tide, so
that the tenders could not get out tho they tried several times,
the Light house fired Signal guns, but all would not do, they
took them in triumph and carried them into Lyn.

Johnny and Charls have the Mumps, a bad disorder, but they
are not very bad. Pray be kind enough to remember me at all
times and write as often as you possibly can to your   Portia

NEW JERSEY STATE CONSTITUTION

Voter Qualifications

JULY 2, 1776

On July 2, 1776, New Jersey became the fourth colony to adopt a constitution declaring independence from Great Britain. The same day, the Continental Congress in Philadelphia separately voted to declare independence for all thirteen colonies; the declaration was ratified two days later. New Jersey state legislators assumed their constitution would be temporary, but it remained in force for sixty-eight years. While other state constitutions defined voter qualifications with terms such as "white male inhabitants" or "free white men," Article IV of the New Jersey state constitution offered the vote to "inhabitants" who held property worth fifty pounds and who had lived there for a year. "Inhabitants" was construed to include women, although only single women qualified; at the time, married women could not hold property in their own names. This expansive view of the voting franchise remained in force for several decades. In 1807, however, the New Jersey legislature passed a law that defined voters as adult white taxpaying men. The change was caused not by unease about women voting but by partisan concerns that led politicians to conclude that women voters were more of a liability than an asset. Women were purged from the polls along with blacks and aliens (non-citizens). But certain property-holding New Jersey women (the exact numbers are impossible to pin down) actively participated in the political process and voted in the early years of the American republic.

IV. That all Inhabitants of this Colony of full Age, who are worth *Fifty Pounds*, Proclamation Money, clear Estate in the same, and have resided within the County in which they claim a Vote for twelve Months immediately preceding the Election, shall be entitled to vote for Representatives in Council and Assembly; and also for all other publick Officers that shall be elected by the People of the County at Large.

MARIA W. STEWART

Lecture at the Franklin Hall
SEPTEMBER 21, 1832

"Who shall go forward, and take off the reproach that is cast upon the people of color? Shall it be a woman?" Maria W. Stewart (1803–1879) raised that powerful rhetorical question in this public lecture in Boston in 1832. The circumstances of her delivery were as provocative as the content of her address: Stewart was the first American woman, black or white, to speak in public about politics and women's rights before a mixed-sex (or, in the terminology of the time, "promiscuous") gathering. While the audience, like Stewart herself, was predominantly free African Americans living in Boston, there was also a sizeable minority of whites. In her lecture Stewart issued a double challenge: for African Americans to aim higher and overcome the barriers placed in their path, and for white Bostonians to confront their complicity in the oppression of blacks. Threaded throughout was an affirmation of the essential role that African American women should play in the larger freedom struggle.

When Maria W. Stewart stepped forward to embody "the woman question" by speaking in public, she was a twenty-nine-year-old widow. In all she gave four lectures in 1832 and 1833 before leaving her public career behind to settle in New York and later Washington, D.C. Her early advocacy of what can be seen as a black feminist stance confirms the central role African American women played from the beginning in the struggle for women's rights.

Why sit ye here and die? If we say we will go to a foreign land, the famine and the pestilence are there, and there we shall die. If we sit here, we shall die. Come let us plead our cause before the whites: if they save us alive, we shall live—and if they kill us, we shall but die.

Methinks I heard a spiritual interrogation—"Who shall go forward, and take off the reproach that is cast upon the people of color? Shall it be a woman?" And my heart made this reply—"If it is thy will, be it even so, Lord Jesus!"

I have heard much respecting the horrors of slavery; but may Heaven forbid that the generality of my color throughout these United States should experience any more of its horrors than to be a servant of servants, or hewers of wood and drawers of water! Tell us no more of southern slavery; for with few exceptions, although I may be very erroneous in my opinion, yet I consider our condition but little better than that. Yet, after all, methinks there are no chains so galling as the chains of ignorance—no fetters so binding as those that bind the soul, and exclude it from the vast field of useful and scientific knowledge. O, had I received the advantages of early education, my ideas would, ere now, have expanded far and wide; but, alas! I possess nothing but moral capability—no teachings but the teachings of the Holy Spirit.

I have asked several individuals of my sex, who transact business for themselves, if providing our girls were to give them the most satisfactory references, they would not be willing to grant them an equal opportunity with others? Their reply has been—for their own part, they had no objection; but as it was not the custom, were they to take them into their employ, they would be in danger of losing the public patronage.

And such is the powerful force of prejudice. Let our girls possess what amiable qualities of soul they may; let their characters be fair and spotless as innocence itself; let their natural taste and ingenuity be what they may; it is impossible for scarce an individual of them to rise above the condition of servants. Ah! why is this cruel and unfeeling distinction? Is it merely because God has made our complexion to vary? If it be, O shame to soft, relenting humanity! "Tell it not in Gath! publish it not in the streets of Askelon!" Yet, after all, methinks were the American free people of color to turn their attention more assiduously to moral worth and intellectual improvement, this would be the result: prejudice would gradually diminish, and the whites would be compelled to say, unloose those fetters!

> Though black their skins as shades of night,
> Their hearts are pure, their souls are white.

Few white persons of either sex, who are calculated for any thing else, are willing to spend their lives and bury their talents in performing mean, servile labor. And such is the horrible idea that I entertain respecting a life of servitude, that if I conceived of there being no possibility of my rising above the condition of a servant, I would gladly hail death as a welcome messenger.

O, horrible idea, indeed! to possess noble souls aspiring after high and honorable acquirements, yet confined by the chains of ignorance and poverty to lives of continual drudgery and toil. Neither do I know of any who have enriched themselves by spending their lives as house-domestics, washing windows, shaking carpets, brushing boots, or tending upon gentlemen's tables. I can but die for expressing my sentiments; and I am as willing to die by the sword as the pestilence; for I am a true born American; your blood flows in my veins, and your spirit fires my breast.

I observed a piece in the Liberator a few months since, stating that the colonizationists had published a work respecting us, asserting that we were lazy and idle. I confute them on that point. Take us generally as a people, we are neither lazy nor idle; and considering how little we have to excite or stimulate us, I am almost astonished that there are so many industrious and ambitious ones to be found; although I acknowledge, with extreme sorrow, that there are some who never were and never will be serviceable to society. And have you not a similar class among yourselves?

Again. It was asserted that we were "a ragged set, crying for liberty." I reply to it, the whites have so long and so loudly proclaimed the theme of equal rights and privileges, that our souls have caught the flame also, ragged as we are. As far as our merit deserves, we feel a common desire to rise above the condition of servants and drudges. I have learnt, by bitter experience, that continual hard labor deadens the energies of the soul, and benumbs the faculties of the mind; the ideas become confined, the mind barren, and, like the scorching sands of Arabia, produces nothing; or, like the uncultivated soil, brings forth thorns and thistles.

Again, continual hard labor irritates our tempers and sours our dispositions; the whole system becomes worn out with toil and fatigue; nature herself becomes almost exhausted, and we care but little whether we live or die. It is true, that the free people of color throughout these United States are neither bought nor sold, nor under the lash of the cruel driver; many obtain a comfortable support; but few, if any, have an opportunity of becoming rich and independent; and the employments we most pursue are as unprofitable to us as the spider's web or the floating bubbles that vanish into air. As servants, we are respected; but let us presume to aspire any higher, our employer regards us no longer. And were it not that the King eternal has declared that Ethiopia shall stretch forth her hands unto God, I should indeed despair.

I do not consider it derogatory, my friends, for persons to live out to service. There are many whose inclination leads them to aspire no higher; and I would highly commend the performance of almost any thing for an honest livelihood; but where constitutional strength is wanting, labor of this kind, in its mildest form, is painful. And doubtless many are the prayers that have ascended to Heaven from Afric's daughters for strength to perform their work. Oh, many are the tears that have been shed for the want of that strength! Most of our color have dragged out a miserable existence of servitude from the cradle to the grave. And what literary acquirements can be made, or useful knowledge derived, from either maps, books or charts, by those who continually drudge from Monday morning until Sunday noon? O, ye fairer sisters, whose hands are never soiled, whose nerves and muscles are never strained, go learn by experience! Had we had the opportunity that you have had, to improve our moral and mental faculties, what would have hindered our intellects from being as bright, and our manners from being as dignified as yours? Had it been our lot to have been nursed in the lap of affluence and ease, and to have basked beneath the smiles and sunshine of fortune, should we not have naturally supposed that we were never made to toil? And why are not our forms as delicate, and our constitutions as slender, as yours? Is not the workmanship as curious and complete? Have pity upon us, have pity upon us, O ye who have hearts to feel for other's woes; for the hand of God has touched us. Owing to the disadvantages under which we labor, there are many flowers among us that are

> "———born to bloom unseen,
> And waste their fragrance on the desert air."

My beloved brethren, as Christ has died in vain for those who will not accept of offered mercy, so will it be vain for the advocates of freedom to spend their breath in our behalf, unless with united hearts and souls you make some mighty efforts to raise your sons and daughters from the horrible state of servitude and degradation in which they are placed. It is upon you that woman depends; she can do but little besides using her influence; and it is for her sake and yours that I have come forward and made myself a hissing and a reproach among the people; for I am also one of the wretched and miserable daughters of the descendants of fallen Africa. Do you ask, why are you wretched and miserable? I reply, look at many of the most worthy and interesting of us doomed to spend our lives in gentlemen's kitchens. Look at our young men, smart, active and energetic, with souls filled with ambitious fire; if they look forward, alas! what are their prospects? They can be nothing but the humblest laborers, on account of their dark complexions; hence many of them lose their ambition, and become worthless. Look at our middle-aged men, clad in their rusty plaids and coats; in winter, every cent they earn goes to buy their wood and pay their rents; their poor wives also toil beyond their strength, to help support their families. Look at our aged sires, whose heads are whitened with the frosts of seventy winters, with their old wood-saws on their backs. Alas, what keeps us so? Prejudice, ignorance and poverty. But ah! methinks our oppression is soon to come to an end; yea, before the Majesty of heaven, our groans and cries have reached the ears of the Lord of Sabaoth. As the prayers and tears of Christians will avail the finally impenitent nothing; neither will the prayers and tears of the friends of humanity avail us any thing, unless we possess a spirit of virtuous emulation within our breasts. Did the pilgrims, when they first landed on these shores, quietly compose themselves, and say, "the Britons have all the money and all the power, and we must continue their servants forever?" Did they sluggishly sigh and say, "our lot is hard, the Indians own the soil, and we cannot cultivate it?" No; they first made powerful efforts to raise themselves, and then God raised up those illustrious patriots, WASHINGTON and LAFAYETTE, to assist and defend them. And, my brethren, have you made a powerful effort? Have you prayed the Legislature for mercy's sake to grant you all the rights and privileges of free citizens, that your daughters may rise to that degree of respectability which true merit deserves, and your sons above the servile situations which most of them fill?

SARAH MOORE GRIMKÉ

from *Letters on the Equality of the Sexes*
SEPTEMBER 6, 1837

From July to October 1837, abolitionist and budding women's rights activist Sarah Moore Grimké (1792–1873) penned a series of letters to Mary S. Parker, the president of the Boston Female Anti-Slavery Society. The fifteen letters, each signed with the evocative closing "Thine in the bonds of womanhood," circulated widely and were later collected in a book. Covering a wide range of religious, political, and cultural topics, Grimké challenged the notions that women's insubordination had been decreed by God and that women's influence should be confined solely to the domestic sphere. Instead she made the case that women should be able to participate in all spheres equally with men, at the time a truly radical claim. This letter concerns the legal status of women, which she repeatedly compares to that of slaves, and starts with the statement of British jurist William Blackstone that "by marriage, the husband and wife are one person in law."

Born the daughter of a wealthy Charleston, South Carolina, planter and slaveowner, Grimké had long been troubled by the morality of slavery (her attempt to teach her personal slave to write provoked a severe reaction from her father) as well as frustrated by the lack of educational opportunities such as her brothers enjoyed. She left the South, became a Quaker, and settled in Philadelphia in the 1820s, joined by her younger sister Angelina in 1829. As she became more deeply absorbed in the abolitionist cause, she found that to speak out against slavery she also had to assert her rights as a woman, confirming how the two controversial causes were closely intertwined.

Letter xii.

LEGAL DISABILITIES OF WOMEN.

Concord, 9th Mo., 6th, 1837.

My Dear Sister,—There are few things which present greater obstacles to the improvement and elevation of woman to her appropriate sphere of usefulness and duty, than the laws which have been enacted to destroy her independence, and crush her individuality; laws which, although they are framed for her government, she has had no voice in establishing, and which rob her of some of her *essential rights.* Woman has no political existence. With the single exception of presenting a petition to the legislative body, she is a cipher in the nation; or, if not actually so in representative governments, she is only counted, like the slaves of the South, to swell the number of law-makers who form decrees for her government, with little reference to her benefit, except so far as her good may promote their own. I am not sufficiently acquainted with the laws respecting women on the continent of Europe, to say anything about them. But Prof. Follen, in his essay on "The Cause of Freedom in our Country," says, "Woman, though fully possessed of that rational and moral nature which is the foundation of all rights, enjoys amongst us fewer legal rights than under the civil law of continental Europe." I shall confine myself to the laws of our country. These laws bear with peculiar rigor on married women. Blackstone, in the chapter entitled "Of husband and wife," says:—

"By marriage, the husband and wife are one person in law; that is, *the very being, or legal existence of the woman* is suspended during the marriage, or at least is incorporated and consolidated into that of the husband under whose wing, protection and cover she performs everything." "For this reason, a man cannot grant anything to his wife, or enter into covenant with her; for the grant would be to suppose her separate existence, and to covenant with her would be to covenant with himself; and therefore it is also generally true, that all compacts made between husband and wife when single, are voided by the intermarriage. A woman indeed may be attorney for her husband, but that implies no separation from, but is rather a representation of, her love."

Here now, the very being of a woman, like that of a slave, is absorbed in her master. All contracts made with her, like those made with slaves by their owners, are a mere nullity. Our kind defenders have legislated away almost all our legal rights, and in the true spirit of such injustice and oppression, have kept us in ignorance of those very laws by which we are governed. They have persuaded us, that we have no right to investigate the laws, and that, if we did, we could not comprehend them; they alone are capable of understanding the mysteries of Blackstone, &c.

But they are not backward to make us feel the practical operation of their power over our actions.

> "The husband is bound to provide his wife with necessaries by law, as much as himself; and if she contracts debts for them, he is obliged to pay for them; but for anything besides necessaries, he is not chargeable."

Yet a man may spend the property he has acquired by marriage at the ale-house, the gambling table, or in any other way that he pleases. Many instances of this kind have come to my knowledge; and women, who have brought their husbands handsome fortunes, have been left, in consequence of the wasteful and dissolute habits of their husbands, in straitened circumstances, and compelled to toil for the support of their families.

> "If the wife be indebted before marriage, the husband is bound afterwards to pay the debt; for he has adopted her and her circumstances together."

The wife's property is, I believe, equally liable for her husband's debts contracted before marriage.

> "If the wife be injured in her person or property, she can bring no action for redress without her husband's concurrence, and his name as well as her own: neither can she be sued, without making her husband a defendant."

This law that "a wife can bring no action," &c., is similar to the law respecting slaves. "A slave cannot bring a suit against his master, or any other person, for an injury—his master, must bring it." So if any damages are recovered for an injury committed on a wife, the husband pockets it; in the case of the slave, the master does the same.

> "In criminal prosecutions, the wife may be indicted and punished separately, unless there be evidence of coercion from the fact that the offence was committed in the presence, or by the command of her husband. A wife is excused from punishment for theft committed in the presence, or by the command of her husband."

It would be difficult to frame a law better calculated to destroy the responsibility of woman as a moral being, or a free agent. Her husband is supposed to possess unlimited control over her; and if she can offer the flimsy excuse that he bade her steal, she may break the eighth commandment with impunity, as far as human laws are concerned.

> "Our law, in general, considers man and wife as one person; yet there are some instances in which she is separately considered, as inferior to him and acting by his compulsion. Therefore, all deeds executed, and acts done by her during her coverture (i. e. marriage,) are void, except it be a fine, or like matter of record, in which case she must be solely and secretly examined, to learn if her act be voluntary."

Such a law speaks volumes of the abuse of that power which men have vested in their own hands. Still the private examination of a wife, to know whether she accedes to the disposition of property made by her husband is, in most cases, a mere form; a wife dares not do what will be disagreeable to one who is, in his own estimation, her superior, and who makes her feel, in the privacy of domestic life, that she has thwarted him. With respect to the nullity of deeds or acts done by a wife, I will mention one circumstance. A respectable woman borrowed of a female friend a sum of money to relieve her son from some distressing pecuniary embarrassment. Her husband was from home, and she assured the lender, that as soon as he returned, he would gratefully discharge the debt. She gave her note, and the lender, entirely ignorant of the law that a man is not obliged to discharge such a debt, actually borrowed the money, and lent it to the distressed and weeping mother. The father returned home, refused to pay the debt, and the person who had loaned the money was obliged to pay both principal and interest to the friend who lent it to her. Women should certainly know the laws by which they are governed, and from which they frequently suffer; yet they are kept in ignorance, nearly as profound, of their legal rights, and of the legislative enactments which are to regulate their actions, as slaves.

> "The husband, by the old law, might give his wife moderate correction, as he is to answer for her misbehavior. The law thought it reasonable to entrust him with this power of restraining her by domestic chastisement. The courts of law will still permit a husband to restrain a wife of her liberty, in case of any gross misbehavior."

What a mortifying proof this law affords, of the estimation in which woman is held! She is placed completely in the hands of a being subject like herself to the outbursts of passion, and therefore unworthy to be trusted with power. Perhaps I may be told respecting this law, that it is a dead letter, as I am sometimes told about the slave laws; but this is not true in either case. The slaveholder does kill his slave by moderate correction, as the law allows; and many a husband, among the poor, exercises the right given him by the law, of degrading woman by personal chastisement. And among the higher ranks, if actual imprisonment is not resorted to, women are not unfrequently restrained of the liberty of going to places of worship by irreligious husbands, and of doing many other things about which, as moral and responsible beings, *they* should be the *sole* judges. Such laws remind me of the reply of some little girls at a children's meeting held recently at Ipswich. The lecturer told them that God had created four orders of beings with which he had made us acquainted through the Bible. The first was angels, the second was man, the third beasts; and now, children, what is the fourth? After a pause, several girls replied, "WOMEN."

"A woman's personal property by marriage becomes absolutely her husband's, which, at his death, he may leave entirely away from her."

And farther, all the avails of her labor are absolutely in the power of her husband. All that she acquires by her industry is his; so that she cannot, with her own honest earnings, become the legal purchaser of any property. If she expends her money for articles of furniture, to contribute to the comfort of her family, they are liable to be seized for her husband's debts: and I know an instance of a woman, who by labor and economy had scraped together a little maintenance for herself and a do-little husband, who was left, at his death, by virtue of his last will and testament, to be supported by charity. I knew another woman, who by great industry had acquired a little money which she deposited in a bank for safe keeping. She had saved this pittance whilst able to work, in hopes that when age or sickness disqualified her for exertion, she might have something to render life comfortable, without being a burden to her friends. Her husband, a worthless, idle man, discovered this hid treasure, drew her little stock from the bank, and expended it all in extravagance and vicious indulgence. I know of another woman, who married without the least idea that she was surrendering her rights to all her personal property. Accordingly, she went to the bank as usual to draw her dividends, and the person who paid her the money, and to whom she was personally known as an owner of shares in that bank, remarking the change in her signature, withdrew the money, informing her that if she were married, she had no longer a right to draw her dividends without an order from her husband. It appeared that she intended having a little fund for private use, and had not even told her husband that she owned this stock, and she was not a little chagrined, when she found that it was not at her disposal. I think she was wrong to conceal the circumstance. The relation of husband and wife is too near and sacred to admit of secrecy about money matters, unless positive necessity demands it; and I can see no excuse for any woman entering into a marriage engagement with a design to keep her husband ignorant that she was possessed of property. If she was unwilling to give up her property to his disposal, she had infinitely better have remained single.

The laws above cited are not very unlike the slave laws of Louisiana.

"All that a slave possesses belongs to his master; he possesses nothing of his own, except what his master chooses he should possess."

"By the marriage, the husband is absolutely master of the profits of the wife's lands during the coverture, and if he has had a living child, and survives the wife, he retains the whole of those lands, if they are estates of inheritance, during his life; but the wife is entitled only to one third if she survives, out of the husband's estates of inheritance. But this she has whether she has had a child or not." "With regard to the property of women, there is taxation without representation; for they pay taxes without having the liberty of voting for representatives."

And this taxation, without representation, be it remembered, was the cause of our Revolutionary war, a grievance so heavy, that it was thought necessary to purchase exemption from it at an immense expense of blood and treasure, yet the daughters of New England, as well as of all the other States of this free Republic, are suffering a similar injustice—but for one, I had rather we should suffer any injustice or oppression, than that my sex should have any voice in the political affairs of the nation.

The laws I have quoted, are, I believe, the laws of Massachusetts, and, with few exceptions, of all the States in this Union. "In Louisiana and Missouri, and possibly, in some other southern States, a woman not only has half her husband's property by right at his death, but may always be considered as possessed of half his gains during his life; having at all times power to bequeath that amount." That the laws which have generally been adopted in the United States, for the government of women, have been framed almost entirely for the exclusive benefit of men, and with a design to oppress women, by depriving them of all control over their property, is too manifest to be denied. Some liberal and enlightened men, I know, regret the existence of these laws; and I quote with pleasure an extract from Harriet Martineau's Society in America, as a proof of the assertion. "A liberal minded lawyer of Boston, told me that his advice to testators always is to leave the largest possible amount to the widow, subject to the condition of her leaving it to the children; but that it is with shame that he reflects that any woman should owe that to his professional advice, which the law should have secured to her as a right." I have known a few instances where men have left their whole property to their wives, when they have died, leaving only minor children; but I have known more instances of "the friend and helper of many years, being portioned off like a salaried domestic," instead of having a comfortable independence secured to her, while the children were amply provided for.

As these abuses do exist, and women suffer intensely from them, our brethren are called upon in this enlightened age, by every sentiment of honor, religion and justice, to repeal these unjust and unequal laws, and restore to woman those rights which they have wrested from her. Such laws approximate too nearly to the laws enacted by slaveholders for the government of their slaves, and must tend to debase and depress the mind of that being, whom God created as a help meet for man, or "helper like unto himself," and designed to be his equal and his companion. Until such laws are annulled, woman never can occupy that exalted station for which she was intended by her Maker. And just in proportion as they are practically disregarded, which is the case to some extent, just so far is woman assuming that independence and nobility of character which she ought to exhibit.

The various laws which I have transcribed, leave women very little more liberty, or power, in some respects, than the slave. "A slave," says the civil code of Louisiana, "is one who is in the power of a master, to whom he belongs. He can possess nothing, nor acquire anything, but what must belong to his master." I do not wish by any means to intimate that the condition of free women can be compared to that of slaves in suffering, or in degradation; still, I believe the laws which deprive married women of their rights and privileges, have a tendency to lessen them in their own estimation as moral and responsible beings, and that their being made by civil law inferior to their husbands, has a debasing and mischievous effect upon them, teaching them practically the fatal lesson to look unto man for protection and indulgence.

Ecclesiastical bodies, I believe, without exception, follow the example of legislative assemblies, in excluding woman from any participation in forming the discipline by which she is governed. The men frame the laws, and, with few exceptions, claim to execute them on both sexes. In ecclesiastical, as well as civil courts, woman is tried and condemned, not by a jury of her peers, but by beings, who regard themselves as her superiors in the scale of creation. Although looked upon as an inferior, when considered as an intellectual being, woman is punished with the same severity as man, when she is guilty of moral offences. Her condition resembles, in some measure, that of the slave, who, while he is denied the advantages of his more enlightened master, is treated with even greater rigor of the law. Hoping that in the various reformations of the day, women may be relieved from some of their legal disabilities, I remain,

Thine in the bonds of womanhood,

SARAH M. GRIMKÉ.

ANGELINA GRIMKÉ

Address to the Massachusetts Legislature
FEBRUARY 21, 1838

In her letter on the legal disabilities of women, Sarah Grimké bemoaned that women had no political existence: "With the single exception of presenting a petition to the legislative body, she is a cipher in the nation." Six months later, on February 21, 1838, Angelina Grimké (1805–1879), her younger sister, seized that opening to present petitions gathered by the women of Massachusetts to the Legislative Committee on Slavery of the Massachusetts General Assembly. She also delivered a speech that, because she had so much to say, took two more days (February 23 and March 2) to complete; it was the first address by an American woman to a legislative body. Only the opening of the extemporaneous speech survives.

Grimké was already well known in abolitionist circles for her masterful pamphlet, *Appeal to the Christian Women of the South* (1836). It was published by the American Antislavery Society, which asked her to become its first female lecturer. Soon joined by Sarah, the two sisters drew large, mixed-sex audiences in New York, New Jersey, and New England. As Maria W. Stewart had found in 1832, the practice of women speaking in public, especially to "promiscuous" audiences, remained highly controversial. Several months after this address, Angelina married Theodore Weld (1803–1895), a noted abolitionist. They shared their New Jersey home with Sarah while raising their family. After the Civil War, they moved to Hyde Park, Massachusetts, where both sisters were active in the Massachusetts suffrage movement.

———————

MR. CHAIRMAN—

More than 2000 years have rolled their dark and bloody waters down the rocky, winding channel of Time into the broad ocean of Eternity, since woman's voice was heard in the palace of an eastern monarch, and woman's petition achieved the salvation of millions of her race from the edge of the sword. The Queen of Persia—if Queen she might be called, who was but the mistress of her voluptuous lord,—trained as she had been in the secret abominations of an oriental harem, had studied too deeply the character of Ahasuerus not to know that the sympathies of his heart could not be reached, except through

27

the medium of his sensual appetites. Hence we find her arrayed in royal apparel, and standing in the inner court of the King's house, hoping by her personal charms to win the favor of her lord. And after the golden sceptre had been held out, and the inquiry was made, "What wilt thou, Queen Esther, and what is thy request? it shall be given thee to the half of the kingdom"—even then she dared not ask either for her own life, or that of her people. She *felt* that if her mission of mercy was to be successful, *his* animal propensities must be still more powerfully wrought upon—the luxurious feast must be prepared, the banquet of wine must be served up, and the favorable moment must be seized when, gorged with gluttony and intoxication, the king's heart was fit to be operated upon by the pathetic appeal, "If *I* have found favor in thy sight, O King, and if it please the King, let *my* life be given at my petition, and *my* people at my request." It was thus, through personal charms, and sensual gratification, and individual influence, that the Queen of Persia obtained the precious boon she craved,—her own life, and the life of her beloved people. Mr. Chairman, it is my privilege to stand before you on a similar mission of life and love; but I thank God that we live in an age of the world too enlightened and too moral to admit of the adoption of the same *means* to obtain as holy an end. I feel that it would be an insult to this Committee, were I to attempt to win their favor by arraying my person in gold, and silver, and costly apparel, or by inviting them to partake of the luxurious feast, or the banquet of wine. I understand the spirit of the age too well to believe that *you* could be moved by such sensual means—means as unworthy of you, as they would be beneath the dignity of the cause of humanity. Yes, I feel that if you are reached at all, it will not be by me, but by the truths I shall endeavor to present to your understandings and your hearts. The heart of the eastern despot was reached through the lowest propensities of his animal nature, by personal influence; yours, I know, cannot be reached but through the loftier sentiments of the intellectual and moral feelings.

I stand before you as a citizen, on behalf of the 20,000 women of Massachusetts, whose names are enrolled on petitions which have been submitted to the Legislature, of which you are the organ. These petitions relate to the great and solemn subject of American slavery,—a subject fraught with the deepest interest to this republic, whether we regard it in its political, moral, or religious aspects. And because it is a *political* subject, it has often been tauntingly said, that *women* had nothing to do with it. "Are we aliens, because we are *women*? Are we bereft of citizenship, because we are the mothers, wives and daughters of a mighty people? Have women *no* country—*no* interests staked in public weal—no liabilities in common peril—no partnership in a nation's guilt and shame?" Let the history of the world answer these queries. Read the denunciations of Jehovah against the follies and crimes of Israel's daughters. Trace the influence of woman as a courtezan and a mistress in the destinies of nations, both ancient and modern, and see her wielding her power too often to debase and destroy, rather than to elevate and save. It is often said that women rule the world, through their influence over men. If so, then may we well hide our faces in the dust, and cover ourselves with sackcloth and ashes. It has not been by moral power and intellectual, but through the baser passions of man.—*This* dominion of women *must* be resigned—the sooner the better; "in the age which is approaching, she should be something *more*—she should be a *citizen*; and this title, which demands an increase of knowledge and of reflection, opens before her a new empire." I hold, Mr. Chairman, that American women have to do with this subject, not only because it is moral and religious, but because it is *political*, inasmuch as we are citizens of this republic, and as such, *our* honor, happiness, and well being, are bound up in its politics, government and laws.

I stand before you as a southerner, exiled from the land of my birth, by the sound of the lash, and the piteous cry of the slave. I stand before you as a repentant slaveholder. I stand before you as a moral being, endowed with precious and inalienable rights, which are correlative with solemn duties and high responsibilities; and as a moral being I feel that I owe it to the suffering slave, and to the deluded master, to my country and the world, to do all that I can to overturn a system of complicated crimes, built up upon the broken hearts and prostrate bodies of my countrymen in chains, and cemented by the blood and sweat and tears of my sisters in bonds.

[The orator then proceeded to discuss the merits of the petitions.]

MARGARET FULLER

from *"The Great Lawsuit"*
JULY 1843

Born in Cambridge, Massachusetts, Margaret Fuller (1810–1850) was an avid reader and was recognized early for her brilliant mind. As a woman, however, she was restricted from the educational and intellectual opportunities open to men of comparable talent. Fuller began to find her voice in 1839 when leading a series of "Conversations" for Boston-area women. Her public profile increased the next year when she became the editor of *The Dial*, a magazine that published the works of important thinkers and philosophers such as Ralph Waldo Emerson, Theodore Parker, and Henry David Thoreau. In 1843 she laid out her ideas about women, men, intellect, and nature in *The Dial* in the essay "The Great Lawsuit. Man versus Men. Woman versus Women," which is excerpted here. In 1845 an expanded version of the essay was published as *Woman in the Nineteenth Century*, which is now widely recognized as a key feminist text. In 1844 Fuller became the first female correspondent on the staff of the *New-York Tribune*, and two years later she journeyed to Europe where she had a firsthand view of the revolutions that were sweeping the continent. In 1850 her brilliant career was cut short when she, together with her Italian husband Giovanni Angelo Ossoli and their young child, drowned in a shipwreck just off Fire Island, New York, when returning to America.

———————

It is not surprising that it should be the Anti-Slavery party that pleads for woman, when we consider merely that she does not hold property on equal terms with men; so that, if a husband dies without a will, the wife, instead of stepping at once into his place as head of the family, inherits only a part of his fortune, as if she were a child, or ward only, not an equal partner.

We will not speak of the innumerable instances, in which profligate or idle men live upon the earnings of industrious wives; or if the wives leave them and take with them the children, to perform the double duty of mother and father, follow from place to place, and threaten to rob them of the children, if deprived of the rights of a husband, as they call them, planting themselves in their poor lodgings, frightening them into paying tribute by taking from them the children, running into debt at the expense of these otherwise so overtasked helots. Though such instances abound, the public opinion of his own sex is against the man, and when cases of extreme tyranny are made known, there is private action in the wife's favor. But if woman be, indeed, the weaker party, she ought to have legal protection, which would make such oppression impossible.

And knowing that there exists, in the world of men, a tone of feeling towards women as towards slaves, such as is expressed in the common phrase, "Tell that to women and children;" that the infinite soul can only work through them in already ascertained limits; that the prerogative of reason, man's highest portion, is allotted to them in a much lower degree; that it is better for them to be engaged in active labor, which is to be furnished and directed by those better able to think, &c. &c.; we need not go further, for who can review the experience of last week, without recalling words which imply, whether in jest or earnest, these views, and views like these? Knowing this, can we wonder that many reformers think that measures are not likely to be taken in behalf of women, unless their wishes could be publicly represented by women?

That can never be necessary, cry the other side. All men are privately influenced by women; each has his wife, sister, or female friends, and is too much biassed by these relations to fail of representing their interests. And if this is not enough, let them propose and enforce their wishes with the pen. The beauty of home would be destroyed, the delicacy of the sex be violated, the dignity of halls of legislation destroyed, by an attempt to introduce them there. Such duties are inconsistent with those of a mother; and then we have ludicrous pictures of ladies in hysterics at the polls, and senate chambers filled with cradles.

But if, in reply, we admit as truth that woman seems destined by nature rather to the inner circle, we must add that the arrangements of civilized life have not been as yet such as to secure it to her. Her circle, if the duller, is not the quieter. If kept from excitement, she is not from drudgery. Not only the Indian carries the burdens of the camp, but the favorites of Louis the Fourteenth accompany him in his journeys, and the washerwoman stands at her tub and carries home her work at all seasons, and in all states of health.

As to the use of the pen, there was quite as much opposition to woman's possessing herself of that help to free-agency as there is now to her seizing on the rostrum or the desk; and she is likely to draw, from a permission to plead her cause that way, opposite inferences to what might be wished by those who now grant it.

As to the possibility of her filling, with grace and dignity, any such position, we should think those who had seen the great actresses, and heard the Quaker preachers of modern times, would not doubt, that woman can express publicly the fulness of thought and emotion, without losing any of the peculiar beauty of her sex.

As to her home, she is not likely to leave it more than she now does for balls, theatres, meetings for promoting missions, revival meetings, and others to which she flies, in hope of an animation for her existence, commensurate with what she sees enjoyed by men. Governors of Ladies' Fairs are no less engrossed by such a charge, than the Governor of the State by his; presidents of Washingtonian societies, no less away from home than presidents of conventions. If men look straitly to it, they will find that, unless their own lives are domestic, those of the women will not be. The female Greek, of our day, is as much in the street as the male, to cry, What news? We doubt not it was the same in Athens of old. The women, shut out from the market-place, made up for it at the religious festivals. For human beings are not so constituted, that they can live without expansion; and if they do not get it one way, must another, or perish.

And, as to men's representing women fairly, at present, while we hear from men who owe to their wives not only all that is comfortable and graceful, but all that is wise in the arrangement of their lives, the frequent remark, "You cannot reason with a woman," when from those of delicacy, nobleness, and poetic culture, the contemptuous phrase, "Women and children," and that in no light sally of the hour, but in works intended to give a permanent statement of the best experiences, when not one man in the million, shall I say, no, not in the hundred million, can rise above the view that woman was made *for man*, when such traits as these are daily forced upon the attention, can we feel that man will always do justice to the interests of woman? Can we think that he takes a sufficiently discerning and religious view of her office and destiny, ever to do her justice, except when prompted by sentiment; accidentally or transiently, that is, for his sentiment will vary according to the relations in which he is placed. The lover, the poet, the artist, are likely to view her nobly. The father and the philosopher have some chance of liberality; the man of the world, the legislator for expediency, none.

Under these circumstances, without attaching importance in themselves to the changes demanded by the champions of woman, we hail them as signs of the times. We would have every arbitrary barrier thrown down. We would have every path laid open to woman as freely as to man. Were this done, and a slight temporary fermentation allowed to subside, we believe that the Divine would ascend into nature to a height unknown in the history of past ages, and nature, thus instructed, would regulate the spheres not only so as to avoid collision, but to bring forth ravishing harmony.

Yet then, and only then, will human beings be ripe for this, when inward and outward freedom for woman, as much as for man, shall be acknowledged as a right, not yielded as a concession. As the friend of the negro assumes that one man cannot, by right, hold another in bondage, so should the friend of woman assume that man cannot, by right, lay even well-meant restrictions on woman. If the negro be a soul, if the woman be a soul, apparelled in flesh, to one master only are they accountable. There is but one law for all souls, and, if there is to be an interpreter of it, he comes not as man, or son of man, but as Son of God.

Were thought and feeling once so far elevated that man should esteem himself the brother and friend, but nowise the lord and tutor of woman, were he really bound with her in equal worship, arrangements as to function and employment would be of no consequence. What woman needs is not as a woman to act or rule, but as a nature to grow, as an intellect to discern, as a soul to live freely, and unimpeded to unfold such powers as were given her when we left our common home. If fewer talents were given her, yet, if allowed the free and full employment of these, so that she may render back to the giver his own with usury, she will not complain, nay, I dare to say she will bless and rejoice in her earthly birth-place, her earthly lot.

ELEANOR VINCENT, LYDIA A. WILLIAMS, LYDIA OSBORN, SUSAN ORMSBY, AMY ORMSBY, ANNA BISHOP

Petition to the Constitutional Convention of the State of New York

AUGUST 8, 1846

In the summer of 1846, six women from rural Jefferson County in upstate New York drafted a petition to the upcoming state constitutional convention "asking for the extension of the elective franchise to women." The petition is not the least bit deferential—it makes the case for the extension of equal civil and political rights to women in straightforward, unequivocal language that asserts their claim as an inalienable right. Moreover, the petition takes for granted the women's shared belief that they had a right to express their opinions not just in the privacy of their homes but in public venues. Who were these potential rabble-rousers who raised this issue two years before the Seneca Falls Convention in 1848? Five of the six women were married, and all were linked by family, friendship, and physical proximity. Except for this petition, they seem to have led totally ordinary lives. And yet they collectively believed in the idea of full political rights for women—and said so publicly by way of a petition presented to their government by a local representative.

———————

Your Memorialists inhabitants of Jefferson county, believing that civil government has its foundation in the laws of our existence, as moral and social beings, that the specific object and end of civil government is to protect all in the exercise of all their natural rights, by combining the strength of society for the defence of the individual—believing that the province of civil government is not to create new rights, but to declare and enforce those which originally existed. Believing likewise that all governments must derive their just powers from the consent of the governed "from the great body of society, and not from a favored class, although that favored class may be even a majority of the inhabitants," therefore respectfully represent: That

34

the present government of this state has widely departed from the true democratic principles upon which all just governments must be based by denying to the female portion of community the right of suffrage and any participation in forming the government and laws under which they live, and to which they are amenable, and by imposing upon them burdens of taxation, both directly and indirectly, without admitting them the right of representation, thereby striking down the only safeguards of their individual and personal liberties. Your Memorialists therefore ask your honorable body, to remove this just cause of complaint, by modifying the present Constitution of this State, so as to extend to women equal, and civil and political rights with men. In proposing this change, your petitioners ask you to confer upon them no new right but only to declare and enforce those which they originally inherited, but which have ungenerously been withheld from them, rights, which they as citizens of the state of New York may reasonably and rightfully claim. We might adduce arguments both numerous and decisive in support of our position, but believing that a self evident truth is sufficiently plain without argument, and in view of our necessarily limited space, we forbear offering any and respectfully submit it for consideration.

ELEANOR VINCENT,   SUSAN ORMSBY,
LYDIA A. WILLIAMS,   AMY ORMSBY,
LYDIA OSBORN,   ANNA BISHOP.
Aug. 8th, 1846.

SENECA FALLS CONVENTION

Declaration of Sentiments and Resolutions
JULY 19–20, 1848

On July 19–20, 1848, approximately three hundred people, including forty men, gathered in the local Methodist church in the small upstate village of Seneca Falls, New York. They came in response to a call to discuss "the social, civil and religious condition of Woman," which had been drafted by Elizabeth Cady Stanton (1815–1902), Lucretia Mott (1793–1880), and Martha Coffin Wright (1806–1875) (but not Susan B. Anthony [1820–1906], who did not join the movement for another two years). Stanton was the group's wordsmith and she boldly restated the central concept of the Declaration of Independence in this memorable way: "All men and women are created equal." The Declaration of Sentiments presented eighteen instances of "repeated injuries and usurpations on the part of man toward woman," including the lack of married women's property rights, their exclusion from profitable employment, women's subordination in organized religion, and lack of access to education. Eleven resolutions followed, all of which passed easily, with the exception of the call "to secure to themselves their sacred right to elective franchise," which passed by only a small majority. The Seneca Falls Convention was not, as is often asserted, the first conference ever held on the question of women's rights, nor (as the Jefferson County petition confirms) was it the first public demand for the vote. Still, thanks in part to the later efforts of Elizabeth Cady Stanton and Susan B. Anthony to promote it as the foundational moment of the women's rights movement, the Seneca Falls Convention has earned an iconic place in the history of American feminism.

Declaration of Sentiments.

When, in the course of human events, it becomes necessary for one portion of the family of man to assume among the people of the earth a position different from that which they have hitherto occupied, but one to which the laws of nature and of nature's God entitle them, a decent respect to the opinions of mankind requires that they should declare the causes that impel them to such a course.

We hold these truths to be self-evident: that all men and

women are created equal; that they are endowed by their Creator with certain inalienable rights; that among these are life, liberty, and the pursuit of happiness; that to secure these rights governments are instituted, deriving their just powers from the consent of the governed.—Whenever any form of Government becomes destructive of these ends, it is the right of those who suffer from it to refuse allegiance to it, and to insist upon the institution of a new government, laying its foundation on such principles, and organizing its powers in such form as to them shall seem most likely to effect their safety and happiness. Prudence, indeed, will dictate that governments long established should not be changed for light and transient causes; and accordingly, all experience hath shown that mankind are more disposed to suffer, while evils are sufferable, than to right themselves by abolishing the forms to which they are accustomed. But when a long train of abuses and usurpations, pursuing invariably the same object, evinces a design to reduce them under absolute despotism, it is their duty to throw off such government, and to provide new guards for their future security. Such has been the patient sufferance of the women under this government, and such is now the necessity which constrains them to demand the equal station to which they are entitled.

The history of mankind is a history of repeated injuries and usurpations on the part of man toward woman, having in direct object the establishment of an absolute tyranny over her. To prove this, let facts be submitted to a candid world.

He has never permitted her to exercise her inalienable right to the elective franchise.

He has compelled her to submit to laws, in the formation of which she had no voice.

He has withheld from her rights which are given to the most ignorant and degraded men—both natives and foreigners.

Having deprived her of this first right of a citizen, the elective franchise, thereby leaving her without representation in the halls of legislation, he has oppressed her on all sides.

He has made her, if married, in the eye of the law, civilly dead.

He has taken from her all right in property, even to the wages she earns.

He has made her, morally, an irresponsible being, as she can commit many crimes with impunity, provided they be done in the presence of her husband. In the covenant of marriage, she is compelled to promise obedience to her husband, he becoming, to all intents and purposes, her master—the law giving him power to deprive her of her liberty, and to administer chastisement.

He has so framed the laws of divorce, as to what shall be the proper causes of divorce; in case of separation, to whom the guardianship of the children shall be given; as to be wholly regardless of the happiness of women—the law, in all cases, going upon the false supposition of the supremacy of man, and giving all power into his hands.

After depriving her of all rights as a married woman, if single and the owner of property, he has taxed her to support a government which recognizes her only when her property can be made profitable to it.

He has monopolized nearly all the profitable employments, and from those she is permitted to follow, she receives but a scanty remuneration.

He closes against her all the avenues to wealth and distinction, which he considers most honorable to himself. As a teacher of theology, medicine, or law, she is not known.

He has denied her the facilities for obtaining a thorough education—all colleges being closed against her.

He allows her in Church as well as State, but a subordinate position, claiming Apostolic authority for her exclusion from the ministry, and, with some exceptions, from any public participation in the affairs of the Church.

He has created a false public sentiment, by giving to the world a different code of morals for men and women, by which moral delinquencies which exclude women from society, are not only tolerated but deemed of little account in man.

He has usurped the prerogative of Jehovah himself, claiming it as his right to assign for her a sphere of action, when that belongs to her conscience and her God.

He has endeavored, in every way that he could to destroy her confidence in her own powers, to lessen her self-respect, and to make her willing to lead a dependant and abject life.

Now, in view of this entire disfranchisement of one-half

the people of this country, their social and religious degradation,—in view of the unjust laws above mentioned, and because
women do feel themselves aggrieved, oppressed, and fraudu-
lently deprived of their most sacred rights, we insist that they
have immediate admission to all the rights and privileges which
belong to them as citizens of these United States.

In entering upon the great work before us, we anticipate no
small amount of misconception, misrepresentation, and ridicule; but we shall use every instrumentality within our power
to effect our object. We shall employ agents, circulate tracts,
petition the State and national Legislatures, and endeavor to
enlist the pulpit and the press in our behalf. We hope this Convention will be followed by a series of Conventions, embracing
every part of the country.

Firmly relying upon the final triumph of the Right and the
True, we do this day affix our signatures to this declaration.

Lucretia Mott,	Hannah Plant,
Harriet Cady Eaton,	Lucy Jones,
Margaret Pryor,	Sarah Whitney,
Elizabeth Cady Stanton,	Mary H. Hallowell,
Eunice Newton Foote,	Elizabeth Conklin,
Mary Ann M'Clintock,	Sally Pitcher,
Margaret Schooley,	Mary Conklin,
Martha C. Wright,	Susan Quinn,
Jane C. Hunt,	Mary L. Minor,
Amy Post,	Phebe King,
Catharine F. Stebbins,	Mary Gilbert,
Mary Ann Frink,	Sophronia Taylor,
Lydia Mount,	Cynthia Davis,
Delia Mathews,	Mary Martin,
Catharine C. Paine,	M. A. Culver,
Elizabeth W. M'Clintock,	Susan R. Doty,
Malvina Seymour,	Rebecca Race,
Phebe Mosher,	Sarah A. Mosher,
Catharine Shaw,	Mary E. Vail,
Deborah Scott,	Lucy Spalding,
Sarah Hallowell,	Lavinia Latham,
Mary M'Clintock,	Sarah Smith,

Julia Ann Drake,
Charlotte Woodward,
Martha Underhill,
Dorothy Mathews,
Eunice Barker,
Sarah R. Woods,
Lydia Gild,
Sarah Hoffman,
Elizabeth Leslie,
Martha Ridley,
Rachel D. Bonnel,
Betsey Tewksbury,
Rhoda Palmer,
Margaret Jenkins,
Cynthia Fuller,
Eliza Martin,
Maria E. Wilbur,
Elizabeth D. Smith,
Caroline Barker,
Ann Porter,
Experience Gibbs,
Antoinette E. Segur,
Hannah J. Latham,
Sarah Sisson.

The following are the names of the gentlemen present in favor of the movement:

Richard P. Hunt,
Samuel D. Tillman,
Justin Williams,
Elisha Foote,
Frederick Douglass,
Henry W. Seymour,
Henry Seymour,
David Spalding,
William G. Barker,
Elias J. Doty,
John Jones,
William S. Dell,
James Mott,
William Burroughs,
Robert Smalldridge,
Jacob Mathews,
Charles L. Hoskins,
Thomas M'Clintock,
Saron Phillips,
Jacob Chamberlain,
Jonathan Metcalf,
Nathan J. Milliken,
S. E. Woodworth,
Edward F. Underhill,
George W. Pryor,
Joel Bunker,
Isaac Van Tassel,
Thomas Dell,
E. W. Capron,
Stephen Shear,
Henry Hatley,
Azaliah Schooley.

Resolutions.

Whereas, the great precept of nature is conceded to be, "that man shall pursue his own true and substantial happiness." Blackstone, in his Commentaries, remarks, that this law of Nature being coeval with mankind, and dictated by God himself, is of course superior in obligation to any other. It is binding over all the globe, in all countries, and at all times; no human laws are of any validity if contrary to this, and such of them as are valid, derive all their force, and all their validity, and all their authority, mediately and immediately, from this original; Therefore,

Resolved, That such laws as conflict, in any way, with the true and substantial happiness of woman, are contrary to the great precept of nature, and of no validity; for this is "superior in obligation to any other."

Resolved, That all laws which prevent woman from occupying such a station in society as her conscience shall dictate, or which place her in a position inferior to that of man, are contrary to the great precept of nature, and therefore of no force or authority.

Resolved, That woman is man's equal—was intended to be so by the Creator, and the highest good of the race demands that she should be recognized as such.

Resolved, That the women of this country ought to be enlightened in regard to the laws under which they live, that they may no longer publish their degradation, by declaring themselves satisfied with their present position, nor their ignorance, by asserting that they have all the rights they want.

Resolved, That inasmuch as man, while claiming for himself intellectual superiority, does accord to woman moral superiority, it is pre-eminently his duty to encourage her to speak, and teach, as she has an opportunity, in all religious assemblies.

Resolved, That the same amount of virtue, delicacy, and refinement of behavior, that is required of woman in the social state, should also be required of man, and the same transgressions should be visited with equal severity on both man and woman.

Resolved, That the objection of indelicacy and impropriety, which is so often brought against woman when she addresses a public audience, comes with a very ill grace from those who encourage, by their attendance, her appearance on the stage, in the concert, or in the feats of the circus.

Resolved, That woman has too long rested satisfied in the circumscribed limits which corrupt customs and a perverted application of the Scriptures have marked out for her, and that it is time she should move in the enlarged sphere which her great Creator has assigned her.

Resolved, That it is the duty of the women of this country to secure to themselves their sacred right to the elective franchise.

Resolved, That the equality of human rights results necessarily from the fact of the identity of the race in capabilities and responsibilities.

Resolved, therefore, That, being invested by the Creator with the same capabilities, and the same consciousness of responsibility for their exercise, it is demonstrably the right aud duty of woman, equally with man, to promote every righteous cause, by every righteous means; and especially in regard to the great subjects of morals and religion, it is self-evidently her right to participate with her brother in teaching them, both in private and in public, by writing and by speaking, by any instrumentalities proper to be used, and in any assemblies proper to be held; and this being a self-evident truth, growing out of the divinely implanted principles of human nature, any custom or authority adverse to it, whether modern or wearing the hoary sanction of antiquity, is to be regarded as self-evident falsehood, and at war with the interests of mankind.

Resolved, That the speedy success of our cause depends upon the zealous and untiring efforts of both men and women, for the overthrow of the monopoly of the pulpit, and for the securing to woman an equal participation with men in the various trades, professions and commerce.

SOJOURNER TRUTH

Speech to Ohio Woman's Rights Convention
MAY 28, 1851

Born and raised as a slave in New York State, Sojourner Truth (c. 1797–1883) renamed herself after she was freed, around 1827, and embarked on a career as an itinerant speaker and activist. In the years after Seneca Falls, she was a frequent participant at woman's rights conventions, including a memorable appearance at the Ohio Woman's Rights Convention, which convened in Akron on May 28, 1851. After asking permission to address the meeting, she gave a short but powerful speech, which was summarized by her friend Marius Robinson, who served as the secretary of the convention, and published in the Salem *Anti-Slavery Bugle* on June 21, 1851. Twelve years later, Frances Dana Gage (1808–1884), who had presided over the Akron convention, circulated her own version of that address. Written in a white woman's problematic approximation of black dialect ("Well, chillen, whar dar's so much racket de must be som'ting out o' kilter"), Gage's version contained the refrain "And ar'n't I a woman?" not once but four times, a phrase that historian Nell Irvin Painter claims was invented by Gage. Even though Robinson's account is far more credible because it was written at the time, Gage's much embellished version is still often uncritically presented as Sojourner Truth's words.

———————

May I say a few words? Receiving an affirmative answer, she proceeded; I want to say a few words about this matter. I am a woman's rights. I have as much muscle as any man, and can do as much work as any man. I have plowed and reaped and husked and chopped and mowed, and can any man do more than that? I have heard much about the sexes being equal; I can carry as much as any man, and can cut as much too, if I can get it. I am as strong as any man that is now. As for intellect, all I can say is, if woman have a pint and man a quart—why cant she have her little pint-full? You need not be afraid to give us our rights for fear we will take too much,—for we cant take more than our pint'll hold. The poor men seem to be all in confusion, and dont know what to do. Why children, if you have woman's rights give it to her and you will feel better. You will have your own rights, and they wont be so much trouble. I cant read, but I can hear. I have heard the bible and have learned that Eve caused man to sin. Well if woman upset the world, do give her a chance to set it right side up again. The Lady has spoken about Jesus, how he never spurned woman from him, and she was right. When Lazarus died, Mary and Martha came to him with faith and love and besought him to raise their brother. And Jesus wept—and Lazarus came forth. And how came Jesus into the world? Through God who created him and woman who bore him. Man, where is your part? But the women are coming up blessed be God and a few of the men are coming up with them. But man is in a tight place, the poor slave is on him, woman is coming on him, and he is surely between a hawk and a buzzard.

ERNESTINE L. ROSE

Speech to the Second National Woman's Rights Convention
OCTOBER 15–16, 1851

One of the most effective orators for women's rights in the 1850s was a Jew, an atheist, and a foreigner. Ernestine L. Rose (1810–1892) was born in Poland and emigrated to the United States by way of England, where she was deeply influenced by Robert Owen's communitarian socialism. Once in this country, she embraced free thought, the antislavery cause, and women's rights, lecturing widely in the 1840s and 1850s. Her most famous speech, an hour-long oration that later circulated widely in print, was given at the Second National Woman's Rights Convention, held in Worcester, Massachusetts, on October 15–16, 1851. More than one thousand people attended this convention, a dramatic increase over the first national convention held in Worcester the year before, showing how this young movement was sparking interest and public support. Rose's thesis that women deserved equal rights as human beings was captured in this formulation: "Humanity recognizes no sex—virtue recognizes no sex—mind recognizes no sex." Like many early women's rights activists, she focused on women's, especially married women's, lack of legal rights. But she also called on women to think for themselves and challenge ingrained notions that women were inferior by nature. As the only foreigner among the first generation of native-born leaders of the women's rights movement, Rose brought an international perspective to her activism. After the Civil War she returned to England, where she continued to be active in reform causes until her death.

After having heard the letter read from our poor incarcerated sisters of France, well might we exclaim, Alas! poor France! where is thy glory? Where the glory of the Revolution of 1848, in which shone forth the pure and magnanimous spirit of an oppressed nation, struggling for Freedom? Where the fruits of that victory that gave to the world the motto, Liberty, Equality, and Fraternity? A motto destined to hurl the tyranny of kings and priests into the dust, and give freedom to the enslaved millions of the earth. Where, I again ask, is the result of these noble achievements, when Woman, ay, one half of the nation, is deprived of her rights? Has Woman then been idle during the contest between Right and Might? Has she been wanting in ardor and enthusiasm? Has she not mingled her blood with that of her husband, son, and sire? Or has she been recreant in hailing the motto of Liberty floating on your banners as an omen of justice, peace, and freedom to man, that at the first step she takes practically to claim the recognition of her Rights, she is rewarded with the doom of a martyr? But Right has not yet asserted her prerogative, for Might rules the day; and as every good cause must have its martyrs, why should Woman not be a martyr for her cause? But need we wonder that France, governed as she is by Russian and Austrian despotism, does not recognize the rights of humanity in the recognition of the Rights of Woman, when even here, in this far-famed land of freedom, under a Republic that has inscribed on its banner the great truth that all men are created free and equal, and endowed with inalienable rights to life, liberty, and the pursuit of happiness,—a declaration borne, like the vision of hope, on wings of light to the remotest parts of the earth, an omen of freedom to the oppressed and downtrodden children of man,—when, even here, in the very face of this eternal truth, woman, the mockingly so called "better half" of man, has yet to plead for her rights, nay, for her life; for what is life without liberty, and what is liberty without equality of rights? And as for the pursuit of happiness, she is not allowed to pursue any line of life that might promote it; she has only thankfully to accept what man in his magnanimity decides as best for her to do, and this is what he does not choose to do himself. Is she then not included in that declaration? Answer, ye wise men of the nation, and answer truly; add not hypocrisy to oppression! Say that she is not created free and equal, and therefore (for the sequence follows on the premises) that she is not entitled to life, liberty, and the pursuit of happiness. But with all the audacity arising from an assumed superiority, you dare not so libel and insult humanity as to say, that she is not included in that declaration; and if she is, then what right has man, except that of might, to deprive woman of the rights and privileges he claims for himself? And why, in the name of reason and justice, why should she not have the same rights? Because she is woman? Humanity recognizes no sex—virtue recognizes no sex—mind recognizes no sex—life and death, pleasure and pain, happiness and misery recognize no sex. Like man, woman comes involuntarily into existence; like him she possesses physical and mental and moral powers, on the proper cultivation of which depends her happiness; like him she is subject to all the vicissitudes of life; like him she has to pay the penalty for disobeying nature's laws, and far greater penalties has she to suffer from ignorance of her far more complicated nature than he; like him she enjoys or suffers with her country. Yet she is not recognized as his equal! In the laws of the land she has no rights, in government she has no voice. And in spite of another principle, recognized in this Republic, namely, that "taxation without representation is tyranny," yet she is taxed without being represented. Her property may be consumed by taxes to defray the expenses of that unholy, unrighteous custom called war, yet she has no power to give her veto against it. From the cradle to the grave she is subject to the power and control of man. Father, guardian, or husband, one conveys her like some piece of merchandise over to the other. At marriage she loses her entire identity, and her being is said to have become merged in her husband. Has nature thus merged it? Has she ceased to exist and feel pleasure and pain? When she violates the laws of her being, does her husband pay the penalty? When she breaks the moral laws, does he suffer the punishment? When he supplies his wants, is it enough to satisfy her nature? And when at his nightly orgies, in the grog-shop and the oyster cellar, or at the gaming-table, he squanders the means she helped by her coöperation and economy to accumulate, and she awakens to penury and destitution, will it supply the wants of her children to tell them, that owing to the superiority of man she had no redress by law; and that as her being was merged in his, so also ought theirs to be? What an inconsistency, that from the moment she enters that compact, in which she assumes the high responsibility of wife and mother, she ceases legally to exist, and becomes a purely submissive being. Blind submission in woman is considered a virtue, while submission to wrong is itself wrong, and resistance to wrong is virtue alike in woman as in man.

But it will be said that the husband provides for the wife, or in other words, he feeds, clothes, and shelters her! I wish I had the power to make every one before me fully realize the degradation contained in that idea. Yes! he *keeps* her, and so he does a favorite horse; by law they are both considered his property. Both may, when the cruelty of the owner compels them to run away, be brought back by the strong arm of the law, and according to a still extant law of England both may be led by the halter to the market-place and sold. This is humiliating indeed, but nevertheless true; and the sooner these things are known and understood, the better for humanity. It is no fancy sketch. I know that some endeavor to throw the mantle of romance over the subject, and treat woman like some ideal existence, not liable to the ills of life. Let such deal in fancy, that have nothing better to deal in; we have to do with sober, sad realities, with stubborn facts.

Again, I shall be told that the law presumes the husband to be kind, affectionate, and ready to provide for and protect his wife. But what right, I ask, has the law to presume at all on the subject? What right has the law to intrust the interest and happiness of one being into the hands of another? And if the merging of the interest of one being into the other is a necessary consequence on marriage, why should woman always remain on the losing side? Turn the tables. Let the identity and interest of the husband be merged in the wife. Think you she would act less generously towards him, than he towards her? Think you she is not capable of as much justice, disinterested devotion, and abiding affection, as he is? Oh, how grossly you misunderstand and wrong her nature! But we desire no such undue power over man; it would be as wrong in her to exercise it as it now is in him. All we claim is an equal legal and social position. We have nothing to do with individual man, be he good or bad, but with the laws that oppress woman. We know that bad and unjust laws must in the nature of things make man so too. If he is kind, affectionate, and consistent, it is because the kindlier feelings, instilled by a mother, kept warm by a sister, and cherished by a wife, will not allow him to carry out these barbarous laws against woman.

But the estimation she is generally held in, is as degrading as it is foolish. Man forgets that woman cannot be degraded without its re-acting on himself. The impress of her mind is stamped on him by nature, and the early education of the mother which no after-training can entirely efface; and therefore, the estimation she is held in falls back with double force upon him. Yet, from the force of prejudice against her, he knows it not. Not long ago, I saw an account of two offenders, brought before a Justice of New York. One was charged with stealing a pair of boots, for which offense he was sentenced to six months' imprisonment; the other crime was assault and battery upon his wife: he was let off with a reprimand from the judge! With my principles, I am entirely opposed to punishment, and hold, that to reform the erring and remove the causes of evil is much more efficient, as well as just, than to punish. But the judge showed us the comparative value which he set on these two kinds of *property*. But then you must remember that the boots were taken by a stranger, while the wife was insulted by her legal owner! Here it will be said, that such degrading cases are but few. For the sake of humanity, I hope they are. But as long as woman shall be oppressed by unequal laws, so long will she be degraded by man. We have hardly an adequate idea how all-powerful law is in forming public opinion, in giving tone and character to the mass of society. To illustrate my point, look at that infamous, detestable law, which was written in human blood, and signed and sealed with life and liberty, that eternal stain on the statute book of this country, the Fugitive Slave Law. Think you that before its passage, you could have found any in the free States—except a few politicians in the market—base enough to desire such a law? No! no! Even those who took no interest in the slave question, would have shrunk from so barbarous a thing. But no sooner was it passed, than the ignorant mass, the rabble of the self-styled Union Safety Committee, found out that we were a law-loving, law-abiding people! Such is the magic power of Law. Hence the necessity to guard against bad ones. Hence also the reason why we call on the nation to remove the legal shackles from woman, and it will have a beneficial effect on that still greater tyrant she has to contend with, Public Opinion.

Carry out the republican principle of universal suffrage, or strike it from your banners and substitute "Freedom and Power to one half of society, and submission and slavery to the other." Give woman the elective franchise. Let married women have the same right to property that their husbands have; for whatever the difference in their respective occupations, the duties of the wife are as indispensable and far more arduous than the

husband's. Why then should the wife, at the death of her husband, not be his heir to the same extent that he is heir to her?
In this inequality there is involved another wrong. When the
wife dies, the husband is left in the undisturbed possession of all
there is, and the children are left with him; no change is made,
no stranger intrudes on his home and his affliction. But when
the husband dies, not only is the widow, as too often is the case,
deprived of all, and at best receives but a mere pittance, while
strangers assume authority denied to the wife. The sanctuary
of affliction must be desecrated by executors; everything must
be ransacked and assessed, lest she should steal something out
of her own house; and to cap the climax, the children must be
placed under guardians. When the husband dies poor, to be
sure, no guardian is required, and the children are left for the
mother to care and toil for them, as best she may. But when
anything is left for their maintenance, then it must be placed in
the hands of strangers for safe keeping! The bringing up and
safety of the children is left with the mother, and safe they are
in her hands. But a few hundred or thousand dollars cannot be
intrusted with her! But, say they, "in case of a second marriage,
the children must be protected in their possession." Does that
reason not hold as good in the case of the husband as in that
of the wife? Oh, no! When *he* marries again, he still retains his
identity and power to act; but *she* becomes merged once more
into a mere nonentity; and therefore the first husband must
rob her to prevent the second from doing so! Make the laws
then, (if any are required,) regulating property between husband and wife, equal for both, and all these difficulties would
be removed.

According to a late act, the wife has a right to the property
she brings at marriage, or receives in any way after marriage.
Here is some provision for the favored few; but for the laboring
many, there is none. The mass of the people commence life with
no other capital than the union of heads, hearts and hands.
To the benefit of this best of capital, the wife has no right.
If they are unsuccessful in married life, who suffers more the
bitter consequences of poverty than the wife? But if successful,
she cannot call a dollar her own. The husband may will away
every dollar of the personal property, and leave her destitute
and penniless, and she has no redress by law. And even where

real estate is left, she receives but a life-interest in a third part of it, and at her death, she cannot leave it to any one belonging to her, it falls back even to the remotest of his relatives. This is law, but where is the justice of it? Well might we say that laws were made to prevent, not to promote, the ends of justice. Or, in case of separation, why should the children be taken from the protecting care of the mother? Who has a better right to them than she? How much do fathers generally do towards the bringing of them up? When he comes home from business, and the child is in good humor and handsome trim, he takes the little darling on his knee and plays with it. But when the wife, with the care of the whole household on her shoulders, with little or no help, is not able to put them in the best order or trim, how much does he do towards it? Oh, no! Fathers like to have children good-natured, well-behaved, and comfortable, but how to put them in that desirable condition is out of their philosophy. Children always depend more on the tender, watchful care of the mother, than of the father. Whether from nature, habit, or both, the mother is much more capable of administering to their health and comfort than the father, and therefore she has the best right to them. And where there is property, it ought to be divided equally between them, with an additional provision from the father towards the maintenance and education of the children. Much is said about the burdens and responsibilities of married men. Responsibilities indeed there are, if they but felt them; but as to burdens, what are they? The sole province of man seems to be centered in that one thing, attending to some business. I grant that owing to the present unjust and unequal reward for labor, many have to work too hard for a subsistence; but whatever his vocation, he has to attend as much to it before as after marriage. Look at your bachelors, and see if they do not strive as much for wealth, and attend as steadily to business, as married men. No! the husband has little or no increase of burden, and every increase of comfort after marriage; while most of the burdens, cares, pains, and penalties of married life fall on the wife. How unjust and cruel, then, to have all the laws in his favor! If any difference should be made, by law, between husband and wife, reason, justice, and humanity—if their voices were heard—would dictate that it should be in her favor.

It is high time to denounce such gross injustice, to compel

man by the might of right to give to woman her political, legal, and social rights. Open to her all the avenues of emolument, distinction, and greatness; give her an object for which to cultivate her powers, and a fair chance to do so, and there will be no need to speculate as to her proper sphere. She will find her own sphere in accordance with her capacities, powers, and tastes; and yet she will be woman still. Her rights will not change, but strengthen, develop, and elevate her nature. Away, then, with that folly and absurdity, that a possession of her rights would be detrimental to her character; that if she is recognized as the equal to man, she would cease to be woman. Have his rights as citizen of a republic, the elective franchise with all its advantages, so changed man's nature, that he has ceased to be man? Oh, no! But woman could not bear such a degree of power; what has benefited him, would injure her; what has strengthed him, would weaken her; what has prompted him to the performance of his duties, would make her neglect hers! Such is the superficial mode of reasoning—if it deserves that name—which is brought against the doctrine of woman's equality with man. It reminds me of two reasons given by a minister of Milton, on the North River. Having heard that I had spoken on the Rights of Woman, he took the subject up on the following Sunday; and in order to prove that woman should not have equal rights with man, he argued, first, that Adam was created before Eve, and secondly, that man was compared to the fore wheels, and woman to the hind wheels of a wagon. These reasons are about as philosophical as any that can be brought against the views we advocate.

But here is another difficulty. In point of principle, some say it is true that woman ought to have the same rights as man; but in carrying out this principle in practice, would you expose her to the contact of rough, rude, drinking, swearing, fighting men at the ballot-box? What a humiliating confession lies in this plea for keeping woman in the background! Is the brutality of some men, then, a reason why woman should be kept from her rights? If man, in his superior wisdom, cannot devise means to enable woman to deposit her vote without having her finer sensibilities shocked by such disgraceful conduct, then there is an additional reason, as well as necessity, why she should be there to civilize, refine, and purify him, even at the ballot-box.

Yes, in addition to the principle of right, this is one of the reasons, drawn from expediency, why woman should participate in all the important duties of life; for, with all due respect to the other sex, she is the true civilizer of man. With all my heart do I pity the man who has grown up and lives without the benign influence of woman. Even now, in spite of being considered the inferior, she exerts a most beneficial influence on man. Look at your annual festivities where woman is excluded, and you will find more or less drunkenness, disorder, vulgarity, and excess, to be the order of the day. Compare them with festive scenes where woman is the equal participant with man, and there you will see rational, social enjoyment and general decorum prevailing. If this is the case now—and who can deny it?—how much more beneficial would be woman's influence, if, as the equal with man, she should take her stand by his side, to cheer, counsel, and aid him through the drama of life, in the Legislative halls, in the Senate chamber, in the Judge's chair, in the jury box, in the Forum, in the Laboratory of the arts and sciences, and wherever duty would call her for the benefit of herself, her country, her race. For at every step she would carry with her a humanizing influence.

Oh! blind and misguided man! you know not what you do in opposing this great reform. It is not a partial affair confined to class, sect, or party. Nations have ever struggled against nations, people against despotic governments; from the times of absolute despotism to the present hour of comparative feedom, the weak have had to struggle against the strong, and right against might. But a new sign has appeared in our social zodiac, prophetic of the most important changes, pregnant with the most beneficial results, that have ever taken place in the annals of human history. We have before us a novel spectacle, an hitherto unheard-of undertaking, in comparison to which all others fall into insignificance, the grandest step in the onward progress of humanity. *One half of the race* stands up against the injustice and oppression of the other, and demands the recognition of its existence, and of its rights. Most sincerely do I pity those who have not advanced far enough to aid in this noble undertaking; for the attainment of woman's coequality with man is in itself not the *end*, but the most efficient *means* ever at the command of mankind towards a higher state of human elevation, without which the race can never attain it. Why should one half of the race keep the other half in subjugation? In this country it is considered wrong for one nation to enact laws and force them upon another. Does the same wrong not hold good of the sexes? Is woman a being like man? Then she is entitled to the same rights, is she not? How can he legislate rightfully for a being whose nature he cannot understand, whose motives he cannot appreciate, and whose feelings he cannot realize? How can he sit in judgment and pronounce a verdict against a being so entirely different from himself?

No! there is no reason against woman's elevation, but there are deep-rooted, hoary-headed prejudices. The main cause of them is, a pernicious falsehood propagated against her being, namely, that she is inferior by her nature. Inferior in what? What has man ever done, that woman, under the same advantages, could not do? In morals, bad as she is, she is generally considered his superior. In the intellectual sphere, give her a fair chance before you pronounce a verdict against her. Cultivate the frontal portion of her brain as much as that of man is cultivated, and she will stand his equal at least. Even now, where her mind has been called out at all, her intellect is as bright, as capacious, and as powerful as his. Will you tell us, that women have no Newtons, Shakspeares, and Byrons? Greater natural powers than even these possessed may have been destroyed in woman for want of proper culture, a just appreciation, reward for merit as an incentive to exertion, and freedom of action, without which, mind becomes cramped and stifled, for it cannot expand under bolts and bars; and yet, amid all blighting, crushing circumstances—confined within the narrowest possible limits, trampled upon by prejudice and injustice, from her education and position forced to occupy herself almost exclusively with the most trivial affairs—in spite of all these difficulties, her intellect is as good as his. The few bright meteors in man's intellectual horizon could well be matched by woman, were she allowed to occupy the same elevated position. There is no need of naming the De Staëls, the Rolands, the Somervilles, the Wollstonecrafts, the Sigourneys, the Wrights, the Martineaus, the Hemanses, the Fullers, Jagellos, and many more of modern as well as ancient times, to prove her mental powers, her patriotism, her self-sacrificing devotion to the cause of humanity, and the eloquence that gushes from her pen, or from her tongue. These things are too well known to require repetition. And do you ask for fortitude, energy, and perseverance? Then look at woman under suffering, reverse of fortune, and affliction, when the strength and power of man have sunk to the lowest ebb, when his mind is overwhelmed by the dark waters of despair. She, like the tender ivy plant, bent yet unbroken by the storms of life, not only upholds her own hopeful courage, but clings around the tempest-fallen oak, to speak hope to his faltering spirit, and shelter him from the returning blast of the storm.

Wherein then, again I ask, is man so much woman's superior, that he must for ever remain her master? In physical strength? Allow me to say, that therein the inmates of the forest are his superior. But even on this point, why is she the feeble, sickly, suffering being we behold her? Look to her most defective and irrational education, and you will find a solution of the problem. Is the girl allowed to expand her limbs and chest in healthful exercise in the fresh breezes of heaven? Is she allowed to inflate her lungs and make the welkin ring with her cheerful voice like the boy? Who ever heard of a girl committing such improprieties? A robust development in a girl is unfashionable, a healthy, sound voice is vulgar, a ruddy glow on the cheek is coarse; and when vitality is so strong within her as to show itself in spite of bolts and bars, then she has to undergo a bleaching process, eat lemons, drink vinegar, and keep in the shade.

And do you know why these irrationalities are practised? Because man wishes them to be delicate; for whatever he admires in woman will she possess. That is the influence man has over woman, for she has been made to believe that she was created for his benefit only. "It was not well for man to be alone," therefore she was made as a plaything to pass away an idle hour, or as a drudge to do his bidding; and until this falsehood is eradicated from her mind, until she feels that the necessities, services, and obligations of the sexes are mutual, that she is as independent of him as he is of her, that she is formed for the same aims and ends in life that he is—until, in fact, she has all rights equal with man, there will be no other object in her education, except to get married, and what will best promote that desirable end will be cultivated in her. Do you not yet understand what has made woman what she is? Then see what the sickly taste and perverted judgment of man now admires in woman. Not physical and mental vigor, but a pale, delicate face; hands too small to grasp a broom, for that were treason in a lady; a voice so sentimental and depressed, that what she says can be learned only by the moving of her half parted lips; and above all, that nervous sensibility which sees a ghost in every passing shadow, that beautiful diffidence which dares not take a step without the protecting arm of man to support her tender frame, and that shrinking mock-modesty that faints at the mention of a leg of a table. I know there are many noble exceptions, who see and deplore these irrationalities; but as a general thing, the facts are as I state, or else why that hue and cry of "mannish," "unfeminine," "out of her sphere," etc., whenever woman evinces any strength of body or mind, and takes interest in anything deserving of a rational being? Oh! the crying injustice towards woman. She is crushed at every step, and then insulted for being what a most pernicious education and corrupt public sentiment have made her. But there is no confidence in her powers, nor principles.

After last year's Woman's Convention, I saw an article in the *Christian Inquirer*, a Unitarian paper, edited by the Rev. Mr. Bellows, of New York, where, in reply to a correspondent on the subject of woman's rights, in which he strenuously opposed her taking part in anything in public, he said: "Place woman unbonneted and unshawled before the public gaze, and what becomes of her modesty and her virtue?" In his benighted mind, the modesty and virtue of woman is of so fragile a nature, that when it is in contact with the atmosphere, it evaporates like chloroform. But I refrain to comment on such a sentiment. It carries with it its own deep condemnation. When I read the article, I earnestly wished I had the ladies of the writer's congregation before me, to see whether they could realize the estimation their pastor held them in. Yet I hardly know which sentiment was strongest in me, contempt for such foolish opinions, or pity for a man that has so degrading an opinion of woman—of the being that gave him life, that sustained his helpless infancy with her ever watchful care, and laid the very foundation for the little mind he may possess—of the being he took to his bosom as the partner of his joys and sorrows—the one whom, when he strove to win her affection, he courted, as all such men court woman, like some divinity. Such a man deserves our pity; for I cannot realize that a man purposely and willfully degrades his Mother, Sister, Wife, and Daughter. No! my better nature, my best knowledge and conviction forbid me to believe it.

It is from ignorance, not malice, that man acts towards woman as he does. In ignorance of her nature, and the interest and happiness of both sexes, he conceived ideas, laid down rules, and enacted laws concerning her destiny and rights. The same ignorance, strengthened by age, sanctified by superstition, ingrafted into his being by habit, makes him carry these convictions out to the detriment of his own as well as her happiness; for is he not the loser by his injustice? Oh! how severely he suffers. Who can fathom the depth of misery and suffering to society from the subjugation and injury inflicted on woman? The race is elevated in excellence and power, or kept back in progression, in accordance with the scale of woman's position in society. But so firmly has prejudice closed the eyes of man to the light of truth, that though he feels the evils, he knows not their cause. Those men who have their eyes already open to these facts, earnestly desire the restoration of woman's rights, as the means of enabling her to take her proper position in the scale of humanity. If all men could see the truth, all would desire to aid this reform, as they desire their own happiness; for the interest and happiness of the sexes cannot be divided. Nature has too closely united them to permit one to oppress the other with impunity. I cast no more blame or reproach on man, however, than on woman, for she, from habit based on the same errors, is as much opposed to her interest and happiness as he is. How long is it, indeed, since any of us have come out of the darkness into the light of day? how long since any of us have advocated this righteous cause? The longest period is but, as it were, yesterday. And why has this been? From the same reason that so many of both sexes are opposed to it yet— ignorance. Both men and women have to be roused from that deathly lethargy in which they slumber. That worse than Egyptian darkness must be dispelled from their minds before the pure rays of the sun can penetrate them. And therefore, while I feel it my duty, ay, a painful duty, to point out the wrong done to woman and its consequences, and would do all in my power to aid in her deliverance, I can have no more ill feelings towards man than, for the same error, I have towards her. Both are the victims of error and ignorance, both suffer. Hence the necessity for active, earnest endeavors to enlighten their minds; hence the necessity for this, and many more Conventions, to protest against the wrong and claim our rights. And in so acting, we must not heed the taunts, ridicule, and stigmas cast upon us. We must remember that we have a crusade before us, far holier and more righteous than led warriors to Palestine—a crusade, not to deprive any one of his rights, but to claim our own. And as our cause is a nobler one, so also should be the means to achieve it. We therefore must put on the armor of charity, carry before us the banner of truth, and defend ourselves with the shield of right against the invaders of our liberty. And yet, like the knight of old, we must enlist in this holy cause with a disinterested devotion, energy, and determination never to turn back until we have conquered, not, indeed, by driving the Turk from his possession, but by claiming our rightful inheritance, for his benefit as well as for our own. To achieve this glorious victory of right over might, woman has much to do. Man may remove her legal shackles, and recognize her as his equal, which will greatly aid in her elevation; but the law cannot compel her to cultivate her mind and take an independent stand as a free being. She must cast off that mountain weight, that intimidating cowardly question, which like a nightmare presses down all her energies, namely, "What will people say? what will Mrs. Grundy say?" Away with such slavish fears! Woman must think for herself, and use for herself that greatest of all prerogatives—judgment of right and wrong. And next she must act according to her best convictions, irrespective of any other voice than that of right and duty. The time, I trust, will come, though slowly, yet surely, when woman will occupy that high and lofty position, for which nature has so eminently fitted her, in the destinies of humanity.

NEW YORK HERALD

The Woman's Rights Convention—
The Last Act of the Drama

SEPTEMBER 14, 1852

The year after Ernestine L. Rose gave her "unsurpassed" speech in Worcester, activists gathered in Syracuse for the third national woman's rights convention. From the beginning the movement drew derision and ridicule in the press, a harbinger of the hostile coverage it would receive throughout its long struggle. This editorial from the *New York Herald* encapsulates practically all of the themes and tropes used to belittle women's rights activists: they were "old maids," women who were unhappily married, mannish women, and henpecked men. Only Rose was signaled out for praise for her "argumentative power." In response to the perennial question of "what do women want?" the editorial writer was aghast that women so forcefully demanded access to the public realm generally ceded to men. Didn't they realize that they were naturally inferior to men, just as "the negro" was inferior to the white race? Then came a litany of the awful things that would happen when women ventured into the public realm, many of which centered on the fanciful idea of women giving birth in the midst of their new duties.

The farce at Syracuse has been played out. We publish, to-day, the last act, in which it will be seen that the authority of the Bible, as a perfect rule of faith and practice for human beings, was voted down; and what are called the laws of nature set up instead of the Christian code. We have also a practical exhibition of the consequences that flow from woman leaving her true sphere where she wields all her influence, and coming into public to discuss questions of morals and politics with men. The scene in which Rev. Mr. Hatch violated the decorum of his cloth, and was coarsely offensive to such ladies present as had not lost that modest "feminine element," on which he dwelt so forcibly, is the natural result of the conduct of the women themselves, who, in the first place, invited discussion about sexes, and in the second place so broadly defined the difference between the male and the female as to be suggestive of anything but purity to the audience. The women of the convention have no right to complain; but for the sake of his clerical character, if no other motive influenced him, he ought not to have followed so bad an example. His speech was sound, and his argument conclusive, but his form of words was not in the best taste. The female orators were the aggressors; but, to use his own language, he ought not to have measured swords with a woman, especially when he regarded her ideas and expressions as bordering upon the obscene. But all this is the natural result of woman placing herself in a false position. As Rev. Mr. Hatch observed, if she ran with horses, she must expect to be betted upon. The whole tendency of these conventions is by no means to increase the influence of woman, to elevate her condition, or to command the respect of the other sex. It is quite the reverse. We do not wonder that, after what has taken place, they should shun the light of New York city, and retreat to the obscurity of Cleveland for their next gathering.

Who are these women?—what do they want?—what are the motives that impel them to this course of action? The *dramatis personæ* of the farce enacted at Syracuse, present a curious conglomeration of both sexes; some of them are old maids, whose personal charms were never very attractive, and who have been sadly slighted by the masculine gender in general; some of them women who have been badly mated, whose own temper, or their husbands, has made life anything but agreeable to them, and they are therefore down upon the whole of the opposite sex; some having so much of the virago in their disposition, that nature appears to have made a mistake in their gender— mannish women like hens that crow; some of boundless vanity and egotism, who believe that they are superior in intellectual ability to "all the world and the rest of mankind," and delight to see their speeches and addresses in print; some silly little girls, of from fifteen to twenty, who are tickled to death with the idea of being one day a great orator, a lawyer, a doctor, a member of Congress, a general in the army, perhaps President of the United States—and some who do not like to work for a living, or to perform the duties of the domestic circle, but to spend their time in talking and gossiping, and longing for a millennium of idleness, when, without any effort of their own, they shall "eat, drink, and be merry," "be clothed in purple and fine linen, and fare sumptuously every day," reigning as queens and potentates all of which shall be but a realization of their rights; and man shall be consigned to his proper sphere, nursing the babies, washing the dishes, mending stockings, and sweeping the house. This is "the good time coming." Besides the classes we have enumerated, there is a class of wild enthusiasts and visionaries—very sincere, but very mad—having the same vein as the fanatical abolitionists, and the majority, if not all of them, being, in point of fact, deeply imbued with the anti-slavery sentiment. Of the male sex who attend these conventions for the purpose of taking a part in them, the majority are hen-pecked husbands, and all of them ought to wear petticoats.

In point of ability, the majority of the women are flimsy, flippant, and superficial. If Lucretia Mott, Mrs. Oakes Smith, Mrs. Paulina Davis, Lucy Stone, and Mrs. Rose, particularly the latter, are exceptions, they but confirm the rule. Even of these Mrs. Rose alone indicates much argumentative power; and in reading Mrs. Oakes Smith's book, of which so much has been said, and which the *Westminster Review* pronounces the ablest work that has been written on the subject, (no great praise after all,) we are wholly at a loss to discover anything beyond smartness, and gracefulness of style, with much that is labored, and smacks of affectation. While it contains a great deal of truth that is not new, in reference to premature marriages and other topics, it carefully avoids all close reasoning upon the real points at issue. In fact, it surrenders the main point contended for at the late convention—the physical and mental equality of woman as the basis of her political equality. Miss Lucy Stone and others contended that there was no difference, physically or mentally, between the sexes, except the bare fact of gender. Mrs. Smith knows better, and accordingly she did not venture to commit herself to that doctrine in her book. In one short sentence we can answer all that has been said for the three days at this Convention, and at all other Conventions:—If it be true that the female sex are equal to the male in point of physical strength and mental power, how is it that from the beginning of the world to the present time, in all ages, in all countries and climes, in every variety of the human species, the male has been predominant, and the female subject, politically, socially, and in the family circle? In no other nation or tribe was woman ever so honored as she is in the United States. If the female sex was ever equal to the male, there would be some record left in history of the women changing places with the men in the work of legislation, and those other objects and pursuits of life that require superior force of body and mind. How did woman first become subject to man as she now is all over the world? By her nature—her sex—just as the negro is and always will be, to the end of time, inferior to the white race, and, therefore, doomed to subjection; but happier than she would be in any other condition, just because it is the law of her nature. The women themselves would not have this law reversed. It is a significant fact, that even Mrs. Swisshelm, who formerly ran about to all such gatherings from her husband, is now "a keeper at home," and condemns these conventions in her paper. How does this happen? Because, after weary years of unfruitfulness, she has at length got her rights in the shape of a baby. This is the best cure for the mania, and we would recommend a trial of it to all who are afflicted.

We are well aware that women of great vigor of mind, and some of immense power of body, have arisen from time to time, while men of weak intellect and mean bodily strength are numerous enough. But individual cases prove nothing—it is the prevailing characteristics of the great mass of each sex that must determine the relative positions of both. Accordingly the very laws of nature, which the Woman's Rights Convention profess to respect, as well as the Bible, whose authority they scout, settle the question for ever.

While man has strength woman has beauty of body and mind, and the result of the union is harmony. In her moral qualities, and in the acuteness of her perceptions, woman is superior to man; but in the high intellectual endowments, and in the attributes of physical power, she is inferior, and hence her domestic, social, and political subordination, and hence also the impossibility of ever accomplishing what Mrs. Oakes Smith, in her speech on the first day of the convention, avowed to be the object and aim of this movement, "an entire subversion of the existing order of society, a dissolution of the whole existing social compact."

What do the leaders of the Woman's Rights Convention want? They want to vote, and to hustle with the rowdies at the polls. They want to be members of Congress, and in the heat of debate to subject themselves to coarse jests and indecent language, like that of Rev. Mr. Hatch. They want to fill all other posts which men are ambitious to occupy—to be lawyers, doctors, captains of vessels, and generals in the field. How funny it would sound in the newspaper, that Lucy Stone pleading a cause took suddenly ill in the pains of parturition, and perhaps gave birth to a fine bouncing boy in court! Or that Rev. Antoinette Brown was arrested in the middle of her sermon in the pulpit from the same cause, and presented a "pledge" to her husband and the congregation; or, that Dr. Harriot K. Hunt, while attending a gentleman patient for a fit of the gout or *fistula in ano*, found it necessary to send for a doctor, there and then, and to be delivered of a man or woman child—perhaps twins. A similar event might happen on the floor of Congress—in a storm at sea—or in the raging tempest of battle, and then what was to become of the woman legislator, the female captain of the ship, or the female general of the army. The bare idea is ludicrous beyond measure.

It is worthy of remark, that the women's rights folks complain that they find women more inimical to their pretensions than men. It is no wonder that all true, discreet, sensible women, would feel that their sex is turned into ridicule by such folly, and that they evince their hostility to it in every shape and form. It is the natural offspring of the silly socialist and abolition doctrines that have agitated this country for a number of years; and we find that the same men and the same women, including Lloyd Garrison, Rev. W. H. Channing, Rev. Mr. May, Gerrit Smith, the Joneses, Lucy Stone, Horace Greeley and Lucretia Mott, that have been actively engaged in those agitations, are equally busy in this. What a pass are we brought to at last!

HARRIOT K. HUNT

Tax Protest

1852

"No taxation without representation," the rallying cry of the American Revolution, continued to resonate in the decades after independence. The women's suffrage movement found it an especially effective argument and deployed it frequently. Starting in 1852, Boston physician Harriot Kezia Hunt (1805–1875) publicly protested the injustice of being assessed for taxes on property she owned without being able to have a say in how that money was allocated and spent. Like many other early suffragists, she contrasted her voteless, taxpaying status—no matter how much property she owned or how upstanding a citizen she was—to other groups she considered undesirable, such as drunkards, felons, "idiots," and "lunatics," who enjoyed the right of voting because they were men. "Wherein," she asked, "is the justice, equality, or wisdom of this?" A successful and well-regarded physician, Hunt was no stranger to controversy. In 1847 she applied to attend lectures at Harvard Medical College but was denied on account of her sex. (Harvard Medical School did not admit women until 1945.) In 1850 she attended the first national woman's rights convention in Worcester and became an active supporter of the cause. Her attempt to gain admission to medical school paved the way for the first generation of women medical graduates in the 1850s and 1860s.

―――――――――

To Frederick U. Tracy, Treasurer, and the Assessors, and other authorities of the City of Boston, and the citizens generally.

Harriot K. Hunt, physician, a native and permanent resident of the City of Boston, and for many years a tax payer therein, in making payment of her city taxes for the coming year, begs leave to protest against the injustice and inequality of levying taxes upon women, and at the same time refusing them any voice or vote in the imposition and expenditure of the same. The only classes of male persons, required to pay taxes, and not at the same time allowed the privilege of voting, are aliens and minors. The objection in the case of aliens, is, their supposed want of interest in our institutions and knowledge of them. The objection in case of minors is, the want of sufficient understanding. These objections certainly cannot apply to women, natives of the city, all whose property and interests are here, and who have accumulated by their own sagacity and industry, the very property on which they are taxed. But this is not all; the alien by going through the forms of naturalization, the minor on coming of age, obtain the right of voting, and so long as they continue to pay a mere poll-tax of a dollar and a half, they may continue to exercise it, though so ignorant as not to be able to *sign* their names, or *read* the very votes they put into the ballot boxes. Even drunkards, felons, idiots, or lunatics of *men*, may still enjoy that right of voting, to which no woman, however large the amount of taxes she pays, however respectable her character, or useful her life, can ever attain. Wherein, your remonstrant would inquire, is the justice, equality, or wisdom of this? That the rights and interests of the female part of community are sometimes forgotten or disregarded in consequence of their deprivation of political rights, is strikingly evinced, as appears to your remonstrant, in the organization and administration of the city public schools. Though there are open in this State and neighborhood, a great multitude of colleges and professional schools, for the education of boys and young men, yet the city has very properly provided two high schools of its own, one Latin, the other English, at which the *male graduates* of the grammar schools may pursue their education still further at the public expense, and why is not a like provision made for the girls? Why is the public provision for *their* education stopped short, just as they have attained the age best fitted for progress, and the preliminary knowledge necessary to facilitate it, thus giving the advantage of superior culture to *sex*, not to mind? The fact that our colleges and professional schools are closed against females, of which your remonstrant has had personal and painful experience, having been in the year 1847, after twelve years of medical practice in Boston, refused permission to attend the lectures of Harvard Medical College, that fact would seem to furnish an additional reason, why the city should provide at its own expense, those means of superior education, which, by supplying our girls with occupation and objects of interest, would not only save them from lives of frivolity and emptiness, but which might open the way to many useful and lucrative pursuits, and so raise them above that *degrading dependence*, so fruitful a source of female misery.

Reserving a more full exposition of the subject to future occasions, your remonstrant in paying her tax for the current year, begs leave to *protest* against the injustice and inequalities above pointed out.

This is respectfully submitted,

HARRIOT K. HUNT, 32 Green street.

BOSTON, Oct. 18, 1852.

ELIZABETH CADY STANTON

Address to the Legislature of New-York
FEBRUARY 1854

Sixteen years after Angelina Grimké addressed the Massachusetts legislature, Elizabeth Cady Stanton delivered an address to the New York State legislature timed to coincide with the state woman's rights convention being held in Albany, which formally adopted Stanton's remarks. Stanton's foray to the state capital was a rare outing away from her bustling household in Seneca Falls, where she raised five children ranging in age from two to twelve while her husband was often away on business. (She would have two more children: a daughter Harriot in 1856, who became an important suffragist in her own right, and a son in 1859, when she was forty-four.) Stanton's address showcased both her familiarity with the law, which is perhaps not so surprising given that she was the daughter of a judge, and her wide-ranging erudition, which was unusual for women at the time. A voracious reader and skilled debater, Stanton benefitted from the formal schooling she received at the Johnstown Academy and then at the Troy Female Seminary run by Emma Willard (1787–1870). As a result of these opportunities as well as her innate intelligence, Stanton knew how to construct a case and relished the chance to make it forcefully in a public setting. This treatise on the status of women, legal and otherwise, was one of her earliest public speeches.

———————

To the Legislature of the State of New-York:

"The thinking minds of all nations call for change. There is a deeplying struggle in the whole fabric of society; a boundless, grinding collision of the New with the Old."

THE tyrant, Custom, has been summoned before the bar of Common Sense. His Majesty no longer awes the multitude—his sceptre is broken—his crown is trampled in the dust—the sentence of death is pronounced upon him. All nations, ranks and classes have, in turn, questioned and repudiated his authority; and now, that the monster is chained and caged, timid woman, on tiptoe, comes to look him in the face, and to demand of her brave sires and sons, who have struck stout blows for liberty, if, in this change of dynasty, she, too, shall find relief.

Yes, gentlemen, in republican America, in the 19th century, we, the daughters of the revolutionary heroes of '76, demand at your hands the redress of our grievances—a revision of your state constitution—a new code of laws. Permit us then, as briefly as possible, to call your attention to the legal disabilities under which we labor.

1st. Look at the position of woman as woman. It is not enough for us that by your laws we are permitted to live and breathe, to claim the necessaries of life from our legal protectors—to pay the penalty of our crimes; we demand the full recognition of all our rights as citizens of the Empire State. We are persons; native, free-born citizens; property-holders, tax-payers; yet are we denied the exercise of our right to the elective franchise. We support ourselves, and, in part, your schools, colleges, churches, your poor-houses, jails, prisons, the army, the navy, the whole machinery of government, and yet we have no voice in your councils. We have every qualification required by the constitution, necessary to the legal voter, but the one of sex. We are moral, virtuous and intelligent, and in all respects quite equal to the proud white man himself, and yet by your laws we are classed with idiots, lunatics and negroes; and though we do not feel honored by the place assigned us, yet, in fact, our legal position is lower than that of either; for the negro can be raised to the dignity of a voter if he possess himself of $250; the lunatic can vote in his moments of sanity, and the idiot, too, if he be a male one, and not more than nine-tenths a fool; but we, who have guided great movements of charity, established missions, edited journals, published works on history, economy and statistics; who have governed nations, led armies, filled the professor's chair, taught philosophy and mathematics to the *savans* of our age, discovered planets, piloted ships across the sea, are denied the most sacred rights of citizens, because, forsooth, we came not into this republic crowned with the dignity of manhood! Woman is theoretically absolved from all allegiance to the laws of the state. Sec. 1, Bill of Rights, 2 R. S., 301, says that no authority can, on any pretence whatever, be exercised over the citizens of this state but such as is or shall be derived from, and *granted by, the people of this state.*

Now, gentlemen, we would fain know by what authority you have disfranchised one-half the people of this state? You who have so boldly taken possession of the bulwarks of this republic, show us your credentials, and thus prove your exclusive right to govern, not only yourselves, but us. Judge Hurlbut, who has long occupied a high place at the bar in this state, and who recently retired with honor from the bench of the Supreme Court, in his profound work on human rights, has pronounced your present position rank usurpation. Can it be that here, where are acknowledged no royal blood, no apostolic descent, that you, who have declared that all men were created equal—that governments derive their just powers from the consent of the governed, would willingly build up an aristocracy that places the ignorant and vulgar above the educated and refined—the alien and the ditch-digger above the authors and poets of the day—an aristocracy that would raise the sons above the mothers that bore them? Would that the men who can sanction a constitution so opposed to the genius of this government, who can enact and execute laws so degrading to womankind, had sprung, Minerva-like, from the brains of their fathers, that the matrons of this republic need not blush to own their sons! Woman's position, under our free institutions, is much lower than under the monarchy of England. "In England the idea of woman holding official station is not so strange as in the United States. The Countess of Pembroke, Dorset and Montgomery held the office of hereditary sheriff of Westmoreland, and exercised it in person. At the assizes at Appleby, she sat with the judges on the bench. In a reported case, it is stated by counsel, and substantially assented to by the court, that a woman is capable of serving in almost all the offices of the kingdom, such as those of queen, marshal, great chamberlain and constable of England, the champion of England, commissioner of sewers, governor of work house, sexton, keeper of the prison, of the gate house of the dean and chapter of Westminster, returning officer for members of parliament, and constable, the latter of which is in some respects judicial. The office of jailor is frequently exercised by a woman. In the United States a woman may administer on the effects of her deceased husband, and she has occasionally held a subordinate place in the post office department. She has therefore a sort of post mortem, post mistress notoriety; but with the exception of handling letters of administration and letters mailed, she is the submissive creature of the old common law." True, the unmarried woman has a right to the property she inherits and the money she earns, but she is taxed without representation. And here again you place the negro, so unjustly degraded by you, in a superior position to your own wives and mothers; for colored males, if possessed of a certain amount of property and certain other qualifications, can vote, but if they do not have these qualifications *they are not subject to direct taxation*; wherein they have the advantage of woman, she being subject to taxation for whatever amount she may possess. (Constitution of N. Y., article 2, sec. 2.) But, say you, are not all women sufficiently represented by their fathers, husbands and brothers? Let your statute books answer the question.

Again we demand, in criminal cases, that most sacred of all rights, trial by a jury of our own peers. The establishment of trial by jury is of so early a date that its beginning is lost in antiquity; but the right of trial by a jury of one's own peers is a great, progressive step of advanced civilization. No rank of men have ever been satisfied with being tried by jurors higher or lower in the civil or political scale than themselves; for jealousy on the one hand, and contempt on the other, has ever effectually blinded the eyes of justice. Hence, all along the pages of history, we find the king, the noble, the peasant, the cardinal, the priest, the layman, each in turn protesting against the authority of the tribunal before which they were summoned to appear. Charles the First refused to recognize the competency of the tribunal which condemned him: For how, said he, can subjects judge a king? The stern descendants of our Pilgrim Fathers refused to answer for their crimes before an English Parliament. For how, said they, can a king judge rebels? And shall woman here consent to be tried by her liege lord, who has dubbed himself law-maker, judge, juror, and sheriff, too?— whose power, though sanctioned by Church and State, has no foundation in justice and equity, and is a bold assumption of our inalienable rights. In England a parliament-lord could challenge a jury where a knight was not empannelled. An alien could demand a jury composed half of his own countrymen; or, in some special cases, juries were even constituted entirely of women. Having seen that man fails to do justice to woman in her best estate, to the virtuous, the noble, the true of our sex, should we trust to his tender mercies, the weak, the ignorant, the morally insane? It is not to be denied that the interests of man and woman in the present undeveloped state of the race, and under the existing social arrangements, are and must be antagonistic. The nobleman cannot make just laws for the peasant; the slaveholder for the slave; neither can man make and execute just laws for woman, because in each case, the one in power fails to apply the immutable principles of right to any grade but his own. Shall an erring woman be dragged before a bar of grim-visaged judges, lawyers and jurors, there to be grossly questioned in public on subjects which women scarce breathe in secret to one another? Shall the most sacred relations of life be called up and rudely scanned by men who, by their own admission, are so coarse that women could not meet them even at the polls without contamination? and yet shall she find there no woman's face or voice to pity and defend? Shall the frenzied mother who, to save herself and child from exposure and disgrace, ended the life that had but just begun, be dragged before such a tribunal to answer for her crime? How can man enter into the feelings of that mother? How can he judge of the mighty agonies of soul that impelled her to such an outrage of maternal instincts? How can he weigh the mountain of sorrow that crushed that mother's heart when she wildly tossed her helpless babe into the cold waters of the midnight sea? Where is he who by false vows thus blasted this trusting woman? Had that helpless child no claims on his protection? Ah, he is freely abroad in the dignity of manhood, in the pulpit, in the bench, in the professor's chair. The imprisonment of his victim and the death of his child, detract not a tithe from his standing and complacency. His peers made the law, and shall law-makers lay nets for those of their own rank? Shall laws which come from the logical brain of man take cognizance of violence done to the moral and affectional nature which predominates, as is said, in woman? Statesmen of New-York, whose daughters, guarded by your affection, and lapped amidst luxuries which your indulgence spreads, care more for their nodding plumes and velvet trains than for the statute laws by which their persons and properties are held—who, blinded by custom and prejudice to the degraded position which they and their sisters occupy in the civil scale, haughtily claim that they already have all rights they want, how, think ye, you would feel to see a daughter summoned for such a crime—and remember these daughters are but human—before such a tribunal? Would it not, in that hour, be some consolation to see that she was surrounded by the wise and virtuous of her own sex; by those who had known the depth of a mother's love and the misery of a lover's falsehood; to know that to these she could make her confession, and from them receive her sentence? If so, then listen to our just demands and make such a change in your laws as will secure to every woman tried in your courts, an impartial jury. At this moment among the hundreds of women who are shut up in prisons in this state, not one has enjoyed that most sacred of all rights—that right which you would die to defend for yourselves—trial by a jury of one's peers.

2d. Look at the position of woman as wife. Your laws relating to marriage—founded as they are on the old common law of England, a compound of barbarous usages, but partially modified by progressive civilization—are in open violation of our enlightened ideas of justice, and of the holiest feelings of our nature. If you take the highest view of marriage, as a Divine relation, which love alone can constitute and sanctify, then of course human legislation can only recognize it. Man can neither bind or loose its ties, for that prerogative belongs to God alone, who makes man and woman, and the laws of attraction by which they are united. But if you regard marriage as a civil contract, then let it be subject to the same laws which control all other contracts. Do not make it a kind of half-human, half-divine institution, which you may build up but cannot regulate. Do not, by your special legislation for this one kind of contract, involve yourselves in the grossest absurdities and contradictions.

So long as by your laws no man can make a contract for a horse or piece of land until he is twenty-one years of age, and by which contract he is not bound if any deception has been practiced, or if the party contracting has not fulfilled his part of the agreement—so long as the parties in all mere civil contracts retain their identity and all the power and independence they had before contracting, with the full right to dissolve all partnerships and contracts for any reason, at the will and option of the parties themselves, upon what principle of civil jurisprudence do you permit the boy of fourteen and the girl of twelve, in violation of every natural law, to make a contract more momentous in importance than any other, and then hold them to it, come what may, the whole of their natural lives, in spite of disappointment, deception and misery? Then, too, the signing of this contract is instant civil death to one of the parties. The woman who but yesterday was sued on bended knee, who stood so high in the scale of being as to make an agreement on equal terms with a proud Saxon man, to-day has no civil existence, no social freedom. The wife who inherits no property holds about the same legal position that does the slave on the southern plantation. She can own nothing, sell nothing. She has no right even to the wages she earns; her person, her time, her services are the property of another. She cannot testify, in many cases, against her husband. She can get no redress for wrongs in her own name in any court of justice. She can neither sue nor be sued. She is not held morally responsible for any crime committed in the presence of her husband, so completely is her very existence supposed by the law to be merged in that of another. Think of it; your wives may be thieves, libellers, burglars, incendiaries, and for crimes like these they are not held amenable to the laws of the land, if they but commit them in your dread presence. For them, alas! there is no higher law than the will of man. Herein behold the bloated conceit of these Petruchios of the law, who seem to say:

> "Nay, look not big, nor stamp, nor stare, nor fret,
> I will be master of what is mine own;
> She is my goods, my chattels; she is my house,
> My household stuff, my field, my barn,
> My horse, my ox, my ass, my anything;
> And here she stands, touch her whoever dare;
> I'll bring my action on the proudest he,
> That stops my way, in Padua."

How could man ever look thus on woman?—She, at whose feet Socrates learned wisdom—she, who gave to the world a Saviour, and witnessed alike the adoration of the Magi and the agonies of the Cross. How could such a being, so blessed and honored, ever become the ignoble, servile, cringing slave, with whom the fear of man could be paramount to the sacred dictates of conscience and the holy love of Heaven? By the common law of England, the spirit of which has been but too faithfully incorporated into our statute law, a husband has a right to whip his wife with a rod not larger than his thumb, to shut her up in a room, and administer whatever moderate chastisement he may deem necessary to insure obedience to his wishes, and for her healthful moral development! He can forbid all persons harboring or trusting her on his account. He can deprive her of all social intercourse with her nearest and dearest friends. If by great economy she accumulates a small sum, which for future need she deposit, little by little, in a savings bank, the husband has a right to draw it out, at his option, to use it as he may see fit.

"Husband is entitled to wife's credit or business talents (whenever their intermarriage may have occurred); and goods purchased by her on her own credit, with his consent, while cohabiting with him, can be seized and sold in execution against him for his own debts, and this, though she carry on business in her own name."—7 *Howard's Practice Reports*, 105, *Lovett agt. Robinson and Witbeck, sheriff, &c.*

"No letters of administration shall be granted to a person convicted of infamous crime; nor to any one incapable by law of making a contract; nor to a person not a citizen of the United States, unless such person reside within this state; nor to any one who is under twenty-one years of age; nor to any person who shall be adjudged incompetent by the surrogate to execute duties of such trust, by reason of drunkenness, improvidence, or want of understanding, nor any married woman; but where a married woman is entitled to administration, the same may be granted to her husband in her right and behalf."

There is nothing that an unruly wife might do against which the husband has not sufficient protection in the law. But not so with the wife. If she have a worthless husband, a confirmed drunkard, a villain or a vagrant, he has still all the rights of a man, a husband and a father. Though the whole support of the family be thrown upon the wife, if the wages she earns be paid to her by her employer, the husband can receive them again. If, by unwearied industry and perseverance, she can earn for herself and children a patch of ground and a shed to cover them, the husband can strip her of all her hard earnings, turn her and her little ones out in the cold northern blast, take the clothes from their backs, the bread from their mouths; all this by your laws may he do, and has he done, oft and again, to satisfy the rapacity of that monster in human form, the rumseller.

But the wife who is so fortunate as to have inherited property, has, by the new law in this state, been redeemed from her lost condition. She is no longer a legal nonentity. This property law, if fairly construed, will overturn the whole code relating to woman and property. The right to property implies the right to buy and sell, to will and bequeath, and herein is the dawning of a civil existence for woman, for now the "femme covert" must have the right to make contracts. So, get ready, gentlemen; the "little justice" will be coming to you one day, deed in hand, for your acknowledgment. When he asks you "if you sign without fear or compulsion," say yes, boldly, as we do. Then, too, the right to will is ours. Now what becomes of the "tenant for life?" Shall he, the happy husband of a millionaire, who has lived in yonder princely mansion in the midst of plenty and elegance, be cut down in a day to the use of one-third of this estate and a few hundred a year, as long as he remains her widower? And should he, in spite of this bounty on celibacy, impelled by his affections, marry again, choosing for a wife a woman as poor as himself, shall he be thrown penniless on the cold world—this child of fortune, enervated by ease and luxury, henceforth to be dependent wholly on his own resources? Poor man! He would be rich, though, in the *sympathies* of many women who have passed through just such an ordeal. But what is property without the right to protect that property by law? It is mockery to say a certain estate is mine, if, without my consent, you have the right to tax me when and how you please, while I have no voice in making the tax-gatherer, the legislator or the law. The right to property will, of necessity, compel us in due time to the exercise of our right to the elective franchise, and then naturally follows the right to hold office.

3d. Look at the position of woman as widow. Whenever we attempt to point out the wrongs of the wife, those who would have us believe that the laws cannot be improved, point us to the privileges, powers and claims of the widow. Let us look into these a little. Behold in yonder humble house a married pair, who, for long years, have lived together, childless and alone. Those few acres of well-tilled land, with the small white house that looks so cheerful through its vines and flowers, attest the honest thrift and simple taste of its owners. This man and woman, by their hard days' labor, have made this home their own. Here they live in peace and plenty, happy in the hope that they may dwell together securely under their own vine and fig tree for the few years that remain to them, and that under the shadow of these trees, planted by their own hands, and in the midst of their household gods, so loved and familiar, here may take their last farewell of earth. But, alas for human hopes! the husband dies, and without will, and the stricken widow, at one fell blow, loses the companion of her youth, her house and home, and half the little sum she had in bank. For the law, which takes no cognizance of widows left with twelve children and not one cent, instantly spies out this widow, takes account of her effects, and announces to her the startling intelligence that but one-third of the house and lot, and one-half the personal property, are hers. The law has other favorites with whom she must share the hard-earned savings of years. In this dark hour of grief, the coarse minions of the law gather round the widow's hearthstone, and, in the name of justice, outrage all natural sense of right; mock at the sacredness of human love, and with cold familiarity proceed to place a monied value on the old arm chair, in which, but a few brief hours since, she closed the eyes that had ever beamed on her with kindness and affection; on the solemn clock in the corner, that told the hour he passed away; on every garment with which his form and presence were associated, and on every article of comfort and convenience that the house contained, even down to the knives and forks and spoons—and the widow saw it all—and when the work was done, she gathered up what the law allowed her and went forth to seek her another home! This is the much talked of widow's dower. Behold the magnanimity of the law in allowing the widow to retain a life interest in one-third the landed estate, and one-half the personal property of her husband, and taking the lion's share to itself! Had she died first, the house and land would all have been the husband's still. No one would have dared to intrude upon the privacy of his home or to molest him in his sacred retreat of sorrow.

How, I ask you, can that be called justice, which makes such a distinction as this between man and woman?

By management, economy and industry, our widow is able, in a few years, to redeem her house and home. But the law never loses sight of the purse, no matter how low in the scale of being its owner may be. It sends its officers round every year to gather in the harvest for the public crib, and no widow who owns a piece of land two feet square ever escapes this reckoning. Our widow, too, who has now twice earned her home, has her annual tax to pay also—a tribute of gratitude that she is permitted to breathe the free air of this republic, where "taxation without representation," by such worthies as John Hancock and Samuel Adams, has been declared "intolerable tyranny." Having glanced at the magnanimity of the law in its dealings with the widow, let us see how the individual man, under the influence of such laws, doles out justice to his helpmate. The husband has the absolute right to will away his property as he may see fit. If he has children, he can divide his property among them, leaving his wife her third only of the landed estate, thus making her a dependent on the bounty of her own children. A man with thirty thousand dollars in personal property, may leave his wife but a few hundred a year, as long as she remains his widow.

The cases are without number where women, who have lived in ease and elegance, at the death of their husbands have, by will, been reduced to the bare necessaries of life. The man who leaves his wife the sole guardian of his property and children is an exception to the general rule. Man has ever manifested a wish that the world should indeed be a blank to the companion whom he leaves behind him. The Hindoo makes that wish a law, and burns the widow on the funeral pile of her husband; but the civilized man, impressed with a different view of the sacredness of life, takes a less summary mode of drawing his beloved partner after him; he does it by the deprivation and starvation of the flesh, and the humiliation and mortification of the spirit. In bequeathing to the wife just enough to keep soul and body together, man seems to lose sight of the fact that woman, like himself, takes great pleasure in acts of benevolence and charity. It is but just, therefore, that she should have it in her power to give during her life, and to will away at her death, as her benevolence or obligations might prompt her to do.

4th. Look at the position of woman as *mother*. There is no human love so generous, strong and steadfast as that of the mother for her child; yet behold how cruel and ruthless are your laws touching this most sacred relation.

Nature has clearly made the mother the guardian of the child; but man, in his inordinate love of power, does continually set nature and nature's laws at open defiance. The father may apprentice his child, bind him out to a trade or labor, without the mother's consent—yea, in direct opposition to her most earnest entreaties, her prayers and tears.

He may apprentice his son to a gamester or rumseller, and thus cancel his debts of *honor*. By the abuse of this absolute power, he may bind his daughter to the owner of a brothel, and, by the degradation of his child, supply his daily wants; and such things, gentlemen, have been done in our very midst. Moreover, the father, about to die, may bind out all his children wherever and to whomsoever he may see fit, and thus, in fact, will away the guardianship of all his children from the mother. The Revised Statutes of New-York provide that "every father, whether of full age or a minor, of a child to be born, or of any living child under the age of twenty-one years, and unmarried, may by his *deed or last will*, duly executed, dispose of the custody and tuition of such child during its minority, or for any less time, to any person or persons, in possession or remainder." 2 R. S., page 150, sec. 1.

Thus, by your laws, the child is the absolute property of the father, wholly at his disposal in life or at death.

In case of separation, the law gives the children to the father; no matter what his character or condition. At this very time we can point you to noble, virtuous, well educated mothers in this state, who have abandoned their husbands for their profligacy and confirmed drunkenness. All these have been robbed of their children, who are in the custody of the husband, under the care of his relatives, whilst the mothers are permitted to see them but at stated intervals. But, said one of these mothers, with a grandeur of attitude and manner worthy the noble

Roman matron in the palmiest days of that republic, I would rather never see my child again, than be the medium to hand down the low, animal nature of its father, to stamp degradation on the brow of another innocent being. It is enough that one child of his shall call me mother. If you are far sighted statesmen, and do wisely judge of the interests of this commonwealth, you will so shape your future laws as to encourage woman to take the high moral ground that the father of her children must be great and good.

Instead of your present laws, which make the mother and her children the victims of vice and license, you might rather pass laws prohibiting to all drunkards, libertines and fools, the rights of husbands and fathers. Do not the hundreds of laughing idiots that are crowding into our asylums, appeal to the wisdom of our statesmen for some new laws on marriage—to the mothers of this day for a higher, purer morality?

Again, as the condition of the child always follows that of the mother, and as by the abuse of your laws the father may beat the mother, so may he the child. What mother cannot bear me witness to untold sufferings which cruel, vindictive fathers have visited upon their helpless children? Who ever saw a human being that would not abuse unlimited power? Base and ignoble must that man be, who, let the provocation be what it may, would strike a woman; but he who would lacerate a trembling child is unworthy the name of man. A mother's love can be no protection to a child; she cannot appeal to you to save it from a father's cruelty, for the laws take no cognizance of the mother's most grievous wrongs. Neither at home nor abroad can a mother protect her son. Look at the temptations that surround the paths of our youth at every step; look at the gambling and drinking saloons, the club rooms, the dens of infamy and abomination that infest all our villages and cities— slowly but surely sapping the very foundations of all virtue and strength.

By your laws, all these abominable resorts are permitted. It is folly to talk of a mother moulding the character of her son, when all mankind, backed up by law and public sentiment, conspire to destroy her influence. But when woman's moral power shall speak through the ballot-box, then shall her influence be seen and felt; then, in our legislative debates, such questions as the canal tolls on salt, the improvement of rivers and harbors, and the claims of Mr. Smith for damages against the state, would be secondary to the consideration of the legal existence of all these public resorts, which lure our youth on to excessive indulgence and destruction.

Many times and oft it has been asked us, with unaffected seriousness, "what do you women want? What are you aiming at?" Many have manifested a laudable curiosity to know what the wives and daughters could complain of in republican America, where their sires and sons have so bravely fought for freedom and gloriously secured their independence, trampling all tyranny, bigotry and caste in the dust, and declaring to a waiting world the divine truth that all men are created equal. What can *woman* want under such a government? Admit a radical difference in sex and you demand different spheres—water for fish, and air for birds.

It is impossible to make the southern planter believe that his slave feels and reasons just as he does—that injustice and subjection are as galling as to him—that the degradation of living by the will of another, the mere dependent on his caprice, at the mercy of his passions, is as keenly felt by him as his master. If you can force on his unwilling vision a vivid picture of the negro's wrongs, and for a moment touch his soul, his logic brings him instant consolation. He says, the slave does not feel this as I would. Here, gentlemen, is our difficulty: When we plead our cause before the law makers and *savans* of the republic, they cannot take in the idea that men and women are alike; and so long as the mass rest in this delusion, the public mind will not be so much startled by the revelations made of the injustice and degradation of woman's position as by the fact that she should at length wake up to a sense of it.

If you, too, are thus deluded, what avails it that we show by your statute books that your laws are unjust—that woman is the victim of avarice and power? What avails it that we point out the wrongs of woman in social life; the victim of passion and lust? You scorn the thought that she has any natural love of freedom burning in her breast, any clear perception of justice urging her on to demand her rights.

Would to God you could know the burning indignation that fills woman's soul when she turns over the pages of your statute books, and sees there how like feudal barons you freemen hold your women. Would that you could know the humiliation she feels for her sex, when she thinks of all the beardless boys in your law offices, learning these ideas of one-sided justice—taking their first lessons in contempt for all womankind—being indoctrinated into the incapacities of their mothers, and the lordly, absolute rights of man over all women, children and property, and to know that these are to be our future Presidents, Judges, Husbands and Fathers; in sorrow we exclaim, alas! for that nation whose sons bow not in loyalty to woman. The mother is the first object of the child's veneration and love, and they who root out this holy sentiment, dream not of the blighting effect it has on the boy and the man. The impression left on law students, fresh from your statute books, is most unfavorable to woman's influence; hence you see but few lawyers chivalrous and high-toned in their sentiments towards woman. They cannot escape the legal view which, by constant reading, has become familiarized to their minds: "*Femme covert*," "dower," "widow's claims," "protection," "incapacities," "incumbrance," is written on the brow of every woman they meet.

But if, gentlemen, you take the ground that the sexes are alike, and, therefore, you are our faithful representatives—then why all these special laws for woman? Would not one code answer for all of like needs and wants? Christ's golden rule is better than all the special legislation that the ingenuity of man can devise: "Do unto others as you would have others do unto you." This, men and brethren, is all we ask at your hands. We *ask* no better laws than those you have made for yourselves. We need no other protection than that which your present laws secure to you.

In conclusion, then, let us say, in behalf of the women of this state, we ask for all that you have asked for yourselves in the progress of your development, since the *May Flower* cast anchor side Plymouth rock; and simply on the ground that the rights of every human being are the same and identical. You may say that the mass of the women of this state do not make the demand; it comes from a few sour, disappointed old maids and childless women.

You are mistaken; the mass speak through us. A very large majority of the women of this state support themselves and

their children, and many their husbands too. Go into any village you please, of three or four thousand inhabitants, and you
will find as many as fifty men or more, whose only business is
to discuss religion and politics, as they watch the trains come
and go at the depot, or the passage of a canal boat through a
lock; to laugh at the vagaries of some drunken brother, or the
capers of a monkey, dancing to the music of his master's organ.
All these are supported by their mothers, wives or sisters.

Now, do you *candidly* think these wives do not wish to
control the wages they earn—to own the land they buy—the
houses they build? to have at their disposal their own children,
without being subject to the constant interference and tyranny of an idle, worthless profligate? Do you suppose that any
woman is such a pattern of devotion and submission that she
willingly stitches all day for the small sum of fifty cents, that she
may enjoy the unspeakable privilege, in obedience to your laws,
of paying for her husband's tobacco and rum? Think you the
wife of the confirmed, beastly drunkard would consent to share
with him her home and bed, if law and public sentiment would
release her from such gross companionship? Verily, no! Think
you the wife, with whom endurance has ceased to be a virtue,
who through much suffering has lost all faith in the justice of
both Heaven and earth, takes the law in her own hand, severs
the unholy bond and turns her back forever upon him whom
she once called husband, consents to the law that in such an
hour tears her child from her—all that she has left on earth
to love and cherish? The drunkards' wives speak through us,
and they number 50,000. Think you that the woman who has
worked hard all her days, in helping her husband to accumulate
a large property, consents to the law that places this wholly at
his disposal? Would not the mother, whose only child is bound
out for a term of years, against her expressed wishes, deprive
the father of this absolute power if she could?

For all these, then, we speak. If to this long list you add all
the laboring women, who are loudly demanding remuneration
for their unending toil—those women who teach in our semi-
naries, academies and common schools for a miserable pittance;
the widows, who are taxed without mercy; the unfortunate
ones in our work houses, poor houses and prisons; who are they
that we do not now represent? But a small class of fashionable

butterflies, who, through the short summer days, seek the sunshine and the flowers; but the cool breezes of autumn and the hoary frosts of winter will soon chase all these away; then, they too will need and seek protection, and through other lips demand, in their turn, justice and equity at your hands.

LUCY STONE AND HENRY BROWNE BLACKWELL

Marriage Protest
MAY 1, 1855

This protest—signed by Lucy Stone (1818–1893) and Henry Browne Blackwell (1825–1909) on the occasion of their marriage and then widely circulated after it was published in the *Worcester Spy* and *The Liberator*—is the reason why married women who keep their given names are referred to as "Lucy Stoners": the bride refused to take her husband's name on principle and for the rest of her life was known simply as Lucy Stone. After meeting in the antislavery movement, it took Henry two years of steady courtship before he could overcome Lucy's deeply held objections to the marital state. By that point she had already begun to forge a career as a public speaker and activist, an unusual ambition for a nineteenth-century woman. A key influence had been her education at Oberlin College in Ohio, which welcomed both genders as well as African Americans. After her graduation in 1847, she became an antislavery lecturer and, in the 1850s, one of the best-known leaders of the emerging women's rights movement. The couple's only child, Alice Stone Blackwell, was born in 1857 and, like both her parents, devoted her life to suffrage and other progressive causes.

MARRIAGE OF LUCY STONE UNDER PROTEST.

T. W. Higginson sends to the Worcester *Spy* the following:

It was my privilege to celebrate May-Day by officiating at a wedding, in a farm-house among the hills of West Brookfield. The bridegroom was a man of tried worth, a leader in the Western Anti-Slavery movement; and the bride was one whose fair fame is known throughout the nation—one whose rare intellectual qualities are excelled by the private beauty of her heart and life.

I never perform the marriage ceremony without a renewed

sense of the iniquity of our present system of laws, in respect to marriage;—a system by which "man and wife are one, and that one is the husband." It was with my hearty concurrence, therefore, that the following protest was read and signed, as a part of the nuptial ceremony, and I send it to you, that others may be induced to do likewise.

PROTEST.

While we acknowledge our mutual affection, by publicly assuming the sacred relationship of husband and wife, yet in justice to ourselves and a great principle, we deem it a duty to declare that this act on our part implies no sanction of, nor promise of voluntary obedience to, such of the present laws of marriage, as refuse to recognise the wife as an independent rational being, while they confer upon the husband an injurious and unnatural superiority, investing him with legal powers which no honorable man would exercise, and which no man should possess.

We protest especially against the laws which give to the husband—

1. The custody of his wife's person.
2. The exclusive control and guardianship of their children.
3. The sole ownership of her personal, and use of her real estate, unless previously settled upon her, or placed in the hands of trustees, as in the case of minors, lunatics and idiots.
4. The absolute right to the product of her industry.
5. Also against laws which give to the widower so much larger and more permanent an interest in the property of his deceased wife, than they give to the widow in that of her deceased husband.
6. Finally, against the whole system by which "the legal existence of the wife is suspended during marriage," so that in most States she neither has a legal part in the choice of her residence, nor can she make a will, nor sue or be sued in her own name, nor inherit property.

We believe that personal independence and equal human rights can never be forfeited, except for crime; that marriage should be an equal and permanent partnership, and so recognized by law; that until it is so recognized, married partners should provide against the radical injustice of present laws, by every means in their power.

We believe that where domestic difficulties arise, no appeal should be made to legal tribunals under existing laws, but that all difficulties should be submitted to the equitable adjustment of arbitrators mutually chosen.

Thus reverencing law, we enter our protest against rules and customs which are unworthy of the name, since they violate justice, the essence of Law.

(Signed,)

HENRY B. BLACKWELL,
LUCY STONE.

☞ We are very sorry (as will be a host of others) to lose LUCY STONE, and certainly no less glad to gain LUCY BLACKWELL. Our most fervent benediction upon the heads of the parties thus united!

LUCY STONE

Address to the Seventh National Woman's Rights Convention

NOVEMBER 25–26, 1856

At the 1855 national convention held in Cincinnati, a heckler interrupted the proceedings by calling the speakers a "few disappointed
women." Lucy Stone replied that she was, in fact, a disappointed
woman: "In education, in marriage, in religion, in everything, disappointment is the lot of woman. It shall be the business of my life
to deepen this disappointment in every woman's heart until she bows
down to it no longer." Stone was in a more upbeat mood when she
addressed the national convention in New York City in this speech
from 1856, practically giddy with all that had been accomplished since
the movement had begun "in a small room in Boston" in 1850. (Note
that unlike later efforts by Elizabeth Cady Stanton and Susan B. Anthony to claim credit for Seneca Falls, Stone does not designate the
1848 convention as the movement's founding moment.) The greatest
successes were the revisions of laws related to women's legal status
passed by various states, but Stone also cheered the progress for wom-
en's rights occurring in England. All this was part of what she called
the "great truth": "that all human rights inhere in each human being."

―――――――――

I am sure that all present will agree with me that this is a day
of congratulation. It is our Seventh Annual National Woman's
Rights Convention. Our first effort was made in a small room
in Boston, where a few women were gathered, who had learned
woman's rights by woman's wrongs. There had been only one
meeting in Ohio, and one in New York. The laws were yet
against us, custom was against us, prejudice was against us, and
more than all, women were against us. We were strong only "in
the might of our right"—and, now, when this seventh year has
brought us together again, we can say as did a laborer in the
Republican party, though all is not gained, "we are without a
wound in our faith, without a wound in our hope, and stronger
than when we began." We have indeed reason to thank God
and take courage. Never before has any reformatory movement
gained so much in so short a time. Looking over the past seven

years, it seems almost a miracle that so much has been wrought, which is traceable directly to our efforts. When we began, the statute books were covered with laws against women, which an eminent jurist (Judge Walker) said would be a disgrace to the statute books of any heathen nation.

Now almost every Northern State has more or less modified its laws. The Legislature of Maine, after having granted nearly all other property rights to wives, found a bill before it asking that a wife should be entitled to what she earns, but a certain member grew fearful that wives would bring in bills for their daily service, and by an eloquent appeal to pockets, the measure was lost for the time, but that which has secured other rights *will* secure *this*. In Massachusetts, by the old laws, a wife owned nothing but the fee simple in her real estate. And even for that, she could not make a will without the written endorsement of her husband, permitting her to do so. Two years ago the law was so changed that she now holds the absolute right to her entire property, earnings included. Vermont, New Hampshire, and Rhode Island, have also very much amended their statutes.

New York, the proud Empire State, has, by the direct effort of this movement, secured to wives every property right except earnings. During two years a bill has been before the Legislature, which provides that if a husband be a drunkard, a profligate, or has abandoned his wife, she may have a right to her own earnings. It has not passed. Two hundred years hence that bill will be quoted as a proof of the barbarism of the times. Now it is a proof of progress.

Ohio, Illinois, and Indiana have also very materially modified their laws. And Wisconsin—God bless these young states!— has granted almost all that has been asked except the right of suffrage. And even this, Senator Sholes, in an able and manly minority report on the subject, said "is only a question of time, and as sure to triumph as God is just." It proposed, that the convention which meets in two years to amend the constitution of the State should consider the subject.

In Michigan, too, it has been moved that *women should have a right to their own babies*—which none of you, ladies, have here in New York. The motion caused much discussion in the Legislature, and it would probably have been carried had not a disciple of Brigham Young's, a Mormon member, defeated the bill. In Nebraska everything is bright for our cause. Mrs. Bloomer is there, and she has circulated petitions, claiming for women the right to vote. A bill to that effect passed the House of Representatives, and was lost in the Senate, only because of the too early closing of the session. That act of justice to woman would be gained in Nebraska first, and scores of women would go there that they might be made citizens, and be no longer subjects.

In addition to these great legal changes, achieved so directly by this reform, we find also that women have entered upon many new, and more remunerative industrial pursuits; thus being enabled to save themselves from the bitterness of dependent positions, or from lives of infamy.

Our demand that Harvard and Yale Colleges should admit women, though not yielded, only waits for a little more time. And while they wait, numerous petty "female colleges" have sprung into being, indicative of the justice of our claim that a college education should be granted to women. Not one of these female colleges (which are all second or third rate, and their whole course of study only about equal to what completes the sophomore year in our best colleges) meets the demand of the age, and so will eventually perish. Oberlin and Antioch Colleges in Ohio admit women on terms nearly equal with men.

Thus briefly I have mentioned some of the cheering results of our labors in this country.

In England the claims of women are making considerable progress. The most influential papers in London have urged the propriety of women physicians. Also a petition was sent to Parliament last year, signed by the Brownings, the Howitts, Harriet Martineau, Mrs. Gaskell, and Mrs. Jameson, asking for just such rights as we claim here. It was presented by Lord Brougham, and was respectfully received by Parliament.

Thus at home and abroad this great question of human equality is taking root, and bearing its own legitimate fruit. Everything has helped us. Everything will help us. The ballot is not yet yielded; but it cannot be far off when, as in the last Presidential contest, women were urged to attend political meetings, and a woman's name was made one of the rallying cries of the party of progress.

The enthusiasm which everywhere greeted the name of

JESSIE was so far a recognition of a woman's right to partici-pate in politics. Encouraged by the success of these seven years of effort, let us continue with unfailing fidelity to labor for the practical recognition of the great truth, that all human rights inhere in each human being. We welcome to this platform, men and women irrespective of creed, country or color; those who dissent from us as freely as those who agree with us.

WOMAN'S LOYAL NATIONAL LEAGUE

Call, Resolutions, and Debate
MAY 14, 1863

When the Civil War broke out in 1861, women's rights advocates put their activism on hold to concentrate on ending slavery. Yet the two causes were always intertwined, as the formation of the Woman's Loyal National League demonstrates. (Stanton and Anthony's *The History of Woman Suffrage* incorrectly refers to it as the Woman's National Loyal League, but the correct title as found on its letterhead is Woman's Loyal National League.) When delegates gathered in New York City on May 14, 1863, activists such as Susan B. Anthony, Ernestine L. Rose, and Angelina Grimké Weld engaged in spirited debate about whether their primary goal should be freedom for enslaved people or a broader commitment to political and civil rights irrespective of race and gender. In the end the disputed resolution 5 ("There never can be a true peace in this Republic until the civil and political rights of all citizens of African descent and all women are practically established") passed. The next step of the Woman's Loyal National League was to initiate a petition drive to Congress calling for a constitutional amendment to abolish slavery, which netted more than 400,000 signatures and helped build popular support for the passage of the Thirteenth Amendment in 1865. Women's rights activists always saw their "loyal" war work as part of an expansive vision of freedom that implied equal rights for women alongside newly freed slaves.

Call for a Meeting of the Loyal Women of the Nation.

In this crisis of our Country's destiny, it is the duty of every citizen to consider the peculiar blessings of a republican form of government and decide what sacrifices of wealth and life are demanded for its defense and preservation.

The policy of the war, our whole future life, depend on a universal, clearly defined idea of the end proposed, and the immense advantages to be secured to ourselves and all mankind by its accomplishment.

No mere party or sectional cry, no technicalities of Constitution or military law, no mottoes of craft or policy, are big enough to touch the great heart of a nation in the midst of revolution. A grand idea, such as freedom or justice, is needful to kindle and sustain the fires of a high enthusiasm.

At this hour, the best word and work of every man and woman are imperatively demanded. To man, by common consent, is assigned the forum, camp, and field. What is woman's legitimate work, and how she may best accomplish it, is worthy our earnest counsel one with another.

We have heard many complaints of the lack of enthusiasm among Northern Women; but, when a mother lays her son on the altar of her country, she asks an object equal to the sacrifice. In nursing the sick and wounded, knitting socks, scraping lint, and making jellies, the bravest and best may weary if the thoughts mount not in faith to something beyond and above it all. Work is worship only when a noble purpose fills the soul.

Woman is equally interested and responsible with man in the final settlement of this problem of self-government; therefore let none stand idle spectators now. When every hour is big with destiny, and each delay but complicates our difficulties, it is high time for the daughters of the revolution, in solemn council, to unseal the last will and testament of the Fathers,—lay hold of their birthright of freedom, and keep it a sacred trust for all coming generations.

To this end, we ask the Loyal Women of the Nation to meet in New York, on Thursday, the 14th of May next.

Let the Women of every State be largely represented, both by person and by letter.

There will be two sessions—the first at 10 o'clock A.M., at the Church of the Puritans, (Dr. Cheever's,) admittance free—the second at the Cooper Institute—at 7½ o'clock P.M., admittance 25 cents.

On behalf of the Woman's Central Committee,

ELIZABETH CADY STANTON.

N.B.—Communications relative to and for the meeting should be addressed to SUSAN B. ANTHONY, 48 Beekman Street, New York.

Resolved, 1. That the present war between slavery and freedom is but one phase of the irrepressible conflict between the aristocratic doctrine that power, not humanity, is statute-maker, and the democratic principle that self-government is the inalienable right of the people.

Resolved, 2. That we heartily approve that part of the President's Proclamation which decrees freedom to the slaves of rebel masters, and we earnestly urge him to devise measures for emancipating all slaves throughout the country.

Resolved, 3. That the national pledge to the freedmen must be redeemed, and the integrity of the Government in making it vindicated at whatever cost.

Resolved, 4. That while we welcome to legal freedom the recent slaves, we solemnly remonstrate against all state or national legislation which may exclude them from any locality, or debar them from any rights or privileges as free and equal citizens of a common Republic.

Resolved, 5. That it is in the same class favoring aristocratic interest that the property, the liberty, and the lives of all slaves, all citizens of African descent, and all women, are placed at the mercy of a legislation in which they are not represented. There never can be a true peace in this Republic until the civil and political equality of every subject of the Government shall be practically established.

Resolved, 6. That if Northern women lack enthusiasm in this war, it is because they have not seen its real nature and purport. If the wife or mother cheerfully lays her loved ones on the altar, she must be impelled to it by a living faith in the justice of her cause.

Resolved, 7. That the women of the Revolution were not wanting in heroism and self-sacrifice, and we, their daughters, are ready in this war to pledge our time, our means, our talents, and our lives, if need be, to secure the final and complete consecration of America to freedom.

SUSAN B. ANTHONY:—Mrs. President, there is great fear expressed on all sides lest this war shall be made a war for the negro. I am willing that it shall be; I am ready to admit that it is a war for the negro. It is a war to found an empire on the negro in slavery, and shame on us if we make it not a war to establish the negro in freedom! It is a war for the elevation of humanity. And the negro, the portion of humanity most down-trodden in this country—the negro, against whom the whole nation, North and South, East and West, in one mighty conspiracy, has been combined from the beginning—must now be made the exponent of the war. There is no name given under heaven wherewith to break, and for ever crush out this wicked conspiracy, save that of the negro.

Great care has been taken, ever since the war began, to keep the negro and slavery out of sight and hearing. But my position has ever been, that instead of thus suppressing the real cause of the war, it should have been proclaimed, not only by the people, but by the President, Congress, Cabinet, and every Military Commander. And when the Government, military and civil, and the people, acknowledged slavery to be the cause of the war, they should have simultaneously, one and all, decreed its total overthrow. Instead of President Lincoln's waiting two long years before calling into the field and to the side of the Government the four millions of allies whom we have had within the territory of rebeldom, it was the first duty of the first decree he sent forth. Every hour's delay has been a sin and a shame registered against him, and every life sacrificed to the Moloch of war, up to the Proclamation that called the slave to freedom and to arms, was nothing less than downright murder by the Government. For by all the laws of common sense—to say nothing of laws military or national—if the President, as Commander-in-Chief of the Army and Navy, could have devised any possible means whereby he might hope to suppress the rebellion, without the sacrifice of the life of one loyal citizen, without the sacrifice of one dollar of the loyal North, it was clearly his duty to have done so. Every interest of the insurgents, every dollar of their property, every institution, however peculiar, every life in every rebel state, even, if necessary, should have been sacrificed, before one dollar or one man should have been drawn from the free States. How much more, then, was it the President's duty to confer freedom on the four million slaves, transform them into a peaceful army for the Union, cripple the rebellion, and establish justice, the only sure foundation of peace! I therefore hail the day when the President, the Government, and the people shall recognize that it is a war for the negro and for his freedom.

For if there is a God in heaven, if there is a law of justice in the earth, if there is a law of cause and effect in the universe, this war can never be suppressed, this nation can never know peace, until slavery—the cause of the war—is wholly and for ever removed. (Applause.) It is impossible. We talk about returning to the old Union—"the Union as it was," and "the Constitution as it is"—about "restoring our country to peace and prosperity—to the blessed conditions that existed before the war!!" I ask you what sort of peace, what sort of prosperity, have we had in this country? We have had no peace, but constant war from the beginning. Since the first slave-ship sailed up the James River with its human cargo, and there, on the soil of the *Old* Dominion, it was sold to the highest bidder, we have had nothing but war. When that pirate captain landed on the shores of Africa, and there kidnapped the first stalwart negro, and fastened the first manacle, the struggle between that captain and that negro was the commencement of the terrible war in the midst of which we are to-day. Between the slave and the master there has been war, and war only, from the beginning. This is only a new form of the war. No, no; we ask for no return to the old conditions. We ask for something better than the old. We want a Union that is a Union in fact—a Union in spirit, not a sham Union. (Applause.) I just remember me that it is the women of the North who are assembled here to-day—the women who have been wont to consider themselves irresponsible for the conduct of the affairs of the nation. And indeed they have no direct responsibility, for they have been content to accept whatever conditions of politics or morals the ruling class has been pleased to make. From the commencement of the Government, political intriguers have given to the entire nation not only its political code, but its moral and religious codes.

By the Constitution as it is—that is, as it has been interpreted and executed from the beginning—the North has stood pledged to protect slavery in the states where it existed. We have been bound, in case of slave insurrections, to go to the aid, not of those struggling for liberty, but to the aid of the oppressors. It was politicians who made the pledge at the beginning, and who have renewed it from year to year to this day.

These same politicians have had control of the churches, the Sabbath-schools, and all religious influences; and the women, in this department, have been a part and party in complicity with slavery. The women have made the large majority in all the different religious organizations throughout the country, and have without protest even, in obedience to the behests of politics and trade, fellowshipped the slaveholder as a Christian, accepted pro-slavery preaching from their pulpits, suffered the words "slavery a crime" to be expurgated from all the lessons taught their children, listened to the perversion of the Golden Rule, "Do unto others as you would that others should do unto you." For all these years, women, mothers, have thus sat silent lookers-on, while their sons and daughters were being educated in forgetfulness of every law of right and justice to the slave. They have had no right to vote in their churches, and, like slaves, have merely accepted whatever of morals and religion the selfish interest of politics and trade dictated.

The point I wish to make here is this, that the hour is fully come, when woman shall no longer be the passive recipient of whatever morals and religion the trade and politics of the nation may decree; but that she shall now assume her God-given responsibilities, and make herself what she is clearly designed to be, the educator of the race. Let her no longer be the mere reflector, the echo of the worldly pride and ambition of the other half of the race. (Applause.) Had the women of the North studied to know and to teach their sons the law of justice to the black man, as the white, regardless of the frown or the smile of pro-slavery priest and politician, they would not now be called upon to offer the loved of their households to the bloody Moloch of war.

And now, women of the North, I ask you to rise up with earnest, honest purpose, to speak the true word and do the just work, in season and out of season. I ask you to forget that you are women, and go forward in the way of right, fearlessly, as independent human beings, responsible to God alone for the discharge of every duty, for the faithful use of every gift, for the multiplying tenfold every talent the good Father has given you. Forget conventionalisms; forget what the world will say, whether you are in your place or out of your place; think your best thoughts, speak your best words, do your best works, looking only to suffering humanity, your own conscience, and God for approval.

ERNESTINE L. ROSE:—I rise simply to make one remark, and I know my friend who has just taken her seat will have no objection. I know what she meant, but some may misunderstand her. No. Woman should never forget herself that she is a woman. It is because she remembers that she is a woman that she is in duty bound to go for everything that is right, for everything that is just, for everything that is grand and noble, and consequently for human freedom. (Applause.)

MRS. HOYT of Wisconsin:—Thus far this meeting has been conducted in such a way as would lead one to suppose that it was an anti-slavery convention. There are ladies here who have come hundreds of miles to attend a business meeting of the Loyal Ladies of the North; and good as anti-slavery conventions are, and anti-slavery speeches are, in their way, I think that here we should attend to our own business.

SPEECH OF MRS. CHALKSTONE.

MRS. CHALKSTONE of California:—My speech shall be as brief as possible, and I ask for an excuse for my broken language. But the lady speaker before me made a few remarks to which, as a woman and a mother, I feel it my duty to respond. And as the cause is such a great one that assembles us together, I think we should be well aware of what we say, and of what it is our duty to do. Let us never forget that we are women, and that we are mothers. It needs something new in these hard times to raise women out of their idleness and inaction. It is the mother who forms the character of the child, and especially of her sons. Woman may raise herself and perform her duty without forgetting that she is a woman. Our field is very small, and God has given us character and abilities to follow it out. We do not need to stand at the ballot-boxes and cast our votes, neither to stand and plead as lawyers; but in our homes we have a great office. I consider women a great deal superior to men. (Laughter and applause.) Men are physically strong, but women are morally better. I speak of pure women, good women. It is woman who keeps the world in the balance.

I am from Germany, where my brothers all fought against the Government and tried to make us free, but were unsuccessful. My only son, seventeen years old, is in our great and noble army of the Union. He has fought many of the battles now, and I only came from California to see him once more. I have not seen him yet. Though I was down in the camp, I could not get any pass. But I am willing to lay down all this sacrifice for the cause of liberty. We foreigners know the preciousness of that great, noble gift a great deal better than you, because you never were in slavery, but we are born in it. Germany pines for freedom. In Germany we sacrificed our wealth and ornaments for it, and the women in this country ought to do the same. We cannot fight in the battles, but we can do this for the great cause, and it is all that we can do. Then, the speaker before me made a remark that Abraham Lincoln was two years before he emancipated slaves. She thought it wrong. It took eighteen hundred years in Europe to emancipate the Jews, and they are not emancipated now. Among great intelligent peoples like Germany and France, until 1814, no Jew had the right to go on the pavement; they had to go in the middle of the street, where the horses walked! And it took eighteen hundred years to emancipate them. It took more than two years to emancipate the people of the North from the idea that the negro was not a human being, and was not capable to be our equal. He has a right to be a free man, but only time can make him an equal. A great many will find fault in the resolution that the negro shall be free and our equal, because our equal not every human being can be; but free every human being has a right to be. He can only be equal in his rights. (Applause.)

ERNESTINE L. ROSE called for the reading of the resolutions, and their consideration *seriatim*. All were adopted unanimously save the fifth, which had a large majority.

The following discussion took place on the fifth resolution, commenced by Mrs. HOYT of Wisconsin:

SPEECH OF MRS. HOYT.
MRS. PRESIDENT:—I object to the passage of this resolution, not because I object to the sentiment expressed, I wish to be

distinctly understood; but I do not think it is a time to bring before this Ladies' Loyal Meeting, assembled for the purpose of devising the best ways and means by which women may properly assist the Government in its struggle against treason, anything which could in the least prejudice the interest in this cause which is so dear to us all. We all know that Woman's Rights as an *ism* has not been received with entire favor by the women of the country, and I know that there are thousands of earnest, loyal, and able women who will not go into any movement of this kind, if this idea is made prominent. (Applause.) I came here from Wisconsin hoping to meet the earnest, loyal women of the country. I hoped that nothing that would in any way damage the cause so dear to us all would be brought forward by any of the members of this meeting, and I am sorry to see it has been done to some extent. (Applause.)

I object to this, because our idea and principal object should be to help maintain, as women properly may, the integrity of our Government; to help vindicate its authority; to re-establish it upon a far more enduring basis than it is established now. The way is open for us. We can do this if we do not involve ourselves in any purely political matter, or any *ism* which is peculiarly obnoxious to the people—I will not say to a majority, but to very many. The one idea should be the maintenance of the authority of the Government as it is, and the integrity of the Republican idea. For this, women may properly work, and I hope this resolution will not pass.

MRS. SARAH HALLOCK:—I would make the suggestion that those women of us who approve of this resolution can afford to give way so far as to allow that part of it which is objected to to be passed by, and to mention in it only the negro. The negroes have suffered more than the women, and the women, perhaps, can afford to give them the preference. Let it stand as regards them, and blot out the word "woman." It may possibly be woman's place to suffer. At any rate, let her suffer, if, by that means, *man*kind may suffer less.

A VOICE:—You are too self-sacrificing.

ERNESTINE L. ROSE:—I always sympathize with those who

seem to be in the minority. I know it requires a great deal of moral courage to object to anything that appears to have been favorably received. I know very well from long experience how it feels to stand in a minority of one; and I am glad that that friend on the other side (Mrs. Hallock) has already added one to make a minority of two, though that is by far too small to be comfortable. I, for one, object to throw women out of the race for freedom. (Applause.) And do you know why? Because she needs freedom for the freedom of man. (Applause.) Our ancestors made a great mistake in not recognizing woman in the rights of man. It has been justly stated that the negro at present suffers more than woman, but it can do him no injury to place woman in the same category with him. I, for one, object to having that term stricken out, for it can have no possible bearing against anything that we want to promote, for we desire to promote human rights and human freedom. It can do no injury, but must do good, for it is a painful fact that woman under the law, until very recently, has been entirely in the same category with the slave. Of late years she has had some small rights conceded to her. Now, mind, I say *conceded*; for publicly it has not yet been recognized by the laws of the land that she has a right to an equality with man. In that resolution it simply states a fact, that in a republic based upon freedom, woman, as well as the negro, should be recognized as an equal with the whole human race. (Applause.)

SPEECH OF MRS. ANGELINA G. WELD.

ANGELINA G. WELD:—Mrs. President, I rejoice exceedingly that that resolution should combine us with the negro in the desire for our rights. I feel that we have been with him; that the iron has entered into our souls. True, we have not felt the slaveholder's lash; true, we have not had our hands manacled; but our *hearts* have been crushed. Was there a single institution in this country that would throw open its doors to the acknowledgment of woman's equality with man in the race for science and the languages, until Oberlin, Antioch, and a very few others opened their doors, twenty years ago? Have I not heard women say—I said thus to my own brother, as I used to receive from him instruction and reading: "Oh, brother, that I could go to college with you! that I could have the doors of instruction opened before me! but I am crushed! I hear nothing, I know nothing, except in the fashionable circle."

A teacher said to a young lady, who had been studying for several years, on the day she finished her course of instruction, "I thought you would be very glad that you were so soon to go home, so soon to leave your studies."

She looked up, and said, "What was I made for? When I go home I shall live in a circle of fashion and folly. I was not made for embroidery, dancing, and folly; I was made a woman; but I cannot be a true woman." And she could not be a full-grown woman in America.

Now, my friends, I do not want to find fault with the past at all. I really believe that men did for women the best that they knew how to do. They did not know their own rights; they did not recognize the rights of any man who had a black face. We cannot wonder that, in their tenderness for woman, they wanted to shelter and protect her, and they made those laws from true, human, generous feelings. Woman was then too undeveloped to demand anything else. But woman is woman to-day, whether man knows it or not; woman is equal to her rights, and equal to the responsibilities of the hour. I want to be identified with the negro—until he gets his rights, we never shall have ours. (Applause.)

SUSAN B. ANTHONY:—I want to make one statement with regard to this resolution. It brings in no question, no *ism*, it seems to me. It merely makes the assertion that in a true democracy, in a genuine republic, every citizen who lives under the government must have the right of representation in that government. You will remember that the maxim upon which our Government is founded is that "Governments derive their just powers from the consent of the governed." This is the fundamental, underlying, vital principle of democracy; and before our Government can possibly be a true democracy—before our republic can be placed upon lasting and enduring foundations—the civil and political rights of every citizen thereof must be recognized and practically established. This only is the assertion of the resolution. It is a philosophical statement. It is not because women suffer, it is not because slaves suffer, it is not because of any individual rights or wrongs—it is the simple assertion of the great fundamental truth of democracy that was proclaimed by our Revolutionary fathers.

I hope the discussion will no longer be continued as to the rights or wrongs of one class or another. The question before us is, Is it possible that peace and union shall be established in this country; is it possible for this Government to be a true democracy, a genuine republic, while one-sixth or one-half of the people are disfranchised? The resolution is simply an assertion of principle, again I repeat; and again I express the hope that we shall not run off into side-issues.

MRS. HOYT:—I do not object—and I wish distinctly to have it understood—to the philosophy of these resolutions. I believe in the advancement of the human race, and certainly not in a retrograde movement of the Woman's Rights question; but at the same time I do insist that nothing that has become obnoxious to a portion of the people of the country shall be dragged into this meeting. (Applause.) The women of the loyal North were invited here to meet in convention the loyal ladies of New York, not to hold a Temperance meeting, not to hold an Anti-Slavery meeting, not to hold a Woman's Rights convention, but to meet here to consult as to the best practical way for the advancement of the loyal cause. To my certain knowledge there are ladies in this house who have come hundreds of miles, who will withdraw from this convention, who will have nothing to do with it, who will go home disappointed, and be thrown back on their own resources, and form other plans of organization; whereas they would much prefer to co-operate with the National Convention if this matter were not introduced. This movement must be sacred to the one object of assisting our Government. I would add one more remark, that though the women of the Revolution did help our Government in that early struggle, they did not find it necessary to set forth in any theoretical or clamorous way their right to equal suffrage or equal political position, though doubtless they believed, as much as any of us, in the advancement of woman.

A LADY:—I want to ask the lady who just spoke if the women of the Revolution found it necessary to form Loyal Leagues?

We are not bound to do just as the women of the Revolution did. (Applause and laughter.)

MRS. HALLOCK:—Although I am very willing and proud to acknowledge myself to have had the common sense to belong to the radical portion of the Woman's Rights Society, still I feel not only willing to take this objection into consideration, but I hope that this resolution will be omitted. Let it pass, if we can promote any good thereby. If we form a League, the very term itself of forming a League I think suggests that we are not one—that we need not all of us profess the same politics. I, for one, am willing to have the resolution omitted.

SPEECH OF LUCY N. COLMAN.

LUCY N. COLMAN:—I wish to say, in the first place, something a little remote from the point, which I have in my mind just now. A peculiar sensitiveness seems to have come over some of the ladies here in reference to the anti-slavery spirit of the resolutions. It seems to me impossible that a company of women could stand upon this platform without catching something of the anti-slavery spirit, and without expressing, to some extent, their sympathy with the advancement of human rights. It is the Anti-Slavery women and the Women's Rights women who called this meeting, and who have most effectually aided in this movement. Their hearts bled to the very core that our nation is to-day suffering to its depths, and they concluded to call a meeting of the loyal women of the nation, to come together and devise means whereby we shall help the country in its great calamity. I respect the woman who opposed this resolution, for daring to say so much. It is really a brave thing for a woman to dare to do anything. She says that it is an Anti-Slavery convention that is in session. So it is, and something more. (Applause.) She says it is a Woman's Rights Convention. So it is, and even more than that; it is a World's Convention. (Applause.) Another woman—I rejoice to hear that lisping, foreign tongue—says that our sphere is so narrow that we should be careful to keep within it. All honor to her, that she dared to say even that. I recognize for myself no narrow sphere. (Applause.) Where you may work, my brother, I may work, and to-day the God of heaven—if such exists—(hisses)—knows that I would willingly stand on the battle-field. (Continued hisses.) My friends, hiss, if you please; but I remembered, after uttering that expression, that I might hurt the feelings of some persons not thinking just as I do, and I beg always to be just. I say, I would willingly stand upon the battle-field, and would be glad to receive the balls in my person, if I could feel that in that way I could do more for my country's good than in any other. I recognize no right of any man or of any woman to say that I should not stand there. Our sphere is *not* narrow—it is broad, it is wide.

Now, in reference to this resolution, Mrs. Hallock—than whom there is no person I more respect—thinks it might be well to leave out woman. No, no, I will not allow it—that is, I will speak against it. Do you remember, friends, long, long ago—I think it was in New York—that an Anti-Slavery convention broke up in high dudgeon because a woman was put upon a committee? But that Anti-Slavery society, notwithstanding those persons who felt so sensitive withdrew from it, has lived thirty years, and to-day it has the honor of being credited as the cause of this war. Perhaps if the principle which was then at stake—that a woman had a right to be on that committee— had been waived, from the very fact that the principle of right was overruled, that society would have failed. And I would not yield one iota, one particle, to this clamor for compromise. Be it understood that it is a Woman's Rights matter; for the Woman's Rights women have the same right to dictate to a Loyal League that the Anti-Woman's Rights women have, and the side that is strongest will carry the resolution, of course. But do not withdraw it. Do not say, "We will take it away because it is objectionable."

I have another point which I wish to make. It is a very long time since I have talked in public. Of course, my thoughts don't come as consecutively as I could wish; but you will excuse the lack of arrangement, and believe me earnest, I know. I want the people to understand that this Loyal League—because it is a Loyal League—must of necessity bring in Anti-Slavery and Woman's Rights. (Applause.) Is it possible that any of you believe that there is such a being in this country to-day as a loyal man or woman who is not anti-slavery to the backbone. (Applause.) It is a contradiction of terms. Neither is there a loyal man or woman who understands himself or herself, and whose intellect is clear enough to take in a broad, large idea, who is not to the very core a Woman's Rights man or woman. (Applause.)

MRS. HOYT:—As I have said before, I wish it distinctly understood, that I am not opposed to Anti-Slavery. I stand here an Abolitionist from the earliest childhood, and a stronger anti-slavery woman lives not on the soil of America. (Applause.) I voted Yea on the anti-slavery resolution, and I would vote it ten times over. But, at the same time, in the West, which I represent, there is a very strong objection to Woman's Rights; in fact, this Woman's Rights matter is odious to some of us from the *manner* in which it has been conducted; not that we object to the philosophy—we believe in the philosophy—but object to this matter being tacked on to a purely loyal convention. I know I stand here in about a minority of one. I see that this Convention is in the hands of ladies who have been prominent in that movement. I am sorry to see it, because I know women from our State are present this morning who will take no part if these ideas prevail, and who will go home disappointed, and feel that the object of their mission has not been accomplished. I speak for a good many others besides myself. If it is desired to have a Woman's Rights convention, a convention for that purpose may be called afterwards, purely for that purpose. I would have no objection to it at all, I would glory in it; but I *do* object to have anything tacked on or mixed up with this that will prevent any true, loyal woman from taking part in the proceedings, and going into it heartily. (Applause.) I will make one more statement which bears upon the point which I have been trying to make. I have never before spoken except in private meetings, and therefore must ask the indulgence of the audience. The women of Madison, Wisconsin, feeling the necessity and importance of doing something more than women were doing to assist the Government in this struggle, organized a Ladies' Union League, which has been in operation some time, and is very efficient.

A VOICE:—What are they doing? Please state.

MRS. HOYT:—When I come to that, I will tell. In Madison we had a very large and flourishing Soldiers' Aid Society. We were the headquarters for that part of the State. A great many ladies worked in our Aid Society, and assisted us, who utterly refused to join with the Loyal League, because, they said, it would damage the Aid Society. We recognized that fact, and kept it purely distinct as a Ladies' Loyal League, for the promotion of the loyal sentiment of the North, and to reach the soldiers in the field by the most direct and practical means which were in our power. If you mix up things a good deal, and bring a great many objects into any association, it detracts from its usefulness. In the West we have labored to keep the Aid Society sacred to the hospital service, and we have succeeded. We have a great many very flourishing Ladies' Loyal Leagues throughout the West, and we have kept them sacred from Anti-Slavery, Woman's Rights, Temperance, and everything else, good though they may be. We have kept them for the one purpose of uniting and strengthening the loyal sentiment of the people. Of course, in coming to New York, I did not expect to do anything more than advise with our lady friends here. In our League we have three objects in view. The first is, retrenchment in household expenses, to the end that the material resources of the Government may be, so far as possible, applied to the entire and thorough vindication of its authority. Second, to strengthen the loyal sentiment of the people at home, and instill a deeper love of the national flag. The third and most important object is, to write to the soldiers in the field, thus reaching nearly every private in the army, to encourage him and stimulate him in the way that ladies know how to do. I state again, it is not an anti-slavery objection. I will vote for every anti-slavery movement in this Convention. I object to the Woman's Rights resolutions, and nothing else.

ERNESTINE L. ROSE:—It is exceedingly amusing to hear persons talk about throwing out Woman's Rights, when, if it had not been for Woman's Rights, that lady would not have had the courage to stand here and say what she did. (Applause.) Pray, what means "loyal?" Loyal means to be true to one's highest conviction. Justice, like charity, begins at home. It is because we are loyal to truth, loyal to justice, loyal to right, loyal to humanity, that woman is included in that resolution. Now, what does this discussion mean? The lady acknowledges that it is not against Woman's Rights itself; she is *for* Woman's Rights. We are here to endeavor to help the cause of human rights and human freedom. We ought not to be afraid. You may depend upon it, if there are any of those who are called copperheads—but I don't like to call names, for even a copperhead is better than no head at all—(laughter)—if there are any copperheads here, I am perfectly sure that they will object to this whole Convention; and if we want to consult them, let us adjourn *sine die*. If we are loyal to our highest convictions, we need not care how far it may lead. For truth, like water, will find its own level. No, friends; in the name of consistency let us not wrangle here simply because we associate the name of woman with human justice and human rights. Although I always like to see opposition on any subject, for it elicits truth much better than any speech, still I think it will be exceedingly inconsistent if, because some women out in the West are opposed to the Woman's Rights movement—though at the same time they take advantage of it—that therefore we shall throw it out of this resolution.

MRS. SPENCE:—I didn't come to this meeting to participate—only to listen. I don't claim to be a Northerner or a Southerner; but I claim to be a human being, and to belong to the human family. (Applause.) I belong to no sect or creed of politics or religion; I stand as an individual, defending the rights of every one as far as I can see them. But now it seems to me on this occasion we have met here—taking it into consideration that there are no gentlemen in the house—(laughter)—we ladies are met here, as I understand it, to come to some unity of action. If we attempt to bring in religious, political, or moral questions, we all must of necessity differ, for the grand panorama of life shows us that we are all progressive, and necessarily must occupy different standings. Some of us have larger spheres than others, and we are necessarily different; consequently we must leave, if possible, our highest ideas on those great questions that we call religious and moral, and see if we cannot come to one platform where we can assimilate together, and unite our sentiment in behalf of what we call our highest idea of liberty. We come here believing, if we have any patriotism in our hearts, we shall be inspired by each other, and our efforts should be to inspire each other with a unity of feeling—that inspiration going forth from the hearts of women, shall inspire the whole nation. We are to send forth the voice of encouragement. This meeting is to lay some plan by which we can unite our inspirations in the form of practical action. I have not heard such a proposition made; but I anticipate that it will be made. (Hear, hear.) Then if we are to unite our feelings on some practical proposition which is to be presented, it seems to me that our resolutions should be practical and directed to the main business. Let the public take them for what they are worth; but let the object of the meeting be a unity of action and expression and spirit in behalf of what we feel to be the highest right. Let the object of this meeting be practical, and when we see it gaining control of what we feel to be moral right, we will then lift up our voices and render our veto against it.

THE PRESIDENT:—Every good cause can afford to be just. The lady from Wisconsin, who differs from some of us here, says she is an anti-slavery woman. We ought to believe her. She accepts the principles of the Woman's Rights movement, but she does not like the way in which it has been carried on. We ought to believe her. It is not, then, that she objects to the idea of the equality of women and negroes, but because she does not wish to have anything "tacked on" to the Loyal League that, to the mass of the people, does not seem to belong here. She seems to me to stand precisely in the position of those good people just at the close of the war of the Revolution. The people then, as now, had their hearts aching with the memory of their buried dead. They had had years of war from which they had garnered out sorrows as well as hopes; and when they came to establish a Union, they found that one black, unmitigated curse of slavery rooted in the soil. Some men said, "We can have no true Union where there is not justice to the negro. The black man is a human being, made by God like us, with the same equal rights." They had given to the world the Declaration of Independence, grand and brave and beautiful, with the word which to-day we mean to ring in the people's ears until the theory of the Government shall be applied practically. They said, "How can we form a true Union?" Some people representing the class that Mrs. Hoyt represents, answered, "Let us have a Union. We are weak; we have been beset for seven long years; do not let us meddle with the negro question. What we are for is a Union; let us have a Union at all hazards." They were earnest men, men of talent, and could speak well and earnestly, and they persuaded the others to silence. So they said nothing about slavery, and let the wretched monster live. To-day, over all our land, the unburied bones of our fathers and sons and brothers tell the sad mistake that those men made when long ago they left this one great wrong in the land. They could not accomplish good by passing over a wrong. If the right of one single human being is to be disregarded by us, we fail in our loyalty to the country. All over this land women have no political existence. Laws pass over our heads that we cannot make or unmake. Our property is taken from us without our consent. The babes we bear in anguish and carry in our arms are not ours. The few rights that we have, have been wrung from the Legislature by the Woman's Rights movement. We come to-day to say to those who are administering our Government and fighting our battles, "While you are going through this valley of humiliation, do not forget that you must be true alike to the women and the negroes." We can never be truly "loyal" if we leave them out. Leave them out, and we take the same backward step that our fathers took when they left out slavery. If justice to the negro and to woman is right, it cannot hurt our loyalty to the country and the Union. If it is not right, let it go out of the way; but if it is right, there is no occasion that we should reject it or ignore it. We make the statement that the Government derives its just powers from the consent of the governed, and that all human beings have equal rights. This is not an *ism*—it is simply an assertion that we shall be truly true to the highest truth.

A MAN IN THE AUDIENCE:—The question was asked, as I entered this house, "Is it right for women to meet here and intermeddle in our public affairs?" It is the greatest possible absurdity for women to stand on that platform and talk of loyalty to a Government in which nine-tenths of the politicians of the land say that she has no right to interfere, and still oppose

Woman's Rights. The very act of standing there is an indorsement of Woman's Rights.

A VOICE:—I believe this is a woman's meeting. Men have no right to speak here.

THE GENTLEMAN CONTINUED:—It is on woman more than on man that the real evils of this war settle. It is not the soldier on the battle-field that suffers most; it is the wife, the mother, the daughter. (Applause. Cries of "Question, question.")

A VOICE:—You are not a woman, sit down.

SUSAN B. ANTHONY:—Some of us who sit upon this platform have many a time been clamored down, and told that we had no right to speak, and that we were out of our places in public meetings; and God forbid, when women assemble, and a man has a thought in his soul, burning for utterance, that we should retaliate upon him. (Laughter and applause.)

The resolution was then put to vote.

A VOICE:—Allow me to inquire if men have a right to vote on this question?

THE PRESIDENT:—I suppose men who are used to business know that they should not vote here. We give them the privilege of speaking.

The resolution was carried by a majority.

SUSAN B. ANTHONY:—I desire to say that the resolution recommending the practical work to be done, has not yet been prepared. We have now a grand platform on which to stand, and I hope we shall be able to present work equally grand. But, Mrs. President, if we should fail to present a practical work at this Convention which should meet the approbation of all the loyal women of the North, we shall not fail in the one grand and great work which was needed to be done at this hour, and that was for women to enunciate the fundamental principles of democracy and republicanism, which underlie the structure of a free government. When the heads and hearts of the women of the North are fully imbued with the true idea of freedom and republicanism, their hands will find a way in which to work to secure the accomplishment of the grand idea.

There evidently is very great earnestness on the part of the women who are present here to settle upon some practical work for us of the North to do. I therefore ask that the women from every State of the Union, who are delegates here from Loyal Leagues and Aid Societies, shall retire, at the close of this meeting, to the lecture-room of this church, and there we will endeavor to fix upon the best possible thing which we can gather from the counsels of the many. I hope this enthusiasm of the women of the North, which is now manifesting itself, may be directed to good and legitimate ends, and not be allowed to evaporate into thin air, and go for nothing. I hope it will be used to good purpose, and will aid greatly in the establishment of this Government on the everlasting foundation of truth.

FRANCES ELLEN WATKINS HARPER

Speech at the Eleventh National Woman's Rights Convention

MAY 10, 1866

When the women's rights movement resumed its practice of holding national conventions after the Civil War, Frances Ellen Watkins Harper (1825–1911) was a featured speaker at the 1866 gathering. Born to free parents in the slave state of Maryland and orphaned at age three, Harper made a name for herself in the 1840s and 1850s as a poet and antislavery lecturer, though she had only recently allied herself with the cause of women. Her epiphany came when she was widowed in 1864 and found herself at the mercy of a legal system that stripped her and her four children of their property and belongings not because of their race but because she was a woman. She realized that if she had died instead of her husband, the outcome would have been completely different. When Harper addressed the convention, she spoke from an intersectional vision that stressed that "we are all bound up together in one great bundle of humanity, and society cannot trample on the weakest and feeblest of its members without receiving the curse in its own soul." This convention resulted in the formation of the American Equal Rights Association, which was dedicated to supporting universal suffrage (or in Elizabeth Cady Stanton's words, "burying the black man and the woman in citizen") in the fraught political landscape following the Civil War.

———————

I feel I am something of a novice upon this platform. Born of a race whose inheritance has been outrage and wrong, most of my life had been spent in battling against those wrongs. But I did not feel as keenly as others, that I had these rights, in common with other women, which are now demanded. About two years ago, I stood within the shadows of my home. A great sorrow had fallen upon my life. My husband had died suddenly, leaving me a widow, with four children, one my own, and the others stepchildren. I tried to keep my children together. But my husband died in debt; and before he had been in his grave three months, the administrator had swept the very milk-crocks and wash tubs from my hands. I was a farmer's wife and made butter for the Columbus market; but what could I do, when they had swept all away? They left me one thing—and that was a looking glass! Had I died instead of my husband, how different would have been the result! By this time he would have had another wife, it is likely; and no administrator would have gone into his house, broken up his home, and sold his bed, and taken away his means of support.

I took my children in my arms, and went out to seek my living. While I was gone; a neighbor to whom I had once lent five dollars, went before a magistrate and swore that he believed I was a non-resident, and laid an attachment on my very bed. And I went back to Ohio with my orphan children in my arms, without a single feather bed in this wide world, that was not in the custody of the law. I say, then, that justice is not fulfilled so long as woman is unequal before the law.

We are all bound up together in one great bundle of humanity, and society cannot trample on the weakest and feeblest of its members without receiving the curse in its own soul. You tried that in the case of the negro. You pressed him down for two centuries; and in so doing you crippled the moral strength and paralyzed the spiritual energies of the white men of the country. When the hands of the black were fettered, white men were deprived of the liberty of speech and the freedom of the press. Society cannot afford to neglect the enlightenment of any class of its members. At the South, the legislation of the country was in behalf of the rich slaveholders, while the poor white man was neglected. What is the consequence to-day? From that very class of neglected poor white men, comes the man who stands to-day, with his hand upon the helm of the nation. He fails to catch the watchword of the hour, and throws himself, the incarnation of meanness, across the pathway of the nation. My objection to Andrew Johnson is not that he has been a poor white man; my objection is that he keeps "poor whits" all the way through. [Applause.] That is the trouble with him.

This grand and glorious revolution which has commenced, will fail to reach its climax of success, until throughout the length and breadth of the American Republic, the nation shall be so color-blind, as to know no man by the color of his skin or the curl of his hair. It will then have no privileged class, trampling upon and outraging the unprivileged classes, but will be then one great privileged nation, whose privilege will be to produce the loftiest manhood and womanhood that humanity can attain.

I do not believe that giving the woman the ballot is immediately going to cure all the ills of life. I do not believe that white women are dew-drops just exhaled from the skies. I think that like men they may be divided into three classes, the good, the bad, and the indifferent. The good would vote according to their convictions and principles; the bad, as dictated by prejudice or malice; and the indifferent will vote on the strongest side of the question, with the winning party.

You white women speak here of rights. I speak of wrongs. I, as a colored woman, have had in this country an education which has made me feel as if I were in the situation of Ishmael, my hand against every man, and every man's hand against me. Let me go to-morrow morning and take my seat in one of your street cars—I do not know that they will do it in New York, but they will in Philadelphia—and the conductor will put up his hand and stop the car rather than let me ride.

A Lady—They will not do that here.

Mrs. Harper—They do in Philadelphia. Going from Washington to Baltimore this Spring, they put me in the smoking car. [Loud Voices—"Shame."] Aye, in the capital of the nation, where the black man consecrated himself to the nation's defence, faithful when the white man was faithless, they put me in the smoking car! They did it once; but the next time they tried it, they failed; for I would not go in. I felt the fight in me; but I don't want to have to fight all the time. To-day I am puzzled where to make my home. I would like to make it in Philadelphia, near my own friends and relations. But if I want to ride in the streets of Philadelphia, they send me to ride on the platform with the driver. [Cries of "Shame."] Have women nothing to do with this? Not long since, a colored woman took her seat in an Eleventh Street car in Philadelphia, and the conductor stopped the car, and told the rest of the passengers to get out, and left the car with her in it alone, when they took it back to the station. One day I took my seat in a car, and the conductor came to me and told me to take another seat. I just screamed "murder." The man said if I was black I ought to behave myself.

I knew that if he was white he was not behaving himself. Are there not wrongs to be righted?

In advocating the cause of the colored man, since the Dred Scott decision, I have sometimes said I thought the nation had touched bottom. But let me tell you there is a depth of infamy lower than that. It is when the nation, standing upon the threshold of a great peril, reached out its hands to a feebler race, and asked that race to help it, and when the peril was over, said, You are good enough for soldiers, but not good enough for citizens. When Judge Taney said that the men of my race had no rights which the white man was bound to respect, he had not seen the bones of the black man bleaching outside of Richmond. He had not seen the thinned ranks and the thickened graves of the Louisiana Second, a regiment which went into battle nine hundred strong, and came out with three hundred. He had not stood at Olustee and seen defeat and disaster crushing down the pride of our banner, until word was brought to Col. Hallowell, "The day is lost; go in and save it;" and black men stood in the gap, beat back the enemy, and saved your army. [Applause.]

We have a woman in our country who has received the name of "Moses," not by lying about it, but by acting it out [applause]—a woman who has gone down into the Egypt of slavery and brought out hundreds of our people into liberty. The last time I saw that woman, her hands were swollen. That woman who had led one of Montgomery's most successful expeditions, who was brave enough and secretive enough to act as a scout for the American army, had her hands all swollen from a conflict with a brutal conductor, who undertook to eject her from her place. That woman, whose courage and bravery won a recognition from our army and from every black man in the land, is excluded from every thoroughfare of travel. Talk of giving women the ballot-box? Go on. It is a normal school, and the white women of this country need it. While there exists this brutal element in society which tramples upon the feeble and treads down the weak, I tell you that if there is any class of people who need to be lifted out of their airy nothings and selfishness, it is the white women of America. [Applause.]

SOJOURNER TRUTH

Address to the First Annual Meeting of the American Equal Rights Association

MAY 9, 1867

Sojourner Truth continued to be an active participant in the women's suffrage movement after the Civil War. In 1867 Susan B. Anthony invited her to address the first annual meeting of the American Equal Rights Association in New York. When Frances Ellen Watkins Harper had addressed the National Woman's Rights Convention the year before, she chided white women for being complicit in the daily discrimination that black women faced. Sojourner Truth chose a different approach, making the case for why black women must be part of all discussions about the future of ex-slaves: "There is a great stir about colored men getting their rights, but not a word about the colored women; and if colored men get their rights, and not colored women theirs, you see that the colored men will be masters over the women, and it will be just as bad as it was before." But she was wrong to imply that she was the only one raising this issue. African American women were very much part of the national discussion about suffrage and rights in the immediate aftermath of the Civil War and for years afterward. Sojourner Truth always supported women's suffrage in tandem with black male suffrage, and in 1867 it was still possible to straddle the issue without having to choose. Soon that would no longer be an option.

My friends, I am rejoiced that you are glad, but I don't know how you will feel when I get through. I come from another field—the country of the slave. They have got their liberty—so much good luck to have slavery partly destroyed; not entirely. I want it root and branch destroyed. Then we will all be free indeed. I feel that if I have to answer for the deeds done in my body just as much as a man, I have a right to have just as much as a man. There is a great stir about colored men getting their rights, but not a word about the colored women; and if colored men get their rights, and not colored women theirs, you see the colored men will be masters over the women, and it will be just as bad as it was before. So I am for keeping the thing going while things are stirring; because if we wait till it is still, it will take a great while to get it going again. White women are a great deal smarter, and know more than colored women, while colored women do not know scarcely anything. They go out washing, which is about as high as a colored woman gets, and their men go about idle, strutting up and down; and when the women come home, they ask for their money and take it all, and then scold because there is no food. I want you to consider on that, chil'n. I call you chil'n; you are somebody's chil'n, and I am old enough to be mother of all that is here. I want women to have their rights. In the Courts women have no right, no voice; nobody speaks for them. I wish woman to have her voice there among the pettifoggers. If it is not a fit place for women it is unfit for men to be there. I am above eighty years old; it is about time for me to be going. I have been forty years a slave and forty years free and would be here forty years more to have equal rights for all. I suppose I am kept here because something remains for me to do; I suppose I am yet to help to break the chain. I have done a great deal of work; as much as a man, but did not get so much pay. I used to work in the field and bind grain, keeping up with the cradler; but men doing no more, got twice as much pay; so with the German women. They work in the field and do as much work, but do not get the pay. We do as much, we eat as much, we want as much. I suppose I am about the only colored woman that goes about to speak for the rights of the colored woman. I want to keep the thing stirring, now that the ice is cracked. What we want is a little money. You men know that you get as much again as women when you write, or for what you do. When we get our rights we shall not have to come to you for money, for then we shall have money enough in our own pockets; and may be you will ask us for money. But help us now until we get it. It is a good consolation to know that when we have got this battle once fought we shall not be coming to you any more. You have been having our right so long, that you think, like a slaveholder, that you own us. I know that it is hard for one who has held the reins for so long to give up; it cuts like a knife. It will feel all the better when it closes up again. I have been in Washington about three years, seeing about these colored people. Now colored men have the right to vote; and what I want is to have colored women have the right to vote. There ought to be equal rights now more than ever, since colored people have got their freedom. I am going to talk several times while I am here; so now I will do a little singing. I have not heard any singing since I came here.

Accordingly, suiting the action to the word, Sojourner sang, "We are going home." There, children, said she, after singing, we shall rest from all our labors; first do all we have to do here. There I am determined to go, not to stop short of that beautiful place, and I do not mean to stop till I get there, and meet you there too.

DEBATES AT THE
AMERICAN EQUAL RIGHTS
ASSOCIATION MEETING

MAY 12–14, 1869

The women's rights conventions were often characterized by long speeches and acrimonious debate, and none more so than the gathering of the American Equal Rights Association in New York City in 1869, which was attended by most of the leading activists: Susan B. Anthony, Elizabeth Cady Stanton, Lucy Stone, Henry Blackwell, Frederick Douglass, Ernestine L. Rose, Paulina Wright Davis, and Mary Livermore, among others. Delegates faced a question that would ultimately split the movement in two: Should they rally behind the proposed Fifteenth Amendment, which guaranteed the right to vote irrespective of race, color, or previous condition of servitude, even if it did not include the desired category of sex? The amendment had been proposed by Congress in February and sent to the states for ratification. Many former abolitionists and suffragists agreed that linking what Wendell Phillips called "the negro's hour" with women's suffrage would irrevocably damage the amendment's chances. Susan B. Anthony, Elizabeth Cady Stanton, and others adamantly disagreed, arguing that women deserved the vote just as much if not more than formerly enslaved men. Right after this convention, Stanton and Anthony formed the National Woman Suffrage Association. Six months later, Lucy Stone, Julia Ward Howe, and Henry Blackwell took the lead in organizing the American Woman Suffrage Association. The rival groups did not disagree about whether women should vote, just when and how that goal could be won. So bitter were the divisions between the competing organizations that the women's suffrage movement did not reunite until 1890. The debates were reported in Stanton and Anthony's weekly newspaper, *The Revolution*.

The anniversary exercises of this Association commenced on Wednesday morning of last week at Steinway Hall, in this city. The opening session was very largely attended, the spacious Hall being nearly full, showing that the era of anniversaries of important and useful Societies, is by no means passed away.

In the absence of the president, Mrs. Lucretia Mott, the chair was taken by Mrs. Elizabeth Cady Stanton, First Vice-President. Rev. Mrs. Hanaford, of Massachusetts, opened the meeting with prayer.

On the platform were seated Elizabeth Cady Stanton, Ernestine L. Rose, of New York; Susan B. Anthony of THE REVOLUTION; Mary A. Livermore of Chicago; Phoebe Cozzens, of St. Louis; Lily Peckham, of Milwaukee; Madam Anneke, of Milwaukee; Madam de Hericourt, of Chicago; Mrs. M. E. J. Gage, of Syracuse; Frederick Douglass; Lucy Stone, of New Jersey; Olive Logan of New York; Josephine Griffing, of Washington; Mrs. Paulina W. Davis; Mrs. Abby H. Patton; Mrs. Kate Doggett; Eleanor Kirk; Mrs. Bachelder, of Boston; Mrs. Mary Macdonald, of Mount Vernon; Rev. Mrs. Hanaford; Rev. Antoinette L. Brown Blackwell, of New Jersey; Mrs. Heath, of Kansas; Mrs. Newman, of Binghamton, New York; Mrs. Wendt (German), of New York; Andrew Jackson Davis; Mary F. Davis; Mrs. Holmes, of Union Village, New York; Mrs. Phelps, of the Woman's Bureau, New York; Senator Pomeroy; Mrs. Longley, of Cincinnati; Mrs. Amelia Bloomer, of Council Bluffs, Iowa (the original Bloomer); Lizzie Boynton, of Ohio; Mary A. Gage, of Brooklyn; Mrs. Sarah Norton, of the New York Working Women's Association, and others.

Mrs. Stanton then made a brief opening address. She remarked that the cry of many in the present day, both here and in England, is that republicanism is a failure. But republicanism, that is to say the equal rights of all before the law—black and white, men and women—has never been yet tried in this country or anywhere else, and till it is fairly tried it cannot be called a failure. The danger, the weakness, of our present system is that it is only part republican. We never can have a true republicanism till the whole idea of aristocracy, of sex or anything else is abandoned. This is the only safety of the country, and the Woman's Rights movement is therefore a great patriotic movement. It is not only merely the right of woman to drop a ballot into a box that is fought for; it is the safety and perpetuity of our government. This cause is now intrusted to the women of this nation. All the nations of the earth are looking to this country. We have the destinies of the world in our hands. Let us be true to ourselves and realize on this Western continent a genuine republicanism, a true manhood and true womanhood, and then set up a beacon light to the nations by which they may safely be guided.

Lucy Stone presented verbally the report of the Executive Committee for the last year, running over the various petitions in favor of Woman Suffrage presented during the year to State Legislatures and the various conventions held in different parts of the country, and remarked upon the greater respect shown to the petitions over former years. Formerly, she said, they were laughed at, and frequently not at all considered. This last year they were referred to committees, and often debated at great length in the legislatures, and in some cases motions to submit to the people of the state an amendment to the State constitution doing away with the distinction of sex in the matter of suffrage was rejected by very small majorities indeed. In one state, that of Nevada, such a motion was carried; and the question will shortly be submitted to the people of the state. A number of important and very successful conventions, in various parts of the country, have also been held, and have made a decided impression. But what is most significant is, that public attention is so called to this subject that newspapers of all shades of opinion are giving a great deal of space to it. The question is recognized as taking its place among the great questions of the age, which cannot be put down until it is settled upon the great basis of immutable justice and right. The report was unanimously accepted and adopted.

The following committees, on motion of Miss Susan B. Anthony, were appointed by the Chair: Committee on Nominations—Edwin S. Bunker, Lydia Mott, Edwin A. Studwell, Abby H. Gibbons, Lucy Stone, Charles C. Burleigh, and Lilie Peckham. Committee on Resolutions—Ernestine L. Rose, Henry B. Blackwell, Anna C. Field, Mary A. Livermore, S. S. Foster, Josephine S. Griffing, Madam Anneke, Madam Hericourt, and Phebe A. Hanaford. Committee on Finance—Susan B. Anthony, Anna C. Field, Mary Gage, and R. J. Johnston.

Rev. Mr. Frothingham, of this city, was then introduced, and said he wondered why an invitation had been sent to him; there was no reluctance in his coming, but it seems against the laws of logic that any man should stand upon the platform to advocate woman's cause. This is woman's opportunity and woman's privilege. It is her time to show what she has to show, and to say her word, and speak her own thought to vindicate her own title, and to demonstrate her own claim. It is not for Mr. Phillips or any other distinguished man to add anything to the importance and dignity of this occasion. I would not pay so poor a compliment to the ladies who ask us here, as to say that they need us to advocate their cause; still less will I accuse them of asking us here to set off their brilliance in contrast to our addresses. But they ask us here to obtain our sympathy, and welcome us to the platform became it is a strong platform. They desire that we should share in their earnestness, and share also in their triumph. Having themselves been shut out from all platforms upon which men have argued, they wish now to play the Christian part and ask us to share theirs. I am not here this morning thinking that I can add anything to the strength of the cause, but thinking that perhaps I may gain something from the generous, sweet atmosphere that I am sure will prevail. This is a meeting, if I understand it, of the former Woman's Rights Association, and the subjects which come before us properly are the subjects which concern woman living under laws that concern woman in all her social, civil, and domestic life. But the one question which is of vital moment and of sole prominence, is the question of Suffrage. All other questions have been virtually decided in favor of woman. She has the *entree* to all the fields of labor, she is beginning to have, and will soon have, all her rights. She is now the teacher, preacher, artist, she has a place in the scientific world—in the literary world. She is a journalist, a maker of books, a public reader; in fact, there is no position which woman, as woman, is not entitled to hold and is freely welcomed to possess. She has overcome all the prejudices relating to these positions; but there is one position alone that woman, as woman, does not occupy, and that is the position of a voter. One field alone she does not possess, and that is the political field; one work she is not permitted, even as a woman, to perform, and that is the work of making laws. This question goes down to the bottom—it touches the vital matter of woman's relation to the state. Lucretia Mott said, at the very beginning of this movement, that she feared the worst enemy of our movement would be woman herself. Her love of ease, her fondness for show, her passion for extravagance, her love of pleasure, the subtle spirit of worldliness which has been forced upon woman in the course of ages, cannot easily be thrown off. I believe that thoughtful men, men of culture, men of earnestness, men of aspiration, men of purpose, men of any scientific acquirements, men who are liberal, are ready for Female Suffrage. (Applause.) They may not go the length of women who advocate it; they may not believe that woman is better, or wiser, or more virtuous, more pure, earnest, more devoted than men are. They may not believe that women are any more proof against the seductions of power, against the temptations of political life; they may not believe that politics would be greatly ennobled by the admission of women to the ballot. The question is, is there anything in the constitution of the female mind, of character, and disposition, as to disqualify her for the exercise of the franchise. Has she nothing to say in regard to war and peace; on questions of finance? Is it nothing to her who is sent to European courts? Is it nothing to her how the laws relating to property are enacted? As long as there are fifty, thirty, ten, or even one woman who is capable of exercising this trust or holding this responsibility, it demonstrates that sex, as a sex, does not disfranchise, and the whole question is granted. (Applause.) Here our laws are made by irresponsible people—people who demoralize and debauch society; people who make them live in a large measure by the upholding the institutions that are inherently, forever, and always corrupt. (Applause.) Laws that are made by the people who own dramshops, who keep gambling-saloons, who minister to the depraved passions and vices of either sex. Laws made by the idler, the dissipated, by the demoralized—are they laws? I believe that it is among men an impression that the government of the city would be better if forty thousand or fifty thousand could be disfranchised. If they were prevented from putting a halter round their own necks, it would be well. Let all have a chance and see who are able to take their position among the law-makers. It is true that this government is founded upon caste. Slavery is abolished, but sex is not. I regard this movement as a conservative one. The object is not to extend the ballot especially, but it is to purify the ballot—it is to raise it. This society takes an interest in the temperance movement, and hygenic reforms, and the anti-slavery reform. One reason that the Suffrage is not conceded to woman is that those who refuse to do so, do not appreciate it themselves. (Applause.) As long as the power of Suffrage means the power to steal, to tread down the weak, and get the rich offices into their own hands, those who have the key of the coffers will wish to keep it in their own pockets. (Applause.)

The next speaker was Mrs. Stanton whose address we were able to give last week, it being about all of the proceedings we had time for, before going to press.

Rev. Antoinette Brown Blackwell followed Mrs. Stanton in a few remarks. She said she could understand that all ignorant men would vote to keep them out of the franchise, but all intelligent men would out-vote them. Would not all men come up and see that their wives and daughters receive their rights? It was safe always to concede rights wherever they were found, and to whomsoever they may belong. (Applause.)

The Committee on Organization then made their report. They recommended as the officers and committees of the society for the ensuing year:

President—Lucretia Mott.

Vice-Presidents at Large—Mrs. Elizabeth Cady Stanton and Ernestine L. Rose.

Vice-Presidents for the States—John Neal, Maine; Armenia White, New Hampshire; James Hutchinson, Jr., Vermont; William Lloyd Garrison, Julia Ward Howe, Massachusetts; Elizabeth B. Chase, Rhode Island; Isabella B. Hooker, Connecticut; Henry Ward Beecher, Frederick Douglass, Martha C. Wright, of New York; Portia Gage, New Jersey; Robert Purvis, Pennsylvania; Mary A. Livermore, Illinois; George W. Julian, Iowa; Benjamin F. Wade, Ohio; Gilbert Haven, Michigan; Rev. A. L. Lindsley, Oregon; Joseph H. Moore, California; Hon. E. Nye, Nevada; Hon. A. P. K. Safford, Arizona; Hon. James H. Ashley, Montana; Josephine S. Griffing, District of Columbia; Thomas Garrett, Delaware; Ellen M. Harris, Maryland; John C. Underwood, Virginia; Mrs. J. K. Miller, North Carolina; Mrs. Pillsbury, South Carolina; Elizabeth Wright, Texas; Mrs. Dr. Hawkes, Florida; Hon. Guy Wines, Tennessee; Mrs. Francis Minor, Missouri; Hon. Charles Robinson, Kansas; Governor Fairchild and Madam Anneke, Wisconsin; Mrs. Harriet Bishop, Minnesota; Hon. Mr. Loughridge, Iowa.

Executive Committee—Elizabeth R. Tilton, Lucy Stone, Edwin Studwell, Susan B. Anthony, Antoinette Brown Blackwell, Thomas W. Higginson, Anna C. Field, Edward S. Bunker, Abby Hutchinson Patton, Oliver Johnson, Elizabeth Smith Miller, Margaret E. Winchester, Edward Cromwell, Robert J. Johnston, Mary A. Davis.

Corresponding Secretaries—Mary E. Gage, Harriet Purvis, Henry B. Blackwell.

Treasurer—John J. Merritt.

The Rev. Stephen Foster rose and made a lengthy speech, in which he laid down the principle that when any person, on account of strong objections against them in the minds of some, prevented harmony in a society and efficiency in its operations, those persons should retire from prominent positions in that society. He related how he had taken that course when, as agent of the Anti-Slavery Society, he became obnoxious on account of the course he took on certain questions. He objected, he said, to certain nominations made by the Committee for various reasons. The first was that the persons nominated had publicly repudiated the principles of the society. One of these was the presiding officer.

Mrs. Stanton—I would like you to say in what respect.

Mr. Foster—I will with pleasure, for, ladies and gentlemen, I admire our talented President with all my heart, and love the woman. (Great laughter.) But I believe she has publicly repudiated the principles of the society.

Mrs. Stanton—I would like Mr. Foster to state in what way.

Mr. Foster—What are these principles? The equality of men—universal suffrage. Now, these ladies stand at the head of a paper, which has adopted as its motto Educated Suffrage. Now, I put myself on this platform as an enemy of educated suffrage, as an enemy of white suffrage, as an enemy of man suffrage, as an enemy of every kind of suffrage except universal suffrage. THE REVOLUTION lately had an article headed "That infamous Fifteenth Amendment." It is true it was not written by our President; yet it comes from a person whom she has over and over again publicly indorsed. Now, I am not willing to take George Francis Train on this platform with his ridicule of the negro and opposition to his enfranchisement.

Mrs. Mary A. Livermore—Is it quite generous to bring George Francis Train on this platform when he has retired from THE REVOLUTION entirely?

Mr. Foster—If THE REVOLUTION, which has so often

indorsed George Francis Train, will repudiate him because of his course in respect to the negro's rights, I have nothing further to say. But they do not repudiate him. He goes out; they do not cast him out.

Miss Anthony—Of course we do not.

Mr. Foster—My friend says yes to what I have said. I thought it was so. Then I have other objections to these women being officers of this society. When we organized this society, we appointed a committee for the purpose of having a body which should be responsible for the funds of the society, and we appointed a treasurer to take care of the funds. But if you look into that committee's report, you will find that it shirked its duty. That committee put its funds into the hands of an individual person, and let her run the machine.

Miss Anthony—That is true.

Mr. Foster—And she never kept any books or account of the expenditures.

Miss Anthony (with energy)—*That is false.* Every dollar received by me and every dollar expended, item by item, was presented to the Trust Fund committee of Boston, of which this gentleman is a member. The account was audited, and has been reported to me, by Wendell Phillips, Parker Pillsbury, Abby Kelley Foster, and Charles K. Whipple and they voted me a check of a thousand dollars to balance the account. If my accounts were not straight, these men, not a woman, uneducated, were to blame.

Mr. Foster—I would be glad to believe Miss Anthony, but her statement is not reliable, for Wendell Phillips and Abby Kelley Foster told me differently.

Mrs. Stanton—When any man comes on to this platform and says that a woman does not speak the truth, he is out of order. I shall put the question to the Convention.

Mrs. Stanton then took the vote on the point of order. It was decided by the audience that Mr. Foster was out of order.

Miss Anthony—I want to say—

Mr. Foster (who still kept the floor)—Susan, you are out of order. (Laughter.)

Miss Anthony—I want to say that I have been in council several times of late with persons for the purpose of bringing about a reconciliation in this matter, so that there might be no feud brought before the public. You hear this. I do not bring it forward.

Mr. Frederick Douglass—Of course the vote of the Society just passed does not prevent Mr. Foster proceeding in order, if he was out of order. If, however, a different understanding is to be given to it—that no one is to be allowed to criticise the list of officers proposed, it is out of the question for me to utter a word on such a platform. We are used to freedom of speech, and there is a profound conviction in the minds of reformers in general, that error may be safely tolerated, while truth is left free to counteract it. What if Mr. Foster does go on with his criticism on Miss Anthony, and Mrs. Stanton and THE REVOLUTION. While Miss Anthony and Mrs. Stanton and THE REVOLUTION have tongues to speak, why not have free speech here about them?

Mr. Foster—Miss Anthony was allowed to charge me with making a false statement and the President did not interfere. When I returned the compliment I was called to order, for contradicting a woman. (Great applause.) But you cannot draw me into a quarrel. Now I only wanted to tell you why the Massachusetts society cannot coalesce with the party here and why we want these women to retire and leave us to nominate officers who can receive the respect of both parties. The Massachusetts abolitionists cannot co-operate with this society as it is now organized. There are certain persons who could serve the cause, if they only loved it better than themselves. If you choose to put officers here that ridicule the negro, and pronounce the Fifteenth Amendment infamous, why I must retire; I cannot work with you. You cannot have my support, and you must not use my name. I cannot shoulder the responsibility of electing officers who publicly repudiate the principles of the society.

Mr. Blackwell said: I have been associated with the negotiation mentioned for the reconciliation of these two parties. I want to call your attention to the fact that these scenes on this platform never originate with the women. The facts of the case are these: During the early portion of the society Miss Anthony was given full power over the funds of the society to spend them as she thought best. Some of us thought her expenditures were not judicious; no one doubted the purity of her motives. The whole financial matter, however, has been settled, and in this way. Miss Anthony brought in a statement of her expenditures to the society. No one doubts that all the expenditures were actually made as she reported. Her statement made due to herself from the society a thousand dollars. Now, Miss Anthony, for the sake of harmony and the good of the cause, has given up her claim for this one thousand dollars. In regard to this we have to say that we are entirely satisfied with the settlement thus made. When a person, for the good of a cause, will make a pecuniary sacrifice of expenditures made, which expenditures many might well consider perfectly wise, although some of us did not, it shows such a spirit that I think that this question might well have been kept back. In regard to the criticisms on our officers, I will agree that many unwise things have been written in THE REVOLUTION by a gentleman who furnished part of the means by which that paper has been carried on. But that gentleman has withdrawn, and you, who know the real opinions of Miss Anthony and Mrs. Stanton on the question of negro suffrage, do not believe that they mean to create antagonism between the negro and the woman question. If they did disbelieve in negro suffrage, it would be no reason for excluding them. We should no more exclude a person from our platform for disbelieving negro suffrage than a person should be excluded from the anti-slavery platform for disbelieving woman suffrage. But I know that Miss Anthony and Mrs. Stanton believe in the right of the negro to vote. We are united on that point. There is now no question of either money or principle between us.

The vote on the report of the Committee on Organization was now taken and the report was adopted by a large majority.

Mr. Douglass—I came here more as a listener than to speak, and I have listened with a great deal of pleasure to the eloquent address of the Rev. Mr. Frothingham and the splendid address of the President. There is no name greater than that of Elizabeth Cady Stanton in the matter of Woman's Rights and Equal Rights, but my sentiments are tinged a little against THE REVOLUTION. There was in the address to which I allude, a sentiment in reference to employment and certain names, such as "Sambo," and the gardener and the bootblack and the daughter of Jefferson and Washington, and all the rest that I cannot coincide with. I have asked what difference there is between the daughters of Jefferson and Washington and other daughters. (Laughter.) I must say that I do not see how any one can pretend that there is the same urgency in giving the ballot to woman as to the negro. With us, the matter is a question of life and death. It is a matter of existence, at least, in fifteen states of the Union. When women, because they are women, are hunted down through the cities of New York and New Orleans; when they are dragged from their houses and hung upon lamp-posts; when their children are torn from their arms, and their brains dashed out upon the pavement; when they are objects of insult and outrage at every turn; when they are in danger of having their homes burnt down over their heads; when their children are not allowed to enter schools; then they will have an urgency to obtain the ballot equal to our own. (Great applause.)

A Voice—Is that not all true about black women?

Mr. Douglass—Yes, yes, yes, it is true of the black woman, but not because she is a woman but because she is black. (Applause.) Julia Ward Howe at the conclusion of her great speech delivered at the convention in Boston last year, said, "I am willing that the negro shall get it before me." (Applause.) Woman! why she has ten thousand modes of grappling with her difficulties. I believe that all the virtues of the world can take care of all the evil. I believe that all the intelligence can take care of all the ignorance. (Applause.) I am in favor of Woman's Suffrage in order that we shall have all the virtue and all vice confronted. Let me tell you that when there were few houses in which the black man could have put his head, this woolley head of mine found a refuge in the house of Mrs. Elizabeth Cady Stanton, and if I had been blacker than sixteen midnights, without a single star, it would have been the same. (Applause.)

Miss Anthony—I want to say a single word. The old anti-slavery school and others have said that the women must stand back and wait until the other class shall be recognized. But we say that if you will not give the whole loaf of justice and suffrage to an entire people, give it to the most intelligent first. (Applause.) If intelligence, justice, and morality are to be placed in the government, then let the question of woman be brought up first and that of the negro last. (Applause.) While I was canvassing the state with petitions in my hand and had them filled with names for our cause and sent them to the legislature, a man dared to say to me that the freedom of women was all a theory and not a practical thing. (Applause.) When Mr. Douglass mentioned the black man first and the women last, if he had noticed he would have seen that it was the men that clapped and not the women. There is not the woman born who desires to eat the bread of dependence, no matter whether it be from the hand of father, husband or brother; for any one who does so eat her bread places herself in the power of the person from whom she takes it. (Applause.) Mr. Douglass talks about the wrongs of the negro; how he is hunted down, and the children's brains dashed out by mobs; but with all the wrongs and outrages that he to-day suffers, he would not exchange his sex and take the place of Elizabeth Cady Stanton. (Laughter and applause.) No matter, there is a glory— (Loud applause, completely drowning the speaker's voice.)

Mr. Douglass—Will you allow me—

Miss Anthony—Yes, anything; we are in for a fight to-day. (Great laughter and applause.)

Mr. Douglass—I want to know if granting you the right of Suffrage will change the nature of our sexes. (Great laughter.)

Miss Anthony—It will change the pecuniary position of women, it will place her in a position where she can earn her own bread. (Loud Applause.) She will not then be compelled to take hold of such employments that man chooses for her.

Why, Mr. Douglass, in our Working Women's Association we discussed a certain question, and then one woman proposed that at the next meeting we should discuss the question "Why marriages are on the decline." When women are thrown upon their own resources without proper education, their alternatives are starvation or prostitution, and then society turns round upon them. Marriage all over the country is regarded as too expensive a luxury. A man cannot afford to marry. What we demand is, that we shall have the ballot; we shall never get our rights until we have it. The object of this Society is to acquire this right and privilege. (Applause.)

Mrs. Norton said that there was one thing that Mr. Douglass's remarks left it open for her to say, and that was to defend the government from the inferred inability to grapple with the two questions at once. It legislates upon many questions of landed and other interests at one and the same time, and it has the power to decide the Woman question and the Negro question at one and the same time. (Applause.)

Mrs. Lucy Stone then said: Mrs. Stanton will, of course, advocate the precedence for her sex, and Mr. Douglass will strive for the first position for his, and both are perhaps right. If it be true that the government derives its authority from the consent of the governed, we are safe in trusting that principle to the uttermost. If one has a right to say that you cannot read and cannot vote, then it may be said that you are a woman and cannot vote. We are lost if we turn away from the middle principle and argue for one class. I was once a teacher among fugitive slaves. There was one old man, and every tooth was gone, his hair was white, and his face was full of wrinkles, yet, day after day and hour after hour, he came up to the school-house and tried with patience to learn to read, and by-and-by, when he had spelled out the first few verses of the first chapter of the Gospel of St. John, he said to me, "Now I want to learn to write." I tried to make him satisfied with what he had acquired, but the old man said, "Mrs. Stone, somewhere in the wide world I have a son; I have not heard from him in twenty years; if I should hear from him, I want to write to him, so take hold of my hand and teach me." I did, but before he had proceeded in many lessons, the angels came and gathered him up and bore him to his Father. Let any man speak of an educated suffrage. The gentleman who addressed you claimed that the negroes had the first right to the Suffrage, and drew a picture which only his great word-power can do. He again in Massachusetts, when she had cast a majority in favor of Grant and negro suffrage, stood upon the platform and said that women had better wait for the negro; that is, that both could not be carried, and that the question of the negro had better be that one. But I freely forgave him because he felt as he spoke. But the Woman Suffrage is more imperative than his own; and I want to remind the audience that when he says what the Ku-Kluxes did all over the south, the Ku-Kluxes here in the north in the shape of men, take away the children from the mother, and separate them as completely as if done on the block of the auctioneer. Over in New Jersey they have a law which says that *any* father—he might be the most brutal man that ever existed—*any* father, it says, whether he be under age or not, may by his last will and testament dispose of the custody of his child, born or to be born, and that such disposition shall be good against all persons, and that the mother may not recover her child; and that law modified in form exists over every state in the Union except in New York and Kansas. Now, I really forget what I was going to say, having thus digressed, but—

Mr. Douglass—Perhaps you were going to explain to the audience how much better it would be if women, instead of being compelled to support their own children—suppose it was imposed upon the woman to support her own children—and when they separated take charge of them and relieve us of all responsibility in the matter.

Mrs. Stone—Mr. Wendell Phillips told us in his lecture on Daniel O'Connell how the Irishman is treated in the way of sale, but the husbands of this day have the right to appropriate to themselves all the fruits of the labor of their wives. The woman has an ocean of wrong too deep for any plummet, and the negro, too, has an ocean of wrongs that cannot be fathomed. There are two great oceans; in the one is the black man, and in the other is the woman. But I thank God for the Fifteenth Amendment, and hope that it will be adopted in every state. I will be thankful in my soul if *any* body can get out of the terrible pit, and if the other party can succeed better than we, then let them do it. (Applause.) Another need for Woman Suffrage is, because our government is full of corruption and fraud, and so the men hate the idea of women having anything to do with it. (Applause.)

But I believe that the national safety of the government would be more promoted by the admission of women as an element of restoration and harmony than the other. I believe that the influence of woman will save the country before every other influence. (Applause.) I see the signs of the times pointing to this consummation, and I believe that in some parts of the country women will vote for the President of these United States in 1872. (Applause.)

EVENING SESSION.—At the opening of the evening session Mr. Henry B. Blackwell presented a series of resolutions, after which the Rev. Antoinette Brown Blackwell made a speech of considerable length, in which she went over considerable ground to that delivered by her in the preceding part of the day.

ADDRESS OF MISS OLIVE LOGAN.

Miss Logan was received with loud applause. She was beautifully dressed upon the occasion in a handsome gray silk dress, with scarlet facings and borders, and pompadour corsage. Her hair was fastened *a la Eugenie*. She said: I see some faces in this room which I did not expect to see here—the features of certain friends who have known me in another sphere of life than this, and who have evidently come here to hear what I shall have to say about Woman's Rights. I am glad to see these faces here, and wish I could induce all my old friends to follow me in that new sphere of life which I have chosen since I have said farewell to the mimic stage. But if, perchance, they have come here to scoff, I hope they will remain until they are ready to pray that God will speed the cause of Woman's Rights. (Applause.) It was my purpose this evening to define my position upon the subject of Woman's Rights, and say what I have to approve of in this movement, and what I disapprove of, and to speak as heartily as I please in praise of the conduct of some of the apostles, and to express my sorrow, my disgust even, at the conduct of certain others who have lost all respect and have trampled upon culture and self-respect in the endeavor to widen woman's field for liberty. (Applause.) But the presence of these friends has induced me to say a few words in explanation of how I became that dreadful creature, a Woman's Rights woman. (Applause.) It has been my custom to talk about the subject with which I am most familiar. When it comes to talking about woman, of course, here is a theme with which I am most familiar; and that reminds me of an old adage, which I thus disprove, about "Familiarity breeding contempt." (Laughter and applause.) I am going to relate my experience, as our Methodist friends say. I had long been on the anxious seat in embracing the religion of woman's rights, though I reject the idiosyncracies of many of its followers and some of the tenets of this religion. I stand here to-night full of faith, inborn faith, in the right of women to advance boldly in all ennobling paths, and full of faith in her right to do with her hands all that she is able to do, and what her brain and intellect are equal to, and to reject all the drudgeries that men dislike and thus think and say that women are peculiarly made to do. I have full faith in her right to enter into the arena of politics and set something right in politics which is now all wrong. (Applause.) This is my text, and it goes no further. It does not include woman's right to infringe the decencies of life and to outrage propriety, or to do anything that can lower her sex—(applause)—and when any woman presumes upon the esteem of these rights so far as to unsex herself, I will be the first to point the finger of scorn. (Great applause.) I am not ready yet to see women wear trousers (great laughter and applause)— nor men wear petticoats (renewed applause)—but that is a branch of the subject on which I am going to speak more fully at a future time. I set out now to relate my experience, and if there are any here who do not take any interest in the relation, they can take a nap until Mrs. Stanton and Miss Anthony speak, and they will wake them up pretty soon. (Laughter.) In my former sphere of life, the equality of woman was fully recognized so far as the form of labor and the amount of reward for her labor are concerned. As an actress, there was no position in which I was not fully welcomed if I possessed the ability and industry to reach it. For if I could become a Ristori, my earnings would be as great as hers, and if I was a man and could become a Kean, a Macready, or a Booth, the same reward would be obtained. If I reach no higher rank than what is called a "walking lady," I am sure of the same pay as a man who occupies the position of a "walking gentleman." In that sphere of life, be it remembered, I was reared from childhood; to that place I was so accustomed that I had no idea it was a privilege denied my sex to enter into almost every other field of endeavor. Whatever evils are attached to the theatrical world—and no one deplores them more deeply than I—I bade farewell to the mimic stage four years ago. What my reasons were it is unnecessary to state at length, but one of them certainly was not a hope of better pay in any other field of labor. As an actress, the money I earned was more evenly proportioned to the labor performed than it has ever been since; but my hope to succeed in literature was strong, and I entered upon my new scene of labor with hope and desire, though knowing well I should not earn in literature what I had been earning. But I found myself in this line on an equality with man again. If I wrote a good article, I got as good pay as a man; and Heaven knows the pay to man or woman was small enough. (Applause.) In that field, for a long time, I did not yet feel an interest in the subject of Women's Rights, and

stood afar off, looking at the work of those revolutionary creatures, Mrs. Stanton and Miss Anthony. The idea of identifying
myself with them was as far removed from my thoughts as becoming a female gymnast and whirling upon a trapeze. But
once I wrote a lecture, and one night I delivered it. Adhering
to my practice of speaking about that which was most familiar,
my lecture was about the stage. I lectured, not because I had a
shadow of a woman's right to lecture, but simply because I
thought the pay would be better in that department; the idea
that I was running counter to anybody's prejudice, never entered my head. And I was so far removed that I never read a
page of THE REVOLUTION in my life, and, what is more, I did
not want to; and when Miss Anthony passed down Broadway
and saw the bills announcing my lecture she knew nothing
about me, and what is more, *she* did not want to. (Laughter.)
She made a confession to me afterwards. She said to herself,
"Here is a lady going to lecture about the stage," looking
through her blessed spectacles, as I can see her (laughter)—and
I can hear her muttering contemptuously "a woman's rights
woman." (Laughter.) That is not so very long ago, a little over
a year. I met a lady the other day who thought I was a speaker
for ten years. But I am only fifteen months old in this business,
but the greater length I go in it the more I find myself enabled
to do. Since this great question of woman's rights was thrust
upon me, I am asked to define my position; wherever I have
travelled in the fifteen months I have had to do so. A lady of
society asked me "Are you in favor of Woman's Rights?" I had
either to answer yes or no, and "Yes," I said. (Applause.) I have
met this sort of bigotry in almost every community where I
lectured. In the city of Norwich, Connecticut, there was a man,
whose name I will not tell—(laughter)—I will call him Mr.
Smith, that is vague enough. (Laughter.) Well, Mr. Smith is a
good church member, and has a wife and daughter. On the
morning after my lecture the daughter went to the neighboring
town by railroad. She took the same train I did, and sat in the
seat directly behind me. She was a loud talker, and presently a
nice young man of her acquaintance also came in and sat down
beside her. I said that she was a loud talker, and he was a loud
talker too. (Laughter.) Presently I heard her say, "Did you go
to that lecture last night?" "What, that Olive Logan? no, I don't

approve of woman lectures," (the speaker imitating a rough voice that induced great laughter.) This was very interesting to me, so I turned round in my seat, and sat myself comfortably, so that I could look them in the face. They did not seem to mind me in the least. "Pau went to that lecture," said the young lady. "You don't say so; I thought your pau did not approve of it. What made him go?" "Well, he did not mean to go, for I wanted him to go and take mau and me; but he was going down to the post-office, and he just looked in at the door and he saw Deacon Croaker there, and he thought that if Deacon Croaker could go in he could." (Great laughter.) This was a revelation to me. It awakened in my mind two ideas: first, that there was a prejudice against a woman as a lecturer, and second, it is a prejudice which leads men to act just as Deacon Croaker. I did not know who Deacon Croaker saw within the hall that he went in—(laughter)—at any rate, from that moment forth I was prepared for that species of bigotry, and being prepared I acted accordingly. Frankly, my chief regret was that I did not get my eyes opened before I went to Boston to lecture; there I distinguished him for the first time, and it almost demoralized me and nearly robbed me of the power of speech. In that audience in Boston Deacon Croaker was present—(laughter)—and unfortunately for me Deacon Croaker did not approve of me, and rose to his feet, heaved a deep sigh, and walked out. (Laughter.) Immediately Mr. Smith—half a dozen Mr. Smiths—who had followed Deacon Croaker in, rose to their feet, heaved deep sighs, and followed him out. (Laughter.) Some of my friends, on the strength of my Boston encounter with Deacon Croaker, placed me on a basis of antagonism with Boston—a position which I decline to occupy. The influences of a lifetime are not to be eradicated so easily, and my esteem for Boston is as strong as it always was. (Applause.) But my experience of Deacon Croaker was a trifling thing in comparison with what I met and saw in other places. I found, in my travels, in a New England town, an educated, cultivated woman, who found herself obliged to earn her livelihood, after living a life of luxury and ease. Her husband, who had provided her with every material comfort, had gone to the grave. All his property was taken to pay his debts, and she found herself penniless. What was that woman to do? She has turned to teaching school for the present, but that will hardly provide her with bread. Besides, she is ambitious of nobler things. In man ambition for nobler things is commended; why not in woman? She appeals to me what I would advise her to do; asks if I would advise her to go upon the stage. Alas! no; I cannot advise any woman to go upon the stage with the demoralizing influences which seem there to prevail more every day, when its greatest rewards are won by brazen-faced, stained, yellow-haired, padded-limbed creatures—(applause)—while actresses of the old school, well trained, well qualified, decent, cannot earn a living. (Applause.) But this woman wants to do something. She looks abroad among the usual employments of women, and her only resource seems to be that little bit of steel around which cluster so many associations—the needle—and by the needle, with the best work and the best wages, the most she can get is two dollars a day. With this, poor as it is, she will be content; but she finds an army of other women looking for the same, and most of them looking in vain. These things have opened my eyes to a vista such as I never saw before. They have touched my heart as it never before was touched. They have aroused my conscience to the fact that this woman question is the question of the hour, and that I must take part in it. (Applause.) I take my stand boldly, proudly, with such earnest, thoughtful women as Susan B. Anthony, Mrs. Stanton and Anna Dickinson, to work together with them for the enfranchisement of women, for her elevation personally and socially, and above all for her right and opportunity to work at such employments as she can follow, with the right to such pay as men get for the same. (Applause.) Those young friends, for the especial benefit of whom I have related my experience, I feel, will sympathise with us in these views. But if they, being women, are not moved to join with us, labor for the advancement of woman—if they will not do this for the sake of those who are not able to fight for themselves, at least do not throw obstacles in our way. There are thousands of women who have no vital interest in this question. They are happy wives and daughters, and may they ever be so; but they cannot tell how soon their husbands and brothers may be lost to them, and then they will find, as so many have found themselves, destitute and penniless with no resources in themselves against misfortune. Then it will be for such that we labor.

(Applause.) Our purpose is to help those who need help, helpless widows and orphan girls. There is no need to do battle in this matter. In all kindness and gentleness we urge our claims. There is no need to declare war upon man, for the best of men in this country are with us heart and soul. (Applause.) These are with us in greater numbers even than our own sex. (A Voice— "That is true." Great applause.) Do not say that we seek to break up family peace and fireside joy; far from it. (Applause.) We interfere not with the wife or daughter who is happy in the strong protection thrown around her by a father or husband, but it is cowardice for such to throw obstacles in the way of those who need help. More than this, for the sake of the helpless woman, to whose unhappiness in the loss of beloved ones is added the agony of hard and griping want. For the sake of the poor girl who has no power to cope with the hard actualities of a desolate life, while her trembling feet tread the crumbling edge of the dark abyss of infamy. For the sake of this we are pleading and entertaining this great question, and withhold your answer till at least you have learned to say, "God speed."

The next speaker was Miss Phoebe Cozzens, a young law student from St. Louis, who gave, in a most agreeable and forcible manner, one of the best addresses of the evening, a report of which is promised for THE REVOLUTION next week.

Mrs. Mary A. Livermore, the proprietor of the *Agitator*, a Woman's Rights organ published in Chicago, closed the evening session with a long address, the principal portion of which was a relation of her knowledge of the hardships endured by women on account of their legal disabilities, and of the incompetency and utter selfishness of politicians and men generally, as seen by her in her experiences as a nurse during the war, and during some time spent in Washington. Mrs. Livermore was heard with the deepest attention, no impatience being manifested by the very large audience, although it was nearly ten o'clock before she took the platform.

SECOND DAY'S PROCEEDINGS.

THE Association met again in convention at Steinway Hall, on Thursday morning, May 13th, the President, Mrs. E. Cady Stanton, in the chair.

Mrs. Lucy Stone read letters to the convention from John Stuart Mill, Wm. Lloyd Garrison, Rev. Samuel Johnson, of Lynn Mass., and others.

James W. Stillman, a member of the Rhode Island Legislature, was then introduced. He said he could not hold his peace while he saw the burdens under which the women of this country were laboring. John Stuart Mill said that there were three steps through which every reform had to pass; the first was ridicule, the second argument, and the third adoption. If he had not greatly mistaken, this question had passed through the first stage, and had come to the second. The time was now passed away for ridicule and contempt: the question is demanding attention, and, like Banquo's ghost, it will not down.

Mrs. Livermore said that they had delegations from the west, and she did not want them to go home and say that they had not been heard because they had not a chance. In Chicago, when they had a convention, the newspapers gave up all their editions for three days and gave them correct reports. But here, judging from the papers that morning, they were thought of no account. Then, too, they were reported to have said what they did not say.

The President—That is rather severe upon our New York reporters. They are doing their best. (Great applause.)

Mrs. Rose—If those who live in Chicago are best, who made them so, or made Chicago what it was? The experience of the child is derived from the parent. What made Chicago but the City of New York? (Great applause.)

Mrs. Livermore—We illustrate the truth of Dr. Watt's hymn which says that "we are grown wiser than our teachers, and better know the Lord." (Great laughter.)

Dr. Mercy B. Jackson recounted the difficulties that had to be met in gaining admission to our colleges for young ladies, and proceeded to argue that if the government depends upon the consent of the governed, woman should not be subject to any laws which she had not a hand in enacting. Women should not be deprived of the trial by a jury of her peers. This freest and best government on the face of the earth is yet open to the objection that a portion of its inhabitants are subject to partial enactments.

Fred. Douglass said that as there is a most important

question submitted to the American people, he wanted to have a vote upon it from that audience. He then read the following resolutions:

Resolved, That the American Equal Rights Association, in loyalty to its comprehensive demands for the political equality of all American citizens, without distinction of race or sex, hails the extension of suffrage to any class heretofore disfranchised, as a cheering part of the triumph of our whole idea.

Resolved, therefore, That we gratefully welcome the pending fifteenth amendment, prohibiting disfranchisement on account of race, and earnestly solicit the State Legislatures to pass it without delay.

Resolved, furthermore, That in view of this promised and speedy culmination of one-half of our demands, we are stimulated to redouble our energy to secure the further amendment guaranteeing the same sacred rights without limitation to sex.

Resolved, That until the constitution shall know neither black nor white, neither male nor female, but only the equal rights of all classes, we renew our solemn indictment against that instrument as defective, unworthy, and an oppressive charter for the self-government of a free people. (Applause and hisses.)

A Lady—I move that these resolutions be laid upon the table for future consideration.

The President—Of course. You see these resolutions require discussion; therefore, they had better be laid upon the table for future consideration.

Mr. Burleigh—I do not think that they should be laid upon the table, because they are not before the meeting. To lay them upon the table will make it necessary to have a vote to bring them before the meeting.

No action being taken on the above resolutions,

The Rev. Gilbert Haven, editor of *Zion's Herald*, was introduced. He said: Ladies and gentlemen—As I believe that is the way to address you, or shall I merge you into one and call you fellow-citizens——

Miss Anthony—Let me tell you how to say it. It is perfectly right for a gentleman to say "ladies and gentlemen," but a lady should say, "gentlemen and ladies." (Great applause.) You mention your friend's name first before you do your own. (Applause.) I always feel like rebuking any lady who says, "ladies and gentlemen." It is a lack of good manners to say so. (Laughter and great applause.)

Mr. Haven (continuing)—I thank the lady for the rule she has laid down. Now, Mr. Beecher has said that a minister is composed of the worst part of man and woman, and there are wealthy men who say that the pulpit should be closed against the introduction of politics, but I am glad this sentiment is not a rule; I rejoice that the country has emancipated the ministry so that a minister can speak politics. Now, I go further than saying that it is the mere right of the women to achieve their end—I say it is an obligation imposed upon the American people to grant their views to this large and influential class of the commonwealth. The legislation of the country concerns the woman as much as the man. Is not the wife as much interested in the preservation of property as her husband? Another reason is, that the purity of politics depends upon the admission of woman to the franchise, for without her influence the morality of politics is not to be obtained. (Applause.)

Mrs. Gage, of Onondaga, New York, presented herself as a delegate to the convention from Onondaga, and read the following report passed at the meeting which appointed her to that office:

Resolved, That this convention calls upon the convention to be convened in the city of New York to recommend and favor a system of organization which shall reach every town, village and hamlet in the United States, presenting a plan in detail, which, by its uniformity, shall render it easy for the whole people to co-operate in the reform.

Mr. Schienhoeff moved a resolution, the purport of which was that the convention should recommend and sanction the formation of co-operative societies as the means of securing to working women just compensation for their labors and the protection and help which they so much need.

This resolution was strongly opposed by Mrs. Livermore and others, on the ground that the question of labor and capital was not within the province of the convention. They thought the whole subject was a separate one, and a very extensive one, and ought to be left to another convention. Mrs. Stanton, Miss Anthony, and others took a different view, contending that any proposition for the amelioration of the condition of working-women was peculiarly appropriate to be discussed by the convention.

Mrs. Dr. L. S. Batchelder, a delegate appointed by the Boston Working Women's Association, said that she represented ten thousand working women of New England, and they had instructed her, as their representative, to introduce a resolution looking to the amelioration of the condition of the working women. All the talk here, so far, has been in favor of the ballot and in the interest of the heiress. She was in favor of inserting a resolution in the series which would look to the interest of the poor working-girl, that she might be enabled to earn her daily bread without resorting to the last means of obtaining it. She then began to read a series of resolutions passed at the recent New England Working women's Convention in Boston, and which were to the effect that industrial schools, instead of alms-houses, should be built, and that the talents of women should be so far recognized that they be accorded the same compensation for their labor that is given to men.

AFTERNOON SESSION.—After some remarks by Lilie Peckham, of Milwaukee, Senator Wilson was called upon, and spoke as follows:

This is a rather new place for me to stand in, and yet I am very glad to say that I have no new views in regard to this question. I learned, fifteen or twenty years ago, something about this reform in its earliest days, when the excellent people who have labored so long with so much earnestness and fidelity first launched it before the country. I never knew the time in the last fifteen or twenty years that I was not ready to give my wife the right to vote, if she wanted to. I believe in the Declaration of Independence in its full scope and meaning, believing it was born of Christianity, that it came from the teachings of the New Testament; and I am willing to trust the New Testament and the Declaration of Independence anywhere on God's earth, and to adopt their doctrine in the fullest and broadest manner. I do not know that all the good in the world be accomplished when the women of the United States will have the right to vote. But that is sure to come. Truth is truth, and will stand.

Mrs. Ernestine L. Rose, in a stirring address, referred to the assertion of the Rev. Mr. Haven, that the seeds of the Woman's Rights reform were sown in Massachusetts, and proceeded to disprove it. Thirty-two years ago she went round in New York city with petitions to the legislature to obtain for married women the right to hold property in their own names. She only got five names the first year, but she and others persevered for eleven years, and finally succeeded. Who, asked Mrs. Rose, was the first to call a national convention of women, New York or Massachusetts? (Applause.) I like to have justice done and honor given where it is due.

Mrs. Sarah F. Norton, of the New York Working Woman's Association, referring to the former attempt to exclude the discussion of the relations of capital and labor in the convention, argued that the question was an appropriate one in any Woman's Rights Convention, and proposed that some member of the New York Working Women's Association be heard on that point.

Mrs. Eleanor Kirk accordingly described the beginning, progress and operations of the association. She also replied to the recent criticism of the *World* upon the semi-literary, semi-Woman's Rights nature of the meetings of their associations, and contended that they had a perfect right to debate and read essays, and do anything else that other women might do.

Mrs. Mary F. Davis—This lady proceeded to speak in behalf of the rights of her own sex, but she expressed her willingness to see the negro guaranteed in his rights, and would wait if only one question could be disposed of. But she thought they would not have to wait long, for the Hon. Mr. Wilson had assured them that their side is to be strongly and successfully advocated. Every step in the great cause of human rights helps the next one forward. In 1848 Mrs. Stanton called the first Convention at Seneca Falls.

Miss Anthony—And Lucretia Mott.

Mrs. Davis—Yes; and Lucretia Mott, and I love to speak of them in association. Mrs. Rose has alluded to the primary steps she took, and there were Susan B. Anthony, Mrs. Lucy Stone, Mrs. Blackwell, and Paulina Davis, and a great galaxy who paved the way; and we stand here to proclaim the immortal principle of woman's freedom. (Great applause.) The lady then referred to the great work that lay before them in lifting out of misery and wretchedness the numbers of women, in this city and elsewhere, who were experiencing all the fullness of human degradation. Even when they had finished their present work, a large field was still before them in the elevation of their sex. (Applause.)

Miss Anthony said, that before they proceeded any further, she would like to hear from Mrs. Paulina W. Davis, who had lately come from the South. (Applause.)

Mrs. Paulina W. Davis then came forward. She would not be altogether satisfied to have the Fifteenth Amendment passed without the Sixteenth, for they would have a race of tyrants raised above them in the South, and the black women of that country would also receive worse treatment than if the Amendment was not passed. Take any class that have been slaves and you will find that they are the worst when free, and become the hardest masters. The colored women of the South say they do not want to get married to the negro, as their husbands can take their children away from them, and also appropriate their earnings. The black women are more intelligent than the men, because they have learned something from their mistresses. She then related a story of how the black men whip and abuse their wives in the South. One of her sister's servants whipped his wife every Sunday regularly. (Laughter.) She thought that sort of men should not have the making of the laws for the governance of the women throughout the land. (Applause.)

Mr. Douglass then stepped forward and was received with great applause. He said that all disinterested spectators would concede that this Equal Rights meeting had been pre-eminently a Woman's Rights meeting. (Applause.) They had just heard an argument with which he could not agree—that the suffrage to the black men should be postponed to that of the women. Here is a woman who, since the day that the snake talked with our mother in the garden—from that day to this, I say, she has been divested of political rights. What may we not expect, according to that reasoning, when woman, when—— (Loud laughter and applause.)

Miss Anthony hereupon rose from her seat and made towards Mr. Douglass, saying something which was drowned in the applause and laughter which continued. Mr. Douglass was heard to say, however, "No, no, Susan," which again set the audience off in another audible smile, and Miss Anthony took her seat.

When silence was somewhat restored, Mr. Douglass continued, saying "You see when women get into trouble how they act. Miss Anthony comes to the rescue—(laughter)—and these good people have not yet learned to hear people through. (Laughter.) When anything goes against them they are up right away. Now I do not believe the story that the slaves who are enfranchised become the worst of tyrants. (A Voice—"Neither do I." Applause.) I know how this theory came about. When a slave was made a driver he made himself more officious than the white driver, so that his master might not suspect that he was favoring those under him. But we do not intend to have any master over us. (Applause.)

The President then took the floor and argued that not another man should be enfranchised until enough women are admitted to the polls to outweigh those who have the franchise. (Applause.) She did not believe in allowing ignorant negroes and ignorant and debased Chinamen to make laws for her to obey. (Applause.)

Mrs. Harper (colored) asked Mr. Blackwell to read the fifth resolution of the series he submitted, and contended that that covered the whole ground of the resolutions of Mr. Douglass.

Miss Anthony—Then I move that that resolution be reconsidered.

Mr. Douglass—Oh! no; you cannot do that while the floor is occupied.

Mrs. Harper then proceeded with her remarks, saying that when it was a question of race she let the lesser question of sex go. But the white women all go for sex, letting race occupy a minor position. She liked the idea of working-women, but she would like to know if it was broad enough to take colored women?

Miss Anthony and several others—Yes, yes.

Mrs. Harper said that when she was at Boston, there were sixty women who rose up and left work because one colored woman went to gain a livelihood in their midst. (Applause.) If the nation could only handle one question, she would not have the black women put a single straw in the way if only the race of men could obtain what they wanted. (Great applause.)

Mr. C. C. Burleigh attempted to speak, but was received with some disapprobation by the audience, and confusion ensued.

Miss Anthony said she protested against the Fifteenth Amendment because it *wasn't Equal Right.* It put two million more men in position of tyrants over two millions women who had until now been the *equals* of the men at their side.

Mr. Burleigh again essayed to speak. The confusion was so great that what could be reported only were the words: "This fifteenth—does not—any person—bar against the enfranchisement of women."

Mrs. Stone now appealed for order, and her first appearance caused the most respectful silence, as did the words of every one of the ladies who addressed them. Mr. Burleigh again ventured, but with no better result, and Miss Anthony made another appeal to hear him. He tried again to get a word in, but was once more unsuccessful.

Mrs. Livermore then came in front, and said that she would have a pretty story to tell her Chicago friends. She then proceeded to speak a few words in advocacy of the resolutions of Mr. Douglass.

A motion was then made to lay the resolutions upon the table, and Mr. Blackwell moved the "previous question."

Miss Anthony hoped that this, the first attempt at gagging discussion would not be countenanced. (Applause.) She then made a strong appeal for silence to hear Mr. Burleigh.

Sufficient silence was then obtained for that gentleman to say that he had finished all he had to say; but he was determined that they should hear the last word in silence. (Hisses, laughter, and yells.) He now took his seat.

The motion to lay upon the table for discussion in the evening was then carried, and the session adjourned until the evening.

EVENING SESSION.—The Association met in the large hall of the Cooper Institute. A letter from Jules Favre, the celebrated French advocate and *literateur,* was read, after which addresses were delivered by Madame Anneke, of Milwaukee (in German), and by Madame d'Hericourt (in French). Both of these ladies are of revolutionary tendencies, and left their native countries because they had rendered themselves obnoxious by a too free expression of their political opinions. Madame d'Hericourt proposed in her address a league of women in all countries in

the world, whose object should be the triumph of right principles everywhere. On motion of Mrs. Livermore, the convention
adopted and recommended Madame d'Hericourt's scheme.

After a short speech by the Rev. J. F. Lovey, of Concord, and
some singing by the Hutchinsons, who were present,

Ernestine L. Rose made an address, at the close of which she
moved that the name of the Society should be changed from
the "American Equal Rights Association" to the "National
Woman's Suffrage Association."

Lucy Stone said she must oppose this till the colored man
gained the right to vote. If they changed the name of the Association for such a reason as it was evident it was proposed,
they would lose the confidence of the public. I hope you will
not do it.

A gentleman—Mrs. President, I hope you will do it; I move
that the name of the association be changed to the "Universal
Franchise Association."

Mrs. Stanton—The question is already settled by our constitution, which requires a month's notice previous to the annual
meeting before any change of name will be made. We will now
have a song. (Laughter.)

Mr. Blackwell said that he had just returned from the south,
and that he had learned to think that the test oath required of
white men at the south who had been rebels must be abolished
before the vote be given to the negro. He was willing that the
negro should have the suffrage, but not under such conditions
that he should rule the South.

At the allusion of Mr. Blackwell to the test oath the audience
hissed loudly the hint at abolishing that oath.

Mrs. Stanton said—Gentlemen and Ladies, I take this as
quite an insult to me. It is as if you were invited to dine with
me and you turned up your nose at everything that was set on
the table.

Mrs. Livermore, the editress of the *Agitator*, was then introduced. She said—It certainly requires a great amount of nerve
to talk before you, for you have such a frankness of expressing
yourselves that I am afraid of you. (Laughter and applause.) If
you do not like the dish, you turn up your nose at it and say
"take it away, take it away." (Laughter.) Now, I was brought up

in the west, and it is a good place to get rid of any superfluous modesty, but I am afraid of you. (Applause.) It seems that you are more willing to be pleased than to hear what we women have to say, but it appears to me that the men of the community cannot do less than to hear what we have got to say. (Applause.) Throughout the day the men who have attended our convention have been turbulent. (Applause.) I say it frankly, that the behavior of the majority of men has not been respectful. (Applause.) We felt as if we were talking to the side of a house. (Laughter.) The lady then proceeded to give a pathetic narration of the sorrow she had seen among the depraved and destitute of our great cities, and said that the work of the coming year would be to get up a monster petition of a million of names asking the Legislature for Suffrage. (Applause.)

After a song from the Hutchinson family, who had come from Chicago to entertain the audiences of the Association, the meeting adjourned.

FREDERICK DOUGLASS

Woman and the Ballot

OCTOBER 27, 1870

At the 1869 American Equal Rights Association meeting, Frederick Douglass (c. 1818–1895) passionately compared the urgency of giving the ballot to African Americans versus women: "When women, because they are women, are hunted down through the cities of New York and New Orleans; when they are dragged from their houses and hung upon lamp-posts; when their children are torn from their arms, and their brains dashed out upon the pavement . . . then they will have an urgency to obtain the ballot equal to our own." What about black women, he was challenged. "Yes, yes, yes, it is true of the black woman but not because she is a woman, but because she is black." An escaped slave who became a powerful abolitionist orator, Douglass had long supported women's rights, speaking in favor of the controversial resolution calling for women's enfranchisement at the Seneca Falls Convention in 1848. Even though he split irrevocably with his former ally Elizabeth Cady Stanton over the Fifteenth Amendment, Douglass remained a staunch supporter of votes for women. Here he lays out a reasoned case why women should have the right to participate in government and public life on equal terms with men. Frederick Douglass continued his advocacy of women's suffrage right up until his death, which occurred hours after he had attended a meeting of the National Council of Women in Washington, D.C.

━━━━━━━━━━

In the number preceding the present the natural right of woman to a voice in the Government under which she lives and to which she is assumed to owe allegiance, and for the support of which she is compelled like male citizens to pay taxes, was briefly discussed. It is proposed now to adduce some reasons resting on other facts why woman should be allowed to exercise her indisputable natural right to participate in government through the same channels and instrumentalities employed by men. That society has a right to employ for its preservation and success all the mental, moral, and physical power it thus possesses and can make available, is a truth requiring no argument to make it clear. Not less clear is it, at least to some minds, that society, through its forms of government, ought to exercise that right. It has many rights and duties; but the right and duty to cripple and maim itself, or to deprive itself of any power it naturally possesses, are not among them. A man may cut off his arms and feet, pluck out his eyes, and society may deprive itself of its natural powers for guidance and well-being, but enlightened reason assents neither to the action of the one nor of the other. In this respect nations and individuals stand upon the same footing. The highest good is the supreme law for both, and each after his kind must bear the penalty attached to transgression. The Chinese woman may cripple her feet in obedience to custom, and the Hindoo woman throw herself in the consuming flame for superstition, but nature's laws exact their full measure of pain from whatever motive or through whatever ignorance her mandates are violated.

The grand idea of American liberty is coupled with that of universal suffrage; and universal suffrage is suggested and asserted by universal intelligence. Without the latter the former falls to the ground; and unless suffrage is made co-extensive with intelligence something of the natural power of society essential to its guidance and well-being is lost. To deny that woman is capable of forming an intelligent judgment concerning public men and public measures, equally with men, does not meet the case; for, even if it were granted, the fact remains the same that woman, equally with men, possesses such intelligence; and that such as it is, and because it is such as it is, woman, in her own proper person, has a right for herself to make it effective. To deprive her of this right is to deprive her of a part of her natural dignity, and the State of a part of its mental power of direction, prosperity, and safety; and thus a double wrong is perpetrated.

Man in his arrogance has hitherto felt himself fully equal to the work of governing the world without the help of woman. He has kept the reins of power securely in his own hands, and the history of nations and the present experience of the world show the woeful work he has made of governing. He has made human history a history of war and blood even until now. The world to-day seems as fierce, savage, and bloody as a thousand years ago, and there is not one of all the civilized nations of the earth which has not mortgaged the energies of unborn generations to pay debts contracted by the crimes and blunders of its Government. Whether the case would have been different had woman's voice been allowed in national affairs, admits of little debate. War is among the greatest calamities incident to the lives of nations. They arrest the progress of civilization, corrupt the sources of morality, destroy all proper sense of the sacredness of human life, perpetuate national hate, and weigh down the necks of after coming generations with the burdens of debt. To nothing more than to war is woman more instinctively opposed. If the voices of wives, sisters, and mothers could be heard, no standing armies would menace the peace of the world to-day, and France and Prussia would not be bathing their hands in each others warm blood. NAPOLEON told us the "Empire means peace," and we say that Republics mean peace, but neither Empires, Republics, nor Monarchies can mean peace while men alone control them. The vote of woman is essential to the peace of the world. Her hand and voice naturally rises against the shedding of human blood. Against this conclusion cases may be cited, but they are exceptional and abnormal. Woman as woman, far more than man as man, is for peace. That slavery imparted something of its own bloodthirsty spirit to the women of the South—that superstition and fanaticism have led some women to consent to the slaughter of their children and to the destruction of themselves—cannot be taken against the natural gentleness and forbearance of the sex as a whole. She naturally shudders at the thought of subjecting her loved ones to the perils and horrors of war, and her vote would be a peace guaranty to the world. While society consents to exclude women from all participation in the guidance of its Government, it must consent to standing armies, preparations for war calculated to bring them on, and smite itself into blood and death.

But whatever may be thought as to the consequences of allowing women to vote, it is plain that women themselves are divested of a large measure of their natural dignity by their exclusion from such participation in Government. Power is the highest object of human respect. Wisdom, virtue, and all great moral qualities command respect only as powers. Knowledge and wealth are nought but powers. Take from money its purchasing power, and it ceases to be the same object of respect.

We pity the impotent and respect the powerful everywhere. To deny woman her vote is to abridge her natural and social power, and deprive her of a certain measure of respect. Everybody knows that a woman's opinion of any law-maker would command a larger measure of attention had she the means of making that opinion effective at the ballot-box. We despise the weak and respect the strong. Such is human nature. Woman herself loses in her own estimation by her enforced exclusion from the elective franchise just as slaves doubted their own fitness for freedom, from the fact of being looked upon as only fit for slaves. While, of course, woman has not fallen so low as the slave in the scale of being, (her education and her natural relation to the ruling power rendering such degradation impossible,) it is plain that, with the ballot in her hand, she will ascend a higher elevation in her own thoughts, and even in the thoughts of men, than without that symbol of power. She has power now—mental and moral power—but they are fettered. Nobody is afraid of a chained lion or an empty gun.

It may be said that woman does already exercise political power—that she does this through her husband, her father and others related to her, and hence there is no necessity for extending suffrage to her, and allowing her to hold office. This objection to the extension of suffrage, is true in the same sense, that every disfranchised people, especially if intelligent, must exert some influence and compel a certain degree of consideration among governing classes, but it is no conclusive argument. If a man is represented in part by another, there is no reason in that why he may not represent himself as a whole, or if he is represented by another, there is no reason in that why he may not represent himself—and the same is true of woman. The claim is that she is represented by man, and that she does therefore indirectly participate in Government. Suppose she does, and the question at once comes if it be right for woman to participate in government indirectly how can it be wrong for her to do so directly? That which is right in itself, is equally right whether done by the principal or the agent especially if equally well done. So far as ability to perform the mere act of voting is concerned woman is as well qualified to do that as to drop a letter in the post office, or to receive one at the window. Let her represent herself. This is the simplest and surest mode of representation. The old slaveholders used to represent the slaves, the rich landowners of other countries represent the poor, and the men in our country claim to represent woman, but the true doctrine of American liberty plainly is, that each class and each individual of a class should be allowed to represent himself—that taxation and representation should go together. Woman having intelligence, capable of an intelligent preference for the kind of men who shall make the laws under which she is to live, her natural dignity and self-respect coupled with the full enjoyment of all her rights as a citizen, her welfare and happiness equally the objects of solicitude to her as to others, affected as deeply by the errors, blunders, mistakes and crimes committed by the Government, as any part of society, especially suffering from the evils of war, drunkenness and immoralities of every kind, instinctively gentle, tender, peaceful, and orderly. She needs the ballot for her own protection, and men as well as women need its concession to her for the protection of the whole. Long deprived of the ballot, long branded as an inferior race—long reputed as incapable of exercising the elective franchise, and only recently lifted into the privileges of complete American citizenship, we cannot join with those who would refuse the ballot to women or to any others of mature age and proper residence, who bear the burdens of the Government and are obedient to the laws.

PART TWO

1870–1900

VICTORIA WOODHULL

Address to the House Judiciary Committee
JANUARY 11, 1871

Victoria Claflin Woodhull (1838–1927), a flamboyant personality with
a propensity to make advantageous liaisons with prominent men, established the first women's brokerage firm on Wall Street in 1870 with
her sister Tennessee Claflin (1845–1923). In January 1871 she became
the first woman to address the House Judiciary Committee, arguing
that women were "persons" under the Fourteenth Amendment and,
as such, national citizens already entitled to the right to vote. Woodhull had not previously allied herself with the women's suffrage movement, but her address coincided with the third annual convention of
the National Woman Suffrage Association being held in Washington,
D.C., and the suffragists, especially Elizabeth Cady Stanton, enthusiastically welcomed her to their ranks. Soon they had reason for regret
when Woodhull publicly endorsed free love and inserted herself into
a messy scandal involving well-known preacher Henry Ward Beecher
and Elizabeth Tilton, one of his parishioners. Woodhull ran for president on the Equal Rights Party ticket in 1872, despite the fact that
at age thirty-four she was constitutionally ineligible. The suffragists
quickly distanced themselves from the controversial public figure, and
Woodhull faded from public view. In 1877 she moved to England,
where she married a prominent banker and lived until her death.

———————

TO THE HON. THE JUDICIARY COMMITTEES OF THE SENATE
AND THE HOUSE OF REPRESENTATIVES OF THE CONGRESS OF
THE UNITED STATES:
 The undersigned, VICTORIA C. WOODHULL, having most
respectfully memorialized Congress for the passage of such laws
as in its wisdom shall seem necessary and proper to carry into
effect the rights vested by the Constitution of the United States
in the citizens to vote, without regard to sex, begs leave to submit to your honorable body the following in favor of her prayer
in said Memorial which has been referred to your Committee:
 The public law of the world is founded upon the conceded fact that sovereignty cannot be forfeited or renounced.
The sovereign power of this country is perpetual in the
politically-organized people of the United States, and can

neither be relinquished nor abandoned by any portion of them. The people in this Republic who confer sovereignty are its citizens: in a monarchy the people are the subjects of sovereignty. All citizens of a republic by rightful act or implication confer sovereign power. All people of a monarchy are subjects who exist under its supreme shield and enjoy its immunities.

The subject of a monarch takes municipal immunities from the sovereign as a gracious favor; but the woman citizen of this country has the inalienable "sovereign" right of self-government in *her own proper person*. Those who look upon woman's status by the dim light of the common law, which unfolded itself under the feudal and military institutions that establish right upon physical power, cannot find any analogy in the status of the woman citizen of this country, *where the broad sunshine of our Constitution has enfranchised all.*

As sovereignty cannot be forfeited, relinquished or abandoned, those from whom it flows—the citizens—are equal in conferring the power, and should be equal in the enjoyment of its benefits and in the exercise of its rights and privileges.

One portion of citizens have no power to deprive another portion of rights and privileges such as are possessed and exercised by themselves. The male citizen has no more right to deprive the female citizen of the free, public, political expression of opinion than the female citizen has to deprive the male citizen thereof.

The sovereign will of the people is expressed in our written Constitution, which is the supreme law of the land. The Constitution makes no distinction of sex. The Constitution defines a woman born or naturalized in the United States, and subject to the jurisdiction thereof, to be a citizen. It recognizes the right of citizens to vote. It declares that the right of citizens of the United States to vote shall not be denied or abridged by the United States or by any State on account of "race, color or previous condition of servitude."

Women, white and black, belong to races; although to different races. A race of people comprises all the people, male and female. The right to vote cannot be denied on account of race. All people included in the term race have the right to vote, unless otherwise prohibited.

Women of all races are white, black or some intermediate

color. Color comprises all people, of all races and both sexes. The right to vote cannot be denied on account of color. All people included in the term color have the right to vote unless otherwise prohibited.

With the right to vote sex has nothing to do. Race and color include all people of both sexes. All people of both sexes have the right to vote, unless prohibited by special limiting terms less comprehensive than race or color. No such limiting terms exist in the Constitution.

Women, white and black, have from time immemorial groaned under what is properly termed in the Constitution "previous condition of servitude."

Women are the equals of men before the law, and are equal in all their rights as citizens.

Women are debarred from voting in some parts of the United States, although they are allowed to exercise that right elsewhere.

Women were formerly permitted to vote in places where they are now debarred therefrom.

The Naturalization Laws of the United States expressly provide for the naturalization of women.

But the right to vote has only lately been distinctly declared by the Constitution to be inalienable, under three distinct conditions—in all of which woman is distinctly embraced.

The citizen who is taxed should also have a voice in the subject matter of taxation. "No taxation without representation" is a right which was fundamentally established at the very birth of our country's independence; and by what ethics does any free government impose taxes on women without giving them a voice upon the subject or a participation in the public declaration as to how and by whom these taxes shall be applied for common public use?

Women are free to own and to control property, separate and apart from males, and they are held responsible in their own proper persons, in every particular, as well as men, in and out of court.

Women have the same inalienable right to life, liberty and the *pursuit of* happiness that men have. Why have they not this right politically, as well as men?

Women constitute a majority of the people of this country

—they hold vast portions of the nation's wealth and pay a proportionate share of the taxes. They are intrusted with the most holy duties and the most vital responsibilities of society; they bear, rear and educate men; they train and mould their characters; they inspire the noblest impulses in men; they often hold the accumulated fortunes of a man's life for the safety of the family and as guardians of the infants, and yet they are debarred from uttering any opinion, by public vote, as to the management by public servants of these interests; they are the secret counsellors, the best advisers, the most devoted aids in the most trying periods of men's lives, and yet men shrink from trusting them in the common questions of ordinary politics. Men trust women in the market, in the shop, on the highway and the railroad, and in all other public places and assemblies, but when they propose to carry a slip of paper with a name upon it to the polls, they fear them. Nevertheless, as citizens women have the right to vote; they are part and parcel of that great element in which the sovereign power of the land had birth: and it is by usurpation only that men debar them from their right to vote. The American nation, in its march onward and upward, cannot publicly choke the intellectual and political activity of half its citizens by narrow statutes. The will of the entire people is the true basis of republican government, and a free expression of that will by the public vote of all citizens, without distinctions of race, color, occupation or sex, is the only means by which that will can be ascertained. As the world has advanced in civilization and culture; as mind has risen in its dominion over matter; as the principle of justice and moral right has gained sway, and merely physically organized power has yielded thereto; as the might of right has supplanted the right of might, so have the rights of women become more fully recognized, and that recognition is the result of the development of the minds of men, which through the ages she has polished, and thereby heightened the lustre of civilization.

It was reserved for our great country to recognize by constitutional enactment that political equality of all citizens which religion, affection and common sense should have long since accorded; it was reserved for America to sweep away the mist of prejudice and ignorance, and that chivalric condescension of a darker age, for in the language of Holy Writ, "The night is far spent, the day is at hand, let us therefore cast off the work of darkness, and let us put on the armor of light. Let us walk honestly as in the day."

It may be argued against the proposition that there still remains upon the statute books of some States the word "male" to an exclusion, but as the Constitution in its paramount character can only be read by the light of the established principle, *ita lex Scripta est*; and as the subject of sex is not mentioned and the Constitution is not limited either in terms or by necessary implication in the general rights of citizens to vote, this right cannot be limited on account of anything in the spirit of inferior or previous enactments upon a subject which is not mentioned in the supreme law. A different construction would destroy a vested right in a portion of the citizens, and this no legislature has a right to do without compensation, and nothing can compensate a citizen for the loss of his or her suffrage—its value is equal to the value of life. Neither can it be presumed that women are to be kept from the polls as a mere police regulation: it is to be hoped, at least, that police regulations in their case need not be very active. The effect of the amendments to the Constitution must be to annul the power over this subject in the States whether past, present or future, which is contrary to the amendments. The amendments would even arrest the action of the Supreme Court in cases pending before it prior to their adoption, and operate as an absolute prohibition to the exercise of any other jurisdiction than merely to dismiss the suit.

3 Dall., 382; 6 Wheaton, 405; 9 Id., 868; 3d Circ., Pa., 1832.

And if the restrictions contained in the Constitution as to color, race or servitude, were designed to limit the State governments in reference to their own citizens, and were intended to operate also as restrictions on the Federal power, and to prevent interference with the rights of the State and its citizens, how then can the State restrict citizens of the United States in the exercise of rights not mentioned in any restrictive clause in reference to actions on the part of those citizens having reference solely to the necessary functions of the General Government, such as the election of representatives and senators to Congress, whose election the Constitution expressly gives Congress the power to regulate?

S. C., 1847: Fox vs. Ohio, 5 Howard, 410.

Your memorialist complains of the existence of State Laws, and prays Congress, by appropriate legislation, to declare them, as they are, annulled, and to give vitality to the Constitution under its power to make and alter the regulations of the States contravening the same.

It may be urged in opposition that the Courts have power, and should declare upon this subject.

The Supreme Court has the power, and it would be its duty so to declare the law; but the Court will not do so unless a determination of such point as shall arise make it necessary to the determination of a controversy, and hence a case must be presented in which there can be no rational doubt. All this would subject the aggrieved parties to much dilatory, expensive and needless litigation, which your memorialist prays your Honorable Body to dispense with by appropriate legislation, as there can be no purpose in special arguments "ab inconvenienti," enlarging or contracting the import of the language of the Constitution.

Therefore, Believing firmly in the right of citizens to freely approach those in whose hands their destiny is placed, under the Providence of God, your memorialist has frankly, but humbly, appealed to you, and prays that the wisdom of Congress may be moved to action in this matter for the benefit and the increased happiness of our beloved country.

Most respectfully submitted,

VICTORIA C. WOODHULL.

Dated NEW YORK, January 2, 1871.

MINOR v. HAPPERSETT Ruling

1875

Victoria Woodhull's assertion that women already possessed the right to vote as citizens was originally proposed by a St. Louis lawyer named Francis Minor (1820–1892) in 1869. Suffragists, including, in 1872, Susan B. Anthony and fourteen other women in Rochester, New York, quickly jumped on the bandwagon of what they called "The New Departure" by spontaneously attempting to vote in their communities. But it was Virginia Minor (1824–1894), Francis's wife, whose test case reached the Supreme Court. When Minor was barred from registering to vote in St. Louis, she sued the local registrar, Reese Happersett. The Minors' case (Francis sued for both of them because married women in Missouri could not bring suits on their own behalf until 1889) lost in state court, but the Supreme Court took the case on appeal because it addressed a constitutional question about federal versus state power (voting rights were generally considered a matter for states to decide). The case was argued in February 1875 and the unanimous decision announced seven weeks later—a total defeat for the suffragists' New Departure strategy. The court found the argument without merit, conceding that Minor was a citizen but affirming that voting was not a constitutional right, effectively divorcing voting from citizenship. With no hope of legal recourse for the foreseeable future, the suffrage movement had only two options: try to amend state constitutions to enfranchise women, or work for a federal amendment to the U.S. Constitution. Those two strategies defined the next half century of suffrage activism.

The CHIEF JUSTICE delivered the opinion of the court.

The question is presented in this case, whether, since the adoption of the fourteenth amendment, a woman, who is a citizen of the United States and of the State of Missouri, is a voter in that State, notwithstanding the provision of the constitution and laws of the State, which confine the right of suffrage to men alone. We might, perhaps, decide the case upon other grounds, but this question is fairly made. From the opinion we find that it was the only one decided in the court below, and it is the only one which has been argued here. The case was undoubtedly brought to this court for the sole purpose of having that question decided by us, and in view of the evident propriety there is of having it settled, so far as it can be by such a decision, we have concluded to waive all other considerations and proceed at once to its determination.

It is contended that the provisions of the constitution and laws of the State of Missouri which confine the right of suffrage and registration therefor to men, are in violation of the Constitution of the United States, and therefore void. The argument is, that as a woman, born or naturalized in the United States and subject to the jurisdiction thereof, is a citizen of the United States and of the State in which she resides, she has the right of suffrage as one of the privileges and immunities of her citizenship, which the State cannot by its laws or constitution abridge.

There is no doubt that women may be citizens. They are persons, and by the fourteenth amendment "all persons born or naturalized in the United States and subject to the jurisdiction thereof" are expressly declared to be "citizens of the United States and of the State wherein they reside." But, in our opinion, it did not need this amendment to give them that position. Before its adoption the Constitution of the United States did not in terms prescribe who should be citizens of the United States or of the several States, yet there were necessarily such citizens without such provision. There cannot be a nation without a people. The very idea of a political community, such as a nation is, implies an association of persons for the promotion of their general welfare. Each one of the persons associated becomes a member of the nation formed by the association. He owes it allegiance and is entitled to its protection. Allegiance and protection are, in this connection, reciprocal obligations. The one is a compensation for the other; allegiance for protection and protection for allegiance.

For convenience it has been found necessary to give a name to this membership. The object is to designate by a title the person and the relation he bears to the nation. For this purpose the words "subject," "inhabitant," and "citizen" have been used, and the choice between them is sometimes made to depend upon the form of the government. Citizen is now more commonly employed, however, and as it has been considered better suited to the description of one living under a republican government, it was adopted by nearly all of the States upon their separation from Great Britain, and was afterwards adopted in the Articles of Confederation and in the Constitution of the United States. When used in this sense it is understood as conveying the idea of membership of a nation, and nothing more.

To determine, then, who were citizens of the United States before the adoption of the amendment it is necessary to ascertain what persons originally associated themselves together to form the nation, and what were afterwards admitted to membership.

Looking at the Constitution itself we find that it was ordained and established by "the people of the United States,"* and then going further back, we find that these were the people of the several States that had before dissolved the political bands which connected them with Great Britain, and assumed a separate and equal station among the powers of the earth,† and that had by Articles of Confederation and Perpetual Union, in which they took the name of "the United States of America," entered into a firm league of friendship with each other for their common defence, the security of their liberties and their mutual and general welfare, binding themselves to assist each other against all force offered to or attack made upon them, or any of them, on account of religion, sovereignty, trade, or any other pretence whatever.‡

Whoever, then, was one of the people of either of these States when the Constitution of the United States was adopted, became *ipso facto* a citizen—a member of the nation created by its adoption. He was one of the persons associating together to form the nation, and was, consequently, one of its original citizens. As to this there has never been a doubt. Disputes have arisen as to whether or not certain persons or certain classes of persons were part of the people at the time, but never as to their citizenship if they were.

Additions might always be made to the citizenship of the United States in two ways: first, by birth, and second, by naturalization. This is apparent from the Constitution itself, for it

* Preamble, I Stat. at Large, IO.
† Declaration of Independence, Ib. I.
‡ Articles of Confederation, § 3, I Stat. at Large, 4.

provides* that "no person except a natural-born citizen, or a citizen of the United States at the time of the adoption of the Constitution, shall be eligible to the office of President,"† and that Congress shall have power "to establish a uniform rule of naturalization." Thus new citizens may be born or they may be created by naturalization.

The Constitution does not, in words, say who shall be natural-born citizens. Resort must be had elsewhere to ascertain that. At common-law, with the nomenclature of which the framers of the Constitution were familiar, it was never doubted that all children born in a country of parents who were its citizens became themselves, upon their birth, citizens also. These were natives, or natural-born citizens, as distinguished from aliens or foreigners. Some authorities go further and include as citizens children born within the jurisdiction without reference to the citizenship of their parents. As to this class there have been doubts, but never as to the first. For the purposes of this case it is not necessary to solve these doubts. It is sufficient for everything we have now to consider that all children born of citizen parents within the jurisdiction are themselves citizens. The words "all children" are certainly as comprehensive, when used in this connection, as "all persons," and if females are included in the last they must be in the first. That they are included in the last is not denied. In fact the whole argument of the plaintiffs proceeds upon that idea.

Under the power to adopt a uniform system of naturalization Congress, as early as 1790, provided "that any alien, being a free white person," might be admitted as a citizen of the United States, and that the children of such persons so naturalized, dwelling within the United States, being under twenty-one years of age at the time of such naturalization, should also be considered citizens of the United States, and that the children of citizens of the United States that might be born beyond the sea, or out of the limits of the United States, should be considered as natural-born citizens.‡ These provisions thus enacted have, in substance, been retained in all the naturalization

* Article 2, § 1.
† Article 1, § 8.
‡ 1 Stat. at Large, 103.

laws adopted since. In 1855, however, the last provision was somewhat extended, and all persons theretofore born or there-after to be born out of the limits of the jurisdiction of the United States, whose fathers were, or should be at the time of their birth, citizens of the United States, were declared to be citizens also.*

As early as 1804 it was enacted by Congress that when any alien who had declared his intention to become a citizen in the manner provided by law died before he was actually natural-ized, his widow and children should be considered as citizens of the United States, and entitled to all rights and privileges as such upon taking the necessary oath,† and in 1855 it was further provided that any woman who might lawfully be naturalized under the existing laws, married, or who should be married to a citizen of the United States, should be deemed and taken to be a citizen.‡

From this it is apparent that from the commencement of the legislation upon this subject alien women and alien minors could be made citizens by naturalization, and we think it will not be contended that this would have been done if it had not been supposed that native women and native minors were al-ready citizens by birth.

But if more is necessary to show that women have always been considered as citizens the same as men, abundant proof is to be found in the legislative and judicial history of the country. Thus, by the Constitution, the judicial power of the United States is made to extend to controversies between citizens of different States. Under this it has been uniformly held that the citizenship necessary to give the courts of the United States ju-risdiction of a cause must be affirmatively shown on the record. Its existence as a fact may be put in issue and tried. If found not to exist the case must be dismissed. Notwithstanding this the records of the courts are full of cases in which the jurisdiction depends upon the citizenship of women, and not one can be found, we think, in which objection was made on that account. Certainly none can be found in which it has been held that

* 10 Id. 604.
† 2 Id. 293.
‡ 10 Stat. at Large, 604.

women could not sue or be sued in the courts of the United States. Again, at the time of the adoption of the Constitution, in many of the States (and in some probably now) aliens could not inherit or transmit inheritance. There are a multitude of cases to be found in which the question has been presented whether a woman was or was not an alien, and as such capable or incapable of inheritance, but in no one has it been insisted that she was not a citizen because she was a woman. On the contrary, her right to citizenship has been in all cases assumed. The only question has been whether, in the particular case under consideration, she had availed herself of the right.

In the legislative department of the government similar proof will be found. Thus, in the pre-emption laws,* a widow, "being a citizen of the United States," is allowed to make settlement on the public lands and purchase upon the terms specified, and women, "being citizens of the United States," are permitted to avail themselves of the benefit of the homestead law.†

Other proof of like character might be found, but certainly more cannot be necessary to establish the fact that sex has never been made one of the elements of citizenship in the United States. In this respect men have never had an advantage over women. The same laws precisely apply to both. The fourteenth amendment did not affect the citizenship of women any more than it did of men. In this particular, therefore, the rights of Mrs. Minor do not depend upon the amendment. She has always been a citizen from her birth, and entitled to all the privileges and immunities of citizenship. The amendment prohibited the State, of which she is a citizen, from abridging any of her privileges and immunities as a citizen of the United States; but it did not confer citizenship on her. That she had before its adoption.

If the right of suffrage is one of the necessary privileges of a citizen of the United States, then the constitution and laws of Missouri confining it to men are in violation of the Constitution of the United States, as amended, and consequently void. The direct question is, therefore, presented whether all citizens are necessarily voters.

* 5 Stat. at Large, 455, § 10.
† 12 Id. 392.

The Constitution does not define the privileges and immunities of citizens. For that definition we must look elsewhere. In this case we need not determine what they are, but only whether suffrage is necessarily one of them.

It certainly is nowhere made so in express terms. The United States has no voters in the States of its own creation. The elective officers of the United States are all elected directly or indirectly by State voters. The members of the House of Representatives are to be chosen by the people of the States, and the electors in each State must have the qualifications requisite for electors of the most numerous branch of the State legislature.[*] Senators are to be chosen by the legislatures of the States, and necessarily the members of the legislature required to make the choice are elected by the voters of the State.[†] Each State must appoint in such manner, as the legislature thereof may direct, the electors to elect the President and Vice-President.[‡] The times, places, and manner of holding elections for Senators and Representatives are to be prescribed in each State by the legislature thereof; but Congress may at any time, by law, make or alter such regulations, except as to the place of choosing Senators.[§] It is not necessary to inquire whether this power of supervision thus given to Congress is sufficient to authorize any interference with the State laws prescribing the qualifications of voters, for no such interference has ever been attempted. The power of the State in this particular is certainly supreme until Congress acts.

The amendment did not add to the privileges and immunities of a citizen. It simply furnished an additional guaranty for the protection of such as he already had. No new voters were necessarily made by it. Indirectly it may have had that effect, because it may have increased the number of citizens entitled to suffrage under the constitution and laws of the States, but it operates for this purpose, if at all, through the States and the State laws, and not directly upon the citizen.

It is clear, therefore, we think, that the Constitution has not

[*] Constitution, Article 1, § 2.
[†] Ib. Article 1, § 3.
[‡] Ib. Article 2, § 2.
[§] Ib. Article 1, § 4.

added the right of suffrage to the privileges and immunities of citizenship as they existed at the time it was adopted. This makes it proper to inquire whether suffrage was coextensive with the citizenship of the States at the time of its adoption. If it was, then it may with force be argued that suffrage was one of the rights which belonged to citizenship, and in the enjoyment of which every citizen must be protected. But if it was not, the contrary may with propriety be assumed.

When the Federal Constitution was adopted, all the States, with the exception of Rhode Island and Connecticut, had constitutions of their own. These two continued to act under their charters from the Crown. Upon an examination of those constitutions we find that in no State were all citizens permitted to vote. Each State determined for itself who should have that power. Thus, in New Hampshire, "every male inhabitant of each town and parish with town privileges, and places unincorporated in the State, of twenty-one years of age and upwards, excepting paupers and persons excused from paying taxes at their own request," were its voters; in Massachusetts "every male inhabitant of twenty-one years of age and upwards, having a freehold estate within the commonwealth of the annual income of three pounds, or any estate of the value of sixty pounds;" in Rhode Island "such as are admitted free of the company and society" of the colony; in Connecticut such persons as had "maturity in years, quiet and peaceable behavior, a civil conversation, and forty shillings freehold or forty pounds personal estate," if so certified by the selectmen; in New York "every male inhabitant of full age who shall have personally resided within one of the counties of the State for six months immediately preceding the day of election . . . if during the time aforesaid he shall have been a freeholder, possessing a freehold of the value of twenty pounds within the county, or have rented a tenement therein of the yearly value of forty shillings, and been rated and actually paid taxes to the State;" in New Jersey "all inhabitants . . . of full age who are worth fifty pounds, proclamation-money, clear estate in the same, and have resided in the county in which they claim a vote for twelve months immediately preceding the election;" in Pennsylvania "every freeman of the age of twenty-one years, having resided in the State two years next before the election, and within that time paid a State or county tax which shall have been assessed at least six months before the election;" in Delaware and Virginia "as exercised by law at present;" in Maryland "all freemen above twenty-one years of age having a freehold of fifty acres of land in the county in which they offer to vote and residing therein, and all freemen having property in the State above the value of thirty pounds current money, and having resided in the county in which they offer to vote one whole year next preceding the election;" in North Carolina, for senators, "all freemen of the age of twenty-one years who have been inhabitants of any one county within the State twelve months immediately preceding the day of election, and possessed of a freehold within the same county of fifty acres of land for six months next before and at the day of election," and for members of the house of commons "all freemen of the age of twenty-one years who have been inhabitants in any one county within the State twelve months immediately preceding the day of any election, and shall have paid public taxes;" in South Carolina "every free white man of the age of twenty-one years, being a citizen of the State and having resided therein two years previous to the day of election, and who hath a freehold of fifty acres of land, or a town lot of which he hath been legally seized and possessed at least six months before such election, or (not having such freehold or town lot), hath been a resident within the election district in which he offers to give his vote six months before said election, and hath paid a tax the preceding year of three shillings sterling towards the support of the government;" and in Georgia such "citizens and inhabitants of the State as shall have attained to the age of twenty-one years, and shall have paid tax for the year next preceding the election, and shall have resided six months within the county."

In this condition of the law in respect to suffrage in the several States it cannot for a moment be doubted that if it had been intended to make all citizens of the United States voters, the framers of the Constitution would not have left it to implication. So important a change in the condition of citizenship as it actually existed, if intended, would have been expressly declared.

But if further proof is necessary to show that no such change was intended, it can easily be found both in and out of the

Constitution. By Article 4, section 2, it is provided that "the citizens of each State shall be entitled to all the privileges and immunities of citizens in the several States." If suffrage is necessarily a part of citizenship, then the citizens of each State must be entitled to vote in the several States precisely as their citizens are. This is more than asserting that they may change their residence and become citizens of the State and thus be voters. It goes to the extent of insisting that while retaining their original citizenship they may vote in any State. This, we think, has never been claimed. And again, by the very terms of the amendment we have been considering (the fourteenth), "Representatives shall be apportioned among the several States according to their respective numbers, counting the whole number of persons in each State, excluding Indians not taxed. But when the right to vote at any election for the choice of electors for President and Vice-President of the United States, representatives in Congress, the executive and judicial officers of a State, or the members of the legislature thereof, is denied to any of the male inhabitants of such State, being twenty-one years of age and citizens of the United States, or in any way abridged, except for participation in the rebellion, or other crimes, the basis of representation therein shall be reduced in the proportion which the number of such male citizens shall bear to the whole number of male citizens twenty-one years of age in such State." Why this, if it was not in the power of the legislature to deny the right of suffrage to some male inhabitants? And if suffrage was necessarily one of the absolute rights of citizenship, why confine the operation of the limitation to male inhabitants? Women and children are, as we have seen, "persons." They are counted in the enumeration upon which the apportionment is to be made, but if they were necessarily voters because of their citizenship unless clearly excluded, why inflict the penalty for the exclusion of males alone? Clearly, no such form of words would have been selected to express the idea here indicated if suffrage was the absolute right of all citizens.

And still again, after the adoption of the fourteenth amendment, it was deemed necessary to adopt a fifteenth, as follows: "The right of citizens of the United States to vote shall not be denied or abridged by the United States, or by any State, on account of race, color, or previous condition of servitude."

The fourteenth amendment had already provided that no State should make or enforce any law which should abridge the privileges or immunities of citizens of the United States. If suffrage was one of these privileges or immunities, why amend the Constitution to prevent its being denied on account of race, &c.? Nothing is more evident than that the greater must include the less, and if all were already protected why go through with the form of amending the Constitution to protect a part?

It is true that the United States guarantees to every State a republican form of government.* It is also true that no State can pass a bill of attainder,† and that no person can be deprived of life, liberty, or property without due process of law.‡ All these several provisions of the Constitution must be construed in connection with the other parts of the instrument, and in the light of the surrounding circumstances.

The guaranty is of a republican form of government. No particular government is designated as republican, neither is the exact form to be guaranteed, in any manner especially designated. Here, as in other parts of the instrument, we are compelled to resort elsewhere to ascertain what was intended.

The guaranty necessarily implies a duty on the part of the States themselves to provide such a government. All the States had governments when the Constitution was adopted. In all the people participated to some extent, through their representatives elected in the manner specially provided. These governments the Constitution did not change. They were accepted precisely as they were, and it is, therefore, to be presumed that they were such as it was the duty of the States to provide. Thus we have unmistakable evidence of what was republican in form, within the meaning of that term as employed in the Constitution.

As has been seen, all the citizens of the States were not invested with the right of suffrage. In all, save perhaps New Jersey, this right was only bestowed upon men and not upon all of them. Under these circumstances it is certainly now too late to contend that a government is not republican, within the

---

* Constitution, Article 4, § 4.
† Ib. Article 1, § 10.
‡ Ib. Amendment 5.

meaning of this guaranty in the Constitution, because women are not made voters.

The same may be said of the other provisions just quoted. Women were excluded from suffrage in nearly all the States by the express provision of their constitutions and laws. If that had been equivalent to a bill of attainder, certainly its abrogation would not have been left to implication. Nothing less than express language would have been employed to effect so radical a change. So also of the amendment which declares that no person shall be deprived of life, liberty, or property without due process of law, adopted as it was as early as 1791. If suffrage was intended to be included within its obligations, language better adapted to express that intent would most certainly have been employed. The right of suffrage, when granted, will be protected. He who has it can only be deprived of it by due process of law, but in order to claim protection he must first show that he has the right.

But we have already sufficiently considered the proof found upon the inside of the Constitution. That upon the outside is equally effective.

The Constitution was submitted to the States for adoption in 1787, and was ratified by nine States in 1788, and finally by the thirteen original States in 1790. Vermont was the first new State admitted to the Union, and it came in under a constitution which conferred the right of suffrage only upon men of the full age of twenty-one years, having resided in the State for the space of one whole year next before the election, and who were of quiet and peaceable behavior. This was in 1791. The next year, 1792, Kentucky followed with a constitution confining the right of suffrage to free male citizens of the age of twenty-one years who had resided in the State two years or in the county in which they offered to vote one year next before the election. Then followed Tennessee, in 1796, with voters of freemen of the age of twenty-one years and upwards, possessing a freehold in the county wherein they may vote, and being inhabitants of the State or freemen being inhabitants of any one county in the State six months immediately preceding the day of election. But we need not particularize further. No new State has ever been admitted to the Union which has conferred the right of suffrage upon women, and this has never been considered a valid objection to her admission. On the contrary, as is claimed in the argument, the right of suffrage was withdrawn from women as early as 1807 in the State of New Jersey, without any attempt to obtain the interference of the United States to prevent it. Since then the governments of the insurgent States have been reorganized under a requirement that before their representatives could be admitted to seats in Congress they must have adopted new constitutions, republican in form. In no one of these constitutions was suffrage conferred upon women, and yet the States have all been restored to their original position as States in the Union.

Besides this, citizenship has not in all cases been made a condition precedent to the enjoyment of the right of suffrage. Thus, in Missouri, persons of foreign birth, who have declared their intention to become citizens of the United States, may under certain circumstances vote. The same provision is to be found in the constitutions of Alabama, Arkansas, Florida, Georgia, Indiana, Kansas, Minnesota, and Texas.

Certainly, if the courts can consider any question settled, this is one. For nearly ninety years the people have acted upon the idea that the Constitution, when it conferred citizenship, did not necessarily confer the right of suffrage. If uniform practice long continued can settle the construction of so important an instrument as the Constitution of the United States confessedly is, most certainly it has been done here. Our province is to decide what the law is, not to declare what it should be.

We have given this case the careful consideration its importance demands. If the law is wrong, it ought to be changed; but the power for that is not with us. The arguments addressed to us bearing upon such a view of the subject may perhaps be sufficient to induce those having the power, to make the alteration, but they ought not to be permitted to influence our judgment in determining the present rights of the parties now litigating before us. No argument as to woman's need of suffrage can be considered. We can only act upon her rights as they exist. It is not for us to look at the hardship of withholding. Our duty is at an end if we find it is within the power of a State to withhold.

Being unanimously of the opinion that the Constitution of

the United States does not confer the right of suffrage upon any one, and that the constitutions and laws of the several States which commit that important trust to men alone are not necessarily void, we

AFFIRM THE JUDGMENT.

NATIONAL WOMAN SUFFRAGE ASSOCIATION

Declaration of Rights of the Women of the United States

JULY 4, 1876

As the country planned a lavish celebration of its centennial in 1876 in Philadelphia, leaders from the National Woman Suffrage Association asked for a place on the program, but their request was denied. Instead the Centennial Commission offered suffragists five general admission tickets. On an oppressively hot July 4, Susan B. Anthony, Matilda Joslyn Gage, Sara Andrews Spencer, Lillie Devereux Blake, and Phoebe Couzins chose the moment when the crowd rose to recognize the Emperor of Brazil, the somewhat incongruous honored guest, to march to the platform and present a "Declaration of Rights of the Women" to the startled master of ceremonies. The women did not try to speak but did scatter copies of the protest to the crowd. After exiting the festivities, the suffragists took over an empty bandstand in Independence Square and Susan B. Anthony read their declaration aloud to the curious crowd. While the Centennial ceremonies were designed to celebrate what had been accomplished in the last hundred years, the suffrage activists wanted to draw attention to what the country had failed to do: give women full civil and political rights, including the right to the voting franchise.

While the Nation is buoyant with patriotism, and all hearts are attuned to praise, it is with sorrow we come to strike the one discordant note, on this hundredth anniversary of our country's birth. When subjects of Kings, Emperors, and Czars, from the Old World, join in our National Jubilee, shall the women of the Republic refuse to lay their hands with benedictions on the nation's head? Surveying America's Exposition, surpassing in magnificence those of London, Paris, and Vienna, shall we not rejoice at the success of the youngest rival among the nations of the earth? May not our hearts, in unison with all, swell with pride at our great achievements as a people; our free speech, free press, free schools, free church, and the rapid progress we have made in material wealth, trade, commerce, and the inventive arts? And we do rejoice, in the success thus far, of our experiment of self-government. Our faith is firm and unwavering in the broad principles of human rights, proclaimed in 1776, not only as abstract truths, but as the corner stones of a republic. Yet, we cannot forget, even in this glad hour, that while all men of every race, and clime, and condition, have been invested with the full rights of citizenship, under our hospitable flag, all women still suffer the degradation of disfranchisement.

The history of our country the past hundred years, has been a series of assumptions and usurpations of power over woman, in direct opposition to the principles of just government, acknowledged by the United States at its foundation which are:

First. The natural rights of each individual.

Second. The exact equality of these rights.

Third. That these rights, when not delegated by the individual, are retained by the individual.

Fourth. That no person can exercise the rights of others without delegated authority.

Fifth. That the non-use of these rights does not destroy them.

And for the violation of these fundamental principles of our Government, we arraign our rulers on this 4th day of July, 1876,—and these are our

ARTICLES OF IMPEACHMENT.

BILLS OF ATTAINDER have been passed by the introduction of the word "male" into all the State constitutions, denying to woman the right of suffrage, and thereby making sex a crime—an exercise of power clearly forbidden in Article 1st, Sections 9th and 10th of the United States Constitution.

THE WRIT OF HABEAS CORPUS, the only protection against *lettres de cachet*, and all forms of unjust imprisonment, which the Constitution declares "shall not be suspended, except when in cases of rebellion or invasion, the public safety demands it," is held inoperative in every State in the Union, in case of a married woman against her husband,—the marital rights of the husband being in all cases primary, and the rights of the wife secondary.

THE RIGHT OF TRIAL BY A JURY OF ONE'S PEERS
was so jealously guarded that States refused to ratify the original
Constitution, until it was guaranteed by the 6th Amendment.
And yet the women of this nation have never been allowed a
jury of their peers—being tried in all cases by men, native and
foreign, educated and ignorant, virtuous and vicious. Young
girls have been arraigned in our courts for the crime of infan-
ticide; tried, convicted, hung—victims, perchance, of judge,
jurors, advocates—while no woman's voice could be heard in
their defence. And not only are women denied a jury of their
peers, but in some cases, jury trial altogether. During the war,
a woman was tried and hung by military law, in defiance of the
5th Amendment, which specifically declares: "no person shall be
held to answer for a capital or otherwise infamous crime, unless
on a presentment or indictment of a grand jury, except in cases
* * * * * of persons in actual service in time of war." During the
last Presidential campaign, a woman, arrested for voting, was
denied the protection of a jury, tried, convicted and sentenced
to a fine and costs of prosecution, by the absolute power of a
judge of the Supreme Court of the United States.

TAXATION WITHOUT REPRESENTATION, the imme-
diate cause of the rebellion of the Colonies against Great Britain, is one of the grievous wrongs the women of this country
have suffered during the century. Deploring war, with all the
demoralization that follows in its train, we have been taxed to
support standing armies, with their waste of life and wealth.
Believing in temperance, we have been taxed to support the
vice, crime, and pauperism of the Liquor Traffic. While we suffer its wrongs and abuses infinitely more than man, we have no
power to protect our sons against this giant evil. During the
Temperance Crusade, mothers were arrested, fined, imprisoned, for even praying and singing in the streets, while men
blockade the sidewalks with impunity, even on Sunday, with
their military parades and political processions. Believing in
honesty, we are taxed to support a dangerous army of civilians,
buying and selling the offices of government and sacrificing
the best interests of the people. And, moreover, we are taxed
to support the very legislators, and judges, who make laws, and
render decisions adverse to woman. And for refusing to pay
such unjust taxation, the houses, lands, bonds, and stock of

women, have been seized and sold within the present year, thus proving Lord Coke's assertion, "that the very act of taxing a man's property without his consent, is, in effect, disfranchising him of every civil right."

UNEQUAL CODES FOR MEN AND WOMEN. Held by law a perpetual minor, deemed incapable of self-protection, even in the industries of the world, woman is denied equality of rights. The fact of sex, not the quantity or quality of work, in most cases, decides the pay and position; and because of this injustice thousands of fatherless girls are compelled to choose between a life of shame and starvation.

Laws catering to man's vices have created two codes of morals in which penalties are graded according to the political status of the offender. Under such laws, women are fined and imprisoned if found alone in the streets, or in public places of resort, at certain hours. Under the pretence of regulating public morals, police officers seizing the occupants of disreputable houses, march the women in platoons to prison, while the men, partners in their guilt, go free.

While making a show of virtue in forbidding the importation of Chinese women on the Pacific coast for immoral purposes, our rulers, in many states, and even under the shadow of the National Capitol, are now proposing to legalize the sale of American womanhood for the same vile purposes.

SPECIAL LEGISLATION FOR WOMAN has placed us in a most anomalous position. Women invested with the rights of citizens in one section—voters, jurors, office-holders—crossing an imaginary line, are subjects in the next. In some states, a married woman may hold property and transact business in her own name; in others, her earnings belong to her husband. In some states, a woman may testify against her husband, sue and be sued in the courts; in others, she has no redress in case of damage to person, property, or character. In case of divorce, on account of adultery in the husband, the innocent wife is held to possess no right to children, or property, unless by special decree of the court. But in no state of the Union has the wife the right to her own person, or to any part of the joint earnings of the co-partnership, during the life of her husband. In some States women may enter the law schools and practice in the courts; in others they are forbidden. In some universities, girls enjoy equal educational advantages with boys, while many of the proudest institutions in the land deny them admittance, though the sons of China, Japan and Africa are welcomed there.

But the privileges already granted in the several states are by no means secure. The right of suffrage once exercised by women in certain States and Territories, has been denied by subsequent legislation. A bill is now pending in Congress to disfranchise the women of Utah, thus interfering to deprive United States citizens of the same rights, which the Supreme Court has declared the National Government powerless to protect anywhere. Laws passed after years of untiring effort, guaranteeing married women certain rights of property, and mothers the custody of their children, have been repealed in States where we supposed all was safe. Thus have our most sacred rights been made the football of legislative caprice, proving that a power which grants, as a privilege, what by nature is a right, may withhold the same as a penalty, when deeming it necessary for its own perpetuation.

REPRESENTATION FOR WOMAN has had no place in the nation's thought. Since the incorporation of the thirteen original states, twenty four have been admitted to the Union, not one of which has recognized woman's right of self-government. On this birthday of our national liberties, July 4th, 1876, Colorado, like all her elder sisters, comes into the Union, with the invidious word "male" in her Constitution.

UNIVERSAL MANHOOD SUFFRAGE, by establishing an aristocracy of sex, imposes upon the women of this nation a more absolute and cruel despotism than monarchy; in that, woman finds a political master in her father, husband, brother, son. The aristocracies of the old world are based upon birth, wealth, refinement, education, nobility, brave deeds of chivalry; in this nation, on sex alone; exalting brute force above moral power, vice above virtue, ignorance above education, and the son above the mother who bore him.

THE JUDICIARY OF THE NATION has proved itself but the echo of the party in power, by upholding and enforcing laws that are opposed to the spirit and letter of the Constitution. When the slave power was dominant, the Supreme Court decided that a black man was not a citizen, because he had not the right to vote; and when the Constitution was so amended as to make all persons citizens, the same high tribunal decided that a woman, though a citizen, had not the right to vote. Such vascillating interpretations of constitutional law unsettle our faith in judicial authority, and undermine the liberties of the whole people.

THESE ARTICLES OF IMPEACHMENT AGAINST OUR RULERS we now submit to the impartial judgment of the people.

To all these wrongs and oppressions woman has not submitted in silence and resignation. From the beginning of the century, when Abigail Adams, the wife of one President and the mother of another, said, "we will not hold ourselves bound to obey laws in which we have no voice or representation," until now, woman's discontent has been steadily increasing, culminating nearly thirty years ago in a simultaneous movement among the women of the nation, demanding the right of suffrage. In making our just demands, a higher motive than the pride of sex inspires us; we feel that national safety and stability depend on the complete recognition of the broad principles of our government. Woman's degraded, helpless position is the weak point in our institutions to-day; a disturbing force everywhere, severing family ties, filling our asylums with the deaf, the dumb, the blind, our prisons with criminals, our cities with drunkenness and prostitution, our homes with disease and death.

It was the boast of the founders of the republic, that the rights for which they contended, were the rights of human nature. If these rights are ignored in the case of one half the people, the nation is surely preparing for its own downfall. Governments try themselves. The recognition of a governing and a governed class is incompatible with the first principles of freedom. Woman has not been a heedless spectator of the events of this century, nor a dull listener to the grand arguments for the equal rights of humanity. From the earliest history of our country, woman has shown equal devotion with man to the cause of freedom, and has stood firmly by his side in its defence. Together, they have made this country what it is. Woman's wealth, thought and labor have cemented the stones of every monument man has reared to liberty.

And now, at the close of a hundred years, as the hour hand of the great clock that marks the centuries points to 1876, we declare our faith in the principles of self-government; our full equality with man in natural rights; that woman was made first for her own happiness, with the absolute right to herself—to all the opportunities and advantages life affords, for her complete development; and we deny that dogma of the centuries, incorporated in the codes of all nations—that woman was made for man—her best interests, in all cases, to be sacrificed to his will.

We ask of our rulers, at this hour, no special favors, no special privileges, no special legislation. We ask justice, we ask equality, we ask that all the civil and political rights that belong to citizens of the United States, be guaranteed to us and our daughters forever.

LUCRETIA MOTT,	MATHILDE FRANCESKE ANNEKE,
ELIZABETH CADY STANTON,	MATHILDE F. WENDT,
PAULINA WRIGHT DAVIS,	ADELAIDE THOMSON,
ERNESTINE L. ROSE,	LAURA DE FORCE GORDON,
CLARINDA I. H. NICHOLS,	ELLEN C. SARGENT,
MARY ANN McCLINTOCK,	VIRGINIA L. MINOR,
AMY POST,	SARA ANDREWS SPENCER,
SARAH PUGH,	LILLIE DEVEREUX BLAKE,
SUSAN B. ANTHONY,	PHEBE W. COUZINS,
MATILDA JOSLYN GAGE,	JANE GRAHAM JONES,
CLEMENCE S. LOZIER,	A. JANE DUNNIWAY,
OLYMPIA BROWN,	BELVA A. LOCKWOOD,

N. B. This Declaration is engrossed in the Centennial Books of the National Woman Suffrage Association. Friends wishing to sign it are invited to call; those at a distance will please send their signatures on a slip of thin paper, to be pasted in the book. Address NATIONAL WOMAN SUFFRAGE PARLORS, No. 1431 CHESTNUT STREET, PHILADELPHIA, PA.

N. B.—And with your name for the Declaration of Rights, please do not fail to send a Contribution, a Dollar, or at least enough to equal the cost of the paper, the printing and posting of the documents you so gladly receive from us.

Address

SUSAN B. ANTHONY,

National Woman Suffrage Parlors,

1431 Chestnut Street, Philadelphia, Pa.

SUSAN B. ANTHONY

Woman Wants Bread, Not the Ballot!
C. 1870–1880

One of Susan B. Anthony's most popular stump speeches in the 1870s was "Woman Wants Bread, Not the Ballot!" Marshaling examples from the history of the British working class as well as the experiences of recently emancipated African Americans, she made a compelling case for the link between disfranchisement and degradation: "Wherever, on the face of the globe or on the page of history, you show me a disfranchised class, I will show you a degraded class of labor." This problem was especially acute for working women, who often lacked the resources and ability to control the circumstances of their lives. As a self-supporting woman who never married, Anthony had firsthand knowledge of the challenges of wage-earning women and the need for economic independence paired with political rights. Despite her empathy for the working class (she consistently supported workers' right to join unions and organize strikes), Anthony still harbored a somewhat naive faith in the dignity of wage labor at a time when industrial conditions were abysmal, especially for women, who tended to be restricted to low-paying, low-status jobs. But she never wavered in her belief that access to the ballot would benefit the lives of working women.

My purpose tonight is to demonstrate the great historical fact that disfranchisement is not only political degradation, but also moral, social, educational and industrial degradation; and that it does not matter whether the disfranchised class live under a monarchial or a republican form of government, or whether it be white workingmen of England, negroes on our southern plantations, serfs of Russia, Chinamen on our Pacific coast, or native born, tax-paying women of this republic. Wherever, on the face of the globe or on the page of history, you show me a disfranchised class, I will show you a degraded class of labor. Disfranchisement means inability to make, shape or control one's own circumstances. The disfranchised must always do the work, accept the wages, occupy the position the enfranchised assign to them. The disfranchised are in the position of the pauper. You remember the old adage, "Beggars must not be choosers;" they must take what they can get or nothing! That is exactly the position of women in the world of work today; they can not choose. If they could, do you for a moment believe they would take the subordinate places and the inferior pay? Nor is it a "new thing under the sun" for the disfranchised, the inferior classes weighed down with wrongs, to declare they "do not want to vote." The rank and file are not philosophers, they are not educated to think for themselves, but simply to accept, unquestioned, whatever comes.

Years ago in England when the workingmen, starving in the mines and factories, gathered in mobs and took bread wherever they could get it, their friends tried to educate them into a knowledge of the causes of their poverty and degradation. At one of these "monster bread meetings," held in Manchester, John Bright said to them, "Workingmen, what you need to bring to you cheap bread and plenty of it, is the franchise;" but those ignorant men shouted back to Mr. Bright, precisely as the women of America do to us to-day, "It is not the vote we want, it is bread;" and they broke up the meeting, refusing to allow him, their best friend, to explain to them the powers of the franchise. The condition of those workingmen was very little above that of slavery. Some of you may remember when George Thompson came over to this country and rebuked us for our crime and our curse of slavery, how the slaveholders and their abettors shouted back to Mr. Thompson, "Look at home, look into your mines and your factories, you have slavery in England."

You recollect a book published at that time entitled, "The Glory and Shame of England." Her glory was the emancipation of slaves in the British West Indies, and her shame the degraded and outraged condition of those very miners and factory men. In their desperation, they organized trades unions, went on strike, fought terrible battles, often destroying property and sometimes even killing their employers. Those who have read Charles Reade's novel, "Put Yourself in his Place," have not forgotten the terrible scenes depicted. While those starving men sometimes bettered their condition financially, they never made a ripple on the surface of political thought. No member ever championed their cause on the floor of Parliament. If spoken of at all, it was as our politicians used to speak of the negroes before the war, or as they speak of the Chinese today—as nuisances that ought to be suppressed.

But at length, through the persistent demands of a little handful of reformers, there was introduced into the British Parliament the "household suffrage" bill of 1867. John Stuart Mill not only championed that bill as it was presented, but moved an amendment to strike out the word "man" and substitute therefor the word "person," so that the bill should read, "every person who shall pay a seven-pound rental per annum shall be entitled to the franchise." You will see that Mr. Mill's motive was to extend the suffrage to women as well as men. But when the vote was taken, only seventy-four, out of the nearly seven hundred members of the British Parliament, voted in its favor.

During the discussion of the original bill, the opposition was championed by Robert Lowe, who presented all the stock objections to the extension of the franchise to "those ignorant, degraded workingmen," as he called them, that ever were presented in this country against giving the ballot to the negroes, and that are today being urged against the enfranchisement of women. Is it not a little remarkable that no matter who the class may be that it is proposed to enfranchise, the objections are always the same? "The ballot in the hands of this new class will make their condition worse than before, and the introduction of this new class into the political arena will degrade politics to a lower level." But notwithstanding Mr. Lowe's persistent opposition, the bill became a law; and before the session closed, that same individual moved that Parliament, having enfranchised these men, should now make an appropriation for the establishment and support of schools for the education of them and their sons. Now, mark you his reason why! "Unless they are educated," said he, "they will be the means of overturning the throne of England." So long as these poor men in the mines and factories had not the right to vote, the power to make and unmake the laws and law-makers, to help or hurt the government, no measure ever had been proposed for their benefit although they were ground under the heel of the capitalist to a condition of abject slavery. But the moment this power is placed in their hands, before they have used it even once, this bitterest enemy to their possessing it is the first man to spring to his feet and make this motion for the most beneficent measure possible in their behalf—public schools for the education of themselves and their children.

From that day to this, there never has been a session of the British Parliament that has not had before it some measure for the benefit of the working classes. Parliament has enacted laws compelling employers to cut down the number of hours for a day's work, to pay better wages, to build decent houses for their employes, and has prohibited the employment of very young children in the mines and factories. The history of those olden times records that not infrequently children were born in the mines and passed their lives there, scarcely seeing the sunlight from the day of their birth to the day of their death.

Sad as is the condition of the workingmen of England today, it is infinitely better than it was twenty years ago. At first the votes of the workingmen were given to the Liberal party, because it was the leaders of that party who secured their enfranchisement; but soon the leaders of the Conservative party, seeing the power the workingmen had, began to vie with the Liberals by going into their meetings and pledging that if they would vote the Tory ticket and bring that party into control, it would give them more and better laws even than the Liberals. In 1874 enough workingmen did go over to bring that party to the front, with Disraeli at its head, where it stood till 1880 when the rank and file of the workingmen of England, dissatisfied with Disraeli's policy, both domestic and foreign, turned and again voted the Liberal ticket, putting that party in power with Gladstone as its leader. This is the way in which the ballot in the hands of the masses of wage-earners, even under a monarchial form of government, makes of them a tremendous balance of power whose wants and wishes the instinct of self-interest compels the political leaders to study and obey.

The great distinctive advantage possessed by the workingmen of this republic is that the son of the humblest citizen, black or white, has equal chances with the son of the richest in the land if he take advantage of the public schools, the colleges and the many opportunities freely offered. It is this equality of rights which makes our nation a home for the oppressed of all the monarchies of the old world.

And yet, notwithstanding the declaration of our Revolutionary fathers, "all men created equal," "governments derive their just powers from the consent of the governed," "taxation and representation inseparable"—notwithstanding all these grand enunciations, our government was founded upon the blood and bones of half a million human beings, bought and sold as chattels in the market. Nearly all the original thirteen States had property qualifications which disfranchised poor white men as well as women and negroes. Thomas Jefferson, at the head of the old Democratic party, took the lead in advocating the removal of all property qualifications, as so many violations of the fundamental principle of our government—"the right of consent." In New York the qualification was $250. Martin Van Buren, the chief of the Democracy, was a member of the Constitutional Convention held in Buffalo in 1821, which wiped out that qualification so far as white men were concerned. He declared, "The poor man has as good a right to a voice in the government as the rich man, and a vastly greater need to possess it as a means of protection to himself and his family." It was because the Democrats enfranchised poor white men, both native and foreign, that that strong old party held absolute sway in this country for almost forty years, with only now and then a one-term Whig administration.

In those olden days Horace Greeley, at the head of the Whig party and his glorious New York Tribune, used to write long editorials showing the workingmen that they had a mistaken idea about the Democratic party; that it was not so much the friend of the poor man as was the Whig, and if they would but vote the Whig ticket and put that party in power, they would find that it would give them better laws than the Democrats had done. At length, after many, many years of such education and persuasion, the workingmen's vote, native and foreign, was divided, and in 1860 there came to the front a new party which, though not called Whig, was largely made up of the old Whig elements. In its turn this new party enfranchised another degraded class of labor. Because the Republicans gave the ballot to negroes, they have been allied to that party and have held it solid in power from the ratification of the Fifteenth Amendment, in 1870, to the present day. Until the Democrats convince them that they will do more and better for them than the Republicans are doing, there will be no appreciable division of the negro vote.

The vast numbers of wage-earning men coming from Europe to this country, where manhood suffrage prevails with no limitations, find themselves invested at once with immense political power. They organize their trades unions, but not being able to use the franchise intelligently, they continue to strike and to fight their battles with the capitalists just as they did in the old countries. Neither press nor politicians dare to condemn these strikes or to demand their suppression because the workingmen hold the balance of power and can use it for the success or defeat of either party.

[Miss Anthony here related various timely instances of strikes where force was used to prevent non-union men from taking the places of the strikers, and neither the newspapers nor political leaders ventured to sustain the officials in the necessary steps to preserve law and order, or if they did they were defeated at the next election.]

It is said women do not need the ballot for their protection because they are supported by men. Statistics show that there are 3,000,000 women in this nation supporting themselves. In the crowded cities of the East they are compelled to work in shops, stores and factories for the merest pittance. In New York alone, there are over 50,000 of these women receiving less than fifty cents a day. Women wage-earners in different occupations have organized themselves into trades unions, from time to time, and made their strikes to get justice at the hands of their employers just as men have done, but I have yet to learn of a successful strike of any body of women. The best organized one I ever knew was that of the collar laundry women of the city of Troy, N. Y., the great emporium for the manufacture of shirts, collars and cuffs. They formed a trades union of several hundred members and demanded an increase of wages. It was refused. So one May morning in 1864, each woman threw down her scissors and her needle, her starch-pan and flat-iron, and for three long months not one returned to the factories. At the end of that time they were literally starved out, and the majority of them were compelled to go back, but not at their old wages, for their employers cut them down to even a lower figure.

In the winter following I met the president of this union, a bright young Irish girl, and asked her, "Do you not think if you had been 500 carpenters or 500 masons, you would have succeeded?" "Certainly," she said, and then she told me of 200 bricklayers who had the year before been on strike and gained every point with their employers. "What could have made the difference? Their 200 were but a fraction of that trade, while your 500 absolutely controlled yours." Finally she said, "It was because the editors ridiculed and denounced us." "Did they ridicule and denounce the bricklayers?" "No." "What did they say about you?" "Why, that our wages were good enough now, better than those of any other workingwomen except teachers; and if we weren't satisfied, we had better go and get married." "What then do you think made this difference?" After studying over the question awhile she concluded, "It must have been because our employers bribed the editors." "Couldn't the employers of the bricklayers have bribed the editors?" She had never thought of that. Most people never do think; they see one thing totally unlike another, but the person who stops to inquire into the cause that produces the one or the other is the exception. So this young Irish girl was simply not an exception, but followed the general rule of people, whether men or women; she hadn't thought. In the case of the bricklayers, no editor, either Democrat or Republican, would have accepted the proffer of a bribe, because he would have known that if he denounced or ridiculed those men, not only they but all the trades union men of the city at the next election would vote solidly against the nominees advocated by that editor. If those collar laundry women had been voters, they would have held, in that little city of Troy, the "balance of political power" and the editor or the politician who ignored or insulted them would have turned that balance over to the opposing party.

My friends, the condition of those collar laundry women but represents the utter helplessness of disfranchisement. The question with you, as men, is not whether you want your wives and daughters to vote, nor with you, as women, whether you yourselves want to vote; but whether you will help to put this power of the ballot into the hands of the 3,000,000 wage-earning women, so that they may be able to compel politicians to legislate in their favor and employers to grant them justice.

The law of capital is to extort the greatest amount of work for the least amount of money; the rule of labor is to do the smallest amount of work for the largest amount of money. Hence there is, and in the nature of things must continue to be, antagonism between the two classes; therefore, neither should be left wholly at the mercy of the other.

It was cruel, under the old regime, to give rich men the right to rule poor men. It was wicked to allow white men absolute power over black men. It is vastly more cruel, more wicked to give to all men—rich and poor, white and black, native and foreign, educated and ignorant, virtuous and vicious—this absolute control over women. Men talk of the injustice of monopolies. There never was, there never can be, a monopoly so fraught with injustice, tyranny and degradation as this monopoly of sex, of all men over all women. Therefore I not only agree with Abraham Lincoln that, "No man is good enough to govern another man without his consent;" but I say also that no man is good enough to govern a woman without her consent, and still further, that all men combined in government are not good enough to govern all women without their consent. There might have been some plausible excuse for the rich governing the poor, the educated governing the ignorant, the Saxon governing the African; but there can be none for making the husband the ruler of the wife, the brother of the sister, the man of the woman, his peer in birth, in education, in social position, in all that stands for the best and highest in humanity.

I believe that by nature men are no more unjust than women. If from the beginning women had maintained the right to rule not only themselves but men also, the latter today doubtless would be occupying the subordinate places with inferior pay in the world of work; women would be holding the higher positions with the big salaries; widowers would be doomed to a "life interest of one-third of the family estate;" husbands would "owe service" to their wives, so that every one of you men would be begging your good wives, "Please be so kind as to 'give me' ten cents for a cigar." The principle of self-government can not be violated with impunity. The individual's right to it is sacred—regardless of class, caste, race, color, sex or any other accident or incident of birth. What we ask is that you shall cease to imagine that women are outside this law, and that you shall come into the knowledge that disfranchisement means the same degradation to your daughters as to your sons.

Governments can not afford to ignore the rights of those holding the ballot, who make and unmake every law and law-maker. It is not because the members of Congress are tyrants that women receive only half pay and are admitted only to inferior positions in the departments. It is simply in obedience to a law of political economy which makes it impossible for a government to do as much for the disfranchised as for the enfranchised. Women are no exception to the general rule. As disfranchisement always has degraded men, socially, morally and industrially, so today it is disfranchisement that degrades women in the same spheres.

Again men say it is not votes, but the law of supply and demand which regulates wages. The law of gravity is that water shall run down hill, but when men build a dam across the stream, the force of gravity is stopped and the water held back. The law of supply and demand regulates free and enfranchised labor, but disfranchisement stops its operation. What we ask is the removal of the dam, that women, like men, may reap the benefit of the law. Did the law of supply and demand regulate work and wages in the olden days of slavery? This law can no more reach the disfranchised than it did the enslaved. There is scarcely a place where a woman can earn a single dollar without a man's consent.

There are many women equally well qualified with men for principals and superintendents of schools, and yet, while three-fourths of the teachers are women, nearly all of them are relegated to subordinate positions on half or at most two-thirds the salaries paid to men. The law of supply and demand is ignored, and that of sex alone settles the question. If a business man should advertise for a book-keeper and ten young men, equally well qualified, should present themselves and, after looking them over, he should say, "To you who have red hair, we will pay full wages, while to you with black hair we will pay half the regular price;" that would not be a more flagrant violation of the law of supply and demand than is that now perpetrated upon women because of their sex.

And then again you say, "Capital, not the vote, regulates labor." Granted, for the sake of the argument, that capital does control the labor of women, Chinamen and slaves; but no one with eyes to see and ears to hear, will concede for a moment that capital absolutely dominates the work and wages of the free and enfranchised men of this republic. It is in order to lift the millions of our wage-earning women into a position of as much power over their own labor as men possess that they should be invested with the franchise. This ought to be done not only for the sake of justice to the women, but to the men with whom they compete; for, just so long as there is a degraded class of labor in the market, it always will be used by the capitalists to checkmate and undermine the superior classes.

Now that as a result of the agitation for equality of chances, and through the invention of machinery, there has come a great revolution in the world of economics, so that wherever a man may go to earn an honest dollar a woman may go also, there is no escape from the conclusion that she must be clothed with equal power to protect herself. That power is the ballot, the symbol of freedom and equality, without which no citizen is sure of keeping even that which he hath, much less of getting that which he hath not. Women are today the peers of men in education, in the arts and sciences, in the industries and professions, and there is no escape from the conclusion that the next step must be to make them the peers of men in the government—city, State and national—to give them an equal voice in the framing, interpreting and administering of the codes and constitutions.

We recognize that the ballot is a two-edged, nay, a many-edged sword, which may be made to cut in every direction. If wily politicians and sordid capitalists may wield it for mere party and personal greed; if oppressed wage-earners may invoke it to wring justice from legislators and extort material advantages from employers; if the lowest and most degraded classes of men may use it to open wide the sluice-ways of vice and crime; if it may be the instrumentality by which the narrow, selfish, corrupt and corrupting men and measures rule—it is quite as true that noble-minded statesmen, philanthropists and reformers may make it the weapon with which to reverse the above order of things, as soon as they can have added to their now small numbers the immensely larger ratio of what men so love to call "the better half of the people." When women vote, they will make a new balance of power that must be weighed and measured and calculated in its effect upon every social and moral question which goes to the arbitrament of the ballot-box. Who can doubt that when the representative women of thought and culture, who are today the moral backbone of our nation, sit in counsel with the best men of the country, higher conditions will be the result?

Insurrectionary and revolutionary methods of righting wrongs, imaginary or real, are pardonable only in the enslaved and disfranchised. The moment any class of men possess the ballot, it is their weapon and their shield. Men with a vote have no valid excuse for resorting to the use of illegal means to fight their battles. When the masses of wage-earning men are educated into a knowledge of their own rights and of their duties to others, so that they are able to vote intelligently, they can carry their measures through the ballot-box and will have no need to resort to force. But so long as they remain in ignorance and are manipulated by the political bosses they will continue to vote against their own interests and turn again to violence to right their wrongs.

If men possessing the power of the ballot are driven to desperate means to gain their ends, what shall be done by disfranchised women? There are grave questions of moral, as well as of material interest in which women are most deeply concerned. Denied the ballot, the legitimate means with which to exert their influence, and, as a rule, being lovers of peace, they have recourse to prayers and tears, those potent weapons of women and children, and, when they fail, must tamely submit to wrong or rise in rebellion against the powers that be. Women's crusades against saloons, brothels and gambling-dens, emptying kegs and bottles into the streets, breaking doors and windows and burning houses, all go to prove that disfranchisement, the denial of lawful means to gain desired ends, may drive even women to violations of law and order. Hence to secure both national and "domestic tranquillity," to "establish justice," to carry out the spirit of our Constitution, put into the hands of all women, as you have into those of all men, the ballot, that symbol of perfect equality, that right protective of all other rights.

MATILDA JOSLYN GAGE

Indian Citizenship
MAY 1878

In 1877–78, a bill was debated in the United States Senate that proposed to naturalize some American Indians; it was opposed by representatives of the Choctaw, Chickasaw, Creek, and Seminole nations for impinging on the sovereignty and jurisdiction of Indian nations and was not passed. Suffragist Matilda Joslyn Gage (1826–1898), who had written admiringly about the large roles Iroquois women played in tribal governance, suspected the bill was part of "the grasping avarice of the white man" for tribal land they desired for settlement. Yet even as she spoke up for honoring treaties and respecting tribal customs, Gage deployed racist comparisons between the educated, white, Christian women who were denied full citizenship and American Indian "savages" who did not want it. That strand of racism runs through much of suffrage history (see the 1893 poster "American Woman and Her Political Peers" in the insert to this volume) and is on display even in the writings of suffragists like Gage, who considered herself a friend and supporter of the Indian cause. Gage first encountered the nascent women's rights movement at age twenty-six when she attended the third annual convention in Syracuse, and later joined forces with Elizabeth Cady Stanton and Susan B. Anthony to edit the first three volumes of the *History of Woman Suffrage* (1881–86). Always committed to a broader view of women's rights than just the vote, she is most noted for *Women, Church, and State* (1893), a critical examination of the status of women under Christianity, which predated Stanton's *Woman's Bible* by two years.

While the United States is trying to force citizenship upon the Indians the latter are everywhere protesting against it. The famous Iroquois, or "Six Nations," held a council at Onondaga the last of March, upon the old, original council grounds, where, before the advent of Columbus, they were wont to meet in settlement of grave questions.

No such important questions ever came up during their old barbaric life as were discussed at the council in March. First among them was the bill recently introduced in the United States Senate by Mr. Kernan of N. Y., to give those tribes the rights of citizenship and allow them to sell their lands in this State.

The Indians decline the gift of citizenship and although Judge Wallace of the Northern District of New York, recently decided in favor of the right of an Oneida Indian who voted at the presidential election of 1876, Chief Skenandoah of the Oneidas, was one of the principal speakers against this innovation.

The Mahommedans have a saying that one hour of justice is worth seventy years of prayer; the Indians seems to think one hour of justice worth a thousand years of citizenship, as the drift of their talk was against any law that should either *allow or compel* them to become citizens, as such a course would open wide the door to the grasping avarice of the white man. They discussed plans to compel the payment due them for lands once deeded them by the United States in treaty, but which were afterwards seized and sold for the benefit of our government.

Over one hundred chiefs and warriors of the different nations took part in this discussion. This council of Indians at Onondaga Castle, in the center of the great Empire State, and the convention of the women of the country at Washington in January, the one protesting against citizenship about to be forced upon them, because with it would come further deprivation of their rights,—the other demanding citizenship denied them, in order to protect their rights, are two forcible commentaries upon our so-called republican form of government. Can woman's political degradation reach much lower depth? She, educated, enlightened, Christian, in vain begs for the crumbs cast contemptuously aside by savages. While some of these red men are educated Christians, others still cling to their pagan rites, yearly celebrating the Green Corn Dance, yearly burning the White Dog.

After close of the council its younger members indulged in a war-dance, and, scalping knife in hand, with painted faces, whirling tomahawk and shrieking war-whoop, recounted their old time prowess.

That the Indians have been oppressed,—are now, is true, but the United States has treaties with them, recognizing them as distinct political communities, and duty towards them demands *not an enforced citizenship* but a faithful living up to its obligations on the part of the Government.

Our Indians are in reality foreign powers, though living among us. With them our country not only has treaty obligations, but pays them, or professes to, annual sums in consideration of such treaties; the U. S. Government paying the Iroquois their annuities in June, the State of New York in September. One great aversion the Iroquois have to citizenship is that they would then be compelled to pay taxes, which they look upon as a species of tribute. From an early day they were accustomed to receiving tribute, sending among the conquered tribes of Long Island for their annual dues of wampum. As poor, as oppressed as they are, surrounded as they now are by the conquering white man, they still preserve their olden spirit of independence, still look upon themselves as distinct nations and in the payment of their annuities, fancy they are receiving, as of old, tribute from their enemies. Compelling them to become citizens would be like the forcible annexation of Cuba, Mexico or Canada to our government, and as unjust.

A delegation of Indians called at the White House on New Year's day. As a sarcasm of justice, on their "Happy New Year" cards were inscribed extracts from various treaties made with them, and disregarded rights guaranteed them in treaty, by the Government.

The women of the nation might take hint from the Indians and on July 4th, send to the legislative, judicial and executive bodies, cards inscribed with such sentiments as "Governments derive their *just* powers from the *consent* of the governed." "Taxation without representation is tyranny," and others of like character.

The black man had the right of suffrage conferred upon him without his asking for it, and now an attempt is made to force it upon the red man in direct opposition to his wishes, while women citizens, already members of the nation, to whom it rightfully belongs, are denied its exercise. Truly, consistency is a jewel so rare its only abode is the toad's head.

MARY TAPE

Letter to the San Francisco Board of Education
APRIL 8, 1885

"Is it a disgrace to be Born a Chinese?" Mary Tape (1857–1934) challenged the San Francisco Board of Education in 1885 after it balked at admitting her eight-year-old daughter Mamie to their neighborhood school. Raised in a Shanghai orphanage and brought to the United States by missionaries at age eleven, Mary learned English, adopted Western dress, and married Joseph Tape, a Chinese American interpreter, with whom she had four children. When her daughter was denied admission to the local public school out of fears of mixing Chinese and American children, the Tapes sued the school board and won in both Superior Court and the California Supreme Court. But in a move that paralleled how southerners found ways to prevent black children from attending white schools, the school superintendent hastily established a separate school for Chinese students. This letter was written at the height of the dispute. Mamie and her brother did in fact enroll at the segregated Chinese Primary School, which counted only three girls among its thirty-eight students in its first year. *Tape v. Hurley* (1885) established the right of Chinese American students to an elementary public education; only in the 1920s were they allowed to attend integrated high schools.

———————

1769 GREEN STREET,
SAN FRANCISCO, April 8, 1885.
To the Board of Education—DEAR SIRS: I see that you are going to make all sorts of excuses to keep my child out off the Public schools. Dear sirs, Will you please to tell me! Is it a disgrace to be Born a Chinese? Didn't God make us all!!! What right! have you to bar my children out of the school because she is a chinese Decend. They is no other worldly reason that you could keep her out, except that. I suppose, you all goes to churches on Sundays! Do you call that a Christian act to compell my little children to go so far to a school that is made in purpose for them. My children don't dress like the other Chinese. They look just as phunny amongst them as the Chinese dress in Chinese look amongst you Caucasians. Besides, if

I had any wish to send them to a chinese school I could have sent them two years ago without going to all this trouble. You have expended a lot of the Public money foolishly, all because of a one poor little Child. Her playmates is all Caucasians ever since she could toddle around. If she is good enough to play with them! Then is she not good enough to be in the same room and studie with them? You had better come and see for yourselves. See if the Tape's is not same as other Caucasians, except in features. It seems no matter how a Chinese may live and dress so long as you know they Chinese. Then they are hated as one. There is not any right or justice for them.

You have seen my husband and child. You told him it wasn't Mamie Tape you object to. If it were not Mamie Tape you object to, then why didn't you let her attend the school nearest her home! Instead of first making one pretense Then another pretense of some kind to keep her out? It seems to me Mr. Moulder has a grudge against this Eight-year-old Mamie Tape. I know they is no other child I mean Chinese child! care to go to your public Chinese school. May you Mr. Moulder, never be persecuted like the way you have persecuted little Mamie Tape. Mamie Tape will never attend any of the Chinese schools of your making! Never!!! I will let the world see sir What justice there is When it is govern by the Race prejudice men! Just because she is of the Chinese decend, not because she don't dress like you because she does. Just because she is decended of Chinese parents I guess she is more of a American then a good many of you that is going to prewent her being Educated.

MRS. M. TAPE.

MORMON WOMEN OF UTAH

Protest

MARCH 6, 1886

When Utah became a territory in 1870, women in this overwhelmingly Mormon settlement received the right to vote alongside men. Mormon women were proud of their status as voters, but the support of the Church of Jesus Christ of Latter-day Saints for celestial (or plural) marriage posed complicated challenges for the national women's suffrage movement, which had to decide whether to embrace or disown polygamous Mormon women voters. The American Woman Suffrage Association distanced itself from the controversial practice, but the National Woman Suffrage Association was more welcoming, at least at first. Emmeline Wells (1828–1921), the editor of the Salt Lake City periodical *Woman's Exponent* and herself a plural wife, served as a representative of Utah on the NWSA board in the late 1870s and early 1880s. By the time of this mass protest meeting in 1886, whose preamble and resolutions are included here, the national political climate had turned much more chilly, with the federal government stepping up its campaign against polygamy. "Being forced to disclose their personal conditions" referred to wives who were compelled by federal authorities to testify against their polygamous husbands. All territorial Utah women lost the right to vote in 1887 but regained it when Utah became a state in 1896, six years after the church officially renounced the practice of polygamy. Among other outcomes, the removal of the issue of polygamy helped to facilitate the reunification of the suffrage movement, which resulted in the creation of the National American Woman Suffrage Association (NAWSA) in 1890.

PREAMBLE AND RESOLUTIONS OF THE WOMEN
OF UTAH IN MASS MEETING ASSEMBLED.

Whereas, The rights and liberties of women are placed in jeopardy by the present cruel and inhuman proceedings in the Utah courts, and in the contemplated measure in Congress to deprive the women voters in Utah of the elective franchise; and,

Whereas, Womanhood is outraged by the compulsion used in the courts of Utah to force mothers on pain of imprisonment to disclose their personal condition and that of their friends in relation to anticipated maternity, and to give information as to the fathers of their children; and,

Whereas, These violations of decency have now reached the length of compelling legal wives to testify against their husbands without their consent, in violation both of written statutes and the provisions of the common law, therefore, be it

Resolved, By the women of Utah in mass meeting assembled, that the suffrage originally conferred upon us as a political privilege, has become a vested right by possession and usage for fifteen years, and that we protest against being deprived of that right without process of law, and for no other reason than that we do not vote to suit our political opponents.

Resolved, That we emphatically deny the charge that we vote otherwise than according to our own free choice, and point to the fact that the ballot is absolutely secret in Utah as proof that we are protected in voting for whom and what we choose with perfect liberty.

Resolved, That as no wife of a polygamist, legal or plural, is permitted to vote under the laws of the United States, to deprive non-polygamous women of the suffrage is high-handed oppression for which no valid excuse can be offered.

Resolved, That the questions concerning their personal condition, the relationship they bear to men marked down as victims to special law, and the paternity of their born and unborn children, which have been put to women before grand juries and in open courts in Utah, are an insult to pure womanhood, an outrage upon the sensitive feelings of our sex and a disgrace to officers and judges who have propounded and enforced them.

Resolved, That we honor those noble women who, standing upon their rights and refusing to reply to improper and insulting questions, such as no true man nor any court with any regard for propriety would compel them to answer, have gone to prison and suffered punishment without crime, rather than betray the most sacred confidence and yield to the brutal mandates of a little brief authority.

Resolved, That the action of the District Attorney and the Chief Justice of Utah, in compelling a lawful wife to testify for the prosecution in a criminal case involving the liberty of her husband and in face of her own earnest protest, is a violation of laws which those officials have sworn to uphold, is contrary to precedent and usage for many centuries, and is an invasion of family rights and of that union between husband and wife which both law and religion have held sacred from time immemorial.

Resolved, That we express our profound appreciation of the moral courage exhibited by Senators Call, Morgan, Teller, Brown and others, and also by Mrs. Belva H. Lockwood, who, in the face of almost overwhelming prejudice, have defended the constitutional rights of the people of Utah.

Resolved, That we extend our heartfelt thanks to the ladies of the Woman Suffrage Association assembled in Boston, and unite in praying that God may speed the day when both men and women shall shake from their shoulders the yoke of tyranny.

Resolved, That we call upon the wives and mothers of the United States to come to our help in resisting these encroachments upon our liberties and these outrages upon our peaceful homes and family relations, and that a committee be appointed at this meeting to memorialize the President and Congress of the United States in relation to our wrongs, and to take all necessary measures to present our views and feelings to the country.

THE NEW YORK TIMES

They Enter a Protest

OCTOBER 28, 1886

To the New York State Woman Suffrage Association, unveiling a statue representing liberty as a woman in a country where women were denied basic political rights was too great a hypocrisy to ignore. The copper statue was originally to have been presented to the people of the United States by the people of France in honor of the country's centennial, but fundraising lagged and the statue was not completed until 1886. As plans went forward for the dedication of the Statue of Liberty in New York harbor on October 28, 1886, suffragists demanded to be included on the program. When their request was denied, they mounted a public protest of their own. They chartered a cattle barge and joined the nautical flotilla that was descending on Bedloe's Island (now called Liberty Island) for the ceremony. Among the leaders of this protest were Lillie Devereux Blake (1833–1913) and Matilda Joslyn Gage, both veterans of the demonstration at the 1876 Centennial in Philadelphia.

WOMAN SUFFRAGISTS THINK THE CEREMONIES AN EMPTY FARCE.

The members of the New-York State Woman Suffrage Association were the only people who looked with disfavor upon the grand pageant yesterday in celebration of Liberty's unveiling. They had been denied a part in the ceremonies on Bedlow's Island, and when they applied for a position in the naval parade had been advised to go on the same boat with the Cercle Français de l'Harmonie. To emphasize their disgust at this treatment by the male managers of the pageant the women hired a boat for themselves, and without asking anybody's leave took up one of the most favorable positions for viewing the ceremonies on the island. They chartered the steamer John Lenox, and it started from the West Twenty-first-street pier at 1 o'clock with 200 members of the association and their friends. There were 25 men on board besides the crew. Among the company were Mrs. Lillie Devereux Blake, Mrs. Caroline Gilkey Rogers, Mrs. Mary Seymour Howell, Mrs. Marguerite Moore, Matilda

Joslyn Gage, Harriet R. Shattuck, Miss Ray Hall, Mrs. Margaret A. Parker, and Mrs. Belle Thompson.

Immediately after the veil had been drawn from before Liberty's face Mrs. Blake called an indignation meeting on the lower deck. After denouncing the ceremonies just witnessed as a farce she offered resolutions declaring "that in erecting a statue of Liberty embodied as a woman in a land where no woman has political liberty men have shown a delightful inconsistency which excites the wonder and admiration of the opposite sex," and other sentiments of a like sort. The resolutions were unanimously carried, and were followed by speeches from Mrs. Moore, Mrs. Rogers, and Mrs. Howell in a similar strain. Mrs. Shattuck read a poem and Miss Ray Hall, of Brooklyn, sang an anthem prepared specially for the occasion.

GEORGE VEST

Remarks on the Amendment to Extend
Suffrage to Women
JANUARY 25, 1887

What came to be known as the Susan B. Anthony Amendment was first introduced in Congress on January 10, 1878, by Aaron A. Sargent (1827–1887), the Republican senator from California. The text, which was modeled on the Fifteenth Amendment, read as follows: "The right of citizens of the United States to vote shall not be denied or abridged by the United States or by any state on account of sex." The Senate Committee on Privileges and Elections held yearly hearings, usually timed to the annual convention of the National Woman Suffrage Association, but the amendment was not considered on the Senate floor until January 25, 1887. George Vest (1830–1904), the Democratic senator from Missouri, was one of those who spoke against it. In remarks reprinted in the *Congressional Record*, his speech encapsulated the arguments politicians used against giving women the vote: they were too emotional, they would be degraded by their association with politics, they would be inconvenienced by their civic duties, and they belonged on a pedestal. Bringing it down to the personal level, Senator Vest confessed, "For my part I want when I go to my home . . . not to be received in the masculine embrace of some female ward politician, but to the earnest, loving look and touch of a true woman." The final vote was 16 yeas, 34 nays, with 25 absent. The Senate would not vote again on the amendment until 1914.

Mr. President, any measure of legislation which affects popular government based on the will of the people as expressed through their suffrage is not only important but vitally so. If this Government, which is based on the intelligence of the people, shall ever be destroyed it will be by injudicious, immature, or corrupt suffrage. If the ship of state launched by our fathers shall ever be destroyed, it will be by striking the rock of universal, unprepared suffrage. Suffrage once given can never be taken away. Legislatures and conventions may do everything else; they never can do that. When any particular class or portion of the community is once invested with this privilege it is fixed, accomplished, and eternal.

The Senator who last spoke on this question refers to the successful experiment in regard to woman-suffrage in the Territories of Wyoming and Washington. Mr. President, it is not upon the plains of the sparsely-settled Territories of the West that woman suffrage can be tested. Suffrage in the rural districts and sparsely settled regions of this country must from the very nature of things remain pure when corrupt everywhere else. The danger of corrupt suffrage is in the cities, and those masses of population to which civilization tends everywhere in all history. Whilst the country has been pure and patriotic, the cities have been the first cancers to appear upon the body-politic in all ages of the world.

Wyoming Territory! Washington Territory! Where are their large cities? Where are the localities in those Territories where the strain upon popular government must come? The Senator from New Hampshire, who is so conspicuous in this movement, appalled the country some months since by his ghastly array of illiteracy in the Southern States. He proposes that $77,000,000 of the people's money be taken in order to strike down the great foe to republican government, illiteracy. How was that illiteracy brought upon this country? It was by giving the suffrage to unprepared voters. It is not my purpose to go back into the past and make any partisan or sectional appeal, but it is a fact known to every intelligent man that in one single act the right of suffrage was given without preparation to hundreds of thousands of voters who to-day can scarcely read. That Senator proposes now to double, and more than double, that illiteracy. He proposes to give the negro women of the South this right of suffrage, utterly unprepared as they are for it.

In a convention some two years and a half ago in the city of Louisville an intelligent negro from the South said the negro men could not vote the Democratic ticket because the women would not live with them if they did. The negro men go out in the hotels and upon the railroad cars. They go to the cities and by attrition they wear away the prejudice of race; but the women remain at home, and their emotional natures aggregate and compound the race-prejudice, and when suffrage is given them what must be the result?

Mr. President, it is not my purpose to speak of the inconveniences, for they are nothing more, of woman suffrage. I trust that as a gentleman I respect the feelings of the ladies and their advocates. I am not here to ridicule. My purpose only is to use legitimate argument as to a movement which commands respectful consideration, if for no other reason than because it comes from women. But it is impossible to divest ourselves of a certain degree of sentiment when considering this question.

I pity the man who can consider any question affecting the influence of woman with the cold, dry logic of business. What man can, without aversion, turn from the blessed memory of that dear old grandmother, or the gentle words and caressing hand of that blessed mother gone to the unknown world, to face in its stead the idea of a female justice of the peace or township constable? For my part I want when I go to my home—when I turn from the arena where man contends with man for what we call the prizes of this paltry world—I want to go back, not to be received in the masculine embrace of some female ward politician, but to the earnest, loving look and touch of a true woman. I want to go back to the jurisdiction of the wife, the mother; and instead of a lecture upon finance or the tariff, or upon the construction of the Constitution, I want those blessed, loving details of domestic life and domestic love.

I have said I would not speak of the inconveniences to arise from woman suffrage—I care not—whether the mother is called upon to decide as a juryman or jury-woman rights of property or rights of life, whilst her baby is "mewling and puking" in solitary confinement at home. There are other considerations more important, and one of them to my mind is insuperable. I speak now respecting women as a sex. I believe that they are better than men, but I do not believe they are adapted to the political work of this world. I do not believe that the Great Intelligence ever intended them to invade the sphere of work given to men, tearing down and destroying all the best influences for which God has intended them.

The great evil in this country to-day is in emotional suffrage. The great danger to-day is in excitable suffrage. If the voters of this country could think always coolly, and if they could deliberate, if they could go by judgment and not by passion, our institutions would survive forever, eternal as the foundations of the continent itself; but massed together, subject to the excitements of mobs and of these terrible political contests that come upon us from year to year under the autonomy of our Government, what would be the result if suffrage were given to the women of the United States?

Women are essentially emotional. It is no disparagement to them they are so. It is no more insulting to say that women are emotional than to say that they are delicately constructed physically and unfitted to become soldiers or workmen under the sterner, harder pursuits of life.

What we want in this country is to avoid emotional suffrage, and what we need is to put more logic into public affairs and less feeling. There are spheres in which feeling should be paramount. There are kingdoms in which the heart should reign supreme. That kingdom belongs to woman. The realm of sentiment, the realm of love, the realm of the gentler and the holier and kindlier attributes that make the name of wife, mother, and sister next to that of God himself.

I would not, and I say it deliberately, degrade woman by giving her the right of suffrage. I mean the word in its full signification, because I believe that woman as she is to-day, the queen of home and of hearts, is above the political collisions of this world, and should always be kept above them.

Sir, if it be said to us that this is a natural right belonging to women, I deny it. The right of suffrage is one to be determined by expediency and by policy, and given by the State to whom it pleases. It is not a natural right; it is a right that comes from the state.

It is claimed that if the suffrage be given to women it is to protect them. Protect them from whom? The brute that would invade their rights would coerce the suffrage of his wife, or sister, or mother as he would wring from her the hard earnings of her toil to gratify his own beastly appetites and passions.

It is said that the suffrage is to be given to enlarge the sphere of woman's influence. Mr. President, it would destroy her influence. It would take her down from that pedestal where she is to-day, influencing as a mother the minds of her offspring, influencing by her gentle and kindly caress the action of her husband toward the good and pure.

ALICE C. FLETCHER

The Legal Conditions of Indian Women
MARCH 25–APRIL 1, 1888

From March 25 to April 1, 1888, representatives of fifty-three women's organizations from nine countries convened in Washington, D.C., for the inaugural meeting of the International Council of Women. One of the featured speakers was Alice Cunningham Fletcher (1838–1923), a specialist in American Indian cultures, especially music. An amateur ethnologist affiliated with Harvard's noted Peabody Museum, Fletcher had traveled extensively throughout the West gaining familiarity with the Omaha, Pawnee, Sioux, Arapaho, and Cheyenne nations, and she often found herself serving as an intermediary between tribes and government agencies. While she respected Indian customs and traditions, she nevertheless promoted efforts to assimilate American Indians into mainstream American culture through legislation like the Dawes Act of 1887, which broke up shared tribal holdings by dividing them into individually held allotments and offered citizenship to individuals who chose to live separately from their tribe. In this talk she surveys the status of Indian women, challenging the popular perception of them as slaves or drudges by focusing on the matrilineal networks that structured tribal life. Tasked with explaining the legal conditions of tribal women, she found it hard not to conclude, as did many Indian women, "I was better as an Indian woman than under white law."

The popular impression concerning Indian women is, that they are slaves, possessing neither place, property, nor respect in the tribe. This impression is confirmed by observing that women are the workers and the burden-carriers; that upon them falls all the drudgery of life. They are also said to be bought and sold as wives, and their life is without honor or happiness. In the face of this generally accepted picture of the Indian woman, I can hardly hope to greatly modify this opinion by the statement of facts. I must, therefore, ask you to receive what I say as from one who, having lived among the people, sharing their poverty in summer and in winter, has thus learned their social and religious customs.

The Indian tribe is not a mere collection of men and women;

it is a completely organized body, girt about by laws, unwritten, it is true, but rooted in the religion and time-honored customs of the people. The tribe is divided into clans or gens, each division having its location in the camp, and duties in the tribe. These clans are organized and subdivided, having appropriate officers to fulfill their rites and customs. These clans are based upon kinship, and are the fundamental units of the tribe. A man is born into his clan, into this family of kindred. In a large proportion of our Indian tribes the mother carries the clan—that is, the man belongs to the clan or kindred of his mother, not to that of his father. It is a general law among a large portion of the tribes that a man may not marry in his own clan. The family, as we understand it, can not exist in the tribe, as the husband and wife represent two distinct political bodies, so to speak, which can never coalesce, for neither the man nor the woman by marrying lose or change any of their rights in their respective clans. There are no family names in an Indian tribe. Of course, I do not refer to the customs which have been introduced by our race in many of the tribes, but to the native conditions unmodified by the white man, which conditions are to-day more or less potent in every Indian community.

The man is given in his infancy one of the names belonging to his clan. These names are generally mythologic in their origin. He frequently takes other names later in life, marking his career, but he never forgets or loses his clan name. The woman is similarly named, and bears her birthright name to her grave. Her children, if the clan follows the mother, are given names proper to her clan, and are identified with her kindred and not with that of their father. The child is never the heir of both his parents, since the claim of the clan into which he is born is primal, and that of the family, as we know it, secondary. For the same reason the wife never becomes entirely under the control of her husband. Her kindred have a prior right, and can use that right to separate her from him or to protect her from him, should he maltreat her. The brother who would not rally to the help of his sister would become a by-word among his clan. Not only will he protect her at the risk of his life from insult and injury, but he will seek help for her when she is sick and suffering. When I last saw the Sun Dance, one of the young men who went through all the tortures did it to redeem a vow he had made when his sister lay ill. At that time he went out of her lodge, and, lifting his hand to the sun, he promised that if she might recover he would tie his body to the tree and suffer for her. The woman never, from her birth to her death, is without the strong protecting arm of her kindred, to whom she can appeal in the case of injury. This is the general law. There are, however, circumstances in which a woman loses by her own act this right of appeal to her kindred, and there is in some tribes a strong superstition concerning witchcraft, from the dread suspicion of which there is no more protection for the Indian accused, than there was for our own ancestors not many centuries ago.

In marriage the woman, as a rule, is free to choose her husband if she so desires. Whether or no she is forced to marry a man against her will to gratify her family, depends upon the individual woman. Still, matches are made all the world over. The gifts made by the man to the family of his wife are not a price paid for her, but the recognition of certain claims and demands upon him. The equivalent of these gifts is returned to the wife, within a few months after her marriage, by her father or near of kin. Custom demands that the man should serve his father-in-law for a few years prior to setting up a separate establishment. Should the husband prove tyrannical or lazy in providing for his family, the wife tells him to go back to his kindred, or if the pair are living in a lodge apart from her family she takes down the lodge and departs, leaving her husband to watch the dying embers of the fire. Her kindred will not send her back, nor would her husband be allowed to coerce her to live with him.

It is true that Indian women are the laborers and burden-bearers. That is not because they are slaves, but because they belong to the non-combatant portion of society. All that part of any society which is not demanded for war is more or less engaged in labor. This is true among us, but the line is not drawn on sex. We set aside a class of men to defend us by arms, another class to defend us by laws, still another to execute the law, and so on; the remainder are employed in the industries and arts of peace. These labors are shared by both sexes and do not belong to women alone, because our society has become co-ordinated. In the Indian tribe you see a much simpler form of society.

No international courtesy or law holds tribes in peace or neutrality, and, until within a few years, every Indian village or camp was hourly in danger of war parties. The Indian man had to sleep on his arms, to be ready at any instant to defend his mother and sisters, his wife and children. This condition of affairs made it impossible for the Indian to become a laborer, and to this was added the necessity of hunting to procure meat and clothing. The Indian man was the sole provider and protector, and the Indian woman the conservor, of the home. He must ride free that he may strike the needed game or the dreaded enemy. He could not be hampered by the *impedimenta* of family bundles and burdens. Since all men were needed to protect all women and children, to the women fell the ax, the hoe, and the burden-strap, and, as a logical consequence, all the property belonged to the women.

In olden times the women claimed the land. In the early treaties and negotiations for the sale of land, the women had their voice, and the famous Chief Cornplanter was obliged to retract one of his bargains because the women forbade, they being the land-holders, and not the men. With the century, our custom of ignoring women in public transactions has had its reflex influence upon Indian custom. At the present time all property is personal; the man owns his own ponies and other belongings which he has personally acquired; the woman owns her horses, dogs, and all the lodge equipments; children own their own articles, and parents do not control the possessions of their children. There is really no family property, as we use the term. A wife is as independent in the use of her possessions as is the most independent man in our midst. If she chooses to give away or sell all of her property, there is no one to gainsay her.

When I was living with the Indians, my hostess, a fine looking woman, who wore numberless bracelets, and rings in her ears and on her fingers, and painted her face like a brilliant sunset, one day gave away a very fine horse. I was surprised, for I knew there had been no family talk on the subject, so I asked: "Will your husband like to have you give the horse away?" Her eyes danced, and, breaking into a peal of laughter, she hastened to tell the story to the other women gathered in the tent, and I became the target of many merry eyes. I tried to explain how a white woman would act, but laughter and contempt met my explanation of the white man's hold upon his wife's property.

It has been my task to explain to the Indian woman her legal conditions under the law. In bringing our legal lines down upon her independent life I have been led to realize how much woman has given of her own freedom to make the strong foundation of the family and to preserve the accumulation and descent of property. All this was necessary, that the pressure of want should be removed, time for mental culture secured, and the development of civilization made possible to the race—a sacrifice needful, but nevertheless a sacrifice. As I have tried to explain our statutes to Indian women, I have met with but one response. They have said: "As an Indian woman I was free. I owned my home, my person, the work of my own hands, and my children could never forget me. I was better as an Indian woman than under white law." Men have said: "Your laws show how little your men care for their women. The wife is nothing of herself. She is worth little but to help a man to have one hundred and sixty acres." One day, sitting in the tent of an old chief, famous in war, he said to me: "My young men are to lay aside their weapons; they are to take up the work of the women; they will plow the field and raise the crops; for them I see a future, but my women, they to whom we owe everything, what is there for them to do? I see nothing! You are a woman; have pity on my women when everything is taken from them." Not only does the woman under our laws lose her independent hold on her property and herself, but there are offenses and injuries which can befall a woman which would be avenged and punished by the relatives under tribal law, but which have no penalty or recognition under our laws. If the Indian brother should, as of old, defend his sister, he would himself become liable to the law and suffer for his championship.

I have been considering strictly the legal conditions of Indian women under tribal and under our own laws. I have not touched upon customs which bear heavily upon them. Many of these customs can not be reached by the law. Their amelioration must depend upon other influences which it is the function of Christian philanthropy to exercise. I would have you, my friends and sisters, take pity on the Indian woman. Her old-time individual independence is gone. She has fallen under the edge of our laws—an edge few of us have ever felt. We do not live under the letter of the law, but in the midst of a growing, broadening Christian spirit that is each year making its mark upon our statute-books and emphasizing the right of every human being to life, liberty, and the pursuit of happiness. Meanwhile our Indian sisters are called to enter our civilization, and for them the path is full of difficulty and hardship. They must lose much they hold dear and suffer wrongs at the hands of those whose added legal powers, when untempered by an unselfish, cultured spirit, makes the legal conditions of woman akin to the cruelest slavery. I crave for my Indian sisters, your help, your patience, and your unfailing labors, to hasten the day when the laws of all the land shall know neither male nor female, but grant to all equal rights and equal justice.

ANNA J. COOPER

from *A Voice from the South,*
by a Black Woman of the South
1892

Anna J. Cooper (1858–1964) was a black feminist intellectual who
never doubted the central role that African American women played
in the struggle for racial and gender advancement: "Only the BLACK
WOMAN can say 'when and where I enter in the quiet, undisputed
dignity of my womanhood, without violence and without suing or
special patronage, then and there the whole race enters with me.'"
That bold vision provided the core of her 1892 book, *A Voice from the
South, by a Black Woman of the South.* This excerpt, from the chapter
"The Status of Woman in America," calls on black women to take
wider social responsibilities in their communities as a way of uplifting
both themselves and the entire black population. The daughter of a
slave woman and her mother's white slave master, Cooper was born
enslaved in Raleigh, North Carolina. Married at nineteen to a much
older man and widowed two years later, she enrolled at Oberlin College, where she received her BA in 1884. An educator as well as a writer
and intellectual, she taught for many years at the prestigious but segregated M Street High School in Washington, D.C. Like many African
American women of her generation, she was an active supporter of
the proliferation of black women's clubs that coalesced into a national
movement by the 1890s.

———————————

The colored woman of to-day occupies, one may say, a unique
position in this country. In a period of itself transitional and
unsettled, her status seems one of the least ascertainable and
definitive of all the forces which make for our civilization. She
is confronted by both a woman question and a race problem,
and is as yet an unknown or an unacknowledged factor in both.
While the women of the white race can with calm assurance
enter upon the work they feel by nature appointed to do, while
their men give loyal support and appreciative countenance to
their efforts, recognizing in most avenues of usefulness the propriety and the need of woman's distinctive co-operation, the
colored woman too often finds herself hampered and shamed
by a less liberal sentiment and a more conservative attitude

on the part of those for whose opinion she cares most. That this is not universally true I am glad to admit. There are to be found both intensely conservative white men and exceedingly liberal colored men. But as far as my experience goes the average man of our race is less frequently ready to admit the actual need among the sturdier forces of the world for woman's help or influence. That great social and economic questions await her interference, that she could throw any light on problems of national import, that her intermeddling could improve the management of school systems, or elevate the tone of public institutions, or humanize and sanctify the far reaching influence of prisons and reformatories and improve the treatment of lunatics and imbeciles,—that she has a word worth hearing on mooted questions in political economy, that she could contribute a suggestion on the relations of labor and capital, or offer a thought on honest money and honorable trade, I fear the majority of "Americans of the colored variety" are not yet prepared to concede. It may be that they do not yet see these questions in their right perspective, being absorbed in the immediate needs of their own political complications. A good deal depends on where we put the emphasis in this world; and our men are not perhaps to blame if they see everything colored by the light of those agitations in the midst of which they live and move and have their being. The part they have had to play in American history during the last twenty-five or thirty years has tended rather to exaggerate the importance of mere political advantage, as well as to set a fictitious valuation on those able to secure such advantage. It is the astute politician, the manager who can gain preferment for himself and his favorites, the demagogue known to stand in with the powers at the White House and consulted on the bestowal of government plums, whom we set in high places and denominate great. It is they who receive the hosannas of the multitude and are regarded as leaders of the people. The thinker and the doer, the man who solves the problem by enriching his country with an invention worth thousands or by a thought inestimable and precious is given neither bread nor a stone. He is too often left to die in obscurity and neglect even if spared in his life the bitterness of fanatical jealousies and detraction.

And yet politics, and surely American politics, is hardly a

school for great minds. Sharpening rather than deepening, it develops the faculty of taking advantage of present emergencies rather than the insight to distinguish between the true and the false, the lasting and the ephemeral advantage. Highly cultivated selfishness rather than consecrated benevolence is its passport to success. Its votaries are never seers. At best they are but manipulators—often only jugglers. It is conducive neither to profound statesmanship nor to the higher type of manhood. Altruism is its *mauvais succes* and naturally enough it is indifferent to any factor which cannot be worked into its own immediate aims and purposes. As woman's influence as a political element is as yet nil in most of the commonwealths of our republic, it is not surprising that with those who place the emphasis on mere political capital she may yet seem almost a nonentity so far as it concerns the solution of great national or even racial perplexities.

Fifty years ago woman's activity according to orthodox definitions was on a pretty clearly cut "sphere," including primarily the kitchen and the nursery, and rescued from the barrenness of prison bars by the womanly mania for adorning every discoverable bit of china or canvass with forlorn looking cranes balanced idiotically on one foot. The woman of to-day finds herself in the presence of responsibilities which ramify through the profoundest and most varied interests of her country and race. Not one of the issues of this plodding, toiling, sinning, repenting, falling, aspiring humanity can afford to shut her out, or can deny the reality of her influence. No plan for renovating society, no scheme for purifying politics, no reform in church or in state, no moral, social, or economic question, no movement upward or downward in the human plane is lost on her. A man once said when told his house was afire: "Go tell my wife; I never meddle with household affairs." But no woman can possibly put herself or her sex outside any of the interests that affect humanity. All departments in the new era are to be hers, in the sense that her interests are in all and through all; and it is incumbent on her to keep intelligently and sympathetically *en rapport* with all the great movements of her time, that she may know on which side to throw the weight of her influence. She stands now at the gateway of this new era of American civilization. In her hands must be moulded the strength, the wit, the statesmanship, the morality, all the psychic force, the social and economic intercourse of that era. To be alive at such an epoch is a privilege, to be a woman then is sublime.

In this last decade of our century, changes of such moment are in progress, such new and alluring vistas are opening out before us, such original and radical suggestions for the adjustment of labor and capital, of government and the governed, of the family, the church and the state, that to be a possible factor though an infinitesimal in such a movement is pregnant with hope and weighty with responsibility. To be a woman in such an age carries with it a privilege and an opportunity never implied before. But to be a woman of the Negro race in America, and to be able to grasp the deep significance of the possibilities of the crisis, is to have a heritage, it seems to me, unique in the ages. In the first place, the race is young and full of the elasticity and hopefulness of youth. All its achievements are before it. It does not look on the masterly triumphs of nineteenth century civilization with that *blasé* world-weary look which characterizes the old washed out and worn out races which have already, so to speak, seen their best days.

Said a European writer recently: "Except the Sclavonic, the Negro is the only original and distinctive genius which has yet to come to growth—and the feeling is to cherish and develop it."

Everything to this race is new and strange and inspiring. There is a quickening of its pulses and a glowing of its self-consciousness. Aha, I can rival that! I can aspire to that! I can honor my name and vindicate my race! Something like this, it strikes me, is the enthusiasm which stirs the genius of young Africa in America; and the memory of past oppression and the fact of present attempted repression only serve to gather momentum for its irrepressible powers. Then again, a race in such a stage of growth is peculiarly sensitive to impressions. Not the photographer's sensitized plate is more delicately impressionable to outer influences than is this high strung people here on the threshold of a career.

What a responsibility then to have the sole management of the primal lights and shadows! Such is the colored woman's office. She must stamp weal or woe on the coming history of this people. May she see her opportunity and vindicate her high prerogative.

COLORADO EQUAL SUFFRAGE ASSOCIATION

Suffrage Referendum Leaflet
1893

In 1893 Colorado became the first state to enfranchise women by popular referendum (the territorial legislatures in Wyoming and Utah had granted women the right to vote, which then carried over into their statehood in 1890 and 1896, respectively). A key factor in Colorado's referendum was a provision in the 1876 state constitution that provided a pathway to enfranchisement by a simple majority of voters rather than the two-thirds usually required for a constitutional amendment. A previous suffrage referendum had been defeated in 1877, but political conditions were much more favorable sixteen years later. Colorado women already possessed school suffrage, politicians from the Republican and Populist Parties were competing for women's political support, Colorado newspapers endorsed the measure by a 3 to 1 margin, and suffrage organizations such as the Colorado Non-Partisan Equal Suffrage Association were well organized and active. So too was the opposition, led by the Denver Brewers' Association. As election day neared, voters found themselves bombarded by leaflets from both sides. Supporters appealed to "every true daughter of Colorado" to embrace her new civic responsibilities while opponents cited vague and unspecified "dangerous consequences." The Colorado referendum passed by a margin of 6,000 votes out of 65,000 cast, a decisive victory.

———————

TO THE WOMEN OF COLORADO.

Women of Colorado, do you know the opportunity that is before you this fall? Do you know that on November 7 the voters of the state will decide whether or not you are to have the ballot hereafter? Do you know that there is a possibility you may rise to legal equality with man? Are you working for this great end? Are you alive to its importance? Are you willing to be classed politically with idiots, criminals and insane, when your own enfranchisement is offered you? Have you no interest in good government, in your town, your country, your state? Have you no interest in the making of good laws, and the election of good men to execute them? Does not your heart swell with patriotism as you see the best interests of Colorado struck down and our fair state lying prostrate under the blow? Do you not wish your voice to count hereafter in the tremendously important choice of the men who are to guard the interests of Colorado in congress? Are you not interested in politics when in spite of the strictest economy want creeps into the household, when the mother is forced to pinch and save and deny her children; when the self-supporting woman sees her wages reduced, and when on every side arises a long, low undertone of sorrow, the cry of the suffering poor? No matter how hardly economic conditions press upon men, except in the cases of a few favored ones they press harder on women. It is the duty of every true daughter of Colorado to come to the rescue; to bend every power of mind and heart to the solving of the social problems that surround us. Charity can never do it. Philanthropy can never do it. Only right laws, rightly executed, can reform social conditions. The ballot is the greatest power and protection of this day and age. All that renders it valuable to men will make it valuable to women. If the circumstances of your life have been such that you have never seen the need of it, it is your duty to aid your less fortunate sisters to attain it. Think of the 16,000 self-supporting women in Colorado. Awake from your indifference. Send for literature; solicit the vote of every man of your acquaintance. Nine out of ten will vote for it if we but ask them. And be assured that in helping to carry Colorado for suffrage this fall you are helping to make history. New Mexico and Arizona are trembling in the balance. Suffrage sentiment there is strong. Should Colorado grant it, they will come into the union with equal suffrage in their constitutions. Should Colorado grant it, the victory in Kansas is assured in 1894. With five great western states in line, one generation will see the women of America enfranchised. Great issues are at stake. Drop all other things from now till November 7 to work for suffrage. Nothing else is so important. Every vote counts, and every vote you make will just so much hasten the day of full liberty for women.

Colorado Non-Partisan Equal Suffrage Association, Room 11, Opera House Block.

COMMITTEE ON PROTEST
AGAINST WOMAN SUFFRAGE

To the Constitutional Convention
of New York State
APRIL–MAY 1894

In the 1890s, women began to organize groups to speak out against their own enfranchisement, with women in New York State leading the way. A key impetus was the New York State Constitutional Convention called for August 1894. While delegates were primarily concerned with the issue of reapportionment, suffragists mounted a public campaign to remove the word "male" from the state constitution's description of eligible voters, which would have effectively opened the franchise to women. When Susan B. Anthony was asked at the height of the campaign whether women in fact did want the vote, she fudged her answer by stating, "They do not oppose it." It turned out they did and were willing to say so publicly. This petition from a group of women in Brooklyn, New York, summarizes the key points of women's antisuffrage stance: women didn't want the vote, the vote threatened women's special privileges and duties, and enfranchisement would inevitably lead to women holding public office. The constitutional convention retained the word "male" and in 1895 antisuffragists formally chartered the New York State Association Opposed to Woman Suffrage, restricting its membership to women only.

To the Constitutional Convention:
The attention of this Honorable Body is called to a Protest against the proposition to eliminate the word "male" from Article II., Sec. I. of the Constitution of the State of New York.
The history of this Protest is briefly as follows:
On April 18th, 1894, a few women met at a private house in Brooklyn. A committee of twenty-one (21) women was formed, who gave to the public on April 21st the Preamble and Protest. These Protests were in circulation until May 16th.
The movement has been carried on without organization, without systematic canvassing, without public meetings.
It has been taken up spontaneously throughout the State by

individuals here and there who have worked with energy and interest.

The names herein presented are largely those of women experienced in the philanthropic work of this State and alive to its civic and governmental interests, as becomes true citizenship.

A noticeable proportion of signatures are those of the bread-winners, the respected and intelligent working-women.

The committee of twenty-one women, who bring the matter to your attention, have, from a studious contemplation of the governmental principles involved, come to a firm conviction, to which this protest gives expression, that woman suffrage would be against the best interests of the State, its women and the home.

The following facts are of significance:

Signatures of women only have been accepted; great care being exercised that only those women legally entitled as citizens and residents of the State should sign.

The whole represents the effort of but twenty-five (25) days, in which space of time signatures have been collected from ninety-four (94) cities, towns and villages situated in thirty-five (35) different counties of the State, which places are enumerated below:

COUNTIES.

Albany.	Jefferson.	Queens.
Alleghany.	Kings.	Rensselaer.
Broome.	Monroe.	Richmond.
Columbia.	Montgomery.	Rockland.
Clinton.	Niagara.	Suffolk.
Cayuga.	New York.	Saratoga.
Chautauqua.	Orange.	Schuyler.
Chemung.	Otsego.	Tompkins.
Dutchess.	Oneida.	Ulster.
Delaware.	Oswego.	Wayne.
Erie.	Onondaga.	Westchester.
Greene.	Ontario.	

CITIES, TOWNS AND VILLAGES.

Albany.

Astoria.

Auburn.

Audubon.

Amondale.

Aurora.

Balmville.

Ballston Spa.

Bartow-on-the-Sound.

Bath Beach.

Bay View.

Brighton.

Bensonhurst.

Binghamton.

Bronxville.

Brooklyn.

Buffalo.

Bridgehampton.

Canandaigua.

Catskill.

Charlotte Centre.

Cooperstown.

Clifton Springs.

Cold Spring.

College Point.

Cornwall.

Cutchogue.

Dobbs' Ferry.

East Rockaway.

East Williston.

Flatbush.

Flushing.

Fostertown.

Geneva.

Gerry.

Glen Cove.

Hempsted.

Hicksville.

Hollis.

Hoosick Falls.

Horseheads.

Irvington.

Ithaca.

Jamestown.

Kingston.

Lansingburgh.

Lockport.

Luther.

Margaretsville.

Morris Park.

Mount Vernon.

Newburgh.

New Windsor.

New Brighton.

New Rochelle.

New York City.

North Chatham.

Northside.

Nyack.

Oyster Bay.

Oswego.

Palatine Bridge.

Palmyra.

Patchogue.

Peconic.

Pelham.

Plattsburgh.

Poughkeepsie.

Richmond Hill.

Ridgedale.

Riverdale.

Rochester.

Saratoga.

Sheepshead Bay.

Shortsville.

Sinclairsville.

Southold.

Spuyten Duyvil.

Stapleton.

Stockport.

Suffern.

Syracuse.

Troy.

Utica.

Watertown.

Watkins.

Wellsville.

Westhampton.

Westfield.

West Mattituck.

Woodbury.

Woodhaven.

Woodside.

Yonkers.

Copy of Preamble and Protest.

We, American women, citizens of the State of New York, protest against the proposal to impose the obligation of suffrage upon the women of this State, for the following, among other reasons:

1. Because suffrage is to be regarded not as a privilege to be enjoyed but as a duty to be performed.

2. Because hitherto the women of this State have enjoyed exemption from this burdensome duty, and no adequate reason has been assigned for depriving them of that immunity.

3. Because conferring suffrage upon the women who claim it would impose suffrage upon the many women who neither desire it as a privilege nor regard it as their duty.

4. Because the need of America is not an increased quantity, but an improved quality, of the vote, and there is no adequate reason to believe that woman's suffrage by doubling the vote will improve its quality.

5. Because the household, not the individual, is the unit of the State and the vast majority of women are represented by household suffrage.

6. Because the women not so represented suffer no practical injustice which giving the suffrage will remedy.

7. Because equality in character does not imply similarity in function, and the duties and life of men and women are divinely ordered to be different in the State, as in the home.

8. Because the energies of women are engrossed by their present duties and interests, from which men cannot relieve them, and it is better for the community that they devote their energies to the more efficient performance of their present work than to divert them to new fields of activity.

9. Because political equality will deprive women of special privileges hitherto accorded to her by the law.

10. Because suffrage logically involves the holding of public office, and office holding is inconsistent with the duties of most women.

Mrs. WILLIAM A. PUTNAM, 70 Willow St., Brooklyn.

Mrs. GEORGE WHITE FIELD, 110 E. 18th St., New York.

Mrs. LYMAN ABBOTT, 110 Columbia Heights, Brooklyn.

Mrs. THOMAS S. MOORE, 91 Willow St., Brooklyn.

Mrs. THOMAS E. STILLMAN, 95 Joralemon St., Brooklyn.
Mrs. TUNIS G. BERGEN, 127 Pierrepont St., Brooklyn.
Mrs. S. B. CHITTENDEN, 212 Columbia Heights, Brooklyn.
Mrs. CHARLES W. IDE, 43 Remsen St., Brooklyn.
Mrs. W. S. P. PRENTICE, 44 Remsen St., Brooklyn.
Miss LILIAN M. HAINES, 70 Willow St., Brooklyn.
Mrs. JOHN TASKER HOWARD, 174 Hicks St., Brooklyn.
Mrs. LINDLEY MURRAY, JR., 6 Clark St., Brooklyn.
Mrs. DAVID M. MORRISON, 18 Monroe Place, Brooklyn.
Mrs CARLL H. DE SILVER, 43 Pierrepont St., Brooklyn.
Mrs. GEORGE H. SOUTHARD, 85 Remsen St., Brooklyn.
Mrs. CHAS. CUTHBERT HALL, 128 Henry St., Brooklyn.
Mrs. JOHN E. LEECH, 94 Remsen St., Brooklyn.
Mrs. GEORGE H. RIPLEY, 140 Columbia Heights, Brooklyn.
Mrs. WILLIAM C. BEECHER, 123 Columbia Heights, Brooklyn.
Mrs. JAMES MCKEEN, 136 Henry St., Brooklyn.
Mrs. R. MAYO-SMITH, 144 Columbia Heights, Brooklyn.

Therefore, this Committee ask all women, citizens of the State of New York, to join with them in sending the following protest to the Constitutional Convention to meet in Albany, May, 1894.
Dated April 20, 1894.

PROTEST.
To the Constitutional Convention of the State of New York,
to meet in Albany, May, 1894:

GENTLEMEN:

We, women, citizens of the State of New York (twenty-one years of age), believing that it will be against the best interests of the State to impose the obligations of the ballot upon the women of the State, protest against striking out the word "male" from Article II, Section 1, of the Constitution.

FANNIE BARRIER WILLIAMS

Women in Politics
NOVEMBER 1894

Fannie Barrier Williams (1855–1944), born in Brockport, New York, and the first African American to graduate from Brockport Normal School, quickly became part of Chicago's black elite when she moved there with her lawyer husband in 1887. The only African American woman appointed to a position on the Board of Lady Managers that oversaw the Woman's Building at the 1893 World's Columbian Exhibition in Chicago, Williams spoke to its World's Congress of Representative Women, one of the few African American women offered a public role at the world's fair. Her speech, "The Intellectual Progress of Colored Women," presented a sweeping survey of black women's aspirations and accomplishments but said little about formal politics. In this 1894 article, Williams challenged women to use their newfound political power wisely: "We ought not to put ourselves in the humiliating position of being loved only for the votes we have." More specifically, she worried that if black women voted along strict party lines, such a stance might benefit the interests of whites in power more than the general interests of African Americans. To avoid that outcome she called on women "to array themselves, when possible, on the side of the best, whether that best be inside or outside of party lines." For African Americans traditionally loyal to the Republican Party for its role in ending slavery, the invitation to jump party lines on matters of principle was a fraught issue.

───────────

American women are beginning to see the end of their years of struggle for equality of suffrage. The arguments are nearly all in and the signs of a favorable verdict are everywhere apparent to those who understand the trend of things.

Fragmentary suffrage, now possessed by women in nearly all the states of the union, carries with it the triumph of the principle contended for, and its extension to complete and national suffrage is as logically certain as any thing can be. Just how soon the complete enfranchisement of women will be realized depends largely upon the use we make of our present gains. The false reasoning of the opposition having been overcome, we have now to fight only the prejudices in opposition. When

228

the opposing man sees women actually voting, and looks in vain for the evils predicted, his prejudices will yield and he will gladly join the forces that are fast making for their complete emancipation.

Nothing in the whole social progress of humanity is more interesting and more suggestive of the persistency of rightness than the steady gain of womankind in those larger relationships of human life and civilization, in which the stronger, as well as the gentler virtues, are tending to increase her importance.

Are women ready to assume the responsibilities of this new recognition of their worth? This question is of immense importance to colored women. For the first time in our history we are to receive public attention and have our womanly worth tested by the high standards of important public duties.

Must we begin our political duties with no better or higher conceptions of our citizenship than that shown by our men when they were first enfranchised? Are we to bring any refinement of individuality to the ballot box? Shall we learn our polities from spoilsmen and bigoted partisans, or shall we learn it from the school of patriotism and an enlightened self-interest? If our enfranchisement means only a few more votes added to the republican and democratic sides, respectively, of political issues, there certainly has been no gain for the cause of principle in American politics. If our enfranchisement is to contribute nothing to the corrective forces of independence in American politics, there will be much disappointment among those who believed that the cause of temperance, municipal reform and better education would be more surely advanced when the finer virtues of women became a part of the political forces of the country.

Our women in Chicago are now, for the first time, getting a taste of politics. By virtue of a recent act of wholesome generosity of our legislators, women are permitted to vote for trustees of the state university. Two women have been duly nominated on the republican and democratic tickets respectively for this office. Fortunately, the nominees are equally meritorious candidates. Although the offices to be filled are purely nonpartisan, our newly fledged suffragists are ranging themselves eagerly in the democratic and republican camps and are campaigning for their respective sides on purely party grounds. So far the campaign speeches and methods have not been elevated in the least degree above the dead level of partisanship. Our own women, too, have gone into the fight with a party zeal that would be satisfactory to the most exacting "boss." Without wishing to discredit the good motives of our women, or to criticise captiously their conduct in the campaign, I believe this new opportunity for self-help and advancement ought not to be lost sight of in our thirst for public favors, or in our eagerness to help any grand old "party." We ought not to put ourselves in the humiliating position of being loved only for the votes we have. The sincerity of white women, who have heretofore so scorned our ambitions and held themselves aloof from us in all our struggles for advancement, should be, to a degree, questioned. It would be much more to our credit if we would seek, by all possible uses of our franchise, to force these ambitious women candidates and women party managers to relent their cruel opposition to our girls and women in the matter of employment and the enjoyment of civil privileges. We should never forget that the exclusion of colored women and girls from nearly all places of respectable employment is due mostly to the meanness of American women, and in every way that we can check this unkindness by the force of our franchise should be religiously done. If, however, we burden our hearts and minds solely with the anxiety for the success of a party ticket for party reasons, we shall be guilty of the same folly and neglect of self-interest that have made colored men for the past twenty years vote persistently more for the special interests of white men than for the peculiar interests of the colored race.

There is no good reason why our women should not be made to feel sufficiently independent not only to make their peculiar interests a motive in the exercise of the franchise, but also to array themselves, when possible, on the side of the best, whether that best be inside or outside of party lines. Much more ought to be expected of colored women in 1894 in the exercise of their suffrage than was expected of the colored men who first voted under the 15th Amendment.

It is now a good time in woman's clubs and organizations of all kinds for women to prepare themselves, by the best lessons of citizenship, to exert a wholesome influence in the politics of the future. The importance of the suffrage, as a means to complete emancipation from the impositions of prejudice should be eagerly taught, and brought home to the conscience of our women everywhere. It is more than probable that issues of immeasurable importance to the weal of our country, and requiring for their adjustment a larger amount of intelligent patriotism than has yet been exacted from the American conscience, will make demands on us by the time universal suffrage becomes one of the organic laws of the land.

JOSEPHINE ST. PIERRE RUFFIN

Address at the First National Conference of
Representatives of Black Women's Clubs

AUGUST 1895

The women's club movement, like suffrage activism, generally ran on separate but parallel tracks for black and white women. Josephine St. Pierre Ruffin (1842–1924) was a leading African American clubwoman in Boston. In addition to serving as the publisher of *The Woman's Era*, the first national black women's newspaper, she founded the New Era Club in 1894. Realizing that black women's clubs were forming across the country, the New Era Club put out a call for a national conference, which resulted in the formation of the National Federation of Afro-American Women in 1895. The next year that organization merged with the Colored Women's League to form the National Association of Colored Women, which under the motto "Lifting as We Climb" pursued a broad agenda that foregrounded women's roles in confronting the "race problem." Ruffin took a similar stance in this 1895 address, articulating black women's reasons for coming together as "earnest, intelligent, progressive" American women to work collectively for the good of humanity as well as their race. African American clubwomen especially looked forward to demonstrating their "purity and mental worth" to a white world that often did not acknowledge that black women possessed those traits.

It is with especial joy and pride that I welcome you all to this, our first conference. It is only recently that women have waked up to the importance of meeting in council, and great as has been the advantage to women *generally*, and important as it is and has been that they should confer, the necessity has not been nearly so great, matters at stake not nearly so vital, as that *we*, bearing peculiar blunders, suffering under especial hardships, enduring peculiar privations, should meet for a "good talk" among ourselves. Although rather hastily called, you as well as I can testify how long and how earnestly a conference has been thought of and hoped for and even prepared for. These women's clubs, which have sprung up all over the country, built and run upon broad and strong lines, have all been a preparation, small conferences in themselves, and their spontaneous birth and enthusiastic support have been little less than inspirational on the part of our women and a general preparation for a large union such as it is hoped this conference will lead to. Five years ago we had no colored women's clubs outside of those formed for special work; to-day, with little over a month's notice, we are able to call representatives from more than twenty clubs. It is a good showing, it stands for much, it shows that we are truly American women, with all the adaptability, readiness to seize and possess our opportunities, willingness to do our part for good as other American women.

The reasons why we should confer are so apparent that it would seem hardly necessary to enumerate them, and yet there is none of them but demand our serious consideration. In the first place we need to feel the cheer and inspiration of meeting each other, we need to gain the courage and fresh life that comes from the mingling of congenial souls, of those working for the same ends. Next, we need to talk over not only those things which are of vital importance to us as women, but also the things that are of especial interest to us as *colored* women, the training of our children, openings for our boys and girls, how they can be prepared for occupations and occupations may be found or opened for them, what *we* especially can do in the moral education of the race with which we are identified, our mental elevation and physical development, the home training it is necessary to give our children in order to prepare them to meet the peculiar conditions in which they shall find themselves, how to make the most of our own, to some extent, limited opportunities, these are some of our own peculiar questions to be discussed. Besides these are the general questions of the day, which we cannot afford to be indifferent to: temperance, morality, the higher education, hygienic and domestic questions. If these things need the serious consideration of women more advantageously placed by reason of all the aid to right thinking and living with which they are surrounded, surely we, with everything to pull us back, to hinder us in developing, need to take every opportunity and means for the thoughtful consideration which shall lead to wise action.

I have left the strongest reason for our conferring together until the last. All over America there is to be found a large and growing class of earnest, intelligent, progressive colored women, women who, if not leading full useful lives, are only waiting for the opportunity to do so, many of them warped and cramped for lack of opportunity, not only to do more but to *be* more; and yet, if an estimate of the colored women of America is called for, the inevitable reply, glibly given, is, "For the most part ignorant and immoral, some exceptions, of course, but these don't count."

Now for the sake of the thousands of self-sacrificing young women teaching and preaching in lonely southern backwoods, for the noble army of mothers who have given birth to these girls, mothers whose intelligence is only limited by their opportunity to get at books, for the sake of the fine cultured women who have carried off the honors in school here and often abroad, for the sake of our own dignity, the dignity of our race, and the future good name of our children, it is "mete, right and our bounden duty" to stand forth and declare ourselves and principles, to teach an ignorant and suspicious world that our aims and interests are identical with those of all good aspiring women. Too long have we been silent under unjust and unholy charges; we cannot expect to have them removed until we disprove them through *ourselves.* It is not enough to try to disprove unjust charges through individual effort, that never goes any further. Year after year southern women have protested against the admission of colored women into any national organization on the ground of the immorality of these women, and because all refutation has only been tried by individual work the charge has never been crushed, as it could and should have been at the first. Now with an army of organized women standing for purity and mental worth, we in ourselves deny the charge and open the eyes of the world to a state of affairs to which they have been blind, often willfully so, and the very fact that the charges, audaciously and flippantly made, as they often are, are of so humiliating and delicate a nature, serves to protect the accuser by driving the helpless accused into mortified silence. It is to break this silence, not by noisy protestations of what we are not, but by a dignified showing of what we are and hope to become that we are impelled to take this step, to make of this gathering an object lesson to the world. For many and apparent reasons it is especially fitting that the *women* of the race take the lead in this movement, but for all this we recognize the necessity of the sympathy of our husbands, brothers and fathers.

Our woman's movement is woman's movement in that it is led and directed by women for the good of women and men, for the benefit of *all* humanity, which is more than any one branch or section of it. We want, we ask the active interest of our men, and, too, we are not drawing the color line; we are women, American women, as intensely interested in all that pertains to us as such as all other American women; we are not alienating or withdrawing, we are only coming to the front, willing to join any others in the same work and cordially inviting and welcoming any others to join us.

If there is any one thing I would especially enjoin upon this conference it is union and earnestness. The questions that are to come before us are of too much import to be weakened by any trivialities or personalities. If any differences arise let them be quickly settled, with the feeling that we are all workers to the same end, to elevate and dignify colored American womanhood. This conference will not be what I expect if it does not show the wisdom, indeed the absolute necessity of a national organization of our women. Every year new questions coming up will prove it to us. This hurried, almost informal convention does not begin to meet our needs, it is only a beginning, made here in dear old Boston, where the scales of justice and generosity hang evenly balanced, and where the people "dare be true" to their best instincts and stand ready to lend aid and sympathy to worthy strugglers. It is hoped and believed that from this will spring an organization that will in truth bring in a new era to the colored women of America.

ELIZABETH CADY STANTON

Significance and History of the Ballot
FEBRUARY 15, 1898

In the midst of the acrimonious debates over the Reconstruction amendments after the Civil War, Elizabeth Cady Stanton repeatedly described African American men in cringe-worthy terms that made clear her horror that they would be enfranchised rather than elite white women like herself. In the 1890s she made comparable statements against recent immigrants, questioning why they were allowed to vote while native-born women lacked the franchise. In this 1898 address to the Senate Select Committee on Woman Suffrage on the effects of mass immigration, Stanton's nativism is on full display. Her solution to the "ignorant vote" is educated suffrage, requiring that recent immigrants be able to speak and write English. At base Stanton was an elitist, never able to see beyond her privileged class and racial position. First with recently freed slaves and later with the foreign-born, she never got over that people she considered inferior could vote, and she could not.

Since our demand for the right of suffrage under the Fourteenth amendment, which was denied by Congress and the courts, the only discussions in Congress have been our appeals for a sixteenth amendment until the recent bills on immigration, by Senator Lodge of Massachusetts, and Senator Kyle of South Dakota, indirectly involving this question, and affecting the interests of woman. Their proposition to demand a reading and writing qualification on landing, strikes me as arbitrary and equally detrimental to our mutual interests. The danger is not in their landing and living in this country, but in their speedy appearance at the ballot box; there becoming an impoverished and ignorant balance of power in the hands of wily politicians.

While we should not allow our country to be a dumping ground for the refuse population of the Old World, still we should welcome all hardy, common-sense laborers here, as we have plenty of room and work for them. Here they can improve their own condition and our surroundings, developing our immense resources and the commerce of the country. The one demand I would make for this class is that they should not become a part of our ruling power until they can read and write the English language intelligently, and understand the principles of republican government. To make a nation homogeneous, its people should all speak one tongue. The dominion of Francis Joseph in Austria, where fifteen different languages are spoken, illustrates its perils. The officers of the army can be understood by only a small per cent of the soldiers. One can readily imagine the confusion and consequent dangers this would cause in time of war.

To prevent the thousands of immigrants daily landing on our shores marching from the steerage to the polls, the National Government should prohibit the States from allowing them to vote in less than five years, and not then unless the applicant could read and write the English language. This is the only restrictive legislation we need to protect ourselves against foreign domination. To this end, Congress should pass a bill for "educated suffrage" for our native-born as well as foreign rulers, alike ignorant of our institutions.

With free schools and compulsory education, no one has an excuse for not understanding the language of the country. As women are governed by a "male aristocracy," we are doubly interested in having our rulers able at least to read and write. See with what care in the Old World the prospective heirs to the throne are educated. There was a time when the members of the British Parliament could neither read nor write, but those accomplishments are now required of the Lords and Commons, and even of the king and queen, while we have rulers, native and foreign, voting for laws, who do not understand the letters of the alphabet; and this in a Republic supposed to be based on the virtue and intelligence of the people!

Much as we need these measures for the stability of our Government, we need them still more for the best interests of women. This ignorant vote is solid against woman's emancipation. In States where amendments to their constitutions are proposed for the enfranchisement of women, this vote has been in every case against the measure. We should ask for national protection against this hostile force playing football with the most sacred rights of one-half of the people. I have long felt that an educational qualification for the exercise of the right of suffrage is a question of such vital consequence that it should be exhaustively discussed by the leaders of thought among our people.

The great political parties fear to propose this measure lest it should insure their defeat. No aspiring politician as an individual would dare express such an opinion, lest it should blast his chance for official position. Hence, only those guided by principle rather than policy are in a position to discuss the merits of this question. Such an amendment to our national Constitution should go into effect at the dawn of the next century.

As all who prize this right sufficiently to labor to attain it can easily do so, an educational qualification in no way conflicts with our cherished idea of universal suffrage. According to our theory of government, all our citizens are born voters, but they must be of age before they can exercise the right. To say they must also read and write the English language is equally logical and fair. We do not propose to withhold this right from any citizen exercising it, but to apply the restriction to all new claimants. Some say that the ignorant classes need the ballot for their protection more than the rich. Well, they have had it and exercised it, and what have they done to protect their own interests? Absolutely nothing, because they did not know in what direction their interests lay, or by what system of legislation they could be lifted out of poverty, vice, and ignorance to enjoy liberty, justice, and equality.

A gun is a good weapon for a man's protection against his enemy, but, if he does not know how to use it, it may prove a danger rather than a defense. There is something lacking in our science of industrial economics when multitudes in this land of plenty are suffering abject poverty. Yet by their ignorant votes they have helped to establish the very conditions from which they suffer. The ballot is of value only in the hands that know how to use it. In establishing free schools, our forefathers said to us in plain words: "The stability of a republic depends on the virtue and intelligence of the people."

"Universal suffrage" with us is a mere pretense, a party cry, as thus far we have had "male suffrage" and nothing more. In most of the States qualifications of property, education, and color have been abolished, but in only four States have our rulers had the courage and conscience to abolish that of sex. A republic based on the theory of universal suffrage, in which a large class of educated women, representing the virtue, intelligence, and wealth of the nation, are disfranchised, is an anomaly in government, especially when all men, foreign and native, black and white, ignorant and educated, vicious and virtuous, by their votes decide the rights and duties of this superior class.

In all national conflicts it is ever deemed the most grievous accident of war for the conquered people to find themselves under a foreign yoke, yet this is the position of the educated women of this Republic to-day. Foreigners are our judges and jurors, our legislators and municipal officials, and decide all questions of interest to us, as to the discipline in our schools, charitable institutions, jails, and prisons. Woman has no voice as to the education of her children or the environments of the unhappy wards of the State. The love and sympathy of the mother soul have but an evanescent influence in all departments of human interest until coined into law by the hand that holds the ballot. Then only do they become a direct and effective power in the Government.

As women have no voice in the laws and lawmakers under which they live, they surely have the right to demand that their rulers, foreign and native, shall be able to read and write the English language. As it would take the ordinary immigrant at least five years to learn our language, we should be sure he had been here the prescribed time before exercising his right to vote. An educational qualification would also stimulate our native population to avail themselves of all the opportunities for learning. In basing suffrage on sex we have defeated the intentions of our ancestors and made their principles of government mere glittering generalities.

The popular objection to woman suffrage is that it would "double the ignorant vote." The patent answer to this is, "Abolish the ignorant vote." Our legislators have this power in their own hands. There have been serious restrictions in the past for men. We are willing to abide by the same for women, provided the insurmountable qualifications of sex be forever removed. In the discussion of this question educated women must now lead the way. Some reformers do not see the wisdom of the measure, so the few who do must take the initiative in arousing public thought and creating a widespread agitation of this important step in woman's emancipation.

During the past month the supreme court of Wyoming has handed down an important and far-reaching decision. The court decided that foreign-born citizens of the State of Wyoming must be able to read the constitution of the State in the English language in order to vote, and that the ability to read the constitution in a foreign language is not a compliance with the requirements of the constitution.

Some of the opponents talk as if educated suffrage would be invidious to the best interests of the laboring masses, whereas it would be most beneficial in its ultimate influence. You who can read and write, and enjoy hours in a library, gleaning there the history of the past as well as advancing civilization; you who can visit the galleries of art, and with your knowledge of the classics, poetry, and mythology, appreciate what the pictures say, little realize the starved condition of the uncultured mind. Blot this knowledge from your mind, and you may then understand the solitude of ignorance. Who can measure its misery? Surely, when we compel all classes to learn to read and write, and thus open to themselves the door to knowledge, not by force, but by the promise of a privilege all intelligent citizens enjoy, we are benefactors and not tyrants. To stimulate them to climb the first rounds of the ladder that they may reach the divine heights where they shall be as Gods, knowing good and evil, by witholding the citizen's right to vote for a few years, is a blessing to them as well as to the State.

The condition of the laboring masses to-day, without adequate shelter, food, and clothes, is the result of their own ignorance of the manner in which the broad distinctions in society have been created. I am fully aware that simply reading and writing will not secure the key to the whole situation, but it is the first necessary step, without which the laboring man can never make and control his own environments.

We must inspire our people with a new sense of their sacred duties as citizens of a republic, and place new guards around our ballot box.

Walking in Paris one day I was deeply impressed with an emblematic statue in the square Chateau d'Eau, placed there in 1883 in honor of the Republic. On one side is a magnificent bronze lion with his forepaw on the electoral urn, which answers to our ballot box, as if to guard it from all unholy uses. Having overturned all pretensions to royalty, nobility, and all artificial distinctions in class, and declared the right of the people to a voice in the making of their laws and the selection of their rulers, they exalted the idea of republican government and universal suffrage with this magnificent monument—the royal lion guarding the sacred treasures within the electoral urn.

As I turned away I thought of the American Republic and our ballot box with no guardian or sacred reverence for its contents among the people. Ignorance, poverty, and vice crowd its precincts, thousands from every incoming steamer march from the steerage to the polls, while educated women, representing the virtue and intelligence of the nation, are driven away.

I would like to see a monument to "educated suffrage" in front of our National Capitol, guarded by the goddess Minerva, her right hand resting on the ballot box, her left hand on the spelling book, the Declaration of Rights, and the National Constitution.

It would be well for us to ponder the Frenchman's idea, but instead of the royal lion, representing force, let us substitute wisdom and virtue in the form of Woman.

FRANCES E. WILLARD

The Ballot for the Home
MARCH 1898

In 1884 the Woman's Christian Temperance Union (WCTU), the largest women's organization of its time, endorsed women's suffrage. That decision was largely driven by its charismatic national leader, Frances E. Willard (1839–1898), who became president of the organization in 1879, five years after its founding. The WCTU grew out of women's grassroots crusades against the power of liquor interests and saloon-keepers and the deleterious effect of drunken men on their families and communities, but Willard widened its focus by adopting a "Do Everything" strategy that embraced a wide range of social reforms, such as prison reform, labor activism, international peace, and the establishment of kindergartens, as well as suffrage. The WCTU was somewhat more racially inclusive than most women's organizations at the time, welcoming black women but still segregating them into a "Department of Colored Temperance." In "The Ballot for the Home," published just months before her premature death in 1898, Willard summarizes the case for the vote through the lens of temperance, stressing how women can deploy the power of the ballot to challenge "the liquor traffic and its accompanying abominations."

Doubtless the strongest points in favor of woman suffrage are:

1. That it is founded on the unchanging principles of justice. Every reasonable man knows that it is not right to tax a class without representing that class, to inflict penalties upon a class that had no hand in determining what those penalties should be, to govern one-half of the human race by the other half. All injustice to one class works harm to every other.

2. The best government known to the race is found in a home where father and mother have equal power, as is the case in an enlightened modern Christian family. No other place is so free from temptation, and no other conserves so completely the best interest of all who dwell therein. Reasoning from analogy, the larger home of society, and that largest home of all called government, might be more like this typical home, and

in proportion as they are made like unto it, society and government will more thoroughly conserve the interest of all, and shut out the pests of civilization.

3. The two most strongly marked instincts of woman are those of protection for herself and little ones, and of love and loyalty to her husband and her son. On the other hand, the two strongest instincts that to-day defend the liquor traffic and drink habit are avarice in the dealer and appetite in the drinker. It has been said that civilization has nothing with which it can offset these two tremendous forces. But may it not be found that in the home, through the reserve power never yet called into government on a large scale, woman's instincts of self-protection and of love are a sufficient offset to appetite and avarice, and will out-vote both at the polls? For it must be remembered that, in a republic, all questions of morality sooner or later find their way to the ballot-box, and are voted up or down.

4. Women constitute more than two-thirds of our church-members, and less than one-fifth of our criminals. As a class women hold the balance of power morally in the republic.

5. There is no enemy dreaded so much by liquor-dealers and saloon-keepers as a woman with the ballot in her hand. Secret circulars sent out by them, and intercepted by our temperance leaders, state this explicitly. One of these is addressed to a legislator, and reads to this effect: "Set your heel upon the woman suffrage movement every time, for the ballot in the hand of woman means the downfall of our trade." When the bill by which the women of Washington Territory had the ballot and secured local option, was declared unconstitutional by the Supreme Court of the Territory, there were bonfires, bell-ringings, and beer on tap in the public square of many a town and village, where the saloon-keepers celebrated their jubilee because the women had lost their right to vote.

6. Wherever women have had the ballot, they have used it in the interest of the home and against the saloons, the gambling-houses, and the haunts of infamy.

In Wyoming, women obtained full suffrage in 1869. Rev. Dr. B. F. Crary, presiding elder of the M. E. churches in that State, wrote years ago of the equal suffrage law, "Liquor-sellers and gamblers are unanimous in cursing it." Chief Justice Groesbeck, of Wyoming, wrote in 1897: "The influence of the women voters has always been on the side of temperance, morality and good government, and opposed to drunkenness, gambling and immorality." Wyoming was the first State in the Union to raise the age of protection for girls to eighteen.

Colorado granted full suffrage to women in 1893. Equal suffrage has raised the age of protection to eighteen; has equalized the property laws between husband and wife; has secured a law making fathers and mothers equal guardians of their children; has greatly increased the number of women serving on educational boards; and has more than quadrupled the number of no-license towns in Colorado.

Kansas gave municipal suffrage to women in 1887. Several years ago the Chief Justice of Kansas and all the judges of the Supreme Court united in paying tribute to the good results. All concurred in substance with Judge W. A. Johnston, who wrote: "In consequence, our elections are more orderly and fair, a higher class of officers are chosen, and we have cleaner and stronger city governments."

After seven years' experience of municipal suffrage, Kansas submitted to the voters, for the second time, an amendment to extend full suffrage to women. The liquor interest organized from one end of the State to the other, to fight it—a sure proof that the women had used their municipal vote well. The amendment was defeated, but received an affirmative vote more than ten times as large as when a similar amendment was first submitted, some years before.

In 1880, Arkansas passed a law that the opening of a saloon within three miles of a church or schoolhouse might be prevented by a petition from a majority of the adult inhabitants, men and women. The liquor dealers contested the constitutionality of the law. Their attorney, in his argument before the Supreme Court, said:

> None but male persons of sound mind can vote; but their rights are destroyed, and the idiot, alien and females step in and usurp their rights in popular government. Since females, idiots, and aliens cannot vote, they should not be permitted to accomplish the same purpose by signing a petition; for the signature of an adult to a petition is the substance of a ballot in taking the popular sense of the community. It merely changes the form, and is identical in effect.

The Supreme Court, however, upheld the constitutionality of the law. Under it, the saloons have been cleared out of three-fourths of the counties in Arkansas.

In Idaho, full suffrage was granted to women in 1896. William Balderston, of Boise, editor of one of Idaho's principal dailies, writes:

> An interesting result of the new law was observed during the session of the Legislature last winter. In Idaho there had been a law legalizing gambling. Up to the time of the adoption of equal suffrage, it would have been impracticable to repeal it; but when a bill was introduced last winter for that purpose, it went through with a large majority. The majority for it was universally credited to the addition of the woman element to the electorate.

In Canada, five provinces give a restricted municipal suffrage to women, and the concurrent testimony of all parties is that the result is altogether in the interest of temperance and morality.

Even at the antipodes, women stand for the home. Equal suffrage has been given to the women of New Zealand, and now comes the news of a movement in New Zealand to put down gambling. "Sweepstakes" have been declared illegal, and a bill to legalize them has been defeated on the avowed ground that the large associations of women, whose votes would be needed at the next election, were against the bill.

The Woman's Christian Temperance Union, while fully convinced that the ballot is the right of every woman in the nation, just as much as it is the right of every man, does not base its line of argument upon this fact, but upon the practical value that woman's vote will have in helping the nation to put away the liquor traffic and its accompanying abominations. We do not ask it for ourselves alone; we are impartial friends of the whole human race in both its fractions, man and woman, and hence we are not more in earnest for this great advance because of the good it brings to the gentler, than because of the blessing that it promises to the stronger sex. It is for these practical reasons that we claim that woman's ballot should be one of the planks in the platform of every righteous party in America.

NATIONAL AMERICAN WOMAN SUFFRAGE ASSOCIATION

On Behalf of Hawaiian Women
JANUARY 1899

After the Spanish-American War of 1898 and the subsequent annexation of Hawaii, the country passionately debated the pros and cons of the new American empire. Suffragists tacitly endorsed the imperial project as a way to demand that women be given the same political rights as men in any new territorial governments. Suffrage was generally seen as a question of states' rights; here was a chance to insert it squarely onto the national political agenda. The logic of this strategy is on full display in the "Hawaiian Appeal" presented to every member of Congress in January 1899 by the National American Woman Suffrage Association. According to suffragists, annexation of the Hawaiian Islands presented an opportunity to extend the benefits of civilization to people "emerging from barbarism." And since one measure of civilization was the status of women, why should these new possessions be saddled with antiquated restrictions that limited the vote to men, when so many American women were already voting? The suffragists did not prevail on this issue—the Hawaiian constitution included the word "male" in its description of voter qualifications, and Hawaiian women could not vote until 1920—but their strategy shows how questions of gender and citizenship got wrapped into turn-of-the-century political discussions about U.S. imperialism and territorial expansion in sometimes unexpected ways.

The following is the memorial sent by the officers of the National American W.S.A. to Congress, and a copy has been personally addressed to each Senator and Member:

To the Senate and House of Representatives:

We respectfully request that, in the qualifications for voters in the proposed constitution for the new Territory of Hawaii, the word "male" be omitted.

The declared intention of the United States in annexing the Hawaiian Islands is to give them the benefits of the most advanced civilization, and it is a truism that the progress of civilization in every country is measured by the approach of women toward the ideal of equal rights with men.

Under barbarism, the struggle for existence is entirely on the physical plane. The woman enters freely the arena, and her failure or success depends wholly upon her own strength. When life rises to the intellectual plane, public opinion is expressed in law. Justice demands that we shall not offer to women emerging from barbarism the ball and chain of a sex disqualification while we hold out to men the crown of self-government.

The trend of civilization is closely in the direction of equal rights for women. Even where equal suffrage measures have been defeated, as in South Dakota and Washington last November, the vote shows a marked gain over former years. Thus, in 1889, Washington defeated woman suffrage by 19,386 majority; in 1898 by a majority of only 9,882, although there had been a large increase of population.

In South Dakota, in 1890, the adverse majority was 23,610; in 1898, only 3,285.

Sixty years ago women could not vote anywhere. In 1838 Kentucky gave school suffrage to widows. In 1861 Kansas gave it to all women. In 1869 England gave municipal suffrage to single women and widows, and Wyoming gave full suffrage to all women. School suffrage was granted in 1875 by Michigan and Minnesota, in 1870 by Colorado, in 1878 by New Hampshire and Oregon, in 1879 by Massachusetts, in 1880 by New York and Vermont. In 1881 municipal suffrage was extended to the single women and widows of Scotland. Nebraska gave school suffrage in 1883, and Wisconsin in 1885. In 1886 school suffrage was given in Washington, and municipal suffrage to single women and widows in New Brunswick and Ontario. In 1887 municipal suffrage was extended to all women in Kansas and school suffrage in North and South Dakota, Montana, Arizona, and New Jersey. In the same year, Montana gave taxpaying women the right to vote upon all questions submitted to the taxpayers. In 1889 municipal suffrage was extended to single women and widows in the Province of Quebec. In 1891 school suffrage was granted in Illinois. In 1893 school suffrage was granted in Connecticut, and full suffrage in Colorado and New Zealand. In 1894 school suffrage was granted in Ohio, bond suffrage in Iowa, and parish and district suffrage in England to women, both married and single. In 1895 full suffrage was granted in South Australia to women, both married and single. In 1896 full suffrage was granted in Utah and Idaho. In 1897 the legislatures of Washington and South Dakota passed full suffrage amendments, in each case by more than a two-thirds vote. In 1898 municipal and county suffrage were granted to the single women and widows of Ireland, and Louisiana gave taxpaying women the right to vote upon all questions submitted to the taxpayers.

Hon. John D. Long, Secretary of the Navy, calls the opposition to woman suffrage a "slowly melting glacier of bourbonism and prejudice." The melting is going on steadily all over our country, and it would be inopportune to impose upon our new possessions abroad the antiquated restrictions which we are fast discarding at home.

We, therefore, petition your honorable body that, upon whatever conditions and qualifications the right of suffrage is granted to Hawaiian men, it shall be granted to Hawaiian women.

> SUSAN B. ANTHONY, *Pres.*
> ANNA H. SHAW, *Vice-Pres.*
> RACHEL FOSTER AVERY, *Cor. Sec.*
> ALICE STONE BLACKWELL, *Rec. Sec.*
> HARRIET TAYLOR UPTON, *Treas.*
> LAURA CLAY, *Auditor.*
> CATHARINE WAUGH MCCULLOCH.
> CARRIE CHAPMAN CATT,
> *Chairman Organization Com.*

ABIGAIL SCOTT DUNIWAY

How to Win the Ballot
1899

Born in Illinois, Abigail Scott Duniway (1834–1915) made the overland journey to Oregon with her family at the age of fifteen, married and raised a family, and for sixteen years edited a newspaper called the *New Northwest*. Of the causes that Duniway promoted in her newspaper and her frequent public speaking, none was more prominent than women's rights. Duniway quickly assumed a dominant role in the Oregon suffrage movement but often clashed with more conservative, eastern-based national leaders. This speech, "How to Win the Ballot," was delivered to the 1899 NAWSA convention in Grand Rapids, Michigan. In Duniway's words, it was "the shortest way at my command for telling many truths that Eastern readers ought to hear." Those "truths" included the reminder that the votes of men were needed to extend the franchise, but what really comes through in Duniway's speech is her sense of regional pride. The upcoming state referendum that she references failed to pass, and Oregon women had to wait thirteen years for their enfranchisement. In 1912, seventy-eight-year-old Duniway would become the state's first registered female voter.

The following address was delivered by myself before the National Convention of the National American Woman Suffrage Association, May 2nd, 1899, at Grand Rapids, Michigan, and is given here as the shortest way at my command for telling many truths that Eastern readers ought to read:

Coming as I do from the far Pacific, where the sun at night sinks into the sea, to greet a convocation of co-workers from the far Atlantic, where the sun at morn rises out of the sea; and standing here, upon the central swell of the Middle West, where the sun at high noon kisses the heaving bosom of the mighty inland sea that answers back to East and West the echoing song of liberty, I realize the importance of my desire to speak to the entire continent, such tempered words as shall help to further unite our common interests in the great work that convenes us.

The first fact to be considered, when working to win the ballot, is that there is but one way by which we may hope to obtain it, and that is by and through the affirmative votes of men. We may theorize, organize, appeal, argue, coax, cajole and threaten men till doomsday; we may secure their pettings, praises, flattery, and every appearance of acquiescence in our demands; we may believe with all our hearts in the sincerity of their promises to vote as we dictate, but all of this will avail us nothing unless they deposit their affirmative votes in the ballot box.

Every man who stops to argue the case, as an opponent, tells us that he "loves women," and, while wondering much that he should consider such a declaration necessary, I have always admired the loyal spirit that prompts its utterance. But, gentlemen,—and I am proud indeed to see such a fine audience of you here tonight—there is another side to this expression of loyalty. Not only is our movement not instigated in a spirit of warfare between the sexes, but it is engendered, altogether, in the spirit of harmony, and inter-dependence between men and women, such as was the evident design of the great Creator when he placed fathers and mothers, brothers and sisters, in the same home and family. We are glad to be assured that you "love women," but we are doubly glad to be able, on proper occasions, and in every suitable way, to return the compliment. No good Equal Suffragist will any longer permit you to monopolize all the pretty speeches about the other sex. Every good woman in the world likes men a great deal better than she likes women, and there isn't a wise woman in all this goodly land who isn't proud to say so. We like you, gentlemen, and you cannot help it. We couldn't help it if we would; we wouldn't help it if we could. You like us, also, because you cannot help it. God made the sexes to match each other. Show me a woman who doesn't like men, and I will show you a sour-souled, vinegar-visaged specimen of unfortunate femininity, who owes the world an apology for living in it at all; and the very best thing she could do for her country, provided she had a country, would be to steal away and die, in the company of the man who doesn't like women. In order to gain the votes of men, so we can win the ballot, we must show them that we are inspired by the same patriotic motives that induce them to prize it. A home without a man in it, is only half a home. A government without women in it, is only half a government. Man without a woman is like one-half of a pair of dislocated shears. Woman without man is like the other half of the same disabled implement. Male and female created He them, saith the Higher Law, and to them God gave dominion "over every living thing upon the earth"—except each other.

Thirty years ago, when I began my humble efforts for securing the enfranchisement of women, away out upon the singing shores of the Pacific Sea, men everywhere imagined, at first, that the movement was intended to deprive them of a modicum of their liberties. They ought to have known this idea was absurd even then, as they have always had the power to both oppose or allow themselves to be ruled by women. But they thought legal supremacy over them was what women were after, and they met their own theory with hoarse guffaws of laughter. I had previously had much experience with the genus masculine, not only with my good husband, but with a large family of sons.

It is needless for me to tell you, after this confession, that I am not young, and you can see for yourselves that I am no longer handsome.

The fact that men, for the most part, contented themselves in those early days of the Suffrage Movement, with exhibitions of ridicule, I accepted as a good omen. If you wish to convince a man that your opinion is logical and just, you have conquered the outer citadel of his resentment when he throws back his head and opens his mouth to laugh. Show me a solemn-visaged voter, with a face as long as the Pentateuch, and I will show you a man with a soul so little that it would have ample room to dance inside of a hollow mustard seed. Having tickled your opponent with a little nonsense, that at first was necessary to arrest his attention, you must then be careful to hold the ground you have gained. Your next step must be to impress upon all men the fact that we are not intending to interfere, in any way, with their rights; and all we ask is to be allowed to decide, for ourselves, also as to what our rights should be. They will then, very naturally, ask what effect our enfranchisement will have upon their politics. Visions of riotous scenes in political conventions will arise, to fill them with apprehension, as the possibility occurs that women, if enfranchised, will only double the vote and augment the uproar. They will recall partisan banquets, at which men have tarried over cups and pipes until they rolled under the table, or were carried off to bed on shutters. Very naturally, men, everywhere, object to seeing reputable women, and especially their own wives, engaged in such excesses. But our mighty men of the Pacific Northwest are troubled very little by these vagaries. They realize, as they sleep off the results of their latest political banquet, that at every public function in which their wives participate, there is a notable absence of any sort of dissipation. They remember that in former times, before good women had joined them, in the mining camps, mountain towns, and on the bachelor farms, that such scenes as sometimes transpire today, at men's great gatherings, were once so common as to excite little comment. It was the advent of good women in the border territories that changed all this, and eliminated the bad woman from social life, just as the ballot will eventually eliminate the bad woman from political life, where she now reigns supreme among men, having everything her own way. By the very charm of good women's presence they brought these changes about on the Pacific Coast, in social life, till men began to wonder how they had endured the old conditions, before the women joined them. Now, quite naturally, they are learning to apply this rule to politics; and so our men of the Pacific Coast are not alarmed, as many men are in other states, lest women, if allowed to become equal with themselves before the law, will forget their natural duties and natural womanliness. If, however, any man grows timid, and exhibits symptoms of alarm, as they sometimes do (even in Oregon), lest the balloted woman will forsake the kitchen sink, at which she has always been "protected" (without wages), or abandon the cooking stove, the rolling pin, the wash tub and the ironing board, at which she has always been shielded (without salary), we remind him that housekeeping and homemaking are, like everything else, undergoing a complete process of evolution. We show him that there is no more reason why every loaf of bread should be baked in a different kitchen than there is why every bushel of wheat should be ground in a different mill. We show him that the laundry is destined, hereafter, to keep pace with the threshing machine; the creamery with the spinning jenny and power loom; the fruit cannery with the great flour mill; the dish washer with the steam-driven mangle, and the bakery with the ready-made clothing store.

When women have been voters long enough to have acquired recognition of their own equal property rights with
men, the servant girl problem will settle itself. When that time
comes there will be no more work left to do in the home than
the wife and mother can perform with comfort to herself and
household; and the servant girls of today will then find systematic employment in the great factories, where food and clothing
are manufactured by rule. This evolution has already begun
with the woman typewriter. You see her everywhere; pretty,
tidy, rosy with a ribbon or flower at her throat, intent upon
her work and sure to get her pay. Then can the mother, for the
sake of herself, her husband, and children, preserve her health,
her beauty, and her mental vigor. Then can she be an adviser
in the home, the state, the church, and the school, remaining
so to a ripe old age.

But women can never have the opportunity, or the power, to
achieve these results, except in isolated cases, till they are voters
and lawmakers; and never even then, till they have had time to
secure, by legislation, the equal property rights that they have
earned with men from the beginning.

All evolution proceeds slowly. Women, under normal conditions, are evolutionists, and not revolutionists, as is shown
by their conduct, as voters, in Wyoming, Colorado, Utah and
Idaho. Your ideal, hysterical reformer, whose aim in life is to
put men in leading strings, like little children, doesn't hail from
any state where women vote.

Mary A. Livermore, at the head of the Sanitary Commission
during our great internecine war; Clara Barton, President of the
National Red Cross Society, and Oregon's own Mrs. Creighton, President of the National White Cross Association, have
each proved the capacity of the American woman for rescuing
the race from the awful consequences of war; while every soldier proves, by the very fact of his existence, that some mother
has borne a son at her peril, perhaps to be shot in battles that
woman might help to avoid.

The very best housekeepers and homemakers in America
are among the Equal Suffrage platform workers, the editor of
the "Ladies' Home Journal" to the contrary notwithstanding. They may know better than to ruin their eyes over Mr.
Bok's latest fad in "Battenburg" or shatter their nerves over

his mental creations in crazy stitches, but they can, and do, raise men and women, like the sons and daughters of Lucretia Mott, Mary A. Livermore, Emily B. Ketchum, Elizabeth Cady Stanton, Lilly Devereaux Blake, Abigail Scott Duniway, Lucy Stone Blackwell, Elizabeth Boynton Harbert, Harriet Beecher Stowe and Julia Ward Howe.

But, your most important point, if you hope to win the ballot at all, is to convince the average voter, that, in seeking your liberties, you are equally anxious that he shall preserve his own. You may drive, or lead, a horse to water, but you cannot make him drink. Nor can you lead any man to vote for your enfranchisement till you have first convinced him that by so doing, he is not placing you in a position where you may, if you choose, trample upon any of his rights, whether they may be fancied or real, healthful or harmful. Every woman knows she cannot rule her husband. The man who would be ruled by his wife would not be worth corralling in the chimney corner after she had driven him home. What is true of men in the abstract, is equally true of men in the aggregate. I cannot too strongly impress upon you, good sisters, the fact that we will never get the ballot till the crack of doom, if we persist in demanding it as a whip, with which to scourge the real or apparent vices of the present voting classes. If we can make men willing to be reformed, they will then reform themselves.

Here is where woman has, in the last two decades, made her greatest blunder. Whenever she demands the ballot, not simply because it is her right to possess it, but because by its use, she expects to reconstruct the genus man by law, on a basis of her own choosing, she only succeeds in driving nails into the closed coffin lid of her own and other women's liberties.

Men know, intuitively, that the right to representation in the legislature is a right as inestimable to us as to them; that it is formidable to tyrants only. They do not believe themselves to be tyrants, and will resent the implication that they are such to the bitter end. They also know that women, in giving existence to the soldiers, suffer their full share of the penalties and perils of existence, equaling all the horrors of war. So, when they say, "Women must fight if they vote," it is easy, in the awful glare of the tragedies of the present year, to convince them in the words of Joaquin Miller, Oregon's greatest poet, that "The bravest battles that ever are fought, are fought by the mothers of men."

When men claim to represent us, it is not difficult, if we are always careful not to make them angry, to prove to them that men never say, if any woman is accused of crime, "May it please the Court and the jury, I represent this woman, punish me."

No man, save Jesus of Nazareth, our divinely commissioned Elder Brother, has ever yet appeared before the bar of God, or man, and offered himself as propitiation for the sins, debts, or taxes of women.

Many good men object to women doing jury duty. They often frighten timid women by saying, "How would you like to be locked up in the Jury Room with eleven men?" I can't understand why so many men imagine that if women should once be allowed their right to vote, they would never, thereafter, do anything else but vote, vote, vote, vote! Nor can I comprehend another fancy, equally absurd, that, just as soon as women are voters, they will all be compelled to sit all the time on juries; and everyone of those unfortunate jurors will always have as many little children as poor John Rogers of historical memory; and no matter what the state of her health and the needs of her neglected husband, and "nine small children," etc., she will still be on the jury; and that jury will always be composed of one woman and eleven men. Such assumptions are too absurd for refutation; but for the fact that they sometimes bring out negative votes, we would not notice them. Men and women always have been, and always will be, excused from jury duty—for cause.

Again, we can never win the ballot by demanding it in the interests of any particular "ism," union, party, sect or creed. In our Pacific Northwest, the majority of the voters stand ready to grant us the ballot whenever we demand it on the broad basis of individual and collective liberty for ourselves; and we will never get it otherwise.

Our friends east of the Rocky Mountains were amazed and electrified, in the autumn of 1883, by the announcement that the Legislature of Washington Territory had extended the ballot to women.

Less than four years later, after a few self-imported agitators had made strong attempts to use the women's ballots for the enforcement of sumptuary legislation, to which the men objected (even while pretending to approve it, till they got the women into a trap), women everywhere were dumfounded by the action of the politicians of the Territory, who retaliated by shutting down the iron gates of a State Constitution in the women's faces, leaving them as ex-voters on the outside of the temple of liberty, with their hands tied.

The men of Washington are not yet over their scare, nor will they be till women have made an effort to convince them that the eyes of the great majority are now open, and they will never be entrapped in such a way again.

I pray you do not misunderstand me, friends. I wage no war upon any organization, or upon any person's political or religious faith. Catholics have just as good right to their religious opinions as Protestants. Republicans have just as good right to their political bias as Democrats, and Socialists have just as good a right to their reformatory fancies as Prohibitionists. Yet, if any one of these great armies of opposing opinions should claim Equal Suffrage as its chief dependence for success, and the great National American Woman Suffrage Association, or the Suffrage Association of any State, should become the champion of its special "ism," we should, henceforth, be unable to rally to our standard any appreciable vote, save that of the particular sect or party with which the voters of opposing sects or parties should believe us allied. We need all the votes we can get from all parties to win.

If I, as a member of the Presbyterian Church, for instance, should have gone before the legislature of Oregon, seeking the submission of our Suffrage amendment as a measure for enforcing the Presbyterian creed, think you that the members of the Catholic Church, or of the Protestant Churches of other denominations, sitting in that assembly, would have electrified the suffragists of this nation by voting almost solidly for our amendment, as allies of the Westminster catechism?

A year ago, when our second semi-annual convention of the Oregon Congress of Women was in session, it was boldly proclaimed by a zealous advocate of sumptuary legislation, that Susan B. Anthony, the venerable and venerated President of the National Woman Suffrage Association, had declared herself a worker for the ballot as the sworn advocate of only one idea. I wrote at once to our beloved President, who never fails us at a critical period, asking for facts over her own signature, and received for answer, her unequivocal denial of the allegation that she was allied, in the Equal Suffrage work, with any sort of sumptuary legislation, or any other side issue under the sun. This declaration, which I caused to be published in the secular papers, set the minds of the voters at rest on that score, and enabled Dr. Annice F. Jeffreys and myself to go before the legislature free from all handicaps.

When the question of sumptuary legislation confronted us at the capitol, we explained that equal suffragists everywhere believed with Gail Hamilton that the only way to reform a man is to begin with his grandmother. This frank announcement removed the last vestige of legislative hostility, and gave us the submission of our Equal Suffrage amendment, practically without opposition. Potential grandmothers do not trouble our politicians overmuch. The present possible rewards of office drive remote probabilities to the wall.

The year 1900 is the period fixed by law for the final vote upon our pending Suffrage amendment, and we need have no fear for the result, if we can keep the fact before our voters that our demand for the ballot is not engendered by emotional insanity.

The men of our Pacific Northwest are a noble lot of freemen. The spirit of enterprise which led them across the untracked continent to form a new empire, beside our sundown sea, was a bold and free spirit; and the patient heroism of the few women who originally shared their lot had in it the elements of grandeur.

There are lessons of liberty in the rockribbed mountains that pierce our blue horizon with their snow-crowned heads, and laugh to scorn the warring elements of the earth, the water and the air. There are lessons of freedom in our broad prairies that roll away into illimitable distances. There are lessons of equality in the gigantic, evenly-crested forest trees that rear their hydra heads to the vaulted zenith and touch the blue horizon with extended arms. There are lessons of truth and justice in the very air we breathe, and lessons of irresistible progress in the mighty waters that surge and sweep, with superhuman power, between the overhanging bluffs of our own Columbia, the "River of the West."

My state is the only one represented this year, in this great Convention, in which an Equal Suffrage Amendment is pending. The opportunity has come to us, as to the women of no other state, to claim the dawn of the 20th century as our year of jubilee. To work in unison with each other, and with the women of the older states, crystallized with constitutions hoary with the encrustations of long-vanished years, and compel them to look to the free, young, elastic West, for the liberties they cannot get at home, is the proud ambition that commands my presence here tonight. Help us with your wisdom, your sympathy, your co-operation, good friends; and when we shall have been successful at the ballot boxes of our state, thus adding a star of the first magnitude to the already bright constellation of our four free states, which now illumine our Northwestern heavens, we will entertain you with a national jubilee to celebrate our liberties, as the most fitting accompaniment to the dawn of the 20th century which patriotism can devise. Then shall liberty, newly born, be christened with a new name, selected for her by an octogenarian Oregonian, now confined with the infirmities of age in a New York hospital, who sent our Equal Suffrage Association as a message of congratulation, when the telegraph proclaimed the news that our amendment had passed the Legislature, the magical greeting, "A child is born, and her name is Alleluia."

(We failed to win the ballot in all of our Pacific Coast States till thirteen years after the above address was given; but its facts appeal, today, with even greater force, to men and women in every state where votes of men are needed to secure the blessings of liberty and responsibility, or the right of self-government for all the people, "by no means excluding women.")

PART THREE

1900–1920

BELLE KEARNEY

The South and Woman Suffrage

MARCH 25, 1903

Starting in the 1890s both northern and southern suffragists attempted to exploit what was euphemistically referred to as "the negro problem" to benefit women's suffrage. In a conservative region known for its devotion to the ideal of the Southern Lady, politicians would never have embraced women's suffrage on its own merits, but they were receptive to a politically expedient argument based on numbers: white women outnumbered black voters, and thus could help prop up white supremacy in the region. Historian Marjorie Spruill Wheeler calls the 1903 NAWSA convention in New Orleans the "high-water mark of the Southern strategy based on exploitation of 'the Negro problem.'"

Increasingly frustrated by their inability to build support on the federal level, suffrage leaders focused their attention on the states, hoping to find allies there that were absent in national politics. Doing business with the South came with the price of endorsing explicitly racist tactics in pursuit of the vote. NAWSA accepted the offer of Louisiana suffragists (and sisters) Kate M. Gordon (1861–1932) and Jean Gordon (1865–1931) to meet in New Orleans in 1903, but in deference to their racist views, African Americans were excluded from attendance. In an even more troubling capitulation, NAWSA passed a states' rights resolution that gave state organizations the freedom to determine their membership (a clear invitation to exclude African Americans) and allowed them to determine on what terms to ask for suffrage, which could include literacy and property requirements specifically designed to exclude black voters. How southern suffragists played the race card to make the case for women's suffrage is on full display in "The South and Woman Suffrage," the keynote address of Mississippi suffragist Belle Kearney (1863–1939). Her speech was a paean to Anglo-Saxon superiority not just as practiced in the South but as a model for the country as a whole. When faced with "4,500,000 ex-slaves, illiterate and semi-barbarous," women's suffrage would ensure "immediate and durable white supremacy."

To-day one third of the population of the South is of the negro race, and there are more negroes in the United States than there are inhabitants in "Mexico, the third Republic of the world." In some Southern States the negroes far outnumber the whites, and are so numerous in all of them as to constitute what is called a "problem." Until the present generation, they have always lived here as slaves.

The race question is national in its bearing. Still, as the South has the bulk of the negro population, the burden of the responsibility for the negro problem rests here.

The world is scarcely beginning to realize the enormity of the situation that faces the South in its grapple with the race question which was thrust upon it at the close of the Civil War, when 4,500,000 ex-slaves, illiterate and semi-barbarous, were enfranchised. Such a situation has no parallel in history. In forging a path out of the darkness, there were no precedents to lead the way. All that has been and is being accomplished is pioneer statecraft. The South has struggled under its death-weight for nearly forty years, bravely and magnanimously.

The Southern States are making a desperate effort to maintain the political supremacy of Anglo-Saxonism by amendments to their constitutions limiting the right to vote by a property and educational qualification. If the United States government had been wise enough to enact such a law when the negro was first enfranchised, it would have saved years of bloodshed in the South, and such experiences of suffering and horror among the white people here as no other were ever subjected to in an enlightened nation.

The present suffrage laws in the different Southern States can be only temporary measures for protection. Those who are wise enough to look beneath the surface will be compelled to realize the fact that they act as a stimulus to the black man to acquire both education and property, but no incentive is given to the poor whites; for it is understood, in a general way, that any man whose skin is fair enough to let the blue veins show through, may be allowed the right of franchise.

The industrial education that the negro is receiving at Tuskegee and other schools is only fitting him for power, and when the black man becomes necessary to a community by reason of his skill and acquired wealth, and the poor white man, embittered by his poverty and humiliated by his inferiority, finds no place for himself or his children, then will come the grapple between the races.

To avoid this unspeakable culmination, the enfranchisement

of women will have to be effected, and an educational and property qualification for the ballot be made to apply, without discrimination, to both sexes and to both races. It will spur the poor white to keep up with the march of progression, and enable him to hold his own. The class that is not willing to measure its strength with that of an inferior is not fit to survive.

The enfranchisement of women would insure immediate and durable white supremacy, honestly attained; for, upon unquestionable authority, it is stated that "in every Southern State but one, there are more educated women than all the illiterate voters, white and black, native and foreign, combined." As you probably know, of all the women in the South who can read and write, ten out of every eleven are white. When it comes to the proportion of property between the races, that of the white outweighs that of the black immeasurably. The South is slow to grasp the great fact that the enfranchisement of women would settle the race question in politics.

The civilization of the North is threatened by the influx of foreigners with their imported customs; by the greed of monopolistic wealth, and the unrest among the working classes; by the strength of the liquor traffic, and by encroachments upon religious belief.

Some day the North will be compelled to look to the South for redemption from these evils, on account of the purity of its Anglo-Saxon blood, the simplicity of its social and economic structure, the great advance in prohibitory law, and the maintenance of the sanctity of its faith, which has been kept inviolate. Just as surely as the North will be forced to turn to the South for the nation's salvation, just so surely will the South be compelled to look to its Anglo-Saxon women as the medium through which to retain the supremacy of the white race over the African.

I have heard it said in the South, "Oh, well, suffrage may be a very good thing for women in other sections of the United States, but not here. Our women are different." How are they unlike those of their own sex elsewhere? They are certainly as intelligent as any upon the face of the earth; they have the same deep love for the home, the same devotion to their country.

"Oh, yes; but, you see, if the white women were allowed to vote, the negro women would have the same privilege, and that would mean the humiliation of having to meet them at the polls on a basis of equality."

That difficulty would be settled by having separate polling places. When the ballot is given to the women of the South, you will find that these distinct voting precincts for the two races will be quickly established.

It is useless for me to attempt, at this late day, to refute the objections raised against woman suffrage, for every obstacle to its progress has been met years ago, and every argument for its existence justified. It is no longer a question of right with the people, for that old battle has been fought; it is now only one of expediency and opposition by prejudice.

To defend woman suffrage before a Louisiana audience would be a work of extreme supererogation, for this noble State has the *éclat* of having empowered by constitutional law, all taxpaying women to vote upon all questions submitted to the taxpayers. Women are permitted to exercise the right of voting in some form in forty-three foreign countries and provinces. Complete enfranchisement is enjoyed by women in the Isle of Man, New Zealand, and Federated Australia.

The passion for individual liberty, so characteristic of the Anglo-Saxon race, has been strongly demonstrated in the women of the United States.

Over 250 years ago, a woman, for the first time in America, asked the privilege of being allowed to vote. That was Margaret Brent, of Maryland, a kinswoman of Lord Baltimore. The next was the wife of John Adams, who begged for the same power over 125 years later; also Mercy Warren, and the sister of Richard Henry Lee, of Virginia. This impulse toward citizenship has been transmitted through the generations of American women.

On July 2, 1776, two days before the Declaration of Independence was adopted, the women of New Jersey were enfranchised by the State Convention held in that commonwealth; but this right was afterwards taken from them. Kentucky was the next State to allow women to vote in any degree; that boon was granted in 1838.

In 1869 full political equality was given to the women of Wyoming. Colorado, Utah and Idaho have since followed, granting unlimited suffrage to women. Besides these four States, with their full enfranchisement, there are 25 other States in this country that have partial suffrage for women. Surprising victories are constantly being gained.

Mississippi was the first State in the Union to have a State Institute and College for Girls. Mississippi claims the honor of being the first State in the Union to bestow upon married women the right of full control of their property. It is my firm belief that, before many decades, the South will astonish the world by giving complete enfranchisement to its women. As a stepping-stone to this blessed consummation, let us now make a determined effort to secure from the next Legislatures of the Southern States the recognition of the right of women to presidential suffrage. The Constitution of the United States confers upon the Legislatures of the different States the undoubted power to enable their women citizens to vote at presidential elections.

If any State, by a simple change in its election law, permits all women who can read and write and who pay a tax on property, to vote at the presidential election of 1904, the general acceptance of the women in that State would settle the question of the wisdom of woman suffrage, for the result would be vastly to increase the majority of the dominant party. Public sentiment would undergo such a revolution as to make a subsequent amendment to the State constitution, bestowing unlimited enfranchisement upon women, easy to obtain.

The South, which has wrought so splendidly in the past, surely will measure up to its responsibility in taking the forward step of woman's enfranchisement in order to render justice to its own firesides and to fix the status of the white race for future years.

Anglo-Saxonism is the standard of the ages to come. It is, above all else, the granite foundation of the South. Upon that its civilization will mount; upon that it will stand unshaken.

The white people of the North and South are children of the same heroic souls who laid the foundations of civil and religious liberty in this new world, and built thereon this great Republic. We call to you, men and women, across that invisible line that divides the sections, across the passage of deathless years, to unite with us in holding this mighty country safe for the habitation of the Anglo-Saxon.

Thank God the black man was freed! I wish for him all

possible happiness and all possible progress, but not in encroachments upon the holy of holies of the Anglo-Saxon race.

The Old South, with its romantic ideals, its grace, its sorrow, has passed into history. Upon the ashes of its desolation has arisen a New South, strong and beautiful, full of majesty and of power. The ambition of the Old was for States' rights, for local supremacy; that of the New is for a limitless sweep of vision, and with the elixir in its veins of an intense patriotic enthusiasm. The destiny of the South is the destiny of the Republic. It will eventually become totally merged in the being of our imperial nation.

Even now, as dearly as I love my people, sacred as I hold their traditions, loyal as I am to their interests, I say with infinitely less pride that I am a Southern woman than that I am an American.

Our sectionalism must broaden without reservation into nationalism that means sovereignty, and that points to immortality.

ANNIE NATHAN MEYER

Woman's Assumption of Sex Superiority

January 1904

Writer and playwright Annie Nathan Meyer (1867–1951) loved to poke
fun at suffragists, including her sister Maud Nathan (1862–1946), who
was a well-respected leader in New York. Meyer was, among other
things, one of the founders of Barnard College, but she publicly embraced the antisuffrage cause, using her caustic wit to poke holes in
many of suffragists' most popular arguments. In this article, Meyer
challenged the notion that women were uniquely qualified to uplift
public life. If a woman can't stand up to her volatile dressmaker, she
asked, how is she going to take on Tammany Hall? And she punctured
the logic that the vote of an educated woman ("Mrs. Thus-and-So")
would offset the vote of an "ignorant hod-carrier" by pointing out
that "Mrs. Hod-carrier" would also presumably be heading to the
polls. What Meyer grasped was the fundamental truth that women
would vote as individuals, not as a sex, rendering many of the exaggerated claims that women would stop prostitution, end war, and clean up
politics patently false. Meyer did not dislike women—she dotted her
antisuffrage writings with tributes to "fine, true women" who would
no doubt cast their votes wisely—but offered a strong caution to the
notion that women voters would change the world.

One of the most charming of the women orators in the late
municipal campaign in New York, in a burst of eloquence for
which she was applauded, pointed to the lady who stood as the
emblem of the Fusion party, and to the tiger of Tammany, and
asked if it were possible to hesitate in the choice: "The lady or
the tiger confronts you. Which shall it be?" Fortunately, the
audience was with the speaker. Questions are admittedly dangerous political weapons. The picture of the voter trembling
before the gates was cleverly drawn; yet it might have been awkward had one ventured to suggest that it was not at all certain
before which gate one would more violently tremble. It is not
difficult to imagine circumstances in which one might pray for
the tiger. My own experience is somewhat limited—on the side
of the tiger. But I fancy an angry tiger kills quickly.

I am quite sure that, in the political arena, I should dread the advent of women as voters and office-holders a little more than that of the tiger. Of course, to the speaker, Woman typified and summed up all that was honorable, pure, noble, uplifting. To her, even the fact that the emblematic "lady" referred to was really a goddess was in no way disconcerting. It was assumed by many campaigners that the interest taken in the campaign by the women was in itself a conclusive arraignment of Tammany, was in itself a proof that the Fusion party stood for honest government. Of course, such an assumption when it is made by a man is not to be seriously challenged; but when it is made by a large proportion (still, I am persuaded, happily, by a minority) of women, then it becomes worth while to examine woman's claim to moral superiority, to examine it soberly and seriously.

The exercise by woman of the power to vote has been held up by these women again and again as a panacea for the chief evils, if not all the evils, that now threaten to undermine the moral life of America. As even these women must be aware that in voting the majority prevails, this is clearly an assumption that the majority of women may be counted upon as a force that would make for political righteousness. It is strangely difficult to keep this inference before the public. The popular method of argument is: "Mrs. Thus-and-So is a splendid woman; would she not give us a more intelligent vote than the ignorant hod-carrier?" The fact that the vote of Mrs. Thus-and-So will be pitted against that of Mrs. Hod-carrier, never seems to be considered. It must be remembered that the suffrage—at least in America—is almost certain to be refused to all women, or given to all women; that a vote to one woman will be a vote to all women, vicious and virtuous, ignorant and educated, lowest and highest.

Let me say right here, as emphatically as possible, that while I challenge the assumption that women as a sex could contribute a regenerative force to the body politic, yet I do not deny the fact that there are many fine, true women who could be relied upon to cast their votes every time for the right. That I further think that most of these women do not wish the suffrage, that they have a clearer idea of their sex as a whole and a profounder appreciation of their real duties, does not concern us at present. The question, shorn of all disingenuousness, of all sentimentality, is just this: What could the sex bring to the service of the state to offset the degeneration of public life, to offset the indifference, the sloth, the moral cowardice, the greed, the dishonesty that are seriously menacing the moral life of our Republic?

When a man is chosen by his party as a candidate for office, his career is scrutinized, the question is asked, What has he done in his private career that implies a promise of success in a public career? Similarly, when women offer themselves for political duty (and in no spirit of humility, but with smug self-satisfaction and assumption of superior virtue), is it not just to scrutinize their past, to ask, What special character, what special force, what special talent have they shown in fulfilling their apportioned duties in the past? Is there anything to warrant a faith that they would discharge this new duty faithfully and ably? It is idle for women to say that it is not fair to scrutinize their past, because it was not a past of their own seeking; to claim that incompetency in domestic life bears no relation to incompetency in political life, that the shirking of disagreeable duties would not mean the shirking of (supposedly) agreeable ones. Idle, and futile, I say, because we are probing deeper than that! We do not wish to know if their heads are equal to the problems of government; it does not concern us if they are not fitted for domestic duties—if they dislike them; it is not brains, nor aptitudes, nor even ability that are vital, it is character. Character is the one force needed in American life to-day. And character may be more safely judged from the way in which we perform disagreeable duties than from the way in which we perform agreeable ones. The question is not so much whether certain tasks allotted to women in the past have been well or ill performed; but it is—it doubly, trebly, is: Having been confronted with these tasks, in what manner have they approached them? Have they shirked them, or have they done their best? Have they done the work they found to be done, willingly, conscientiously, patiently, uncomplainingly? Have they been satisfied to do it without applause, without public reward? Have they brought to bear on this work the best they had, the best they could become? Have they never reached forth to grasp the more spectacular work of others, while turning their backs on their own? In short, have they any claim to such characteristics as, if contributed to American public life to-day, could purify and ennoble it?

I have spoken of the lack of character as the real lack in American public life to-day. Is there any question of this? To what is due the general neglect of the disagreeable part of political duty, but to a lack of character? What explains the too common custom of paying for concessions instead of fighting for one's just dues, but a lack of character? What, the yielding to blackmail, the seeking of the line of least resistance? What, the venality, the greed, and the acceptance of a double standard of honesty—political and commercial? What does all this signify, but a lack of character?

Perhaps the enlarged opportunities enjoyed by women during the past forty years have qualified them in some directions for the suffrage. Certainly, their mental qualifications will not be so sweepingly questioned as when the subject first arose for debate. But it is my firm conviction that the development of woman's character has by no means kept step with that of her intellect. I think this is a serious arraignment of the women's colleges, one to which several of the leading colleges are awakening, and to the correction of which the best friends of woman's education are addressing themselves. There is no longer question of the capacity of woman's brain to be trained to wield the suffrage. But, alas! it can never be repeated often enough that it is not brains that are needed just now. There is a cry welling up from the surcharged hearts of those who tremble for the steadfastness of American government: but it is not a cry for brains—it is a cry for character.

"Put United Womanhood," they say, (a resounding phrase much made use of—as if all women could be united on anything save puffed sleeves or pocketless skirts!), "Put United Womanhood into politics, and we shall have character. You will no longer see the Boss one instant the epitome of all that is evil, and the next, worthy to fold his legs under your mahogany." But is this true? Is there even a shadow of truth in it? Have women, then, as a sex been so brave in fighting the conventional standpoint? Show me that more than a handful of women have the courage to ostracize the "great catch" that they know has no right to associate with their daughters, and I shall take heart. Give me the slightest inkling that women will fight the tyrannous hand of the Labor-Unions, now stifling the manhood of our business as well as of our laboring world. Give me the faintest hope that women will refuse to pay for what should come to them freely, that women will resist all favoritism, all unfairness! What is there in the past that can vouch for the future? Will the woman who quails before the departing cook, stand firm before the District Leader? Will the woman who submits to the tyranny of her volatile dressmaker, resist the voluble walking delegate? Will the woman who has made a mess of the domestic question, straighten out the tangles of the industrial and financial world? And, finally, will a woman who has shirked the noblest duty on God's earth, not shirk the lesser duties to which she, strangely enough, aspires? I hope I am not unduly severe. I am not more severe than are the women themselves who decry the moral weakness of the average man. In the very charge of inferiority launched against men by the women, they present the strongest possible indictment of their own sex. These men, who are so weak, so corrupt, so far below the standard of the women—had they no mothers? With so many grafters, so many "respectable" tools of a machine, is it possible that a great many women have not betrayed their trust? Do not tell me that the casting of a bit of paper in a box once a year can offset the daily influence of a mother, or that votes can be better gained from a political platform than at the home fireside.

I fail to see in women any evidence of the character that is needed in our public life. I fail to see that they are even on the right track to attain it. I think there is no school so eminently unfit for the development of character as that of the public platform, which women are seeking more and more. I think there is a grave danger to the moral force of womanhood in woman's increasing participation in organized effort, in public life. To say nothing of the wire-pulling, of the unscrupulousness in attaining an end, of the unfairness, of the love of office, of the insincerity which reveal themselves in the large organizations of women, with discouraging and startling resemblance to the methods of their weaker brethren, I hold that there is certain to come a deterioration which I like to name "Platform Virtue." One who feeds on applause learns how easily it is gained, grows impatient of any task which does not win it, is apt to scorn such work as is not in the public eye. The most subtle moral danger lies in the fact that it is so easy to be noble, to be generous, to be unselfish, on the public platform,—in one's typewritten Confession of Faith. How is the strength to be given to work on, to fight on quietly, unknown, uninterviewed, unrewarded, certainly unapplauded, when the enunciation of a few well-rounded periods yields such delightful recognition! An audience is the most good-natured, indifferent censor in the world. It seldom probes below the surface; in the rare cases in which it does, its memory is conveniently short. Just as the kindergarten methods, in the opinion of some educators, have lost for our children a certain sturdiness, a certain grim power of overcoming difficulties, so the platform habit, the club habit, the President and Secretary habit have entailed upon our women serious losses. The daily uncomplaining attention to household details that make for comfort and a restful home atmosphere; the tender, unseen care given to the children; the brooding over, watching and painstaking upbuilding of character; the brave, inspiring encouragement of the wearied wage-earner—for these things has not taste been lost?

It is so perilously easy, on the one hand, to be an angel of loving-kindness to some class of workers for whom one has founded a protecting organization, and, on the other, in the privacy of one's home, to withhold from one's servants the most ordinary human consideration. It is so easy to appeal on the platform to the highest, purest motives, to implore others to do their duty, and in the home to shrink from the most elementary duties, not only of motherhood, but of wifehood. It is so easy to be suave and delightful, gracious and charming, on the platform, and at home nervous, unstrung, impatient, fretful. The hardening processes of the age may be exemplified most strongly in the evolution of the very newest new woman. She who, twenty-five years ago, refused marriage in favor of her so-called "career," at least was willing to make a sacrifice of her emotional needs. She of to-day has no idea of renouncing marriage, but remoulds its old-fashioned idea of obligation—at times with an overriding of nature that would be comic if it were not tragic.

Are we, then, to throw over entirely our cherished idea, that woman is the morally superior sex? Well, I think the women have been banking a little too heavily upon certain claims. I think that, if they had lived for centuries in the same freedom and under the same temptations as men, they would have shown far less self-control and power of resistance; and this opinion might find support in some of the conditions known to exist in the social life of our own community. Perhaps some brave twentieth-century Fielding will arise and write an up-to-date parody of "Pamela": it will be instructive.

Even of so masculine a vice as drunkenness, there is something to be said. The assertion of sex superiority is not proven because there are fewer drunkards among women than men. Dare any one affirm that, since women have entered into industrial competition, into public life with its drain on the nervous strength, there has been less drunkenness than before? On the contrary, every one knows that the use of stimulants among women is increasing rapidly.

Notwithstanding the usual tone that pervades the speeches at a Woman's Rights Meeting (and there is a degree of bitterness, of contempt, of positive enmity against men that is not dreamed of by the average person), I believe that the work now done by the men would not be improved by being done by women.

It may seem so on the surface, but I am not wholly reactionary. I do not think that all virtue or all character is buried in the graves of our ancestresses. There is much that may be gained from all the discussion, all the unrest and change of the past half century, if only the trained women who should be the leaders will take their covetous eyes from the careers of the men, and, casting them backward over the past, will say: "Let us see how much better we can do the woman's work in the future. Let us see what training and science can do to make that work more helpful and more intelligent." I have hope for the future, because I know there are many strong women working quietly for this end. They are not the women who are supposed to represent us; they are certainly not those who periodically assure the Legislature that they do. They are seldom found on a platform. They are not presidents of clubs. They are not be-badged "chairmen" of committees; they do not belong to Mothers' Congresses, but they are accomplishing their end in a sincere, an unspectacular, the only lasting way, through the weight of personal character, the effect of personal example, through the divine influence that is so dangerously slipping away from this organization-worshipping, this number-idolizing, world of ours—I mean, the impulse of the *personal touch*. I have hope, because many of the excesses of women will be righted after women have grasped a little longer the baubles they have yearned for, after they have seen how valueless are these baubles in their hands. Then, I cannot but think, they will learn to value the things they have so blithely let go.

MARY CHURCH TERRELL

The Progress of Colored Women
JUNE 13, 1904

When Mary Church Terrell journeyed to Berlin in 1904 to address the International Council of Women, she realized that she would represent not just the American suffrage movement but the experiences of African American women as well. Like many other black women active in the public sphere, in her speech, "The Progress of Colored Women," she displayed a strong intersectional vision that acknowledged the connections between race, class, and gender oppression in shaping the experiences of African American women. In Berlin, Terrell used her platform to give the delegates a tutorial in African American women's history, contrasting the days of "oppression and despair" under slavery with the "true miracle" of the progress since then. And she did so in German, being fluent in the language from her travels abroad after her graduation from Oberlin in 1884. Women's international networks were especially vibrant in the late nineteenth and early twentieth centuries, and Terrell was far from the only American who made the trip to Berlin. Susan B. Anthony, Anna Howard Shaw (1847–1919) and Carrie Chapman Catt (1859–1947), were also in attendance, and they used the occasion to found the International Woman Suffrage Alliance, a separate transnational organization that fed the growth of the suffrage movement worldwide.

If it had not been for the War of the Rebellion, which resulted in victory for the Union forces in 1865, my friends, instead of addressing you as a free woman to night, in all human probability I should be on some plantation in one of the southern states of my country, manacled body and soul in the fetters of a slave. In all this great world gathering of women I take it I am unique in two respects. In the first place I am the only woman participating in these exercises who represents a race which has been free for as short a time as forty years. In the second place I am the only woman who will speak from this platform whose parents were actually held as chattels and who but for the kindly intervention of a beneficent Providence would herself have been a slave. As you fasten your eyes on me therefore, you are truly beholding a rare, rare bird.

And so, as I stand here to night, the cause of my happiness is two fold, rejoicing, as I do, not only in the emancipation of my race, but in the almost universal elevation of my sex. If any one had had the courage to predict fifty years ago that a woman with African blood in her veins would journey from the United States to Berlin Germany to address an International Congress of Women in the year 1904, he would either have been laughed to scorn or he would have been immediately confined in an asylum for the hopelessly insane. For in the days of our oppression and despair, colored women were not only refused admission to institutions of learning, but the laws of all but two of the states in which the majority lived made it a crime to teach them to read. Not only could they possess no property, but even their bodies were not their own. Nothing in short which could degrade or brutalize the womanhood of my race was lacking in that system from which colored women fifty years ago had but little hope of escape. So gloomy were their prospects, so pernicious were the customs, so fatal the laws, so hard the heart of the masters only fifty years ago. But from the day their fetters were broken and their minds released from the darkness of ignorance in which they had been shrouded for nearly three hundred years, from the day they could stand erect in the dignity of womanhood, no longer bond but free, till to night, colored women have forged steadily ahead in the acquisition of knowledge and in the cultivation of those graces of character which make for good. To use a thought of the illustrious Frederick Douglass, if judged by the depths from which they have come, rather than by the heights to which those blessed with centuries of opportunities have attained, colored women need not hang their heads in shame. Not only are colored women handicapped on account of their sex, but they are almost everywhere baffled and mocked on account of their race. Desperately and continuously they are forced to fight an opposition born of a cruel, unreasonable prejudice which neither their merit nor their necessity seems able to remove.

But in spite of the almost insurmountable obstacles which block their path, the progress made by colored women along all lines is a veritable miracle of modern times. Mentally, morally and financially they are advancing at a rapid rate. From the most renowned universities, as well as the best colleges and high schools throughout the United States, colored girls have graduated with honor and have thus forever settled the question of their capacity and worth. A few years ago a large number of young men and women of the dominant race and only one colored girl competed for a scholarship, entitling the successful competitor to an entire course through the Chicago University. As a result of the examination which was held, the only colored girl stood first and thus captured this great prize. Wherever colored girls have studied their instructors bear testimony to their intelligence, their diligence and their skill. Of the colored teachers engaged in instructing our youth about 80% are women. Ever since a book was published in 1776, entitled Poems on Various Subjects, Religious and Moral by Phyllis Wheatley, Negro Servant of Mr. John Wheatley of Boston, Colored Women have from time to time given abundant evidence of literary ability. In sculpture we are represented by a woman upon whose chisel Italy has set her seal of approval; in painting by one of Bouguereau's pupils, whose work was exhibited a few years ago in a Paris salon and in music by young women who hold diplomas from the best conservatories in the land. In the professions we have several lawyers, together with a goodly number of dentists and doctors whose practice is lucrative and large.

In business Colored women have achieved signal success. A few years ago the largest ice plant in Halifax Nova Scotia was owned by a Colored woman, who sold it recently for a large amount. In the State of Alabama there is a large milling and cotton business belonging to and controlled by a colored woman, who has sometimes as many as 75 men in her employ. Although conditions prevailing in that part of my country in which the Afro-American was formerly held as a slave are not always conducive to the moral elevation of Colored women, although safeguards usually thrown around maidenly youth and innocence are frequently withheld from colored girls who are protected in this section neither by public sentiment nor by law, according to statistics compiled by men who would certainly not falsify in favor of my race, immorality among the Colored women of the United States is not so great as among women with similar environment and temptations in certain foreign lands.

Indefatigably in public work of all kinds Colored Women engage in order to improve their own condition as well as elevate their race. By banding themselves together in the interest of education and morality and by adopting the most practical means to this end during the past thirty years Colored women have exerted a powerful infuence for good. Through the instrumentality of various organizations both in the Church and out and through the National Association of Colored Women, of which it is my privilege to be the Honorary president, and which has at least 10,000 members at the present time, kindergartens have been established and successfully maintained, day nurseries for the infants of working women have been opened, object lessons in the best way to sweep, dust, cook, wash and iron have been given, classes in German, English Literature and other branches have been formed, efforts have been made to establish rescue homes and retreats for fallen women and tempted girls, and charity of all kinds has been dispensed. In short, what our hands have found to do, that we have done with all our might. In their earnest endeavor to work out their own salvation colored women have often been generously aided and encouraged by their more fortunate sisters of the dominant race, many of whom are broad in their views on the race problem, just and kind in their treatment of their sisters of a darker hue, and strong in their determination to render them any assistance in their power. In the United States of America there is a good number of women of the dominant race, who approach as near the ideal of perfect womanhood as can be found anywhere in the civilized world. Without the sympathy and hearty cooperation of such women the lot of colored women would be sad and hard indeed. It is a great pleasure, therefore, for me to express in this public way on a foreign soil my heartfelt gratitude and that of the 3,000,000 colored women in whose name I speak to night, to the white women of the United States, who could not possibly have more capable or more noble representatives than Susan B. Anthony, the veritable Abraham Lincoln in the emancipation of women, May Wright Sewall, Anna Howard Shaw, Hanna G. Solomon, Mary Wood Swift and Ida Husted Harper who are present with us to night.

Industrially, Colored women are heavily handicapped in the United States. There are comparatively few avocations and trades in which they are permitted to engage. So overcrowded are the pursuits in which it is possible for them to secure employment and so poor is the pay in consequence that only the barest livelihood can be eked out by the rank and file. Generally speaking, Colored women are school teachers, dressmakers, nurses for children and invalids, laundresses, chambermaids and cooks. Beyond these pursuits it is difficult for them to secure anything to do.

Ever since their emancipation Colored people have striven assiduously to emulate the example of their more highly civilized white brothers, upon whom they have always looked as veritable paragons and ideals. In one respect, at least, they have achieved success. Certainly in one particular Colored women are absolutely the equals of their sisters in white. That is to say, as domestic servants in some sections of my country, they are equally difficult to have and to hold, they are equally hard to placate and please. Generally speaking, the virtues and vices ascribed to the maids of other nationalities who ply their trade in the U.S. may be safely imputed to their colaborers of a darker hue. It would be a useless waste of your valuable time, therefore, and a needless strain upon your nerves, if I should dissertate upon the defects of the domestic servants of my race, when they are, in the main, common to those of your own. For no matter whether they hail from Greenland's icy mountains or from India's coral strands, no matter whether they call themselves German, Dane, English, Irish or Swede, no matter whether they be as fair as Solomon's lily or as black as Kaiser's tinte; in the United States all maids are equally hard to capture and to keep. In nearly every state of our glorious Republic it is much easier to catch a humming bird than it is to corral a maid.

In spite of this dearth of servants, however, Colored people in the U.S. are rapidly losing ground in what is called the menial pursuits and trades. This is sometimes the result of their own negligence, but it is more often caused by the bitter, cruel prejudice against their race. So long as the labor federations in the U.S. are so hostile to colored people as they are at the present time, it will be impossible for them to make much headway in the various trades. Alarmed at this tide of industrial hostility which is setting so strong against them, Colored people of intelligence and foresight are doing everything in their power to stem it—first by preaching the dignity of labor in season and out, and second by urging their youth to cultivate more assiduously habits of industry, proficiency and skill. Affable and amiable by nature, easy to imitate and learn, grateful and faithful to his employer, the Afro-American is surpassed by none as a servant and is equalled by very few. There is no reason, therefore why he should fail. The more carefully I study the servant problem in the U.S. and out, the more firmly am I convinced that this vexed question will never be justly and satisfactorily settled anywhere in the civilized world, until more of that patience and perfection so imperiously demanded of servants shall be acquired by the masters and mistresses themselves. To one who has lain awake nights studying this subject it is perfectly clear that the solution of this vexed question will never be achieved, until mistresses study their own imperfections more and ventilate their servants less.

Because I wished to present as many facts about the women of my race as could be compressed within ten minutes I have thought best to leave the discussion of the servant problem to brighter and more philosophical intellects than my own. If it has been possible to interest even a few women in foreign lands in the struggle which Colored women in the U.S. are making to rise from the degradation and ignorance forced upon them for nearly 300 years, my mission here in Berlin has been gloriously fulfilled. If I have presented facts about the progress of Colored women, not generally known, the object of my voyage has been fully attained.

Thanks to the pernicious activity of our enemies, the vices and defects of the Afro-American are far better known abroad than are his virtues, his achievements and his good deeds. The evil we do as a race is paraded and exaggerated from the Cape of Good Hope to the North Pole, while the good is borne on the wings of Dame Rumor and is carried in the columns of the press only a few short roods. If I can convince you that the Afro-American is not so black as he is frequently painted, and that he is waging a desperate and courageous warfare to secure the highest and best things in life; if I can convince you that, as a race, we are striving with all our heart, soul, mind and strength to quit us like women and men, my voyage of more than 3000 miles has not been made in vain.

In spite of opposition relentless and obstacles almost insurmountable the Afro-American can present to night such a record of progress in education, industry, finance and trade as has never been made in the same length of time under such discouraging circumstances, since the world began. If you should ask me what special phase of the Afro-AMERICAN's development makes me most hopeful of his ultimate triumph over present difficulties, I should answer unhesitatingly it is the magnificent work our women are doing to regenerate and uplift the race. And no people need ever despair, whose women are fully aroused to the duties which rest upon them and are willing to shoulder responsibilities which they alone can successfully assume.

So long as there sits in the White House (and as a race, we are going to do everything in our power to keep him there four years more,) a man whose mind is as broad, whose heart is as generous and whose courage is as great as that of Theodore Roosevelt, my despised and struggling race will not despair.

GROVER CLEVELAND

Would Woman Suffrage be Unwise?

OCTOBER 1905

Under the editorship of Edward W. Bok (1863–1930), the *Ladies' Home Journal* built a strong popular base of readers (in 1903 it became the first magazine to reach a million subscribers) but generally shied away from addressing contentious public issues like women's suffrage, only doing so in a way that upheld the status quo. That certainly was the agenda of Grover Cleveland (1837–1908) here. A Democratic politician who had the distinction of being the only president elected to nonconsecutive terms (1885–89 and 1893–97), Cleveland offered a strong endorsement of traditional gender roles, where "actual strife and battle" were allotted to men while women aspired to "lofty aims and purposes." The natural equilibrium of these roles, he argued, would be fundamentally upset by such a radical change as women's suffrage. Cleveland even expressed doubts about women's clubs, seeing them as potential stepping-stones to subversive ideas and practices.

———————

No standard of advanced civilization can receive intelligent sanction that fails to yield to genuine womanhood the highest place among the social agencies that refine humanity and make the world better. And of course it is equally certain that the nearer social conditions approach perfect excellence the more tender and careful will be the homage and consideration accorded by all decent men to unperverted womanhood. If, however, these sentiments are to indicate a spirit of true and sterling manliness they must rest upon something better than the shallow gallantry which, while professing admiration for womankind, indulges in a sort of pitying toleration of feminine subordination and frailty.

Thoughtful and right-minded men base their homage and consideration for woman upon an instinctive consciousness that her unmasculine qualities, whether called weaknesses, frailties, or what we will, are the sources of her characteristic and especial strength within the area of her legitimate endeavor. They know that if she is not gifted with the power of clear and logical reasoning she has a faculty of intuition which by a shorter route leads her to abstract moral truth; that if she deals mistakenly with practical problems it is because sympathy or sentiment clouds her perception of the relative value of the factors involved; that if she is unbusinesslike her trustfulness and charitableness stand in the way of cold-blooded calculation; that if she is occasionally stubborn it is because her beliefs take a strong hold upon her; and that if she is sometimes fitful and petulant it is but the prelude to bright smiles and sunny endearments. They know she is loving, long-suffering, self-sacrificing and tender, because God has made her so; and with it all they gratefully realize that whatever she has or lacks, the influence and ministrations of woman give firm rooting and sure growth to man's best efforts.

THE PLACES ASSIGNED TO MEN AND WOMEN

It is a mistake to suppose that any human reason or argument is needful or adequate to the assignment of the relative positions to be assumed by man and woman in working out the problems of civilization. This was done long ago by a higher intelligence than ours. I believe that trust in Divine wisdom, and ungrudging submission to Divine purposes, will enable dutiful men and women to know the places assigned to them, and will incite them to act well their parts in the sight of God. It should also be easy for such as these to see how wisely the work of human progress has been distributed, and how exactly the refining, elevating influence of woman, especially in her allotted sphere of home and in her character of wife and mother, supplements man's strenuous struggles in social and political warfare. In actual war it is the men who go to battle, enduring hardship and privation, and suffering disease and death for the cause they follow. They are deservedly praised for bravery and patriotism. It is the mothers, wives and maids betrothed, who, neither following the camp nor fighting in battle, constitute at home an army of woman's constancy and love, whose yearning hearts make men brave and patriotic. They teach from afar lessons of patient fortitude, and transmit through mysterious agencies, to soldiers in the field, the spirit of endurance and devotion. Soldiers who have fought, and those who praise or eulogize them, never forget to accord to woman the noble service of inspiration she has thus wrought with womanly weapons wielded in her appointed place.

WOMAN'S TRUEST INFLUENCE IN POLITICS

So in political warfare, it is perfectly fitting that actual strife and battle should be apportioned to man, and that the influence of woman, radiating from the homes of our land, should inspire to lofty aims and purposes those who struggle for the right. I am thoroughly convinced that woman can in no better way than this usefully serve the cause of political betterment, and preserve her present immeasurable power of good. It is sane intelligence, and not sentimental delusion, that discovers between the relative duties and responsibilities of man and woman, as factors in the growth of civilization, a natural equilibrium, so nicely adjusted to the attributes and limitations of both that it cannot be disturbed without social confusion and peril. It is therefore not surprising that a multitude of good American men and women, who certainly are not lacking in solicitude for their country's welfare, are troubled lest this equilibrium should be jostled out of balance by the dissemination of notions which present a distorted view of the saving grace of womanhood as a constructive influence and a potent force in our homes, and in the moral activities of our nation. These good people believe that this saving grace cannot be protected and perpetuated in its ordained beauty and strength, except by protecting and perpetuating in their ordained loyalty and purity all the distinctive traits and attributes of woman's nature. They repudiate the idea that these things have been outrun by advance and progress and are no longer worth saving. On the contrary, their patriotic thoughtfulness and clear intelligence lead them to see that, now and for all time to come, the work and mission of women within the sphere to which God has adjusted them, must constitute the immutable and unchangeable foundations of all that human enlightenment can build.

FALSE DOCTRINES TAUGHT BY CERTAIN WOMEN

None of us can deny that we have unhappily fallen upon a time when doctrines are taught by women, and to women, which tend with more or less directness to the subversion of sane and wholesome ideas of the work and mission of woman-hood, and lead to a fanciful insistence upon sharing in the stern, rugged and unwomanly duties and responsibilities allotted to man. As is usually the case when a radical and unnatural change is the object of effort, those most extreme and pronounced in opinion have forged to the front and assumed leadership. In outspoken discontent with the station and opportunity American women now enjoy, these clamorous leaders openly demand their equal participation with men in the right of suffrage and in every other political right and privilege. Many other women, more considerate and conservative, who refuse to indorse these demands, nevertheless by amiably tolerating them, or by ad-vocating other less direct attempts to enlarge the character of woman's endeavor, encourage and aid, perhaps unconsciously and unintentionally, female suffrage radicalism.

In this magazine, a few months ago, I ventured to publish some views I entertain touching woman's clubs and their ten-dencies. I am afraid a portion of what I wrote has been a little misunderstood by some women of genuine disposition, whose good opinion I would be glad to retain. Nevertheless I have no intention of attempting to make my meaning plainer, or of modifying the opinions I have expressed relating specifically to woman's clubs. I desire to supplement those opinions by declaring that, while they have elicited considerable approval from women, I have been hardly less gratified to discover in the expressions of many who have dissented a tone of charming womanliness and moderation, which has confirmed me in the belief that there need be no apprehension that such women are prepared deliberately and willfully to undermine woman's legit-imate mission; but what I fear more and more is the result of their good-natured and indirect affiliation with those more rad-ically disposed—who, with noisy discontent and possibly with not too much disinclination for notoriety, exploit in the news-papers their unpleasant temper, and their indifferent attempts to commend woman suffrage, accompanied occasionally by something very like unwomanly abuse and misrepresentation.

GENERAL WOMAN SUFFRAGE IS INEXPEDIENT

I desire here to make a statement which I am willing to have regarded somewhat in the light of a confession. In my former article in THE JOURNAL a reference was made in the following terms to the movement on foot to secure for woman the right to vote and otherwise participate in public affairs:

"Let it here be distinctly understood that no sensible man has fears of injury to the country on account of such participation. It is its dangerous undermining effect on the characters of the wives and mothers of our land that we fear." The subject under discussion was the unfavorable effect of woman's clubs on American womanhood; and it is tolerably apparent, from what immediately followed the above-quoted indulgent allusion to female participation in public affairs, that such allusion was incidental and illustrative of the main topic. So far as I am concerned, although I then saw no prospect of the accomplishment of this participation, as appears from other parts of the same article, I believed that general woman suffrage would be an inexpedient and venturesome experiment. I am willing, however, to admit that it was only after a more thorough appreciation of what female suffrage really means that I became fully convinced that its inauguration would vastly increase the unhappy imperfections and shortcomings of our present man-voting suffrage, and that it was only after a better knowledge of the spirit and disposition that stand behind it, gained from recent experience and observation, that I was entirely persuaded that its especial susceptibility to bad leadership and hurtful influences would constitute it another menacing condition to those which already vex and disturb the deliberate and intelligent expression of the popular will.

It will not do to suppose that a majority of the sensible and responsible women of the land desire suffrage and admittance to the activities of politics. On the contrary, there is now a great preponderance of these who either actively oppose all movements in this direction or are contentedly indifferent. A few years ago the question of allowing municipal suffrage in Massachusetts to women was submitted to all the voters of that State who were eligible to vote for school committees. The number of women at that time qualified to register and ballot on the question was about 575,000. Of these, more than 550,000 declined to vote. The total woman's vote cast in favor of the proposition was smaller than had sometimes been cast in school elections. There were forty-seven towns in which not one woman's ballot was cast in the affirmative, and in each of one hundred and thirty-eight other towns fifteen women or less so voted.

I think twenty States which refuse to women all other suffrage privileges permit them to vote for school officers, either without restriction or under certain conditions. It is alleged, however, that the number who avail themselves of this privilege is commonly very small. It is said with apparent authority that at the elections for school officers, which ought to interest all women who in good faith desire to be really useful by means of their suffrage, the proportion of women who vote in the State of New York is estimated at two per cent., in Connecticut at from one to two and a half per cent., and in Massachusetts ordinarily at not more than three or four per cent. The decrease of their desire to vote on this question is indicated by such statistics as these: in the city of Chicago 29,815 women registered as voters in 1894; but in 1898 the number was only 1488. In the year 1895, in the city of Cleveland, 5831 women registered; but in 1898 this number was reduced to 82.

THE WOMAN'S CLUB AS AN ALLY OF FEMALE SUFFRAGE

In the face of such an adverse majority and such indifference among their own sex it is not unreasonable to assume that the propagandists of female suffrage who continue to goad on the cause, rely considerably for final success upon the aid of the numerous woman's clubs, which, whatever their declared objects may be, are apt to pave the way to the reception of woman-suffrage radicalism. I have lately received a letter from a thoroughly conscientious lady which illustrates the gradation from membership in a moderate woman's club to the most extreme affiliations. While protesting in a delightfully womanly way against my views in regard to woman's clubs she frankly admitted the consequences, in her own case, of acquiring the club habit. She first joined a literary club for the "mutual improvement and culture" of its members, then an art club, then a civic club, and finally, having thus been brought within the influence of certain missionaries in the cause of female municipal suffrage, she became, and continues to be, an ardent convert to that doctrine. I do not claim that many instances have fallen under my observation which so completely demonstrate how apparently innocent club membership leads to unanticipated extremity. It is not unusual, however, for women in all stages of such membership to admit that the formation of the club habit is one of its frequent accompaniments. Our knowledge of human nature does not permit us to discredit the shrewdness of the advocates of female suffrage, who frequently encourage all sorts of woman's clubs, perfectly understanding how this habit can be utilized to open the female mind to the acceptance of their creed.

Another encouragement to those who propagate the doctrine of woman suffrage grows out of their reliance upon the chivalric consideration which the men of our nation, in the halls of legislation and everywhere, have for the female sex. A woman speaking in opposition to female suffrage before a Senate Committee a few years ago said:

"It is not the tyranny but the chivalry of men that we American women have to fear. The men of America want to give us everything we really need; and the danger is that they will mistake a minority for a majority."

A distinguished writer in dealing with the question declared:

"A woman has the inalienable right of attacking without being attacked in turn. She may strike, but must not be struck either literally or figuratively."

This is precisely as it should be—especially when women are within the sacred precincts of true womanhood. But after all is said or conceded, the question remains, whether, when woman deliberately breaks away from womanly environments and enters the arena of challenge and disputation, man's duty and reason should be silenced in deference to her demands and his mental forces given over to easy-going and undutiful gallantry.

THE BALLOT IS NOT WOMAN'S INHERENT RIGHT

Nothing can be more palpable than that a safe regulation of our suffrage lies at the very foundation of American free institutions; and of course nothing more important than this can engage the attention of those who make our laws. Legislators should never neglect the dictates of chivalry in their treatment of woman; but this does not demand that a smirking appearance of acquiescence should conceal or smother a thoughtful lawmaker's intelligent disapproval of female suffrage. It is one of the chief charms of women that they are not especially amenable to argument; but that is not a reason why, when they demand the ballot as an inherent right, they should not be reminded that suffrage is a privilege which attaches neither to man nor to woman by nature. Nor could it be deemed discourteous if, when they claim the right to vote because women are taxed as owners of property, it is pointed out to them that they are not the only persons taxed as property-holders from whom the ballot is withheld, and that under present conditions there is always a complete willingness to do every possible thing, by way of legislation, to secure and protect their property rights. Our statute books are full of proof of this.

I suppose it was only a willingness to indulge in flattering pleasantry that led a distinguished jurist, when lately addressing a large audience of young women at one of our prominent female colleges, to intimate that within the present generation the suffrage might be extended to women in every State, and to excite the enthusiastic applause of his emotional hearers by the hint that before they became gray-haired there might "sit in the White House a woman who, like Queen Victoria, will shed lustre upon this country as Victoria shed lustre upon England."

SOME RESULTS IN WOMAN-SUFFRAGE STATES

Those most active in pushing the demand for woman suffrage point in its vindication to what they deem wholesome legislation accomplished in the few States where such suffrage has been granted. I am afraid, however, that in dealing with this feature of the question these advocates occasionally take a mistaken view of the relationship between cause and effect. I believe it will be found that, if the wise and progressive legislation in these woman-suffrage States is weighed against such legislation in States where woman suffrage is withheld, the balance will certainly not be found against the latter. As bearing upon the credit due to woman voters for legislation where full female suffrage has been adopted, it is worth noting that the male voters exceptionally outnumber the female voters in all these localities.

It is sometimes claimed that woman suffrage would have the effect of elevating and refining politics. Neither its short trial in four States containing in the aggregate a population very slightly in excess of one-third the population of the city of New York nor our political experience or observation supports this claim. The States in which full female suffrage prevails are Colorado, Utah, Idaho and Wyoming. In the first two of these States the proportion of female voters is considerably greater than in the others; and yet the voters of Utah have lately elected through their Legislature to the United States Senate a man whose fitness is now the subject of a pending Senatorial investigation, and not long ago they elected to Congress another man whom that body rejected. These incidents may not go far toward discrediting woman suffrage, but they certainly do not indicate its invariably refining and elevating tendency.

NOT A CREDITABLE SHOWING IN COLORADO

I hope it will not be deemed ungracious if I refer to another circumstance which is at least interesting as a coincidence. Of the four States permitting full woman suffrage, Colorado should certainly be regarded as affording the best illustration of its results, as this State is most like the older States of the East in point of urban population, in the variety and extent of its business interests, and in the proportion of women to men among its residents of voting age. Less than two years ago a member of the House of Representatives from that State, holding his place by virtue of an apparent majority of the direct votes of the men and women of his district, resigned his seat for the reason, as he openly declared, that fraudulent votes had been cast for him in the election. An investigation of the case by a Congressional Committee developed the fact that some of the most glaring frauds were committed by women. A New York newspaper in February, 1904, published a summary of the evidence taken by the committee, from which it appeared that one woman, admitting her participation in these frauds, confessed among other political sins that she gave directions to the women who were to do repeating at the polls, and that two other women were associated with her in the manipulation of ballots, one of whom arranged to have a fight started at the election place, to afford opportunity to throw out the watchers and challengers of the other party. The resigning Congressman, with a show of characteristic masculine gallantry, gave it as his opinion that of the persons implicated very few were women—"not more than one in ten at the outside." It seems to me that this statement falls far short of mitigating the situation. The most gluttonous suffrage corruptor in the world ought to be a happy scoundrel if he could "implicate" in bringing about his ends ten out of every hundred voters.

ONE DELUSION OF FEMALE SUFFRAGE

I have sometimes wondered if the really good women who are inclined to approve this doctrine of female suffrage are not deluding themselves with purely sentimental views of the subject. Have they not in some way allowed the idea to gain a place in their minds that if the suffrage were accorded to women it would be the pure, the honest, the intelligent and the patriotic of the sex who would avail themselves of it? If they are drifting on the smooth surface of such a pleasing conceit as this it behooves them to take soundings and locate landmarks. They can perhaps thus bring themselves to a realization of the fact that among women, as is, unfortunately, the case now among men, it would not be the best and most responsible that would most diligently use their voting powers, and that, even if every woman in the land should exercise the suffrage, the votes of the thoughtful and conscientious would almost certainly be largely outweighed by those of the disreputable, the ignorant, the thoughtless, the purchased and the coerced. It is not to the purpose to say that even with all this the condition among women with the suffrage would be no worse than it now is among men. We need something better for the improvement of our suffrage, not an addition of the bad already existing. Do respectable and public-spirited women who favor female suffrage have a vague idea that all women endowed with the franchise can be taught to exercise the privilege intelligently and honestly? Who is to undertake this duty, and how? They may rely upon it that the condition of civic fitness in which the suffrage finds the great mass of women will grow worse instead of better. Vested with the power of suffrage equally with the best of their sex, the unintelligent and characterless would be inclined to resist the approach of those who assume with an air of superiority to give them instruction in voting duty. Nor could such approach be expected to end with mere resistance to teaching and influence. We all know how much further women go than men in their social rivalries and jealousies. Woman suffrage would give to the wives and daughters of the poor a new opportunity to gratify their envy and mistrust of the rich. Meantime these new voters would become either the purchased or cajoled victims of plausible political manipulators, or the intimidated and helpless voting vassals of imperious employers.

This phase of the suffrage question cannot better be presented than in the following words of another: "Women change politics less than politics change women."

THE EFFECT OF THE BALLOT ON WOMAN

I take the following quotation from a book I have lately read, written by a very painstaking and conscientious woman who has spent much time in personal investigation of all questions pertaining to woman's welfare and improvement. She is zealously in favor of woman's clubs, and, it seems to me, would be glad to advocate woman suffrage if she could; but not being a theorist, but a careful, practical investigator, her experience and observation do not permit her to go to that length. After spending considerable time and mingling with all sorts of people in Colorado, where the problem of woman suffrage can be better studied than anywhere else in the United States, she presents the result of her examination in language which I appropriate as my concluding words:

"However suffrage may be regarded as an abstract problem, it is not to be denied that in Colorado its use by women has, whatever else it may have done or failed to do, brought grave disaster upon those women. The possession of the ballot and the employment of that possession have hurt the women of Colorado as women can least afford to be hurt. . . . . Her ideals have been lowered; the delicacy of her perception of right and wrong has been dulled. Whatever good she may be able to render to her State and to the Nation by her vote, can that good, however great, compensate for the injury which she has wrought to that State and to the Nation by reason of the blow she has dealt her own womanhood?"

FINLEY PETER DUNNE

Mr. Dooley on Woman's Suffrage

JUNE 1909

Finley Peter Dunne (1867–1936) was an Irish American journalist who began his career at a Chicago newspaper. Starting in 1892, he began a weekly column under the guise of a character named Martin Dooley, who delivered monologues in dialect on a range of topics to a fictitious politician named John McKenna or to a millworker named Malachi Hennessey. In 1900 Dunne relocated to New York, where Mr. Dooley became one of the most popular characters in American journalism. In this piece published in *The American Magazine*, Mr. Dooley rambles at length on the topic of women's suffrage, recycling old tropes that dominated popular discussion at the time. But as Mr. Dooley holds forth, he actually exposes the hypocrisy of many of these arguments and builds sympathy for the cause. When Mr. Hennessey says he would no more talk to his wife about voting than she would to him about trimming a hat, Mr. Dooley says that maybe women getting the vote wouldn't be such a bad thing: "What this country needs is voters that knows something about housekeeping," precisely the point suffragists had been making for years.

"Well sir," said Mr. Dooley, "fr'm th' way this here female sufferage movement is sweepin' acrost th' counthry it won't be long befure I'll be seein' ye an' ye'er wife shthrollin' down th' shtreet to vote together."

"Niver," said Mr. Hennessy with great indignation. "It will niver come. A woman's place is in th' home darnin' her husband's childher. I mean——"

NO LONGER "FOR GENTLEMEN ONLY"

"I know what ye mean," said Mr. Dooley. "'Tis a favrite argymint iv mine whin I can't think iv annything to say. But ye can't help it, Hinnessy. Th' time is near at hand whin iliction day will mean no more to ye thin anny other day with th' fam'ly. Up to th' prisint moment it has been a festival marked: 'For gintlemen on'y.' It's been a day whin shtrong men cud go foorth, unhampered be th' prisince iv ladies, an' f'r th' honor iv their counthry bite each other. It was a day whin it was proper an' right f'r ye to slug ye'er best frind.

"But th' fair sect are goin' to break into this fine, manly spoort an' they'll change it. No more will ye leap fr'm ye'er bed on iliction mornin', put a brick in ye'er pocket an' go out to bounce ye'er impeeryal vote against th' walls iv inthrenched privilege. No more will ye spind th' happy mornin' hours meetin' ye'er frinds an' th' akelly happy avenin' hours receivin' none but inimies.

"No sir, in a few years, as soon as ye've had ye'er breakfast, ye'er fellow citizen who, as th' pote says, doubles ye'er expinses an' divides ye'er salary, will say to ye: 'Well, it's about time we wint down to th' polls an' cast my votes. An' I do wish ye'd tie ye'er necktie sthraight. Honorya, bring me me new bonnet an' me Cashmere shawl an' get papa his stove pipe hat.' Thin ye'll be walked down th' sthreet, with a procission iv other married men in their best clothes an' their wanst a week shoes that hurt their feet. Th' sthreets will look like Easter Sundah. Ye'll meet ye'er frinds an' their wives comin' fr'm th' pollin' place an' talk with thim on th' corner.

"'Good morning, Michael.'

"'Ah, good morning, Cornelius.'

"'A delightful morning is it not f'r th' exercise iv th' franchise.'

"'Perfect! Howiver, I fear that such a morning may bring out a large republican vote.'

"'I hope our frind Baumgarten will succeed in his candydacy.'

"'I heartily agree with ye—he will make an excellent coroner, he's such good company.'

"'Yes, indeed, a charming fellow f'r a Dutchman. Cud I prevail on ye an' ye'er lady to come an' have a tub iv ice cream sody with us?'

"'Thank ye, Cornelius, we wud be delighted, but three is all I can hold. Shall I see ye at th' magic lanthern show to-night?'

"'Th' pollin' place won't be in th' office iv a livry stable or a barber shop, but in a pleasant boodwar. As ye enter th' dure ye won't say to th' polisman on jooty: 'Good mornin', Pete; anny murdhers so far?'"

OUR RECENT IMPORTATIONS IN BALLOTS

"But wan iv th' judges will come forward an' bow an' say: 'Madam, can I show ye annything in ballots? This blue is wan iv our recent importations, but here is a tasty thought in ecru. F'r th' gintleman I'd ricommind something in dark brown to match th' socks. Will that be all? Th' last booth on th' right is unoccypied. Perhaps ye'er husband wud like to look at a copy iv th' *Ladies Home Journal* while ye'er preparin' th' ballots.'

"Ye needn't get mad about it, Hinnessy. Ye might as well face it. It's sure to come now that I see be th' pa-apers that female suffrage has been took up be ladies in our best s'ciety. It used to be diff'rent. Th' time was whin th' on'y female sufferigists that ye iver see were ladies, Gawd bless thim, that bought their millinery th' same place I buy mine, cut their hair short, an' discarded all iv their husband's names excipt what was useful f'r alimony.

"A fine lot iv rugged pathrites they were.

"I used to know wan iv thim—Docthor Arabella Miggs—as fine an' old gintleman as ye iver see in a plug hat, a long coat an' bloomers. She had ivry argymint in favor iv female suffrage that ye iver heerd, an' years ago she made me as certain that women were entitled to a vote as that ye are entitled to my money.

"Ye are entitled to it if ye can get it. They ain't anny argymint against female suffrage that wudden't make me lible to arrest ivry time I'm seen near a pollin' place. But it isn't argymints or statistics that alters things in th' wurruld. Th' thick end iv a baseball bat will change a man's mind quicker an' more permanently thin anny discoorse.

"So th' first iv thim lady sufferigists had a hard time iv it, an' little boys used to go to their meetings to hoot at thim, an' they were took up in th' sthreet be polismen f'r pretindin' to look like gintlemen, an' th' pa-apers wud no more think iv printin' their speeches thin iv printin' a sermon in a church.

"Now, be hivens, 'tis diff'rent. 'Tis far diff'rent. I pick up th' pa-apers an' read:

"'Gr-reat suffrage revival. Society queens take up th' cause. In th' magnificent L. Quince dhrawin' rooms iv Mrs. Percy Lumley's mansion in Mitchigan avnoo yesterdah afthernoon wan iv th' most successful suffrage teas iv th' season was held. Mrs. Lumley, who presided, was perfectly ravishing in a blue taffeta which set off her blonde beauty to perfection. She wore pearls an' carried a bunch iv American beauty roses. On th' platform with her were Mrs. Archibald Fluff, in green bombyzine with a pink coal scuttle hat, Mrs. Alfonso Vanboozen in a light yellow creation cut demi thrain an' manny other leaders iv th' smart set.'"

SENDING YOUR VOTE BY THE FOOTMAN

"'A spirited debate was held over th' pint whether something shudden't be done to induce th' department stores to put in polling places. Wan dhream iv beauty asked whether if it rained iliction day wud th' iliction be held or postponed f'r betther weather. Th' chairman ruled that th' iliction wud have to go on rain or shine. "Iv coorse," says she, "in very bad weather we cud sind th' footman down with our votes. But we must not expict to gain this great reform without some sacrifice. (Applause.) In anny case th' tillyphone is always handy."

"'A lady in th' aujeence wanted to know how old a lady wud have to be befure she cud vote. Says th' chairman: "To be effective th' reform must be thorough. I am in favor iv makin' it legal f'r ivry woman to vote no matther how old she is an' I, therefore, wud put th' maximum age at a lib'ral figure, say thirty years. This gives all iv us a chance." (Cheers.) Afther th' meetin', a few voters dhropped in f'r an informal dance. Among those presint was.'

"An' there ye are. Ain't I again female sufferage? Iv coorse I am. Th' place f'r these spiled darlings is not in th' hurly burly iv life but in th' home, be th' fireside or above th' kitchen range. What do they know about th' vast machinery iv governmint? Ye an' I, Hinnissy, are gifted with a supeeryor intilligence in these matthers. Our opposition to a tariff is based on large pathriotic grounds. We have thought th' subjick out carefully, applyin' to it minds so sthrong that they cud crush a mountain an' so delicate that they cud pick up a sheet iv gold foil. We are in favor iv abolishin' th' tariff because it has thrown around this counthry a Chinese wall; because we are bribed be British goold fr'm th' Parsee merchant who riprisints th' Cobden Republican Marchin' Club iv London, England; because th' foreigner does or does not pay th' tax; because Sam'l J. Tilden was again th' tariff; because th' ultimate consumer must be proticted.

"Larkin on th' other hand, blessed with a republican intelleck since eighteen eighty four whin he become a protectionist because James G. Blaine was a fine man, annyway ye took him, is in favor iv a tariff on borax, curled hair, copra, steel ingots, an' art because cheap clothes makes a cheap man; because th' star spangled banner an long may it wag; because th' party that put down th' rebellyon an' stormed th' heights iv Lookout Mountain an' sthrewed th' bloody field iv Anteetam is th' same party (applause) that to-day is upholdin' th' tax on hides undher th' leadership iv th' incomp'rable hero Seerinio D. Payne. Often have I set here listenin' to ye an' Larkin discussin' this here question, wan moment thinkin' that I was as fine a pathrite as th' goose that saved Rome, be payin' more f'r me pants thin they were worth an' another moment fearin' I was a thraitor to th' flag f'r buyin' pants at all undher this accursed tariff. Both iv ye want to do what's best f'r th' counthry.

"But if ye put th' question up to th' ladies, if women undherstood th' tariff, which th' poor crathers don't, ye'd find they were against it f'r no higher reason thin that it made thim pay too much f'r th' childher's shoes an' stockin's. Can ye imagine annything baser thin that, to rejooce a great question like th' tariff down to a personal level, take all th' music an' pothry out iv it an' say: 'I'm again it, not because it has lowered th' morality iv ivrywan that it has binifitted, but because it's a shame that I have to pay eighty-six cints a pair f'r stockin's.'"

LIFE SPENT AT THE BARGAIN COUNTER

"Women take a selfish view iv life. But what can ye expict fr'm a petted toy iv man's whim that has spent most iv her life thryin' to get four dollars worth iv merchandise f'r two dollars an' a half? Th' foolish, impractical little fluffy things! It wud be a shame to let thim hurl thimsilves into th' coorse battles iv pollyticks. How cud ye explain to wan iv these ideelists why we have th' Phlippeens an' th' Sandwich Islands, an' why we keep up a navy to protict Denver, Colorado.

"We don't hear much about sufferage up our way in Ar-rchy road an' th' ladies that have got out their noblest hats in behalf iv th' cause complain that they can't stir up anny excitement among th' more numerous ladies that prefer to wear a shawl on their heads. Maybe th' reason is that these fair dhreamers haven't been able to figure out that a vote is goin' to do thim anny good. P'raps if ye asked ye'er wife about it she'd say:

"'Well, ye've had ye'er vote f'r forty years. F'r forty years ye've governed this counthry be a freeman's ballot an' ye'er salary an' perquisites at th' mills still amounts to a dollar an' eighty-five cints a day. If a vote hasn't done ye anny more good thin that I don't think I can spare time fr'm me domestic jooties to use wan. I will continue to look afther th' fam'ly, which is th' on'y capital a poor man can accumylate to protict him fr'm poverty in his old age. I'll stay at home an' see that th' boys an' girls are saved up ontil they are old enough to wurruk f'r us. An' if ye want to amuse ye'erself be votin' go on an' do it. Ye need recreation wanst in a while, an' ye'er vote don't do anny wan no harm.'

"I wudden't talk to me wife about votin' anny more thin she'd talk to me about thrimmin' a hat," said Mr. Hennessy.

"Well," said Mr. Dooley, "if she gets a vote maybe she'll thrim it to please ye. Annyhow it won't be a bad thing. What this country needs is voters that knows something about housekeeping."

ALICE HILL CHITTENDEN

The Counter Influence to Woman Suffrage
JULY 29, 1909

Alice Hill Chittenden (1869–1945) first surfaced in suffrage history in 1894 when she attended an antisuffrage meeting with her mother. Twenty-five years old at the time, she devoted the next twenty-five to the antisuffrage cause. Born in Brooklyn to an elite family that sent her to Miss Porter's school in Farmington, Connecticut, Chittenden bridged the conservatism of antisuffragism's late nineteenth-century beginnings with its increasing activism in the twentieth. Here she rises to the challenge advanced in a 1909 magazine editorial: "If you don't agree with them (the suffragists) you ought to think of some way of stemming the rising tide in favor of woman suffrage." To that end Chittenden marshaled evidence, mainly from the western states, demonstrating a pattern of defeats and setbacks that belied the notion that giving women the vote was inevitable or beneficial. Chittenden even drew a causal relation between the founding of the organized antisuffrage movement in 1894 and the lack of success since then. But the year 1909 was about the last time that antisuffragists could claim to be holding the suffrage movement in check. In 1910 Washington State passed a suffrage referendum, followed the next year by California; by 1914, Arizona, Kansas, Oregon, Nevada, and Montana had enfranchised women. When Chittenden became president of the National Association Opposed to Woman Suffrage in January 1913, she confronted a vastly changed political landscape.

———————

In a recently published magazine article on the subject of the woman suffrage propaganda, this challenge was thrown down in an editorial note, "If you don't agree with them (the suffragists) you ought to think of some way of stemming the rising tide in favor of woman suffrage."

Lists of woman suffrage "gains" are published from time to time in our daily papers, but a careful study of these statistics will disclose the fact that during the past decade these "gains" have been made chiefly in countries where monarchical government prevails, while here in our own republic only a few minor woman suffrage measures have been enacted during the same period. On the other hand, a study of some of the recent defeats and checks which woman suffrage has received in this country will not only disprove the theory that the tide is rising in its favor, but will confirm the statement made by so close an observer of social conditions as Mrs. Humphry Ward, who, after her visit here last spring, said: "After half a century of agitation, the woman suffrage movement in the United States is obviously declining, put down by the common sense of the women themselves." What are some of the facts upon which Mrs. Ward based this statement, which is sure to be challenged by those who mistake a campaign of English suffragette methods for an increasing sentiment in favor of granting women the elective franchise?

The vote on this question in the State of Oregon a year ago last June, when compared with the vote there in previous years, furnishes considerable proof of the truth of her assertion. Situated as it is in comparatively close proximity to the four suffrage States—Wyoming, Utah, Colorado and Idaho—the suffragists have continuously claimed that Oregon would soon "fall in line" and become the fifth star in the suffrage flag. Working with untiring energy, they have succeeded in bringing this question before the voters of that State to vote upon three times in the past eight years, with the following results:

In 1900, a constitutional amendment in favor of woman suffrage having passed the legislature, was submitted to the people at the polls. At that time 28,402 votes were cast against the measure and 26,265 in its favor, there being an unrecorded vote on this particular question of 27,283. The provisions of the act of initiative and referendum, which Oregon adopted soon after that, enabled the suffragists in 1906 to simply file a petition with the Secretary of State for a constitutional amendment without first appealing to the Legislature. In full confidence that this easy method of bringing the question before the people would assure their success, the suffragists waged a vigorous campaign in every county of the State, and sent twelve of their best speakers into the field. The official count showed that 47,075 votes were registered against the amendment, while 36,902 were recorded in favor of it, making a majority of 10,173, or almost five times as large a majority against the question as in the previous election of 1900. Ten counties went on record as being in favor of woman suffrage, while twenty-three opposed it. Disappointed, but not disheartened, the suffragists started in almost immediately on another campaign, and succeeded in bringing this question again before the people to vote upon. The official returns from the election held June 4, 1908, must dispel every shadow of doubt from the minds of the unprejudiced regarding the sentiment which prevails in Oregon on the question of giving the ballot to women, for while the amendment this year polled 36,858 affirmative votes, 58,670 were recorded against it, a significant majority of 21,812, while only four counties instead of ten were carried by the suffragists.

These figures when studied as a whole show that over 30,000 more votes were cast against granting the franchise to women in 1908 than were recorded against it in 1900, while in the same length of time, and despite their three campaigns of unceasing vigor, the suffragists only succeeded in increasing the votes in their favor by a little over 10,000. To what counter influence then was this steadily increased sentiment against women suffrage in Oregon due?

Wholly to a campaign of education along the broadest sociological lines, carried on quietly and persistently by a small number of intelligent, clear-visioned women in Oregon, who earnestly believe, with many others of their sex thruout the country, that a sovereign state recognizes the natural law of the differentiation of sex activity when it exempts its women citizens from certain duties which it imposes upon its male citizens, and, furthermore, that this law should not be abrogated merely because a few women desire to add political responsibilities to their already manifold duties.

But Mrs. Ward did not base her statement that woman suffrage is obviously declining in the United States solely on the figures of the three elections in Oregon. She had an array of other facts to prove the truth of her conclusions—facts to which the general public should give heed when they hear it said, that woman suffrage is inevitable and that all opposition to it is futile. What are some of them?

In four States, as has already been stated, women exercise the full power of the elective franchise. The history of how suffrage came to be granted to women in those States is closely interwoven with the development, at one time and another, of various populistic doctrines in that section of the country.

Woman suffrage existed in Utah and Wyoming in the days when they were still Territories. The suffragists are not very proud of Utah, and do not like to be reminded that the women voters of that State helped to send Mr. Brigham H. Roberts, a Mormon with three wives, to the House of Representatives in Washington. Every one remembers that Mr. Roberts was not allowed to take his seat, and it was said at the time that the protests against seating him which the Congressmen received from the non-voting women of the other States were largely responsible for his exclusion by a vote of 268 to 50.

The women of Colorado obtained the ballot in 1892 by the small majority of 5,000 out of a vote of 200,000, while in Idaho in 1896 the result was so close it had to be referred to the Supreme Court for decision. Since that date, thirteen years ago, no State has granted either full suffrage or even municipal suffrage to women. In fact, the suffragists can only point to a few measures of minor importance which have been enacted in their favor in any of the forty-six States during this period. Delaware, for instance, had school suffrage to tax-paying women in 1898, and since then Louisiana and New York have granted suffrage to women taxpayers under certain conditions, but in the latter State this only applies in towns and villages. A new clause in Michigan's constitution entitles women who own property to vote upon questions of appropriations, but the proposition to admit women to full suffrage was defeated in the constitutional convention.

If these are the suffrage gains in this country since 1896, what are some of the defeats which the movement has suffered during the same length of time? In the same year in which Idaho, with its small and widely scattered population, became a "suffrage State," the voters of California, the great State of the Pacific Coast, defeated a constitutional amendment for women suffrage. In South Dakota and Washington a similar measure was defeated in 1898. New Hampshire voted against woman suffrage in 1903, and we have seen how the question has been lost three times at the polls in Oregon. Last year the constitutional convention of the new State, Oklahoma, refused to embody in their constitution a provision granting women the ballot.

In addition to these defeats when this question has been

taken to the polls, there is the long list of legislative defeats of woman suffrage measures in the several States year after year. In 1908 the legislatures of eight States either rejected or defeated such bills, and in 1907 similar bills were defeated in sixteen States.

In twenty-nine States women exercise a more or less limited form of school suffrage, but the indifference of women to this form of voting is evidenced by the following figures: At the legislative hearing on a municipal suffrage bill in the State House at Boston last winter, the facts were brought out, that whereas 700,000 women in Massachusetts were qualified to vote for school committees, the number actually voting thruout the State fell from 18,483 in 1906 to 13,619 in 1907. In 189 towns in Massachusetts in 1907, where 3,068 women were registered as voters, not one woman voted. The Bridgeport (Connecticut) *Farmer* of November 5, 1908, said:

> "Despite the prominence of the woman suffrage movement in New York, there was not a single woman who cared to exercise her rights during the last election to vote on the school question in this city. The town clerk provided the necessary ballot boxes and ballots in each district, and after the city had gone to this great expense, not a single member of the fair sex came out to vote."

In Cleveland, Ohio, 6,681 women qualified to vote for school officers in 1904, while three years later, in 1907, only 3,179 registered, showing a decrease of 2,502. A leading paper of that city comments on "the surprising lack of interest shown by women in the school board election." These facts in regard to school suffrage are now so widely known, that within three years five States have refused to grant this form of suffrage to women, and in two States, Ohio and Connecticut, the question of repealing this law has been seriously considered.

Kansas holds a unique position on this question. In 1887 municipal suffrage was granted to the women of that State, but since that time every effort to extend the full franchise to them has failed. Even when it was submitted to the people at the polls to vote upon, a majority of 34,827 was recorded against it. It is our municipal government which is today almost a national disgrace, and the advocates of woman suffrage are prone to argue that a ballot in woman's hands would purify politics. After twenty-one years of municipal suffrage in Kansas, have women voters there wrought any great changes in the government of its cities? If so, the knowledge of it has not reached the outside world.

These statistics do not furnish much evidence of a rising tide in favor of woman suffrage in the United States, but, on the contrary, show that the movement has received a severe check, and that this check, as Mrs. Ward truly says, has come from the women themselves.

During the past sixty years a swift current of varied forces has swept woman away from the quiet moorings of home and turned her adrift on the turbulent sea of economic independence. During this period colleges and universities have likewise opened their doors to her, and today there is scarcely a recognized profession or trade which does not number women in its ranks. A study of the statute books of any State shows how many laws have been enacted in woman's favor, until now she has many legal privileges to which no man may lay claim. All these movements have developed without any serious opposition, because thoughtful men and women have recognized that they were largely due to natural causes. But the fact that within recent years the agitation in favor of woman suffrage has met with organized opposition at once differentiates it and sets it apart from all the other so-called woman's movements.

There is undeniable magic in the word progress, and the phrase, "When you oppose the extension of suffrage to women you retard woman's progress," appeals to many as an argument in its favor. But progress to be genuine must accord with natural laws, and the demand that woman shall now assume the burden of political responsibility is at distinct variance with two natural laws. First, the essential and intended difference in sex activity, and, secondly, the great law of evolution which teaches that the development of the race has been a continuous growth in specialization. A recent writer has said:

> "Either sex is an appalling blunder or else it must have been intended that each sex should have its own work to do, not merely in the physical economy of the race, but also in the social and intellectual world."

There is no economy in having two people do the same work. This leads to diffusion, or a tendency to weaken the forces, while concentrated effort or specialization strengthens the natural powers.

The open opposition to woman suffrage in the country started in the early nineties, or shortly after the ballot had been given to the women of Colorado. A few thoughtful women in New York, Massachusetts and Illinois began to consider the woman suffrage question seriously and to study some of the sociological principles which it involved. Of what benefit will the ballot be to women themselves, and what possible advantage will accrue to the State by doubling its voting population? These were two of the questions asked, and in 1894, when the constitutional convention met in New York State, an answer to these questions was formulated and placed at the head of the protest against woman suffrage which was sent to the constitutional convention by a committee of Brooklyn women:

> "The women who bring this matter to your attention have, from a studious contemplation of governmental principles involved, come to a firm conviction that woman suffrage would be against the best interests of the State, its women and the home."

This is the platform upon which the anti-suffragist in the United States stands today, and in opposing the extension of the suffrage to her sex she is animated by the highest motives of patriotism. The personal element is entirely eliminated from her view of the question. She does not oppose giving the ballot to women, because, as is so often asserted, she herself does not wish to vote, but because she sincerely believes that in the ideal State the duties of man and woman should not be similar, but rather correlated. As these fundamental sociological principles which underlie the woman suffrage question are becoming more widely recognized, the old time semi-chivalrous argument, "If the women want to vote, we will let them," is less often heard, and the suffragists are having a harder time convincing the general public that they are suffering from disabilities and wrongs which the ballot would right.

Even their oft repeated claim that a working woman's pay would advance if she had the ballot cannot be substantiated by facts. The ballot never raised men's wages, and it is nothing less than a delusion to suppose or expect that it would have the least effect on the wages of the working girl. The law of supply and demand will be the controlling factor in the regulation of wages of the working woman as long as there are more applicants for the positions in factories and commercial houses than there are available places. Furthermore, the temporary character of woman's work tends to keep her wages down. The girl enters a factory or business house with the idea, in nine cases out of ten, that she will stay there a few years until she is married. Her work is therefore largely unskilled, and as such cannot command high wages. No one can close his eyes to the fact that the road traveled by the woman who has been forced into a position of economic independence is hard and difficult, but it is a false notion to suppose that the ballot will be the panacea to bring about the much needed changes in the conditions under which she works.

It is easier to pull down than to build up, and it is this present day tendency toward destructive principles rather than constructive ones which the anti-suffragists are combating with much earnestness and with a firm conviction of the truth of their contentions, when they oppose the extension of the suffrage to their sex. The fact that since the public enunciation of their principles in the early nineties there has not been a single suffrage gain of any importance in any State in this country shows that there is considerable strength in this counter movement to woman suffrage.

BROOKLYN, N. Y.

FLORENCE H. LUSCOMB

Our Open-Air Campaign

1909

The women's suffrage movement had long relied on tactics such as gathering signatures on petitions, lobbying legislators for suffrage bills, organizing women's suffrage organizations on the local, state, and national levels, and trying to win favorable publicity for the women's cause. But decades of such agitation had not brought the movement much closer to success, so around 1909, suffrage leaders began to experiment with new ways to reach voters and stimulate interest in the cause. Brazenly discarding any lingering notions of protected Victorian womanhood and influenced by the tactics of militant British suffragists, Massachusetts women began holding open-air meetings and selling suffrage newspapers on street corners like newsboys. Florence H. Luscomb (1887–1985), who had just graduated from the Massachusetts Institute of Technology with a degree in architecture, was one of these brave women. Here she recounts what it was like to speak at an open-air meeting, right down to the small boys and inevitable dogs who filled out the crowd.

Equal Suffrage is not held back by opposition. That helps us. We are handicapped by indifference and its resulting ignorance. However unjustly, the burden of proof is laid upon us. We, being shut out of the franchise, are required to prove our case in order to get in. Now, just because we live in a semi-republic we have got to prove our case, not to a small body of lawmakers, but to a large body of the people, those who elect the lawmakers, and to prove it to them we must make them listen. How? They are not interested in Woman Suffrage, do not expect to appeal to them through the subject, but reach them by curiosity, by the commendable human desire to be well informed on the affairs of the day. If they are uninterested it is because you have not made the subject interesting. Make it so. Make it picturesque. This is what the English women have accomplished. Then when you have made it picturesque there is one other step; make it easy. Remember that you are dealing with the average human being, busy and tired. Is it not a trifle arrogant to expect him, at the end of a day's work, to come to you, to hear you speak on your chosen topic? At any rate he certainly does not come. It follows that you must go to him.

I do not decry indoor meetings. Once you have caught their attention, the semi-interested and the semi-converted will flock in. An outdoor meeting is sketchy, only partially heard, and intended merely to lay down the fundamental principles of the justice and expediency of our cause. It requires more solid stuff to build earnest convictions and ardent supporters. This is the field of the meetings in halls and parlors. But for the large number of our new recruits and for the stirring of public interest you must rely largely on the out-of-door campaign. Realizing this, several Boston ladies, members of the Equal Suffrage Association, organized themselves independently under the title of the VOTES FOR WOMEN COMMITTEE to carry on the out-of-door work. This has been three-fold. First, meetings held from Boston as headquarters covering all nearby towns. Second, the trip covering the whole State. Third, work at the various county fairs. The latter was carried on chiefly by the Boston Equal Suffrage Association for Good Government.

The meetings carried on from Boston were all which were at first contemplated. These were to be held on Saturday afternoons, and the speaking party was to go out in an automobile loaned by one of the members. A tentative meeting at Bedford (near Lexington) was first undertaken to see how the new scheme would work. Two days before the meeting all the surrounding towns and country were thoroughly billed with large yellow posters which were placed in store windows, nailed to telegraph poles, and spread upon the sign post of every country crossroad. Saturday came, and with it came the deluge. The speakers, indeed, were there, but only the dripping elms of the old Town Common stood round for audience. Not to be foiled, the committee planned a second meeting for the next Saturday. More bills were printed and posted as before. This time the women were rewarded for their perseverance by a beautiful June day. Three o'clock was the hour set, and by three were assembled half a dozen Suffragists, twenty children under twelve years of age, and one policeman. Mrs. Fitzgerald, Secretary of the B.E.S.A. for G. G. offers herself as victim to set the ball rolling. She opened by remarking that we were highly gratified to see that this subject was attracting such attention and receiving such serious consideration from so many of the younger generation, to whom it was of such paramount importance. A very few minutes of this sufficed while a less juvenile audience was gathering and then the serious arguments were taken up. There were about five speakers, talking about ten or fifteen minutes apiece. Meanwhile, helpers circulated the petition on the outskirts of the crowd. Our audience at this first meeting totalled a hundred, and thirteen signatures were obtained.

Right here I want to tell you what outdoor speaking is *not* like. The majority of people who have never been to our open air meetings have already decided what they are like, down to the minutest detail as to what variety of vegetable is thrown at the speaker. Although every one knows from experience that an American woman can stand in a hall and address American men with dignity and earnestness on her part, and courtesy and interest on theirs, yet, presto, remove the roof and the same woman must become a ranting fanatic, the same men are jeering hooligans. Now I have spoken at more than a score of sky-roofed meetings this summer, to audiences varying from twenty-five to two thousand, at mill gates and at fashionable summer resorts, but have never seen anything which would disgrace an indoor meeting.

The open air meetings promising so well, they were continued throughout the summer. It was found best to hold two meetings in nearby towns each Saturday; one at four o'clock and the other at seven-thirty. The time and strength required were but little more than one meeting consumed, and far less than would be needed to make two separate trips. Meetings were also held on Wednesday afternoons at various beaches. This being the marketman's day off, the seashore is almost as well attended on that day as on Saturday.

From the success of these meetings around Boston Mrs. Fitzgerald gradually developed the idea of sending out a party which should spend the month of August touring the State and speaking in all the more important towns. The route as laid out went Westerly through the Northern towns, swung around and returned through the Southern part of the State, taking in the Marshfield and Barnstable County Fairs. We aspired to go by automobile; we went by trolley. We spoke three times a day, generally in three separate towns, except as an entire day was devoted to such cities as Fall River and New Bedford. The party was made up of four ladies,—Mrs. Fitzgerald, commander-in-chief and orator-in-chief, went for the whole month, as did also Miss Edith Haynes, a Boston lawyer. For the first half of the trip Mrs. Dennett (Mary Ware Dennett) and Miss Alfretta McClure accompanied them; and for the last two weeks Miss Katherine Tyng, Radcliffe '09, and I had the pleasure of being the other two members.

The paraphernalia of the trip consisted of one large yellow banner six feet long inscribed in black, "Votes for Women," a jointed flagstaff for the same made to fold in to three pieces, and a heavy, heavy suitcase of literature and buttons. Besides this, each member had her individual suitcase, and there was a bundle of umbrellas.

Picture our party unloading from a street-car in the central square of some little country town. This in itself is a lengthy operation. Then we make for the nearest drug store, deposit all our luggage in one corner, and to compensate for its storage all of us are in duty bound to buy sodas. We have consumed innumerable soft drinks for the sake of the cause, and have become authorities upon the drugstores of Massachusetts. While we drink, the drug clerk is cross-examined as to where the best audience can be collected, time of trolleys, hotel for the night, union or non-union, what they manufacture, and a few dozen other similar things. Meanwhile, if the town is large enough for us to require a permit to speak, Mrs. Fitzgerald has interviewed the police. Our leaflets are then unpacked, our flag erected, we borrow a Moxie box from the obliging drug clerk and proceed to the busiest corner of the town square. Our chief mounts the box, the banner over her shoulder, and starts talking to the air, three assorted dogs, six kids, and the two loafers in front of the grocery store just over the way. The rest of us give handbills to all the passersby and to all the nearby stores. Within ten minutes our audience has increased to from twenty-five to five hundred, according to the time and place. We speak in turn for an hour or more, answer questions, sell buttons, and circulate the petition. Then we leave, generally in undignified haste, to catch our car for the next meeting. At New Bedford, all loaded down as we were, we fairly charged for a block down the middle of a street lined on either side by people waiting for their cars.

Such were the afternoon and evening meetings. The noon ones were slightly different in character. These were held at the mill gates in factory towns. If there were several mills in town, or several entrances to the same mill, our party was divided so that sometimes each of the four held an independent meeting. As the workers came out at noon we gave out the bills and announced speaking at half past. They returned early from dinner, and we had a half hour of speaking. These meetings were very interesting. The audience was there ready to be entertained, often sympathetic in advance; and I know some of us enjoyed the experience of being thrown on our own resources, with the entire subject to handle in that short time.

Ordinarily, of course, the arguments were divided up between us to prevent repetition and insure completeness.

During the speaking we circulated the petition as quietly as possible on the outskirts of the crowd. We found it best not to attempt to get many signatures during the speaking as it created too much disturbance. Whenever we had time to stop after the meeting we did canvas the audience pretty thoroughly, but this was not often. For this reason we averaged a smaller percentage of signatures on the trip than at the meetings carried on around Boston, where we were not so hurried.

The trip was by no means all hard work. The first week, while the party was passing through the Berkshires, meetings were far apart, and time for rest and meals scant. Later on, however, in the more thickly settled regions, travelling was not so hard although we never had much time to spare. The motto adopted to describe the trip was, "plain thinking, hard talking, any old kind of living." One other of our collection was, "Gather ye rosebuds while ye may," which being interpreted read, "Sit down every time you get a chance." Nevertheless it was a pleasant trip to travel in the fresh air through pleasant country and picturesque towns.

We were an inexhaustible source of wonder and interest to the small boy. He dogged our footsteps clamouring for literature; he audibly surmised whether we were Salvation Army or Anti-tuberculosis, and the climax of his joy was attained when we allowed him to carry our banner.

Our other constant admirers were the dogs. I feel hardly at home now at a meeting at which there is not at least one dog present, preferably yellow; and when there are a dozen dogs of assorted sizes, colors, and howls, Oh, that is bliss! We even reveled in dog-fights; for, as our chief remarked while we were enjoying one such experience, "After all, there is nothing to draw a crowd like a dog-fight."

Several times we found ourselves competing with the Salvation Army. In New Bedford they had even begun a meeting on the spot where they generally met, but which our permit allowed to us for that evening. They were very nice, indeed, when it was explained to them, and cheerfully adjourned to another square. They left some of their audience to us, however, so the saying was reversed, and those who came to pray remained to scoff. In one city we were rivalled by a Mormon meeting, but they were soon persuaded to withdraw to a comfortable distance. Once we were permitted to speak on a certain street, the only stipulation by the police being that we should not block the entrance to the hotel bar.

Our only real sacrifices came at night. Those of you who have stopped at the ordinary hotel of the small mill town know whereof I speak. Sometimes they were fairly good; sometimes not. Never shall I forget our room of the smell. It was really amusing to see us down on our hands and knees crawling around the room, stopping once in a while to smell of the carpet or furniture. It was of no avail. No concentrate and removable odor was discovered,—only the general permeation which could not be thrown out of the window. Once we thought we had found our skeleton in the closet, but the door was locked and vigorous sniffing at the keyhole failed to fasten the crime there, so we went to bed and endeavored to drown all our discomforts in sleep. We called that our dead dog room.

Experiences such as this made us appreciate our treatment in Fall River. A Mrs. Hyde, hearing that we were to reach town that night walked the street near the car-station until we arrived, near midnight, and then bore the whole party off to her own home. She slept on a sofa that we might have a comfortable bed and sent us off in the morning rested, and cheered by a good breakfast.

We spent one day at the Marshfield Fair, and one at the

Barnstable Fair. This work was of the kind done at all the county fairs this fall. We found speechmaking to be impracticable; the people were there solely to be amused, and we could not compete with the noise and confusion of the other clamorous entertainments. Instead, we carried on individual work. We approached anyone who was not engrossed with one of the fakirs, handed out our leaflets, and asked for a signature to the petition. Whenever it seemed worthwhile we stopped and argued the matter, answering objections and stating our case. We often got signatures in this way from persons at first unfavorable, or at least left behind us a more serious and impartial thought on the matter. We found that each one of us could obtain about fifty signatures by a day of hard work.

Mrs. Fitzgerald was inspired with the plan of winding up our tour by a grand meeting on Boston Common. The newspapers announced that the state trolley-trippers would arrive at a certain hour and march in a torchlight parade to the Common, which was going us one better and served to arouse even more public interest. On the eventful evening an audience of two thousand assembled. We spoke in turn, standing on an empty waste-paper barrel, which, as one speaker remarked, was an indication that women in politics might be expected to interest themselves in civic housecleaning. So large was the audience that we had speaking simultaneously from two platforms, and smaller meetings on the outskirts gathered around the different workers. The crowd was most deeply interested, and lingered after the speaking in knots of discussion while we passed the petition,—lingered indeed, even after we were forced to leave.

I am continually hearing echoes of this meeting in odd and interesting ways, such as the following. When making a purchase in a store one day, the clerk said to me, "Didn't I hear you speak on the Common one night?" I pleaded guilty, and asked if he were interested in the subject. "Why, yes," he rejoined, "I am, and my wife is very much interested indeed. Before that night I didn't know very much about it and I had always thought that there were a few cranks pushing it. But that night I saw that it was earnest, intelligent, refined women, who had convictions and were not afraid to stand up and say so."

Was our summer campaign successful? Did it pay? A few figures will answer. We have spoken to 24,900 people, and given literature to thousands of others. The expense of the trolley trip was about one hundred dollars a week, which includes fares and living expenses for four, cost of literature, press notices, and all other incidentals. We held sixty-eight meetings,—fifteen of them at factories. Altogether this summer we have held 97 meetings at an average cost of $6.62 a meeting, with an average audience of 257, and have obtained over 2000 signatures to the National Petition. I think you will agree with me that it was a splendid success.

JANE ADDAMS

Why Women Should Vote
January 1910

Jane Addams (1860–1935) founded Hull House in Chicago in 1889, a pioneering social experiment that brought college-educated reformers and activists to inner-city neighborhoods where they lived, worked, and learned from the poor firsthand. Soon settlement houses sprang up in cities across the country. Addams used her Hull House plat-form to engage with a wide range of turn-of-the-century progressive reforms, including lobbying for juvenile courts and playgrounds and agitating for laws to improve working conditions in factories as well as urban sanitation. She also belonged to the National Child Labor Committee, the National Association for the Advancement of Col-ored People, and, not surprisingly, the National American Woman Suffrage Association, where she served as an officer. In this article for the *Ladies' Home Journal* in 1910, Addams makes a "municipal housekeeping" argument for the ballot: women can't fulfill their duties to their homes and families in isolation. They must engage with the structures of politics and government whose decisions affect the home, and fundamental to that civic engagement is access to the ballot.

For many generations it has been believed that woman's place is within the walls of her own home, and it is indeed impossible to imagine the time when her duty there shall be ended or to forecast any social change which shall release her from that paramount obligation.

This paper is an attempt to show that many women today are failing to discharge their duties to their own households properly simply because they do not perceive that as society grows more complicated it is necessary that woman shall extend her sense of responsibility to many things outside of her own home if she would continue to preserve the home in its entirety. One could illustrate in many ways. A woman's simplest duty, one would say, is to keep her house clean and wholesome and to feed her children properly. Yet if she lives in a tenement house, as so many of my neighbors do, she cannot fulfill these simple obligations by her own efforts because she is utterly dependent upon the city administration for the conditions which render decent living possible. Her basement will not be dry, her stairways will not be fireproof, her house will not be provided with sufficient windows to give light and air, nor will it be equipped with sanitary plumbing, unless the Public Works Department sends inspectors who constantly insist that these elementary decencies be provided. Women who live in the country sweep their own dooryards and may either feed the refuse of the table to a flock of chickens or allow it innocently to decay in the open air and sunshine. In a crowded city quarter, however, if the street is not cleaned by the city authorities no amount of private sweeping will keep the tenement free from grime; if the garbage is not properly collected and destroyed a tenement-house mother may see her children sicken and die of diseases from which she alone is powerless to shield them, although her tenderness and devotion are unbounded. She cannot even secure untainted meat for her household, she cannot provide fresh fruit, unless the meat has been inspected by city officials, and the decayed fruit, which is so often placed upon sale in the tenement districts, has been destroyed in the interests of public health. In short, if woman would keep on with her old business of caring for her house and rearing her children she will have to have some conscience in regard to public affairs lying quite outside of her immediate household. The individual conscience and devotion are no longer effective.

Chicago one spring had a spreading contagion of scarlet fever just at the time that the school nurses had been discontinued because business men had pronounced them too expensive. If the women who sent their children to the schools had been sufficiently public-spirited and had been provided with an implement through which to express that public spirit they would have insisted that the schools be supplied with nurses in order that their own children might be protected from contagion. In other words, if women would effectively continue their old avocations they must take part in the slow upbuilding of that code of legislation which is alone sufficient to protect the home from the dangers incident to modern life. One might instance the many deaths of children from contagious diseases the germs of which had been carried in tailored clothing. Country doctors testify as to the outbreak of scarlet fever in remote neighborhoods each autumn, after the children have begun to wear the winter overcoats and cloaks which have been sent from infected city sweatshops. That their mothers mend their stockings and guard them from "taking cold" is not a sufficient protection when the tailoring of the family is done in a distant city under conditions which the mother cannot possibly control. The sanitary regulation of sweatshops by city officials is all that can be depended upon to prevent such needless destruction. Who shall say that women are not concerned in the enactment and enforcement of such legislation if they would preserve their homes?

Even women who take no part in public affairs in order that they may give themselves entirely to their own families, sometimes going so far as to despise those other women who are endeavoring to secure protective legislation, may illustrate this point. The Hull-House neighborhood was at one time suffering from a typhoid epidemic. A careful investigation was made by which we were able to establish a very close connection between the typhoid and a mode of plumbing which made it most probable that the infection had been carried by flies. Among the people who had been exposed to the infection was a widow who had lived in the ward for a number of years, in a comfortable little house which she owned. Although the Italian immigrants were closing in all around her she was not willing to sell her property and to move away until she had finished the education of her children. In the mean time she held herself quite aloof from her Italian neighbors and could never be drawn into any of the public efforts to protect them by securing a better code of tenement-house sanitation. Her two daughters were sent to an Eastern college; one June, when one of them had graduated and the other still had two years before she took her degree, they came to the spotless little house and to their self-sacrificing mother for the summer's holiday. They both fell ill, not because their own home was not clean, not because their mother was not devoted, but because next door to them and also in the rear were wretched tenements, and because the mother's utmost efforts could not keep the infection out of her own house. One daughter died and one recovered but was an invalid for two years following. This is, perhaps, a fair illustration of the futility of the individual conscience when woman insists upon isolating her family from the rest of the community and its interests. The result is sure to be a pitiful failure.

One of the interesting experiences in the Chicago campaign for inducing the members of tbe Charter Convention to recommend municipal franchise for women in the provisions of the new charter was the unexpected enthusiasm and help which came from large groups of foreign-born women. The Scandinavian women represented in many Lutheran Church societies said quite simply that in the old country they had had the municipal franchise upon the same basis as men since the seventeenth century; all the women formerly living under the British Government, in England, Australia or Canada, pointed out that Chicago women were asking now for what the British women had long had. But the most unexpected response came from the foreign colonies in which women had never heard such problems discussed and took the prospect of the municipal ballot as a simple device—which it is—to aid them in their daily struggle with adverse city conditions. The Italian women said that the men engaged in railroad construction were away all summer and did not know anything about their household difficulties. Some of them came to Hull-House one day to talk over the possibility of a public wash-house. They do not like to wash in their own tenements; they have never seen a washing-tub until they came to America, and find it very difficult to use it in the restricted space of their little kitchens and to hang the clothes within the house to dry. They say that in the Italian villages the women all go to the streams together; in the town they go to the public wash-house; and washing, instead of being lonely and disagreeable, is made pleasant by cheerful conversation. It is asking a great deal of these women to change suddenly all their habits of living, and their contention that the tenement-house kitchen is too small for laundry-work is well taken. If women in Chicago knew the needs of the Italian colony they would realize that any change bringing cleanliness and fresh clothing into the Italian household would be a very sensible and hygienic measure. It is, perhaps, asking a great deal that the members of the City Council should understand this, but surely a comprehension of the needs of these women and efforts toward ameliorating their lot might be regarded as matters of municipal obligation on the part of voting women.

The same thing is true of the Jewish women in their desire for covered markets which have always been a municipal provision in Russia and Poland. The vegetables piled high upon the wagons standing in the open markets of Chicago become covered with dust and soot. It seems to these women a violation of the most rudimentary decencies and they sometimes say quite simply: "If women had anything to say about it they would change all that."

If women follow only the lines of their traditional activities here are certain primary duties which belong to even the most conservative women, and which no one woman or group of women can adequately discharge unless they join the more general movements looking toward social amelioration through legal enactment.

The first of these, of which this article has already treated, is woman's responsibility for the members of her own household that they may be properly fed and clothed and surrounded by hygienic conditions. The second is a responsibility for the education of children: (*a*) that they may be provided with good schools; (*b*) that they may be kept free from vicious influences on the street; (*c*) that when working they may be protected by adequate child-labor legislation.

(*a*) The duty of a woman toward the schools which her children attend is so obvious that it is not necessary to dwell upon it. But even this simple obligation cannot be effectively carried out without some form of social organization as the mothers' school clubs and mothers' congresses testify, and to which the most conservative women belong because they feel the need of wider reading and discussion concerning the many problems of childhood. It is, therefore, perhaps natural that the public should have been more willing to accord a vote to women in school matters than in any other, and yet women have never been members of a Board of Education in sufficient numbers to influence largely actual school curriculi. If they had been kindergartens, domestic science courses and school playgrounds would be far more numerous than they are. More than one woman has been convinced of the need of the ballot by the futility of her efforts in persuading a business man that young children need nurture in something besides the three r's. Perhaps, too, only women realize the influence which the school might exert upon the home if a proper adaptation to actual needs were considered. An Italian girl who has had lessons in cooking at the public school will help her mother to connect the entire family with American food and household habits. That the mother has never baked bread in Italy—only mixed it in her own house and then taken it out to the village oven—makes it all the more necessary that her daughter should understand the complications of a cooking-stove. The same thing is true of the girl who learns to sew in the public school, and more than anything else, perhaps, of the girl who receives the first simple instruction in the care of little children, that skillful care which every tenement-house baby requires if he is to be pulled through his second summer. The only time, to my knowledge, that lessons in the care of children were given in the public schools of Chicago was one summer when the vacation schools were being managed by a volunteer body of women. The instruction was eagerly received by the Italian girls, who had been "little mothers" to younger children ever since they could remember.

As a result of this teaching I recall a young girl who carefully explained to her Italian mother that the reason the babies in Italy were so healthy and the babies in Chicago were so sickly was not, as her mother had always firmly insisted, because her babies in Italy had goat's milk and her babies in America had cow's milk, but because the milk in Italy was clean and the milk in Chicago was dirty. She said that when you milked your own goat before the door you knew that the milk was clean, but when you bought milk from the grocery store after it had been carried for many miles in the country "you couldn't tell whether or not it was fit for the baby to drink until the men from the City Hall, who had watched it all the way, said that it was all right." She also informed her mother that the "City Hall wanted to fix up the milk so that it couldn't make the baby sick, but that they hadn't quite enough votes for it yet." The Italian mother believed what her child had been taught in the big school; it seemed to her quite as natural that the city should be concerned in providing pure milk for her younger children as that it should provide big schools and teachers for her older children. She reached this naïve conclusion because she had never heard those arguments which make it seem reasonable that a woman should be given the school franchise, but no other.

(*b*) But women are also beginning to realize that children need attention outside of school hours; that much of the petty vice in cities is merely the love of pleasure gone wrong, the overrestrained boy or girl seeking improper recreation and excitement. It is obvious that a little study of the needs of children, a sympathetic understanding of the conditions under which they go astray, might save hundreds of them. Women traditionally have had an opportunity to observe the plays of children and the needs of youth, and yet in Chicago, at least, they had done singularly little in this vexed problem of juvenile delinquency until they helped to inaugurate the Juvenile Court movement a dozen years ago. The Juvenile Court Committee, made up largely of women, paid the salaries of the probation officers connected with the court for the first six years of its existence, and after the salaries were cared for by the county the same organization turned itself into a Juvenile Protective League, and through a score of paid officers are doing valiant service in minimizing some of the dangers of city life which boys and girls encounter.

This Protective League, however, was not formed until the women had had a civic training through their semi-official connection with the Juvenile Court. This is, perhaps, an illustration of our inability to see the duty "next to hand" until we have become alert through our knowledge of conditions in connection with the larger duties. We would all agree that social amelioration must come about through the efforts of many people who are moved thereto by the compunction and stirring of the individual conscience, but we are only beginning to understand that the individual conscience will respond to the special challenge largely in proportion as the individual is able to see the social conditions because he has felt responsible for their improvement. Because this body of women assumed a public responsibility they have seen to it that every series of pictures displayed in the five-cent theater is subjected to a careful censorship before it is produced, and those series suggesting obscenity and criminality have been practically eliminated. The police department has performed this and many other duties to which it was oblivious before simply because these women have made it realize that it is necessary to protect and purify those places of amusement which are crowded with young people every night. This is but the negative side of the policy pursued by the public authorities in the fifteen small parks of Chicago, each of which is provided with halls in which young people may meet nightly for social gatherings and dances. The more extensively the modern city endeavors on the one hand to control and on the other hand to provide recreational facilities for its young people the more necessary it is that women should assist in their direction and extension. After all, a care for wholesome and innocent amusement is what women have for many years assumed. When the reaction comes on the part of taxpayers women's votes may be necessary to keep the city to its beneficent obligations toward its own young people.

(c) As the education of her children has been more and more transferred to the school, so that even children four years old go to the kindergarten, the woman has been left in a household of constantly-narrowing interests, not only because the children are away, but also because one industry after another is slipping from the household into the factory. Ever since steam power has been applied to the processes of weaving and spinning woman's traditional work has been carried on largely outside of the home. The clothing and household linen are not only spun and woven, but also usually sewed, by machinery; the preparation of many foods has also passed into the factory and necessarily a certain number of women have been obliged to follow their work there, although it is doubtful, in spite of the large number of factory girls, whether women now are doing as large a proportion of the world's work as they used to do. Because many thousands of those working in factories and shops are girls between the ages of fourteen and twenty-two there is a necessity that older women should be interested in the conditions of industry. The very fact that these girls are not going to remain in industry permanently makes it more important that some one should see to it that they shall not be incapacitated for their future family life because they work for exhausting hours and under insanitary conditions.

If woman's sense of obligation had enlarged as the industrial conditions changed she might naturally and almost imperceptibly have inaugurated the movements for social amelioration in the line of factory legislation and shop sanitation. That she has not done so is doubtless due to the fact that her conscience is slow to recognize any obligation outside of her own family circle, and because she was so absorbed in her own household that she failed to see what the conditions outside actually were. It would be interesting to know how far the consciousness that she had no vote and could not change matters operated in this direction. After all, we see only those things to which our attention has been drawn, we feel responsibility for those things which are brought to us as matters of responsibility. If conscientious women were convinced that it was a civic duty to be informed in regard to these grave industrial affairs, and then to express the conclusions which they had reached by depositing a piece of paper in a ballot-box, one cannot imagine that they would shirk simply because the action ran counter to old traditions.

To those of my readers who would admit that although woman has no right to shirk her old obligations, that all of these measures could be secured more easily through her influence upon the men of her family than through the direct use of the ballot, I should like to tell a little story. I have a friend in Chicago who is the mother of four sons and the grandmother of twelve grandsons who are voters. She is a woman of wealth, of secured social position, of sterling character and clear intelligence, and may, therefore, quite fairly be cited as a "woman of influence." Upon one of her recent birthdays, when she was asked how she had kept so young, she promptly replied: "Because I have always advocated at least one unpopular cause." It may have been in pursuance of this policy that for many years she has been an ardent advocate of free silver, although her manufacturing family are all Republicans! I happened to call at her house on the day that Mr. McKinley was elected President against Mr. Bryan for the first time. I found my friend much disturbed. She said somewhat bitterly that she had at last discovered what the much-vaunted influence of woman was worth; that she had implored each one of her sons and grandsons, had entered into endless arguments and moral appeals to induce one of them to represent her convictions by voting for Bryan! That, although sincerely devoted to her, each one had assured her that his convictions forced him to vote the Republican ticket. She said that all she had been able to secure was the promise from one of the grandsons, for whom she had an especial tenderness because he bore her husband's name, that he would not vote at all. He could not vote for Bryan, but out of respect for her feeling he would refrain from voting for McKinley. My friend said that for many years she had suspected that women could influence men only in regard to those things in which men were not deeply concerned, but when it came to persuading a man to a woman's view in affairs of politics or business it was absolutely useless. I contended that a woman had no right to persuade a man to vote against his own convictions; that I respected the men of her family for following their own judgment regardless of the appeal which the honored head of the house had made to their chivalric devotion. To this she replied that she would agree with that point of view when a woman had the same opportunity as a man to register her convictions by vote. I believed then as I do now, that nothing is gained when independence of judgment is assailed by "influence," sentimental or otherwise, and that we test advancing civilization somewhat by our power to respect differences and by our tolerance of another's honest conviction.

This is, perhaps, the attitude of many busy women who would be glad to use the ballot to further public measures in which they are interested and for which they have been working for years. It offends the taste of such a woman to be obliged to use indirect "influence" when she is accustomed to well-bred, open action in other affairs, and she very much resents the time spent in persuading a voter to take her point of view, and possibly to give up his own, quite as honest and valuable as hers, although different because resulting from a totally different experience. Public-spirited women who wish to use the ballot, as I know them, do not wish to do the work of men nor to take over men's affairs. They simply want an opportunity to do their own work and to take care of those affairs which naturally and historically belong to women, but which are constantly being overlooked and slighted in our political institutions.

In a complex community like the modern city all points of view need to be represented; the resultants of diverse experiences need to be pooled if the community would make for sane and balanced progress. If it would meet fairly each problem as it arises, whether it be connected with a freight tunnel having to do largely with business men, or with the increasing death rate among children under five years of age, a problem in which women are vitally concerned, or with the question of more adequate street-car transfers, in which both men and women might be said to be equally interested, it must not ignore the judgments of its entire adult population.

To turn the administration of our civic affairs wholly over to men may mean that the American city will continue to push forward in its commercial and industrial development, and continue to lag behind in those things which make a city healthful and beautiful. After all, woman's traditional function has been to make her dwelling-place both clean and fair. Is that dreariness in city life, that lack of domesticity which the humblest farm dwelling presents, due to a withdrawal of one of the naturally coöperating forces? If women have in any sense been responsible for the gentler side of life which softens and blurs some of its harsher conditions, may they not have a duty to perform in our American cities?

In closing, may I recapitulate that if woman would fulfill her traditional responsibility to her own children; if she would educate and protect from danger factory children who must find their recreation on the street; if she would bring the cultural forces to bear upon our materialistic civilization; and if she would do it all with the dignity and directness fitting one who carries on her immemorial duties, then she must bring herself to the use of the ballot—that latest implement for self-government. May we not fairly say that American women need this implement in order to preserve the home?

HARRIOT STANTON BLATCH

from *"The Women's Political Union"*
1910

Harriot Stanton Blatch (1856–1940) proved herself as indispensable to the women's suffrage movement in the early twentieth century as her mother, Elizabeth Cady Stanton, had been in the nineteenth. A born politician who was also one of the most class-conscious of elite white suffragists, Blatch played an especially large role in New York State politics. In 1907 she formed the Equality League of Self-Supporting Women, which linked industrial and professional women in a single organization (it renamed itself the Women's Political Union in November 1910). While the Equality League was not the first to imitate the British open-air meetings and parades (that distinction belongs to a little-known group called the American Suffragettes in 1907–8), in 1910 it took the lead in organizing the first large-scale suffrage parade, in New York City. Blatch's tongue-in-cheek account, from her 1940 memoir *Challenging Years*, of how many suffrage leaders suddenly took to their beds with feigned illnesses rather than march in a public spectacle underscores what a radical departure the parade was. Don't even think about riding in automobiles rather than facing the crowds, she chastised them: after the first year it was "on foot or no parade."

————————

Convinced as I was that mankind is moved to action by emotion, not by argument and reason, I saw the possibilities in a suffrage parade. What could be more stirring than hundreds of women, carrying banners, marching—marching—marching! The public would be aroused, the press would spread the story far and wide, and the interest of our own workers would be fired.

And so we prepared for a parade on May 21, 1910, a parade of protest against the Legislature for its indifference to our demands for woman suffrage.

We needed the support of all the suffrage organizations, and as we tried to enlist their aid, we ran into difficulties. Some disapproved. Some wanted to ride. The Equality League of Self-Supporting Women wanted to march. But we compromised, for it was important that we stage this one parade; then more would follow as a matter of course.

The press of Friday, May 5, set forth the fluttering in suffrage dove-cots, and quoted Mrs. Richard Stevens of New Jersey, in view of women marching in the street, as resigning from the Equal Franchise Society and foreswearing suffrage. Mrs. Mackay was described as greatly shocked and Mrs. Belmont as furious and retiring to Long Island; Anna Howard Shaw as having grave doubts as to the necessity of "so radical a demonstration, but would march." She rode. Mrs. Belmont told a reporter of the *Sun* that ill health prevented her participation in the demonstration.

We were told by the New York State Suffrage Association and by the National American Woman Suffrage Association that a parade would set suffrage back fifty years.

When a member of Mrs. Mackay's executive board moved that the Equal Franchise Society form a section of the parade, Mrs. Mackay instantly became voluble. In no measured tones, she expressed her views on street parades, and as she grasped the fact that her board was against her, she beat the table with her hands, and in uncontrolled fury, as one after another voted to join the procession, buried her face in her hands. It well illustrated her quickly varying moods and her generosity that she later joined in the discussion of banners and regalia, and seemed to desire her organization to make a good appearance even though she highly disapproved of the occasion and would not attend.

There was an unspoken gentleman's agreement between Mrs. Mackay and me. She never mentioned parades, Votes-for-Women balls, and other beating of the drums of public propaganda. And I, on my part, never suggested she might wander forth on these thorny paths. I knew how she felt and imagined she would not take the pricking calmly.

"Flying their banners and wearing yellow Votes-for-Women sashes, the greatest suffrage parade and demonstration ever seen in New York moved on Union Square thousands strong this afternoon," reported the *Evening Telegram* of May 21.

Starting at Fifty-ninth Street, the Woman's Suffrage League of New York represented by women from sixty-three districts led the parade in automobiles. At Thirty-third Street it was re-inforced by the Collegiate Equal Suffrage League marching in caps and gowns—200 strong, carrying banners of buff, green, and violet. The Equality League of Self-Supporting Women joined the march at Twenty-second Street. Banners flying over the heads of the marchers carried such sentiments as these: "We Protest Against the Inaction of the New York State Leg-islature"; "New York State Denies the Vote to Idiots, Lunatics, Criminals, and Women"; "Not Favor but Justice"; "Taxation Without Representation Is Tyranny." Along the way, houses of sympathizers were decorated with flags and bunting. A body of mounted police guarded the parade and there was no disorder. Shortly after three, the rain began to fall, but it did not dampen the ardor of the marchers, or of the speakers, or of the crowds at Union Square, where platforms had been erected and con-tinuous meetings were held until seven o'clock. Mrs. James Lee Laidlaw acted as chairman for the Woman's Suffrage League on one of the platforms in the place of Carrie Chapman Catt, who "was too ill to be present." Among the many speakers were Dr. Anna Howard Shaw, Mrs. Jessica Finch of the Finch School, Jessie Ashley, Elizabeth Ellsworth Cook, Assemblyman Toombs, Judge William Wood, and Robert Elder, Assistant District Attorney. Some of the younger women, mingling with the crowd, distributed literature and Votes-for-Women buttons.

Our contingent entered Union Square behind a big yellow banner, which I carried. We took possession of the Park cot-tage where we were somewhat sheltered from the heavy rain. Toward evening the hecklers began their work and I was busy for two hours answering questions. The *New York American* was very complimentary saying that I probably made more "votes for women" than were made at any previous meeting in the state. I always took heckling good-naturedly, my sense of humor coming at once to my rescue. When one young man pompously announced that suffragettes would neglect family life and bring forth a race of weaklings, I got a laugh from the crowd by my quick retort, "My dear young man, I am a grandmother. All my progeny, although I was graduated from college, are bouncing and lusty." To the many questions about women bearing arms, I replied, "In the French Revolution women did bear arms. But there was justice there to fight for.

We shall not be like you men who fight in war without knowing what you are killing people for."

The day was a great success but it gave us food for thought. The Woman's Suffrage League of New York City to the last "marcher" had climbed into automobiles, and rushing down the avenue, gave the on-lookers one flash of yellow and were gone. Not at all what the Parade Committee of the Equality League was seeking to accomplish.

Riding in a car did not demonstrate courage; it did not show discipline; it did not give any idea of numbers of "marchers"; it would not show year-by-year growth in adherents. We made mental notes, and very shortly a bold resolve. Our organization, which that autumn became the Women's Political Union, would be the arbiter in all future parades. Very arbitrary! Yes, very, but obviously necessary. We had a definite program, one that could reach its goal only by a long process of training for women. Women were to march on their own two feet out on the streets of America's greatest city; they were to march year by year, better and better.

The Parade Committee would waste no time in the future in trying to have democratic control; it would waste no time trying to build up compromise agreements with those who apparently had no idea of what they were aiming at; it would not attend any more committee meetings to listen to long written communications setting forth the thesis that street meetings and parades would put suffrage back fifty years. The conclusion was we would venture out into the great unknown alone, and thus escape having our enthusiasm lowered by getting streams of cold water poured down our backs. All might join who would submit to the rules laid down:

1. No automobiles in line.
2. Marchers must stick to the procession from start to finish.
3. If possible, marchers should attend classes in the art of walking given free at Women's Political Union headquarters and some of the armories by Josephine Beiderhasse, Director of Physical Training of the Wadley High School.

Never did such an epidemic of diseases break out. Letters told of serious complaints such as no doctor had ever treated.

It seemed as if every daughter of Eve had had an operation. I blushed for the poor health record of my sex. Autos or nothing seemed to be the ultimatum. Even our own forces were demoralized, for moving on rubber tires seemed so comfortable and easy. But the Women's Political Union stuck to its guns. Even if the executive board were deserted by its own members, it would still go on foot every inch of the way. No office dispensing psycho-analytic cures ever had nearly as striking success with suffering humanity as the office of the Women's Political Union with its miraculous pill, "On foot or no parade."

The parades continued year after year. In 1911, on May 6, we marched to the music of brass bands, to a "Women's Political Union March" written for us by Elsa Gregori. Inez Milholland and Sarah McPike led the parade, carrying a large banner with these words:

> Forward out of error,
> Leave behind the night;
> Forward through the darkness,
> Forward into light.

The Suffrage Clubs of the State, the Equal Franchise Society without Mrs. Mackay, the Political Equality League without Mrs. Belmont, delegations from Pennsylvania, Massachusetts, New Jersey, and Connecticut, joined our ranks. Dr. Anna Howard Shaw walked the entire length of the line of march and made many speeches at Union Square. Mrs. Ernest Seton Thompson marched with us, and Mary Austin, Charlotte Perkins Gilman, Fola La Follette, and Beatrice Forbes-Robertson. Eighty-nine men from the Men's League for Woman Suffrage took part, among them John Dewey, James Lees Laidlaw, Witter Bynner, Foster Peabody, George Harvey, Frederick Hazard, Hamilton Holt, and Oswald Garrison Villard. My daughter hurriedly handed Mr. Villard a banner, and when it was unfurled, it was greeted with guffaws by the crowd, for it read, "Men have the vote, Why not we?" The guying of the men who marched was terrific. Mayor Gaynor and City officials refused to review the parade. The press of May 7 gave us much space and pictures galore.

Even the conservative *New York Times*, which did not believe in woman suffrage, gave us an editorial on May 10 which read in part, "There seems to be a general admission that the marchers, instead of injuring their cause by conduct that by all the established conventions was distinctly unfeminine and therefore obnoxious and ridiculous, really accomplished something at least of what they hope to achieve, and did not lose but gained respect. Yet even their own councils were divided, before the parade, as to whether it was advisable or not, and the insistence of their bolder spirits on carrying out the audacious plan caused several alarming desertions from their army. The deserters are probably sorry now, for the event had proved them wrong both as tacticians and prophets."

And *Harpers Weekly*, May 20, 1911, carried many pictures of the parade and a sympathetic article, "The March of 3,000 Women," which gave me credit for being the inspiration of the parade.

In 1912, 1913, and on through the years the parades continued, growing larger and more impressive, giving increasing evidence of women's serious determination to win the ballot.

CHARLOTTE PERKINS GILMAN

Something to Vote For

JUNE 1911

The suffrage career of Charlotte Perkins Gilman (1860–1935) spanned more than thirty years. A leading feminist intellectual and intrepid lecturer, Gilman saw suffrage as part of a larger struggle for human progress in which women would play a leading role. She was also a prolific writer, publishing widely in leading journals, magazines, and newspapers (she is best known today for her short story "The Yellow Wallpaper"). In 1909 she founded her own monthly magazine, *The Forerunner*, for which she served as editor and publisher as well as the sole writer. Gilman published some of her sharpest suffrage commentary in *The Forerunner*, including this fifty-minute parlor theatrical with minimal stage requirements. The play's broad topical sweep features victims, villains, unsung heroes, and even a little romance in a plot about a women's club and a local campaign for pure milk.

———————

A One Act Play

TIME, 50 MINUTES.
PEOPLE IN THE PLAY.

MRS. MAY CARROLL: *A young, beautiful, rich widow; an "Anti"; President of Woman's Club; social leader.*

DR. STRONG: *A woman doctor, from Colorado, interested in Woman Suffrage and pure milk.*

MISS CARRIE TURNER: *Recording Secretary of Club; a social aspirant; agrees with everybody; "Anti."*

MRS. REEDWAY: *Corresponding Secretary of Club; amiable, elderly nonentity; "Anti."*

MRS. WOLVERHAMPTON: *Rich, impressive, middle-aged matron; "Anti."*

MRS. O'SHANE: *A little woman in black; thin, poor.*

LOUISE: *A maid.*

CLUB WOMEN: *Mrs. Black, White, etc.*

MR. HENRY ARNOLD: *A Milk Inspector.*

MR. JAMES BILLINGS: *Head of the Milk Trust.*

PLACE: *A parlor, porch or garden, belonging to Mrs. Carroll.*

PROPERTIES REQUIRED: *Chairs enough, a small table, a small platform covered with a rug, a table bell, two pitchers, a glass, a vase; two milk bottles filled with water, starch and a little black dirt; a yellow-backed bill, some red ink, a small bunch of flowers, two large clean handkerchiefs, a small bottle of iodine, a teacup. Miss Turner has a bag for her papers, and Dr. Strong an instrument bag or something similar, also a large pocket-book.*

SOMETHING TO VOTE FOR.

(*Chairs arranged at right, platform, with table and three chairs at left front. Doors at left, right and center.*)
    (*Enter Miss Turner and Mrs. Reedway, l.*)

MRS. REEDWAY: Dear me! I was so afraid we'd be late!

MISS TURNER: (*Looking at watch.*) Oh, no! The meeting begins at three you know, and it's only quarter past!

MRS. REEDWAY: (*Drawing scarf about her.*) I wish it would get warmer! I do like warm weather!

MISS TURNER: So do I!

MRS. REEDWAY: What a lovely place Mrs. Carroll has! I think we are extremely fortunate to have her for our president.

MISS TURNER: So do I! She's so sweet!

MRS. REEDWAY: I hear she has asked Mr. Billings to this milk discussion.

MISS TURNER: Yes—you're not surprised are you?

MRS. REEDWAY: Oh, no! Every one is talking about them. He's been conspicuously devoted to her for some time now. I think it's her money he's after.

MISS TURNER: So do I! But she's crazy about him!

MRS. REEDWAY: I suppose she thinks he's disinterested—being so rich himself. But I've heard that he'd lose a lot if this milk bill goes through.

MISS TURNER: So have I!

    (*Enter Dr. Strong. l.*)

DR. STRONG: Sorry to be late. I was detained by a patient.

MISS TURNER: Oh, you're not late, Dr. Strong. The ladies are usually a little slow in gathering.

DR. STRONG: I see! And about what time do your meetings really begin?

MISS TURNER: About half past three, usually.

DR. STRONG: Next time I'll come then. I could have seen two more patients—I hate to see women so unpunctual.

MISS TURNER: So do I! This is Mrs. Reedway, our corresponding secretary, Dr. Strong. (*They shake hands.*)

MRS. REEDWAY: You must remember, Dr. Strong, that our members are not—as a whole—professional women.

DR. STRONG: More's the pity!

(*Enter Mrs. Wolverhampton, l.*)

MRS. WOLVERHAMPTON: Well, well! Not started yet? But you're always on hand, Miss Turner. (*Fans herself.*) Bless me, how hot it is! I do hate hot weather.

MISS TURNER: So do I.

MRS. REEDWAY: Have you met our new member, Mrs. Wolverhampton? Dr. Strong, of Colorado. (*Mrs. W. bows. Dr. S. comes forward and shakes hands.*)

MRS. WOLVERHAMPTON: Dear me! From Colorado! And I suppose you have voted!

DR. STRONG: I certainly have. You seem to think I look like it.

MRS. WOLVERHAMPTON: Why, yes; if you'll pardon me, you do.

DR. STRONG: Pardon you? It seems to me a compliment. We're very proud of being voters—in my country.

(*Mrs. R. and Mrs. W. draw aside and converse in low tones. Miss T. fussily arranges papers; she has a large flat bag, and is continually diving into it and fumbling about.*)   (*Enter Mrs. Carroll, c.*)

MRS. CARROLL: Pardon me, ladies! I'd no idea it was so late. (*Greets them all*).

MISS TURNER: Dear Mrs. Carroll! Would you accept these flowers?

MRS. CARROLL: How charming of you, Miss Turner! They are lovely. (*Sweeps toward Dr. S., both hands out, c.*) My *dear* Doctor! I feel so glad and proud to have you with us! (*Turns to others.*) You know, Mrs. Wolverhampton, Dr. Strong saved my mother's life! If she had come here sooner I'm sure she would have saved my baby! And she's going to be *such* a help to our club, aren't you, Doctor?

DR. STRONG: I'm not so sure of that, Mrs. Carroll. I'm afraid this isn't the sort of club I'm used to.

MRS. CARROLL: It's the sort of a club that needs you, Doctor! (*Takes Dr.'s arm and sits down with her.*) Make yourselves quite at home, ladies, the others will be here presently. (*Miss T., Mrs. R. and Mrs. W. go out, c.*) We've got everything arranged, Doctor. I'm going to have a bottle of the Billings Co. milk tested, and Mr. Billings himself is to be here.

DR. STRONG: That may be awkward.

MRS. CARROLL: Oh, no! The milk is all right—I've taken it for years. And I think he's a very fine man.

DR. STRONG: (*Drily.*) So I hear.

MRS. CARROLL: You mustn't believe all you hear, Doctor.

DR. STRONG: I don't. But I hope it isn't true.

MRS. CARROLL: Hope what isn't true?

DR. STRONG: About you and Mr. Billings.

MRS. CARROLL: Never mind about me and Mr. Billings! The question is have you got the new Inspector to come?

DR. STRONG: Yes, he'll be ready on time—but the club won't, I'm afraid.

MRS. CARROLL: Oh, a few moments won't matter, I'm sure. It's a Mr. Arnold you said—do you know his initials?

DR. STRONG: His name's Henry T. Arnold. I believe he's honest and efficient.

MRS. CARROLL: (*Meditatively.*) *I* used to go to school with a boy named Harry Arnold—he was the very nicest boy in the room. I think he liked me pretty well——

DR. STRONG: And I think you liked him pretty well—eh?

MRS. CARROLL: Oh, well! That was years ago!

DR. STRONG: (*Suddenly.*) By the way, Mrs. Carroll, have you any red ink?

MRS. CARROLL: Red ink?

DR. STRONG: Yes, red ink—can you get me some?

MRS. CARROLL: Why, I'm sure I don't know. Let me see—I did have some—it's right here—if there is any. (*Goes out r. and returns with red ink.*)

DR. STRONG: Thank you. (*Takes out a yellow-backed bill, and deliberately marks it.*)

MRS. CARROLL: How exciting! What *do* you do that for, Doctor?

DR. STRONG: Just a habit of mine. Some day I may see that again and then I'd know it.

MRS. CARROLL: Do you mark all your money?

DR. STRONG: Oh, no. Only some of it. And now will you do me a real favor?

MRS. CARROLL: Indeed I will!

DR. STRONG: Please do not make any remark about this bill if you see me change it!!

MRS. CARROLL: How mysterious! I won't say a word.

DR. STRONG: (*Putting away bill.*) You said I might bring along one of my patients, for evidence, and I have. I've got little Mrs. O'Shane here to tell them how it affects the poor people.

MRS. CARROLL: That will be interesting, I'm sure—where is she?

DR. STRONG: Waiting outside—I couldn't induce her to come in.

MRS. CARROLL: I'll bring her in.
(*Exit Mrs. C., l., returns with a small shabby woman in black, who shrinks into the chair farthest back and sits silent.*)

MRS. CARROLL: It's very good of you to come, Mrs. O'Shane; we're so much obliged!
(*Enter Louise, l.*)

LOUISE: Mr. Arnold, Ma'am.

MRS. CARROLL: Show him in, Louise. (*Exit Louise. Enter Mr. Arnold, l.*)

DR. STRONG: Mrs. Carroll—Mr. Arnold.

MRS. CARROLL: It is Harry Arnold, I do believe! But you don't remember me!

MR. ARNOLD: Don't remember little May Terry! The prettiest girl in school! I've never forgotten her. But I did not expect to find you here.

MRS. CARROLL: I'm glad to welcome you to my home, Mr. Arnold, as well as to our club. And how are you—getting on?

MR. ARNOLD: Nothing to boast of Mrs. Carroll, if you mean in dollars and cents. I like public work you see, and the salaries are not high.

MRS. CARROLL: But some of our officials get very rich, don't they?

MR. ARNOLD: Yes, some of them do,—but not on their salaries.

DR. STRONG: If you knew more about politics, Mrs. Carroll, you would think better of Mr. Arnold for not making much. And he an Inspector, too!

MRS. CARROLL: You don't mean that our public men are bribed, surely!

DR. STRONG: It's been known to occur.

MRS. CARROLL: Oh, I can't believe that such things go on— here! Did any one ever bribe you, Mr. Arnold?

MR. ARNOLD: Some have tried.

MRS. CARROLL: Not in this town, surely.

MR. ARNOLD: Not yet.

DR. STRONG: He's only just appointed, Mrs. Carroll.

MR. ARNOLD: Thanks to you, Dr. Strong.

DR. STRONG: Yes, I guess I did help.
   (*Enter Louise, l.*)

LOUISE: Mr. Billings.

MRS. CARROLL: Ask him to come in. (*Exit Louise, l. Enter Mr. Billings, l.*) Good afternoon, Mr. Billings. Let me present you to my dear friend, Dr. Strong—our new member. And Mr. Arnold you probably know—the Milk Inspector. (*Mr. Billings approaches Dr. Strong, who bows stiffly. He shakes hands amiably with Mr. Arnold.*)

MR. BILLINGS: Well, Mr. Arnold, I think we're going to make an impression on these ladies. I trust you'll deal gently with me.

MR. ARNOLD: I'll do the best I can, Mr. Billings. I didn't expect to have the head of the Milk Trust in my audience.

MRS. CARROLL: That is all my fault, Mr. Arnold. I have taken milk of Mr. Billings' company for years, and it's always good. And I want the ladies to know it. Mr. Billings can stand the test.

MR. ARNOLD: I'm glad to hear it, Mrs. Carroll.

MR. BILLINGS: (*Genially.*) You'll show up all of us rascally milk-men I don't doubt.

MR. ARNOLD: I hope not. (*Mr. Billings goes to Mrs. Carroll. They talk apart. Dr. Strong confers with Mr. Arnold.*)

DR. STRONG: (*To Mr. Arnold.*) Now Mr. Arnold watch me, and be sure you play up. Say you can't make change for this bill! (*Goes to Mr. Billings.*) Mr. Billings—can you—and will you— change this bill for me? Mr. Arnold here can't make it.

MR. ARNOLD: I'm sorry, Doctor. But I haven't seen a hundred dollar bill in some time.

MRS. CARROLL: Perhaps I can—

MR. BILLINGS: No indeed, Mrs. Carroll! I shall be delighted, Dr. Strong,—if I have that much about me. (*Brings out bills from pockets and makes up the amount.*)

DR. STRONG: Thank you, Mr. Billings. (*Gives him her marked bill. The club members are seen arriving in background, c. Returning to Mr. A.*) What figures have you brought, Mr. Arnold? I don't want to cross your trail. (*They confer apart.*)

MR. BILLINGS: (*To Mrs. Carroll.*) Isn't it rather a new thing for you to interest yourself in public matters, Mrs. Carroll?

MRS. CARROLL: Oh, but milk is really a domestic matter—don't you think so? So many of our ladies are getting interested in it.

MR. BILLINGS: I suspect that is because you are! I do not think you realize your influence in this town.

MRS. CARROLL: I'm sure you overestimate it.

MR. BILLINGS: Not in the least! Look at the way you swing this club! And these are the society lights—all the other women follow. And the men are yours to command anyhow! I tell you such an influence as yours has Woman Suffrage beaten to a standstill!

MRS. CARROLL: Oh!—Woman Suffrage! (*With great scorn. Enter Mrs. Wolverhampton, c.*)

MRS. WOLVERHAMPTON: Pardon me Mrs. Carroll, but it is half past three.

MRS. CARROLL: Dear me! yes, we must come to order. (*Ladies all come in and take seats. Some polite confusion. Mrs. Carroll in the chair. Mrs. O'Shane and Mr. Billings at extreme right, behind others but near front of stage.*)

(*Platform, table, etc., l. front.*)

MRS. CARROLL: (*Rising.*) Ladies, and—gentlemen,—I—er—as you all know, I can't make a speech,—and I'm not in the least fit to be the president of a club—but you would have it you know! (*Murmur of approval; faint applause.*) I am very glad to welcome you to my home, and I'm sure I hope we shall all enjoy meeting here. (*More faint applause.*) I don't suppose it's very business like—but the very first thing I want to do is to introduce our new member, Dr. Strong of Col. (*Mrs.*

C. sits, Dr. S. rises and bows.) O do come forward to the platform, Doctor, where we can all see you.

DR. STRONG: (*Coming to platform.*) Madam President— Ladies—and gentlemen! I did not expect to be sprung on you until after the reading of the minutes at least. But I am very glad to meet you and to feel that you have honored me with membership in what I understand is the most influential woman's club in this community. I have heard that this is a very conservative club, but I find that you are interesting yourselves in one of the most vital movements of our time—a question of practical politics—Pure Milk. (*The ladies cool and stiffen at the word "politics."*) It is a great question—a most important question—one that appeals to the mother-heart and housekeeping sense of every woman. It is a matter of saving money and saving life—the lives of little children! I do not know of any single issue now before us which is so sure to make every woman want to vote. The ballot is our best protection. (*Cries of "no!" "no!" Much confusion and talking among members. One hiss. Mrs. Wolverhampton rises ponderously.*)

MRS. WOLVERHAMPTON: Madam President! I rise to a point of order! I move you that our new member be informed that all discussion of woman suffrage is forbidden by the by-laws of this club! There is no subject so calculated to disrupt an organization.

MRS. BLACK: Madam President!

MRS. CARROLL: Mrs. Black.

MRS. BLACK: I wish to second the motion! We decided long ago to allow no discussion of woman suffrage! I consider it to be one of the most dangerous movements of our time!

MRS. WHITE: Madam President!

MRS. CARROLL: Mrs. White. Won't you come forward, Mrs. White?

MRS. WHITE: O no, excuse me—no. I'll speak from here. I merely wish to agree with the previous speaker. Woman suffrage breaks up the home.

MRS. GREY: Madam President!

MRS. GREEN: Madam President.

MRS. CARROLL: Mrs. Grey I think spoke first. In a moment, Mrs. Green.

MRS. GREY: I just want to say that I for one should feel obliged to resign if woman suffrage is to be even mentioned in the club!

MRS. GREEN: Madam President!

MRS. BROWN: Madam President!

MRS. &C: Madam President! (*There has been a constant buzz of disapproval.*)

MRS. CARROLL: Ladies! One at a time, please! (*Several ladies are on their feet. All speak together.*)

MRS. GREEN: A woman's place is in the home, Madam President! If she takes good care of the home and brings up her children right—

MRS. BROWN: Women are not fitted for politics, they haven't the mind for it—and my husband says politics is not fit for women, either!

MRS. JONES: This club decided long ago that it was against woman suffrage—et al. Who'd take care of the baby?

Our power is through our feminine influence—

Yes—a woman's influence.—(*Great confusion.*)

MRS. CARROLL: (*Rapping feebly on the table.*) Ladies, ladies, we will adjourn for some refreshments. Won't you please all come and have some tea?

 (*All go out, c. and r. still talking. Mrs. C. and Mr. B. last. Dr. S. and Mr. A remain.*)

MR. ARNOLD: (*To Dr. S.*) Well, Dr. Strong, you did put your foot in it!

DR. STRONG: (*Ruefully.*) Yes—that was unfortunate, wasn't it? I'd no idea they'd fly up like that.

MR. ARNOLD: Never mind. I'll only talk milk to 'em—pure milk!

DR. STRONG: (*Walks up and down, hands behind her, much perturbed.*) I'm right sorry to have annoyed those women. This is an awfully important occasion. Even if they can't vote, they could do something.

MR. ARNOLD: Don't you fret, Doctor, we'll get them interested.

DR. STRONG: You don't know how important this is. The death rate among the babies here is something shameful—it's mostly owing to bad milk—and the bad milk is mostly owing to this man Billings. If this bill passes he's got the whole thing in his hands! And he's crooked!

MR. ARNOLD: I'd about come to that conclusion, myself.

DR. STRONG: He's got her confidence you see—and she swings this town, socially. What's more, he means to marry her—and he's not a fit man to marry any decent woman. We've got to put a spoke in his wheel, Mr. Arnold!

MR. ARNOLD: I'm willing.

DR. STRONG: You'll never get a better opportunity than right now! He'll try to fix you before you speak—I'll promise you that! and do you stick out for that hundred dollar bill—and take it!

MR. ARNOLD: I guess not! What do you think I am?

DR. STRONG: I think you're man enough to see this game through. It's a marked bill, I tell you! You take that hundred and look at it—if there's a speck of red in the middle on the top—on both sides—you take it, and bring it out in evidence after you've shown up the milk!

MR. ARNOLD: But the milk he sends here'll be all right.

DR. STRONG: Of course! But I've brought in another bottle in my bag—and I'm going to substitute it! It's his milk, all right—the common grocery store kind—you'll be safe with the iodine test. Sh! You take that bill!

(*Re-enter Mrs. C. c. bringing tea to Mrs. O'Shane.*)

MRS. CARROLL: (*To Mrs. O.*) We are really much indebted to you for coming, Mrs. O'Shane—I hope you are quite comfortable?

MRS. O'SHANE: Thank you Ma'am, thank you kindly!

MRS. CARROLL: (*Crossing to Dr. S.*) Now Dr. Strong, you musn't be angry because our ladies are not suffragettes.

DR. STRONG: Not a bit—I'm only sorry I mentioned it—I'm here to talk milk—not suffrage.

MRS. CARROLL: That's so nice of you! Now do go out and get some tea, doctor. (*Exit Dr. S. r.*)

MRS. CARROLL: I suppose you're going to be very impressive Mr. Arnold! You were as a boy, you know!

MR. ARNOLD: Was I? I don't remember that.

MRS. CARROLL: Yes, indeed. You used to brush your hair,—when you did brush it—in a way I thought extremely fine.

MR. ARNOLD: And yours was always brushed! Beautiful long soft curls! I used to wish I dared touch them!

MRS. CARROLL: My hair's grown so much darker since then, and I'm getting grey.

MR. ARNOLD: (*Drawing nearer.*) Grey! It's a libel! Not a single one.

MRS. CARROLL: There were—two or three—but, to speak confidentially, I pulled them out.

MR. ARNOLD: It wasn't necessary. You will be still more beautiful with grey hair!

MRS. CARROLL: You didn't make compliments at thirteen.

MR. ARNOLD: No—I didn't dare.

MRS. CARROLL: And how do you dare now.

MR. ARNOLD: The courage of desperation, I suppose. Here you are, still young, more beautiful than ever—the richest woman in the town; the social leader; able to lift and stir all these women—and here am I, a lot older than you are—and nothing but a milk inspector!

MRS. CARROLL: You haven't had much personal ambition, have you?

MR. ARNOLD: No, I haven't. But I might—if I were encouraged.

MRS. CARROLL: Mr. Arnold! I am so glad to find you are my old friend. And to think that you do—perhaps—value my opinion.

MR. ARNOLD: You're right as to that. That's what discouraged me when you married Carroll; and when I heard that you had become a mere society woman—You've got a good mind, always had, but you don't use it.

MRS. CARROLL: You do think I have a mind then?

MR. ARNOLD: Indeed I do! A first-class one!

MRS. CARROLL: Then let me persuade you to speak for this milk bill, Mr. Arnold! And I do hope in your speech—you'll mention the excellent influence—on the milk, you know—of Mr. Billings' company.

MR. ARNOLD: Why—I shall have to tell what I know, Mrs. Carroll; you want the facts.

MRS. CARROLL: Of course we want the facts! But—having Mr. Billings' milk to be tested—and Mr. Billings here—and he being a good friend of mine—I'm particularly anxious to have his reputation thoroughly established.

MR. ARNOLD: I see. And if I said anything against Mr. Billings, we should meet as strangers?

MRS. CARROLL: Not at all, Mr. Arnold! It's the milk we're talking about—not Mr. Billings.

MR. ARNOLD: I beg pardon—I understand! (*Re-enter Mr. B. c. Exit Mr. A. r.*)

MR. BILLINGS: (*Coming to Mrs. C.*) I began to think I shouldn't have a chance to see you at all!

MRS. CARROLL: Why I'm quite conspicuous, I'm sure,—in the chair!

MR. BILLINGS: Ah! But I like best to see you alone!

MRS. CARROLL: No one sees me when I'm alone!

MR. BILLINGS: You can joke about it, Mrs. Carroll; it is a very serious matter to me. You must know how much I care for you—how long I have been devoted to you. You know I'm an ambitious man, Mrs. Carroll. I must be to dare hope for you! There are things I can't speak of yet—big chances in politics—if I had you with me—with your beauty and fascinating ways—By Heavens! There's no place I wouldn't try for. (*Walks up and down excitedly.*) I never wanted anything so much in my life—as I want you. When will you give me an answer?

MRS. CARROLL: Certainly not now, Mr. Billings.

MR. BILLINGS: When the meeting is over?

MRS. CARROLL: Perhaps—when the meeting is over.
(*Enter Miss Turner c. with bag and papers.*)

MRS. CARROLL (*rises, and goes to her. Mr. B. turns away*): Well, Miss Turner, are you going to set us to work again?

MISS TURNER: I hope I don't interrupt—

MRS. CARROLL: Interrupt! Why this is a club meeting, Miss Turner! Are we ready now?

MISS TURNER: Perhaps, if you'd have the maid bring in the sample.

MRS. CARROLL: Oh, yes. (*Rings. Enter maid r.*)

MRS. CARROLL: Bring in the bottle of milk, Louise. (*Exit maid r. Re-enter Dr. S. and Mr. A. c.*)

MR. BILLINGS (*jocularly*): I'm to be the scapegoat for the sins of the whole community, I see!

MRS. CARROLL: You are going to clear the good name of our milk supply, Mr. Billings.
(*Re-enter maid r. with bottle of milk, sets it on table l. f.*)

MRS. CARROLL: Here it is! The best milk in town. (*They all approach table.*)

MR. BILLINGS (*takes it up*): That's mine, all right. Name blown

in the bottle, sealed with paraffine, air-tight from cow to cus-
tomer, Mr. Arnold!

MR. ARNOLD (*examining bottle*): Looks like good milk, Mr.
Billings.

MR. BILLINGS: It *is* good milk, Mr. Arnold; there's none better
in the market! We're not afraid of your examination.

MR. ARNOLD: Do you send out a uniform quality?

MR. BILLINGS: Well, hardly that, of course. We have some with
less butter fat, comes a cent or two lower—but it's all pure
milk.

DR. STRONG (*to A. aside*): Get 'em to look at your papers—call
'em off!

MR. ARNOLD: Have you seen our official cards, Mrs. Carroll?
(*Takes out papers. They turn to him. The doctor whips out bottle
of milk from her bag and changes it for the one on the table.
Billings hears her and turns around. Comes over to table and
takes bottle up. Starts. Others turn also.*)

DR. STRONG: What's the matter?

MR. BILLINGS: Matter? Why—nothing.

DR. STRONG: Name blown in the bottle all right? Paraffine seal
all right? (*All come to look.*)

MR. BILLINGS: Yes, yes, it's all right. (*Moves off evidently
perturbed.*)

MRS. CARROLL: What is it? Anything wrong with the milk?

MR. BILLINGS: No, no, certainly not.

MRS. CARROLL: Well, Miss Turner, I think we must collect our
audience. (*They go out. c.*)

DR. STRONG: Can I be of assistance? (*Follows with a meaning
glance at Mr. A. who is by the table.*)
(*Mr. B. with sudden determination walks swiftly to the table
to take milk bottle. Mr. A. seizes it.*)

MR. BILLINGS: Excuse me, Mr. Arnold—but there's a mistake
here! This is not the milk I sent Mrs. Carroll—by some error
it's a bottle of our second quality. I'd hate to have her find it
out. I've got my car here and I'm just going to run off and
change this—it won't take but a minute!

MR. ARNOLD (*holding the bottle*): I don't think you'd better, Mr.
Billings. It would look badly. There's really no time.

MR. BILLINGS (*agitated*): I guess you're right. See here—this is
a very important matter to me—more important than you

know. . . . This bottle is not my *best* milk—but—but I'd be much obliged to you if it tested well——

MR. ARNOLD (*drily*): I hope it will.

MR. BILLINGS: Look here, Arnold, confound it! They'll all be back in a minute! Here! Quick! (*Passes him a bill.*)

MR. ARNOLD (*takes it. Looks at it, both sides*): I'm not in the habit of taking bribes, Mr. Billings.

MR. BILLINGS: Sh! I can see that—you are so stiff about it! For goodness sake, man, see me through this foolish hen-party and I'll make it well worth your while! Come, put that in your pocket for this one occasion, you understand!

MR. ARNOLD: Well—just for this one occasion! (*Puts bill in pocket.*)

(*Ladies all re-enter r. l. c. and take seats. Meeting called to order. Mrs. C. in chair as before; l. f., bustle, talk.*)

MRS. CARROLL (*rapping on table*): Will the meeting please come to order. I think, since it is already so late—and since we have such important—er—such an important—question to discuss, it will be as well to postpone the regular order of business until our next meeting. I'm sure you will be glad to have our discussion opened with a few words from Mr. Billings. Mr. Billings is the head of the milk business here, and knows more about it than any man in town. It is his milk which we are to have tested this afternoon—and he is proud to have it so—aren't you, Mr. Billings? (*Smiles at him.*)

MR. BILLINGS (*rather constrainedly*): Yes; yes.

MRS. CARROLL: Now, do talk to us a little, Mr. Billings. Won't you please come forward.

MR. BILLINGS (*rising in his place*): Madam President, and ladies, also Mr. Inspector: I feel it to be an honor to be here to-day to meet so many of the leading ladies of our community; to see so many fair faces—hear so many sweet voices—take the hand of so many I am proud to number among my friends. I wish to congratulate this club on its new president (*bows to Mrs. Carroll.*)—a lady whose presence carries a benefaction wherever she goes. (*Applause.*) In these days, when so many misguided and unwomanly women are meeting together for all manner of unnecessary and sometimes utterly mistaken purposes, it is a genuine pleasure to find here so many true women of that innate refinement which always avoids notoriety. (*Takes out large white handkerchief and wipes face.*) The subject upon which I have been asked to address you is one which appeals to the heart of every woman—milk for babes! The favorite food of our children, the mainstay of the invalid, the foundation of all delicate cookery!

It has been my pleasure, ladies, and my pride to have helped in serving this community with pure and healthful milk for many years past.

Our new organization, of which there is now so much discussion in the public press, is by no means the evil some would have you believe. I speak as one who knows. This is not the place for dry financial statistics, but I assure you that through this combination of milk dealers which has been recently effected you will have cheaper milk than has ever been given here before, and a far more regular and reliable service. For the quality we must trust to the opinion of these experts (*waves his hand to Dr. Strong and Mr. Arnold*); but for the wish to serve your best interests, and for a capacity in service developed through years of experience, you may always count upon yours truly. (*Bows and sits. Stir and murmurs of approval. Applause.*)

MRS. A.: Isn't he interesting.

MRS. B.: Just what I think.

MRS. CARROLL: I'm sure we are all very grateful to Mr. Billings for giving us so much of his valuable time. It is so interesting, in this study of large general questions, to get information from the fountain head. And now we shall learn the medical side of it from a most competent authority. Ladies, I take pleasure in introducing my dear friend, Dr. Strong, who will speak to us on—what do you call it, Doctor?

DR. STRONG (*coming forward*): Let us call it The Danger of Impure Milk. (*Stands a moment, looking earnestly at them.*) We all love babies. We love our own babies best of all, naturally. We all want to feed our babies well, and some of us can't do it ourselves. Next to the Mother, the most important food supplier for our children is the Cow. Milk is the most valuable article of food for little children.

I suppose you all know that bottle-fed babies die faster than breast-fed—by far; they die mostly in summer, and from enteric and diarrheal diseases. (*Reads from notes.*) 17,437 babies under a year old died in New York in 1907; 1,315 died in Boston between June 1st and November 30th of that same year—in six months. In Fall River, at that time, more than 300 out of 1,000 died—nearly one-third. In New York, in five years, over 23,000 children of all ages died of measles, scarlet fever and diphtheria combined, and in the same time over 26,000 babies under two years died of diarrheal diseases. Out of 1,943 cases of these infantile diseases, in New York, only three per cent were breast-fed.

Now, ladies, this class of diseases comes from bacteria, and the bacteria come, in the vast majority of cases, from the milk. You see, the bottle-fed baby does not get its supply directly from the source, as when fed by its mother; between the Cow and the Baby stands the Milkman. The Milkman is not a mother. I really believe that if mothers ran the milk business they would not be willing to poison other women's babies even to make money for their own!

The producer and distributor of milk has small thought for the consumers' interests. To protect the consumer, the law now provides the Milk Inspector. But the Milk Inspector has on one side a few alert business men, often ready to pay well to protect their interests, and on the other the great mass of apathetic citizens, who do not take the trouble to protect their own.

The discussion to-day is in the hope of rousing this club to see the vital importance of pure milk for our children, and to urge its members to use their influence to secure it.

By the kind permission of your president I have brought with me a resident of a less fortunate part of the town, that she may give you a personal experience. Mrs. O'Shane, will you please come to the platform? (*The little woman in black rises, hesitates, sits down again.*)

MRS. CARROLL: Won't you please make room, ladies? (*She comes down and escorts Mrs. O'Shane to platform. Mrs. O'Shane much agitated.*)

DR. STRONG: Brace up, Mrs. O'Shane. It's for little Patsy's sake, you know. He's gone, but there are many more.

MRS. O'SHANE: Indade there are, thank Hiven! It's not too late for the others! The street's full ov thim! If ye please, ladies, did any of you ever lose a child?

MRS. CARROLL (*coming to her and taking her hand*): I have, Mrs. O'Shane. (*Sits again.*)

MRS. O'SHANE: There's many, I don't doubt. But ye have the consolation of knowin' that your children had all done that could be done for thim. An' ours dies on us every summer—such a many of thim dies—an' we can't help it. They used to tell us 'twas the Hand o' God, and then they said 'twas the hot weather, and now they're preachin' it to us everywhere that 'tis the milk does it! The hot weather is bad, because thim things that's in the milk shwarms thicker and faster—thim little bugs that kills our babies. . . . If ye could have seen my little Patsy! He was the han'somest child, an' the strongest! Walkin' he was—and him hardly a year old! An' he was all I had—an' me a widder! An', of course, I took the best milk I could get; but all the milk in our parts comes from the Trust—an' sisteen cents a quart for thim fancy brands I could not pay. An', just think of it—even if I could, there's not enough of that sort *to go around!* There's so many of us! We have no choice, and we have no money to pay for the extras, an' we must give our babies the milk that is sold to us—an' they die! . . .

I know I should care most for the hundreds an' thousands of thim—an' for Mrs. Casey's twins that died in a week last summer, an' three of Mrs. Flaharty's, an' even thim little blackies on Bay street; but I care the most for my Little Patsy—havin' but the wan! Ladies, if you could have seen him! The hair on his head was that soft!—an' all in little rings o' curls! An' his cheeks like roses—before he took sick; an' his little feet was that pretty—an' he'd kick out so strong and bold with them! An' he could stand up, and he was beginning to hold on the chairs like—an' he'd catch me by the skirts an' look up at me with such a smile—an' pull on me he would, an' say Mah! Mah! An' what had I to give him but the milk? And the milk killed him. . . . I beg your pardon, ladies, but it breaks my heart! (*She cries. Mrs. Carroll comforts her, crying too. Many handkerchiefs out. Mrs. Carroll rises up, repressing emotion.*)

MRS. CARROLL: Ladies, we will now hear from our new Inspector, Mr. Arnold. (*Mr. Arnold comes forward and bows.*)

MR. ARNOLD: I fear cold facts will make but little impression after this moving appeal. Mrs. O'Shane has given you the main points in the case. Most people are poor. Most milk is poor. And the poorest milk goes to the poorest people. The community must protect itself. The Inspector has no power except to point out defects in the supply. Action must be taken to enforce the law, and unless the public does its duty there is often no action taken. (*Reads from paper.*) Dr. Strong has given you some figures as to the mortality among babies. There is also a heavy death rate for adults from contaminated milk, as in the case of the typhoid fever outbreak in Stamford, Conn., in 1895, when 160 cases were reported in nine days, 147 of which had all used milk from one dairyman. In about six weeks 386 cases were reported; of these 352 took milk from that one dealer, and four more got it from him indirectly. His dairy was closed, and in two weeks the outbreak had practically subsided.

Typhoid fever, scarlet fever and diptheria, as well as many less common diseases, are spread by infected milk.

The inspection service watches both the producer and distributor; examining the dairy farm as to the health of the cattle, the nature of their surroundings, the care given them, the methods of milking, bottling, and so on; and looking to the milkmen in each step of handling, carriage and delivery.

In judging milk there are three main questions to be considered: Its comparative quality as good milk (the percentage of butter-fats, etc.); its cleanliness (dirty milk is always likely to carry disease); and its freedom from adulteration—from the primitive pump-water and starch down to the subtler and more dangerous commercial methods of to-day.

I have been asked to show you a simple test or two—such as might be used at home. These do not require chemical or bacteriological analysis, a microscope or a lactometer; merely a fine cloth (*produces it*) and a little iodine (*produces that*).

(*The ladies lean forward eagerly. Mr. Billings looks indifferent.*)

MR. ARNOLD: Please understand, ladies, that neither of these tests proves anything absolutely harmful. I feel extremely awkward in testing a bottle of the Billings Company milk in the presence of Mr. Billings. Please remember that the Billings Company has many supply dairies. If this one bottle should not prove first-class it is no direct reproach to your guest.

MR. BILLINGS: Ladies, I do not ask any excuses. The Billings Company is reliable.

MRS. CARROLL: We have every confidence in this milk, Mr. Billings; that is why I asked for the test.

MR. ARNOLD: May I ask for another vessel—a pitcher or milk bottle?

(*Mrs. Carroll rings. Enter Louise, r.*)

MRS. CARROLL: Bring another pitcher, Louise, and an empty milk bottle—clean. (*Exit Louise, r., and returns with them, r., while Mr. Arnold continues.*)

MR. ARNOLD: Only two things are to be decided by this little test—whether the milk is clean, and whether it has starch in it. If it is clean milk, according to our standard, there will be but a slight smear on the cloth when it is strained. (*He puts cloth over top of pitcher, pushing it down inside, and fastens it with string or rubber band; then solemnly pours in most of the milk. Buzz among ladies.*)

MR. ARNOLD: While this is straining, I will apply the iodine test to what remains in the bottle. If there is starch in it, it will turn blue. (*Pours water from a glass into the bottle, adds a few drops of iodine, shakes it, holds it up before them. It is blue.*)

MRS. W., MRS. B., MRS. G. (*together*): Oh! Look at that! Just think of it!

(*Mr. Billings much confused, but unable to escape.*)

MR. ARNOLD: I'm afraid one of the supplying dairymen thins his milk and whitens it. Starch is not dangerous. Dirt is. We will now examine our strainer. (*Holds up cloth. A heavy, dark deposit is shown. There is a tense silence.*)

MRS. O'SHANE (*suddenly rising up*): That's what killed my Patsy! (*Points at Mr. Billings.*) An' 'twas him that did it! (*Commotion.*)

MR. BILLINGS (*rising*): Ladies, I demand to be heard! You have all known me for years. Most of you take my milk. You know it is good. There is some mistake; that is not the milk that should have been delivered here.

MRS. CARROLL: Evidently not.

MRS. O'SHANE: No! 'Tis not the milk for the rich—'tis the milk for the poor!

MR. BILLINGS: Ladies, I protest! My standing in this community—my years of service—ought to give me your confidence long enough to look into this matter. I must find out from which of my suppliers this inferior milk has come. We will have a thorough overhauling, I assure you. I had no idea any such milk was being handled by us.

MR. ARNOLD: Then why did you give me this bill? (*Shows marked bill.*) This was handed to me a few moments ago by Mr. Billings to ensure my giving him a favorable test. It is the first time I ever held a bribe—even for evidence.

DR. STRONG (*coming forward*): Ladies, I wish to clear Mr. Arnold of even a moment's suspicion. I knew the Milk Trust would not bear inspection, so I urged Mr. Arnold to take the money, if it was offered, and bring it out in evidence. There it is.

MR. BILLINGS: I suspected as much! This is admitted to be a conspiracy between our new doctor and our new inspector. But I trust, ladies, that more than the word of two strangers will be required to condemn an old friend and fellow-citizen.

DR. STRONG: I gave you that bill, Mr. Billings; it's the one you changed for me just now. That much of a conspiracy I admit.

MR. BILLINGS: So you and your accomplice had it all framed up to knife me! And is your word and his—a man whose very admission proves him a venal scoundrel—to stand against mine? Do you think I had but one hundred-dollar bill about me?

DR. STRONG: I doubt if you had more than one with a red mark in the middle of the top—on both sides! (*Mrs. Carroll suddenly takes up bill and examines it. Rises.*)

MRS. CARROLL: It was a painful surprise to find the quality of milk which has been served to me, but it is more painful to see that it was evidently known to be bad. Ladies, I saw Dr. Strong mark that bill. I saw her give it to him in change for smaller ones.

MRS. O'SHANE: Sure, an' I saw him pass it to the man!

MRS. CARROLL: Ladies, if you will kindly move a little I think Mr. Billings would be glad to pass out. (*They make way for him and he goes out, turns at door and shakes fist at Mr. Arnold.*)

MR. BILLINGS: You'll lose your job, young man! I have some power in this town!

MRS. CARROLL: And so have I, Mr. Billings. I'll see that Mr. Arnold keeps his place. We need him. You said this club could carry the town; that we women could do whatever we wanted to here—with our "influence"! Now we see what our "influence" amounts to! Rich or poor, we are all helpless together unless we wake up to the danger and protect ourselves. That's what the ballot is for, ladies—to protect our homes! To protect our children! To protect the children of the poor! I'm willing to vote now! I'm glad to vote now! I've got something to vote for! Friends, sisters, all who are in favor of woman suffrage and pure milk say Aye!

(*Clubwomen all rise and wave their handkerchiefs, with cries of "Aye!" "Aye!"*)

CURTAIN.

ALICE STONE BLACKWELL

Militant Methods

C. 1911

American suffragists closely followed the actions of their British sisters. Starting in 1905, Emmeline Pankhurst (1858–1928) and the Women's Social and Political Union embarked on a militant campaign to force the British government to act on women's suffrage by smashing windows, heckling government officials, and destroying property. Their militant actions provoked police reprisals and prison terms; when their request for political prisoner status was denied, they went on hunger strikes and were forcibly fed. British suffragettes shared their stirring tales of civil disobedience and mass demonstrations with American audiences as early as 1908, laying the seeds for the embrace of these new tactics in the 1910s. In this NAWSA pamphlet, written around 1911, Alice Stone Blackwell (1857–1950), the longtime editor of the *Woman's Journal*, chronicles the actions of British suffragists while also defending them from what Blackwell sees as distorted representation in the press. When Alice Paul (1885–1977) and the National Woman's Party later embraced militant actions, such as provoking arrest and then going on hunger strikes, they always made it clear that they did not condone violence against private property. For this reason American suffragists shied away from the term "suffragette."

The extraordinary situation that led to the militant suffrage tactics in England could not possibly arise here, and can with difficulty be understood by Americans. It cannot be understood at all by those who have read only the garbled and misleading cablegrams in the daily press.

The fundamental grievance of the English women is that the woman suffrage bill has never in forty years been allowed to come to a decisive vote in Parliament. For more than a generation, a majority of the members of the House of Commons have professed themselves willing to give votes to women. The suffrage bill has passed its second reading over and over again— in the early years by small majorities, of late years by very large ones—but it has never once been allowed to come up for third reading and final vote. The cabinet controls the time of the

House, and the cabinet has always taken the ground that all the time was wanted for more pressing measures.

About six years ago, some of the women got out of patience and made up their minds to convince the cabinet ministers that their question was really pressing. When their bill was blocked in Parliament, they protested from the ladies' gallery. The ladies' gallery was closed. Their male sympathizers then protested from the men's gallery. The men's gallery was closed. The women sent delegations to interview the Prime Minister. An old law, obsolete for more than a century, was revived to stop them. It forbade any procession or public meeting within a mile of the Houses of Parliament. Whether the women went in procession or small groups, they were forcibly turned back, and if they tried to push their way through, they were arrested for "obstructing the police." Great numbers of highly respected and respectable women were sent to prison, and were given heavier sentences for a purely technical offence than culprits who were drunk and disorderly.

Still the women tried to get into the Houses of Parliament with their protests, and, as their peaceful deputations had been stopped by force, they resorted to all kinds of strategy. Furniture vans driving past suddenly opened, and let out a band of women who made a dash for the doors. A steam launch crowded with suffragists came up the Thames to the water side of Parliament House and delivered the suffrage message. Thousands of police guarded Parliament on the land side, while police boats patrolled the water; and still in all sorts of ways the members and the public were kept reminded that women wanted to vote. A monster kite bearing the words "Votes for Women" flew for days over Parliament House. One morning London woke up to find the whole city placarded with invitations to the public to come at a certain hour and help the suffragists "rush" the House of Commons. A huge crowd gathered, and for this Mrs. Pankhurst and her daughter, Christabel, were sent to prison, after a memorable trial at which Christabel conducted the defence, and compelled several cabinet ministers to come into court and be questioned as to whether they had not helped to provoke the riot.

Whenever a cabinet minister addressed any public meeting, he was asked what the cabinet was going to do about woman suffrage. At first the women waited till the end of the speech before putting their question; but as the statesman always hurried away without answering, they began to question him in the middle of his address. Men who asked questions on other subjects received a civil answer, but the women were thrown out of the meetings with great violence.

Finally all women were excluded from public meetings where any cabinet minister was to speak. The women showed endless ingenuity in getting in. For days in advance they hid themselves on the roof, in the cellar, or under the platform; and at the psychological moment they emerged and asked their question. If they could not get in, husbands and brothers in the audience asked the question for them. The cabinet ministers went everywhere under a strong police guard to protect them from women who wanted to question them. The Prime Minister was smuggled out of one meeting with his head under a horse blanket to keep him from being recognized, and on another occasion he had himself shot through the pneumatic tube for parcels in the postoffice, to avoid venturing into the street.

As the leaders of the party in power were responsible for refusing to let the suffrage bill come to a vote, the women fought the candidates of that party at the elections, spoke and electioneered against them, defeated a number of them, and greatly reduced the majority of many others. Mrs. Pankhurst on one occasion was knocked down and brutally kicked by partisans of the defeated candidate, and left in the street half dead. Several times her daughters almost lost their lives.

Upon successive refusals of the cabinet to let the suffrage bill come to a vote, the women smashed the ministers' windows, or the windows of government buildings. This has been the customary way of expressing popular disapproval in England for centuries.

Mr. Asquith refused to receive any deputation of women who wanted to talk to him about suffrage. This led to "the silent siege" of the House of Commons. Women stood in silence at all the doors of the House, holding suffrage petitions as a sign that they wanted to interview the Prime Minister. Many of the most highly esteemed women in England took part in the siege—women socially prominent, women illustrious for good deeds, working women who could ill spare the time and strength—women of all sorts. They stood there day and night, in all weathers, for a length of time aggregating more than 10,000 hours. Mr. Asquith, with true British obstinacy, still refused. No public man in America would keep the most highly-respected women of this country standing at his gate in sun and rain for 10,000 hours rather than allow a deputation of them to interview him for ten minutes. It was as a protest against this refusal that two of the women finally went and poured a mixture of ink and photographic chemicals (falsely described in the cablegrams as corrosive acid) into the ballot boxes at Bermondsey. It was not a wise way to protest; but it did not compare with the foolishness shown by the Prime Minister.

The women sent to prison for suffrage demonstrations claimed that they ought to be given the food and treatment customary for prisoners guilty of political offences. When they were given instead the food of common criminals, they went on a "hunger strike," submitted to the painful ordeal of forced feeding, and in several cases were brought to death's door.

One of the latest deputations of women attempting to see the Prime Minister was both brutally and indecently handled by the police. They had been ordered not to arrest the women, but to drive them away. As the women refused to go without seeing Mr. Asquith, the police for hours knocked them about, kicked and trampled on them, and took personal liberties with them of the most offensive character. In consequence, the nephew of the Postmaster General of England took a dogwhip to Winston Churchill, the Home Secretary, under whose orders the police were believed to have acted. More than a hundred witnesses testified to the outrages. Members of Parliament demanded an investigation. Mr. Churchill refused it. No public man in America would have dared to refuse an investigation under such circumstances.

All this had made woman suffrage not only a pressing but a burning question. A committee of sixty members of Parliament, made up from all parties, had organized themselves into a Suffrage Association within Parliament itself, to try to get the suffrage bill brought to a vote. They called themselves the Conciliation Committee, because they wanted to conciliate the differences of opinion between the Tory, Liberal and Labor members of Parliament as to the form which the woman suffrage bill should take. The Committee made a careful canvass of the House, and found that the largest support would be given to a bill enfranchising women "householders," who have had municipal suffrage in England since 1869. There anyone is classed as a householder who occupies a house, or any part of a house—even a single room—over which he or she has full control. The only exception is when the landlord lives on the premises. Then he is classed as the householder. The poor in England immensely outnumber the rich, and an extensive canvass made several years ago by the Independent Labor Party proved that eighty-two per cent of the women having municipal suffrage were women of the working class.

These sixty members of Parliament drew up a manifesto pointing out that every House of Commons which had met since 1870 had had a majority in favor of woman suffrage, and that the reform was long overdue. They urged that the question should be allowed to come to a decisive vote. The anti-suffragists implored that it should not. Mr. Asquith finally promised to grant time next year for the bill to go to third reading and final vote; and in view of this promise the militant tactics were discontinued.*

Throughout the struggle the trans-Atlantic cablegrams have systematically distorted the facts, and always to the disadvantage of the suffragists. The violence done by them has been grossly exaggerated, the violence done to them passed over without mention, and the nature of their grievance left wholly unexplained.

The most extreme militancy of the women has been nothing to what the men of England have done under far less provocation. The women have neither killed nor seriously hurt anybody. In 1882, when a bill widening the franchise for men was held up in Parliament for a short time, there was widespread rioting and bloodshed. In my father's native city of Bristol alone, the mob burned the custom house, three prisons and forty-two private dwellings. In comparison, as Israel Zangwill truly says,

---

* Since this was written they have been resumed by one of the two militant societies, in consequence of action on Mr. Asquith's part which they regard as a breach of faith.

England has reason to be grateful to the women for "the feminine mildness of their methods."

Almost every cablegram on the subject has been distorted and colored. Take as an example the story about Lady Constance Lytton and her "little hatchet." In almost every daily paper in America, she was represented as something like an exaggerated caricature of Mrs. Carrie Nation, and her supposed assault upon her opponents with a hatchet was made the subject of innumerable anti-suffrage editorials. As a matter of fact, she never used a hatchet. The members of the cabinet had refused to let the woman suffrage bill come to a vote. They were questioned upon the subject by women at every public meeting which they addressed. To avoid answering, they adopted a rule that women should be excluded from the meetings. High wooden barricades were erected and guarded by police to keep the women out. Women who tried to get in were arrested and given severe prison sentences, out of all proportion to the punishments inflicted on men for disorderly political demonstrations.

The women so treated were "commoners." Lady Constance Lytton was indignant against the sentences, which she thought excessive and illegal. She and her friend, Mrs. H. M. Brailsford, resolved to take part in a demonstration themselves, and see if the courts would venture to treat women of high social position in the same way. Lady Constance was the sister of an earl. Mrs. Brailsford was the wife of an influential journalist, was much beloved for her charities, and had distinguished herself in raising a relief fund for the Macedonians, and going out with her husband in person to distribute it. Lady Constance threw a stone at the automobile in which a cabinet minister was riding. She aimed it carefully at the car and not at the inmates, having no wish to injure anyone. Mrs. Brailsford would not throw a stone, because she was doubtful of her aim, and feared she might hurt somebody. Instead, she hid a meat-chopper under a bouquet of chrysanthemums, and made her way through the crowd close up to the wooden barrier that stretched across the street. She chose a spot in full view of the police; then she suddenly dropped her bouquet, made one chop at the barrier, and was immediately arrested. From this mild and trifling incident grew the Great Hatchet Myth, and the descriptions of Lady Constance running amuck with her dangerous weapon.

Many other incidents have likewise "suffered a sea change" in crossing the Atlantic, and have come out fantastically different from the original facts.

In this case the expectation was justified that the drastic sentences imposed on women of the plain people would not be meted out to women of the aristocracy. Lady Constance and Mrs. Brailsford were let off easily, Lady Constance being declared to have a heart trouble which would endanger her life if she were forcibly fed. Later, learning that some suffragist prisoners were being treated with great brutality in the Liverpool jail, Lady Constance cut off her hair, dressed herself in poor clothes, took part in a suffrage demonstration before the same jail, gave her name as Jane Warton, a seamstress, and was promptly sent to prison and subjected, without ceremony, to forcible feeding and other rough usage. The authorities were dismayed when they found out whom they had been abusing, and Lady Constance proved up to the hilt her charge that in dealing with suffrage prisoners there was one law for the rich and another for the poor. This chivalrous lady, represented in the American press as a dangerous and ridiculous virago, is the person to whom Olive Schreiner dedicated her recent book, "Woman and Labor."

"I have inscribed it to my friend, Lady Constance Lytton; not because I think it worthy of her, nor because of the splendid part she has played in the struggle of the women fighting to-day in England for certain forms of freedom for all women. It is, if I may be allowed without violating the sanctity of a close personal friendship, so to say, because she, with one or two other men and women I have known, has embodied for me the highest ideal of human nature, in which intellectual power and strength of will are combined with an infinite tenderness and wide human sympathy."

Another anti-suffrage myth, telegraphed to the press all through the United States, was that the suffragists kicked Augustine Birrell and seriously hurt his knee. According to Mr. Birrell's own statement, he was not kicked, but accidentally twisted his own knee in making for a cab after he had been surrounded by a bevy of protesting suffragettes. The cruelty of kicking and laming an old man was made the subject of editorials by the score. But no mention was made in the press of the fact that Mr. Alfred Hawkins, an old man with a medal for bravery in the royal navy, was fiercely assaulted and had his leg broken by the anti-suffragists for asking a question at a public meeting. He was confined to the hospital for weeks, and was awarded substantial damages. Other suffragists had arms and ribs broken, and women without number were beaten, kicked and subjected to the grossest ill-usage. The press reports have deceived the American public into the belief that the suffragettes have been in the habit of kicking, scratching, biting, hurling hatchets and corrosive acid, and generally conducting themselves like furies; whereas the great bulk of the violence committed has been committed on the other side. If the press despatches had told the truth, the sympathy of the American public, irrespective of their views on suffrage, would be strongly with the women.

LEONORA O'REILLY

*Statement before Joint Congressional
Session of Congress*

MARCH 13, 1912

Working-class women played active and vibrant roles in the women's suffrage movement, especially in the last decade before the passage of the Nineteenth Amendment. These suffragists, who often came out of the trade union movement, were street-smart and politically savvy. Like the intersectional vision of African American suffragists, they contributed a broader theoretical perspective by arguing that class solidarity must always be prominent alongside gender. This testimony given to a Joint Congressional Committee in 1912 by labor activist Leonora O'Reilly (1870–1927) effectively rebutted the criticisms that working women did not want the vote or that the vote was irrelevant to the problems that working-class women faced in their lives. Born into an Irish family on New York's Lower East Side, O'Reilly had started work not at thirteen, as she said in her statement, but at eleven. She initially became involved in the trade union movement through the Knights of Labor and later joined forces with middle-class allies in the Women's Trade Union League. O'Reilly was a charismatic speaker and her passionate commitment to labor and women comes through clearly in this testimony. As she argued to great applause, "We working women want the ballot, not as a privilege but as a right. . . . All the other women ought to have it, but we working women must have it."

───────────

Mr. Chairman and gentlemen of the committee: Yes; I have outdone the lady who went to work at 18 by five years. I have been a wage earner since I was a little over 13. I, too, know whereof I speak; that is the reason I do not want to play a bluff game with you any longer. You can not or will not make laws for us; we must make laws for ourselves. We working women need the ballot for self-protection; that is all there is to it. We have got to have it.

We work long, long hours and we do not get half enough to live on. We have got to keep decent, and if we go "the easy way" you men make the laws that will let you go free and send us into the gutter. [Applause.]

We can not believe in man-made laws any longer. We have gone from one assembly to another, from one State senator to another, and we have heard the same old story. You think only of output; there is not a soul among you who cares to save human beings. We have grown rich, as a nation, but we have grown very rotten. As a people—gentlemen, I use the term "rotten" advisedly—for, as far as the working women are concerned, the foundation we are building on is rotten. To purify the life of the Nation we women know we have got to do our part, political as well as industrial duty. Government, as a whole, rests on industry. You men say to us: "Go back to the home. Your place is in the home," yet as children we must come out of the home at 11, at 13, and at 15 years of age to earn a living; we have got to make good or starve.

"Pay your way" we are taught in school and in church—the greatest thing on earth is to be able to pay your way. Well, if any people on earth pay their way in life we working women do. The return we get is that most of us become physical wrecks along the roadside of life. When you gentlemen hear what it costs a working woman to "pay her way" in life, you sit back in your chairs, say "the story is terrible, but they manage to live somehow." Somehow—that is it, gentlemen. I want to make you realize the *somehow* of life to the hundreds of girls I have seen go down in the struggle. You men do not care. You want this country to get rich, and you do not know the only riches of a nation are its people. [Applause.]

We have gone before legislature after legislature making our pleas for justice. We have seen the game as you play it. What is it? We go there and we are told the same old tommyrot—let men do this for you. I tell you as a bit of business experience if you let anybody do a thing for you they will do you. That is business. [Applause.]

Now, while we have had the colleges opened to women, only one woman in a thousand goes to college, while modern industry claims one woman in every five to-day. It is industrial methods which are teaching the women the facts I am telling you. "Do the other fellow before he gets a chance to do you"— do him so hard that he can not stand up again; that is good business. We know that, and we women are sure that there must be some higher standard for life than business.

We are not getting a square deal; we go before legislature after legislature to tell our story, but they fail to help the women who are being speeded so high in the mills and in factories, from 54 hours to 72 hours in stores in New York, and 92 hours in one week in sub-cellar laundries. Who cares? Nobody! Nobody does; nobody cares about making laws so long as we get cheap and nasty things in the market. Working women come before you and tell you these things and think you will do something for them. Every man listening is convinced that the girls are telling the truth. It is only when you think of them as your own girls that you have the right to make laws for them. Every man listening wants to do the fair thing, but just as soon as our backs are turned, up comes the representative of the big interest and says, "Lad, you are dead politically if you do what those women ask." They know it is true, and we get nothing, because all the votes are owned.

Every vote you cast is owned, and it is the owned vote which has fought our women. Go before legislatures as you will, the only argument that you can bring in to the man in politics—he is there to go up the ladder, decently if he can, but he will go up anyhow, if he can—the only argument that you can bring to that man is the power of the ballot. When we can say to him, "Man, do this and we will return you so many million votes," he will listen and act.

This is what we want, because it is for the good of the women, because it is for the good of the whole people. It is for that reason that the working woman, facing the hard facts of life and having to fight her way, has come to the conclusion that you men in politics—I am not going to give you any taffy—you men in politics are not leaders, you follow what you think is the next step on the ladder. We want you to understand that the next step in politics, the next step in democracy, is to give to the women of your Nation a ballot. [Applause.]

The working women send me to you with the plain, honest truth; because, working beside you in the same mill or factory, we know you with your evening suit off and your tall hat in the box, or wherever it belongs; you are just a competitor with us there; we tell you the truth there, as I have come to tell you the truth here. Let women have the ballot, in order that you may once more throw the burden which you have carried, or thought you carried, onto them; that is the thing you have done since the beginning of time; when the load was too heavy for you you piled it onto Eve's back. [Applause.] You have got us in a devil of a mess, economic and political. It is so rank it smells to Heaven; but we will come in and help you clean house. We will start all over again, because we belong together shoulder to shoulder. We must get on to a better time. It is only because you will not, in your prejudice and your ignorance, let us into the political field with you that the situation is as bad as it is to-day.

We working women want the ballot, not as a privilege but as a right. You say you have only given the ballot as an expediency; you have never given it as a right; then we demand it as an expediency for the 8,000,000 working women. All the other women ought to have it, but we working women must have it. [Applause.]

MAX EASTMAN

Values of the Vote

MARCH 21, 1912

In 1909 a group of prominent New Yorkers organized the Men's League for Woman Suffrage, with George Foster Peabody (1852–1938) serving as president and Max Eastman (1883–1969) as secretary/treasurer. Its charter members, many from the New York intellectual establishment, marched in suffrage parades, attended NAWSA conventions, lobbied in Albany and Washington, and spoke at public forums. This address by Max Eastman, in which he faults former president Theodore Roosevelt for his lukewarm endorsement of women's suffrage, was delivered to a gathering of the New York chapter. Eastman's suffrage advocacy mixed the personal and the political. A graduate of Williams College who studied philosophy under John Dewey (1859–1952) at Columbia, Eastman was part of the lively Greenwich Village scene in the 1910s, serving as the first editor of the influential socialist magazine *The Masses*. His sister Crystal Eastman (1881–1928) was an active suffragist, as was his wife, Ida Rauh (1877–1970); and Inez Milholland (1886–1916), known for leading suffrage parades in New York and Washington, D.C., on horseback, was a close friend.

———————

I have just attended the organization-meeting of a new chapter of the Men's League for Woman Suffrage in a middle western state. A leading capitalist of that state is the president, and a leading Socialist is one of the vice-presidents of the organization—a fact which reminds us that the importance of woman suffrage lies deeper than any special program of reform, or the platform of any political party. It lies deeper than any constitution. It appeals, upon the theoretic side, to those fundamental principles of popular government which underlie our constitution, the principles of rule by the majority—that there *is* no majority with a right to rule, until after a single vote is the property of every single citizen.

It is this profounder basis of our faith that makes us reject with contempt a proposal to submit to a majority vote of all the women, the question whether they would like the suffrage or not, supposing somebody were moved to give it to them. I

365

want to read you this proposal as it appeared in the *Outlook* a
little while ago:

> "I think that it would be well to let the women themselves, and
> only the women, vote at some special election as to whether they
> do or do not wish the vote as a permanent possession. In other
> words, this is peculiarly a case for the referendum to those most
> directly affected—that is, the women themselves. I believe such a
> referendum was held in Massachusetts, in which a majority of the
> women who voted, voted in favor of the ballot. But they included
> only about five per cent. of the women who were entitled to vote,
> and where the vote is so light, those not voting should be held
> to have voted 'No'."

I want to say that the obvious foolishness of that proposal,
in the form in which it is stated there, is not the worst thing
about it. The worst thing about it, in whatever form it may be
stated, is that it gives a glamour of apparent justice to a travesty
of the principle of democratic government. That principle does
not allow that a majority shall decide whether or not a minority
may have the privilege of voting; it demands that everyone shall
be guaranteed the privilege of voting, and *after* that—and not
until after that—the vote of a majority shall rule.

My subject to-night is "Values of the Vote," and I will suggest as a head-line for to-morrow, "Theodore Roosevelt and
Emma Goldman Agree!" Roosevelt believes in woman suffrage,
and you may take what comfort you can out of that; but the
keynote of his recent editorial is the statement, five times repeated, that the suffrage is "not important." There are great
and terrible evils, high problems which confront women in
this country, tragic need of what he calls "reforms" in their
situation; but the suffrage is not important, political standing is
not important. "Life is not saved by politics, but by principles."

Coming from the chief politician of our times, the one who is
best acquainted with American politics at first hand, such statements are interesting. They are more than interesting—they are
illuminating. I want you to get the full force of them, and so I
am going to read you one or two of them.

> "I do not regard the movement as anything like as important as
> either its extreme friends or extreme opponents think. It is so

much less important than many other reforms that I have never been able to take a very heated interest in it."

"Life is not saved by politics, but by principles."*

"To sum up: The point I wish to emphasize is that the supreme importance and high position of the woman of the type of Julia Ward Howe cannot be materially increased by the possession of the ballot."

"I most earnestly desire to emphasize my feeling that the question of woman suffrage is unimportant."

Now, let me call your attention to the things whose supreme importance he does emphasize, in the same editorial:

"The ruin of motherhood and childhood by the merciless exploitation of the labor of women and children is a crime of capital importance."

"Any tendency to permit the man to shirk his duty as breadwinner, as keeper of the household, who owes his best effort to his wife and children, is an evil of capital importance."

"Any force or tendency which lowers the efficiency or the standard of living of either the average man or the average woman, whether on the farm or in the workshop or the store or the counting-room or the professions, is a tremendous evil, an evil of capital importance."

"Motherhood must be protected; and the State should make the security of the mothers its first concern."

You will note that all the things whose "capital importance" is especially emphasized, are problems of our industrial and social life in which women's health, welfare and happiness—in some cases women's very lives—are involved. But the suffrage is not important. "Life is not saved by politics, but by principles."

Now, Emma Goldman goes just one step farther than that. She emphasizes all these vital problems which confront women

* Quoted, with emphatic approval, from Miss Ida Tarbell.

in our society in exactly the same way that he does, and then she says that the suffrage is not only not important, but it is *entirely superfluous.* "Life is not saved by politics, but by principles"— that is her political philosophy exactly!

I don't know whether you have ever read Emma Goldman's essay on woman suffrage. It is published in her book, "Anarchism and Other Essays." It has just the same oracular way, that this editorial has, of belittling citizenship, and obscuring every political issue with a moral platitude. I have read both these essays, one after the other, and I repeat that I can see no difference whatever between the attitude of Theodore Roosevelt and the attitude of Emma Goldman upon the importance of citizenship to people who are confronted with acknowledged economic and social problems—except this, that Emma Goldman goes consistently to the limit.

Now, in exact opposition to these persons who have not an ardent faith in political democracy as the first step toward the solution of such problems, but who believe that the world can be saved only by their particular brand of philanthropic oratory —I want to say that I, for one, have an ardent faith in political democracy. I do believe that suffrage is important. I believe it is important to all people who are confronted and oppressed by social and economic evils.

I believe that when you have said that "the ruin of motherhood and childhood by the merciless exploitation of the labor of women and children is a crime of capital importance," you have already said that woman suffrage is a duty of capital importance.

I believe that when you have said: "Motherhood must be protected; and the State should make the security of the mothers its first concern"—you have already said that *your* first concern is to see to it that, in your State, the mothers are a part of the sovereign power.

Not only do I believe that the suffrage is important to those who are confronted by problems, however, but I believe it is important to those who are genuinely interested in principles. I cannot accept the complete separation of politics from principles which this editorial, and Emma Goldman's essay, suggest! I believe that politics is good for something; and if it is good for anything, then it is good as an opportunity for the effective expression of principles.

So much for the refutation. Now, I want to specify just what the great values of political citizenship are—and especially its values to women, and to women who work for pay. I have these values in my mind under four heads:

First, citizenship is a stimulus. It will tend to wake women up to an active discontent with their situation, and an aggressive, self-respecting intention to better it. And that is the first essential thing.

People say that the fact that women are not greatly awake and active in their own behalf now, that the workers, especially, as a body, are not fighting for citizenship, is a reason for withholding it. But they are just wrong! Citizenship is the stimulus. It is the gift (or the imposition—I don't care!) that will arouse them.

I can prove to you that citizenship is a stimulus by the history of the recent election in Los Angeles. I believe that a majority of the women of that city were opposed to woman suffrage, but after they got it, at the first vital ballot they were called on to cast, they went to the polls in overwhelming majorities.

With no exception, throughout the whole history of this movement, *after* the women of a State or country get citizenship, they value it, they use it, they will not relinquish it. And this is because with the using of it they begin to acquire that knowledge which makes it valuable. They learn the game.

That is the second great value of citizenship to women. It gives them a stimulus, and then it gives them knowledge-by-experience. It teaches them how to act intelligently in their own behalf.

And upon this point, again—people say that the fact that women as a class do not already possess the knowledge which pertains to citizens, is a reason for not making them citizens. And here again they are just wrong! Women as a class have not the knowledge which pertains to citizens, and they never will have under the sun until after they *are* citizens. For no special kind of knowledge ever arose in any group of individuals until after the activity to which that knowledge relates was open to them.

The women who don't want citizenship, don't know enough to want it. And the reason they don't know enough, is that they haven't the kind of knowledge that citizenship begets. Therefore the more they don't want it, the more they need it—the more you ought to want it for them.

Please do not think that what I am saying here is peculiar to women. It is true of mankind. I believe that the general awakening of their spirits and the progressive development of their minds are the two greatest benefits that have so far accrued to men from the possessing of civil liberty. For some time they will be the greatest benefits that will accrue to women.

But there is a third value of citizenship, more obvious, but for those not especially interested in institutions, less important than these two. I mean the power which citizenship gives you of accomplishing things through legislation and government. I do not think this is the chief general value of citizenship. I do not think that what the people can accomplish through their political institutions is the deep reason for having a popular system of government. But it *is* a reason, and for the workers a rapidly growing reason, and let us not be too scornful of it. Suffice it to say that obviously, in order to accomplish anything through the legislature, you have to be able to address the legislators as their constituents. The courtesy of a man to a woman is a lovely and beautiful thing, but for everyday steady reliability it can't compare at all to the courtesy of a legislator to his constituents!

But please remember that the power to promote legislation is not the main argument, it is not the original or basic reason for popular government. Neither are stimulus and education the original and basic reasons. The original reason—the great meaning of democracy in politics—is that it guarantees to every citizen a certain elementary standing in his community, and before the powers of that community. It gives him a little bit of the personal sacredness of a sovereign. It certifies to him that his needs and his wishes shall be of some consequence to the society he dwells in and serves. In this lies the historic origin, and still the radical significance of democracy in politics. Democracy did not arise because certain people sat down and thought it over, and decided that a good way to run a government would be to have all the people vote. It arose out of the gradually developing conviction in the mind of the common man that, though the government should run all to hell, he had a right to *be somebody*. And that is what it still means.

I would rather conclude with an illustration, than an exposition, of this fourth point. And so I recall you again to this illuminating editorial in the *Outlook*. Let us approach it, not logically but psychologically—seeking for the subconscious reason why it is that Theodore Roosevelt thinks that woman suffrage is not important.

When one specially points out that women confront all the great problems that men confront to-day, and then says that woman suffrage is not important—it seems to me he must unconsciously believe one of two things: either that the suffrage in general is not important, or else that women in general are not important.

Now, his worst enemy would not say that Mr. Roosevelt thinks the suffrage is not important; and so I am forced to conclude that it is women who are not important. And I make the conclusion in all seriousness; that, in so far as he is a public character and a man of affairs, his instinctive attitude towards *women in general* is to think that they are not of first-hand importance. That will continue to be his instinctive attitude *until women in general have become his constituents.*

Surely no one will maintain that if women *had* the suffrage in the United States, Theodore Roosevelt would have announced in the *Outlook* just at this time that woman suffrage is not important. And that is how this editorial becomes, upon examination, a strong argument in favor of the importance of woman suffrage—to women.

JOSEPHINE JEWELL DODGE

The Lesson That Came from the Sea—
What it Means to the Suffrage Cause

APRIL 1912

Both the suffragists and the antisuffragists argued that the sinking of the RMS *Titanic* in the frigid waters of the North Atlantic on the morning of April 12, 1912, held a suffrage lesson, although they disagreed about what it was. Antisuffragists pointed to the actions of chivalrous men who honored the timeworn adage of "women and children first" as evidence that men would protect women and therefore women did not need the vote. (The *Titanic*'s lifeboats could only accommodate half the passengers; the men onboard died disproportionately when they gave women and children preference to be saved.) Suffrage leaders emphatically distanced themselves from the "women and children first" tenet, seeing it as a barbarous relic of outmoded ideals. Women didn't want a different standard from men, they argued; they wanted to participate equally in all facets of life. This editorial by antisuffragist Josephine Jewell Dodge (1855–1928) lays out both sides of the argument.

———————

THINKERS WITHOUT REGARD TO POLITICS OR CREED,
SEE IN IT A REFUTATION OF THE ARGUMENTS OF
AGITATORS FOR THE BALLOT—IT POINTS OUT
A "DIFFERENCE."

In the story that came up from the sea there are many lessons. One of those lessons is that when the final crash came men and women alike were unanimous in making the sex distinction. It was not a question of "Voters first," but the cry all over the ship was "Women first!" In acquiescing to that cry the women admitted that they were not fitted for men's tasks. They did not think of the boasted "equality" in all things. This is not an implication that the women are inferior, it just shows an inequality or a difference.

Much has been spoken and written by thinkers on this phase of the disaster and its influence on the eternal cry of some women to be allowed to take up the activities and responsibilities that belong to man just as woman's responsibilities belong to woman. The disaster tends in its terribly grim way to point out the everlasting "difference" of the sexes.

Speaking of the sacrifice of the men aboard the Titanic, the Rev. Dr. Leighton Parks, of St. Bartholomew's Church, said, "The women did not ask for the sacrifice, but it was made. Those women who go shrieking about for their 'rights' want something very different. Put the world on a basis merely of 'rights' and you put it on an inclined plane where it will never stop until it has gone to the lowest level of barbarism and bestiality.

"These men gave up their lives in love, and in so doing they helped to pay the debt we all owe to the mothers who bore and reared us, to the sweethearts that have kept us pure, to the wives and friends who have suffered and sacrificed themselves for us."

Dr. Charles H. Parkhurst, writing in the New York "Journal," an ardent suffrage paper, says:

"One would suppose that those women who are making it a part of their creed to lampoon the members of the other sex and to charge them with all kinds of wanton injustice and coarse barbarity, would wince a little under the superb courtesy accorded to them at the wreck of the Titanic.

"That men will stand back, and, with full knowledge that it means their own death, will, with tender consideration, purchase with their lives the rescue of the women who are aboard ship, is a refutation of the coarse charge hurled against them, which ought to bring the blush of shame and self-contempt upon the cheeks of every one of these cantankerous viragos who are doing so much to bring their sex into discredit.

"We are not arguing for or against the doctrines that are being exploited by these incriminating members of what from our youth up we have been taught to consider the gentler sex.

"But it would seem as though with such an exhibition of chivalry of the finest sort, as was evinced at midnight of April 15th, the great mass of our women, thoroughly feminine at heart, and soundly appreciative of the magnificent spirit of their masculine companions, would rise up in revolt against the vulgar aspersions cast upon us by their libelous and hysterical sisters.

"That they do not openly and concertedly resent the conduct

of their defamatory leaders lays them under the implication of being of the same ilk and infected with the same virus, which we do not believe that they are.

"But people are estimated by the quality of their leaders, and for women to follow on unresistingly at the beck of a termagant argues that they have themselves been contaminated by a bacillus of the same order.

"Nothing would be so promotive of the interests of suffrage or be so likely to win for itself a place in the respect of intelligent and temperate ladies and gentlemen as for the main body of suffragists to decline the farther championship of rampant demagogues and put themselves under the conduct of women who are thoroughly women in manner and methods."

Commenting upon the subject editorially, The New York "Herald" says:

"But the suffragettes, who have been asking for equal rights for women, are using it as an argument that women should take their chances of drowning with the men, and in this they are at least consistent. On the other hand many women who are opposed to suffrage for their sex are also crying out against the sacrifice of male lives, under circumstances of heroism, and numerous letters have been received by the "Herald" insisting that hereafter no preference be given.

"It is really a matter for men to settle for themselves, because the feeling that the weak, whether they vote or not, should be those first protected is deeply implanted by nature. The suffragettes, by placing a plank in their platform abolishing the rule: 'Women and children first,' will probably make no headway so long as manhood shall endure."

Dr. Felix Adler, in a sermon following the disaster, also disagreed with the contention of the suffragettes. In part he said:

"It is necessary to emphasize this because some excellent women who are concerned for the equality of their sex with man have contended that the women should vote and have insisted on an equal number of men in the boats and an equal number of women. They have taken the idea of equality externally and mechanically; they have not understood the principle which Aristotle laid down, that wherever genuine equality existed no accidental inequality for the sake of the equality shall be offset by some counter act and corresponding inequality.

It is the rule of the sea and the land, and it is regrettable that women should try to base their equality, which is ethical, on the assumed equality in physical strength."

Under the caption, "Miss Pankhurst's Silly Talk," the New York "Evening Post" says editorially:

"'Only a matter of rule,' says Miss Sylvia Pankhurst, of the rescue of women on the Titanic, 'and there is no special chivalry about it.'

"Men of much use to the world perished in that catastrophe because their inherent chivalry compelled them to give way to women. But Miss Pankhurst is impudent enough to withhold credit for them. She wants to vote, she wants a voice in public affairs, she wants to hold public office, but she also wants a safe place in a life-boat at the cost of a useful man's life if she happens to be in a wreck, and she wants nothing to be said about chivalry afterward.

"What do the women survivors of the Titanic think of Miss Pankhurst and her views? What do they think of her coadjutor, Mrs. Mansel, who declares that 'the new woman would rather be without exceptional treatment'? Naturally, the British National Union of Women's Suffrage Societies is alarmed. It announces to the public its regret 'that certain suffragists should have made the Titanic disaster a field of controversy.' But 'certain suffragists,' when they are not invading the vestibules of legislatures, bullying politicians or smashing windows, will continue to talk arrant and often wicked nonsense. Miss Pankhurst and her set had already hurt the cause for which they think they are laboring. Now they have given it another setback."

MARIE JENNEY HOWE

An Anti-Suffrage Monologue

1912

Much antisuffrage sentiment boiled down to the argument that voting and engagement with politics would violate woman's essential nature, which should be confined to home, domesticity, and maternity. Suffragists found it fairly easy to punch holes in the often contradictory arguments put forward by the antis, as this satirical monologue by Marie Jenney Howe (1870–1934) demonstrates. Howe cleverly showed the contradictions of antisuffrage propaganda by arranging her arguments in couplets: "if you don't like one you can take the other." Howe, who was a Unitarian minister and writer, wrote this sketch for the drama group of the New York Woman Suffrage Party in 1912 and it gained wide circulation when it was distributed by NAWSA. She was also a founder of Heterodoxy, a Greenwich Village feminist group, whose vision she articulated in the same pointed language she had employed in her suffrage satire: "We intend to be ourselves, not just our little female selves, but our whole big human selves."

———————

Please do not think of me as old-fashioned. I pride myself on being a modern up-to-date woman. I believe in all kinds of broad-mindedness, only I do not believe in woman suffrage because to do that would be to deny my sex.

Woman suffrage is the reform against nature. Look at these ladies sitting on the platform. Observe their physical inability, their mental disability, their spiritual instability and general debility! Could they walk up to the ballot box, mark a ballot and drop it in? Obviously not. Let us grant for the sake of argument that they could mark a ballot. But could they drop it in? Ah, no. All nature is against it. The laws of man cry out against it. The voice of God cries out against it—and so do I.

Enfranchisement is what makes man man. Disfranchisement is what makes woman woman. If women were enfranchised every man would be just like every woman and every woman would be just like every man. There would be no difference between them. And don't you think this would rob life of just a little of its poetry and romance?

Man must remain man. Woman must remain woman. If man goes over and tries to be like woman, if woman goes over and tries to be like man, it will become so very confusing and so difficult to explain to our children. Let us take a practical example. If a woman puts on a man's coat and trousers, takes a man's cane and hat and cigar and goes out on the street, what will happen to her? She will be arrested and thrown into jail. Then why not stay at home?

I know you begin to see how strongly I *feel* on this subject, but I have some reasons as well. These reasons are based on logic. Of course, I am not logical. I am a creature of impulse, instinct and intuition—and I glory in it. But I know that these reasons are based on logic because I have culled them from the men whom it is my privilege to know.

My first argument against suffrage is that the women would not use it if they had it. You couldn't drive them to the polls. My second argument is, if the women were enfranchised they would neglect their homes, desert their families and spend all their time at the polls. You may tell me that the polls are only open once a year. But I know women. They are creatures of habit. If you let them go to the polls once a year, they will hang round the polls all the rest of the time.

I have arranged these arguments in couplets. They go together in such a way that if you don't like one you can take the other. This is my second anti-suffrage couplet. If the women were enfranchised they would vote exactly as their husbands do and only double the existing vote. Do you like that argument? If not, take this one. If the women were enfranchised they would vote against their own husbands, thus creating dissension, family quarrels, and divorce.

My third anti-suffrage couplet is—women are angels. Many men call me an angel and I have a strong instinct which tells me it is true; that is why I am an anti, because "I want to be an angel and with the angels stand." And if you don't like that argument take this one. Women are depraved. They would introduce into politics a vicious element which would ruin our national life.

Fourth anti-suffrage couplet: women cannot understand politics. Therefore there would be no use in giving women political power, because they would not know what to do with it. On the other hand, if the women were enfranchised, they would mount rapidly into power, take all the offices from all the men, and soon we would have women governors of all our states and dozens of women acting as President of the United States.

Fifth anti-suffrage couplet: women cannot band together. They are incapable of organization. No two women can even be friends. Women are cats. On the other hand, if women were enfranchised, we would have all the women banded together on one side and all the men banded together on the other side, and there would follow a sex war which might end in bloody revolution.

Just one more of my little couplets: the ballot is greatly over-estimated. It has never done anything for anybody. Lots of men tell me this. And the corresponding argument is—the ballot is what makes man man. It is what gives him all his dignity and all of his superiority to women. Therefore if we allow women to share this privilege, how could a woman look up to her own husband? Why, there would be nothing to look up to.

I have talked to many woman suffragists and I find them very unreasonable. I say to them: "Here I am, convince me." I ask for proof. Then they proceed to tell me of Australia and Colorado and other places where women have passed excellent laws to improve the condition of working women and children. But I say, "What of it?" These are facts. I don't care about facts. I ask for proof.

Then they quote the eight million women of the United States who are now supporting themselves, and the twenty-five thousand married women in the City of New York who are self-supporting. But I say again, what of it? These are statistics. I don't believe in statistics. Facts and statistics are things which no truly womanly woman would ever use.

I wish to prove anti-suffrage in a womanly way—that is, by personal example. This is my method of persuasion. Once I saw a woman driving a horse, and the horse ran away with her. Isn't that just like a woman? Once I read in the newspapers about a woman whose house caught on fire, and she threw the children out of the window and carried the pillows downstairs. Does that show political acumen, or does it not? Besides, look at the hats that women wear! And have you ever known a successful woman governor of a state? Or have you ever known a really truly successful woman President of the United States? Well, if they could they would, wouldn't they? Then, if they haven't, doesn't that show they couldn't? As for the militant suffragettes, they are all hyenas in petticoats. Now do you want to be a hyena and wear petticoats?

Now, I think I have proved anti-suffrage; and I have done it in a womanly way—that is, without stooping to the use of a single fact or argument or a single statistic.

I am the prophet of a new idea. No one has ever thought of it or heard of it before. I well remember when this great idea first came to me. It waked me in the middle of the night with a shock that gave me a headache. This is it: woman's place is in the home. Is it not beautiful as it is new, new as it is true? Take this idea away with you. You will find it very helpful in your daily lives. You may not grasp it just at first, but you will gradually grow into understanding of it.

I know the suffragists reply that all our activities have been taken out of the home. The baking, the washing, the weaving, the spinning are all long since taken out of the home. But I say, all the more reason that something should stay in the home. Let it be woman. Besides, think of the great modern invention, the telephone. That has been put into the home. Let woman stay at home and answer the telephone.

We antis have so much imagination! Sometimes it seems to us that we can hear the little babies in the slums crying to us. We can see the children in factories and mines reaching out their little hands to us, and the working women in the sweated industries, the underpaid, underfed women, reaching out their arms to us—all, all crying as with one voice, "Save us, save us, from Woman Suffrage." Well may they make this appeal to us, for who knows what woman suffrage might not do for such as these. It might even alter the conditions under which they live.

We antis do not believe that any conditions should be altered. We want everything to remain just as it is. All is for the best. Whatever is, is right. If misery is in the world, God has put it there; let it remain. If this misery presses harder on some women than others, it is because they need discipline. Now, I have always been comfortable and well cared for. But then I never needed discipline. Of course I am only a weak, ignorant woman. But there is one thing I do understand from the ground up, and that is the divine intention toward woman. I *know* that the divine intention toward woman is, let her remain at home.

The great trouble with the suffragists is this; they interfere too much. They are always interfering. Let me take a practical example.

There is in the City of New York a Nurses' Settlement, where sixty trained nurses go forth to care for sick babies and give them pure milk. Last summer only two or three babies died in this slum district around the Nurses' Settlement, whereas formerly hundreds of babies have died there every summer. Now what are these women doing? Interfering, interfering with the death rate! And what is their motive in so doing? They seek notoriety. They want to be noticed. They are trying to show off. And if sixty women who merely believe in suffrage behave in this way, what may we expect when all women are enfranchised?

What ought these women to do with their lives? Each one ought to be devoting herself to the comfort of some man. You may say, they are not married. But I answer, let them try a little harder and they might find some kind of a man to devote themselves to. What does the Bible say on this subject? It says, "Seek and ye shall find." Besides, when I look around me at the men; I feel that God never meant us women to be too particular.

Let me speak one word to my sister women who are here to-day. Women, we don't need to vote in order to get our own way. Don't misunderstand me. Of course I want you to get your own way. That's what we're here for. But do it indirectly. If you want a thing, tease. If that doesn't work, nag. If that doesn't do, cry—crying always brings them around. Get what you want. Pound pillows. Make a scene. Make home a hell on earth, but do it in a womanly way. That is so much more dignified and refined than walking up to a ballot box and dropping in a piece of paper. Can't you see that?

Let us consider for a moment the effect of woman's enfranchisement on man. I think some one ought to consider the men. What makes husbands faithful and loving? The ballot, and the monopoly of that privilege. If women vote, what will become of men? They will all slink off drunk and disorderly. We antis understand men. If women were enfranchised, men would revert to their natural instincts such as regicide, matricide, patricide and race-suicide. Do you believe in race-suicide or do you not? Then, isn't it our duty to refrain from a thing that would lure men to destruction?

It comes down to this. Some one must wash the dishes. Now, would you expect man, man made in the image of God, to roll up his sleeves and wash the dishes? Why it would be blasphemy. I know that I am but a rib and so I wash the dishes. Or I hire another rib to do it for me, which amounts to the same thing.

Let us consider the argument from the standpoint of religion. The Bible says, "Let the women keep silent in the churches." Paul says, "Let them keep their hats on for fear of the angels." My minister says, "Wives, obey your husbands." And my husband says that woman suffrage would rob the rose of its fragrance and the peach of its bloom. I think that is so sweet.

Besides did George Washington ever say, "votes for women?" No. Did the Emperor Kaiser Wilhelm ever say, "Votes for women?" No. Did Elijah, Elisha, Micah, Hezekiah, Obadiah and Jeremiah ever say, "Votes for women?" No. Then that settles it.

I don't want to be misunderstood in my reference to woman's inability to vote. Of course she could get herself to the polls and lift a piece of paper. I don't doubt that. What I refer to is the pressure on the brain, the effect of this mental strain on woman's delicate nervous organization and on her highly wrought sensitive nature. Have you ever pictured to yourself Election Day with women voting? Can you imagine how women, having undergone this terrible ordeal, with their delicate systems all upset, will come out of the voting booths and be led away by policemen, and put into ambulances, while they are fainting and weeping, half laughing, half crying, and having fits upon the public highway? Don't you think that if a woman is going to have a fit, it is far better for her to have it in the privacy of her own home?

And how shall I picture to you the terrors of the day after election? Divorce and death will rage unchecked, crime and contagious disease will stalk unbridled through the land. Oh, friends, on this subject I feel—I feel, so strongly that I can—not think!

LOS ANGELES TIMES

Squaws Beat Militants to Right of Franchise
JANUARY 30, 1913

In early 1913, Marie L. Baldwin (1863–1952), a Turtle Mountain Chippewa who had been an accountant since 1904 at the Bureau of Indian Affairs in Washington, D.C., received an unusual request: Would she organize a float for the upcoming suffrage parade to show the support of American Indian women for the right to vote? When Baldwin was interviewed by the wire services, she said she had not yet made up her mind about whether to comply with the request, but she made it clear that American Indian women had enjoyed the right to vote in their tribes since "time immemorial" and that they were considered full members when it came to making their wishes known. The article reported the existence of equal suffrage among American Indians in a straightforward fashion, but the headline succumbed to the casual racism of the times, referring to Indian women as "squaws," an extremely derogatory term. The March 3, 1913, parade referenced was organized by Alice Paul to coincide with Woodrow Wilson's inauguration. American Indian women were invited to participate in the suffrage parade on what seem to be equal terms, unlike black suffragists, who were told to march in a segregated section at the back so as not to offend the sensibilities of southern white suffragists.

WASHINGTON, Jan. 30.—The Indian woman as a suffragette may be represented in the suffragette parade here March 3. Mrs. Marie L. Baldwin, a Chippewa connected with the Indian bureau, has been asked to arrange for some sort of float which would portray the Indian woman as in favor of the voting right.

"I have not yet decided," Mrs. Baldwin said today, "whether I will obey the request of the parade arrangers or not. As for the Indian women, they have had virtual suffrage, also the power of recall, since time immemorial. Whenever they were dissatisfied with a chief of a tribe, all they had to do was to make their wishes known and he was promptly recalled.

"And as to voting, I do not know that they exercised the right often, but it amounted to the same thing, for they would inform their men what they wanted and the result of the election usually showed that their wishes had prevailed."

ALICE PAUL

Testimony at Suffrage Parade Hearings
MARCH 8, 1913

Alice Paul planned the first major suffrage parade in the nation's capital in just nine weeks. As this testimony to a Senate committee details, she had to haggle with D.C. authorities over the date (she wanted it the day before President Wilson's inauguration on March 4, they suggested the day after), the parade route, and the thorny question of police protection under several overlapping jurisdictions. The suffragists had cause to be concerned about their safety. At 3:00 P.M. on March 3, 1913, almost ten thousand suffrage marchers left the Peace Monument near Capitol Hill and began the fifteen-block procession down Pennsylvania Avenue. Unruly bystanders taunted and physically jostled the marchers while the police stood idly by. Finally the cavalry was called, order was restored, and the parade resumed. Even though newspapers at the time were generally unsympathetic to the suffrage cause, commentators were outraged at the insult and injury inflicted on American women simply trying to exercise their constitutional right to protest. The Senate convened this hearing and concluded that major lapses in police protection had contributed to the near riot. Paul relished the publicity and determined to stage more such militant actions. Within the year she had split from NAWSA and founded the Congressional Union, which later became the National Woman's Party.

The witness was duly sworn by the chairman.

The CHAIRMAN.   Give your full name to the reporter.

Miss PAUL.   Miss Alice Paul.

The CHAIRMAN.   Where do you live, Miss Paul?

Miss PAUL.   Moorestown, N.J.

The CHAIRMAN.   What has been your position in connection with this parade?

Miss PAUL.   I was the chairman of the committee which arranged the procession.

The CHAIRMAN.   As chairman of the committee, you may state to this committee what you did in regard to securing protection for the parade, and just state it in your own way as clearly and concisely as possible.

Miss PAUL.   The first thing we did was to go to President Taft. I think the date was February 4. The reason that we went to President Taft was because it had taken us about a month of very arduous work to secure a permit to march up the Avenue.

The CHAIRMAN.   When did you secure this permit?

Miss PAUL.   We secured it on January 9.

The CHAIRMAN.   On January 9 you secured the permit?

Miss PAUL.   Yes, sir; we began in December, about the middle of December, and we went first to the chief of police and then to the Commissioners of the District, and then to the chairman of the District Committee of Congress, and also to the inaugural committee chairman, and the various members of that committee, trying in every possible way to get the permit.

The CHAIRMAN.   State briefly what difficulties you had and what objections were made to granting the permit.

Miss PAUL.   Maj. Sylvester, when we first went to him, said he would not allow us to have a procession in Washington on March 3. He wanted us to have it on March 5. After considerable argument we finally insisted that we would have it on March 3.

The CHAIRMAN.   What reasons did he have for not wanting to have it on March 3?

Miss PAUL.   What he said was all in the light of advice. He thought March 5 would be so much better for the procession; there would be more people here on March 5, and so on. We did not agree with these reasons, and we determined to have it on the 3d.

The CHAIRMAN.   Did he suggest that there would be a very large crowd here on the 3d, and he didn't have force enough to protect you?

Miss PAUL.   No. The argument he used was that there would be a so much larger crowd on the 5th that it would be so much better for us; that all the people would be here to see us then, and so on.

The CHAIRMAN.   His idea seemed to be to have you parade on the 5th, when you would have a larger crowd?

Miss PAUL.   Yes, sir. When we did finally make him agree to let us have it on the 3d, the question arose as to where the procession would take place. We asked him for the Avenue. He said that would be impossible; that we would have to have it on Sixteenth Street, beginning on Florida Avenue, way out in the country. And his reason then was that there would be such huge crowds he could not possibly protect us on the Avenue. It was exactly contradictory to his first argument.

So we then spent about a month trying to get permission to have it on the Avenue, instead of on Sixteenth Street. He said it was a Democratic victory, and the situation would be worse than it had been for years and years at inauguration time. This would mean that the riff-raff of the South would be here—those are his words—and it would be quite impossible for him to protect us; and he gave very alarming pictures of what Pennsylvania Avenue was at inauguration times.

However, after taking countless delegations of women to Maj. Sylvester and the commissioners of the District, and starting a newspaper campaign of publicity, we finally, on January 9, received this permit from Maj. Sylvester.

At the time he gave the permit he stated to newspaper men that he had never opposed our marching on Pennsylvania Avenue, excepting that he had thought we should not do it in the evening; if we wanted it in the afternoon, he was quite willing for us to do so. Of course, in our formal application we stated that we wanted to march in the afternoon.

The CHAIRMAN. You judged that by reported interviews in the newspapers—not from anything he said to you?

Miss PAUL. He said that to a great number of people who went to him. He said it to Miss Jeanette Richards.

The CHAIRMAN. You were not with Miss Richards when he said it?

Miss PAUL. No; but the point was that finally on January 9 we received the permit, after about a month's struggle for it.

Then, having been told how very dangerous it was to march on the Avenue on March 3, and that he was entirely unable to protect us, as he said, we thought it might be well to appeal to the President for protection, and we went then to President Taft. He said, of course we must be protected; that if a permit had been given, the Avenue must be kept clear; but the request for any protection outside of what the District could give us must come from the District officials.

I then went back to Maj. Sylvester and related this to him, and he said that it was preposterous to get troops; he would not dream of asking for them; he could manage the situation—which was exactly opposite to what he had told us before.

The CHAIRMAN. Did you suggest to him then that he might not have sufficient force to handle the crowd?

Miss PAUL. We reminded him of what he had said before.

The CHAIRMAN. What answer did he make to that?

Miss PAUL. He said it would be all right. We were still rather skeptical, and finally we went to the commissioners. Gen. Anson Mills took me to see each one of the commissioners, except Gen. Johnston, who was away, but we saw him afterwards. As the result they said they would ask the Secretary of War for more protection, and they wrote a letter to the Secretary of War, which you have in your record. Then a reply came from the War Department, saying they were unable to grant this aid.

The CHAIRMAN. That is the reply that we have in the record?

Miss PAUL. That is the reply we have in the record. I then asked Mrs. Jenness-Miller to go to the War Department and see if she could do anything. She was unable to see Secretary Stimson. I then went myself to Gen. Johnston to ask if anything could be done, and I told him again all the tales that the commissioners and Maj. Sylvester had told us about the Avenue being difficult to keep cleared on that day. He said perhaps these tales were told us to discourage us in our efforts. He said it was not as bad as they led us to think. He said nothing further could be done, that he felt sure that the Avenue would be protected all right, and that they could not make any further appeals for troops.

The CHAIRMAN. Did he say anything about any shortage of police or officers of the police force?

Miss PAUL. No. Maj. Sylvester at the beginning, when we asked him for protection, said that he had only 100 men to handle the matter, and that that force could not do anything.

The CHAIRMAN. Where did he say he had just a hundred men?

Miss PAUL. Where? He said he had only a hundred men when we first asked him for the permit.

The CHAIRMAN. Did you understand him to mean that he had only a hundred men in the District of Columbia?

Miss Paul. Yes, sir. That is the reason that we went up to the chairman of the District Committee. I said if it is true that Maj. Sylvester has only a hundred men, we would then like to ask for an appropriation to give him more men. Mr. Johnson said whenever Maj. Sylvester didn't want to do anything, he didn't have enough men; that he had enough men, and there was no need for an appropriation.

Then I went to Gen. Johnston who said that nothing could be done.

Commissioner Johnston. Nothing could be done as to troops?

Miss Paul. Yes. I asked Gen. Johnston if there was anything further that we could do, since the War Department had decided that they could not do anything; if there was any further step that we could take which would aid in protecting us that day. He said no, there was nothing more to do.

Mrs. Mills has said that he was very much opposed to our having the procession. Then I went personally to see Secretary Stimson, as we had already gotten this letter from the War Department, and I related at length the very inadequate and incompetent policing of the city at the time of the arrival of Mrs. Rosalie Jones. Secretary Stimson said that undoubtedly if the permit had been given we must be protected; that the only question would be should it come from him or from the District officials, and that he would communicate with the District officials and would let me know in the morning. So in the morning I asked Mrs. Moller to go around and get his reply, which was that he had not received a definite request from the District of Columbia officials.

I then called up the President's office to ask if anything in that direction could be done, and they said, "No: the recommendation must come from the Secretary of War."

I sent Dr. Monroe Hopkins around to see Maj. Sylvester and the commissioner—this was on Sunday, and we were getting very short on time—to ask them to make a definite request on the War Department.

The Chairman. Who was that?

Miss Paul. Dr. Monroe Hopkins. He is in Philadelphia. I talked to him last night by long distance phone, and he sent me this telegram. Would you like to see his telegram? He then told me, as he represents in that telegram, that Maj. Sylvester said that he would not ask for troops. He then called up one of the commissioners—it was, I think, Commissioner Rudolph—he mentions it there—and he also said he would not ask for troops.

We also tried then to get troops from the various suffragette States, in case their troops might be here. I sent Mrs. Katherine Woods to see the Senators and Representatives from suffragette States, and we found that no troops would be here from suffragette States.

We also went that evening to see Gov. Sulzer, of New York, and asked him for troops, and he refused the New York troops.

The CHAIRMAN. Of course, he could not very well detail the New York troops.

Miss PAUL. We want to show that we did everything possible, took every possible step. The reason for this was because Capt. Hobson called up and told me he could not get anything from the Commissioners of the District of Columbia or anything from the police department. The troops could be utilized, however; as long as they were outside of the District they could act as an escort. So we did.

We exhausted every possible means of getting protection on that day, and we made it clearly known to every official the immense number of women that were coming, and that they must be prepared.

I would say, too, in regard to getting the Avenue cleared of street cars, and getting the whole Avenue, we met the same constant opposition. That was the reason we had the bill introduced in Congress, because we had been unable to do anything as far, at least, as Maj. Sylvester was concerned.

The CHAIRMAN. Now, with all your requests of the police department you were not able to get a direct request from them to the Secretary of War stating that troops were necessary, and requesting a detail of troops?

Miss PAUL. No; both the War Department and the commissioners and the police department always assured us, after we had gotten the permit, that everything would be all right; that the place would be thoroughly policed. However, they added that if there was any trouble the fault would be with some one else; the War Department said, "If there is any trouble the fault is with the commissioners," and Maj. Sylvester said, "If there is any trouble, of course, it is up to Stimson."

The CHAIRMAN. We have in the record the letters from the Secretary of War, showing the position of the War Department——

Miss PAUL. Yes.

The CHAIRMAN. Showing that they considered it obligatory on them not to send troops unless a request was sent by the city authorities.

Miss PAUL. But that we very carefully pointed out to the city authorities, and they refused, it seemed, to act, and still said, "If trouble does occur it will be Secretary Stimson's fault," though we urged them to make the request if they thought it was needed, but they always assured us that it was not needed.

The CHAIRMAN. That they could take care of it?

Miss PAUL. Quite; and before they gave us this permit they told us it would be impossible.

Senator DILLINGHAM. How many interviews in all did you have with Maj. Sylvester?

Miss PAUL. I could not say.

Senator DILLINGHAM. Give us some idea.

Miss PAUL. You see, I sent so many people——

Senator DILLINGHAM. How many did you have personally?

Miss PAUL. I should imagine about four. I know positively of four at this moment—possibly more.

Senator DILLINGHAM. How many people did you send?

Miss PAUL. Really a tremendous number, I should think; there were a good many people that I called on when they wrote letters or telephoned or passed resolutions at meetings, they went to see him. I mean that during that month it was constant.

Senator DILLINGHAM. It was a sort of bombardment?

Miss PAUL. That is what we endeavored to make it, but it did not work. Would you like to see the permit?

Senator DILLINGHAM. I would, yes.

Miss Paul here handed a paper to Senator Dillingham.

The CHAIRMAN. This telegram should not be put into the record. It is not sworn to and possibly it would not give us any more information than we already have because the Secretary of War this morning set out fully the position of the Federal Government and the request of the District authorities.

Miss PAUL. The only point in this is that we went personally to Maj. Sylvester and Maj. Sylvester refused to act.

The CHAIRMAN. Probably he would not act in any way where the Secretary of War should act, so that would not add anything to the record.

HELEN HAMILTON GARDENER

Woman Suffrage, Which Way?

NOVEMBER 1913

Helen Hamilton Gardener (1853–1925), a writer and lecturer, first gained notoriety in the 1880s for publicly challenging the notion that women's brains were inferior to men's. Her scientific conclusions had political connotations, and she soon found herself in demand as a lecturer on women's rights. After moving to Washington, D.C., she joined the Congressional Committee of the National American Woman Suffrage Association. Instead of following Alice Paul when Paul seceded to found what became the National Woman's Party, Gardener stuck with NAWSA, where she served as a key liaison to President Woodrow Wilson. This pamphlet was published by NAWSA in 1915, but its genesis was a speech that Gardener gave to the Southern States Suffrage Conference in New Orleans in November 1913. In a region generally unsympathetic to women's suffrage, Gardener appealed to southern men to match the chivalry of western men who had already enfranchised their women. While Gardener stressed the inevitability of suffrage, it was still not at all clear which way—federal amendment or state action—would guarantee that outcome, although by 1915 efforts were coalescing around the federal route.

The time is past when there is any question as to whether or not we are to have woman suffrage. Already in eleven of our States and in twenty-eight countries it is in operation. The question before us now is, *Which way* do we prefer to have it come—State by State, as it has so far come, or all at one time by constitutional amendment?

The South has had some rather trying experiences with the vote being conferred upon its citizens by the latter method.

With that experience in mind the question now is: Is the South willing to delay so long, in this new movement in popular government, that it will again have the matter taken out of its own hands?

Is it not far better that the men (as well as the women) of the South recognize that a *real* Democracy is at hand? That a *real* (and the *first*) Republic is about to be born where

391

government shall, in deed and in truth, rest upon the consent of the governed? Where there shall not be taxation without representation?

The South is famed for its chivalry, yet the men of eleven of our Western States have past them in this race for chivalry which is based upon justice. A chivalry which says to the women of their households: "We do not want to hold you in legal subjection. You must and shall have every legal and political right which we claim as ours. A country cannot be free with its mothers a subject class before the law, with half of its people political paupers, dependent upon the other half for justice. We want our commissions as law-makers to come from the homes as well as from the street and the office. We do not want the great principles of Democracy to be too small to extend to both sexes. Women stood by our sides and helped to conquer the wilderness. They bore the hardships as well as the men. We refuse to take for ourselves alone the best and highest results of the struggle—Liberty, Equality, Fraternity."

Is not that a far finer chivalry than is mere word-flattery?

Are you willing that the Western men outdo you, surpass the Southern men in justice, courtesy and respect for the women of their States? Have you Southern men less confidence to repose in the mothers who bore you, the wives who bear your children, the daughters of whom you are so proud, than have the men of Illinois, or California or Colorado? Are you willing that your women shall appeal in vain to you for citizenship, for self-government, and that they shall receive it at the hands of men more just than you—through Constitutional Amendment? Is it not far better that you put your own house in order? Will not this insure to *you* the gratitude, co-operation of the new citizens far more surely than the other way?

I can assure you, that the Western women are almost as proud of their men for having given them the franchise without a serious struggle by them to secure it, as they are of their new dignity of citizenship itself.

These men never fail to express their belief and knowledge that it has worked good, and only good, to their States.

And you must remember that it is no longer an experiment in some of them.

In Colorado, the most populous of them, where the women

have been voters for so long (20 years) a time as to make it beyond question a good test, a State where there are large cities and vast wealth, it is the universal testimony of the public men that the votes and the help of the women have been of inestimable value in bringing that State to the high civilization to which it has attained. These men have found the advice, the insight and the co-operation of the women of the State invaluable.

And it has done something even finer than this. It has made of those men and women real friends, real comrades. They respect each other. They trust each other in a better and finer sense. They realize that they are equally responsible for the defects of their government. The women are not resentful or petty in their judgments, holding the men to account for all the wrongs and mistakes and holding themselves as "judges after the fact," without responsibility and without understanding of the needs, the difficulties and the possible remedies.

They work together for the things they want. If they find they have made a mistake they work together to correct it. This leaves no place for sex antagonism. It enlarges the outlook of the women. It makes them realize that the price of liberty is eternal vigilance, and that the governing of a city or a State is simply a larger home-making, for, after all, what is the State and city but your home?

The house you live in is only a small part of your home, just as the room you sleep in is a smaller part of that home—as the kitchen or the dining-room is your "home" but surely not *all* of it. No woman is doing all of her home-making if she keeps only her own room attractive. She is not a good homemaker if she thinks of nothing but her kitchen.

It is equally true of the city and the state. The woman has the homemaker's instinct. What man ever makes a real home? He may pay for chairs and tables and cook-stoves, but the quality which transforms these things into a home (whether of high or low estate) is the woman's part. She wants permanency, cleanliness, and order. She wants beauty and harmony of surroundings. The State needs these and the other qualities which women bring to their work. Men do not see, or, seeing, do not care much for many of the things which make for the higher civilization, the cleaner, more ordered life. Garbage cans in the street, raw meat hung in the dust, milk cans washed in polluted water, these things are the housekeeper's problem. They appeal to women. Men are thinking of stocks, bonds, crops of cotton or grain—then the epidemic comes along, the typhoid gathers in a few loved ones, and some woman's club comes forward and finds out that the water supply of the town is polluted.

But we must all understand that this "Feminist movement" is not local. It is world-wide. It began with the education of girls and it cannot and will not stop until woman stands as a human unit, even as her brother is a human unit.

Throughout history he has looked upon himself as the Unit and upon her as the cipher that stood back of him.

From his point of view, of itself, the cipher was valueless. In its relation to him only did it achieve value. It multiplied him tenfold.

If he chose to remove himself, she became once more the cipher.

If this condition was to remain, the first fatal blunder was made when women were allowed (not so long ago, either) to learn the alphabet.

And, after all, it has taken a very brief time, as history goes, to lift the women of the world, compared with the eons of time that it required to do the same thing for different classes of men.

Up to a few hundred years ago the masses of men were the pawns that Barons and Kings used to play with.

Men were the ciphers then, used by brute force and inherited rank to give fictitious value to the privileged men.

Those in power then, like some of them now, laughed at the idea of "the average man" having the same legal rights and political opportunities as were held by the privileged class of men.

They said it wasn't his place. He was unfit for self-government. He would wreck the State.

Well, he changed the State, it is true, but he bettered it, and what was more important still, he *bettered himself*. He grew up to his new dignity and status of a human unit. Women will do the same.

There never was in all history so well prepared a new electorate in education and intelligence as the women of America.

We must remember that every struggle made by man for

his own emancipation from bondage has worked for woman's liberty, also. Every blow that was struck for his own human status helped to weaken the bonds on the woman who stood encouraging him in his upward struggle.

She has earned your help now.

It would be ingratitude, unspeakable, for man to refuse to her the help which she so faithfully gave to him. Never an argument used by man in the interest of his own liberty but applies with added force to women.

Listen! Let me quote from three of your Democratic leaders of today. Then you shall say whether what they say is true, whether they meant what they said.

In a very remarkable article written recently by that distinguished Democrat, Mr. William Randolph Hearst, in speaking of the founders of this Nation, he said;

"On the one hand were the Democratic Republicans, who believed both in the letter and in the spirit of the Declaration of Independence, who were convinced that a new order of things was both advisable and advantageous; that the old established systems of government *by a superior class* were *failures*, and that the government by all the people was not only the most just and righteous, but the most practical and the most successful form of government that could be devised."

Did he mean it? Government by all the people, and that there should be no class? And, then, are women people?

In speaking before a great patriotic body of women recently in Washington our silver-tongued Secretary of State, the Hon. William Jennings Bryan, used these words:

"We established an independent nation in order that men might enjoy a new kind of happiness and a new kind of dignity. That kind which a man has when he respects every other man's and woman's individuality as he respects his own; where he is not willing to draw distinctions between classes; where he is not willing to shut the door of privilege in the face of anyone."

Again, he said before the same distinguished body of patriotic women, of whom I was one:

"The *problems* are *different*, but the *principles* are the *same*. Turn back to the Declaration of Independence and the Constitution and apply the principles found in them to our modern questions.

"This spirit must lead you to work for the preservation *to each individual* of his inalienable rights and to keep this a Government of the people, for the people, by the people. Then, and then only, will you be true Daughters of the American Revolution."

Now, are women individuals? Are they people? Did the Secretary of State really mean those words at their par value?

The arguments against woman suffrage are, in point of fact, simply arguments against self-government. They are the arguments which have been used by king to serf in all the ages past, with women now the disqualified unit or "lower class."

If government is to rest upon suffrage at all—that is, upon the expressed will of anybody not a "king by divine right"—who is to decide that men are born with the divine right to vote, and that I am not?

When and how did they get the right and where and how did I lose it?

That always puzzles me. I can not remember when I lost it. If it is a divine right, what particular streak of divinity has been discovered in men that women lack?

If it is not a natural, inherent, human right, then they say it is a "conferred privilege." Now, who conferred it? Where did they get it to confer?

Is not special privilege in government a wrong and an outrage against which people have been fighting since history began?

Again, I want to point a moral here, and so I am going to quote from President Wilson:

"As for other men setting up as a Providence over myself, I seriously object. I will not live under trustees if I can help it. If any part of our people want to be wards; if they want to have guardians put over them; if they want to be taken care of; if they want to be children patronized by the Government; why I am sorry, because it will sap the manhood of America."

There never was a truer thing written than that. And it has already sapped the womanhood of America to such an extent that there are women willing to travel around the country telling other women that their place is at home; that they ought to stay inside of four walls, where guardians and trustees will keep them in perpetual tutelage, and take care of them like children.

These traveling ladies, who insist that woman's place is

the home, assert that this movement of ours is one of sex antagonism.

Was it "sex antagonism" that made President Wilson object to having guardians set over him? There isn't even anything new about the cry of "stirring up sex antagonism." It is the same old argument used against Thomas Jefferson and against every other man who has stood for *real* Democracy. It is the cry of Power against People. It is the argument of those who have, against those who have not the benefits which all must pay for. Absolutely the only change in it is that to-day they use the word "sex," while in our father's day they used "class antagonism" to cover the same old selfish abuse of Privilege.

Again, in a recent speech, President Wilson emphasized in the strongest possible words the fact that the sacred part of America's heritage is her claim to be governed by the *consent* of all of her people.

He even went so far as to say that he "would like to believe that nowhere could a Government *endure* which is supported by anything but the consent of the governed."

But, lest you think I have misquoted the President, I want to read his own words.

He was speaking of the great size of our country, then he said;

"But the extent of the American conquest is not what gives America distinction in the annals of the world. It is the professed *purpose* of the conquest, which was to see to it that every foot of that land should be the home of *free, self-governed people*, who should have no government whatever which did not rest upon the consent of the governed. I would like to believe that all this hemisphere is devoted to the same *sacred purpose*, and that nowhere can any Government endure which is stained by blood or *supported by anything but the consent of the governed*." Pres. Wilson's address, Swarthmore College, Pa., Oct. 25, 1913. (Washington Post.)

In a recent book Senator John Sharp Williams has collected and commented upon the strongest and best writings and acts of the father of Democracy, Thomas Jefferson. There is hardly a page of the volume which is not, an unanswerable argument for woman suffrage. And this holds good in regard to the words of both Thomas Jefferson and Senator Williams.

It is quite possible that neither of these men realized that their words were quite as strong arguments for women and their liberty and self-government as they were for these same desirable things for men.

Possibly neither Thomas Jefferson nor Senator Williams so much as thought of one-half of all these "people" or "citizens" who must obey the laws when they propounded the "self-evident facts" about "inalienable rights," "rights derived from God," that *could* not be alienated *even by their own consent*, etc., etc. How did all these terms get to be the property of one-half of mankind? Rights are not masculine only, and Justice knows no sex.

Now, assuming that these and other distinguished Democrats (as well as Republicans and Progressives) said what they meant, assuming that they are sincere when they speak or write for the public (and I would not wish to be guilty of assuming anything else in their cases), I ask you in which way the South is going to meet this question: State by State, controling the details itself, or by a National Constitutional Amendment?

The passage of such an amendment to the United States Constitution is no longer a remote contingency. In the Sixty-third Congress the following resolution was introduced in both the Senate and the House:

"RESOLVED by the Senate and the House of Representatives of the United States of America in Congress assembled (two-thirds of each House concurring therein), That the following article be proposed to the legislatures of the several States as an amendment to the Constitution of the United States, which, when ratified by three-fourths of the said legislatures, shall be valid as part of said Constitution, namely:

"Article—Section 1. The right of citizens of the United States to vote shall not be denied or abridged by the United States or by any State on account of sex.

"Section 2. Congress shall have power by appropriate legislation to enforce the provisions of this article."

For the first time since 1892, the amendment was favorably reported to the Senate in 1913, and on March 19, 1914, it received a vote of 35 to 34 in favor, lacking only 11 votes of the necessary two-thirds majority. It was reported to the House by the Judiciary Committee without recommendation—the first time since 1894 that it has been reported out of committee in the House of Representatives. On January 12th, 1915, it received a vote of 174 in favor to 204 opposed—lacking 78 of the necessary two-thirds majority. In view of this showing of strength in Congress for a woman suffrage amendment, it behooves the Southern States to arouse themselves if they would secure that Southern women shall be enfranchised by the action of their own Southern men, and by amendment of their own State Constitutions.

Already there are over four million women in America who have the Presidential vote, who vote for their Senators and Representatives. What right have these four million to a higher and firmer citizenship than have the other women of the country? Why should a woman who lives in Colorado or California or Illinois be a citizen, and in South Carolina and Louisiana a voiceless, unconsidered cipher politically?

Why should she be a unit in one State and a cipher in another? Why is she capable of self-government and the dignity of liberty of conscience in Chicago or Denver or San Francisco, and incapable of, or without that dignity, in Charleston or New Orleans? Why can Western men trust the women of their States, and the Southern men not do so? Why are the women of one part of the country helpful in government and useless or dangerous in another part?

And in this connection I want to refer to one thing that is constantly brought up in arguments on this subject. That is whether or not women will better conditions when they vote; whether they will or will not vote for this or that "reform?"

I insist that you have no right to ask just what woman is going to do with her vote when she gets it.

That question is always based on two assumptions: First, that man has a right to dictate to her, to control her vote and make her vote the way he wants to; and the other is that she most likely is going to vote either like a knave or a fool, that she will be prone to use her vote with bad results.

Nobody assumes that attitude when extending the franchise to the young men as they become of age. Now, why should women be asked or required to prove that they are not going to vote unwisely? Are they more corrupt or more foolish than their 21-year-old sons?

There is just one other point which it might be well to consider from a Southerner's outlook, in case the fundamental
principle of self-government and human justice does not appeal
to you when these standards of democracy are being applied
to women.

It is this: You are doubtless aware that there is a strong movement on foot to make the representation of the States in Congress depend upon the number of voters, and not upon the
population.

When that carries (and it has great and strong backing), the
South will need the vote of every patriotic woman as well as
man, unless she is willing to be swamped utterly and hopelessly.

It will be a trifle late to prepare for this situation after the
move is effected.

"*Now* is the accepted time," if the South is to hold its own in
chivalry and justice towards its women—or yield these to the
men of the West.

"*Now* is the accepted time," if the South is to hold its own in
national representation—or yield to the hoards of foreign-born
voters of the East.

"*Now* is the accepted time" to gain the gratitude and respect
of the Southern women and their loyal co-operation—or to
throw these away by allowing the National Government to give
them the dignity of citizenship which you refuse to them.

Woman suffrage is coming, in the South as elsewhere. It is
almost here. The only question now is, WHICH WAY?

MARY JOHNSTON

A Difference of Opinion

1913

Mary Johnston (1870–1936) was one of the country's most popular turn-of-the-century writers. *To Have and To Hold*, a historical romance set in colonial Jamestown, was the nation's best-selling novel in 1900, selling close to half a million copies. So when Johnston's suffrage novel *Hagar* appeared in 1913, offering a fictional account of scenes that might have been occurring in actual households across the South, it caused a stir. Set in a small backwater of rural Virginia called Gilead Balm, it tells the story of Hagar Ashendyne, a product of the Old South who grows up to be a New Woman. That widening perspective sets up the "difference of opinion" confrontation described in this excerpt: in order for women like Hagar to grow and prosper, the old values of the South must give way to more modern views. For a work that is usually referred to as a suffrage novel, *Hagar* is more a general plea for women's emancipation than a suffrage tract. It received only mixed reviews and failed to capture the reading public's attention. Even though Johnston is practically forgotten today as a novelist, she deserves recognition as part of a determined cadre of southern suffragists who raised the issue in a region that was decidedly unreceptive to their message.

———————

But the great Gilead Balm explosion came three days later.

It was nearly sunset, and they were all upon the wide, front porch—the Colonel, Old Miss, Miss Serena, Captain Bob, Mrs. LeGrand, Hagar. Ralph was not there, he had ridden to Hawk Nest, but would return to-night. It had been a beautiful, early September day, the sky high and blue, the air all sunny vigour. Gilead Balm sat and enjoyed the cool, golden, winey afternoon, the shadows lengthening over the hills, the swallows overhead, the tinkle of the cow-bells. It was not one of your families that were always chattering. The porch held rather silent than otherwise. Mrs. LeGrand could, indeed, keep up a smooth, slow flow of talk, but Mrs. LeGrand had been packing to return to Eglantine which would "open" in another week, and she was somewhat fatigued. The Colonel, pending the arrival of yesterday's newspaper, was reviewing that of the day before yesterday. Captain Bob and Lisa communed together. Old Miss knitted. Miss Serena ran a strawberry emery bag through and through with her embroidery needle. Hagar had a book, but she was not reading. It lay face down in her lap; she was hardly thinking; she was dreaming with her eyes upon a vast pearly, cumulus cloud, coming up between the spires of the cedars. A mulatto boy appeared with the mail-bag. "Ha!" said the Colonel, and stretched out his hand.

There was a small table beside him. He opened the bag and turned the contents out upon this, then began to sort them. No one—it was a Gilead Balm way—claimed letter or paper until the Colonel had made as many little heaps as there were individuals and had placed every jot and tittle of mail accruing, ending by shaking out the empty bag. He did all this to-day. Captain Bob had only a county paper—no letters for Old Miss—a good deal of forwarded mail for Mrs. LeGrand— the Colonel's own—letters and papers for Hagar. The Colonel handled each piece, glanced at the superscription, put it in the proper heap. He shook out the bag; then, gathering up Mrs. LeGrand's mail, gave it to her with a smile and a small courtly bow. Miss Serena rose, work in hand, and took hers from the table. Lisa walked gravely up, then returned to Captain Bob with the county paper in her mouth. The Colonel's shrunken long fingers took up Hagar's rather large amount and held it out to her. "Here, Gipsy"—the last time for many a day that he called her Gipsy. A letter slipped from the packet to the floor. Bending, the Colonel picked it up, and in doing so for the first time regarded the printing on the upper left-hand corner—*Return in five days to the——Equal Suffrage League*. The envelope turned in his hand. On its reverse, across the flap, was boldly stamped—VOTES FOR WOMEN.

Colonel Argall Ashendyne straightened himself with a jerk. "Hagar!—What is that? How do you happen to get letters like that?—Answer!"

His granddaughter, who had risen to take her mail, regarded first the letter and then the Colonel with some astonishment. "What do you mean, grandfather? The letter's from my friend, Elizabeth Eden. I wonder if you don't remember her, that summer long ago at the New Springs?"

The Colonel's forefinger stabbed the three words on the back of the envelope. "You don't have friends and correspondents who are working for *that?*"

"Why not? I propose presently actively to work for it myself."

Apoplectic silence on the part of the Colonel. The suddenly arisen storm darted an electric feeler from one to the other upon the porch.

"What's the matter?" demanded Captain Bob. "Something's the matter!"

Old Miss, who had not clearly caught the Colonel's words, yet felt the tension and put in an authoritative foot. "What have you done now, Hagar? Who's been writing to you? What is it, Colonel?"

Ralph, in his riding-clothes, coming through the hall from the back where he had just dismounted, felt the sultry hush. "What's happened? What's the matter, Hagar?"

"Get me a glass of water, Serena!" breathed the Colonel. He still held the letter.

"My dear friend, let me fan you!" exclaimed Mrs. LeGrand, and moved to where she could see the offending epistle. "VOTES FOR—oh, Hagar, you surely aren't one of *those* women!"

Miss Serena, who had flown for the water, returned. The Colonel drank and the blood receded from his face. The physical shock passed, there could be seen gathering the mental lightning. Miss Serena, too, read over his shoulder "VOTES— . . . Oh, *Hagar!*"

Hagar laughed—a cool, gay, rippling sound. "Why, how round-eyed you all are! It isn't murder and forgery. Is the word 'rebellion' so strange to you? May I have my letter, grandfather?"

The Colonel released the letter, but not the situation. "Either you retire from such a position and such activities, or you cease to be granddaughter of mine—"

Old Miss, enlightened by an aside from Mrs. LeGrand, came into action. "She doesn't mean that she's friends with those brazen women who want to be men? What's that? She says she's going to work with them? I don't believe it! I don't believe that even of Maria's daughter. Going around speaking and screaming and tying themselves to Houses of Parliament and interrupting policemen! If I believed it, I don't think I'd ever speak to her again in this life! Women Righters and Abolitionists!—doing their best to drench the country with blood, kill our people and bring the carpet-baggers upon us! Wearing bloomers and cutting their hair short and speaking in town-halls and wanting to change the marriage service!—Yes, they do wear bloomers! I saw one doing it in New York in 1885, when I was there with your grandfather. And she had short hair—"

Mrs. LeGrand, as the principal of a School for Young Ladies, always recognized her responsibility to truth. She stood up for veracity. "Dear Mrs. Ashendyne, it is not just like that now. There are a great many more suffragists now—so many that society has agreed not to ostracize them. Some of them are pretty and dress well and have a good position. I was at a tea in Baltimore and there were several there. I've even heard women in Virginia—women that you'd think ought to know better—say that they believed in it and that sooner or later we'd have a movement here. Of course, you don't hear that kind of talk, but I can assure you there's a good deal of it. Of course, I myself think it is perfectly dreadful. Woman's place is the home. And we can surely trust *everything* to the chivalry of our Southern men. I am sure Hagar has only to think a little—The whole thing seems to me so—so—so *vulgar!*"

Miss Serena broke out passionately. "It's against the Bible! I don't see how any *religious* woman—"

Hagar, who had gone back to her chair, turned her eyes toward Captain Bob.

"Confound it, Gipsy! What do you want to put your feet on the table and smoke cigars for?"

Hagar looked at Ralph.

He was gazing at her with eyes that were burning and yet sullen and angry. "Women, I suppose, have got to have follies and fads to amuse themselves with. At any rate, they have them. Suffrage or bridge, it doesn't much matter, so long as it's not let really to interfere. If it begins to do that, we'll have to put a stop to it. Woman, I take it, was made for man, and she'll have to continue to recognize that fact. Good Lord! It seems to me that if we give her our love and pay her bills, she might be satisfied!"

All having spoken, Hagar spoke. "I should like, if I may, to tell you quietly and reasonably why—" her eyes were upon her grandfather.

"I wish to hear neither your excuses nor your reasons," said the Colonel. "I want to hear a retraction and a promise."

Hagar turned slightly, "Grandmother—"

"Don't," said Old Miss, "talk to me! When you're wrong, you're wrong, and that's all there is to it! Maria used to try to explain, and then she stopped and I was glad of it."

Hagar leaned back in her chair and regarded the circle of her relatives. She felt for a moment more like Maria than Hagar. She felt trapped. Then she realized that she was not trapped, and she smiled. Thanks to the evolving whole, thanks to the years and to her eternal self pacing now through a larger moment than those moments of old, she was not by position Maria, she was not by position Miss Serena. Before her, quiet and fair, opened her Fourth Dimension. Inner freedom, ability to work, personal independence, courage and sense of humour and a sanguine mind, breadth and height of vision, tenderness and. hope, her waiting friends, Elizabeth, Marie, Rachel, Molly and Christopher, Denny, Rose Darragh, many another—her work, the story now hovering in her brain, what other and different work might rise above the horizon—the passion to help, help largely, lift without thinking if it were or were not her share of the weight—the universe of the mind, the growing spirit and the wings of the morning . . . there was her land of escape, real as the hills of Gilead Balm. She crossed the border with ease; she was not trapped. Even now her subtle self was serenely over. And the Hagar Ashendyne appearing to others upon this porch was not chained there, was not riveted to Gilead Balm. Next week, indeed, she would be gone.

A tenderness came over Hagar for her people. All her childhood was surrounded by them; they were dear, deep among the roots of things. She wanted to talk to them; she longed that they should understand. "If you'd listen," she said, "perhaps you'd see it a little differently—"

The Colonel spoke with harshness. "There is no need to see it differently. It is you who should see it differently."

"It comes of the kind of things you've always read!" cried Miss Serena. "Books that I wouldn't touch!"

"Yes, Maria was always reading, too," said Old Miss. For her it was *less* Hagar than Maria sitting there. . . .

"If it was anything we didn't know, we would, of course, listen to you, Hagar dear," said Mrs. LeGrand. "I should be glad to listen anyhow, just as I listened to those two women in Baltimore. But I must say their arguments sounded to me very foolish. Ladies in the South certainly don't need to come into contact with the horrors they talked about. And I cannot consider the discussion of such subjects delicate. I should certainly consider it disastrous if my girls at Eglantine gained any such knowledge. To talk about their being white slaves and things like that—it was nauseating!"

"Would you listen, Ralph?" asked Hagar.

"I'll listen to you, Hagar, on any other subject but this."

Mrs. LeGrand's voice came in again. She was fluttering her fan. "All these theories that you women are advancing now-a-days—if they *paid*, if you stood to gain anything by them, if by advancing them you didn't, so it seems to me, always come out at the little end of the horn—people ridiculing you, society raising its eyebrows, men afraid to marry you—! My dear Hagar, men, collectively speaking—men don't want women to exhibit mind in all directions. They don't object to their showing it in certain directions, but when it comes to women showing it all around the circle they do object, and from my point of view quite properly! Men naturally require a certain complaisance and deference from women. There's no need to overdo it, but a certain amount of physical and mental dependence they certainly do want! Well, what's the use of a woman quarrelling with the world as it's made? Between doing without independent thinking and doing without an establishment and someone to provide for you—! So you see," said Mrs. LeGrand, smoothly argumentative, "what's the use of stirring up the bottoms of things? And it isn't as though we weren't really fond of the men. We are. I've always been fonder of a man, every time, than of a woman. I must confess I can't see any reason at all for all this strenuous crying out against good old usage! Of course a woman with considerable mental power may find it a little limiting, but there are a lot of women, I assure you, who never think of it. If there's a little humbug and if some women suffer, why those things are in the dish, that's all! The dish isn't all poisoned, and a woman who knows what she is about can pick and choose and turn everything to account. I wouldn't know what to do," said Mrs. LeGrand, "with the dish that people like you would set before us. All this crying out about evolution and development and higher forms doesn't touch me in the least! I like the forms we've got. Perhaps they're imperfect, but the thing is, I feel at home with imperfection."

She leaned back, in good humour. Hagar had given her an opportunity to express herself very well. "Don't you, too," she asked, "feel at home with the dear old imperfection?"

Hagar met her eyes. "No," she said.

Mrs. LeGrand shrugged. "Oh, well!" she said, "I suppose each will fight for the place that is home."

Hagar looked beyond her, to her kindred. "You're all opponents," she said. "Alike you worship God as Man, and you worship a static God, never to be questioned nor surpassed. You have shut an iron door upon yourselves. . . . One day you who shut it, you alone—you will open it, you alone. But I see that the day is somewhat far."

She rose. "I was going anyhow you know, grandfather, in four days. But I can take the morning train if you'd rather?"

But Colonel Ashendyne said stiffly that if she had forgotten her duty, he had not his, and that the hospitality of Gilead Balm would be hers, of course, for the four days.

Hagar listened to him, and then she looked once more around the circle. A smile hovered on her lips and in her eyes. It broadened, became warm and sweet. "I'll accept for a time the partial estrangement, but I don't ever mean that it shall be complete! It takes two to make an estrangement." She went up to her grandmother and kissed her, then said that she was going for a walk.—"No, Ralph, you are not coming with me!"

She went down the porch steps, and moved away in the evening glow. The black cedars swallowed her up; then upon the other side, beyond the gate, she was seen mounting the hill to the right. The sun was down, but the hilltop rested against rose-suffused air, and above it swam the evening star.

Ralph spoke with a certain grim fury. "I wish the old times were back! Then a man could do what he wished! Then you didn't feel yourself caught in a net like a cobweb that you couldn't break—"

Mrs. LeGrand again opened her fan. "I am very fond, of course, of dear Hagar, but I must say that she seems to me intensely unwomanly!"

MABEL LEE

The Meaning of Woman Suffrage
MAY 12, 1914

In March 1912, American newspapers reported that women in China had been granted the right to vote. The report was misleading—only Chinese women in Guangdong Province had been promised the vote, and it was quickly rescinded—but it was enough for NAWSA president Anna Howard Shaw to carry a banner that said "N.A.W.S.A. Catching Up With China" in the New York City suffrage parade that May. Also participating in that parade was sixteen-year-old Mabel Ping-hua Lee (1896–1966), who would start her studies at Barnard College in the fall. Lee had been born in China, learned English as a child, and came to the United States in 1905 after winning a scholarship that also provided a visa (at the time there were strict limits on Chinese immigration). At Barnard she joined the Chinese Students' Association and wrote articles for the *Chinese Students' Monthly*, including this 1914 essay. Framing the question of women's suffrage as one of justice and equality, Lee explicitly connects suffrage activism to feminism, a new term just coming into vogue in the 1910s. Lee remained active in the suffrage movement throughout her college years, and later became the first Chinese woman to earn a PhD from Columbia. Ironically, she herself did not benefit from the Nineteenth Amendment. Because the Chinese Exclusion Act of 1882 prevented her from becoming a citizen, she could not vote until the law was rescinded in 1943.

I once heard Professor Kirchwey of Columbia say that although scientists are always telling us that in the midst of life we are in death, we are not as apt to realize it as much as that while in the midst of life we are in the woman suffrage question. And it is a fact that no matter where we go we cannot escape hearing about woman suffrage. Yet there is hardly a question more misunderstood or that has more misapplications. So manifold are its misconceptions that it has come to be a by-word suitable for every occasion. For instance, if when in company one should wish to scramble out of an embarrassing situation, or his more fortunate brother should wish to be considered witty, all that either would have to do would be to mention woman suffrage, and they may be sure of laughter and merriment in response.

The reason for this is that the idea of woman suffrage at first stood for something abnormal, strange and extraordinary, and so has finally become the word for anything ridiculous. The idea that women should ever wish to have or be anything more than their primitive mothers appears at first thought to be indeed tragic enough to be comic; but if we sit down and really think it over, throwing aside all sentimentalism, we find that it is nothing more than a wider application of our ideas of justice and equality. We all believe in the idea of democracy; woman suffrage or the feminist movement (of which woman suffrage is a fourth part) is the application of democracy to women.

Let us briefly consider the field and scope of democracy so as to trace its application to the feminist movement.

The fundamental principle of democracy is equality of opportunity, as distinguished from equality of compensation. It means an equal chance for every man to show what his merits are. To my mind, I conceive it as fourfold, i. e., having four stages in its development, like four waves, one rolling into another. They are: first, moral, religious or spiritual; second, legal; third, political; and, fourth, economic. European history is the realization of the progress of democracy in this progression.

The first or spiritual stage is represented by the early Christian movement. Christ himself makes the democratic statement that slaves had as much as princes in the sight of God. Therefore we get equality of spiritual privileges with primitive Christianity.

The second or legal stage is the fight for equality before the law, and is worked out principally in England, also somewhat in Germany. It began with the fight for the Magna Charta and, we might say, is still going on. Thus with this wave we have an extension of the equality of opportunity in claiming for man equal rights before the law.

The third or political stage is that for the equal right to choose the rulers for making laws, and is summed up in the statement of Thomas Jefferson, "Just government depends on the consent of the governed." It is the fundamental idea of American democracy and is well expressed in the Declaration of Independence. And this idea of political equality is being worked out in this country in spite of the interruptions of the negro question, etc.

The fourth or economic stage stands for economic equality

or full reward of labor, and is commonly known as socialism. With the introduction of machinery since the industrial revolution, there has been created a class of owners of the instruments of production who do not have to work, but make a profit just because they are owners. Thus this class does not work and yet gains the same reward or profit that the poor laborer gets only through the "sweat of his brow." This fourth movement of democracy, therefore, protests against this economic inequality and advocates government ownership of these instruments of production. Were this condition to prevail, there would be none to gain the reward who has not labored. This phase of democracy has but recently appeared and has developed most rapidly in Germany.

There are great documents giving proof of these stages in the development of democracy. For the spiritual, we have the Sermon on the Mount; for the legal, the Magna Charta or Bill of Rights; for the political, mainly the United States' Declaration of Independence (for, although the idea was derived from France through such writers as Rousseau and others, the United States was the first nation to stand for the ideal); for the economic, the Communist Manifesto by Engels and Marx.

Thus we have seen that democracy is fourfold and of four stages of development. The opponents of democracy in every stage have always used the misrepresentation that the democrats want to level the whole thing from good to mediocrity. But the real democratic idea is to have a really natural aristocracy by giving equality of opportunity in order to let every man prove his merits.

And in the feministic movement these opportunities are again applying the same misrepresentation by saying that the feminists wish to make women like men; whereas the feminists want nothing more than the equality of opportunity for women to prove their merits and what they are best suited to do. This is a purely scientific attitude, for we can never determine anything until it has been tried. For instance, it was not so long ago that even Western people thought that woman was not capable of being taught even the three R's. The very thought of a woman knowing how to read or write made them hold up their hands in "holy horror," for it would "entirely unsex the women." But when woman proved that she could go through elementary school, then these same persons said that she could not go through a secondary school—"it was too much for women and they could never be taught such difficult subjects." Again woman proved herself capable, and these people then said that she could not go through college. It is only a short time since she gained the victory of admission to college, and there are still many schools too conservative to open their doors for her instruction. At present there is still the cry that though woman has gone so far, she can go no further, that she cannot succeed in the professions. But this again is being refuted by the success of pioneers of today.

The idea of feminism is to give unto woman what man has successively gained in the different stages. It is the application to her of the fourfold ideal of democracy.

In Christianity woman was not given an equality of privileges because of the ascetic idea that she was the tempter of man. But, on the other hand, its doctrine of sympathy for the weak gave her greater respect. And so the compromise of the two ideas has led to the conception that the wife and mother are to be respected.

In legal rights, even in this country, woman still has some difficulties, as in cases of divorce and ownership of children; yet she may be said to have almost all the legal rights.

The third or political phase of feminism is the question of woman suffrage—the giving of political privileges to woman. Therefore, suffrage is only one fourth of the system of feminism. It is interesting to note that the English militants of today are using exactly the same argument as that of the American Revolution, i. e., if we have no legal means, then we will use illegal means.

The fourth or economic application to woman is that there should be no discrimination in industry because of her sex.

Let us now turn to make a comparison of the importance of these four movements in the application of democracy for woman. We find the legal phase the least important, because it is already won. The political is the most immediately pressing demand and is the most conspicuous, because it is in the forefront. The spiritual or cultural—the movement for freedom of women to any kind of spiritual self-expression, for freedom from conventionalities (to dress as she likes and to study what she likes)—may not seem the most important now, but it will be in the end. Undoubtedly the economic is the most basic, because without it we cannot have the spiritual.

The history of this economic phase divides itself into three stages or conceptions. First, there is the old conception that woman, single or married, should remain at home. Then there comes the industrial revolution, taking the industry out of the home and consequently taking the woman out with it. In order to meet this new condition, there next arises a second conception, that woman must choose from the two prerogatives of either getting married or going out to business, and that as soon as a woman gets married she must leave her profession and stay at home. The second conception is the one we are living under, but there is a third conception on its way which says that woman whether married or not should have economic freedom.

Therefore, the following shall be arguments in favor of economic independence for woman. I have divided them under five heads, namely, those for the interest of the race, the interest of the community, the interest of woman herself, the interest of the husband, and the interest of the child.

FOR THE INTEREST OF THE RACE

Using the argument of President Jordan of Leland Stanford University for universal peace—war is one of the worst things for any race, because the bravest are drained off and killed while the cowards are left to be fathers of the coming generation—we may say that for the interest of eugenics, woman should not be forced to choose between marriage and profession, because then the able professional woman will lead a life of celibacy while the other is left for the mother of the race.

FOR THE INTEREST OF THE COMMUNITY

Since the industrial revolution, less and less of occupation is being left in the home for the mind and body of woman. The kindergarten has gone out of the home, industry has gone out with the incoming of the age of machinery, and the care of children is being more and more recognized as a matter for experts, i. e., just because she is the mother doesn't any longer mean that she is most capable to arrange her child's diet, discipline, etc.

Thus one half of the people is left almost idle; and the increasing cost of living is due to the fact that women of the higher and middle classes are becoming parasites.

FOR THE INTEREST OF WOMAN HERSELF

In the present condition of things, woman is distinctly inferior to man intellectually. This is caused by the lack of having their minds trained in some profession. If man had no systematized work and went idly about the house, except for petty chores, he, too, would be intellectually inferior. Therefore, it is to the interest of woman intellectually to have a profession.

FOR THE INTEREST OF THE HUSBAND

The ideal marriage state is a life of comradeship; but there can be no real comradeship unless the two parties are intellectually congenial, and this can only result from giving professions to woman. Under the old system, after marriage the man continues to develop mentally, while the woman stands still, and the result is that after two or three years the husband feels the lack of companionship at home and rushes to his club or other congenial society at every opportunity. His wife has lost her interest and knowledge of his outside world and has ceased to be his intellectual comrade. Moreover, life would be more ideal if woman should not be made to marry for mercenary purposes; and there would be more courtesy between men and women if they both can be self-supporting.

FOR THE INTEREST OF THE CHILD

Although it must be admitted that a child loses something in not having the mother beside it to supply all its physical needs, nevertheless this is overbalanced by having mothers who are intellectual companions. After all, the real need and beauty of maternal affection consists in being always at hand for sympathy and confidence, and not in the performance of petty chores. Besides, if a mother has some intellectual interest to occupy her for a part of the day, she is much fresher to take care of her children than if she stays in the house and is nagged by them the whole day long.

There have been several solutions presented for bringing about this condition of economic independence for woman, as, for instance, the one for an extension of the school to the most primary work, even to include creches, and the other for new regulations and hours in the industries for woman; but I shall not take the time and space of going into them, as conditions in China are different from those of western countries and will require different solutions.

The writer wishes merely to present true feminism as it is, giving a review of its history, aims and development; and to show that it is nothing more than the extension of democracy or social justice and equality of opportunities to women. The position of woman is in an unwholesome transitional stage at present in the western countries, as testified by the conditions in England and the work for the divorce courts in the United States. The building up of western civilization has, as it were, left every other beam loose in its construction by leaving out its women, and now there naturally has to be a time of difficult and careful readjustment before the structure can be made solid.

As students and patriots of China in this her period of reconstruction, this problem is worthy of our interest and consideration. With the introduction of machinery and Western methods in our country, we cannot keep the women ignorant. Are we going to build a solid structure or are we going to leave every other beam loose for later readjustment in spite of the lesson herein presented?

I cannot too strongly impress upon the reader the importance of this consideration, for the feministic movement is not one for privileges to women, but one for the requirement of women to be worthy citizens and contribute their share to the steady progress of our country towards prosperity and national greatness.

MARY ROBERTS COOLIDGE

Raising the Level of Suffrage in California,
Or What Have They Done With It?

AUGUST 1914

After the decisive defeat of an 1896 suffrage referendum where liquor interests had played an outsize role, the California suffrage movement languished for a decade. Starting around 1910, a more progressive state political climate encouraged the revitalization of the movement, which planned another referendum for October 10, 1911. Organizing campaigns in a state as vast as California posed logistical challenges. Most voters centered in the north, where the California Equal Suffrage Association was dominant. In Southern California the Political Equality League based in Pasadena and the Votes for Women Club headed by Clara Shortridge Foltz (1849–1934) led the fight. To reach widely dispersed voters, suffragists used rallies, picnics, and auto tours, and also distributed suffrage memorabilia like buttons and handbills. Early returns from the San Francisco Bay Area and Los Angeles pointed toward defeat, but when all the votes were counted, suffragists had a margin of victory of 3,587 votes out of 250,000 cast. This 1914 article by Mary Roberts Coolidge (1860–1945), a former professor at both Wellesley and Stanford, looks at what California women did with their new votes, claiming they were more nonpartisan than men and pursued an issue-oriented approach to politics that sounds very similar to the strategy of the League of Women Voters in the 1920s.

The most important thing that the women of California have done has been to raise the level of suffrage itself. And they are doing it in a very natural, inconspicuous and dignified way. In 1911, when they first had the opportunity to vote, women registered as a matter of conscience, rather than to support one party or another, as men usually do. As a class they have shown themselves essentially non-partisan and far more interested in causes than in particular candidates or parties. Their feminine intuitions make them keenly alive to the dangers of machine politics and they are more and more the despair of those politicians who insist upon lining up the voters and herding them ignorantly to the polls.

California women, all over the State during the last two years, have been quietly studying the political issues upon which they have to vote. They have invited the State and local candidates to present themselves and their measures before thousands of club gatherings, and have taken their calibre. They are surprisingly acute in feeling the untrustworthiness of those who try to hypnotize the voters with loud oratory and who dodge straight answers to their questionings.

The non-partisan forum offered by women's clubs and civic leagues is already improving the tone of political campaigns. Women despise personal attacks and the wordy buncombe which is the usual stock of the second-rate politician, and they are suspicious of his sweeping pre-election promises. Nor will the feminine voters support men whose private record is crooked or indecent—an attitude which is compelling the party managers to put up better candidates.

It is a significant fact that the women demand clear issues. They vote up to their registration often when they perfectly understand the issue, but rather than be befogged into voting wrong, when the issue is not clear, they stay away from the polls entirely. This is the explanation of many contradictory figures that have been published by the friends and foes of suffrage with regard to the behavior of California women at the polls.

In their first encounter with the State Legislature in 1913, they showed remarkably good sense in the way in which they brought their political power to bear. Instead of demanding impossible things, the larger bodies of women—the W.C.T.U., the Federated Clubs, the California Civic League and the Juvenile Protective Association—got behind a few measures important to the welfare of women and children and let alone the thousands of other bills whose supporters clamored to secure the "woman vote." They sent a delegate council to the legislative session, but did no lobbying whatever. Every legislator had already heard from the women of his home district what bills they expected him to support, and the council watched him closely to see whether he was fulfilling his duty as their representative. If he tried to shrink he immediately heard from the women at home.

As a result the three measures endorsed by more than 50,000 women, the Equal Guardianship of Children, a Detention

Home for Girls, carrying an appropriation of $200,000, and the (Iowa) Red Light Abatement Law were passed by large majorities in both houses—the latter in spite of tremendous opposition on the part of the liquor and vice interests.

The women who vote in California are chiefly the solid, earnest, domestic middle-class. They vote conscientiously and intelligently and are not easily fooled. They do not wish to hold office, but they demand that candidates shall be decent and shall have some experience to fit them for the offices they seek. And they cannot be held to any party unless the men and the issues of that party suit their ideas of clean, representative government. They have raised and they will continue to raise the whole level of voting citizenship.

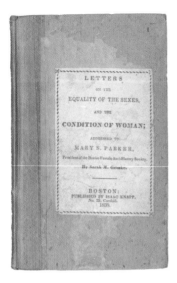

1. In *Letters on the Equality of the Sexes*, published in 1838, Sarah M. Grimké challenged notions of women's subordination in letters to Mary S. Parker, President of the Boston Female Anti-Slavery Society.

2. One of the most widely circulated images in nineteenth-century abolitionist circles was "Am I not a man and a brother?", which was based on a medallion designed by English potter Josiah Wedgwood in 1787. In 1830 Elizabeth Margaret Chandler of Philadelphia adapted the iconography to feature an enslaved woman.

LEADERS OF THE WOMAN'S RIGHTS CONVENTION TAKING AN AIRING

3. One of the first visual documents to refer to the Seneca Falls convention was this color print, published in 1848 by New York lithographer James S. Baillie. The representation of women's rights advocates who cannot control their horses (none seem to be portrayals of actual suffragists) suggests that when women challenge their exclusion from public life, the result will be disorder.

WOMAN'S EMANCIPATION.
(BEING A LETTER ADDRESSED TO MR. PUNCH, WITH A DRAWING, BY A STRONG-MINDED AMERICAN WOMAN.)

4. This engraving from the August 1851 issue of *Harper's New Monthly Magazine* depicts six women wearing bloomer-style outfits and engaging in masculine behaviors such as smoking, wearing top hats, or carrying canes, and speaks to popular fears that women would become like men if they gained political rights.

FRANK LESLIE'S ILLUSTRATED NEWSPAPER

No. 1,732.—Vol. LXVII.] NEW YORK—FOR THE WEEK ENDING NOVEMBER 24, 1888. [Price, 10 Cents.]

WOMAN SUFFRAGE IN WYOMING TERRITORY.—SCENE AT THE POLLS IN CHEYENNE.
From a Photo. by Kirkland.—See Page 256.

5. This wood engraving of women at the polls in Cheyenne, Wyoming, appeared on the cover of *Frank Leslie's Illustrated Newspaper* on November 24, 1888. Unlike satirical depictions mocking women's political aspirations, the scene (made from a photograph) shows well-dressed women decorously casting their ballots.

6. Ida B. Wells was a crusading anti-lynching journalist. In 1913 she founded the first African American women's suffrage club in Chicago.

I Take Her Paper

7. Lucy Stone and her husband Henry Browne Blackwell founded the *Woman's Journal*, an influential suffrage periodical, in Boston in 1870. This badge, offered as a promotion to increase subscriptions after Stone's death, features an image from 1855, when Stone was thirty-seven and recently married.

8. In 1891 Susan B. Anthony (LEFT) and Elizabeth Cady Stanton (RIGHT) sat for a series of studio portraits that captured their lifelong friendship and shared political activism.

Frances Willard

American Woman and Her Political Peers.

9. Henrietta Briggs-Wall created this poster for display at the 1893 World's Columbian Exposition. Functioning as visual propaganda, it argues that Frances Willard, center, the esteemed president of the Woman's Christian Temperance Union, is superior to four categories of men also denied the right to vote: "idiots, convicts, the insane, and Indians."

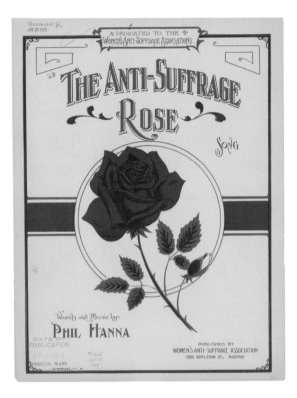

10. Anti-suffragists grasped the power of branding, adopting the red rose as their symbol. That choice inspired composer and lyricist Phil Hanna to create a song titled "The Anti-Suffrage Rose" for the Women's Anti-Suffrage Association in Boston.

11. On April 9, 1912, male voters in Cook County, Illinois, deposited ballots for or against women's suffrage in special ballot boxes. When the votes were counted, the suffrage referendum went down to defeat.

12. For the suffrage procession timed to coincide with Woodrow Wilson's inauguration, Alice Paul commissioned a twenty-page souvenir program. The full-color cover image by Benjamin Moran Dale drew on colors (purple and gold) and images (women on horseback, votes for women banners) associated with the cause.

13. The height of the suffrage movement coincided with what has been called the golden age of campaign buttons. This button, shown actual size, features twelve stars representing the states in which women had full or partial suffrage at the time it was made: Wyoming (1869), Colorado (1893), Utah (1896), Idaho (1896), Washington (1910), California (1911), Kansas, Oregon, and Arizona (all 1912), Illinois (1913), and Montana and Nevada (both 1914).

Since, in this progressive age,
Woman's Suffrage is all the rage,
You strive in this to take the lead,
As if 'twere case of vital need;
When you thus seek excuse among the men to roam,
We're apt to think there's something wrong—at home.

14. Starting in the 1850s, a strong market developed for inexpensive comic valentines. Almost any topic was fair game, including suffrage. This valentine adopts a decidedly skeptical tone about women's forays beyond the domestic sphere.

15. Suffragists often argued that women needed the vote in order to be better mothers. Here children (drawn by artist Rose O'Neill, the creator of the Kewpie doll) make that point on a postcard distributed by the National American Woman Suffrage Association (NAWSA) in 1915.

16. Because suffrage speakers fluent in foreign languages were in short supply, around 1915 NAWSA began to circulate fliers with brief, snappy arguments geared to male voters who were recent immigrants.

VOTES FOR WORKERS

CARL HENTSCHEL L^{TD} 182, 183 & 184 FLEET ST E.C.   PUBLISHED BY ARTISTS' SUFFRAGE LEAGUE.

17. Working women forcefully argued that they needed the vote to improve
their lives. Maybe then they wouldn't fall asleep at a sewing machine after
a long day's work, like the exhausted—and voteless—seamstress depicted
in this lithograph by W. F. Winter.

VOTES FOR WOMEN

18. On October 29, 1864, Sojourner Truth visited Abraham Lincoln at the White House. *The Crisis*, the magazine of the National Association for the Advancement of Colored People, used a composite photograph created by Hinton Gilmore of their iconic meeting for the cover of its August 1915 issue devoted to women's suffrage.

19. African American women used women's clubs and churches as launch pads for political activism, including women's suffrage. Here Nannie Burroughs and eight other delegates gather for the Banner State Woman's National Baptist Convention in 1915.

20. A 1916 cartoon in *The Crisis*, "Woman to the Rescue!", shows an African American woman wielding a bat labeled "federal constitution" to attack instruments of white supremacy such as Jim Crow laws and segregation, a visual representation of the potential results if black women were allowed to vote. In contrast, the disenfranchised African American man fleeing the scene counsels not causing trouble and making do with what they have.

WOMAN TO THE RESCUE!

21. Henry Mayer's striking centerfold, "The Awakening," from the February 20, 1915, issue of *Puck Magazine*, shows a torch-bearing female striding across a map of the United States, symbolizing the importance of women voters in Western states in awakening the rest of the country. Below the illustration is a poem by Alice Duer Miller (see pages 473–74 in this volume).

22. In recognition of the courage of the women jailed for picketing the White House, Alice Paul presented each with a small (1-by-1 ½ inch) metal brooch in the shape of the locked door of a prison cell. Paul modeled the prison pin on the "Holloway Brooch" distributed to members of the British Woman's Social and Political Union who had been jailed for the cause.

23. Carrie Chapman Catt's favorite flowers were blue delphiniums, and her grateful suffrage followers presented her with a huge bouquet of them when she returned to New York City after the official certification of the Nineteenth Amendment on August 26, 1920.

24. Contrary to popular perceptions, "any good suffragist" did not simply roll over and go back to sleep after the ratification of the Nineteenth Amendment. Instead the suffragists drawn by cartoonist Nina E. Allender enthusiastically embraced their new roles as women citizens—after they got a good night's sleep, that is.

Any good Suffragist the morning after.

25. For African American women in the South, the Nineteenth Amendment did little to change the conditions that kept them from the polls. In 1964 Fannie Lou Hamer, a Mississippi sharecropper turned voting rights activist, took that fight to the Democratic National Convention in Atlantic City, New Jersey.

26. Political cartoonist John T. McCutcheon originally published "How high will she go?" in the *Chicago Tribune* on June 29, 1922, just two years after the ratification of the Nineteenth Amendment. This version from 1937 features a slightly different set of steps, but both renditions build to the White House and the presidency as the ultimate step for women in politics.

HAZEL MACKAYE

Pageants as a Means of Suffrage Propaganda

NOVEMBER 28, 1914

As part of Alice Paul's counter inaugural parade in Washington in 1913, theatrical director Hazel MacKaye (1880–1944) produced a classically themed pageant called *Allegory* on the steps of the Treasury building, featuring more than one hundred amateur actors. Pageants, which were extremely popular in early twentieth-century America, proved especially adaptable to town histories and other historical commemorations, but MacKaye reasoned they would work just as well as suffrage propaganda. In this article for *The Suffragist*, she calls pageants a "forceful and vivid form of drama" with "more power to convince people of the truth of our cause than any other means." MacKaye mounted two more suffrage pageants at the height of the suffrage movement: *Six Periods of American Life: Past—Present—Future*, staged for the Men's League for Woman Suffrage in 1914, and a dramatization of the life of Susan B. Anthony to benefit Alice Paul's Congressional Union in 1915. MacKaye's final *Equal Rights Pageant* was staged for the National Woman's Party in Seneca Falls, New York, in 1923 to commemorate the seventy-fifth anniversary of the convention. Combining theatricality with a firm grasp of women's history, the ehnd of the pageant featured a giant sign spelling out "Declaration of Principles" in electric lights, symbolically bringing suffrage history into the modern age.

Four very practical problems must be solved daily by every suffrage organization in the country in its campaign for the vote. These are:

1. To convert people to suffrage.
2. To keep the movement constantly before the public.
3. To stimulate interest and co-operation among members.
4. To make money to carry on the campaign.

Now, I believe that in organized pageantry we find the elements which successfully solve all four of these problems. Let us consider them, one by one.

The first is "to convert people to suffrage." In spite of the fact that it seems preposterous to any good Suffragist today that there can remain a single doubt in the world as to the righteousness of votes for women, there are still many hundreds of thousands of male voters and an equal number of female "subjects" who are skeptical about the subject.

The work of propaganda is still bitterly necessary—alas! in every state in the Union.

I cannot take the time here to enlarge much upon this subject. I can only state my firm belief that a pageant has more power to convince people of the truth of our cause than any other means. A pageant is a forceful and vivid form of drama. It combines the medium of the spoken word, the dance, pantomime, stirring music, masses of people in striking costumes, strong contrasts in situation, in its appeal. It is an intensely moving thing to witness. When our emotions are swayed, our very innermost being is touched. The light comes to us in a single flash, instead of by dim and cautious flickerings.

I do not speak from theory alone, but from actual experience. Perhaps the most striking instance of what a pageant can do to make converts is afforded by the Metropolitan Pageant written by Margaret Tuttle, which was given at the Metropolitan Opera House in May, 1913. I cannot personally speak of what it did on that occasion, but I know what it did when it was repeated in Cleveland in May, 1914. At that performance, people were asked to sign the petitions before the performance began, but many refused to do so. After they had witnessed the spectacle, however, and had breathed in the beauty, the sincerity, the majesty of what had taken place upon the stage, and had been filled to the brim with its spiritual message, those same people, upon leaving the theatre, eagerly asked to be allowed to reconsider their decision and to place their names upon the list. As one man said, "No one could witness that noble spectacle and have a doubt left in his mind that human beings capable of so lofty and beautiful a thing were unworthy of the vote, and that, for his part, he felt that if any man, after witnessing this pageant, should still deny women the right to vote, that such a man should be summarily disposed of then and there." For the purpose of propaganda, a pageant can hardly be surpassed.

Our second problem is "to keep the cause constantly before the public." As a news-provoker a pageant has possibilities second to none save, perhaps, a "hikers" campaign. Two months before the pageant was held in Washington on March 3, 1913, the papers were filled with stories concerning it. Not a day passed without some item of interest being eagerly seized upon by the press. First, there were the women who were organizing the pageant, and all the numerous "stories" attaching to them. Then, came the notables who were to take part, Nordica, Mary Shaw, and the final substituting for these names of those of Hedwig Reicher and Sarah Truax. It was even stated in a New York paper that a Suffragist, whose picture accompanied the statement, was to pose on the Treasury steps as "Hope," and would greet the new President upon his arrival in the city in a beautiful tableau, together with other "suffragettes." This item, although scarcely redounding to the credit of the accuracy of newspaper statements, nevertheless aroused the greatest interest in what the "suffragettes" were proposing to do. Then came the actual event. Newspapers throughout the country gave lengthy "write-ups" of it. It was commented upon everywhere and was even cartooned, the greatest publicity compliment that could be paid.

The problem of publicity, therefore, is successfully solved by a pageant for as many weeks as it takes to prepare it.

Our third problem is "to stimulate interest and co-operation among our members." In other words, to keep everyone busy and to draw in other workers at the same time. What arouses greater interest and enthusiasm among the average woman than to look forward to taking part in a dramatic performance! There is something about the fascination of appearing behind that mysterious curtain we have gazed at so often from the front (if the performance be indoors), that makes our blood tingle—and our hearts begin to beat. To enter to a blaze of trumpets in a sweeping costume with a banner or a wand, or a star upon one's brow, whether it be down lofty steps or through winding paths of greensward, makes the commonplace days of one's ordinary life seem drear and dry, indeed. There is no use in denying that this kind of thing stimulates an interest that no street meeting or convention or any other form of demonstration can possibly arouse.

And it is absolutely necessary to have co-operation in a

pageant, else the whole thing fails. I have known of only one instance where there was the slightest suspicion of the ordinary desire with which amateurs are credited, of seeking the center of the stage, in any of the suffrage pageants that I have had the honor to be associated with. That instance, I am glad to be able to say, was not afforded by a Suffragist, but by a girl with "professional" ambitions who sought this occasion to be before the public eye. Under the most trying conditions of rehearsing, even when there were no costumes at the final dress rehearsal, every participant has stood by his post like a soldier to his gun, with a magnificent performance as the result. Friendships are made in this way, closer and more vital interest in the movement, a keener sense of the "get together" spirit is developed by association in a form of drama where the personal emphasis is subordinated to the larger, more inclusive elements of life.

And now we come to the ever-present, annoying and often arduous problem of raising money to carry on the campaign.

I hardly think that anyone will deny that the pageant solves many of our problems, but when the solving of the money-making problem is looked into, then grave doubts begin to arise. For there is no use in denying that a pageant is an expensive thing to produce. The expense varies naturally with the kind of pageant and the size of pageant that you wish to give. Briefly, pageants may be divided into the following:

1. Outdoor (in a natural amphitheatre, or where seats or stage have to be built).
2. Indoor (in theatre or auditorium with accompanying scenic effects or scenery and lights), and further into:

   1. Requiring one hundred participants.
   2. Requiring three hundred participants.
   3. Requiring five hundred participants.
   A pageant means expenses in regard to
   a. Costumes.
   b. Properties.
   c. Scenery (if indoors).
   d. Lights (if indoors or outdoors in the evening).
   e. Stage hands.
   f. Place for rehearsal.

g. Printing.
h. Publicity.

It needs a number of well-organized committees behind it. In fact, it isn't a thing which can be done in the flash of a pan. It takes organization and devotion. That is why it is difficult for one city or town to undertake a pageant all by itself. It needs co-operation with other places to make a pageant a safe investment. The initial expenses of a pageant are heavy. If, however, the same pageant goes from place to place, the initial expenses of costumes, properties and scenery may be divided between all of these places, so that no one place will have the whole burden to bear. In other words, if Suffragists could be persuaded to look upon pageantry as a part of the organized work of the movement, we could probably enhance our revenue by very substantial sums every year of our lives. But success can only come through organized effort on the part of all, or the greater number of suffrage organizations. It cannot be done by one alone. This was proved conclusively by the experiment tried by the Equal Franchise Society of New York. That society conceived the admirable idea of producing the same pageant in most of the large cities of New York state in order to help win victory in 1915. The organizer was to go in advance and make all the preliminary arrangements, and the director was to follow to put the pageant into rehearsal. But alas! this excellent plan failed through lack of co-operation from the organizations throughout the state. Single-handed, the Equal Franchise Society was unable to cope with the situation. But the society made a splendid try at it.

Now it is my earnest conviction that if we could establish a National Bureau of Suffrage Pageants which should link together all organizations throughout the country by a series of pageants planned to go from coast to coast, we would accomplish surprising things by such a policy. A conference on this subject might be held, attended by delegates from all over the country, and a business-like, vigorous campaign be pushed to further this idea. Does it not seem worse than folly to allow this eminently powerful and appropriate means of aiding our cause to lie fallow? We should wake up! We should use the same energy and persistence and invention in pushing this venture through that we have shown in our slow but steady gain in the states, and our still more encouraging gains in the Senate and the House of Representatives. Let's waste no time, but begin now to make pageantry, the great drama of the people and for the people, serve us in this mighty struggle.

IDA B. WELLS

Seeking the Negro Vote

1914–1915

Not all African American men were disfranchised by Jim Crow re-strictions: a small but growing minority exercised the right to vote outside the South, with Chicago's South Side offering an especially vibrant political community. When Illinois offered presidential and municipal suffrage to women in 1913, African American women joined the ranks of voters. One of Chicago's leading political activists was Ida Wells-Barnett (1862–1931), an anti-lynching crusader and newspa-perwoman. In March 1913 she challenged the racism of the white-led suffrage movement by refusing to march in a segregated parade in Washington, D.C., timed to the inauguration of President Woodrow Wilson—and prevailed. Two months before that confrontation, she founded the first African American suffrage group in Chicago, the Alpha Suffrage Club, a nonpartisan organization whose primary goal was to educate African American women about the duties and respon-sibilities of citizenship and voting. After a successful registration drive, the club's voters became active in the race for alderman in 1914 and the Chicago mayoral race the next year, campaigns that Wells-Barnett describes in this chapter from her posthumously published autobiog-raphy, *Crusade for Justice*.

It was about this time that the Illinois legislature was consider-ing the question of enfranchising the women voters of the state. I had been a member of the Women's Suffrage Association all during my residence in Illinois, but somehow I had not been able to get very much interest among our club women.

When I saw that we were likely to have a restricted suffrage, and the white women of the organization were working like beavers to bring it about, I made another effort to get our women interested.

With the assistance of one or two of my suffrage friends, I organized what afterward became known as the Alpha Suffrage Club. The women who joined were extremely interested when I showed them that we could use our vote for the advantage of ourselves and our race. We organized the block system, and once a week we met to report progress. The women at first were very much discouraged.

They said that the men jeered at them and told them they ought to be at home taking care of the babies. Others insisted that the women were trying to take the place of men and wear the trousers. I urged each one of the workers to go back and tell the women that we wanted them to register so that they could help put a colored man in the city council.

This line of argument appealed very strongly to them, since we had already taken part in several campaigns where men had run independent for alderman. The work of these women was so effective that when registration day came, the Second Ward was the sixth highest of the thirty-five wards of the city.

Our men politicians were surprised because not one of them, not even our ministers, had said one word to influence women to take advantage of the suffrage opportunity Illinois had given to her daughters. At the next primary campaign for alderman, because of the women's vote, Mr. W. R. Cowan, who was running independently, came within 167 votes of beating the ward organization candidate, Mr. Hugh Norris.

This happened on Tuesday. When the Alpha Suffrage Club convened for its regular meeting Wednesday night, we found present Mr. Samuel Ettelson and Mr. Oscar DePriest. These gentlemen came representing the ward organization and asked a chance to say a few words. Mr. Ettelson was hoarse with campaigning and Mr. DePriest was delegated spokesman. The gist of his remarks was to urge the women not to support an independent candidate for alderman since it was feared if they did so, the Democratic candidate might win.

He told us how much they admired the splendid work that had been done by us and assured us that if we would turn in and give our support to the organization candidate, who had won by only 167 votes the day before, the organization, having realized that there was now a demand for a colored man, would itself nominate one at the next vacancy. Mr. Ettelson nodded his head in agreement and asked me to tell the women that Mr. DePriest represented the organization in what he said.

The women began to fire broadcast at him. They wanted to know when there would be another vacancy and were informed that Mr. George Harding, who was our second alderman (for at that time every ward in the city had two aldermen) had said that he was going to try for something else during the year. If he did so, this would make his place vacant for next spring. Another question was asked—How could we be sure that the organization would keep its promise as made by Mr. DePriest? Mr. DePriest suggested that a committee be named, which would include some of our representative people outside of the Suffrage Club, to wait upon the ward organization and get its assurance to that effect.

After a most interesting session the gentlemen withdrew and the club proceeded to act on their suggestions. We sent out letters to representative organizations asking them to name someone to be part of a committee which was to wait upon the Second Ward organization. Most of them ridiculed the idea that the organization meant to do any such thing as suggested and thought we were wasting our time.

In due course of time Mr. Harding was elected state senator which, of course, did make his position as alderman vacant. The very next day after the November election, Mr. Oscar De-Priest called together a group of colored men to a dinner, and informed them that he had already received the endorsement of the Second Ward organization for Mr. Harding's place until the following February and election in April.

For that entire eight months Mr. DePriest interviewed every person of any influence, ringing doorbells and asking their support. Of course he won at the primaries. The next day afterward Mr. Edward H. Wright called a meeting of the Political Equality League executive committee, when Mr. Cowan announced that he had been visited at two o'clock in the morning after the primary and asked to run independently against Mr. DePriest, and that if the parties met his conditions, he was going to run. Evidently the matter was so unpopular that the gentleman gave up the idea.

I was present at the meeting and challenged both Mr. Wright and Mr. Cowan on their action. I told them that the action of this nameless white man had not been prompted by the desire to "secure a better man for the nomination." It simply was to get two colored men to fight against each other, and the result would be that neither one of them would secure the place. Thanks to the loyalty of the women, Mr. DePriest won out hands down. But it was not long before we found that he had quite forgotten those who had helped him to win.

He had asked my support and I had told him that I would give it to him with the understanding that if he won he would use his influence to see that Mr. Barnett realized the dream of his life and was elected judge. "You know that he was elected before, Mr. DePriest, and that he did not have the active support of his own race in order to make that election sure." He promised me solemnly that he would do this, but strange to say, from the day Mr. DePriest was elected until the day he was removed from his office, he never made the slightest effort to keep his promise.

In the meantime Mr. William Hale Thompson decided that he would try to be elected mayor of the city. One Sunday morning I had a telephone call asking if I would be one of a number of persons to meet in the First National Bank building to consider the establishment of an orphanage for colored girls. Because I knew none of the persons named who were to be present, I said I could not promise to be present unless I knew more about the movement.

The speaker then asked if he could come out to see me. He came and spent two hours. His remarks simmered down to this, that Commodore William Hale Thompson wanted to be mayor of the city; that he thought he could win the nomination if he had the labor vote and the Negro vote. He had the labor vote cinched and the speaker was scouting in the Second Ward all summer in the effort to find out who the masses of colored people accepted as leader. He said that he had found that it was not a man but a woman, and that I was that woman.

I inquired what Mr. Thompson proposed to do for colored people in return for their vote, but Mr. Hulit could not answer that question to my satisfaction. He ended up inviting me to attend a meeting at the Sherman Hotel the following Tuesday evening. He said that Commodore William Hale Thompson's friends had set out to get one hundred thousand pledge cards signed, and that Mr. Thompson would not give his consent to allow his name to be used until that number of persons had been pledged to vote for him. The meeting every week was to report progress.

The next day, when I reached home, the girl who lived with

me said that the same gentleman would be back again that afternoon. He came and was greatly excited to let me know that
when he went back and told Mr. Thompson of his interview
with me, Mr. Thompson was very pleased because he said that
my reputation among the people would be a great help to him
if they could get me to come in with them. And his mission
there was not only to bring me tickets for the meeting at the
Sherman Hotel but to tell me that they would want me to
speak.

Mr. Barnett and I both attended the meeting and I was called
on to speak, though I had said the night before that I could
not promise to do so until I had better acquainted myself with
the situation. When called upon I made that same statement
and told them that it would be impossible for me to make any
pledge as had been done by the other speakers until I knew
what Mr. Thompson's program was with reference to colored
people; that I was tired of having white men come out in the
Second Ward just before or on election day and buy up the
votes of Negroes who had no higher conception of the ballot
than to make it a question of barter and sale.

I had always felt that the man who bought votes was just as
much to be condemned as the man who sold them, but the
world at large did not look upon it in that way. Speaking for
those whom I represented, I was sure that we needed greater
interest taken in our welfare; that we needed better chance for
employment in the city work; and that we especially desired
that representation be given us commensurate with our voting
strength.

Mr. William Hale Thompson was seated in the rear of the
room and always wound up his speech by touching upon points
made by the speakers of the evening. He came forward and
launched at once into an answer to the questions I had asked.
Nothing could have been stronger than his endorsement of my
views and his promise that if we helped him to win the election
he would assure us that nobody would be a better friend to our
best interests than he.

That was the beginning of our acquaintance, and for the
next six months I threw my heart and soul into the movement.
The Second Ward added very largely to the result of securing those one hundred thousand names by the first week in

December. We had over twenty thousand pledge cards signed in the Second Ward alone. I sent an appeal to every woman's club and to the heads of other organizations throughout the city assuring them that I believed we had a true friend in this man Thompson and advising them to get pledges for him all over the city. This was done, and when the city woke up William Hale Thompson had two hundred thousand voters pledged to his nomination. This had been accomplished without machine organization and without newspaper assistance.

Things seemed to be going smoothly. It was understood that if Mr. Thompson won, our reading room and social center was to be made an auxiliary of the city, and through our employment agency, colored men were to be given street-cleaning jobs and work in other departments of the city. The Alpha Suffrage Club was the very first organization to endorse Mr. William Hale Thompson for mayor.

Just about the time we felt that the sun was going to shine on our side of the street, and that we were going to have a friend in court who believed in working for the benefit of our people, the regular Republican organization of the city drafted Chief Justice Olson to make the race for mayor against Mr. Thompson. I went at once to Judge Olson's office and asked him why he didn't tell me he was planning to run against Mr. Thompson. I told him I had made speeches all over the town for Mr. Thompson and had gotten everybody I knew to pledge themselves to vote for him; and I had been at this work for six months.

Judge Olson didn't seem to think much of the pledge card idea, and remarked that he had been known to voters for over fifteen years. I did not see how he could overcome Mr. Thompson's lead in three weeks, but I did see that I could make no more speeches for Mr. Thompson and take no more part in his campaign. I called Mr. Fred Lundin and told him of my predicament. He said, "Mrs. Barnett, no one has done more for our cause than you. If you want to go with us to the end there will be no one who will have greater influence with Mr. Thompson's administration than you." "I cannot do it, Mr. Lundin," I said. "To continue to make speeches for Mr. Thompson I will have to discredit Judge Olson. All my life I have been the victim of ingrates. I have constantly affirmed that I agree with the old time Spartans in spirit, anyhow, when they put ingrates to death.

"Judge Olson gave me the place I hold in the courts on a silver salver and I can neither say nor do anything against him; so I am notifying you that you will have to take my name off your speakers' list. I have told him I don't believe he can overcome the six months' work that we have done for Mr. Thompson in so short a time. My work is done and I can go no further with it. I would like, however, to select the person to carry on the hard work I have done." "Anybody you suggest," said Mr. Lundin, "will be acceptable with us."

After consulting with my husband I asked Mr. Edward H. Wright if he would take the place. Mr. Wright had fallen out with the organization when he ran a few years before for alderman against the organization's candidate. He had also been at loggerheads with the Deneen organization, because Governor Deneen had not in the eight years of his incumbency in the state house appointed a colored man to any representative position. Mr. Wright gave me permission to offer his name. I called up Mr. Lundin and told him about our choice and he seemed gratified, for he knew of Mr. Wright's ability and his political strength.

I made an appointment for Mr. Wright to see him the next day at three o'clock in the Union Hotel. The appointment was kept and Mr. Wright took over the management of the affairs of William Hale Thompson among the colored people. From that time his political career rose again. Mr. Thompson won at the primary with the help of the Second Ward, and all of our leading politicians proceeded to get on the bandwagon, with the result that William Hale Thompson was elected to the office of mayor with the largest vote that had ever been cast.

It was also the first time that women had voted for mayor. But from the time he was elected, not only Mr. Thompson but all our leading politicians proceeded to ignore those of us who had helped to make it possible for him to realize his ambition. I have been told that when some suggestion was made about keeping a promise to put me on the school board, our men told the mayor that "he didn't owe Mrs. Barnett anything because she did not go with them to the end."

I have also been reminded hundreds of times that I was

foolish not to have continued with him, since Judge Olson was not able to keep me in the adult probation office to which he had appointed me. In less than six months after Mayor Thompson's election, I had lost my job. And the Negro Fellowship Reading Room and Social Center had again to fall back on what we could make from our employment office.

THE CRISIS

Votes for Women: A Symposium by
Leading Thinkers of Colored America

AUGUST 1915

Founded in 1910, *The Crisis* was the official magazine of the National Association for the Advancement of Colored People. For the August 1915 issue, editor W.E.B. Du Bois (1868–1963) solicited short essays from eleven men and fifteen women on the topic of "Votes for Women." The men included members of the clergy, educational leaders, politicians, and judges, while the women were mostly members of the National Association of Colored Women and other black women's clubs. (Note that, with one exception, the essays of the men ran first, followed by the essays of the women.) Many of the respondents linked the cause of women's suffrage with the denial of voting rights to black men, none more forcefully than Mary Church Terrell: "Even if I believed that women should be denied the right of suffrage, wild horses could not drag such an admission from my pen or my lips, for this reason: precisely the same arguments used to prove that the ballot be withheld from women are advanced to prove that colored men should not be allowed to vote." Du Bois was so proud of the caliber of the contributions that he felt no need to add his editorial voice to what he called "one of the strongest cumulative attacks on sex and race discrimination in politics ever written."

––––––––––––

THE LOGIC OF WOMAN SUFFRAGE

BY REV. FRANCIS J. GRIMKE
Pastor 15th St. Presbyterian Church,
Washington, D. C.

I am heartily in favor of woman suffrage. I did not use to be, but it was simply because I had not given the subject due consideration. The moment I began to think seriously about it, I became convinced that I was wrong, and swung over on the other side, and have been on that side ever since. I do not see how any one who stops to think, who takes a common sense view of things, can be opposed to the franchise for women. What is this right to vote, after all? Is it not simply the right to form an opinion or judgment as to the character and fitness of those who are to be entrusted with the high and responsible duty of making laws and of administering the laws after they are made, and of having that judgment count in the selection of public officials? The ballot is simply the expression of the individual judgment in regard to such matters. Such being the case three things are perfectly clear in my mind:

(1). The interests of women are just as much involved in the enactment of laws, and in the administration of laws, as are the interests of men. In some respects they are even more so. In many things, such as the liquor traffic, the social evil, and other demoralizing influences, which directly affect the peace and happiness of the home, the kind of laws that are enacted, and the character of the men who are to enforce them, have for women a peculiar, a special interest.

(2). The average woman is just as well qualified to form an opinion as to the character and qualifications of those who are to be entrusted with power as the average man. The average man is in no sense superior to the average woman, either in point of intelligence, or of character. The average woman, in point of character, is superior to the average man; and, in so far as she is, she is better fitted to share in the selection of public officials.

(3). To deprive her of the right to vote is to govern her without her consent, which is contrary to the fundamental principle of democracy. That principle is clearly expressed in the Declaration of Independence, where we read: "Governments are instituted among men, deriving their just powers from the consent of the governed." Under this principle, which is a just principle, women have the same right to vote as men have. Are they not governed? And being governed, can the government imposed upon them be justly imposed upon them without their consent? It is simply to treat them as minors and inferiors, which every self-respecting woman should resent, and continue to resent until this stigma is removed from her sex. The time is certainly coming, and coming soon I believe, when this just claim on the part of women will be fully recognized in all truly civilized countries.

CHICAGO AND WOMAN'S SUFFRAGE
BY HON. OSCAR DE PRIEST
Alderman of the City of Chicago

I favor extension of the right of suffrage to women. The experience in Chicago has been that the women cast as intelligent a vote as the men. In the first campaign in which the women voted in Chicago, a certain degree of timidity attended their advent. In the recent campaign, however, the work of the women was as earnest and the interest as keen as that of the men and in some instances the partisanship was almost bitter. As far as the colored men are concerned, in the aldermanic campaign of 1914 the feeling was so high that it penetrated social, church and other circles and some friendships of long standing were threatened. In the campaign of 1915 when colored men were primary candidates for alderman, the women of the race seemed to realize fully what was expected of them, and, with the men, rolled up a very large and significant vote for the colored candidates; and they were consistent at the election, contributing to a plurality of over 3,000 votes for the successful colored candidate in a field of five. Personally, I am more than thankful for their work and as electors believe they have every necessary qualification that the men possess.

POLITICS AND WOMANLINESS
BY BENJAMIN BRAWLEY
Dean of Morehouse College, Atlanta, Ga.

The argument is all for woman suffrage. More and more one who takes the opposing view finds himself looking to the past rather than to the future. Each woman as well as each man is a child of God, and is entitled to all the privileges of that high heritage. We are reminded of the heroine in "A Doll's House:" "Before all else you are a wife and mother," says the husband in Ibsen's play. "No," replies Nora, "before all else I am a human being."

There is one objection which many honestly find it difficult to overcome. There are thousands of men in this country who are theoretically in favor of woman suffrage, but who would be sorry to see their wives and sisters at the polls. They cannot overcome the feeling that woman loses something of her fineness of character when she takes her place with a crowd of men to fight out a live issue. Her very need of a protector calls forth man's chivalry; take away that need and the basis of woman's strongest appeal to man is gone.

Even this last objection, merely a practical one, can be overcome. The finest and deepest culture is not that which keeps its possessor forever enclosed in a Doll's House. It is rather that which looks at life in the large, with a just appreciation of its problems and sorrow, and that labors in the most intelligent manner to right the wrongs that are in existence. When once everywhere woman has entered the fray and helped to clean up some of the graft in our cities and to improve the tone of our voting places, even this last fear will disappear.

CHRISTIANITY AND WOMAN
BY JOHN HURST, D.D.,
Bishop of the African M. E. Church and
Secretary of the Bishops' Council

The earlier civilizations seem to have conspired to limit woman's sphere; her position and functions as member of the community were to extend so far and no further. Intellectual accomplishments and graces could raise her beyond the status of the slave, but not beyond the estimate put upon a toy, a bauble or a common-place ornament. Often she was subjected to systems leading to degradation, stifling her soul and stealing away from her the qualities that make an individual and a woman. The law forbidding her to abstain from the service at the Jewish Synagogue, said she should not be seen. Amidst the civilization of classic antiquity, even down to the enlightened age of Pericles, she was subservient to the caprices and rude passions of the other sex. Her fate was disposed of with little regard to her wishes. She had even no choice as to whom she should marry. The sacred fire of love was not supposed to burn upon the altar of her heart. She was but a commodity, a chattel to be bartered off. Under the Roman law, her status was hardly that of a human being. Whether under the Empire or the Republic, she had not even a first name.

But with the advent of Christianity, the path for a true, honorable and lasting civilization was laid. It discarded and upset the teachings of the past. It gave woman her freedom, and womanhood has been lifted to the place where it justly belongs.

Christianity established equality and community of woman with man in the privileges of Grace, as being heir together with all the great gifts of life; receiving one faith, one baptism and partaking of the same holy table. Its thundering message to all is "There is neither Jew nor Greek, there is neither bond nor free, there is neither male nor female, for we are all one in Christ Jesus," and the echo of its teachings the world over is to "Loose her and let her go."

"ABOUT AUNTIES"
BY HON. J. W. JOHNSON,
Formerly U. S. Consul to Nicaragua

There is one thing very annoying about the cause of Woman Suffrage and that is the absurdity of the arguments against it which one is called upon to combat. It is very much more difficult to combat an absurd argument than to combat a sound argument. The holder of a sound argument is generally a person amenable to reason and open to conviction; whereas, the holder of an absurd argument is always a person blinded by prejudice or bound by some such consideration as custom or sentiment; a person, indeed, to whom it is often impossible to prove that 2 and 2 make 4.

The people who oppose votes for women are divided into two classes:—those who boldly declare that women are inferior beings, neither fit nor capable of becoming fit to exercise the right of suffrage, and those who apologetically contend that the ballot will drag woman down from her domestic throne and rob her of all gentleness, charm, goodness,—this list of angelic qualities may be extended to any length desired.

It takes only a glance to see the striking analogy between these two arguments and the old pro-slavery arguments. The very ease with which they can be disproved makes them exasperating.

But, regardless of all arguments, for or against, woman is going to gain universal suffrage. The wonderful progress made by the sex in the last century and a half places this beyond doubt. This progress is nowhere more graphically indicated than by the fact that in the first edition of the Encyclopedia Britannica (1771) the article "Woman" consisted of eight words, "Woman,—the female of man—See Homo." In the edition of

1910 the article "Woman" takes up seven pages. Besides there are thirty women among the writers of the Encyclopedia, and the work contains articles on more than five hundred women, distinguished in history, literature and art.

Woman has made her place in the arts, she is making her place in the economic world, and she is sure to make her place in the political world.

OUR DEBT TO SUFFRAGISTS

BY HON. ROBERT H. TERRELL,

Justice of the Municipal Court, District of Columbia

Of all the elements in our great cosmopolitan population the Negro should be most ardently in favor of woman suffrage, for above all others, he knows what a denial of the ballot means to a people. He has seen his rights trampled on, he has been humiliated and insulted in public, and he has brooded over his weakness and helplessness in private, all because he did not possess the power given by the vote to protect himself in the same manner as other classes of citizens defend themselves against wrong and injustice. To those who oppose the right of women to vote it may be well to quote the stirring words of Benjamin Wade, of Ohio, uttered on the floor of the United States Senate, when he was advocating Negro Suffrage. He said: "I have a contempt I cannot name for the man who would demand rights for himself that he is not willing to grant to every one else."

Finally, as a matter of sentiment, every man with Negro blood in his veins should favor woman suffrage. Garrison, Phillips, Frederick Douglass and Robert Purvis and the whole host of abolitionists were advocates of the right. I often heard it said when I was a boy in Boston that immediately after the Civil War Susan B. Anthony, Julia Ward Howe, Elizabeth Cady Stanton and other leaders of the women's rights movement at the request of these men devoted all of their efforts towards obtaining the ballot for the Negro, even to the neglect of their own dearly cherished cause, hoping, indeed, that the black man, who would be in some measure the beneficiary of their work and sacrifice, would in turn give them the aid they so sorely needed at that time. Now what our fathers failed to do for these pioneers who did so much for our cause before and after the great war, let us do for those who are now leading the fight for woman suffrage. I believe that in supporting them we will render our country a great and much needed service.

WOMAN IN THE ANCIENT STATE
BY W. H. CROGMAN, LITT.D.,
Professor of Ancient Languages,
Clark University, S. Atlanta, Ga.

Slowly but steadily woman has risen from a state of servile dependence to her legitimate position of respect and consideration, and it needs no prophetic vision to see that the full recognition of her civic rights is near at hand. To form a just estimate of her achievements to date one must necessarily take into consideration the point from which she started, that is to say, the condition of her sex in the ancient state.

For light on this we turn naturally to the two most enlightened nations of antiquity. In the Homeric age woman was treated, we should infer, with tender and affectionate regard, and her virtues were sung by the greatest of poets. Even today, after twenty-seven centuries have rolled by, one cannot read without emotion and a thrill of admiration the story of Penelope's conjugal fidelity to her absent husband. Nor are we less affected by the scene of Hector and Andromache with the babe in her arms. Yet it would not be safe to conclude that these instances were fairly representative of the general status of woman in the ancient state, for at the same period there also existed cruelty, brutality, treachery. Beside the fidelity of Penelope may easily be placed the infidelity of Helen and the perfidy of Paris. Women were captured in war and subjected to the unspeakable. The greatest poem of the ages is but a recital of the fatal quarrel of two brutal men over the disposal of a captive maiden. Woman had practically no part in state affairs. Her duties were chiefly confined to the home. Says one writer:

"At no time of her life could a woman be without a guardian. If her husband was not alive, it would be her nearest male relative, and this person remained her guardian even when she was married. After her husband's death her son was her guardian. She could not legally make any contract beyond a shilling or two—there was no occasion for an Athenian to advertise that he would not be responsible for his wife's debts—and she could not bring actions at law."

And all this in Athens, in Athens at the summit of her greatness!

It is needless to say that a somewhat similar state of things existed at Rome where the father had the right of life and death over every member of the family. Verily it is a far cry from the rostrum of today, graced by the presence of a woman earnestly pleading for her civic rights, to that dismal period when she was a negligible factor in human affairs.

WOMEN'S RIGHTS
BY CHARLES W. CHESNUTT
Author of "The Wife of His Youth,"
"The Marrow of Tradition," etc.

I believe that all persons of full age and sound mind should have a voice in the making of the laws by which they are governed, or in the selection of those who make those laws. As long as the family was the social unit, it was perhaps well enough for the householder, representing the family, to monopolize the vote. But with the broadening of woman's sphere the situation has changed, and many women have interests which are not concerned with the family.

Experience has shown that the rights and interests of no class are safe so long as they are entirely in the hands of another class—the rights and interests of the poor in the hands of the rich, of the rich in the hands of the poor, of one race in the hands of another. And while there is no such line of cleavage between the sexes as exists between other social classes, yet so far as women constitute a class as differentiated from men, neither can their rights be left with entire safety solely in the hands of men. In the gradual extension of statutory rights, women are in many countries, the equals of men before the law. They have always been subject to the burdens of citizenship. The burden of taxation, generally speaking, falls more heavily upon them, perhaps because they are more honest in returning their personal property for taxation, or less cunning in concealing it. They are subject, equally with men, to the criminal laws, though there, I suspect, for sentimental reasons, the burden has not fallen so heavily upon them. Their rights need protection, and they should be guarded against oppression, and the ballot is the most effective weapon by which these things can be accomplished.

I am not in favor of woman suffrage because I expect any great improvement in legislation to result from it. The contrary, from woman's lack of experience in government, might not unreasonably be expected. Women are certainly no wiser or more logical than men. But they enjoy equal opportunities for education, and large numbers of them are successfully engaged in business and in the professions and have the requisite experience and knowledge to judge intelligently of proposed legislation. Even should their judgment be at fault—as men's judgment too often is—they have fine intuitions, which are many times a safe guide to action; and their sympathies are apt to be in support of those things which are clean and honest and just and therefore desirable—all of which ought to make them a valuable factor in government.

STATES' RIGHTS AND THE SUFFRAGE
BY HON. JOHN R. LYNCH
Major, Retired, U. S. Army; formerly Speaker of the House of Representatives of Mississippi; U. S. Representative, 6th District of Mississippi, 43rd, 44th and 47th Congresses; 4th Auditor of the U. S. Treasury, 1889–93; etc.

What the friends and advocates of equal suffrage have to fear more than anything else, is the dangerous and mischievous doctrine of "States' Rights." Those who are opposed to equal suffrage contend that it is a local and not a National question—one that each State must determine for itself. But what is a State? It seems to be an indefinable abstraction. "The United States," the National Constitution declares, "shall guarantee to every state in this Union a republican form of government," but this is a meaningless declaration. It has remained a dead letter since the adoption of the constitution, because some of the so-called states were and are nothing more nor less than despotic oligarchies. We have seen and now see that what is called the "State," in some parts of the country, is simply a part of the white males who obtained (it matters not how), possession of the local machinery which they call, and the National Government recognizes, as the "State Government." This government never allows any of the inhabitants of the "State" who are not identified with the ruling oligarchy to have any voice in its government. The friends of Equal Rights can hope for no favorable action from such governments as these, for they are not only close corporations, but they are determined to allow none to become members of the corporation that the managers can not absolutely and easily control. With a view of perpetuating themselves in power through the local machinery called "the State," some of them have, during the past twenty-five years, practically nullified the fifteenth amendment of the Federal Constitution. The recent decision of the Supreme Court by which some of the different schemes and devices for this purpose were declared unconstitutional and void is a most hopeful and encouraging indication. Let the friends of equal suffrage take on renewed hope. Victory, and that too on a national basis will ultimately be an accomplished fact.

DISFRANCHISEMENT IN THE DISTRICT OF COLUMBIA
BY L. M. HERSHAW
Of the United States Land Office

As regards the ballot, men and women are equal in the District of Columbia; both are deprived of it. Citizens of the District of Columbia have not voted since 1874, the year in which the ballot was taken from them by act of Congress. From time to time since then fitful efforts have been made to recover the lost right, but there has been no properly organized sustained movement with that object in view.

The female population of the District of Columbia exceeds the male population in round numbers by 16,000. In intelligence, in public spirit, in moral influence and in support of established institutions and philanthropies the female population is the equal, and in some instances the superior of the male population. If suffrage is ever restored to the citizens of the District it should be made to include the women. The right of the woman to vote rests on the same basis as the right of the man: her humanity. "Honio sum, et humani a mi nil alienum puto;"—I am a human being, and I consider nothing belonging to the human race foreign to me is the maxim constituting the major premise of the logic of human rights. To deny woman the right to vote is so far forth a denial of her humanity.

In the District of Columbia where neither man nor woman votes, the woman is as worthy a member of the community as the man. If Congress should reenact suffrage in the District it is difficult to see how it could except women from its exercise without fixing upon them an undeserved stigma. The example of women voting in the District would go a long way toward educating the backward and unprogressive throughout the country to the necessity of doing justice to the other half of our common humanity.

VOTES AND LITERATURE
BY MRS. PAUL LAURENCE DUNBAR

Matthew Arnold defined literature as a "criticism of life." By that he meant life in its entirety, not a part of it. Therefore, if a woman is to produce real literature, not pretty phrasing, she needs to have a firm grasp on all that makes life complete. The completion and perfection of life is love—love of home and family, love of humanity, love of country. No person living a mentally starved existence can do enduring work in any field, and woman without all the possibilities of life is starved, pinched, poverty-stricken. It is difficult to love your home and family if you be outcast and despised by them; perplexing to love humanity, if it gives you nothing but blows; impracticable to love your country, if it denies you all the rights and privileges which as citizens you should enjoy.

George Eliot, George Sand, Harriet Beecher Stowe wrote great novels because they looked at life from the point of view of the masculine mind, with a background of centuries of suffrage. Yet each was peculiarly feminine. It is a significant fact that the American and English women who are now doing the real work in literature—not necessarily fiction—are the women who are most vitally interested in universal suffrage.

WOMEN AND COLORED WOMEN
BY MRS. MARY B. TALBERT
Vice President-at-large, National Association
of Colored Women

It should not be necessary to struggle forever against popular prejudice, and with us as colored women, this struggle becomes two-fold, first, because we are women and second, because we are colored women. Although some resistance is experienced in portions of our country against the ballot for women, because colored women will be included, I firmly believe that enlightened men, are now numerous enough everywhere to encourage this just privilege of the ballot for women, ignoring prejudice of all kinds.

The great desire of our nation to produce the most perfect form of government, shows incontestible proofs of advance. Advanced methods in prison reforms are shown by our own state Commissioner, Miss Katherine B. Davis. Advanced methods in school reforms are shown by Mrs. Ella Flagg Young, Superintendent of Education of Chicago. Advanced methods in the treatment of childhood and adolescence, are shown by the bureau of child welfare under Mrs. Julia C. Lathrop. Each of these women have been most kindly toward the colored women. In our own race advanced methods of industrial training are shown by Miss Nannie H. Burroughs, Mrs. Charlotte Hawkins Brown, and Mrs. Mary McLeod Bethune, and numbers of other colored women in various lines have blazed the path of reform.

By her peculiar position the colored woman has gained clear powers of observation and judgment—exactly the sort of powers which are today peculiarly necessary to the building of an ideal country.

"VOTES FOR MOTHERS"
BY MRS. CORALIE FRANKLIN COOK
Member of the Board of Education, District of Columbia

I wonder if anybody in all this great world ever thought to consider *man's* rights as an individual, by his status as a father? yet you ask me to say something about "Votes for Mothers," as if mothers were a separate and peculiar people. After all, I think you are not so far wrong. Mothers *are* different, or ought to be different, from other folk. The woman who smilingly goes out, willing to meet the Death Angel, that a child may be born, comes back from that journey, not only the mother of her own adored babe, but a near-mother to all other children. As she serves that little one, there grows within her a passion to serve humanity; not race, not class, not sex, but God's creatures as he has sent them to earth.

It is not strange that enlightened womanhood has so far broken its chains as to be able to know that to perform such service, woman should help both to make and to administer the laws under which she lives, should feel responsible for the conduct of educational systems, charitable and correctional institutions, public sanitation and municipal ordinances in general. Who should be more competent to control the presence of bar rooms and "red-light districts" than mothers whose sons they are meant to lure to degradation and death? Who knows better than the girl's mother at what age the girl may legally barter her own body? Surely not the men who have put upon our statute books, 16, 14, 12, aye, be it to their eternal shame, even 10 and 8 years, as "the age of consent!"

If men could choose their own mothers, would they choose free women or bond-women? Disfranchisement because of sex is curiously like disfranchisement because of color. It cripples the individual, it handicaps progress, it sets a limitation upon mental and spiritual development. I grow in breadth, in vision, in the power to do, just in proportion as I use the capacities with which Nature, the All-Mother, has endowed me. I transmit to the child who is bone of my bone, flesh of my flesh and *thought of my thought; somewhat* of my own power or weakness. Is not the voice which is crying out for "Votes for Mothers" the Spirit of the Age crying out for the Rights of Children?

"VOTES FOR CHILDREN"
BY MRS. CARRIE W. CLIFFORD
*Honorary President of the Federation of
Colored Women's Clubs of Ohio*

It is the ballot that opens the schoolhouse and closes the saloon; that keeps the food pure and the cost of living low; that causes a park to grow where a dump-pile grew before. It is the ballot that regulates capital and protects labor; that up-roots disease and plants health. In short, it is by the ballot we hope to develop the wonderful ideal state for which we are all so zealously working.

When the fact is considered that woman is the chosen channel through which the race is to be perpetuated; that she sustains the most sacred and intimate communion with the unborn babe; that later, she understands in a manner truly marvelous (and explain only by that vague term "instinct") its wants and its needs, the wonder grows that her voice is not the *first* heard in planning for the ideal State in which her child, as future citizen, is to play his part.

The family is the miniature State, and here the influence of the mother is felt in teaching, directing and executing, to a degree far greater than that of the father. At his mother's knee the child gets his first impressions of love, justice and mercy; and by obedience to the laws of the home he gets his earliest training in civics.

More and more is it beginning to be understood that the mother's zeal for the ballot is prompted by her solicitude for her family-circle.

That the child's food may be pure, that his environment shall be wholesome and his surrounding sanitary—these are the things which engage her thought. That his mind shall be properly developed and his education wisely directed; that his occupation shall be clean and his ideals high—all these are things of supreme importance to her, who began to plan for the little life before it was even dreamed of by the father.

Kindergartens, vacation-schools, playgrounds; the movement for the City Beautiful; societies for temperance and for the prevention of cruelty to children and animals—these and many other practical reforms she has brought to pass, *in spite of not having the ballot.* But as she wisely argues, why should she be forced to use indirect methods to accomplish a thing that could be done so much more quickly and satisfactorily by the direct method—by casting her own ballot?

The ballot! the sign of power, the means by which things are brought to pass, the talisman that makes our dreams come true! Her dream is of a State where war shall cease, where peace and unity be established and where love shall reign.

Yes, it is the great mother-heart reaching out to save her children from war, famine and pestilence; from death degradation and destruction, that induces her to demand "Votes for Women," knowing well that fundamentally it is really a campaign for "Votes for Children."

TRAINING AND THE BALLOT
BY MARY FITZBUTLER WARING, M. D.
*Chairman of the Department of Health
and Hygiene, N. A. C. W.*

In the earlier ages, the thought was common among the nations of the world, that woman was not the equal of man.

Socially, religiously and politically she was compelled to take an inferior position and to submit to the will and wiles of man. In some countries she was not even considered as the legal parent of her own child.

The ability to weigh the merits of the persons to fill office and the value of ordinances which govern the people, requires a knowledge of men and affairs. A trained mind, no matter in what profession, is more capable of making logical deductions; therefore the people naturally turn for information to the enlightened. The question of sex is of no importance.

The work of the professional woman just as that of the professional man places her in a position to help the many with whom she necessarily comes in contact, and therefore her influence is a power to be reckoned with. The ethical relations of the professional woman makes her, ofttimes, the confidant and advisor of others and for that reason she should be well informed on political issues and aspirants for public office.

Trained judgment is needed everywhere and it should always be armed with the ballot.

DEMOCRACY AND ART

BY WILLIAM STANLEY BRAITHEWAITE

Author of Anthologies of Magazine Verse, etc.

We find that at almost every stage of its development Democracy has been betrayed by one or another of its idealist professors, except one. Democracy has its source in political ethics, but neither religion nor social justice have performed towards it, in practice, those strict obligations which are defined by the nature of their idealisms. Art alone has kept her covenant with Democracy.

Art is the embodiment of spiritual ideals. There is no human progress without a previsioning of the aspiration through one of the symbolic languages of art. All the great craving desires of humanity have been promised and attained through the message of art. Art cannot flourish in a democracy, is the critical opinion common to a good many. I say, that in the future, art will not flourish without democracy. All that democracy has gained in the last twenty years it has owed to the ideals of art. Was the social conscience of America vitalized by religion or the justice and wisdom of political enactments? No; but by an art, the art of poetry. The undemocratic methods of industrial power, did the Christian church protest against it? No; it was a poet with a passion and a message. Now, art has seen to it that public opinion consider all the rights and demands that democracy makes towards the justification of its ideals. These have not all been accomplished. It has got to eliminate racial prejudice which has governmental sanction, and it has got to win sufferance for all citizens alike. Art is bringing democracy face to face with beauty, and beauty knows neither race, caste nor sex. The social vision of art is complete. And its light is ever shining upon the luminous figure of Democracy, the ideal Mother of human hopes, the hopes of the rejected, of the denied, of the subjected individual.

The voice of art expressing the spirit of democracy is beautifully illustrated in this passage from Mr. Witter Bynner's recently published poem "The New World:"

> "To stop the wound and heal the scar
> Of time, with sudden glorious aptitude
> Woman assumes her part. Her pity in a flood
> Flings down the gate.
> She has been made to wait
> Too long, undreaming and untaught
> The touch and beauty of democracy.
> But, entering now the strife
> In which her saving sense is due,
> She watches and she grows aware,
> Holding a child more dear than property,
> That the many perish to empower the few,
> That homeless politics have split apart
> The common country of the common heart."

BLACK WOMEN AND REFORM
BY MISS N. H. BURROUGHS
Secretary of the Woman's Auxiliary to the
National Baptist Convention.

The Negro Church means the Negro woman. Without her, the race could not properly support five hundred churches in the whole world. Today they have 40,000 churches in the United States. She is not only a great moral and spiritual asset, but she is a great economic asset. I was asked by a southern white woman who is an enthusiastic worker for "votes for (white) women," "What can the Negro woman do with the ballot?" I asked her, "What can she do without it?" When the ballot is put into the hands of the American woman the world is going to get a correct estimate of the Negro woman. It will find her a tower of strength of which poets have never sung, orators have never spoken, and scholars have never written.

Because the black man does not know the value of the ballot, and has bartered and sold his most valuable possession, it is no evidence that the Negro woman will do the same. The Negro woman, therefore, needs the ballot to get back, by the wise *use* of it, what the Negro man has lost by the *misuse* of it. She needs it to ransom her race. A fact worthy of note is that in every reform in which the Negro woman has taken part, during the past fifty years, she has been as aggressive, progressive and dependable as those who inspired the reform or led it. The world has yet to learn that the Negro woman is quite superior in bearing moral responsibility. A comparison with the men of her race, in moral issues, is odious. She carries the burdens of the Church, and of the school and bears a great deal more than her economic share in the home.

Another striking fact is that the Negro woman carries the moral destiny of two races in her hand. Had she not been the woman of unusual moral stamina that she is, the black race would have been made a great deal whiter, and the white race a great deal blacker during the past fifty years. She has been left a prey for the men of every race, but in spite of this, she has held the enemies of Negro female chastity at bay. The Negro woman is the white woman's as well as the white race's most needed ally in preserving an unmixed race.

The ballot, wisely used, will bring to her the respect and protection that she needs. It is her weapon of moral defence. Under present conditions, when she appears in court in defence of her virtue, she is looked upon with amused contempt. She needs the ballot to reckon with men who place no value upon her virtue, and to mould healthy public sentiment in favor of her own protection.

THE SELF-SUPPORTING WOMAN AND THE BALLOT
BY MISS M. E. JACKSON

Of the Civil Service of the State of Rhode Island, President of the R. I. Association of Colored Women's Clubs

Looked at from a sane point of view, all objections to the ballot for women are but protests against progress, civilization and good sense.

"Woman's place is in the home." Would that the poorly paid toilers in field, work-shop, mill and kitchen, might enjoy the blessed refreshment of their own homes with accompanying assurance that those dependent upon them might be fed, clothed, properly reared and educated.

Each morning's sun beholds a mighty army of 8,000,000 souls marching forth to do battle for daily bread. You inquire who they are? Why, the mothers, wives, sisters and daughters of the men of America. "The weaker vessels," the majority of whom are constrained from necessity.

There is no field of activity in the country where women are not successfully competing with men. In the agricultural pursuits alone, there are over 900,000. In the ministry 7,000 dare preach the gospel with "Heads uncovered." And 1,010 possess the courage to invade the field of the Solons, bravely interpreting the laws, although their brothers in all but twelve of the forty-five States (so far as the ballot is concerned), class them with criminals, insane and feeble-minded.

The self-supporting woman out of her earnings, pays taxes, into the public treasury and through church, club and civic organization gives her moral backing unstintingly to her Country.

Imagine if you can the withdrawal of this marvelous economic force,—the working women of America! It is a fundamental necessity of modern civilization.

The laboring man has discovered beyond peradventure that his most effective weapon of defence is the *ballot in his own hand*. The self-supporting woman asks for and will accept nothing less.

"TRUST THE WOMEN!"
BY MRS. JOSEPHINE ST. PIERRE RUFFIN
Pioneer in the club movement among Colored Women of the United States

Many colored men doubt the wisdom of women suffrage because they fear that it will increase the number of our political enemies. I have been in suffrage work in Massachusetts for forty years and more. I have voted 41 times under the school suffrage laws. I was welcomed into the Massachusetts Woman's Suffrage Association by Lucy Stone, Julia Ward Howe, Ednah Cheney, Abby Morton Diaz and those other pioneer workers who were broad enough to include "no distinction because of race" with "no distinctions because of sex." I feel that a movement inaugurated by men and women of such wisdom and vision as that of the early workers, cannot dwindle or be side-tracked, and that today, as in those early days, the big women, the far seeing women, are in the ranks of the suffragists. We can afford to follow those women. We are justified in believing that the success of this movement for equality of the sexes means more progress toward equality of the races. I have worked, along with other colored women with those pioneers in the Abolition movement, in the various movements to open educational opportunities for women, business opportunities for women and to equalize the laws; the longer I have been associated with them, the more deeply I have been impressed by this farsightedness and broadmindedness of the leaders, both early and late, in the Woman Suffrage Movement.

Y.W.C.A.
BY MRS. A. W. HUNTON
Formerly Adviser to the National Board of Directors, Y.W.C.A.

A membership of more than a half million, representing some seventeen nationalities, makes the Young Women's Christian Association a world movement.

In the United States three hundred thousand members, distributed in 979 college, city and county associations have as their objective the advancement of the "physical, social, intellectual, moral and spiritual interests of young women."

One of the most unique and wonderful characteristics of the association is the adaptability to meet the needs of all types of women, so that its membership is as diversified as women's lives and interests. This diversified membership, constituting at once the governing and sustaining force of the association, is its strongest barrier to any creed save that upon which the movement is founded.

However difficult it is to express any relation between the association and the suffrage movement, it is not difficult to understand that the association spirit dominating womanhood would count for righteousness in the solution of this important question.

Acutely suffering from the wrongs and humiliations of an unjustly restricted suffrage, it is but natural that the colored woman should feel deeply and keenly wherever the question of suffrage arises. But the colored woman within the association, in common with thousands of her sisters who have been touched by other spiritual forces, is animated by a fine spirit of idealism—an idealism not too far removed from everyday existence to find expression in service. Hence she is giving her energy largely to the development of the highest qualities of mind and soul—for these alone can give to the nation the best there is in citizenship.

VOTES FOR TEACHERS
BY MISS MARIA L. BALDWIN
Principal of the Agassiz Public School, Cambridge, Mass.

Women teachers in those states where school suffrage has already been granted them have found out that even so meagre a share of voting power has given them a definite influence, and has brought about a few notable results. In several cases local schools have been kept, by the women's vote, from the control of persons who threatened all that was best in them. Candidates for election to school boards reckon early with the "teacher vote" and hasten to announce their "rightness" on this or that issue supposedly dear to teachers. It is wholly reasonable to infer that the extension of the suffrage will enable teachers to secure more consideration for themselves, and to have an important influence on the quality of the persons chosen to direct the schools.

At the outset teachers will be confronted by the temptation of power—the temptation to use it for personal or selfish ends.

What, as a class, will they do with this temptation! What motives will lie behind their advocacy of men and measures? What tests of fitness will they apply to the candidate for their votes? Will they decline to recognize fine qualities for school service in one who may hold heretical views about increase of salaries, or length of vacations? These questions, which would test any group of workers, I cannot answer. I can only submit what seems an earnest that this group may stand the test.

The profession of teaching has a rich inheritance. These convictions were bequeathed to it, to have and to hold: that the dearest interests of life are in its keeping; that its peculiar service to society is to nourish and perpetuate those noblest aspirations called its ideals; that to do such work one must be devoted and unselfish.

This tradition still inspires the teacher. Some of the unrest, the dissatisfaction with conditions that are everywhere has penetrated her world, but probably no other work is done less in the commercial spirit nor any service more expanded beyond what "is nominated in the bond." Many school rooms are moving pictures of this spirit at work.

One is warranted in thinking that teachers will transfer to their use of the ballot this habit of fidelity to ideals.

WOMAN SUFFRAGE AND SOCIAL REFORM
BY MISS ANNA H. JONES
Chairman of the Department of Education, National Association of Colored Women

Of the four great institutions of human uplift—the home, the school, the church, and the State, woman has a direct controlling force in the first three institutions. In the State her influence at present is indirect. Since her control in the three is unquestioned, should she not have the legal means—the ballot—to widen and deepen her work?

In terms of today, her work is the conservation and improvement of the child; child labor laws, inspection of the health of school children, safeguarding the youth in the home, in the school, in the court, in the street, in the place of amusement. Her work is the prevention of vice with its train of physical and moral evils; the enactment of laws to secure and regulate sanitation, pure food, prohibition, divorce; the care of the aged, the unfortunate, the orphan. All the questions touch in a very direct way the home—woman's kingdom.

When an experiment has been tried for a certain purpose it seems logical to refer to its success or failure. A review of the States in which women have had the ballot will show that their exercise of the franchise has been along the lines of reform mentioned above. Her ballot has not been cast against the forces of right. Is it probable that in the other, the more conservative States, her course will be less judicial?

It may take a little time for woman to learn to make the ballot count for righteousness, but her closer view, and sympathetic touch will be of material assistance in the solution of the social problems that confront her as the homemaker.

The century awaits the "finer issues" of woman's "finely touched spirit."

COLORED WOMEN'S CLUBS
BY MRS. B. K. BRUCE
Editor of the official organ of the National Association of Colored Women

The national club movement among colored women began definitely in 1895, when a call was sent out from Boston by Mrs. Josephine St. P. Ruffin to a number of prominent colored women to meet in conference.

The special object of that conference was to repel and refute a vicious statement by an evil minded individual who had given currency to his false and misleading statements in book form. A national association called The National Federation of Colored Women, was formed at this conference.

The first convention of the new organization was called to meet a year later in July 1896, in Washington, D.C. In August of 1896 the first convention of the National League of Colored Women was held. The two organizations united under the name, National Association of Colored Women. In 1916 this organization will hold its tenth biennial session in Baltimore, Maryland. One year ago in Wilberforce, Ohio, the largest and most successful convention in its history was held. Over four hundred delegates, representing 50,000 women organized in clubs throughout the country, were present. The delegates came from the East, the West, the North, the South. The burden of the song of the numberless reports and addresses was social service not alone for colored people but for humanity. Miss Zona Gale said of the meeting that she had never attended a convention which so confirmed her belief in the possibilities of the common human race.

One thousand clubs are numbered with The National Association of Colored Women. In 1912–13 these clubs raised $82,424. Over $60,000 was spent in purchasing property for Orphans' Homes, Working Girls' Homes, Christian Association Homes, Social Settlements and so on. In 1914 the valuation of the various properties exceeded $100,000.

VOTES FOR PHILANTHROPY

BY MRS. ELIZABETH LINDSAY DAVIS

*National Organizer, National Association
of Colored Women*

The New citizen is no longer a novelty nor an experiment. She is demonstrating at all times her fitness for her duties and responsibilities by study; by insistent investigation of all candidates for public office regardless of party lines; by an intelligent use of the ballot in correcting the evils arising from graft, dishonesty and misappropriation of public funds; by persistent agitation to arouse civic consciousness, until now she is a potent factor in the body politic.

Men recognize her intuitive ability to think and decide for herself, respect her opinions and bid for her vote.

The keynote in the music of the Twentieth Century is Social Service, and in no better way can systematic philanthropy be done than by using the power of the ballot upon the heads of the great corporations and private individuals to direct their attention to the serious consequences of present day industrial and social unrest, the crime, disease, and poverty emanating from bad housing and unwholesome environment, to train their hands to give systematically to the cause of human betterment.

Woman is a pioneer in the forward movement for Social uplift, racial and community development, whether for the abandoned wife, the wage earning girl, the dependent and delinquent child or the countless hordes of the unemployed.

The highest and most successfully developed philanthropical

work depends absolutely upon the control of political influence by the best American citizenship, men and women working in unity and cooperation at the polls.

WOMAN SUFFRAGE AND THE 15TH AMENDMENT
BY MRS. MARY CHURCH TERRELL
Honorary President of the National Association of Colored Women

Even if I believed that women should be denied the right of suffrage, wild horses could not drag such an admission from my pen or my lips, for this reason: precisely the same arguments used to prove that the ballot be withheld from women are advanced to prove that colored men should not be allowed to vote. The reasons for repealing the Fifteenth Amendment differ but little from the arguments advanced by those who oppose the enfranchisement of women. Consequently, nothing could be more inconsistent than that colored people should use their influence against granting the ballot to women, if they believe that colored men should enjoy this right which citizenship confers.

What could be more absurd and ridiculous than that one group of individuals who are trying to throw off the yoke of oppression themselves, so as to get relief from conditions which handicap and injure them, should favor laws and customs which impede the progress of another unfortunate group and hinder them in every conceivable way. For the sake of consistency, therefore, if my sense of justice were not developed at all, and I could not reason intelligently, as a colored woman I should not tell my dearest friend that I opposed woman suffrage.

But how can any one who is able to use reason, and who believes in dealing out justice to all God's creatures, think it is right to withhold from one-half the human race rights and privileges freely accorded to the other half, which is neither more deserving nor more capable of exercising them?

For two thousand years mankind has been breaking down the various barriers which interposed themselves between human beings and their perfect freedom to exercise all the faculties with which they were divinely endowed. Even in monarchies old fetters which formerly restricted freedom, dwarfed the intellect and doomed certain individuals to narrow circumscribed spheres, because of the mere accident of birth, are being loosed and broken one by one. In view of such wisdom and experience the political subjection of women in the United States can be likened only to a relic of barbarism, or to a spot upon the sun, or to an octopus holding this republic in its hideous grasp, so that further progress to the best form of government is impossible and that precious ideal its founders promised it would be it seems nothing more tangible than a mirage.

VOTES FOR HOUSEWIVES
BY MRS. LILLIAN A. TURNER
Honorary President of the Minnesota Association of Colored Women's Clubs

That the housewife, that great reasoner, will vote intelligently, is my happy conclusion, after reading the ponderous decision of a wise man, who protests that voters should be "only those who are able to substitute reason for sentiment." It is such a relief to have an impartial definition even though its close analysis might exclude a large portion of present voters. But my concern is with the housewife, the future voter, as tested by the wise man's definition.

Now, Sentiment is the housewife's most cherished possession; to this assertion all agree—the man, the anti-suffragist and the rest of us. Furthermore, lack of excessive use will keep it so, for the housewife early learns to substitute Reason for Sentiment. When Sentiment wails because husband walks two steps ahead instead of beside her; weeps because Boy's curls are shorn; foolishly resents the absence of the old attentions, and more foolishly dwells on an infinite variety of things, Reason comes nobly to the rescue and teaches her that none of these things are necessary to life. Reason is the constant substitute for her cherished Sentiment. But Reason's assertion, that protection from vice for Son of the Shorn Curls, is impracticable for business reasons, is too difficult for mental gymnastics. Sentiment conquers, and the housewife unreasonably demands the ballot to protect Son! However, Reason being already so well developed through "discipline by substitution" (still quoting the wise man) I have ceased to tremble when I hear dire predictions of the ruin that is expected to follow the rapid approach of woman's franchise.

[Articles were received too late for insertion from President John Hope, Hon. C. W. Anderson, Mrs. G. W. Morgan, Hon. W. H. Lewis and Mrs. N. J. Asberry.]

OREOLA WILLIAMS HASKELL

The Greatest Thing

1920

Banner Bearers: Tales of the Suffrage Campaign by Oreola Williams
Haskell (1875–1953) is a series of fictional sketches "each embodying
one special feature of the many-sided efforts to win the vote." Haskell
put human faces on the collective drama of broader social change by
telling the story through the eyes of ordinary suffrage workers going
about their daily business of the incredibly difficult task of winning
votes for women. In this story, Mrs. John L. Leeds (as was the custom
at the time, married suffrage leaders were often referred to by their
husbands' names) presides over a meeting of suffrage leaders while
contemplating whether she should accept an offer to join the national
leadership team. Haskell's fictional depiction of New York suffrage circles drew on her own experiences as president of the Brooklyn-based
Kings County Political Equality League. At the time of the major New
York State suffrage referendums in 1915 and 1917, she served as head of
the Press Bureau of the New York City Woman Suffrage Party. *Banner
Bearers*, which was published in 1920, was her only book.

The leaders of Manhattan crowded into the Borough Chairman's room and sat down close together on creaking camp
chairs. It was the usual Borough meeting and they exchanged
low-toned remarks about the reports they must give on the
work in their assembly districts. A good-natured rivalry was
shown in their remarks:

"How many members have you now?"

"Most of my canvassing is done. We are on the last lap."

"Don't tell me you are 100 per cent captained?"

"Had six hundred at my last public meeting. Can you say as
much?"

"Does Manhattan still lead the Boroughs. Brooklyn is working overtime."

The Borough Chairman, Mrs. John L. Leeds, tall and dark,
unconsciously made a pretty picture as she sat at her desk.
She was a bit of autumn with all its tints present in the dark
brown of her luxuriant hair, in the red of her cheeks, in the leaf

brownness of her eyes that seemed at times deep pools with the sparkle of sunshine on them. The brown dress she wore with its touch of crimson carried out the autumnal color scheme and set off her beauty in an effective way.

Usually brimming with vivacious life, to-day she seemed strangely subdued and a little distrait. Rather absently she greeted each newcomer with a word and a smile and nervously sorted and arranged the numerous papers on her desk. From time to time, the Borough Secretary, seated beside her, looked at her wonderingly. She did not know that the Borough Chairman was secretly thrashing out a problem. She did not know that a letter just received and held folded in the Chairman's hand was bothering her, and that its phrases kept floating before her inner vision in a detached fashion.

"Your great ability—time you served in a higher capacity— greater opportunities in the national field—relinquish your present duties—urge your acceptance—talents especially fit you for our work—find your successor."

Especially did "find your successor" stick in Hesper Leeds's mind. She looked about the room, appraising each of the leaders silently. Many had great ability, but they lacked either the leisure, the gift of speech needed by a Borough Chairman, or the financial backing required by one who had many demands made upon her pocketbook as well as upon her time, strength and talents. The Borough Officers, too, seemed to yield no goodly candidate. The vice chairman was all that could be desired mentally, but she was physically weak. And when it came to this item, Hesper Leeds was forced to admit that none had her own radiant health. With a kind of wonder, since it was the first time she had really considered the question, she realized that on all counts she seemed made for her present position. She had always vaguely supposed that the selection of herself as Chairman had "just happened." Now she saw its fitness, now that she was about to give it up. For of course, she would give it up. It was a great honor that was offered her, a chance to be a national figure, to assist in the making of suffrage plans and policies for the whole country, to leave the hard and grilling local activities and to travel from state to state and get a deeper knowledge and a wider understanding of the beloved cause and its thousands of adherents. She thrilled a little at the thought and the color deepened in her cheeks.

"I envy Mrs. Leeds her splendid vitality," whispered the leader of the second district to the leader of the sixth. "She spoke at six meetings last night, rushing around all over the city to keep her appointments, and she looks as fresh as a rose to-day. I'd be all in after three meetings if I expended the enthusiasm she puts in every speech."

"What topic are we to discuss after the reports?" asked Mrs. Leeds in a low tone of her secretary.

"What is the Greatest Thing in the Suffrage Cause?" answered the secretary smiling. "The sixth tried it out in a district meeting and it brought out some interesting points. It might be illuminating to find out what the leaders place first and then we'd know on what they would concentrate most strongly."

"Good enough," returned Mrs. Leeds. "It's time to begin."

She took up the gavel, called the meeting to order and proceeded with the usual routine. During the reading of the minutes, the treasurer's report, the reports of the districts on their work, and the speeches of various chairmen of standing committees and of organizers fresh from their labors, a kind of gentle melancholy stole over her, as she realized that this was her last borough meeting. The call to go higher must be accepted promptly. She began to think out a farewell speech. She would tell them the news just before the close of the session, and would express her appreciation of their loyal support, of their unfailing willingness to work, of their unselfish devotion. A lump rose in the Borough Chairman's throat and a mist came across her eyes. Of course, it would be fine to be high up in the councils of the organization, but would she not miss the contact with those bearing the heat and the burden of the campaign? As she looked about on the twenty-three familiar faces of the leaders, they had never seemed so pleasant and so dear.

It came time to broach the subject of raising a fund for a special purpose, and the Borough Chairman took it up with some reluctance. For all of a sudden, she realized how often the demand for money was presented to women who with one or two exceptions were themselves only comfortably placed financially, and represented women in their districts who could contribute largely to no movement. Yet when she made her request, they responded with cheerful alacrity.

"It means another card party for us," said one leader cheerfully. "And I still ache from the last one."

"I'll start my district's quota with a contribution, and that will set a good example," cried another.

"But Mrs. Stevens, you have already done so much," said the Borough Chairman involuntarily, as the modesty of the Stevens income came to her mind.

"Oh, she'll give up the dress she was going to buy. I know her. It's the third one and she's used to it," explained a fellow leader. "It's to be hoped she won't get too shabby to preside at meetings."

"Well, I gave up my maid yesterday," said Mrs. Martin joyously. "She was certain of another place, and I'm going to do my own work, and give all the perfectly good dollars I used to hand out to Norah to the Cause. It's a great idea."

"I had it long ago," laughed little Miss Larcom. "So you're not a bit original."

"When we get this money it means starting a new line of work and it just occurs to me that some of you won't be here," said Mrs. Leeds. "There's Mrs. Penting, going to her country home soon, only to come in occasionally, and there's Miss Marlow who's planned a vacation and—"

"No," cried Mrs. Penting and Miss Marlow together in eager dissent.

"Don't you know?" asked another leader quickly. "Mrs. Penting has sent the family and the servants on to her country place and she's camping out all alone in her apartment. Couldn't keep a maid here in this sizzling weather, but stays herself."

"Oh, but that's different," explained Mrs. Penting. "It's easy for me because I'm doing it for the Cause."

"And you, Miss Marlow," gasped Mrs. Leeds, quite aghast at the idea of the elegant Mrs. Penting for the first time in her life eschewing the country, to which she was devoted, and attending to her own wants in solitary state.

"Oh," said Miss Marlow shyly. "I just changed my mind."

"She couldn't have a vacation and give what she wanted to suffrage, so she's cut out the vacation," said Miss Stanley.

"Well," stammered Miss Marlow, "so many of the women in

my district are giving up every luxury and many a necessity in order to help, I felt like a criminal to think of a vacation."

"After saving for this particular one for two years," added Miss Stanley.

"But, of course, one is glad to sacrifice anything for the Cause," said two or three voices earnestly.

"Yes," replied Mrs. Leeds, and all of a sudden behind the roomful of women she seemed to see the hovering figure of an angel of self-sacrifice and self-denial, and she spoke softly as though in a sacred presence.

"Now that the business part of our program is completed, we shall pass on to the entertaining part and discuss the subject, What is the Greatest Thing in the Suffrage Cause."

There was a little ripple of interest and then Miss Stevens sprang to her feet and declared that it was the canvassing, bolstering up her statement by many convincing arguments. At the end, Mrs. Penting cried:

"I don't agree with you. It's the Speakers." And she in turn gave some snappy reasons for her belief.

"What are speakers to Leaflets?" asked Mrs. Mervin with scorn. "The voice of a speaker reaches at best the ears and minds of a few hundred people, the leaflets go to thousands and work for us silently and effectively."

And Mrs. Mervin provoked great applause by her enthusiastic defense of her contention.

"Speakers and leaflets and canvassing,—what are they in comparison with the Press?" asked Mrs. Benson. "People who don't go to meetings to hear the speakers, who throw the leaflets in the waste-paper basket, and avoid the canvasser, get suffrage thrust at them regularly from their daily paper. It's the editors who are the greatest thing, God bless them, like a long line of Suffrage Knights extending clear across the country."

And Mrs. Benson made one of the hits of the day by her lucid and vivid presentation of her subject.

She was followed by one of the organizers who vaunted the Organization itself, with its power of thousands of people bound together by the ties of a struggling sisterhood, working in marvelous harmony for a common object, presenting to the world and hostile forces the strength of a united and impressive front. "This is the greatest thing we have," contended the speaker.

But she was not left in undisputed possession of the field, for another woman lifted her voice and eulogized the Great Leaders of the movement, "throwing the light of progress and justice across the stormy sea of the world, our lighthouses that warn our suffrage barks from the dangerous places, from the hidden rocks and the narrow channels and the drifting fog-banks." This, too, met with enthusiastic approval.

Through the speeches that went on for some time, Mrs. Leeds sat in a musing silence, oblivious to the voices and the arguments. Face after face before her took on a new aspect. The pallor of Dr. Halsey was no longer pallor, but a beauty that she had acquired working long hours by day among her suffering patients in the tenements and devoting her evenings to suffrage street-meetings and work. The lines in the face of Alice Stevens—what were they but lovely things engraved there by the weariness that comes from working ceaselessly for high ideals? The toil-worn hands of Mrs. Jacobs, of an eastside district spoke eloquently of the extra work that Mrs. Jacobs did, after her duties for a large family were over, and she sat up half the night sewing garments to sell for the cause. Mrs. Brent, with her haggard features—the Borough Chairman remembered how Mrs. Brent cooked and sold preserves to contribute to the Party treasury. And Miss Stirwell's cane that supported her in her lameness, and that Mrs. Leeds knew had gone tapping its way on long journeys in Queens, out to the quiet places of small meetings where waiting for trains often meant weary waits on deserted platforms at night, and even when an automobile was provided, brought long and fatiguing rides through sleeping villages and down dark country roads. While this was varied by lively city meetings, Mrs. Leeds knew that Miss Stirwell, editor as she was of the weekly suffrage paper that sparkled with her wit and pungent comments, never refused a call to speak for the cause, be the inconvenience of dragging about a "game leg," as she valiantly called it, ever so great. Brooding over these things, Mrs. Leeds wondered whether there was not a suffrage halo waiting in some higher region to crown Miss Stirwell's white head. One by one, she studied the women before her and thought of others, toiling, drudging, with no hope of honor and advancement, with no promise of reward, content to be all and give all to what they felt was a righteous and a worthy movement.

And as she looked and pondered, with a feeling of scorn and disgust she wiped out of her mind the farewell speech. To leave them now, having guided them halfway up the rugged pathway of the campaign—what would that be but a crime of desertion, like a captain leaving his troops in a narrow pass, like a mother fleeing from her children. A deep feeling of love and loyalty to those she led swept over the Borough Chairman like an invisible tidal wave.

"There is no greater honor than to stay with these, to guide them and to help them," she said to herself with earnest conviction, and she crushed ruthlessly the letter whose siren words had tempted her for a moment.

She was brought back to the meeting by a voice that said:

"And what does our Borough Chairman think is the greatest thing we have and that the suffrage movement has evolved?"

And a chorus cried:

"Oh yes, Mrs. Leeds, tell us your views?"

Mrs. Leeds rose to her feet with her usual vivacity and vigor.

"While you've been arguing," she said. "I've been wondering how you could all be so blind as not to see what the greatest thing is. What I think may best be preceded by a story, one of the right-behind-the-scenes tales that every movement has. Most of you know of Prudence Harrow, of the second order of pioneers, a woman of strong personality, of a burning oratory and of great devotion to the Cause in the day when in this city one was accounted a freak to advocate suffrage. When the Suffrage Party was formed Prudence had a fine record for converts made, meetings addressed, clubs organized, speeches delivered, and everybody thought her the logical candidate for the position of chairman of her borough. She herself believed she would be selected, and was alive with interest, hope, and happiness, her mind full of plans of what she would do, and of dreams of the honor of joining the inner circle of which Charlotte Chester Cleeves was the center.

But while she was fresh from the congratulations of admiring friends, the organizing committee sent for her, assured her she was fitted for the office and would succeed if she ran, but asked her to stand aside in the interest of the cause, and allow a new and untried woman, who had the prestige, the position, and the influence that Prudence Harrow lacked, to take the office. No one knows what a bitter blow this was, for to her it seemed dealt by those who were unjust, unappreciative and ungrateful. It is a long story of how she struggled with her problem, urged by friends to fight for her just due, by others to capitulate, a struggle that went on for weeks and wore down her spirit and her body. For Prudence Harrow was not an angel, just a very human person, feeling that she had won only humiliation for long and honorable service. But finally her problem was settled. And how do you think?"

"How?" queried the leaders with vivid interest.

"Very simply. It happened she was guided, as we sometimes are. She went to a hotel meeting, fell asleep after it in an alcove, and remaining undiscovered, was roused at length by the voices of a number of antis holding a conference, reviling the Cause, berating its leaders, and making comprehensive plans for a campaign to oppose them in her own city. And then Prudence Harrow felt as a mother does who sees her child lifted on a spear, as a general does who sees his troops massacred, and all at once, the narrow ambition that had consumed her fell from her like a wornout garment. And first she telephoned Mrs. Cleeves and then she went directly to the woman of whom she had been jealous, asked her to run for the office she had desired, and pledged to her a support and help that was later found invaluable. And when somebody, knowing the story, asked her how she felt, she gave an odd answer. 'Like a suffrage banner,' she said. And when her puzzled questioner asked why, she replied 'Like the big banner that hangs on the wall at Headquarters,' And when her bewildered questioner again asked why, she replied: 'The one that reads:

> 'In deeds of daring rectitude,
> In scorn of miserable aims that end in self.'"

The leaders looked at each other in a wondering way. Mrs. Leeds read their unasked question.

"What has this to do with the greatest thing in the suffrage movement? It illustrates it. For the greatest thing is you, dear leaders, you and thousands like you, the devoted, self-sacrificing, hard-working, undaunted and undefeated women that we develop and attract, the women who, like Prudence Harrow, rise above self and selfish things. This is our supreme achievement."

And to the great surprise of the leaders, Mrs. Leeds went round the room and kissed them all with a fervor they could not understand. But the only person to whom she explained the matter was her husband, John L. Leeds, who came from the Men's League for Suffrage to take her home.

"It was my way of thanking them for showing me a great truth which I shall never forget."

ARTHUR RAYMOND BROWN

from *How It Feels to be the Husband of a Suffragette*
1915

How It Feels to be the Husband of a Suffragette was published anonymously in *Everybody's Magazine* in 1914 and in pamphlet form the following year. "You are the party aimed at," it opened, meaning the hecklers who taunted marchers at a suffrage parade in New York City. "You who stood on the sidewalk and urged passionately that we who marched go home and wash the dishes or mind the baby." Those hecklers weren't aiming at women marchers, however. Their target was the delegation from the Men's League for Woman Suffrage. The author of the pamphlet was Arthur Raymond (Ray) Brown (1865–1944), an advertising executive and illustrator who was married to Gertrude Foster Brown (1867–1956), the president of the New York State Woman Suffrage Association. An avid suffragist himself, he put his creative talents to good use to support his wife's cause. The pamphlet was not a closely reasoned pro-suffrage tract. Instead, as this excerpt shows, it used humor and wit to make its points, appealing more to emotion and caricature than to logic and facts. But why use the fraught term *suffragette* in the title? Like most American suffragists, Gertrude Foster Brown would never have referred to herself by that term, so why did her husband? Perhaps he saw it as a term of playful endearment, but probably it was simply another ploy to catch the public's attention.

Getting a suffragette for a wife is no different from obtaining any other kind of a wife. The formula is the same in both cases. There's a certain excitement, though, in the fact that you don't always know she is going to be a suffragette until after you have got her. But that, happily, is getting rarer and rarer. The new crop is finding out that advertising pays, and it is pretty hard nowadays to pick out a discreet and docile suffragette who will absolutely refrain from confiding the fact to you, if you sit up with her long enough.

Personally, we—I and mine—fell into suffrage together and practically made only one splash; but it was long after we were married. You notice that I said *mine*. I meant it. Sharing some common things in common doesn't necessarily prevent the lady from being all yours.

We had been at a nice little dinner-party in a smart suburban town. The dinner was all it should be, with one exception: the star guest refused to perform for the benefit of the company. He was a very clever Irish lawyer, with a name for wit. He came accompanied by a rarely beautiful wife, and her efforts during the evening to have husband jump through the hoop and lie down and roll over and play dead were pathetic. Something had gone wrong business-wise during the day, and Melancholia had claimed him for her own. He would do nothing but grunt and grump.

After dinner, when all were comfortable in the smoking-room library, the hostess made a last stab to draw him out. The papers at that moment were full of the first despatches telling of the astounding performances of the English militants, and the hostess said in her sweetest coo:

"Oh, Mr. Blank, do you think women should vote?"

And in a voice that carried more grouch than any previous grunt during the evening, he answered: "Of course I do, course I do; and if they hadn't been such damn fools, they would have been doing it long ago."

On the way to the station the lady who controls my destinies repeated the hostess's question:

"Do you believe women should vote?"

It was an awful question to have put to one in the darkness and mystery of a station hack. It was so sudden that, I am ashamed to confess, I dived in the hope of avoiding it.

I went down like a mud-hen, deep enough, as I trusted, to let an ocean liner go over my head.

When I came up there was the same old question with both barrels trained full on me.

Did I believe that women should vote?

What did I know about it?

Had I ever given it a single second's thought?

Were the things I thought were my thoughts and liked to advertise as my ideas anything more than a hazy blend of old cartoons, funny men's paragraphs, and an occasional squint at a set of spit curls on an elderly dame who seemed to be discontented with something?

I held my breath for half a minute and thought so hard that I could almost hear my mental processes.

"Yes," I said, "I do believe they should vote."

"Why?" asked the silent partner.

Well, there was the Revolution—no taxation without representation; and there was the Rebellion—no slavery, political or economic. Big wars, both of them, mighty expensive, definitely deciding the questions involved for all the people of these United States.

Then you get down to the proposition: "Are women *people*?"

I believe they must be, or they wouldn't act the way they do. Besides, it's discouraging to try to argue that women aren't people. After you've done your best, you are likely to wind up by merely proving that you yourself are either a Turk or an Ishmaelite. They are the only two varieties of humans who've ever been able to make it stick. They just say blandly that women haven't any souls, and as they believe it and convince their lady friends that they believe it, the argument bogs down right there.

Then you've got the fact that about fifty per cent. of the population is feminine and that in the minds of the other fifty per cent. they certainly represent at least half of the sweetness, truth, and idealism of the nation.

Of course, there may be an odd Schopenhauer here and there who jumps sidewise and has a fit every time he sees a skirt; but most of us aren't nearly as timid as that.

Somewhere along here it became evident that the lady wasn't going to insist on any more reasons, but was inclined to accept meekly the hereditary intellectual dominance of the male.

Lots of good men who have no intellectual objection to women's voting nurse at heart a timidity whenever they visualize the horrible results. You can see it in many a polite, genteel citizen's eye, the moment suffrage talk starts, as if he were wondering just what his own women folks would act like around the house if they knew they were as good as he was and could prove it legally.

Of course it is a false alarm. The percentage of divorces doesn't rise in suffrage states because of suffrage; and logically there is no more reason why two domestic partners who are comrades, mutually acknowledging a pleasant equality, should separate, than there is for the separation of two people of opposite sex who, condemned to live together, are striving diligently to maintain an inequality.

And isn't it quaint that the states which have given suffrage to their women should be almost uniformly the "gun" states—states where the husky male not infrequently tops off his wardrobe with a cartridge belt and a gun or two? But there is a kind of logic in it, after all, because a man with two guns ought not to be so much afraid of his wife as the man who is afraid of firearms. It is the man whose polite soul cleaves to gentle ways who is most likely to dread the possibility of being surrounded by women whom the law has pronounced his equals. To him the possibilities even of verbal rough-house seem appalling, and his gentle spirit quails.

For some odd reason the Wholesale Liquor Dealers' Association doesn't happen to like the idea of female suffrage, either. But this is largely, also, a case of false alarm. For in spite of the activities of the W.C.T.U., the average woman is quite prone to look on drinking largely as a masculine accomplishment, and as long as it is pursued in reasonable moderation is fairly content to have it that way; that is, she neither clamors for the booze herself nor is she insistent on wholly separating man from it; and you will find that few of the states with large feminine vote have made any determined wholesale assault on alcohol.

It is only when alcohol is arrogant and dictates politics or insidiously attempts to wreck homes or ruin young lives that the feminine vote comes across and lights on the alcoholic neck; and even then it is likely to be a measure tending to repress rather than to extirpate.

You may think that all of this is irrelevant. You may want more intimate details. But I was asked to tell "how it feels," and that's what I am trying to tell you—how it feels rather than the daily routine and whether the coffee was good this morning (which it certainly was), and whether she wears good-looking hats (which she most assuredly does).

But you have probably read in the English despatches that Mr. and Mrs. So-and-so were arrested for leading a mob to throw bricks at Mr. Asquith's windows and had to spend the next two years in jail in separate cells; or you may have read in the American press that the distinguished Mrs. Blank, who lives in New York, is delivering a lecture in New Orleans, and immediately your mind conjures up Mr. Blank as a sad-eyed, lonesome, scared-looking tyke, with debilitated side-whiskers, who alternates being neglected most to death with being hustled around the house till he daren't peep.

From the outside, looking in, it may seem to you as if there isn't any inside to the home; but, honestly, there is.

Personally, I believe that a lady with a well-worn latch-key, who has healthy interests outside her home, is better company than one whose view of life is circumscribed by the four walls that the landlord refused to paper last spring. And that pretty clothes as an incidental habit are cheerier to live with than swell raiment as an engrossing topic of conversation and a financial holocaust at the end of the month.

My own pet boss doesn't know how to play bridge. When a friend urges her to learn, she always says she hasn't time. Mind you, she has time to study the economics of Australia and the politics of China; she understands the workings of the Gutenberg liquor law, and she has gone pretty thoroughly into street-cleaning problems with one of the engineers of the department. She also has time to go on long, lazy fishing trips with me, when we rustle our own grub and forget what day of the week it is. And she drives a car a lot better than the lad who draws pay for the job. But she hasn't time for bridge.

You'll say that she is either a remarkable woman or else she has me hypnotized.

All right, say it; get it off your chest.

But you are this far wrong:

She is only remarkable in this, that she didn't stop with the "finishing-school," as so many of them do: she went right on trying to learn things that were worth while, trying to get better acquainted with life, trying to economize the efforts spent in drudgery and utilize the time saved for better things, trying to stop waste in order to enjoy plenty.

I remember when her books were comparatively simple. Now I don't know where her reading is going to take her next. But I don't care. Like the bee, she brings back sweetness from every field. Solomon was eminently correct when he said—speaking of her type of lady—"her price is above rubies."

ALICE DUER MILLER

from *Are Women People?*
1915

Father, what is a Legislature?
A representative body elected by the people of the state.
Are women people?
No, my son, criminals, lunatics and women are not people.
Do legislators legislate for nothing?
Oh, no; they are paid a salary.
By whom?
By the people.
Are women people?
Of course, my son, just as much as men are.

From 1914 to 1917, poet and novelist Alice Duer Miller (1874–1942) published a weekly suffrage column called "Are Women People?" in the *New-York Tribune*. Her witty and pointed poems were widely read and discussed, and the phrase became something of a catchword for the suffrage movement. In 1915 many of these columns were collected in a book called *Are Women People? A Book of Rhymes for Suffrage Times*, for which the poem above served as the introduction. "Why We Oppose Pockets for Women" and "Why We Oppose Votes for Men" both turn antisuffrage reasoning on its head, and "Feminism" encourages women to keep speaking out.

Why We Oppose Pockets for Women

1. Because pockets are not a natural right.

2. Because the great majority of women do not want pockets. If they did they would have them.

3. Because whenever women have had pockets they have not used them.

4. Because women are required to carry enough things as it is, without the additional burden of pockets.

5. Because it would make dissension between husband and wife as to whose pockets were to be filled.

6. Because it would destroy man's chivalry toward woman, if he did not have to carry all her things in his pockets.

7. Because men are men, and women are women. We must not fly in the face of nature.

8. Because pockets have been used by men to carry tobacco, pipes, whiskey flasks, chewing gum and compromising letters. We see no reason to suppose that women would use them more wisely.

Why We Oppose Votes for Men

1. Because man's place is the armory.

2. Because no really manly man wants to settle any question otherwise than by fighting about it.

3. Because if men should adopt peaceable methods women will no longer look up to them.

4. Because men will lose their charm if they step out of their natural sphere and interest themselves in other matters than feats of arms, uniforms and drums.

5. Because men are too emotional to vote. Their conduct at baseball games and political conventions shows this, while their innate tendency to appeal to force renders them peculiarly unfit for the task of government.

Feminism

"Mother, what is a Feminist?"
"A Feminist, my daughter,
Is any woman now who cares
To think about her own affairs
    As men don't think she oughter."

ABBY SCOTT BAKER

Letter to the Editor of The Outlook
AUGUST 23, 1916

As the 1916 election approached, some four million women in twelve states were already eligible to vote—a sizable number, and enough to make politicians take notice. The Woman's Party, a political organization formed in Chicago in June 1916, was determined to harness that clout. In this letter to the editors of *The Outlook*, Abby Scott Baker (1871–1944), the Woman's Party press chairman, detailed the strategy they had in mind, which boiled down to western women using their votes to help enfranchise eastern women by securing a federal amendment. Baker compiled statistics showing how close the balance of political power was in many of the suffrage states—one Senate election was decided by a mere 38 votes—which suggested that organized women could make a difference if they cast their votes strategically. Pledging to "put suffrage first," the Woman's Party urged members to vote against the Democratic Party, which had been "openly unfriendly" to the national amendment. That stance, which derived from the British model of holding the party in power responsible, proved quite controversial in the United States, especially in the West, where many Democrats were in fact suffrage supporters. Despite the Woman's Party's efforts, Democrat Woodrow Wilson easily won reelection in November 1916.

———————————

To the Editor of The Outlook:

Dear Sir—Will you permit me to say, in answer to your editorials in The Outlook of July 19 on "The Women Voters" and "The Issues as Women See Them," that the vote of the Woman's Party must be reckoned with because a small number of votes constitute the balance of power in each of the twelve suffrage States? The Woman's Party is already completely organized in all of these States, and it has an issue which makes an especial appeal to women.

Of course the entire vote of the four million women qualified to vote for President will not be cast solidly for any one candidate. It it absurd to expect that it will be. It is quite possible, as you estimate, that not more than two million or two million five hundred thousand will actually avail themselves of their opportunity to vote. Fortunately, however, for the hopes of the Woman's Party, neither four million nor even two million votes are necessary to make effective the demand for an amendment to the Constitution enfranchising women.

The suffrage States are close and doubtful territory. During the last five Presidential campaigns an average change of only nine per cent of the vote would have altered the result in every election. The percentages for the five elections are as follows:

	1896.	1900.	1904.	1908.	1912.
California	0.3	0.6	17.4	11.2	0.01
Colorado	34.9	6.7	3.0	0.5	7.8
Idaho	28.4	2.1	20.2	8.4	0.5
Illinois	6.5	4.2	14.2	7.7	0.8
Kansas	4.9	3.3	19.4	4.8	3.2
Montana	30.1	9.3	10.2	2.2	3.4
Nevada	28.4	10.9	10.7	1.0	5.9
Oregon	1.0	7.8	23.8	11.0	3.4
Utah	33.3	1.1	14.3	8.5	2.5
Washington	6.7	5.9	25.3	12.9	4.0
Wyoming	0.7	8.5	18.9	7.9	0.9

In 1912 the result in Idaho was determined by 556 votes; in Wyoming, by 376; in California, by 88. In Nevada Senator Newlands was elected to the Senate by 38 votes and Senator Pittman by 88.

It is obvious that the dependence of the Woman's Party need not be in numbers, although, before its campaign has fairly begun, it has tens of thousands of members. Standing apart from and outside of the two great parties, the Woman's Party can hold the balance of power in the States whence come ninety-one electoral votes. The strength of the Woman's Party is not in numbers, but in strategic position.

The Woman's Party is completely organized in each of the twelve suffrage States. It is, in fact, the third party, having possessed itself of the place left vacant by the Progressive Party, but with this advantage—that the Woman's Party vote is concentrated, instead of scattered over the whole United States. The Woman's Party was launched in Chicago, June 5, 6, and 7, at a convention of voting women called by Miss Alice Paul,

National Chairman of the Congressional Union for Woman Suffrage. It is made up of voting women pledged to put "suffrage first" in the fall campaign. Upon coming into being the party, under the leadership of Miss Anne Martin, Chairman of the National Committee, took possession of the State organizations perfected during the last three years in the twelve States by the Congressional Union. Since June 7 organization has gone rapidly forward, until now committees have been formed and are at work in almost every county. It is expected that the organization of every county will be complete by August 10, when the first conference to determine election policies convenes in Colorado Springs.

No one who went West in the Suffrage Special can doubt that the Woman's Party has an issue which makes a special appeal to women. Although it is quite true that women, like men, are interested in the European war, our Mexican policy, prohibition, and international questions, yet it is also true that the National Woman Suffrage amendment, usually known as the Susan B. Anthony Amendment, can be made a paramount issue with thousands and thousands of Western women. The reasons why Western women can be so interested are plain. It is only by a Federal amendment that the inter-State and National discrimination against their own political rights can be removed, that Eastern women can be enfranchised, and that Western women can use their political power to bestow the gift of freedom upon others.

Western women want the Susan B. Anthony Amendment because they resent conditions which disfranchise them if they move East to live. They resent laws which take from them their citizenship if they marry aliens. Great hardship is wrought by such laws. In the State of Washington, for instance, an American woman was denied a mother's pension because her husband, who had deserted her and neither seen her nor supported her for years, had become a Canadian. In Illinois an American woman applying for a pension for the blind was refused because she was married to a foreigner. American women lawyers who marry foreigners can no longer practice in our courts. Western women wish to safeguard their citizenship and their political freedom as men's are safeguarded.

Western women desire more influence in shaping National

policies. This they cannot possess until all American women count politically. But American women cannot be enfranchised within any reasonable length of time except by an amendment to the Constitution of the United States. Amending State Constitutions is slow, burdensome, and in many States hopeless, because of the difficulties to amendment inherent in the Constitutions of the States.

A State constitutional amendment must usually be passed by a two-thirds vote of the State Legislature, and then submitted to a referendum of the male voters of the State. In New Mexico the proposed amendment must receive a three-fourths vote of the entire Legislature, a three-fourths vote of the entire electorate, and a two-thirds vote of all those voting in each county. In New Hampshire an amendment must be submitted by a constitutional convention, which can be called only once in seven years, and the process of calling it is excessively difficult. The proposed amendment requires for ratification two-thirds of the votes of all electors voting. Indiana requires a majority of the votes of all the qualified electors of the State. It has never been possible to amend the Constitution of Indiana.

Seven States fix a term of years after an amendment has failed of adoption before it can be resubmitted. Four States restrict the number of amendments to be submitted at any election. Eleven States require for the approval of an amendment a majority of all the votes cast at an election, not a majority of the votes cast for or against the particular amendment. In two States the final approval of an amendment is left with the legislators even after the electors have approved of it. These are only a few of the difficulties in the way of amending State Constitutions. Moreover, State work is like trying to progress over shifting sand. An advance once made cannot be held. When a State referendum fails, work must start again from the very beginning.

On the other hand, in work for a Federal amendment every step forward is a permanent gain. A Federal amendment once passed by a two-thirds vote of Congress is passed forever, and needs for ratification only a majority vote of three-fourths of the State Legislatures. Once ratified by a State Legislature, the amendment cannot be brought up again; but, if rejected by the State Legislature, it can be immediately reconsidered.

The Federal method is not only easier, it is also fair. A Federal amendment does not infringe on the rights of a State. Such rights cannot be abridged by using a method prescribed by the Constitution and agreed to by the States. A Federal amendment simply applies the principle of majority rule, and objections to it lie equally against our whole system of government. A Federal woman suffrage amendment does not complicate the race problem. There are six million more white than colored women living south of Mason and Dixon's line, and two million more white women than Negro men, women, and children combined.

Nor is the Federal method alarmingly novel. The States have never had exclusive control of suffrage. The original Constitution laid down specifications as to who should vote for members of the Senate and who should vote for members of the House of Representatives. The Seventeenth Amendment declared that United States Senators should be elected by the people. Moreover, the Federal Government alters the electorate through its control of naturalization laws. The United States permits foreigners to become citizens. Under the Fifteenth Amendment, it forbids the disfranchisement of these citizens simply because they are foreigners.

Men may regard with complacency the difficulties of the State-by-State road to enfranchisement, toward which women are blandly waved. But women will not accept this impossible way for their sisters when they have a right to proceed in an easier and better way according to established forms of law. Western women thrill to the thought that they have the power to open to their sisters this way to freedom. They realize that their power can be made effective only in pressure upon the National Government. It is a pregnant fact, and very characteristic of the psychology of women, that work for the freedom of women appeals to thousands of women who did not work for their own enfranchisement. And hundreds of women have contributed to the war chest of the Woman's Party who did not contribute to their own State suffrage campaign.

Why should it be called revenge for women who desire the political freedom of others to vote against a party openly unfriendly to the only method by which Nation-wide suffrage for women can be gained? It is no more revenge to vote in the interests of the freedom of *other women* than to vote in the interests of peace and preparedness. And why should suffrage as an all-absorbing issue be side-tracked by the women of the West for "Americanism"? There never was a greater opportunity to make "suffrage first" the paramount issue. Both great parties are vociferous in claiming the issues of peace and preparedness. President Wilson, who stands for peace, also toured the country in the interests of military preparedness. The Republican party stands for peace, according to the testimony of Governor Glynn. In his keynote speech at the Democratic Convention Governor Glynn, amid shouts of applause and cries for more, recited the many occasions on which under international provocation leaders of the Republican party had in the past written notes! Certainly the Republican party claims preparedness too. Witness the cartoons of Colonel Roosevelt weeping for his stolen issue and not to be comforted.

In this connection, I must confess that I do not know just precisely what Americanism means. But if it means, as I believe it does, the dedication of all that is best in our beloved country to making this Nation, not only strong and peaceful, but also *just*, then surely there is no reason why Western women should not vote as women in woman's cause of freedom.

ABBY SCOTT BAKER,
Press Chairman Woman's Party.

National Headquarters,
    Washington, D. C.

CARRIE CHAPMAN CATT

The Crisis

September 7, 1916

Carrie Chapman Catt took over the presidency of NAWSA from Anna Howard Shaw in December 1915 and stayed at the helm until the ratification of the Nineteenth Amendment five years later. When both the Republican and Democratic national conventions failed to offer strong endorsements of women's suffrage in the lead-up to the 1916 presidential election, Catt took the unusual step of calling an emergency convention of NAWSA that September in Atlantic City. In her lengthy presidential address, she tried to rally her troops to her deeply held conviction that the moment was ripe for action ("The Woman's Hour Has Struck," she said repeatedly) and that securing a federal amendment should be "our ultimate goal." Her passionate speech had its intended impact. Maud Wood Park (1871–1955), who would soon take charge of lobbying Congress for the federal amendment, later wrote of the moment: "I felt like Moses on the mountain top after the Promised Land had been shown to him and he knew the long years of wandering in the wilderness were soon to end."

I have taken for my subject, "The Crisis," because I believe that a crisis has come in our movement which, if recognized and the opportunity seized with vigor, enthusiasm and will, means the final victory of our great cause in the very near future. I am aware that some suffragists do not share this belief; they see no signs nor symptoms today which were not present yesterday; no manifestations in the year 1916 which differ significantly from those in the year 1910. To them, the movement has been a steady, normal growth from the beginning and must so continue until the end. I can only defend my claim with the plea that it is better to imagine a crisis where none exists than to fail to recognize one when it comes; for a crisis is a culmination of events which calls for new considerations and new decisions. A failure to answer the call may mean an opportunity lost, a possible victory postponed.

The object of the life of an organized movement is to secure its aim. Necessarily, it must obey the law of evolution and pass through the stages of agitation and education and finally through the stage of realization. As one has put it: "A new idea floats in the air over the heads of the people and for a long, indefinite period evades their understanding but, by and by, when through familiarity human vision grows clearer, it is caught out of the clouds and crystalized into law." Such a period comes to every movement and is its crisis. In my judgment, that crucial moment, bidding us to renewed consecration and redoubled activity has come to our cause. I believe our victory hangs within our grasp, inviting us to pluck it out of the clouds and establish it among the good things of the world.

If this be true, the time is past when we should say: "Men and women of America, look upon that wonderful idea up there; see, one day it will come down." Instead, the time has come to shout aloud in every city, village and hamlet, and in tones so clear and jubilant that they will reverberate from every mountain peak and echo from shore to shore: "The Woman's Hour Has Struck." Suppose suffragists as a whole do not believe a crisis has come and do not extend their hands to grasp the victory, what will happen? Why, we shall all continue to work and our cause will continue to hang, waiting for those who possess a clearer vision and more daring enterprise. On the other hand, suppose we reach out with united earnestness and determination to grasp our victory while it still hangs a bit too high? Has any harm been done? None!

Therefore, fellow suffragists, I invite your attention to the signs which point to a crisis and your consideration of plans for turning the crisis into victory.

PROPHESIES CHANGE AFTER WAR

FIRST: We are passing through a world crisis. All thinkers of every land tell us so; and that nothing after the great war will be as it was before. Those who profess to know, claim that 100 millions of dollars are being spent on the war every day and that 2 years of war have cost 50 billions of dollars or 10 times more than the total expense of the American Civil War. Our own country has sent 35 millions of dollars abroad for relief expenses.

Were there no other effects to come from the world's war, the transfer of such unthinkably vast sums of money from the usual avenues to those wholly abnormal, would give so severe a jolt to organized society that it would vibrate around the world and bring untold changes in its wake.

But three and a half millions of lives have been lost. The number becomes the more impressive when it is remembered that the entire population of the American Colonies was little more than three and one-half millions. Those losses have been the lives of men within the age of economic production. They have been taken abruptly from the normal business of the world and every human activity from that of the humblest, unskilled labor to art, science and literature has been weakened by their loss. Millions of other men will go to their homes, blind, crippled and incapacitated to do the work they once performed. The stability of human institutions has never before suffered so tremendous a shock. Great men are trying to think out the consequences but one and all proclaim that no imagination can find color or form bold enough to paint the picture of the world after the war. British and Russian, German and Austrian, French and Italian agree that it will lead to social and political revolution throughout the entire world. Whatever comes, they further agree that the war presages a total change in the status of women.

A simple-minded man in West Virginia, when addressed upon the subject of woman suffrage in that State, replied, "We've been so used to keepin' our women down, 'twould seem queer not to." He expressed what greater men feel but do not say. Had the wife of that man spoken in the same clear-thinking fashion, she would have said, "We women have been so used to being kept down that it would seem strange to get up. Nature intended women for 'door-mats.'" Had she so expressed herself, these two would have put the entire anti-suffrage argument in a nut-shell.

EUROPEAN WOMEN RISING

In Europe, from the Polar Circle to the Aegean Sea, women have risen as though to answer that argument. Everywhere they have taken the places made vacant by men and in so doing, they have grown in self-respect and in the esteem of their respective nations. In every land, the people have reverted to the primitive division of labor and while the men have gone to war, women have cultivated the fields in order that the army and nation may be fed. No army can succeed and no nation can endure without food; those who supply it are a war power and a peace power.

Women by the thousands have knocked at the doors of munition factories and, in the name of patriotism, have begged for the right to serve their country there. Their services were accepted with hesitation but the experiment once made, won reluctant but universal praise. An official statement recently issued in Great Britain announced that 660,000 women were engaged in making munitions in that country alone. In a recent convention of munition workers, composed of men and women, a resolution was unanimously passed informing the government that they would forego vacations and holidays until the authorities announced that their munition supplies were sufficient for the needs of the war and Great Britain pronounced the act the highest patriotism. Lord Derby addressed such a meeting and said: "When the history of the war is written, I wonder to whom the greatest credit will be given; to the men who went to fight or to the women who are working in a way that many people hardly believed that it was possible for them to work." Lord Sydenham added his tribute. Said he: "It might fairly be claimed that women have helped to save thousands of lives and to change the entire aspect of the war. Wherever intelligence, care and close attention have been needed, women have distinguished themselves." A writer in the "London Times" of July 18, 1916, said: "But for women, the armies could not have held the field for a month; the national call to arms could not have been made or sustained; the country would have perished of inanition and disorganization. If, indeed, it be true that the people have been one, it is because the genius of women has been lavishly applied to the task of reinforcing and complementing the genius of men. The qualities of steady industry, adaptability, good judgment and concentration of mind which men do not readily associate with women have been conspicuous features."

On fields of battle, in regular and improvised hospitals, women have given tender and skilled care to the wounded and are credited with the restoration of life to many, many thousands. Their heroism and self-sacrifice have been frankly acknowledged by all the governments; but their endurance, their skill, the practicality of their service, seem for the first time, to have been recognized by governments as "war power." So, thinking in war terms, great men have suddenly discovered that women are "war assets." Indeed, Europe is realizing, as it never did before, that women are holding together the civilization for which men are fighting. A great search-light has been thrown upon the business of nation-building and it has been demonstrated in every European land that it is a partnership with equal, but different responsibilities resting upon the two partners.

TO BE "DOOR-MATS" NO LONGER

It is not, however, in direct war work alone that the latent possibilities of women have been made manifest. In all the belligerent lands, women have found their way to high posts of administration where no women would have been trusted two years ago and the testimony is overwhelming that they have filled their posts with entire satisfaction to the authorities. They have dared to stand in pulpits (once too sacred to be touched by the unholy feet of a woman) and there, without protest, have appealed to the Father of All in behalf of their stricken lands. They have come out of the kitchen where there was too little to cook and have found a way to live by driving cabs, motors and street cars. Many a woman has turned her hungry children over to a neighbor and has gone forth to find food for both mothers and both families of children and has found it in strange places and occupations. Many a drawing-room has been closed and the maid who swept and dusted it is now cleaning streets that the health of the city may be conserved. Many a woman who never before slept in a bed of her own making, or ate food not prepared by paid labor, is now sole mistress of parlor and kitchen.

In all the warring countries, women are postmen, porters, railway conductors, ticket, switch and signal men. Conspicuous advertisements invite women to attend agricultural, milking and motor-car schools. They are employed as police in Great Britain and women detectives have recently been taken on the government staff. In Berlin, there are over 3,000 women street car conductors, and 35,000 women are employed on the general railways of Germany. In every city and country, women are doing work for which they would have been considered incompetent two years ago.

The war will soon end and the armies will return to their native lands. To many a family, the men will never come back. The husband who returns to many a wife will eat no bread the rest of his life save of her earning.

What, then, will happen after the war? Will the widows left with families to support cheerfully leave their well-paid posts for those commanding lower wages? Not without protest! Will the wives who now must support crippled husbands give up their skilled work and take up the occupations which were open to them before the war? Will they resignedly say: "The woman who has a healthy husband who can earn for her, has a right to tea and raisin cake, but the woman who earns for herself and a husband who has given his all to his country, must be content with butterless bread"? Not without protest! On the contrary, the economic axiom, denied and evaded for centuries, will be blazoned on every factory, counting house and shop: "Equal pay for equal work"; and common justice will slowly, but surely enforce that law. The European woman has risen. She may not realize it yet, but the woman "door-mat" in every land has unconsciously become a "door-jamb"! She will have become accustomed to her new dignity by the time the men come home. She will wonder how she ever could have been content lying across the threshold now that she discovers the upright jamb gives so much broader and more normal a vision of things. The men returning may find the new order a bit queer but everything else, too, will be strangely unfamiliar, and they will soon grow accustomed to all the changes together. The "jamb" will never descend into a "door-mat" again.

SEES ECONOMIC AND POLITICAL CHANGE

The male and female anti-suffragists of all lands will puff and blow at the economic change which will come to the women of Europe. They will declare it to be contrary to Nature and to God's plan and that somebody ought to do something about it. Suffragists will accept the change as the inevitable outcome of an unprecedented world's cataclysm over which no human agency had any control and will trust in God to adjust the altered circumstances to the eternal evolution of human society.

They will remember that in the long run, all things work together for good, for progress and for human weal.

The economic change is bound to bring political liberty. From every land there comes the expressed belief that the war will be followed by a mighty, oncoming wave of democracy for it is now well known: that the conflict has been one of governments, of kings and Czars, Kaisers and Emperors; not of peoples. The nations involved have nearly all declared that they are fighting to make an end of wars. New and higher ideals of governments and of the rights of the people under them, have grown enormously during the past two years. Another tide of political liberty, similar to that of 1848, but of a thousand fold greater momentum, is rising from battlefield and hospital, from camp and munitions factory, from home and church which, great men of many lands tell us, is destined to sweep over the world. On the continent, the women say, "It is certain that the vote will come to men and women after the war, perhaps not immediately but soon." In Great Britain, which was the storm centre of the suffrage movement for some years before the war, hundreds of bitter, active opponents have confessed their conversion on account of the war services of women. Already, three great provinces of Canada, Manitoba, Alberta and Saskatchewan, have given universal suffrage to their women in sheer generous appreciation of their war work. Even Mr. Asquith, world renowned for his immovable opposition to the Parliamentary suffrage for British women, has given evidence of a change of view. Some months ago, he announced his amazement at the utterly unexpected skill, strength and resource developed by the women and his gratitude for their loyalty and devotion. Later, in reply to Mrs. Henry Fawcett, who asked if woman suffrage would be included in a proposed election bill, he said that when the war should end, such a measure should be considered without prejudice carried over from events prior to the war. A public statement issued by Mr. Asquith in August, was couched in such terms as to be interpreted by many as a pledge to include women in the next election bill.

BRITISH FETTERS BREAKING

In Great Britain a sordid appeal which may prove the last straw to break the opposition to woman suffrage, has been added to the enthusiastic appreciation of woman's patriotism and practical service and to the sudden comprehension that motherhood is a national asset which must be protected at any price. A new voters' list is contemplated. A parliamentary election should be held in September but the voters are scattered far and wide. The whole nation is agitated over the questions involved in making a new register. At the same time, there is a constant anxiety over war funds, as is prudent in a nation spending 50 millions of dollars per day. It has been proposed that a large poll tax be assessed upon the voters of the new lists, whereupon a secondary proposal of great force has been offered and that is, that twice as much money would find its way into the public coffers were women added to the voters' lists! What nation, with compliments fresh spoken concerning women's patriotism and efficiency could resist such an appeal?

So it happens that above the roar of cannon, the scream of shrapnel and the whirr of aeroplanes, one who listens may hear the cracking of the fetters which have long bound the European woman to outworn conventions. It has been a frightful price to pay but the fact remains that a womanhood, well started on the way to final emancipation, is destined to step forth from the war. It will be a bewildered, troubled and grief-stricken womanhood, with knotty problems of life to solve but it will be freer to deal with them than women have ever been before.

"The Woman's Hour Has Struck." It has struck for the women of Europe and for those of all the world. The significance of the changed status of European women has not been lost upon the men and women of our land; our own people are not so unlearned in history, nor so lacking in National pride that they will allow the Republic to lag long behind the Empire, presided over by the descendant of George the Third. If they possess the patriotism and the sense of nationality which should be the inheritance of an American, they will not wait until the war is ended but will boldly lead in the inevitable march of democracy, our own American specialty. Sisters, let me repeat: "The Woman's Hour Has Struck!"

PIONEERS EGGED

SECOND: As the most adamantine rock gives way under the constant dripping of water, so the opposition to woman suffrage in our own country has slowly disintegrated before the increasing strength of our movement. Turn backward the pages of our history! Behold, brave Abbie Kelley rotten-egged because, she, a woman, essayed to speak in public. Behold the Polish Ernestine Rose, startled that women of free America drew aside their skirts when she proposed that they should control their own property. Recall the saintly Lucretia Mott and the legal-minded Elizabeth Cady Stanton, turned out of the World's Temperance Convention in London and conspiring together to free their sex from the world's stupid oppressions. Remember the gentle, sweet-voiced Lucy Stone, egged because she publicly claimed that women had brains capable of education. Think upon Dr. Elizabeth Blackwell, snubbed and boycotted by other women because she proposed to study medicine. Behold Dr. Antoinette Brown Blackwell, standing in sweet serenity before an assembly of howling clergymen, angry that she, a woman, dared to attend a Temperance Convention as a delegate. Revere the intrepid Susan B. Anthony mobbed from Buffalo to Albany because she demanded fair play for women. These are they who, with others, builded the foundation of political liberty for American women.

Those who came after only laid the stones in place. Yet, what a wearisome task even that has been! Think of the wonderful woman who has wandered from village to village, from city to city, for a generation compelling men and women to listen and to reflect by her matchless eloquence. Where in all the world's history has any movement among men produced so invincible an advocate as our own Dr. Anna Howard Shaw? Those whom she has led to the light are Legion. Think, too, of the consecration, the self-denial, the never-failing constancy of that other noble soul set in a frail, but unflinching body,—the heroine we know as Alice Stone Blackwell! A woman who never forgets, who detects the slightest flaw in the weapons of her adversary, who knows the most vulnerable spot in his armor, presides over The Woman's Journal, and, like a lamp in a lighthouse, the rays of her intelligence, far-sightedness and clear-thinking have enlightened the world concerning our cause. The names of hundreds of other brave souls spring to memory when we pause to review the long struggle.

The hands of many suffrage master-masons have long been

stilled; the names of many who laid the stones have been forgotten. That does not matter. The main thing is that the edifice of woman's liberty nears completion. It is strong, indestructible. All honor to the thousands who have helped in the building.

"ALL HANDS, HEAVE TO"

The four corner-stones of the foundation were laid long years ago. We read upon the first: "We demand for women, education; for not a high school or college is open to her"; upon the second, "We demand for women religious liberty for in few churches is she permitted to pray or speak"; upon the third, "We demand for women the right to own property and an opportunity to earn an honest living. Only six, poorly-paid occupations are open to her and if she is married, the wages she earns are not hers"; upon the fourth, "We demand political freedom and its symbol, the vote."

The stones in the foundation have long been overgrown with the moss and mould of time and some there are who never knew they were laid. Of late, four cap-stones at the top have been set to match those in the base and we read upon the first: "The number of women who are graduated from high schools, colleges and universities is legion"; upon the second, "The Christian Endeavor, that mighty undenominational church militant, asks the vote for women and the Methodist Episcopal Church, and many another, joins that appeal"; upon the third, "Billions of dollars' worth of property are owned by women; more than 8 millions of women are wage earners. Every occupation is open to them"; upon the fourth, "Women vote in 12 States; they share in the determination of 91 electoral votes."

After the cap-stones and cornice comes the roof. Across the empty spaces, the roof-tree has been flung and fastened well in place. It is not made of stone but of two planks,—planks in the platforms of the two majority parties and these are well supported by planks in the platforms of all the minority parties.

And we, who are the builders of 1916, do we see no crisis? Standing upon these planks which are stretched across the top-most peak of this edifice of woman's liberty, what shall we do? Over our heads, up there in the clouds, but tantalizingly near, hangs the roof of our edifice,—the vote. What is our duty?

Shall we spend time in admiring the cap-stones and cornice? Shall we lament the tragedies which accompanied the laying of the corner stones? Or, shall we, like the builders of old, chant, "Ho! all hands, all hands, heave to! All hands, heave to!" and while we chant, grasp the overhanging roof and with "a long pull, a strong pull and a pull all together," fix it in place for ever more?

Is the crisis real or imaginary? If it be real, it calls for action, bold, immediate and decisive.

ENEMIES MUST BE OVERCOME

Let us then take measure of our strength. Our cause has won the endorsement of all political parties; every candidate for the presidency is a suffragist. It has won the endorsement of most churches; it has won the hearty approval of all great organizations of women. It has won the support of all reform movements; it has won the progressives of every variety. The majority of the press in most States is with us. Great men in every political party, church and movement are with us. The names of the greatest men and women of art, science, literature, philosophy, reform, religion and politics are on our lists.

We have not won the reactionaries of any party, church or society and we never will. From the beginning of things, there have been Antis. The Antis drove Moses out of Egypt; they crucified Christ, who said: "Love thy neighbor as thyself"; they have persecuted Jews in all parts of the world; they poisoned Socrates, the great philosopher; they cruelly persecuted Copernicus and Galileo, the first great scientists; they burned Giordano Bruno at the stake because he believed the world was round; they burned Savonarola who warred upon church corruption; they burned Eufame McIlyane because she used an anaesthetic; they burned Joan of Arc for a heretic; they have sent great men and women to Siberia to eat their hearts out in isolation; they burned in effigy Wm. Lloyd Garrison; they egged Abbie Kelly and Lucy Stone and mobbed Susan B. Anthony. Yet, in proportion to the enlightenment of their respective ages, these Antis were persons of intelligence and honest purpose. They were merely deaf to the call of Progress and were enraged because the world insisted upon moving on. Antis, male and female, there still are and will be to the end of time. Give to them a prayer of forgiveness for they know not what they do; and prepare for the onward march.

We have not won the ignorant and illiterate and we never can. They are too undeveloped mentally to understand that the institutions of today are not those of yesterday nor will be those of tomorrow.

We have not won the forces of evil and we never will. Evil has ever been timorous and suspicious of all change. It is an instinctive act of self-preservation which makes it fear and consequently oppose votes for women. As the Hon. Champ Clark said the other day: "Some good and intelligent people are opposed to woman suffrage; but all the ignorant and evil-minded are against it."

These three forces are the enemies of our cause.

Before the vote is won, there must and will be a gigantic final conflict between the forces of progress, righteousness and democracy and the forces of ignorance, evil and reaction. That struggle may be postponed but it cannot be evaded or avoided. There is no question as to which side will be the victor.

MOVEMENT LACKS ORGANIZATION

Shall we play the coward, then, and leave the hard knocks for our daughters or shall we throw ourselves into the fray, bare our own shoulders to the blows and thus bequeath to them a politically liberated womanhood? We have taken note of our gains and of our resources and they are all we could wish. Before the final struggle, we must take cognizance of our weakness. Are we prepared to grasp the victory? Alas, no! Our movement is like a great Niagara with a vast volume of water tumbling over its ledge but turning no wheel. Our organized machinery is set for the propagandistic stage and not for the seizure of victory. Our supporters are spreading the argument for our cause; they feel no sense of responsibility for the realization of our hopes. Our movement lacks cohesion, organization, unity and consequent momentum.

Behind us, in front of us, everywhere about us are suffragists,—millions of them, but inactive and silent. They have been "agitated and educated" and are with us in belief. There are thousands of women who have at one time or another been members of our organization but they have dropped out because to them, the movement seemed negative and pointless. Many have taken up other work whose results were more immediate. Philanthropy, charity, work for corrective laws of various kinds, temperance, relief for working women and numberless similar public services have called them. Others have turned to the pleasanter avenues of clubwork, art or literature.

There are thousands of other women who have never learned of the earlier struggles of our movement. They found doors of opportunity open to them on every side. They found well-paid posts awaiting the qualified woman and they have availed themselves of all these blessings; almost without exception they believe in the vote but they feel neither gratitude to those who opened the doors through which they have entered to economic liberty nor any sense of obligation to open political doors for those who come after.

There are still others who, timorously looking over their shoulders to see if any listeners be near, will tell us they hope we will win and win soon but they are too frightened of Mother Grundy to help. There are others too occupied with the small things of life to help. They say they could find time to vote but not to work for the vote. There are men, too, millions of them, waiting to be called. These men and women are our reserves. They are largely unorganized and untrained soldiers with little responsibility toward our movement. Yet these reserves must be mobilized. The final struggle needs their numbers and the momentum those numbers will bring. Were never another convert made, there are suffragists enough in this country, if combined, to make so irresistible a driving force that victory might be seized at once.

"THE WOMAN'S HOUR HAS STRUCK"

How can it be done? By a simple change of mental attitude. If you are to seize the victory, that change must take place in this hall, here and now!

The old belief, which has sustained suffragists in many an hour of discouragement, "woman suffrage is bound to come," must give way to the new, "The Woman's Hour Has Struck." The long drawn out struggle, the cruel hostility which, for years, was arrayed against our cause, have accustomed suffragists to the idea of indefinite postponement but eventual victory. The slogan of a movement sets its pace. The old one counseled patience; it said, there is plenty of time; it pardoned sloth and half-hearted effort. It set the pace of an educational campaign. The "Woman's Hour Has Struck" sets the pace of a crusade which will have its way. It says: "Awake, arise, my sisters, let your hearts be filled with joy,—the time of victory is here. On-ward march."

If you believe with me that a crisis has come to our move-ment,—if you believe that the time for final action is now, if you catch the rosy tints of the coming day, what does it mean to you? Does it not give you a thrill of exaltation; does the blood not course more quickly through your veins; does it not bring a new sense of freedom, of joy and of determination? Is it not true that you, who wanted, a little time ago, to lay down the work because you were weary with long service, now, under the compelling influence of a changed mental attitude, are ready to go on until the vote is won. The change is one of spirit! Aye, and the spiritual effect upon you will come to others. Let me borrow an expression from Hon. John Finlay: what our great movement needs now is a "mobilization of spirit,"—the jubi-lant, glad spirit of victory. Then let us sound a bugle call here and now to the women of the nation: "The Woman's Hour Has Struck." Let the bugle sound from the suffrage headquarters of every State at the inauguration of a State campaign. Let the call go forth again and again and yet again. Let it be repeated in every article written, in every speech made, in every conversa-tion held. Let the bugle blow again and yet again: The political emancipation of our sex calls you women of America, arise! Are you content that others shall pay the price of your liberty?

Women in schools and counting houses, in shops and on the farm, women in the home with babes at their breasts and women engaged in public careers will hear. The veins of Amer-ican women are not filled with milk and water. They are nei-ther cowards nor slackers. They will come. They only await the bugle call to learn that the final battle is on.

Give heed at once to the organization of the reserves; and then to the work that they shall do. Organize in every Assembly District and every voting precinct. It is the only way to make our appeal invincible. Swell the army, then set it upon the trail of every legislator and congressman, for they alone hold the key to our political emancipation. Compel this army of lawmakers to see woman suffrage, to think woman suffrage, to talk woman suffrage every minute of every day until they heed our plea.

All this is mere preparedness for the final drive to victory. The next question is: what shall be our aim?

AIM AT FEDERAL AMENDMENT

We have listened to an exhaustive discussion upon the three-cornered questions: Shall we concentrate on the Federal Amendment; shall we concentrate on State Referenda or shall we proceed as before, supporting both methods. The Convention has voted to continue both forms of activity but there is one further point which should be made clear before we adjourn and that is the exact program to be followed in the support of the two methods. This should be so precisely defined by this convention that every member, every friend and even every foe, may understand it.

We have long known the many obstacles imposed by most State Constitutions and that there are States in which women must wait a probable half century for their enfranchisement if no other avenue of escape is offered than amendment of their State constitutions. But there are other and even graver considerations which, in my judgment, should compel us to make the Federal Amendment our ultimate aim and work in the States a program of preparedness to win nation-wide suffrage by amendment of the National Constitution. I must say, in passing, that this is no new opinion. I have held it for a quarter of a century and the varying suffrage events of the passing years have only served to strengthen and emphasize my conviction. To my mind, the insistence of the enfranchisement of the women of our land by Federal amendment, is the only self-respecting course to pursue. My reasons, I beg the privilege of presenting.

RECALLS EARLY CAMPAIGN

My first campaign was that in South Dakota in the year 1890. Because I was young and all the experiences were new, every event in that campaign stands out in my memory with a vividness which does not mark later and even more important events. My first point was Mitchell, where a two days' suffrage meeting was held prior to the State Republican Convention. Miss Anthony was the leader; Miss Shaw "the star," and the very best women of South Dakota were there. Of course, we wanted a plank in the Republican platform. The great concession was made the suffragists of ten seats on the platform where no one could see or be seen. I was fortunate enough to be one of the ten, and being young, I did not mind standing on a chair in order to see the convention. Peeping over the heads and shoulders of those before me, I saw a man arise and move that a delegation of Sioux Indians be admitted. They had been enfranchised by the National government and the delegate said, their votes must be won. They were admitted to the floor of the house,—three blanketed, long-haired, greasy men of the plains. On the platform sat Miss Anthony, bent with the weight of her seventy years, forty of which had been unceasingly expended to secure education, property rights and the vote for her sex. Upon her face was the expectancy born of "the hope which springs eternal in the human breast." On the floor sat the Indians unmoved and unknowing. The time came when five minutes was given the unenfranchised women, and Miss Shaw was called to speak for them. She has made many powerful addresses but never one quite so wonderful as that. All the men who packed that big skating-rink combined, could not have provided so soul-stirring an appeal for any cause. But it was a prophet whose soul was lighted by a vision of truth, speaking to a mob, who marvelled at the power of the speaker but did not comprehend her message. With the crowd, I passed out of the door stunned by the knowledge I had gained that Americans did not understand the principles of self-government. On either side stood a man handing out papers. They were men of the lowest type and the papers were "The Remonstrance," published by a few rich women in Boston who were, at that date, too timid to have their names printed on the document. What agent secured the men who, every person in the town knew, were henchmen of the local saloons, I never learned.

PROGRESS CHECKED BY CONSPIRACIES

My last point in the State was Aberdeen and there on election day, I, with other women, served as watchers. All day long, at intervals, groups of five or ten Russians filed in to the order of poll workers. They, too, were saloon henchmen. These Russians could not speak English; they were totally illiterate and signed the poll-book with a cross. They had no more comprehension of the sacredness of a vote than a wild man from Borneo. The man who chiefly managed the affair and who must have voted a hundred men that day, grew bold and more than once paid his men their $2 in plain sight.

No king marshaling his army upon a battle-field could bear himself with more triumphant mien than did this political criminal whenever he entered that polling place with a new line of purchased voters. The hatred and contempt of his expression as he led them past us could not have been exceeded by an Apache chief gloating over his conquered foe. There was no remedy. South Dakota had no law to fit the case. These events at the time seemed mere local incidents, but I was to learn later that they were the early manifestation of a nation-wide condition which would remain constant in our campaigns until the end and that they were to grow into an increasingly better organized hostility to be met in every State.

Rich women, protected and serene, or women well paid by rich women, have grown bolder and more skilful in their unspeakable treachery to their sex. There have been those willing to villify their sister women from ocean to ocean and to declare them too incompetent mentally and too unclean morally to be trusted with the privilege of self-government. Their motives suffragists will never understand.

The liquor forces have developed an organized opposition, apparently supported by large funds, which has been an active factor in every campaign except two since 1890, and in those two we won. The Secretary of one of the State Liquor Associations recently said to a man of honor, that they would not allow another State to be carried for suffrage within the next ten years. Still another representative of the same force said to another man that they could gather 10 millions of dollars if necessary to throw into any State which gave indications of a suffrage victory. These are doubtless wild threats, but the fact remains that a powerful force is arrayed against our cause, and it scruples at nothing.

In every precinct, there seem to be a few men willing to

sell their citizen's right and these may be numerous enough to become a balance of power which added to the normal conservative vote may defeat our amendments. This "triple alliance," the women who work in the open, appealing to the respectable conservative element and the liquor forces secretly conniving with the purchasable vote forms a combined foe very difficult to combat since its attack is subterranean.

Opposition in the open which meets our arguments with arguments, our claims with defense, must always be welcome. Truth has ever followed in the wake of free and honest discussion. But an opposition which conspires behind closed doors to buy its victory with money or spoils is a criminal so black, so indescribably hideous that it fills the soul, not with discouragement for our cause but with shame for our Republic. We shall never know how many campaigns have been lost by such conspiracies, but it is my own sincere conviction that there have been several.

BREWERS ALLIED WITH ANTIS

We know that in the Colorado campaign, the brewers of Denver printed false statements and caused them to be put under the door of every house in the city. We know that in the last unsuccessful campaign in Oregon, the order went out from the liquor forces to the saloons of the State to deliver a stated number of votes in opposition to the suffrage amendment. Every suffragist in Michigan seems to agree that the amendment was counted out in the first campaign and that the ballots were stuffed in the second and that the agents were the liquor forces. The Attorney General who was serving at the time of the Nebraska campaign has declared that, he believes the amendment was counted out there, and again, the charge lies at the same door. The wet counties in Iowa certainly defeated the amendment there. The Boston & Maine Railway contributed to defeat the suffrage question in the Constitutional Convention of New Hampshire and afterward it was found that it had been done in collusion with the liquor lobby. The brewers, arrested upon the Federal charge of conspiracy in elections and brought to trial in Pittsburgh this year, are supposed to have contributed large sums to defeat the question in the four Eastern campaign

States and although this remains unproven, it is true that their business was conducted in so irregular a fashion that check books and stubs had been destroyed. It was true in New York that men visited trade unionists and told them that woman suffrage meant the certain loss of positions in all trades allied to the liquor business. It is true that in New Jersey the woman poll workers were appalled at the seemingly endless number of illiterate, drunken and degenerate types who were lined up to vote in opposition to the amendment in that State. It is true that the four men representing Texas, Indiana, Georgia and New Jersey respectively, who signed the minority report of the Resolutions Committee in St. Louis, which would have taken the suffrage plank out of the Democratic platform are all well-known henchmen of the liquor interests. It is well-known that a group of liquor men have issued newspaper plate matter under the imprint of an alleged Farmers' Association and have sent it broadcast to rural papers, its contents purporting to be of interest to farmers but always containing anti-suffrage articles.

The liquor interests have been driven to the aggressive defensive by the inroads of the prohibition movement. They are obsessed by the idea that woman suffrage is only a flank prohibition movement. They have the American's right to fight for their own. We cannot relieve them of their notion that woman suffrage will promote prohibition and hence must accept their opposition as normal. But when that opposition ceases to be honest and resorts to conspiracy and bribery to gain its ends, it becomes criminal.

Since this kind of opposition has occurred to a greater or less extent in all our campaigns, suffragists must be prepared to meet it in future. What, if any, underground connection there may be between the women antis and the liquor antis no one knows. Some of the women are conscientious and honest, I am sure, but the obvious fact remains that these women secure what they want, that is their own disfranchisement by the aid and the evident conjunction of the liquor forces with the purchasable, controllable vote and in several campaigns, their posters, their literature and buttons were circulated through saloons. This may have been done without the knowledge or consent of the women, but the fact remains that the saloons and the women antis agree that votes in the hands of women are a "menace."

NO REDRESS FOR CORRUPTION

Corruption has existed since the beginning of things and will continue so long as there are dishonest men to tempt and weak ones to yield. It is a far more invidious foe to our country's weal than the bugaboos of wars with Germany, Mexico or Japan. A French philosopher said that "The corruption of each form of government commences with the decay of its principles." History proves that statement to be true and in our own land, the careful student should feel genuine anxiety at the ignorance and indifference among our people concerning those truths we have called "American principles."

It is through the departure from loyalty to those principles that corruption has crept into our political life and it is through the weakness created by internal corruption that most of the great dead nations have met their downfall.

If the suffrage amendments are defeated by illegal practices, why not demand redress, asks the novice in suffrage campaigns. Ah, there's the rub. In 25 States no provision has been made by the election law for any form of contest or recount on a referendum. Political corrupters may, in these States, bribe voters, colonize voters and repeat them to their hearts' content and redress of any kind is practically impossible. If clear evidence of fraud could be produced, a case might be brought to the courts and the guilty parties might be punished but the election would stand. In New York, in 1915, the question was submitted to the voters as to whether there should be a constitutional convention. The convention was ordered by a majority of over 1,300. It was estimated that about 800 fraudulent votes were cast. Leading lawyers discussed the question of effect upon the election and the general opinion was that even though the entire majority and more was found to be fraudulent, the election could not be set aside. The convention was held.

In twenty States, contests on referenda seem possible under the law, but in practically every one the contest means a resort to the courts and in only eight of these is reference made to a recount. The law is vague and incomplete in nearly all of these

States. In some of these, including Michigan where the suffrage amendment is declared to have been counted out, application for a recount must be made in each voting precinct. To have secured redress in Michigan, provided the fraud was widespread, as I understand it was, it would have been necessary to have secured definite evidence of fraud in a probable 1,000 precincts and to have instituted as many cases.

In some States, the Courts decide what the redress shall be and in these, no assurance is given by the law that such redress would include a correction of the returns. In at least seven, the applicants must pay all costs if they fail to prove their case.

ILLITERATES BRIBED

The penalties for bribery range from $5 to $2,000 and from 30 days to 10 years, but only one State (Ohio) provides in terms for punishment of bribery as part of the penalty in an election contest. Just as proof of bribery does not throw out the person's vote, so the other way about, the throwing out of the purchased votes in contest cases does not bring with it automatically punishment of the purchased voter. If we may judge from this omission from the contest provisions these bribery cases could be separate actions. Twenty-one States in clear terms disfranchise (or give the Legislature power to disfranchise) bribers and bribed, but few make provision for the method of actually enforcing the law and upon inquiry, the Secretary of State of many of these States reported that so far as he knew, no man had ever been disfranchised for this offense. This was true of States which have been notorious for political corruption.

With a vague, uncertain law to define their punishment in most States and no law at all in 25 States, as a preliminary security, corrupt opponents of a woman suffrage amendment find many additional aids to their nefarious acts. A briber must make sure that the bribed carries out his part of the contract. Whenever it is easy to check up the results of the bribe, corruption may reign supreme and with little risk of being found out. A study of some of the recent suffrage votes results in significant food for reflection. In Wisconsin, the suffrage ballot was separate and pink. It was easy to teach the most illiterate how to vote "No" and to check up returns with considerable accuracy. In New York, there were three ballots. The official ballot had emblems which easily distinguished it. The other two were exactly alike in shape, size and color and each contained three propositions, those which came from the constitutional convention and the other those which came from the Legislature. The orders went forth to vote down the Constitutional provisions and it was done by a majority of 482,000, or nearly 300,000 more than the majority against woman suffrage. On the ballot containing the suffrage amendment which was No. 1, there was proposition No. 3, which all the political parties wanted carried. It could easily be found by all illiterate as it contained more lines of printing, yet so difficult was it to teach ignorant men to vote "no" on suffrage and "yes" on No. 3 that, despite the fact that orders had gone forth to all the State that No. 3 was to be carried, it barely squeezed through.

In Pennsylvania there are no emblems to distinguish the tickets and, on the large ballot, the suffrage amendment would have been difficult to find by an untutored voter. In consequence, as I believe, Pennsylvania polled the largest proportional vote for the amendment of any Eastern State. In Massachusetts, the ballot was small and the suffrage amendment could be easily picked out by a bribed illiterate. In Iowa, the suffrage ballot was separate and yellow, while the main ballots were white. In consequence, there were 35,000 more votes cast on the suffrage proposition than for the nomination of Governor, although the contest was an excited one. In North Dakota, the regular ballot was long and complicated and the suffrage ballot separate and small. It was very easy to teach the dullest illiterate how to vote "No." It might be said that it would be equally easy to teach him to vote "Yes." True, but suffragists never bribe. Both the briber and the illiterate are allies of the Antis.

PARTY MACHINE A SAFEGUARD

The election boards are bi-partisan and each party has its own machinery, not only of election officials but watchers and challengers, to see that the opposing party commits no fraud. The watchfulness of this party machinery, plus an increasingly vigilant public opinion, has corrected many of the election frauds which were once common, and many elections are probably free from all the baser forms of corruption.

When a question on referendum is sincerely espoused by both the dominant parties, it has the advantage of the watchfulness of both party machines and is doubly safe-guarded from fraud. But when such a question has been espoused by no dominant party, it is utterly at the mercy of the worst forms of corruption. The election officers may even agree to wink at fraud even when plainly committed, since it is no affair of theirs. Or, they may even go further and join in the pleasing game of running in as many votes against such an amendment as possible. This has not infrequently been the unhappy experience of suffrage amendments in corrupt quarters. With no one on the election board whose especial business it is to see that honesty is upheld, a suffrage amendment suffers further disaster through the fact that most States do not permit women watchers to stand guard over their own question.

When it is remembered that immigrants may be naturalized after a residence of five years; that, when naturalized they automatically become voters by all our State constitutions; that in nine States, immigrant voters are not even required to be citizens; that the right to vote is limited by an educational qualification in only 17 States and that nine of these are Southern with special intent of disfranchising the negro; that there is an unscrupulous body ready to engage the lowest elements of our population by fraudulent processes to oppose our amendment; that there is no authority on the election board whose business it is to see that we get a square deal; that the method of preparing the ballot is often an advantage to the enemy; that after the fraud is committed, there is practically no redress provided by election laws, it ought to be clear to all that State constitutional amendments when unsponsored by the dominant political parties which control the election machinery, must run the gauntlet of exceedingly unfair conditions. When suffragists have been fortunate enough to overcome the obstacles imposed by the Constitution of their States, they immediately enter upon the task of surmounting the infinitely greater hazards of the election law.

We are justly proud of the nine States which have been won on a referendum but these are not greater monuments to the triumphs of our cause than to the integrity of the elections in those States. I am certain that at least five other States should stand in that list. That they are not there is a reflection upon the inefficiency of the election machinery of those States.

No careful observer of the modern trend of human affairs doubts that "governments of the people" are destined to replace the monarchies of the world. No "listener in" will fail to hear the rumble of the rising tide of democracy. No watcher of events will deny that the women of all civilized lands will be enfranchised as part of "the people" and no American possessed of the least political acumen, doubts woman suffrage in our land as a coming fact.

INDIANS, NEGROES AND IMMIGRANTS VOTE

Bear these items in mind and remember that three-fourths of the men of our nation have received the vote as the direct or indirect gift of the Naturalization laws; that the federal government enfranchised the Indians, assuming its authority upon the ground that they are wards of the nation; that the negroes were enfranchised by federal amendment; that the Constitutions of all States not in the list of the original thirteen, automatically extended the vote to men; that in the original colonial territory, the chief struggle occurred over the elimination of the land-owning qualification and that a total vote necessary to give the franchise to non-landowners, did not exceed 50 or 75 thousand in any State.

Let us not forget that the vote is the free-will offering of our 48 States to any man who chooses to make this land his home. Let us not overlook the fact every five years of late an average of one million immigrant voters are added to our electors' lists,—a million men mainly uneducated and all moulded by European traditions. To these men, women of American birth, education and ideals must appeal for their enfranchisement. No humiliation could be more complete; unless we add the sorrowful fact that leaders of Americanism in Congress and Legislatures are willing to drive their wives and daughters to beg the consent of these men to their political liberty.

Let us return to South Dakota a moment. During the Civil War there was an uprising of the Sioux Indians who occupied a reservation covering a large part of the territory now comprising that State. These Indians instituted one of the cruelest and most savage massacres in our history. They committed atrocities upon women, so indescribably indecent that they were never recorded in ordinary history.

By 1890, the numerous efforts to win them to civilization had culminated in an offer of land in severalty and if accepted in good faith, these land owners were promised the vote. Their blanketed representatives sat in the Republican Convention of that year and took their first lesson in American politics. In 1916, I am reliably informed that there are 5,000 Sioux voters in the State of South Dakota and that they may prove the balance of power in November to decide whether women who have borne the burdens of pioneer life shall be permitted the vote. How much the schools have taught them of human liberty within the last quarter of a century, I do not know but I opine that they will make congenial allies to the antis.

To my mind, the considerations aroused by such facts entirely outweigh any philosophy which supports the theory of suffrage by "State rights."

Again, let us not forget that while our struggle continues in this supposedly democratic land, women have been enfranchised within a year in three provinces of Canada nearly equal in extent to all our territory east of the Mississippi; in Denmark and Iceland by majority vote of their respective Parliaments. All signs indicate the early enfranchisement of the women of Great Britain by the same process.

AMERICAN WOMEN HUMILIATED

Why, then, should American women be content to beg the vote on bended knee from man to man, when no American male voter has been compelled to pay this price for his vote and no woman of other countries is subjected to this humiliation? Shall a Republic be less generous with its womanhood than an Empire? Shall the government be less liberal with its daughters than with its sons?

The makers of the constitution foresaw the necessity of referring important questions of State to a more intelligent body than the masses of the people and so provided for the amendment of the Constitution by referendum to the Legislatures of the various States. Why should we hesitate to avail ourselves of the privileges thus created. We represent one land and one people. We have the same institutions, customs and ideals. It is the advocates of State rights who are championing national prohibition and child labor. It will be a curious kind of logic that can uphold these measures as national and, at the same time relegate woman suffrage to the States. Our cause has been caught in a snarl of constitutional obstructions and inadequate election laws. We have a right to appeal to our Congress to extricate our cause from this tangle. If there is any chivalry left, this is the time for it to come forward and do an act of simple justice.

In my judgment, the women of this land, not only have the right to sit on the steps of Congress until it acts but it is their self-respecting duty to insist upon their enfranchisement by that route.

FEDERAL ACTION NOT A SHORT CUT

But, let me implore you, sister women, not to imagine a Federal Amendment an easy process of enfranchisement. There is no quick, short cut to our liberty. The Federal Amendment means a simultaneous campaign in 48 States. It demands organization in every precinct; activity, agitation, education in every corner. It means an appeal to the voters only little less general than is required in a referendum. Nothing less than this nation-wide, vigilant, unceasing campaigning will win the ratification.

Do not allow my comments to discourage you who represent the States where campaigns are pending. Your campaign may win the promise to safeguard your election from the dominant parties. It may so arouse public sentiment that any fraud may be outvoted. You are doing the best work possible. If you win, you have made Federal action and ratification more certain. If you lose, you have organized an army ready for your ratification campaign and have added testimony to the need of Federal action. What you have done in your State must be done in every State. A few women here and there have dropped out from State work in the fond delusion that there is no need of work if the Federal amendment is to be the aim. I hold such women to be more dangerous enemies of our cause than the known opponent. State work alone can carry the amendment through Congress and through the ratifications. There must be no shirkers, no cowards, no backsliders these coming months. The army in every State must grow larger and larger. The activity must grow livelier and even more lively. The reserves must be aroused and set to work. Let no one labor under the delusion that suffrage can be won in any other way than by the education and organization of the constituencies. Let no woman think the vote will be handed her some bright summer morning "on a golden platter at the foot of a rainbow."

"The Woman's Hour Has Struck." Yet, if the call goes unheeded, if our women think it means the vote without a struggle, if they think other women can and will pay the price of their emancipation, the hour may pass and our political liberty may not be won.

WOMEN ARISE: DEMAND THE VOTE! The character of a man is measured, it is said, by his will. The same is true of a movement. Then, WILL to be free. Demand the vote. Women, ARISE!

BOSTON EQUAL SUFFRAGE ASSOCIATION FOR GOOD GOVERNMENT

Letter Series No. 1–10

1917

Founded in 1901 by Maud Wood Park, Pauline Agassiz Shaw (1841–1917), and Mary Hutcheson Page (1860–1940), the Boston Equal Suffrage Association for Good Government (BESAGG) initially pursued a broad agenda of civic reform but by 1910 had narrowed its focus primarily to women's suffrage. (In 1920 it would reconstitute itself as the Boston League of Women Voters.) The group adopted new tactics like canvassing and open-air meetings (see also Florence Luscomb, pages 307–314 in this volume) but faced an uphill battle in a state like Massachusetts, which was a stronghold of antisuffrage sentiment. After the resounding defeat of a state suffrage referendum in 1915, the suffragists regrouped. One new area of outreach was to the working class, as represented in this series of ten letters drafted by BESAGG's Industrial Department. Suffragists handed out handbills and fliers like these at lunchtime at local factories and mills. The letter series offers a tutorial on the conditions of the 400,000 working women in Massachusetts at the time, making the case that working women needed the vote to improve their lives. And to do that they needed the help of working men. As each flier said at the end, "Please pass it on."

INDUSTRIAL DEPARTMENT—WHO IT IS AND WHAT IT WANTS.

LETTER SERIES
No. 1

Dear Sir and Brother:—

The Industrial Department of the Boston Equal Suffrage Association for Good Government is a committee composed of women who believe in higher industrial standards. We are out to get the vote for the women of this state and as working women we appeal to you as working men to help us get it.

In the State of Massachusetts there are over 400,000 women who must work in order to live.

Women do everything from making cores in foundries, sausages in packing houses, pickles and candies, to working in human hair, chemicals and rags. We scrub floors in offices, wash dishes, prepare vegetables, cook and carry heavy laden trays in restaurants. We sit over electric power machines often speeded up to 3,500 stitches a minute, making garments, and break our backs over mangles and irons in laundries. We work with our hands and often with our feet, using foot pressure sometimes so heavy that we injure ourselves internally. We stand long hours behind counters, often suffering from varicose veins and flat feet, or we sit glued to the telephone using sight, touch and hearing, many times suffering from what is medically known as a telephone ear.

You know, Brother, as well as we that adequate consideration will be given to our demands only when men in public office recognize that they must be responsible to us, as part of their constituency, for protection in our industrial life, and that through the power of the ballot we can express our endorsement or disapproval of their actions.

Can't you see that working women have the same interests as working men in the vote?

Our next letter will tell you about the conditions under which our sisters work, and why, for your sake as well as ours, we need the vote.

Fraternally yours,
Mabel Gillespie
Maud Foley
Rose Sullivan
Committee on Publicity

PLEASE PASS IT ON

WOMEN IN THE TEXTILE MILLS.

LETTER SERIES
No. 2

Dear Sir and Brother:—

Fifty-one thousand, five hundred and eighty-nine women

work in the textile industries in Massachusetts making cotton, woolens, silks, carpets, knit underwear, etc. Our country depends upon the labor of these women to produce clothing, shelter and various kinds of material for our men on the fields of war. The din of the machinery is deafening in many of these factories and often the machinery is so closely placed that there is difficulty in passing without catching the clothing. Women winders stand through a ten-hour day watching from 16 to 25 bobbins, ready to tie up broken threads and on the lookout for any hitch in the machinery.

Women examine woolen cloth to pick out any knots that may occur; their wages are very low, and the work is very hard on the hands while the strain of watching is continuous.

One widow, who is trying to support her children on her meagre wages (she had three of them, 11, 9 and 3 years of age) when asked who cooked their luncheon, replied, "Well, the children eat dry bread the same as I take to the factory to eat. I come home in the evenings and fix it up."

Surely we all remember the strike of the textile workers of Lawrence and the terrible conditions of want and privation that that strike brought to light.

Talk of suffrage destroying the home! Why, whole families of mill workers, father, mother and children, are forced to work in the mill so that body and soul may be kept together. Such industrial conditions destroy the home.

Don't you think that the vote in the hands of the women in the textile mills could do much to help bring about better working conditions and a happier time for all? Of course it would. Give us the vote and see how well we can use it.

Our next letter will deal with the subject of Fire Protection.

Fraternally yours,

Mabel Gillespie
Maud Foley
Rose Sullivan

Committee on Publicity

PLEASE PASS IT ON

FIRE PROTECTION

LETTER SERIES
No. 3

Dear Sir and Brother:—

A constant fear and danger to the working women today is the fire hazard. We have in our industrial centers many shops in which women are employed, where the fire prevention laws of the State of Massachusetts are violated. Occasionally local disturbances unearth these conditions. We women do not like to work in such places but we are often compelled to by circumstances. We have many tragedies in the industrial world and fire has played a heavy part—fires that could have been prevented if the laws were properly enforced.

The 400,000 working women in our state have no vote in determining who shall make the laws or who shall have the power to appoint a sufficient number of inspectors to enforce the laws which protect their lives. There is a constant effort on the part of powerful interests to do away with the protection provided by the present law.

You know, Brother, as well as we that often more consideration is given to property, to the owner of the building and the expenditure of his money, than to the lives of the men and women inside the factories, and shops.

Because men and women are not property, they have no such effective protection as property has.

Do working women need the vote—Yes—a thousand times—Yes! Won't you help give it to her?

Our next letter takes up the subject of Women in the Garment Trades.

> Fraternally yours,
> Mabel Gillespie
> Maud Foley
> Rose Sullivan
> Committee on Publicity

PLEASE PASS IT ON

WOMEN IN THE GARMENT TRADES

LETTER SERIES
No. 4

Dear Sir and Brother:—

There are 25,000 women who work on garments in the State of Massachusetts. They make men's, women's and children's coats, skirts, gloves, dresses, waists, underwear, etc. Many of these women even while they are still young are the bread winners for the families, supporting old or sick parents or younger brothers and sisters.

Guarded machinery, safety, sanitation, light, air, etc., depend upon the laws and their enforcement. That these laws are violated is borne witness to by the number of small, dark, filthy sweat shops still to be found in our great industrial cities and the number of accidents from unguarded machinery.

The laws are made by the legislature elected by the voters and they are enforced by men appointed by the Governor, who is elected by men. These 25,000 women working in the garment factories have nothing to say about who is elected. What they want is not considered because they are without influence, for they have no vote. They have no choice but to work, yet they have no voice to declare who shall make the laws under which they must work and live.

Is that fair? Give these women the chance to elect their representatives. Give them the vote.

Our next letter will tell of the Struggles of the Working Women of Massachusetts to secure a 48-hour Week.

Fraternally yours,

Mabel Gillespie
Maud Foley
Rose Sullivan

Committee on Publicity

PLEASE PASS IT ON

THE EIGHT HOUR DAY

LETTER SERIES
No. 5

Dear Sir and Brother:—

We working women of Massachusetts have been trying for three years to get the 48-hour week for women passed in the Legislature. Women representing the textile, laundry, hotel, candy, jewelry and garment industries and many other trades and crafts, have appeared before the legislative committees stating clearly the conditions in their trades and the need of a shorter work day for women. These women were told that they had proved their case, but—we all understand the reason of the but,—the women had no vote while their employers have, and so each year the women workers bring stronger evidence proving their case more convincingly only to see it unjustly defeated, through circumstances they cannot control.

Have you ever stopped to think what the long work day means to the working women of the state? Medical authorities everywhere say that the fatigue caused by long hours, nerve strain and speeding up is a menace and a danger to the future mothers of the state and to the nation as a whole. And you well know, Brother, that a woman's work is not done when she leaves the factory.

The only states having an eight-hour law for women are: Colorado, California, Washington, Oregon and Arizona. In all these states women vote.

There are 68 laws in 28 states that provide for an eight-hour day in certain industries for men. It is estimated that 500 men to one woman are protected by an eight-hour law.

Don't you think that the vote has something to do with that, Brother?

The subject of the next letter is Working Men's Wives and Mothers.

Fraternally yours,
Mabel Gillespie
Maud Foley
Rose Sullivan
Committee on Publicity

PLEASE PASS IT ON

WORKING MEN'S WIVES AND MOTHERS

LETTER SERIES
No. 6

Dear Sir and Brother:—

What interest has the wife of the working man and the mother of his children in the vote? The question of

FOOD	HOUSING
HEALTH CLOTHES	PLAYGROUNDS

are all involved in politics today, and all affect the home and the children. The wife buys the food and the clothes for her family. If the food is bad, if the milk is watered or impure, she cannot give her children nourishing and good food.

If the prices jump sky high, she cannot meet the cost.

There are pure food laws which must be enforced. Today their enforcement depends upon men.

If dishonest representation of what clothes really are made of is given, the mother finds she pays for wool and gets cotton and the children are cold, not warm.

The health of her child not only depends upon good food and warm clothing but upon the health of the community. We have health laws but if they are not enforced the children suffer.

There is no phase of the child's life from food and clothing to light and air that is not a matter of law. Sunlight and air are as important to the health of a child as pure food. *But sunlight and fresh air as well as fresh food are under political control.* In the big cities sunlight cannot be bought by many working people. Their homes are sunless because of the high buildings all around them. Their streets are sunless for the same reason. Children grow up in sunless homes and streets, and sun is as important to a growing child as it is to a flower to make it healthy and strong.

The mother's interest must be in the kind of men who go to the Legislature, and the kind of men who are elected to be Governor or Mayor.

Give your wives and mothers the vote.

Industrial Disease will be the subject of the next letter.

Fraternally yours,

Mabel Gillespie

Maud Foley
Rose Sullivan
Committee on Publicity

PLEASE PASS IT ON

INDUSTRIAL DISEASES

LETTER SERIES
No. 7

Dear Sir and Brother:—

There are many trades that cause industrial diseases. There are trades in which *poisonous substances* are used and poisonous gases generated which hold within themselves disease.

There are other trades which bring with them disease because of the conditions under which people work. Women as well as men suffer, and there are many trades causing them ill health, in which the majority of the workers are women. For instance, girls working in stores, laundries, paper-box factories, etc., where they are required to stand continually, suffer from varicose veins or flat feet which are very painful; and they are frequently incapacitated for motherhood, especially in some trades where they have to use foot pressure on machines and carry heavy weights. Girls working in certain departments of candy factories are compelled to sit all day in artificially chilled rooms, where they become chilled to the bone, and their physical condition so impaired that they are unable successfully to combat illness. Girls working in textile mills breathing in the fluff-laden air and stooping over their work all day are prone to tuberculosis. Incessant noise and the pressure of speed work are nerve destroying. The telephone operator frequently suffers from throat trouble and nervous breakdown and what is medically known as "telephone ear."

What has the vote to do with these conditions? There are health laws in this State. The State and the Cities have health departments with health officers who are men appointed by the health authorities. The enforcement of the law depends upon these men. Better health laws are necessary. They depend upon legislators elected by men.

The industrial conditions as they exist today in the life of women tend to increase infant mortality, lower birth rate, and weaken the second generation. Should not women, mothers, whose sons will be the manhood of our nation, have the vote to safeguard their lives?

This is your interest as well as ours, Brother. Give her the vote so she can have the power to protect all working women.

Child Labor, the subject of the next letter, concerns every father and mother.

> Fraternally yours,
> Mabel Gillespie
> Maud Foley
> Rose Sullivan
> Committee on Publicity

PLEASE PASS IT ON

CHILD LABOR

LETTER SERIES
No. 8

Dear Sir and Brother:—

Perhaps it would interest you to know that in this great country of ours where natural resources are so abundant more than 2,000,000 childen under the age of sixteen are working their lives away. Before they have had a chance to grow they are harnessed to the wheels of industry where they are crippled body and soul and are old men and women at twenty. Yet one state like Texas could house, feed and clothe the entire population of the country.

At the close of 1916 there were 42,268 of our boys and girls under sixteen years of age at work in the State of Massachusetts.

This number does not include the children working in the tenements of our large cities.

Almost any hour of the day and night, in many of our cities young children can be found vending newspapers, because father works for wages too small to support the family.

Children are held just as dear by the working class fathers and mothers as by the rich. It does seem all wrong that at this stage of civilization we, the workers, should permit our children to be ground into dollars.

When we use our might of numbers we men and women of the working class can get for our children their right to child-hood, their right to grow, their right to play and their right to an education through "*Ballots for Both.*"

The subject of the next letter is "The Development of Self-Government."

Fraternally yours,

Mabel Gillespie

Maud Foley

Rose Sullivan

Committee on Publicity

PLEASE PASS IT ON

THE DEVELOPMENT OF SELF-GOVERNMENT

LETTER SERIES
No. 9

Dear Sir and Brother:—

Many of our brothers look upon the vote as merely a piece of paper not worth bothering with. Yet it gives the right of self-government which men have bled and died to win.

Government began with the rule of a tribal chieftain who later became a king. He had control of all land and property and power of life and death over his subjects. The king was everything, the people nothing.

The king's power was first curbed in England. Then the barons, the great land-owning class, forced King John to sign the Magna Charta in 1215. This event stands as a land mark in the long struggle for human freedom, but it left the masses of the people without political power and their lot remained very miserable.

In those days and for hundreds of years later, manufacturing was carried on by hand labor and there was little class division between master and man. They lived together and worked to-gether and the apprentice could hope to be master in his turn.

But with the introduction of machinery, a new class was born.

The owners of factories grew so rich and powerful that they came to share political power with the great land owners. But the position of the working people became worse and worse.

Only within the last fifty or sixty years did working men gain some political and industrial power. After long and bitter struggles they were granted the vote. Then they were able to wring from the government the right to organize and thus to secure better wages, shorter hours, and some control over their job.

No one denies that the vote is the working man's defense against oppression.

Give women an equal chance with men. Work for equal suffrage.

Our next letter will tell how the working man got the vote in Massachusetts.

Fraternally yours,
Mabel Gillespie
Maud Foley
Rose Sullivan
Committee on Publicity

PLEASE PASS IT ON

HOW THE WORKING MAN GOT THE VOTE IN MASSACHUSETTS

LETTER SERIES
No. 10

Dear Sir and Brother:—

Most working men in the United States take it for granted that they have always had the right to vote. This is not true. Only a century ago the working men were in the same position that the working women are in today.

The two great principles established in the United States after the Revolutionary War and reaffirmed recently in the Senate by President Wilson;—"*That all governments derive their just powers from the consent of the governed*" and that "*taxation without representation is tyranny*," did not apply to the man who toiled with his hands.

In early Massachusetts days only those who were church members or those who could procure a certificate from the majority of the selectmen of the town to the effect that the applicant was a freeholder of something like 120 pounds (about $500.00) value of taxable property, had the right to vote.

In 1691 the church membership was dispensed with as a requirement for voting and a uniform moderate property qualification was established.

In 1820 the Constitution was amended by abolishing the property qualification in voting and substituting merely the payment of the regular taxes for a period of two years. *Now, for the first time, the working man had the vote.*

In 1891 all tax paying qualifications for voters were removed; so that today citizenship, legal residence, and the ability to read English are the only required qualifications.

It was only through constantly agitating and campaigning that our unenfranchised brothers were able to secure after many years of struggle the full rights of suffrage that they now enjoy.

We ask you to be as just to working women as the property owning men have been to the working men. Give us the vote.

Fraternally yours,
Mabel Gillespie
Maud Foley
Rose Sullivan
Committee on Publicity

PLEASE PASS IT ON

MAUD WOOD PARK

To NAWSA Congressional Chairmen
MARCH 21, 1917

The "front door lobby" was the "half-humorous, half-kindly" name one of the press-gallery journalists gave to NAWSA's Congressional Committee in Washington because, he explained, they "never used backstairs methods." Under the able direction of Maud Wood Park, as many as twenty-five regular lobbyists (almost all volunteers) lived at Suffrage House, the Congressional Committee's combined office and living quarters on Rhode Island Avenue. They were supported by the state congressional chairmen in NAWSA's forty-four state branches, as well as by ninety-five congressional aides who were available to stir up constituent and press support targeted at wavering members of Congress. Keeping track of the portfolios of 435 members of Congress and 96 senators was difficult and tedious work—far less glamorous than marching in a suffrage parade or speaking at an open-air meeting—but it was absolutely crucial to the movement's ultimate success. In this letter to congressional chairs in March 1917, Park shows the disciplined attention to detail and depth of organization that the suffrage lobby was noted for. She and her team continued nonstop until the suffrage amendment finally passed both houses of Congress in June 1919.

March 21, 1917

DEAR CONGRESSIONAL CHAIRMAN:

The 65th Congress has been called together on April 2nd. Although we cannot tell what the extra session may bring forth, we hope that the need of political justice for women will be more apparent than ever before and that openings may arise which we had not foreseen. It is imperative that we should take advantage of every possibility in our favor. For that reason, there is urgent need for activity in the home districts of Members of Congress. Will you therefore please give immediate attention to the following requests.

I. REPORTS

There are several new members with regard to whom we have had no word from their own state. Please send us *immediately* a statement, as full as you are able to make it, about the men whose names are enclosed.

CAUTION. Although we are most anxious to know how the Members of Congress stand with regard to the Federal Amendment, we beg you to take the utmost care that no Member is allowed to commit himself *against* the Amendment when he can be prevented from doing so. If you think he is inclined to be opposed, let us know your opinion; but in your letters to him and in your interviews, frame your appeals in such a way that they will not offer opportunity for a negative answer.

II. DELEGATIONS

If time allows and unless you have already done this work, delegations should visit your new Members before they leave for Washington. Delegations should be sent also to the old Members who are reported as "non-committal" or "opposed." Old Members who are in favor should be seen less formally, thanked for their position in the past, and given to understand, in a friendly and cordial way, that we are confident of their continued support.

In this connection, we ought all to remind ourselves constantly that Members expect to be treated as individuals. Do not permit circular letters to be sent them; but in writing or visiting them, be sure to make clear that you differentiate the individual from the group. In the case of friendly men, great harm has been done by writing or speaking as if their previous records were unknown and their support unappreciated.

Care should be taken in forming delegations to choose, if possible, women whose families have political influence in the man's own party and who are representative of the different sections of his district. It is well to have a small group of persons of real importance in the District rather than a large group of less prominent people. Effective use should be made of our recent remarkable gains in Ohio, North Dakota, Indiana and Canada. For example, copies of the maps giving the increase of suffrage territory might be shown and a statement made of our gain in electoral votes.

Please let us know what you are able to do in this matter.

III. Work by Men

INDIVIDUAL CALLS. The best advice that we have been able to get with regard to our work in the coming session bids us lay much more emphasis on *work by men in the home Districts*. We therefore urge you to try to get men of political prominence to call, apparently casually, on your Congressmen before they return to Washington to express to them the hope that they may support the Federal Amendment. The more men you can get to make these calls the better, for they will be enormously effective. They should be quite apart from the delegations.

COMMITTEES OF MEN. While you are seeking men to make these personal calls, it would be well also to start in each Congressional District a committee or group of men prominent in politics or in other ways who will agree to help as the need may arise by sending letters and telegrams to the Congressmen. When such a committee or group has been formed, a list of its members with addresses should be sent to our office with the name of the District Congressional Chairman through whom they can be reached. Mrs. Catt in her letter of March 12th wrote you in this connection. We are merely reminding you and urging you to make every effort to secure as many influential men as possible for these committees.

IV. Completion of State Congressional Committees

Mrs. Catt also urged you to complete your list of District Congressional Chairmen, if such list is not already filled. The Chairman of each District should make herself responsible for the accumulation of all information with regard to her Congressman which could possibly be of use to the workers in Washington. She should know about his political, social and personal standing, what influences effected his election, what pressure he would most quickly feel, his previous record in Congress and any earlier political record he may have. If he is a former member of the State Legislature, she should know what kind of bills he sponsored in the legislature and whether he is progressive or reactionary with regard to social and humanitarian measures. In short, she should know all about him, and most important of all, she should pass that information on to us in Washington in order that we may make the best possible use of it.

SPECIAL. In addition to your chairman for each Congressional District, you should appoint two members "at large" each of whom should hold herself responsible for one of your Senators in the same manner in which the Congressional District Chairman is responsible for the Representative from her District. Will you kindly send us the names of those two members-at-large as soon as possible?

V. STATE ORGANIZATION WORK

When your State is planning its organization work, can you not arrange with the State Organization Committee to put its full force into the Districts whose Representatives in Congress are on your "doubtful" list? It is possible that the reason why that Representative is "doubtful" is that the suffrage organization in his District is weak. If you could send an organizer into that District to stir up new suffrage sentiment or to make articulate and effective the feeling that is already there, the man might be swung into our ranks for the coming session. If you can accomplish this with even one of your "doubtful" men, you will have done much toward the end which we are all hoping to attain in this coming Congress. We look to the State Congressional Chairmen and their lieutenants in the Congressional District to make this hope an accomplished fact.

SUMMARY

We shall then expect from you:

I. An immediate report on the new members whose names are enclosed.

II. An early report of any delegations that you are able to arrange.

III. A list of members of your men's committees with their addresses.

IV. The names of the two members-at-large on your State Congressional Committee and the names of any District Chairmen who may have been appointed since your last report to us.

Your National Committee hopes to hear from you more frequently during the coming year. We are convinced that our fighting strength must lie chiefly in a connection with our state organizations represented by the State Congressional

Chairmen. We urge you, therefore, to share with us freely all the wisdom which you may have. Your suggestions and criticism at any time, as well as your active co-operation, will be heartily appreciated.

     Very cordially yours,
     Maud Wood Park, CHAIRMAN
     Ruth White, SECRETARY
     NATIONAL CONGRESSIONAL COMMITTEE

THE NEW YORK TIMES

"Silent, Silly, and Offensive" and
"Militants Get 3 Days; Lack Time to Starve"

JANUARY 11 AND JUNE 28, 1917

On January 10, 1917, Alice Paul, frustrated by Woodrow Wilson's continued refusal to endorse women's suffrage, took a dramatic step: the National Woman's Party began picketing the White House. Now a standard political tactic, it is often forgotten that suffragists were the first to deploy it. Each day, no matter what the weather, the "Silent Sentinels" took their posts outside the White House, making their case rhetorically with an ever-changing array of banners such as "Mr. President! How Long Will Women Have to Wait for Their Freedom" and "Democracy Should Begin at Home." *The New York Times*, never a friend of the women's suffrage movement, published an editorial the day after the first pickets were deployed, offering a hypothetical case of Socialist leaders deciding to do the same thing, only to declare it impossible "because they are men, and men's minds . . . are not made so that they would work in just this way." Six months later, once D.C. police had begun to arrest the picketers for obstructing traffic and disturbing the peace, the *Times* applauded the short sentences meted out to militant suffragists because they would keep them from going on hunger strikes.

SILENT, SILLY, AND OFFENSIVE.

Suppose this impossible piece of news should be printed to-morrow morning:

WASHINGTON, Jan. 11.—Socialist leaders visited the White House to ask the President to support Socialism. He replied that his views on that subject were unchanged. Upon leaving the White House they held an indignation meeting, at which it was resolved to post Socialist pickets hereafter about the White House grounds and to make it impossible for the President to enter or leave the building without encountering a picket bearing some device pleading the Socialist cause. The pickets will be known as "silent sentinels." At the indignation meeting a fund was started to finance the movement. EUGENE V. DEBS started the fund with $1,000, BOUCK WHITE contributed $100, and a prominent member of the I.W.W. pledged $100 a month.

The popular feeling at this organized harassment of the President can be imagined. It would not have much chance to gather headway, of course, because at the first manifestation of so impudent an attempt to annoy the head of the nation the police would unceremoniously assemble the offenders in a patrol wagon and deposit them in a body in the District jail. However, no one can imagine the Socialists, the Prohibitionists, or any other party conceiving of a performance at once so petty and so monstrous; one could not imagine even the I.W.W. attempting it. Why? Because they are men, and men's minds may be wicked, virtuous, wise, or foolish, but are not made so that they would work in just this way. There is something in the masculine mind that would shrink from a thing so compounded of pettiness and monstrosity, if for no other reason than that he would dimly feel the absurdity and futility of it.

Yet nobody is astonished that woman suffragists should propose such a thing, and therein lies a matter of deep concern in dealing with the whole woman suffrage question. The granting of suffrage would intrude into governmental affairs a great body of voters comprehending many whose minds do work in just that way, a great many to whom that compound of pettiness and monstrosity seems natural and proper. It would introduce into the management of the Government many persons so constituted that they can see nothing wrong in trying to influence the President himself by duress when they cannot convince him by argument. That the female mind is inferior to the male mind need not be assumed; that there is something about it essentially different, and that this difference is of a kind and degree that with votes for women would constitute a political danger is or ought to be plain to everybody.

———————

MILITANTS GET 3 DAYS; LACK TIME TO STARVE

Washington Jail Sentences Adjusted to Object of Preventing Hunger Strike.

Special to The New York Times.

WASHINGTON, June 27.—Six militant suffragists, members of the Woman's Party, are in the District of Columbia Jail tonight serving sentences of three days for obstructing the sidewalk by displaying propaganda banners at the gates of the White House. After a trial of three hours they were convicted and fined $25, with the alternative of spending three days in jail. They accepted the alternative, and, refusing to go in taxicabs, were taken to the jail in the "Black Maria." The women occupy six of the best cells, each fitted with running water and bath facilities.

Those who preferred jail to paying a fine are Miss Mabel Vernon of Nevada, Miss Virginia Arnold and Miss Anne Arneil of Delaware, Miss Katherine Morey of Boston, Miss Lavinia Dock of Pennsylvania, and Miss Maud Jamison of Virginia.

It is supposed that in imposing such a light sentence, Judge Mullowney had in mind that the women intended to attempt a hunger strike. They would hardly starve to death in three days.

In jail tonight the militants held a song service and suffrage meeting for the other forty women inmates. At a little organ in a carpeted corridor sat Miss Mabel Vernon, playing "God be with you till we meet again," and other hymns, while about her stood her companions, singing. Huddled on a stairway, beyond a barred partition, were thirty negro women and a few women who joined in the refrain. The jail matron gave the suffragists permission to address their fellow prisoners, and the meeting which followed developed fervent pleas for the cause of "Votes for Women."

ALICE HILL CHITTENDEN

Woman's Service or Woman Suffrage
MAY 1917

On April 6, 1917, the United States entered World War I by declaring war on Germany. Wilson's decision dramatically changed the playing field for suffrage. Alice Paul and the National Woman's Party refused to support the president and vowed to continue picketing the White House during wartime. In contrast, Carrie Chapman Catt patriotically offered the services of NAWSA to the war effort but refused to put aside suffrage activism. "We must do both," she said, anticipating that women's patriotic contributions would increase political pressure to give women the vote. Antisuffragists took a different stance. Not to be outdone in their commitment to preparedness and defense of the home front, they patriotically threw themselves into efforts like food conservation and selling war bonds at the expense of their organized antisuffrage activities, making it clear that they did not expect any specific payback for their patriotic service. "A truly patriotic woman wants no reward for her work," said Alice Hill Chittenden, the president of the New York State Association Opposed to Woman Suffrage. The increasing focus of antisuffragists on war work, coupled with the determination of New York suffragists to press forward with plans for a women's suffrage referendum, opened a window for a major suffrage victory in the state in November 1917.

———————————

I am sure there are no men or women in this audience to-night who have not within recent weeks rededicated themselves both in spirit and in action to the service of our beloved country. James Russell Lowell said:

> "Once to every man and nation comes the moment to decide
> In the strife of Truth and Falsehood for the good or evil side."

Within the past few weeks this nation has made a tremendous decision on the side of truth and righteousness, and I am sure we are all agreed that we are proud at last to stand just where we belong, by the side of those great nations fighting to uphold the principles for which we fought 140 years ago.

Our Anti-Suffrage Association feels it is especially justified in holding a patriotic meeting at this time, for over a year ago we passed a resolution endorsing the adoption of adequate measures for national defense, and declaring that women everywhere should strive to further the cause of preparedness by the study of the conservation of food supply and by thrift and economy in household management. Within recent months our association took an unqualified stand in favor of universal military service, believing that such service furthers the ideals of democracy and affirms individual responsibility to the State.

It is not necessary for me to dwell upon the war service which the women of this country are prepared to give in this crisis; you have but to read the daily papers to understand the variety of their activities. In all wars true women have always stood back of their men on the firing line and the American woman will not be found wanting in the coming months of stress and strife.

The women are, however, entering upon this service with two different attitudes. The president of the National Woman Suffrage Association announced at a public meeting in New York in March:

"We ask the vote as a war measure just as the emancipation of the slaves was a war measure. We ask it that women may have the feeling that they have been recognized as assets of the nation before that nation falls back upon them for war services," and some male advocates of woman suffrage have likewise expressed this sentiment.

This point of view is not only foreign, but abhorrent to anti-suffragists.

We stand ready to give the best there is in us in the service of our country at this time, without the least desire or expectation of any reward whatever for services rendered.

A truly patriotic woman wants no reward for her work.

Woman's service to the state as to the family is unselfish, unconditional and unremitting.

The suggestion that (the State) shall offer women the political payment of a vote for war services is a direct slur on woman's patriotism.

What the vast majority of women need and desire at this period of national crisis with the extra duties imposed by the war is exemption from political competition with men or with women. To force women into partisan politics is to divert women from non-partisan services.

It has been said the ballot is a symbol of liberty. We claim that its absence is a symbol of something more valuable to the State—the symbol of disinterested service. Think what it means to the State and to the nation, whether in time of peace or in time of war, to have a band of disinterested non-partisan citizens willing to do their "bit" without any thought of political reward or preferment.

We therefore protest most earnestly against the placing of a political price on woman's patriotism and ask the men of New York to vote "No" on the woman suffrage amendment next November.

LAVINIA DOCK

The Young Are at the Gates

JUNE 30, 1917

While the leaders of NAWSA steadily plodded along with their lobbying in Washington, D.C., and their organizational work in the states, the National Woman's Party became increasingly impatient. Their decision to picket the White House in January 1917 marked a bold step, and the NWP kept up the pressure for the next two years, despite increasing retribution from D.C. and federal officials. In this article for *The Suffragist*, Lavinia Dock (1858–1956) captures the uncompromising defiance that characterized many of the militants, contrasting their "spirit of revolt" with the "creeping paralysis of mental old age" of lawmakers and government officials. Ironically Dock was almost sixty years old, which suggests that this spirit of rebellion was not just confined to the chronologically young. Based at the Henry Street Settlement House on New York's Lower East Side, Dock was a trained nurse who played a key role in the professionalization of that field. She first joined Harriot Stanton Blatch's Equality League for Self-Supporting Women in 1907, but later gravitated toward Alice Paul and the National Woman's Party. Dock was one of the first six pickets to be arrested on the trumped-up charge of obstructing traffic in June 1917; when she refused to pay the fine, she spent three days in jail. Altogether Dock spent forty-three days in jail in support of the suffrage cause.

If anyone says to me: "Why the picketing for suffrage?" I should say in reply, "Why the fearless spirit of youth? Why does it exist and make itself manifest?"

Is it not really that our whole social world would be likely to harden and toughen into a dreary mass of conventional negations and forbiddances—into hopeless layers of conformity and caste, did not the irrepressible energy and animation of youth, when joined to the clear-eyed sham-hating intelligence of the young, break up the dull masses and set a new pace for laggards to follow?

What is this potent spirit of youth? Is it not the spirit of revolt, of rebellion against senseless and useless and deadening things? Most of all, against injustice, which is of all stupid things the stupidest?

Such thoughts come to one in looking over the field of the suffrage campaign and watching the pickets at the White House and at the Capitol, where sit the men who complacently enjoy the rights they deny to the women at their gates. Surely, nothing but the creeping paralysis of mental old age can account for the phenomenon of American men, law-makers, officials, administrators and guardians of the peace, who can see nothing in the intrepid young pickets with their banners, asking for bare justice, but common obstructors of traffic, naggers,—nuisances that are to be abolished by passing new, stupid laws forbidding and repressing, to add to the old junk heap of laws which forbid and repress? Can it be possible that any brain cells not totally crystallized could imagine that giving a stone instead of bread would answer conclusively the demand of the women who, because they are young, fearless, eager and rebellious are fighting and winning a cause for all women—even for those who are timid, conventional and inert?

A fatal error—a losing fight. The old stiff minds must give way. The old selfish minds must go. Obstructive reactionaries must move on. The young are at the Gates!

CAROLINE KATZENSTEIN

Prison Experiences with Emphasis on the Night of Terror

NOVEMBER 1917

Caroline Katzenstein (1888–1968) called the treatment of suffrage pickets in Washington, D.C., jails "one of the blackest pages in the history of the United States." For the "crime" of obstructing traffic, suffragists were arrested and thrown into jail for days and weeks at a time. Once incarcerated, suffragists endured horrendous conditions: inedible food, unsanitary cells, lack of legal rights, and casual brutality from prison guards, all designed to break their spirit. When their demand for political prisoner status was denied, many went on hunger strikes and were force-fed by prison authorities, a dangerous and demeaning procedure. The worst night of violence—called the "Night of Terror"—occurred in November 1917 at the Occoquan Workhouse, where a large contingent of suffragists refused to cooperate with authorities. Showing no restraint, the guards beat the women prisoners, inflicting serious bodily harm. When Lucy Burns (1879–1966), Alice Paul's lieutenant, defied the guards, they handcuffed her hands over her head and left her like that all night. Katzenstein herself never spent time in prison, but she later compiled a chilling compendium of what the suffragists endured in *Lifting the Curtain: The State and National Woman Suffrage Campaigns in Pennsylvania as I Saw Them* (1955). By the time her book was published, these sacrifices were a distant memory, but the militants' bravery helped push the suffrage amendment to final victory.

A fast is the sincerest form of prayer. It does not mean coercion of anyone. It does of course exercise pressure on individuals, even on Government, but this is a natural and moral result of an act of sacrifice. It stirs up sluggish consciences and inspires loving hearts to act. Those who have to bring about radical changes in human conditions and surroundings cannot do it without raising a ferment in society.*—*Mahatma Gandhi.*

---

* From "The Women in Gandhi's Life," by Eleanor Morton.

We have now arrived at one of the blackest pages in the history of the United States—the treatment of the suffrage pickets in the several prisons to which they were committed.

It is impossible to believe that the Administration did not know what was happening to the women confined in the District Jail, Occoquan Workhouse, and, later, in the abandoned Workhouse. The National Woman's Party, through its excellent publicity department, had told the story to the whole country and the press had given much space to it. Also, the three Commissioners, who governed the District of Columbia, the police court judges, the Chief of Police, the warden of the jail, and the superintendent of Occoquan Workhouse were all directly or indirectly answerable to the President.

The jail in which the pickets were first imprisoned was unspeakably dirty and was infested with vermin and rats. Julia Emory said the rats were so large and strong that prisoners at night could actually hear the light cell-chairs being moved by them. One night, she beat three of the rats, one after another off her bed.

The constant complaints of the prisoners finally brought action, but no results. The poison used by the prison officials did not decrease the rats, and the dog that was brought in seemed afraid of them.

But as bad as things were at the District Jail, they were much worse in the Workhouse at Occoquan. Occoquan is beautifully situated in picturesque country and its group of white buildings, its cultivated fields, and other attractive outside features tended to give the impression that it was a model institution. But its exterior belied its interior and the place left a sense of horror in the pickets confined in it. Even Lucy Burns, who seemed not to know fear, confessed that while there she suffered nameless and inexplicable terrors.

The women's ward was a long, clean, sunny room with two rows of beds, but those beds served a very mixed group of white and colored prisoners, and often the blankets on them had not been changed since used by the previous occupants. Indeed, the matron, who handled the bedclothes, was compelled to wear rubber gloves, while the Suffragists, even when they were put to painting the lavatories, had no such protection. There seemed to be a premeditated plan to humiliate the Suffragists who were all made to undress in the same bathroom and, without any privacy, to take shower baths one after another.

The punishment cells, situated in another building, were tiny brick rooms with tiny windows very high up. A young relative of one of the jail officials, wearing the uniform of an officer of the United States Army, would come into this building at night and look through the undraped grating of these cells. One time he unlocked the door and entered a room where two young pickets were sleeping. One of the pickets thought quickly enough to ask, "Are you a physician?" When the man said he was not, she covered her head with the bedclothes. He soon left.

In September, 1917, Lucy Burns filed charges with Commissioner Brownlow of the District of Columbia about conditions in the Workhouse. In that complaint, she said:

> The hygienic conditions have been improved at Occoquan since a group of Suffragists were imprisoned there. But they are still bad. The water they drink is kept in an open pail, from which it is ladled into a drinking cup. The prisoners frequently dip the drinking cup directly into the pail.
>
> The same piece of soap is used for every prisoner. As the prisoners in Occoquan are sometimes afflicted with disease, this practice is appallingly negligent.

In September, 1917, Mrs. Virginia Bovee, an officer of the Occoquan Workhouse, was discharged. I shall quote from Mrs. Bovee's affidavit:

> The blankets now being used in the prison have been in use since December without being washed or cleaned. Blankets are washed once a year. Officers are warned not to touch any of the bedding. The one officer who has to handle it is compelled by the regulations to wear rubber gloves while she does so. The sheets for the ordinary prisoners are not changed completely, even when one has gone and another takes her bed. Instead, the top sheet is put on the bottom, and one fresh sheet given them. I was not there when the Suffragists arrived, so I do not know how their bedding was arranged. I doubt whether the authorities would have dared to give them one soiled sheet.
>
> The prisoners with diseases are not always isolated, by any means. In the colored dormitory there are now two women in

advanced stages of consumption. Women suffering from syphilis, who have open sores, are put in the hospital. But those whose sores are temporarily healed are put in the same dormitory with the others. There have been several such in my dormitory.

When the prisoners come, they must undress and take a shower bath. For this they take a piece of soap from a bucket in the storeroom. When they have finished, they throw the soap back into the bucket. The Suffragists are permitted three showers a week, and have only these pieces of soap which are common to all inmates. There is no soap at all in the washrooms.

The beans, hominy, rice, cornmeal (which is exceedingly coarse, like chicken feed), and cereal have all had worms in them. Sometimes the worms float on top of the soup. Often they are found in the corn bread. The first Suffragists sent the worms to Whittaker on a spoon. On the farm is a fine herd of Holsteins. The cream is made into butter, and sold to the tuberculosis hospital in Washington. At the officers' table we have very good milk. The prisoners do not have any butter, or sugar, and no milk except by order of the doctor.

When the Superintendent of Occoquan told Katherine Rolston Fisher that no person under punishment—that is, in solitary confinement—was allowed to see legal counsel, she asked him, "Is that the law of the District of Columbia?" He replied, "It is the law here because it is the rule I make." In Miss Fisher's "From the Log of a Suffrage Picket," in the *Suffragist* of October 13, 1917, she tells more of her experiences and of what she saw while confined in Occoquan:

> We learned what it is to live under a one-man law . . . Our Counsel after one visit was forbidden, upon a pretext, to come again.
>
> On Tuesday, September 18, we were made to exchange our new gingham uniforms for old spotted gray gowns covered with patches upon patches; were taken to a shed to get pails of paint and brushes, and were set to painting the dormitory lavatories and toilets. By this time we were all hungry and more or less weak from lack of food. A large brush wet with white paint weighs at least two pounds. Much of the work required our standing on a table or stepladder and reaching above our heads. I think the wiser of us rested at every opportunity, but we did not refuse to work.
>
> All this time we had been without Counsel for eight days. . . .

The food, which had been a little better, about the middle of the month reached its zenith of rancidity and putridity. We tried to make a sport of the worm hunt, each table announcing its score of weevils and worms. When one prisoner reached the score of fifteen worms during one meal, it spoiled our zest for the game. . . .

We had protested from the beginning against doing any manual labor upon such bad and scanty food as we received. . . .

Mrs. Kendall, who was the most emphatic in her refusal, was promptly locked up on bread and water. The punishment makes a story to be told by itself. It clouded our days constantly while it lasted and we knew not half of what she suffered. . . .

All this time—five days—Mrs. Kendall was locked up, her pallid face visible through the windows to those few Suffragists who had opportunity and ventured to go to her window for a moment at the risk of sharing her fate.

The imprisoned Suffragists managed to have samples of their food smuggled out to the well-known food expert, Dr. Harvey W. Wiley. Dr. Wiley, aroused by these samples, asked the Board of Charities to let him make an investigation of the food. "A Diet of Worms won one revolution, and I expect it will win another," said he.

It was, however, to the group of pickets arrested November 14, 1917, and sentenced to Occoquan, that the most outrageous things happened. They went through an experience that was rightly called *The Night of Terror*. Sixteen of these Suffragists, immediately upon their arrival at the Workhouse, began a hunger-strike as a protest against the Government's refusal to treat them as political offenders. They demanded the privilege of exercising, receiving mail and visitors, buying food and reading matter.

When these prisoners arrived at the Workhouse, Superintendent Whittaker was away; and they were kept in the office of one of the small cottages. Because the Suffragists were still making their demand to be treated as political prisoners, Mrs. Lawrence Lewis, acting as spokesman for the group, refused to answer the usual questions put to them by Mrs. Herndon, the woman at the desk, saying that she would wait and talk to Mr. Whittaker.

"You will sit here all night then," said Mrs. Herndon. After the Suffragists had waited for hours, Mrs. Herndon tried again to get them to register, but they made no reply. Soon several men entered the room.

"You had better answer up, or it will be the worse for you," said one man. Another man said, "I will handle you so you'll be sorry you made me." Still there was no reply.

Suddenly the door was flung open and Superintendent Whittaker rushed in followed by a number of other men. It was later discovered that he had just left a conference of the District of Columbia Commissioners at the White House. The Suffragists had been sitting or lying on the floor. Mrs. Lawrence Lewis rose and began to speak, saying, "We demand to be treated as political pris—" when the Superintendent interrupted with, "You shut up! I have men here glad to handle you!" "Seize her!"

Mrs. Lewis was seized by two men and dragged away from the other Suffragists. Another man sprang at Mrs. Mary A. Nolan, a frail, lame woman over seventy years of age. In describing this experience, Mrs. Nolan said:

> I am used to being careful of my bad foot, and I remember saying: "I will come with you; do not drag me. I have a lame foot." But I was dragged down the steps and away into the dark. I did not have my feet on the ground. I guess that saved me.

All that Mrs. Nolan recalls of the black outside was the approach to a low, dark building from which flew a brilliantly lighted American flag. As she entered the hall, a man wearing the uniform of Occoquan, brandished a stick and called out, "Damn you! Get in there!" Before Mrs. Nolan was shot through the hall, Dorothy Day, a very slight, delicate girl, was brought in by two men who were twisting her arms above her head. She was suddenly lifted by her captors and her body was brought down twice over the back of an iron bench. "The damned Suffrager! My mother ain't no Suffrager! I will put you through hell!" called out one of the men handling Dorothy Day. Then Mrs. Nolan was pulled down a corridor and pushed through a door.

Back of Mrs. Nolan, and dragged along as she had been, came Mrs. Cosu. Mrs. Nolan's fall was broken by the bed, but Mrs. Cosu hit the wall. In a few minutes, Mrs. Lewis, all doubled over, was thrown into the same room. Her head struck the iron bed and she fell senseless to the floor. Mrs. Nolan and Mrs. Cosu, thinking that Mrs. Lewis was dead, began to weep, but they finally revived her. Later, Mrs. Cosu was seized with a heart attack and was desperately ill the rest of the night. Despite the women's repeated calls for medical help, no attention was paid to them by either the woman or the man guard in the corridor. Provided with only two mattresses and two blankets, the prisoners shivered all through the night.

But iron bars did not prevent Lucy Burns from taking charge of the situation as she always did when arrested. In order to find out if all the pickets were alive and there, she began in her clear, beautiful voice to call the roll. To the guard's order to "Shut up!" she paid not the slightest attention. "Where is Mrs. Lewis?" she demanded. Mrs. Cosu replied, "They have just thrown her in here." The guard yelled that he would put them in strait-jackets if they spoke again. This so frightened Mrs. Nolan and Mrs. Cosu that for a time they kept still. Lucy Burns, however, continued to call the roll, and, when at the guard's order she refused to stop, her wrists were handcuffed and the handcuffs were fastened above her head to the cell door. Also she was threatened with a buckle gag. Although little Julia Emory, in her cell opposite Lucy Burns', could do nothing to help, she made a sympathetic protest by putting her hands above her head exactly as Lucy Burns' hands were bound and stood before her door until Lucy Burns was released. The handcuffs were worn by Lucy Burns all night.

In an effort to lower Lucy Burns' morale, the authorities took her clothes away from her. When Mr. O'Brien, the N.W.P. lawyer, visited her, she was lying on a cot in a dark cell, wrapped in blankets. On his return to Headquarters, he was full of admiration for her remarkable spirit and said that she was as much herself as if they had been talking in the drawing room at Headquarters. Also news from Occoquan reached Headquarters through Mrs. Nolan after her release at the end of her six-day sentence. It was these things that made the Suffragists decide on habeas corpus proceedings. Mr. O'Brien applied to the United States District Court at Richmond for this writ. It was granted returnable on November 27. Fearing, however, that the women might by that time have collapsed from harsh treatment and starvation, Mr. O'Brien made a second journey to see Judge Waddill and succeeded in having the date of the hearing advanced to the 23rd of November.

In order to serve the writ on Superintendent Whittaker, Mr. O'Brien had to resort to a ruse. When, on the night of November 21, he called at Mr. Whittaker's home and was told the superintendent was not there, he left and telephoned from a nearby point that he would not return until the morning. Instead, he returned immediately, found Mr. Whittaker at home, and served the papers.

For some reason unknown to the others, Mrs. Henry Butterworth was taken away from the other Suffragists and put in a prison where there were only men.

Mrs. Paula Jakobi gave further details of the Night of Terror and of the days that followed it. Three Suffragists were thrust into each of the cold, unventilated cells that contained a single bed and a mattress on the floor. Both floor and blankets were "filthy." No facilities for washing in the morning were provided, and no food was offered although the women had had nothing to eat since noon of the previous day. Faint and exhausted by the treatment they had received, the women, at eight in the morning, were ordered before the superintendent for questioning.

The Rights of Political Prisoners being denied them, the Suffragists began a hunger strike. The first day's fasting did not make Mrs. Jakobi ill, only weak. The second day brought slight nausea and headache; the third day, fever and dizziness, the fever remaining and causing very dry, peeling skin and swollen lips. By this time, she was both weaker and more nervous and she showed symptoms of aphasia. She could remember no names and found it impossible to read.

The women, she said, were summoned so often and so suddenly from their rooms to see Mr. Whittaker or to be transferred to other rooms that they were never sure when they should be searched and when their few remaining treasures would be taken from them. Conspicuous among these *treasures* were stubs of pencils and bits of writing paper for exchanging messages inside the prison or for smuggling them outside to friends and relatives. Everything in prison seems conducive to concealment, and Mrs. Jakobi was especially ingenious in avoiding discovery. With woman's main tool, a hairpin, she ripped a small hole in the ticking of her pillow and hid stubs of pencils in this innocent-looking object. Her paper she hid behind steam radiator pipes. Dimes and nickels for the trusty she placed in a row over the sill of her door.

One evening a great commotion was heard in the corridor. Doors that did not lock were held, and there were rapid footsteps to and fro. Disturbing sounds came from the adjoining room. Lucy Burns was being forcibly fed. There were more hurried footsteps and the men went to Mrs. Lewis' room. Fifteen minutes later the two women were hurried into an ambulance and taken away—where, neither Mrs. Jakobi nor the other pickets were told. "We had," continued Mrs. Jakobi, "visions of being separated, hurried out of sight to oblivion, somewhere away from everyone we knew."

A note from Lucy Burns, smuggled out of the Washington District Jail to which she and Mrs. Lewis had been transferred, proved that the anxiety expressed by Mrs. Jakobi over their sudden disappearance from Occoquan was justified. As usual, neither of the women was told why they were sent to Washington, but they were simply told that they must go. When they refused to be examined by Dr. Gannon, the District Jail physician, they were dragged through the halls by force, their clothing partly removed by force, and an examination was made—heart tested, blood pressure and pulse taken.

When the pickets from Occoquan arrived at the Alexandria Court House, they learned the reason for the sudden disappearance of Lucy Burns and Mrs. Lewis to "parts unknown." It was to prevent their appearance at Court, despite the pleading of Counsel for the National Woman's Party that they be present at the trial. But Dudley Field Malone cleverly outwitted the authorities. The following day both Lucy Burns and Mrs. Lewis were at the trial.

From all over the country protests were sent to Washington. This public reaction, plus the prospect of forcibly feeding such a large number of women, seems to have had a direct influence on the Government, because three days later all of the imprisoned pickets were released.

Early in December a mass meeting in honor of the released pickets was held in Washington. The Belasco Theatre was crowded, and, despite the bitter cold, an overflow meeting of four thousand stood outside to listen to an address by Elsie Hill. And this time there was ample police protection. The police reserves, who had often in the past arrested the pickets, were on hand to keep order among the thousands of persons gathered in honor of these same Suffragists.

Eighty-one pickets that had served prison sentences marched down the aisles of the Theatre, carrying purple, white, and gold banners, and also banners with messages inscribed on them. They took their places on the stage. Each of these "prisoners of freedom" was presented with a silver pin that was a small replica of the cell doors they had so often faced. The speakers were Maud Younger, Mrs. O. H. P. Belmont, Dudley Field Malone, Mrs. Thomas Hepburn, and Mrs. William Kent.

Eighty-six thousand, three hundred and eighty-six dollars was raised in honor of the pickets that night. This sum included two contributions of thirty cents and fifty cents, which deeply touched the women. These two contributions from Occoquan, sent "because the Suffragettes helped us so much down there," were accepted on behalf of the pickets by Mrs. John Rogers, Jr., who gave "tenderest thanks for this help from our comrades in the Workhouse."

While the Suffragists had done much to improve conditions for their fellow-prisoners, much remained undone. Over and over again, the other prisoners asked whether things might not be improved for them if they, too, should go on a hunger-strike. But the Suffragists had to explain that such a protest would be useless to persons having no organization back of them. In every way open to the Suffragists, however, they tried to lend a helping hand to these unfortunates.

WOODROW WILSON

Address to the Senate on
the Nineteenth Amendment

SEPTEMBER 30, 1918

Few would ever consider Woodrow Wilson a friend of women's suffrage. In fact a good case can be made that women won the vote in spite of the president. A southerner, Wilson held very traditional notions about women, seeing them as helpmates to men, who were supposed to do the more important public work while women presided over home and hearth. Once he left academe for elected office, he tempered his original antisuffragism by saying that he would give women's suffrage "consideration" and approach it with an "open mind," then fudged the issue by saying he supported it as a private citizen in the state of New Jersey but couldn't possibly take a stand as president. He also made sure that the Democratic Party platform (which he controlled) left the issue to the states. But spurred in part by political expediency and in response to unremitting pressure from NWP militants and NAWSA lobbyists, Wilson had a dramatic change of heart. On September 30, 1918, he delivered a speech on the Senate floor in support of a federal suffrage amendment as "a vitally necessary war measure." Doris Stevens called it "a truly beautiful appeal" and Maud Wood Park found it "the most impassioned" speech he had ever uttered, a rare moment of agreement between the two suffrage camps. But it did not change a single vote in the Democratic-controlled Senate, where the next day the measure came up two votes short.

Speaking Copy 30 Sept., 1918.

GENTLEMEN OF THE SENATE: The unusual circumstances of a world war in which we stand and are judged in the view not only of our own people and our own consciences but also in the view of all nations and peoples will, I hope, justify in your thought, as it does in mine, the message I have come to bring you. I regard the concurrence of the Senate in the constitutional amendment proposing the extension of the suffrage to women as vitally essential to the successful prosecution of the great war of humanity in which we are engaged. I have come to urge upon you the considerations which have led me to that conclusion. It is not only my privilege, it is also my duty

543

to apprise you of every circumstance and element involved in this momentous struggle which seems to me to affect its very processes and its outcome. It is my duty to win the war and to ask you to remove every obstacle that stands in the way of winning it.

I had assumed that the Senate would concur in the amendment because no disputable principle is involved but only a question of the method by which the suffrage is to be extended to women. There is and can be no party issue involved in it. Both of our great national parties are pledged, explicitly pledged, to equality of suffrage for the women of the country. Neither party, therefore, it seems to me, can justify hesitation as to the method of obtaining it, can rightfully hesitate to substitute federal initiative for state initiative, if the early adoption of the measure is necessary to the successful prosecution of the war and if the method of state action proposed in the party platforms of 1916 is impracticable within any reasonable length of time, if practicable at all. And its adoption is, in my judgment, clearly necessary to the successful prosecution of the war and the successful realization of the objects for which the war is being fought.

That judgment I take the liberty of urging upon you with solemn earnestness for reasons which I shall state very frankly and which I shall hope will seem as conclusive to you as they seem to me.

This is a peoples' war and the peoples' thinking constitutes its atmosphere and morale, not the predelections of the drawing room or the political considerations of the caucus. If we be indeed democrats and wish to lead the world to democracy, we can ask other peoples to accept in proof of our sincerity and our ability to lead them whither they wish to be led nothing less persuasive and convincing than our actions. Our professions will not suffice. Verification must be forthcoming when verification is asked for. And in this case verification is asked for,—asked for in this particular matter. You ask by whom? Not through diplomatic channels; not by Foreign Ministers. Not by the intimations of parliaments. It is asked for by the anxious, expectant, suffering peoples with whom we are dealing and who are willing to put their destinies in some measure in our hands, if they are sure that we wish the same things that they do. I do not speak by conjecture. It is not alone the voices of statesmen and of newspapers that reach me, and the voices of foolish and intemperate agitators do not reach me at all. Through many, many channels I have been made aware what the plain, struggling, workaday folk are thinking upon whom the chief terror and suffering of this tragic war falls. They are looking to the great, powerful, famous Democracy of the West to lead them to the new day for which they have so long waited; and they think, in their logical simplicity, that democracy means that women shall play their part in affairs alongside men and upon an equal footing with them. If we reject measures like this, in ignorance or defiance of what a new age has brought forth, of what they have seen but we have not, they will cease to believe in us; they will cease to follow or to trust us. They have seen their own governments accept this interpretation of democracy,—seen old governments like that of Great Britain, which did not profess to be democratic, promise readily and as of course this justice to women, though they had before refused it, the strange revelations of this war having made many things new and plain, to governments as well as to peoples.

Are we alone to refuse to learn the lesson? Are we alone to ask and take the utmost that our women can give,—service and sacrifice of every kind,—and still say we do not see what title that gives them to stand by our sides in the guidance of the affairs of their nation and ours? We have made partners of the women in this war; shall we admit them only to a partnership of suffering and sacrifice and toil and not to a partnership of privilege and right? This war could not have been fought, either by the other nations engaged or by America, if it had not been for the services of the women,—services rendered in every sphere,—not merely in the fields of effort in which we have been accustomed to see them work, but wherever men have worked and upon the very skirts and edges of the battle itself. We shall not only be distrusted but shall deserve to be distrusted if we do not enfranchise them with the fullest possible enfranchisement, as it is now certain that the other great free nations will enfranchise them. We cannot isolate our thought or our action in such a matter from the thought of the rest of the world. We must either conform or deliberately reject what they propose and resign the leadership of liberal minds to others.

The women of America are too noble and too intelligent and too devoted to be slackers whether you give or withhold this thing that is mere justice; but I know the magic it will work in their thoughts and spirits if you give it them. I propose it as I would propose to admit soldiers to the suffrage, the men fighting in the field for our liberties and the liberties of the world, were they excluded. The tasks of the women lie at the very heart of the war, and I know how much stronger that heart will beat if you do this just thing and show our women that you trust them as much as you in fact and of necessity depend upon them.

Have I said that the passage of this amendment is a vitally necessary war measure, and do you need further proof? Do you stand in need of the trust of other peoples and of the trust of our own women? Is that trust an asset or is it not? I tell you plainly, as the commander-in-chief of our armies and of the gallant men in our fleets, as the present spokesman of this people in our dealings with the men and women throughout the world who are now our partners, as the responsible head of a great government which stands and is questioned day by day as to its purposes, its principles, its hopes, whether they be serviceable to men everywhere or only to itself, and who must himself answer these questionings or be shamed, as the guide and director of forces caught in the grip of war and by the same token in need of every material and spiritual resource this great nation possesses,—I tell you plainly that this measure which I urge upon you is vital to the winning of the war and to the energies alike of preparation and of battle.

And not to the winning of the war only. It is vital to the right solution of the great problems which we must settle, and settle immediately, when the war is over. We shall need then in our vision of affairs, as we have never needed them before, the sympathy and insight and clear moral instinct of the women of the world. The problems of that time will strike to the roots of many things that we have not hitherto questioned, and I for one believe that our safety in those questioning days, as well as our comprehension of matters that touch society to the quick, will depend upon the direct and authoritative participation of women in our counsels. We shall need their moral sense to pre-serve what is right and fine and worthy in our system of life as well as to discover just what it is that ought to be purified and reformed. Without their counsellings we shall be only half wise.

That is my case. This is my appeal. Many may deny its validity, if they choose, but no one can brush aside or answer the arguments upon which it is based. The executive tasks of this war rest upon me. I ask that you lighten them and place in my hands instruments, spiritual instruments, which I do not now possess, which I sorely need, and which I have daily to apologise for not being able to employ.

THE SUFFRAGIST

Reminding the President When He Landed in Boston

MARCH 1, 1919

Six weeks after Woodrow Wilson's speech to the Senate (see previous document), the November 11, 1918, armistice ended World War I. Wilson spent increasing amounts of his presidency in Europe, his attention focused on negotiations for the peace treaty and his plans for the League of Nations. After Republicans won both houses of Congress in November 1918, suffrage supporters tried one more time to get the amendment through the Democrat-controlled Senate before the new Senate session would begin in March, but came up one vote short. Meanwhile, the National Woman's Party kept the pressure on Wilson by holding public demonstrations that emphasized the disconnect of making the world safe for democracy when half of this nation remained unfree. This protest in Boston on February 24, 1919, reported in *The Suffragist*, resulted in the jailing of local suffragists for the "crime" of speaking on Boston Common without a permit. (One of their banners parroted a quote from Wilson's September 30 speech.) Except for one more demonstration in New York in March, this protest marked the end of NWP's militant actions. From that point on, all attention focused on Congress. President Wilson called a special session for May 19, and the suffrage amendment "galloped" through the House 304–89. On June 4, 1919, it passed the Senate by a margin of two votes. The amendment now had to be ratified by thirty-six states, far more than the number where women currently voted.

Historic Boston! Boston, the "cradle of liberty"—"where men draw in freedom with the very air they breathe," etc., etc. A fitting place, surely, for the emissary of freedom abroad to land on his return to this country from his patriotic mission. A fitting place, too, in which to remind him that he is returning to a nation in fact and deed but one-half free. Yet who is there to point out the fitness in the rest of the story—in the story that there in Boston, before the State House, and on old Boston Common, twenty-five American women were arrested for unfurling the banners of woman's freedom—arrested for asking for liberty?

This is not Czarist Russia of three years ago, of which we

read. It is Boston, in the State of Massachusetts, in the United States of America. Nor is it the Boston of harsh witchcraft days. It is Boston in this year of enlightenment and of triumphant democracy—in this victory year of Nineteen Hundred and Nineteen.

On Monday morning, February 24, all Boston turned out to see President Wilson on his return from European council tables. True to their promise to take part in this big demonstration, a large group of Massachusetts suffragists, members of the National Woman's Party, was of the crowd. Boston papers had several days previously carried large headlines and a front page story about the President's welcome—a large proportion of which space had been devoted to the announced plans of the women for this occasion, and to the counter plans of the police to establish a dead line beyond which no suffragists should be allowed to penetrate to worry the President with their foolish pleas for liberty. The political descendants of old Boston's magistrates and "sires of freedom" were going to see to it that the day should not be marred by any such untoward event as a demand for justice and democracy under the very nose of the world's champion of democracy, and on the sacred soil of old Boston Common, where fighting Colonists rebelled against King George!

But the women were there. Marching through the lines of marines which held the crowds back from the reviewing stand where the President was to appear, they took their station and unfurled their banners. For nearly an hour the line of brave, bright color stood there—then they were all whirled away in patrols to the house of detention. But they were there, and they were seen, and the deep significance of the fact that they should have to be there at all could not be escaped by the most casual passerby.

The lettered banner which addressed the President on this his homecoming from affairs of foreign democracy was composed by Mrs. Samuel Warren and was carried by Mrs. Lois Warren Shaw, of Manchester, N. H., formerly of Massachusetts, and Miss Ruth Small, of Boston, organizer of the Massachusetts Branch of the National Woman's Party. The banner read:

"MR. PRESIDENT, YOU SAID IN THE SENATE ON SEP-
TEMBER 30, 'WE SHALL NOT ONLY BE DISTRUSTED
BUT WE SHALL DESERVE TO BE DISTRUSTED IF WE
DO NOT ENFRANCHISE WOMEN.' YOU ALONE CAN
REMOVE THIS DISTRUST NOW BY SECURING THE
ONE VOTE NEEDED TO PASS THE SUFFRAGE AMEND-
MENT BEFORE MARCH 4."

The American flag held the place of honor at the head of the
line, borne by Miss Katherine Morey, of Boston. On either side
of the stars and stripes were those two lettered banners now
become historic in the drama of women's struggle for freedom.

"MR. PRESIDENT, HOW LONG MUST WOMEN WAIT
FOR LIBERTY?"
"MR. PRESIDENT, WHAT WILL YOU DO FOR WOMAN
SUFFRAGE?"

These were backed up staunchly by more and more banners
of purple, white and gold.

Among the women arrested for taking part in this demon-
stration were many of the most prominent and best known of
Boston. Mrs. Jessica Henderson, Miss Ruth Small, Miss Lou
Daniels, Mrs. Frank Page, Miss Josephine Collins, Miss Berry
Pottier, Miss Wilma Henderson, Mrs. Irving Gross, were all of
Boston; others were Mrs. George Roewer, of Belmont, Mas-
sachusetts; Miss Frances Fowler, of Brookline; Miss Camilla
Whitcomb, of Worcester; Mrs. H. L. Turner, of Allston; Miss
Eleanor Calnan, of Methuen; Miss Betty Connelly, of Newton;
Miss Betty Gram, of Portland, Ore.; Mrs. Lois Warren Shaw,
of Manchester, N. H.; Miss Rose Lewis, of New York; and Mrs.
H. D. Russian, of Detroit.

All of the women arrested were held for some time at the
police station and then sent to the House of Detention to await
trial the next morning. They were charged with "loitering more
than seven minutes."

In the afternoon, undismayed by the result of the morning's demonstration, another demonstration was held, this one
taking the form of a watchfire—such as has made famous the
strip of sidewalk before the White House in Washington—on

Boston Common. While the President was speaking in Mechanics Hall across the square, in this watchfire, before vast crowds which far surpassed any crowd previously gathered to witness a suffrage demonstration, the words of the President on democracy and liberty were burned almost as they were spoken. Mrs. Louise Sykes, of Cambridge, Mass., whose late husband was president of the Connecticut College for Women, presided over the burning. Miss Elsie Hill, of Norwalk, Connecticut, daughter of the late Congressman Hill of that state, Mrs. C. C. Jack, wife of a Harvard Professor, and Mrs. Mortimer Warren, of Boston, whose husband is the head of one of the Base Hospitals in France, were arrested for speaking and were taken off to the house of detention to join their comrades of the morning. Mrs. Robert Treat Whitehouse, of Portland, Maine, State Chairman of the Woman's Party, and Mrs. Agnes H. Morey, Massachusetts State Chairman, each made speeches to the assembled throngs, and were not disturbed by the police. Mrs. Mortimer Warren and Mrs. Jack, after being held by the police for some time, were released. Miss Hill, however, was detained on the charge of speaking without a permit.

In the Hall the President spoke to a great audience about America's part in the fight for Right and Liberty and Democracy, and on the Common, women spoke to another vast audience about the way in which these words were not being carried out in deeds.

The big, the amazing thing about the protest demonstration on Boston Common was the very fact of its bigness, of its immensity. There were the thousands left on the streets and on the Common from the parade, and the thousands who streamed out of Mechanics Hall across the square, and they gathered there about the suffragists and their torches as a center, seething to and fro in vast masses striving to reach a point where they could hear the women speaking and catch a glimpse of the ceremonies of the burning of the President's words.

From three o'clock in the afternoon until six in the evening the women held the center of the vast scene. Not for a long, long time had old Boston witnessed such a spectacle. The population seemed to realize that they were seeing history in the making, that theirs was the opportunity to behold what in after years will be regarded as a remarkable thing—the sight of women forced to a public demonstration to ask for liberty—and they made the most of their opportunity to behold this thing. They stayed, and watched, and listened. And for those three hours of the afternoon the women spoke without interruption to their immense audience; then at six came the order for arrest. Why the long interval, unmolested? Who knows? And the charge? "Speaking on Boston Common without a permit!" A permit had previously been applied for, but had been neither granted nor refused, so the suffragists availed themselves of the ancient American privilege of free speech, of the free right of protest against injustice, and—spoke. Spoke for three hours before their speech became an offence and themselves liable to arrest.

Arrested for speaking for freedom on Boston Common! Shades of the worthy gentlemen of the Teaparty!—And arrested for "loitering more than seven minutes on the public highway."

Said Mrs. Agnes Morey, in charge of the demonstration:

"It is a most extraordinary thing. Thousands loitered from curiosity on the day the President arrived. Twenty-two loitered for liberty, and only those who loitered for liberty were arrested!"

On that day, February 25, the women were sentenced to ten days in jail, and are now serving that sentence. An account of the trial will appear in next week's Suffragist.

SOUTHERN WOMEN'S LEAGUE

*Declaration of Principles for the Rejection of the
Proposed Susan B. Anthony Amendment to the
Constitution of the United States*

DECEMBER 1919

Under Carrie Chapman Catt's "Winning Plan," southern suffrage leaders felt overlooked because state referendums were not a high priority; to their minds, because of the region's deep commitment to states' rights and state sovereignty, especially within the dominant Democratic Party, gaining suffrage by that route was highly preferable to the imposition of a constitutional amendment from outside. But by 1919, most southern suffragists had resigned themselves to the federal route, with Laura Clay (1849–1941) and Kate Gordon the notable holdouts. It was left to the southern antisuffrage forces, mainly led by women, to articulate the reasons why a federal amendment should be rejected. In December 1919, the Southern Women's League for the Rejection of the Proposed Susan B. Anthony Amendment to the Constitution of the United States was formed in Alabama. As the logo on one of their handbills declared, "We Serve that our States May Live, and Living, Preserve the Union." In the end the only southern states to ratify the Nineteenth Amendment were Kentucky, Texas, Arkansas, and Tennessee.

---

1. We believe in the political principle of Local Self Government and that **State Sovereignty is essential** to the Liberty, Happiness, True Progress, and Welfare of the American People.

2. **WE ARE UNALTERABLY OPPOSED TO THE ADOPTION OF THE SUSAN B. ANTHONY AMENDMENT TO THE CONSTITUTION OF THE UNITED STATES**, which Amendment will force the unrestricted ballot upon unwilling majorities in Southern States, and will place the control of the electorate outside the Sovereign State.

3. We deny the Justice of the Compulsory Regulation of the Electorate of our States by a **combination** of other States, who have no sympathetic understanding of our peculiar Social and Racial problems.

4. We oppose any measure that threatens the continuation of **Anglo-Saxon** domination of Social and Political affairs in each and every State of the Union without strife and bloodshed which would inevitably follow an attempt to overthrow it.

5. We oppose **SOCIALISM, BOLSHEVISM, RADICAL-ISM** and all the Social disorders that are now disturbing the world and are rapidly encroaching upon our own Republic, and believe that these disorders will be aided and multiplied and more effectually forced upon the Conservative States such as we represent, through the adoption of the Susan B. Anthony Amendment.

6. We declare that the REJECTION of the Susan B. Anthony Amendment to the Constitution of the United States, in **NO** way affects the rights of the several individual States, **TO SO AMEND THEIR CONSTITUTIONS,** as to enfranchise the women of those States, where a **majority** so elect; and to throw safeguards and limitations upon electoral qualifications as local conditions demand.

7. We believe that in its present form, we live under the fairest and most liberal Government in the world, and desire to see it perpetuated in order that generations coming after us may enjoy the same Liberty in the Pursuit of Happiness we have enjoyed; and to that end we pledge our most earnest and continued efforts in behalf of the **Rejection of the Susan B. Anthony Amendment to the Constitution of the United States,** and call upon **all true Americans** to join us in this fight.

MAUD WOOD PARK

A Perfect Moment

AUGUST 1920

Planning was already well advanced for the ratification fight before the Senate vote on June 4, 1919. The most pressing challenge was the threshold of a two-thirds majority: supporters had to win ratification in thirty-six states, but opponents only had to prevail in thirteen to stop the amendment. It did not have an expiration date for ratification, which helped project a certain sense of inevitability, but the suffragists were determined to have the amendment in place in time for women to vote in the 1920 presidential election. As Maud Wood Park retells the story here, it all came down to Tennessee. After overcoming a few last-minute legal challenges, the Nineteenth Amendment was certified as part of the U.S. Constitution on August 26, 1920, now celebrated as Women's Equality Day.

Ratification by at least thirty-six states—that was the mountainous load that Mrs. Catt took upon her shoulders as soon as the amendment was through the Congress. In fact, she assumed that burden long before the work in Washington was completed. Her plans were therefore all ready—plans that, like her ratification dress, had been made, outdated and remade more than once.

In her own words:

> Every Legislature had been polled, Governors had been interviewed, the press kept informed of the necessary procedure of the campaign, and an expectant, eager army, thoroughly well-equipped and trained, was waiting for the next move. Before the sun set on June 4, telegrams had been sent to all Governors where special legislative sessions would be necessary, urging that such sessions be called. Instructions for still more intensive campaigns with Governors, legislators and the press were wired to State auxiliaries to the National [American Woman] Suffrage Association, and when the sun rose on June 5 the campaign was already under full speed. . . .
>
> The Legislatures of Illinois and Wisconsin being on the eve of adjournment, the Suffrage Amendment was wired to both from

555

Washington for ratification. Thereupon started a lively contest between the two States for first place. Illinois newspapers helped by calling loudly upon the Legislature to be "First"; her Governor, Frank O. Lowden, helped by sending a spirited message to the Legislature; and her Assembly helped by introducing into the Senate a resolution for ratification twenty-four hours after the passage of the amendment and before the receipt of the official notification. Action was taken on June 10.

Two letters in the alphabet came near losing Illinois first place. A sentence in the joint resolution transmitted from the federal Secretary of State's office to the Illinois Governor read "which shall be valid for all events and purposes as part of the constitution." "Events" should have been "intents." Legal authorities said that ratification was not invalidated, but to be safe the Illinois Legislature re-ratified June 17.

Wisconsin ratified on the same day. . . . Wisconsin had the distinction of filing her certificate first.*

Ratification followed in rapid succession in Michigan, Kansas, Ohio and New York: "six ratifications in as many days." Then three states, Pennsylvania, Massachusetts and Texas, in which the antisuffragists had been hopeful of defeat, disappointed them by ratifying; and special sessions in Iowa and Missouri brought the number of ratifications within a month up to eleven. But the total of thirty-six was still a long way off.

Surprisingly, the far-western states, which had been counted on to ratify at once, were dilatory. Some of their political leaders took the selfish ground that inasmuch as their women were already enfranchised by state action, they had nothing to gain by the federal amendment.

In July, in order to get definite pledges of special sessions from governors, Mrs. Catt sent four women as "envoys": two, who were Republicans, to Minnesota, North Dakota, Washington, Oregon, Idaho and Wyoming; and two, who were Democrats, to Nevada, Arizona, New Mexico, Utah and Oklahoma.

That month Arkansas, Nebraska and Montana all ratified by means of special sessions. They were followed in September by Minnesota, New Hampshire and Utah, making seventeen in all.

---

* Carrie Chapman Catt and Nettie Rogers Shuler, *Woman Suffrage and Politics* (New York: Charles Scribner's Sons, 1923), pp. 343–46.

Then came a pause, inexplicable in view of the continued delay of most of the early suffrage states—a delay that led Mrs. Catt to "put on her bonnet" and set forth to hold conferences in twelve states, with "Wake up, America!" as the slogan of her efforts. The trip brought calls for special sessions in California, North Dakota, Colorado, Oregon and Nevada, though in one of those states the suffragists had to get the legislators to agree to pay their own expenses before the governor would consent to call the session. By the end of the year, Maine, California, North Dakota, South Dakota and Colorado brought the total number of ratifications up to twenty-two.

By that time opponents had begun a series of systematic attempts to find legal flaws in the ratifications or to have them held up by a referendum to the voters. The problem of the antisuffragists, who had only to keep thirteen states from ratifying, was far simpler than that of the suffragists, who had to get favorable action from thirty-six. But, in spite of the difficulties that the opposition put in the way, five states ratified in January, 1920: Rhode Island, Kentucky, Oregon, Indiana and Wyoming. Five others followed in February: New Jersey, Idaho, Arizona, New Mexico and Oklahoma.

Mrs. Catt knew that the opposition had grown exceedingly bitter with every one of the later states, and in West Virginia, the thirty-fourth, the outcome was so close that a state senator who was in California when the special session was called and to whom the opponents refused a pair, was obliged to hurry back across the continent in order to cast the deciding vote in favor of ratification. Then, in March, 1920, Washington, the last of the far-western states, by action of a special session, brought the total number of ratifications up to thirty-five. The fight then narrowed down to the crucial thirty-sixth state.

At first Vermont seemed the most promising field, and, to overcome the objection of cost of a special session, the suffragists secured the pledges of a majority of the legislators to pay their own expenses. But even then Governor Percival W. Clement, who was a confirmed opponent, refused to call the session. Governor Marcus H. Holcomb of Connecticut, also an opponent, took a similar course. Efforts were then concentrated upon Delaware, where, after terrific work by both sides, ratification was defeated in the lower House, making Delaware

the tenth state and the only one north of the Mason-Dixon
Line to take adverse action.

Happily for the suffrage forces, their grievous disappointment about Delaware was offset that same week by a decision
of the United States Supreme Court that a referendum on a
federal amendment, such as the antisuffragists were seeking in
several states, would be illegal.

The last hope of getting a thirty-sixth state in time for
women to vote in the presidential election of 1920 rested
then in Tennessee. But there the Governor had refused to call
a special session because he believed that a provision of the
state constitution required action in regard to ratification to
be taken at a regular session. In this emergency the suffragists
appealed to President Wilson, and, through the instrumentality of Helen Gardener, the President asked the Department
of Justice to render an opinion about the applicability of the
Supreme Court's recent decision to the situation in Tennessee.
When the Department rendered an opinion to the effect that
the state constitution could not put an obstacle in the way of
a method of ratification permitted by the federal Constitution,
the President sent a telegram to the Governor urging a special
session of the Tennessee legislature. After considerable delay
the session was called for August 9.

Mrs. Catt, who had gone to Tennessee on June 15 with the
idea of expediting the preparations, stayed on through the dev-
astating heat of the intervening weeks because she realized how
relentless the opposition had become and how unscrupulous its
tactics were likely to be. Her insight proved prophetic, for every
known or imaginable device for preventing or delaying a favorable vote was tried during the twelve days of the special session.

In spite of the excitement, Mrs. Catt held resolutely to her
conviction that her presence during the legislative session debates would be an almost unbearable strain with no corresponding advantage for the cause; but through the open windows of
her room in a nearby hotel, she could often hear cheers and
applause, without knowing until some of the suffrage workers
came to report which side was ahead.

Although the resolution for ratification passed the Senate
with comparatively little difficulty, the struggle in the House

was marked by a long series of dramatic surprises in which first one side and then the other appeared to have the upper hand. Even when a vote of 49 in favor to 47 against was taken on August 18, a motion to reconsider held up the decision for three days longer, during which 38 opposed legislators tried the trick, at that time a novel one, of fleeing to a neighboring state in the hope of preventing a quorum. When that device failed and reconsideration was voted down on August 21, the Speaker of the House, who was the floor leader of the opposition, announced that an injunction against forwarding the certificate of ratification to Washington had been issued by one of the judges of the state Supreme Court. Two days were spent by the suffragists in getting the injunction dissolved, and on the twenty-fourth the certificate was signed by the Governor and started on its way to Washington.

Meanwhile Helen Gardener had arranged with the Department of State to have the certificate examined as soon as it came so that the Secretary of State would be able to take the final step of announcing that the amendment had been adopted. We were fearful that any delay would give opportunity for further injunctions to be brought by the antisuffragists, who were leaving no stone unturned in their efforts to hold up the announcement of ratification.

At four o'clock on the morning of August 26, the certificate from Tennessee reached Washington, and the Solicitor-General, who had sat up all night waiting for it, made the examination needed before the signature of the Secretary of State could be affixed.

Shortly after eight, that same morning, Mrs. Catt, on her way back from Tennessee, arrived in Washington, and the first thing she did was to telephone to the office of the Secretary of State. Mrs. Harriet Taylor Upton and I were in the room with her and heard her ask him whether the Tennessee certificate had been received. In a moment she put down the telephone, turned to us and said, "The Secretary has signed the proclamation, and he wants us to go over to his office and see it before he sends it out."

So quietly as that, we learned that the last step in the enfranchisement of women in the United States had been taken and the struggle of more than seventy years brought to a successful end.

We were all too stunned to make any comment until we were in the cab on our way to the Department of State, where we almost had to stick pins into ourselves to realize that the simple document at which we were looking was, in reality, the long sought charter of liberty for the women of this country.

Then Mrs. Catt had a conference with the Solicitor-General about the legal aspects of the fight in Tennessee, for she anticipated that the antisuffragists would bring suit on that score, as later they did without success.

That evening we had a jubilee meeting at Poli's Theatre, where every seat was taken and standing space was crowded to the last limit permitted by the fire regulations. The greetings and congratulations of the President were presented by the Secretary of State. Mrs. Harriet Taylor Upton and Miss Charl Ormond Williams, who had had important roles in the campaign in Tennessee, told about the "ways that were dark and the tricks that were vain" on the part of the opponents there, and then Mrs. Catt made one of her greatest speeches.

Her journey to New York the next day was as truly a triumphal procession as anything I ever expect to see. At every station at which the train stopped, deputations of women, many of them smiling through tears, were waiting with their arms full of flowers for her. When she reached the Pennsylvania Terminal in New York, Senator William M. Calder, a Republican, was standing at the door of her car; and Governor Alfred E. Smith was waiting on the main floor to voice the official congratulations of the state of New York on the outstanding achievement of its "distinguished citizen, Carrie Chapman Catt." The Woman Suffrage Party of New York City presented her with a huge sheaf of her favorite blue delphinium and then formed a procession, led by mounted police and a fine band, with the other officers of the National American Woman Suffrage Association marching, like a guard of honor, beside her motorcar on its way to the celebration at the Hotel Astor.

There is a beautiful picture of her taken just before the procession started, when she stood in the car, the flowers in her arms and her face alight with the joy of triumphant home-coming.

No one of us who saw her then will ever cease to be thankful for that perfect moment when she must have felt to the full the happiness of a great task completed.

PART FOUR
1918-1965

GERTRUDE FOSTER BROWN

From *Your Vote and How to Use It*
1918

Now that women had won the vote, they needed to learn how to exercise it effectively. That was the premise behind the founding of the League of Women Voters at the final convention of the National American Woman Suffrage Association in February 1920. It was also the premise of *Your Vote and How to Use It*, a book published in 1918 after New York women won the vote in their successful state referendum the year before. Geared to the "busy housewife or the overworked woman in the factory," it offered a basic civics course designed to connect politics and government to women's daily lives, differentiating between the scope of federal, state, and local governments, surveying who could vote and how naturalization laws worked, explaining how political parties and elections operated, and offering short primers on taxation and the legal system. The manual styled itself as "a book for amateur citizens written by an amateur citizen" but its author, Gertrude Foster Brown, was not a typical new voter. A pianist and lecturer who had pursued a successful career on the stage, Brown became president of the New York State Woman Suffrage Association in 1914. Suffrage ran in her family: her husband, Ray Brown, was the author of *How It Feels to be the Husband of a Suffragette* (see pages 468–472 in this volume). Like many other suffrage activists, Brown joined the League of Women Voters after the ratification of the Nineteenth Amendment.

――――――――――

POLITICS AND WOMAN'S INTERESTS

The average woman has never thought of politics as having an intimate relation to her daily life. She has not realized that government has a direct effect on the comfort and happiness of the family in the home, on the successful upbringing of children, and on the health and safety of men and women workers.

She has known vaguely that government controls the fundamental question of war or peace; that it has to do with taxation; that it handles the mail, but that it also plays a large part in domestic and social life is a fact that she has only recently been learning.

With the rapid extension of the vote to women, especially the recent granting of suffrage to the women of New York State, there is a new and wide-spread interest in how government works, and a realization of the importance of good government and the dire peril of bad government. Women are conscientious; they are accepting their new responsibilities with much seriousness. They are eager to learn how to be good citizens. The war also has made everybody think. It has made government seem a more personal affair.

WHAT IS GOVERNMENT?

Government is the management of those common affairs of a people which can be handled in a more effective and more economical way by a community acting together than by each individual acting for himself.

In a sparsely settled community government is less apparent than in a city. Its functions are simple. Sometimes it does not seem very important. But as people congregate closer together it becomes more complicated and comes in closer and closer touch with the individual and family life.

For example, a man living in the country may rely on himself to protect his home and property; but in the city life and property are better protected by a police force than if each individual citizen had to provide his own protection. A woman in a pioneer country may bring up her child as she pleases. She may teach him when and how she chooses. But as population increases and government is established, a large part of the child's training is dictated by it. He must go to school at a certain age; he must stay there so many hours a day; he must study certain things in a certain way. He cannot be put to work until he has reached a certain age. If he contracts a contagious disease the city takes control of the case.

Directly and indirectly the government in a city affects a woman's life and interests in innumerable ways.

She is dependent on it for the light and sunshine that comes into her home. Laws concerning housing and building and tenement departments of government are very important to the health, comfort, and even decency of the family. She is dependent on government for the safety of the milk she has to feed her baby. The health of the family depends as much on the city department of health as on the mother's care. It is of the utmost importance to the city mother that the streets be kept clean, because they are usually the only place that her children have in which to play. The street cleaning department, therefore, touches her closely. It is of vital moment to her that the streets be kept free of criminal influence, therefore the management of the police department is of great importance to her. If the town is run "wide open" it may mean that her husband's wages may be dissipated. The way in which the excise law and the laws against gambling are enforced is a matter which deeply concerns her.

If she lives in the country the relation of government to her life is not so varied, but she is still dependent on it for the education of her child, for the socializing influences of the community, and for much of the business prosperity of the farm. Are telephone connections cheap, are the roads passable at all seasons, are good market facilities provided? These are all questions that greatly affect her welfare, and they depend largely on the government.

It is the business of government to maintain peace and to provide for the common defense.

This is a function of government so fundamental as to need little comment. It is the first essential to the safe existence of the home.

It is the business of government to assure justice and equality of treatment to all citizens.

This becomes more difficult as population increases and life grows more complicated. Nearly every human being to-day is dependent on the work of other people for most of the necessities, as well as the comforts and conveniences, of life. The food that we eat, the cotton and wool in the garments we wear, the coal that heats our houses, we owe to the toil of other people who in return may be dependent on us for something that they use. It is a matter that concerns every one of us that in producing these things that we use human life shall be safeguarded, that living wages shall be paid, and that standards of civilization shall be maintained and advanced.

As individuals we cannot control conditions even for ourselves, as individuals we cannot control them for other people; but all of us working together in government can secure these fundamental necessities for every one of us.

Since government in a democracy is made by the people themselves, it is a responsibility that every one should share to help secure these common needs.

It is also a function of modern government to raise the standard of health, education, and living.

Plato said, "Only that state is healthy and can thrive which unceasingly endeavors to improve the individuals who constitute it."

Society must be protected from vicious and destructive influence; the intelligence and knowledge of all the people are needed for the common good.

As human beings have become dependent on one another, the well-being or the degradation of one individual or family does not stop there. It strongly influences the welfare of other individuals and families. For their own protection people have not only the right, but the obligation to make a government that shall foster and advance the common welfare.

The basis of good government is the golden rule. To help secure for others the protection that you demand for yourself is part of the obligation of good citizenship. The honesty and efficiency of government in a republic like the United States depend on the voters; on their sense of responsibility, and on the intelligence with which they use their power. The feeling of responsibility of each individual, for the public welfare, cannot be too highly developed.

Democracy can only be a success in the degree that the people who make that democracy are determined that it shall deal with justice, and that it shall offer opportunity to every one within its borders. They must also be vigilant to see that it shall deal wisely with their common problems as they develop.

To be a citizen of such a democracy and to have the power to help it grow along these lines, to be able to serve one's country loyally in the full efficiency of citizenship, are great privileges.

FAIRCHILD v. HUGHES and LESER v. GARNETT Rulings

1922

The Nineteenth Amendment faced legal challenges even before ratification. In early 1922, the Supreme Court decided two cases, filed before ratification was completed, that affirmed the validity of the amendment. In *Fairchild v. Hughes* the court ruled that general citizens in a state with women's suffrage lacked the standing to challenge the validity of the constitutional amendment. That suit had been filed in July 1920 and the court rightly saw it as an attempt to circumvent the ratification process then still ongoing. *Leser v. Garnett*, also decided on the same day in 1922, raised more substantive issues about whether the federal government had the power to regulate voting in the states and whether state legislatures could ratify the amendment if their state constitutions prohibited women's voting, but once again, the Supreme Court ruled unanimously in favor of the newest addition to the U.S. Constitution. The next year, the Supreme Court pointed to the dramatic changes in women's citizenship institutionalized by the Nineteenth Amendment as a factor in striking down a federal law requiring a minimum wage for women workers in *Adkins v. Children's Hospital of the District of Columbia* (1923), reasoning in part that women did not need special protection because of their newly won political rights. Unlike the Fourteenth Amendment, which continues to have a profound impact on American jurisprudence, the Nineteenth Amendment has rarely been at the center of key constitutional litigation.

Fairchild v. *Hughes*

MR. JUSTICE BRANDEIS delivered the opinion of the court.

On July 7, 1920, Charles S. Fairchild of New York brought this suit in the Supreme Court of the District of Columbia against the Secretary of State and the Attorney General. The prayers of the bill are that "the so-called Suffrage Amendment [the Nineteenth to the Federal Constitution] be declared unconstitutional and void"; that the Secretary of State be restrained from issuing any proclamation declaring that it has been ratified; and that the Attorney General be restrained from enforcing it. There is also a prayer for general relief and for an interlocutory injunction. The plaintiff, and others on whose behalf he sues, are citizens of the United States, taxpayers and members of the American Constitutional League, a voluntary association which describes itself as engaged in diffusing "knowledge as to the fundamental principles of the American Constitution, and especially that which gives to each State the right to determine for itself the question as to who should exercise the elective franchise therein."

The claim to relief was rested upon the following allegations. The legislatures of thirty-four of the States have passed resolutions purporting to ratify the Suffrage Amendment; and from one other State the Secretary of State of the United States has received a certificate to that effect purporting to come from the proper officer. The proposed Amendment cannot, for reasons stated, be made a part of the Constitution through ratification by the legislatures; and there are also specific reasons why the resolutions already adopted in several of the States are inoperative. But the Secretary has declared that he is without power to examine into the validity of alleged acts of ratification, and that, upon receiving from one additional State the customary certificate, he will issue a proclamation declaring that the Suffrage Amendment has been adopted. Furthermore, "a force bill" has been introduced in the Senate which provides fine and imprisonment for any person who refuses to allow women to vote; and if the bill is enacted, the Attorney General will be required to enforce its provisions. The threatened proclamation of the adoption of the Amendment would not be conclusive of its validity, but it would lead election officers to permit women to vote in States whose constitutions limit suffrage to men. This would prevent ascertainment of the wishes of the legally qualified voters, and elections, state and federal, would be void. Free citizens would be deprived of their right to have such elections duly held; the effectiveness of their votes would be diminished; and election expenses would be nearly doubled. Thus irremediable mischief would result.

The Supreme Court of the District granted a rule to show cause why an interlocutory injunction should not issue. The return was promptly made; and the defendants also moved to dismiss the bill. On July 14, 1920, the rule was discharged; a decree was entered dismissing the bill; and an appeal was taken to the Court of Appeals of the District. The Secretary, having soon thereafter received a certificate of ratification from the thirty-sixth State, proclaimed, on August 26, 1920, the adoption of the Nineteenth Amendment. The defendants then moved to dismiss or affirm. The Court of Appeals affirmed the decree on the authority of *United States* v. *Colby*, 49 App. D. C. 358; 265 Fed. 998, where it had refused to compel the Secretary to cancel the proclamation declaring that the Eighteenth Amendment had been adopted. The grounds of that decision were that the validity of the Amendment could be in no way affected by an order of cancellation; that it depended on the ratifications by the States and not on the proclamation; and that the proclamation was unimpeachable, since the Secretary was required, under Rev. Stats., § 205, to issue the proclamation upon receiving from three-fourths of the States official notice of ratification and had no power to determine whether or not the notices received stated the truth. But we have no occasion to consider these grounds of decision.

Plaintiff's alleged interest in the question submitted is not such as to afford a basis for this proceeding. It is frankly a proceeding to have the Nineteenth Amendment declared void. In form it is a bill in equity; but it is not a case within the meaning of § 2 of Article III of the Constitution, which confers judicial power on the federal courts, for no claim of plaintiff is "brought before the court[s] for determination by such regular proceedings as are established by law or custom for the protection or enforcement of rights, or the prevention, redress, or punishment of wrongs." See *In re Pacific Railway Commission*, 32 Fed. 241, 255, quoted in *Muskrat* v. *United States*, 219 U. S. 346, 356. The alleged wrongful act of the Secretary of State, said to be threatening, is the issuing of a proclamation which plaintiff asserts will be vain but will mislead election officers. The alleged wrongful act of the Attorney General, said to be threatening, is the enforcement, as against election officers, of the penalties to be imposed by a contemplated act of Congress which plaintiff asserts would be unconstitutional. But plaintiff is not an election officer; and the State of New York, of which he is a citizen, had previously amended its own constitution so as to grant the

suffrage to women and had ratified this Amendment. Plaintiff
has only the right, possessed by every citizen, to require that
the Government be administered according to law and that the
public moneys be not wasted. Obviously this general right does
not entitle a private citizen to institute in the federal courts a
suit to secure by indirection a determination whether a statute
if passed, or a constitutional amendment about to be adopted,
will be valid. Compare *Giles* v. *Harris*, 189 U. S. 475; *Tyler* v.
Judges of Court of Registration, 179 U. S. 405.

Decree affirmed.

Leser et al. v. *Garnett et al.*

MR. JUSTICE BRANDEIS delivered the opinion of the court.

On October 12, 1920, Cecilia Streett Waters and Mary D.
Randolph, citizens of Maryland, applied for and were granted
registration as qualified voters in Baltimore City. To have their
names stricken from the list Oscar Leser and others brought
this suit in the court of Common Pleas. The only ground of
disqualification alleged was that the applicants for registration
were women, whereas the constitution of Maryland limits the
suffrage to men. Ratification of the proposed Amendment to
the Federal Constitution, now known as the Nineteenth, 41
Stat. 362, had been proclaimed on August 26, 1920, 41 Stat.
1823, pursuant to Rev. Stats., § 205. The Legislature of Maryland had refused to ratify it. The petitioners contended, on
several grounds, that the Amendment had not become part of
the Federal Constitution. The trial court overruled the contentions and dismissed the petition. Its judgment was affirmed
by the Court of Appeals of the State, 139 Md. 46; and the case
comes here on writ of error. That writ must be dismissed; but
the petition for a writ of certiorari, also duly filed, is granted.
The laws of Maryland authorized such a suit by a qualified
voter against the Board of Registry. Whether the Nineteenth
Amendment has become part of the Federal Constitution is the
question presented for decision.

The first contention is that the power of amendment conferred by the Federal Constitution and sought to be exercised does not extend to this Amendment, because of its character. The argument is that so great an addition to the electorate, if made without the State's consent, destroys its autonomy as a political body. This Amendment is in character and phraseology precisely similar to the Fifteenth. For each the same method of adoption was pursued. One cannot be valid and the other invalid. That the Fifteenth is valid, although rejected by six States including Maryland, has been recognized and acted on for half a century. See *United States* v. *Reese*, 92 U. S. 214; *Neal* v. *Delaware*, 103 U. S. 370; *Guinn* v. *United States*, 238 U. S. 347; *Myers* v. *Anderson*, 238 U. S. 368. The suggestion that the Fifteenth was incorporated in the Constitution, not in accordance with law, but practically as a war measure which has been validated by acquiescence, cannot be entertained.

The second contention is that in the constitutions of several of the thirty-six States named in the proclamation of the Secretary of State there are provisions which render inoperative the alleged ratifications by their legislatures. The argument is that by reason of these specific provisions the legislatures were without power to ratify. But the function of a state legislature in ratifying a proposed amendment to the Federal Constitution, like the function of Congress in proposing the amendment, is a federal function derived from the Federal Constitution; and it transcends any limitations sought to be imposed by the people of a State. *Hawke* v. *Smith, No. 1*, 253 U. S. 221; *Hawke* v. *Smith, No. 2*, 253 U. S. 231; *National Prohibition Cases*, 253 U. S. 350, 386.

The remaining contention is that the ratifying resolutions of Tennessee and of West Virginia are inoperative, because adopted in violation of the rules of legislative procedure prevailing in the respective States. The question raised may have been rendered immaterial by the fact that since the proclamation the legislatures of two other States—Connecticut and Vermont—have adopted resolutions of ratification. But a broader answer should be given to the contention. The proclamation by the Secretary certified that from official documents on file in the Department of State it appeared that the proposed Amendment was ratified by the legislatures of thirty-six States, and that it "has become valid to all intents and purposes as a part of the Constitution of the United States." As the legislatures of Tennessee and of West Virginia had power to adopt the resolutions of ratification, official notice to the Secretary, duly authenticated, that they had done so was conclusive upon him, and, being certified to by his proclamation, is conclusive upon the courts. The rule declared in *Field* v. *Clark*, 143 U. S. 649, 669–673, is applicable here. See also *Harwood* v. *Wentworth*, 162 U. S. 547, 562.

Affirmed.

INDIAN CITIZENSHIP ACT

1924

On June 2, 1924, President Calvin Coolidge (1872–1933) signed legislation extending U.S. citizenship to all American Indians, including American Indian women who had been excluded from the purview of the Nineteenth Amendment because of their noncitizen status. A concern for gender equity was not a driving factor in the action, which was designed to reduce inefficiency and corruption in the Bureau of Indian Affairs. While the language of the bill explicitly stated that granting citizenship would not threaten tribal sovereignty (in effect offering a kind of dual citizenship to indigenous people), this unilateral action was still controversial because it theoretically threatened the integrity of traditional tribal governance structures by incorporating them into the U.S. polity. American Indian women stood on both sides of the debate. According to Yankton Sioux Zitkála-Šá (1876–1938), also known as Gertrude Simmons Bonnin, "The Red man asks for a simple thing—citizenship in the land that was once his own—America." But Wyandotte Jane Zane Gordon (c. 1871–1963) disagreed: "No government organized . . . can incorporate into its citizenship anybody or bodies without the[ir] formal consent." Even with their new citizenship status, American Indians faced widespread barriers to voting on the state and local levels until the passage of the Voting Rights Acts of 1965 and 1975.

Sixty-eighth Congress of the United States of America:
At the First Session,
Begun and held at the City of Washington on Monday,
the third day of December, one thousand
nine hundred and twenty-three.

AN ACT
To authorize the Secretary of the Interior to issue
certificates of citizenship to Indians.

Be it enacted by the Senate and House of Representatives of the United States of America in Congress assembled, That all non-citizen Indians born within the territorial limits of the United States be, and they are hereby, declared to be citizens of the United States: *Provided*, That the granting of such citizenship shall not in any manner impair or otherwise affect the right of any Indian to tribal or other property.

F. H. Gillett
Speaker of the House of Representatives.

A. B. Cummins
Acting President pro tempore of the Senate.

Approved June 2, 1924.

Calvin Coolidge

DORIS STEVENS AND
DR. ALICE HAMILTON

The "Blanket" Amendment—A Debate

AUGUST 1924

One of the most divisive issues for political women in the immediate post-suffrage years was the Equal Rights Amendment, introduced in 1923 by Alice Paul on behalf of the National Woman's Party. The text of the amendment was deceptively simple—"Equality of rights under the law shall not be denied or abridged by the United States or by any state on account of sex"—but it caused a fundamental split between those who supported protective legislation for women workers and those who insisted that men and women be treated equally before the law. In 1924, *The Forum* sponsored a debate on the issue. Doris Stevens (1888–1963), a veteran suffrage organizer, was the principal spokesperson for the National Woman's Party on this issue throughout the 1920s. (The ERA was often called the "blanket amendment" because it would cover all discriminatory laws, rather than dealing with them on a case-by-case basis.) Speaking against the amendment was Dr. Alice Hamilton (1869–1970), a pioneer in the field of industrial medicine and the first woman faculty member at Harvard. Both sides agreed that in an ideal world, men and women would enjoy protection in the workplace, but few courts were likely to extend such benefits to men in the conservative judicial climate of the 1920s.

I—SUFFRAGE DOES NOT GIVE EQUALITY

DORIS STEVENS

When the baby-carriage was invented, the press and the pulpit cried out in alarm, "What is to become of the home, that sacred foundation of the State? Whither will go the morals of women when they no longer have to carry their young in their arms?" And then they answered their own questions. "There will be no limit to the corruption which will follow when women can wheel their offspring far from home. There will be no check on the temptations offered by men to roaming mothers." A whole battalion of sedate mothers, suddenly turned flippant, irresponsible, courting moral hazards, practically racing each other through the lanes to get away from their chosen partners

577

and into amorous difficulties! Such was the picture painted by the male alarmists of that period.

Let us pass over the absurd prediction of sudden and demoralizing change in the habits of mothers when possessed of a new mechanical device. Let us rather deplore that unflattering picture of themselves which men, in their anxiety, inadvertently painted. Did they really wish to keep women unwillingly tied to them by enforced papoosing? Did they really find themselves so unattractive as husbands and fathers that the innocent baby-carriage was all that stood between them and unfaithful, licentious wives and mothers? Is the male, of himself, so insecure that he becomes perennially frantic when he sees the female performing any act of self-direction? If the opponents of baby-carriages had taken to banner bearing, their slogans would doubtless have read: "Some women go astray while wheeling their babies. Therefore abolish perambulators and protect women!"

Now the intellectual calibre of the opposition to the present demand to improve further the position of women is scarcely more distinguished. It has its roots in the same fears, the same prejudices, and the same feelings of insecurity. It is rarely malicious. When articulate at all, it springs from misunderstanding. But whether on a high or a low level, opposition must be met and answered. The fact that we are here engaged in a debate proves that the equality program is not accepted without defense, even by leading periodicals.

When women finally got the right to vote, after seventy-five years of agitation in the United States, many good citizens sighed with relief and said, "Now that's over. The woman problem is disposed of." But was it? Exactly what do women want now? Just this. They ask the same rights, in law and in custom, with which every man is now endowed through the accident of being born a male. Frail and inadequate as these rights may be, compared to those rights we would like to see enjoyed by all men, women are nevertheless still deprived of many of them. To establish equality between men and women in law and in custom is the task undertaken by the National Woman's Party, an organization composed of women diverse in political, religious, and economic faith, but united on the platform of improving the position of women.

There is not a single State in the Union in which men and

women live under equal protection of the law. There is not a State which does not in some respects still reflect toward women the attitude of either the old English Common Law or the Napoleonic Code. Woman is still conceived to be in subjection to, and under the control of the husband, if married, or of the male members of the family, if unmarried. In most of the States the father and mother have been made equal guardians of their children, but many of these States still deny the mother equal rights to the earnings and services of the children. Among the poor this is often a serious handicap to the mother. In New York, fathers are preferred to mothers as controllers of the services, earnings, and real estate of the children. In two States the father can still will away the custody of the child from the mother. In two States the earnings of the wife outside the home belong to the husband. In forty States the husband owns the services of his wife in the home. In most of these States this means that the husband recovers the damages for the loss of these services, should the wife meet with an injury. A wife then cannot collect for her own suffering, for in the eyes of such laws, it is not the wife who is injured, but the husband is assumed to be injured through the loss of her services to him. More than half the States do not permit women to serve on juries. Some legislators oppose jury service for women because of "moral hazard" of deliberating in a room with men. Other legislators favor jury service for women, for it means extending to women a service which men are seldom willing to perform. In only a third of the States is prostitution a crime for the male as well as the female.

With the removal of all legal discriminations against women solely on account of sex, women will possess with men:

Equal control of their children
Equal control of their property
Equal control of their earnings
Equal right to make contracts
Equal citizenship rights
Equal inheritance rights
Equal control of national, state, and local government
Equal opportunities in schools and universities
Equal opportunities in government service
Equal opportunities in professions and industries
Equal pay for equal work

Of course, no law on earth can compel a woman to take her inheritance, for instance, if she prefers to give it to her brother or to some one else. But such an act would then become voluntary, not compulsory. No law can compel a woman to sit in the Cabinet or act as Ambassador if she does not wish to do so. But neither the law nor any other human-made restriction will, under a régime of equality, be able to prevent her from doing either of these things if she so chooses.

The plan of action is the next point to consider. The National Woman's Party, out of its experience in amending the national Constitution granting universal suffrage to women, proposes to secure the adoption of the further amendment now before Congress: "Men and women shall have equal rights throughout the United States and every place subject to its jurisdiction. Congress shall have power to enforce this article by appropriate legislation."

The Federal method is preferred to the State-by-State method for the following reasons. All broad, general principles governing a country should be written into the supreme law of the land. National action is more dignified, and the more intelligent road to pursue; five hundred and thirty-one men in Congress are more easily moved than the entire electorate. A national campaign unites the resources of women, whereas State-by-State action divides the resources of women and makes their work infinitely more wasteful. Time and money are important factors. In a century, with vast sums expended, each separate State statute could eventually be changed to establish legal equality. But why should women take the long, tedious, expensive route when a shorter one lies before them? Each gain by State action in any given State can be taken away by a subsequent legislature through repeal, as has already twice happened in the case of State laws. Gains to be safeguarded and made permanent must be written into the national Constitution. Once passed by Congress and ratified by the State legislatures, all existing discriminatory State laws will have to conform to the new Federal amendment, just as did the existing State laws when the national suffrage amendment was ratified. Furthermore it will prevent new sex discriminations from being written into the law.

In so far as opposition to the foregoing plan has crystallized at all, three main objections stand out. First, that change in the laws should come slowly, statute by statute. Our answer to this objection is found in the preceding paragraph on Federal action. Second, that maternity legislation and widows' pensions will be wiped out. Now maternity legislation is designed to assist a special group of women under special circumstances. It is not special legislation for *women*; it is for *mothers*. All women are not mothers. All mothers are not in constant need of maternity protection. That group of women whom this legislation is written to protect, will still be protected by such special legislation, just as workmen's compensation, written to cover special groups of men, and soldiers' bonuses and funds for invalided soldiers, are written to protect them. The amendment under consideration will in no way affect such special legislation, for the simple reason that it is not based on sex, but upon the special need of a given group under certain circumstances. The same is true of widows' pensions. Such pensions are written for the benefit of the child, and are being given more and more to whichever parent of the child survives, widow or widower. In Colorado the law already provides that such pensions shall be administered either by widow or widower. Is there any reason to believe that a needy widower should not have that same protection for the child that a deserving widow has? The final objection says: Grant political, social, and civil equality to women, but do not give equality to women in industry.

Here lies the heart of the whole controversy. It is not astonishing, but very intelligent indeed, that the battle should center on the point of woman's right to sell her labor on the same terms as man. For unless she is able equally to compete, to earn, to control, and to invest her money, unless in short woman's economic position is made more secure, certainly she cannot establish equality in fact. She will have won merely the shadow of power without essential and authentic substance.

Those who would limit only women to certain occupations and to certain restricted hours of work, base their program of discrimination on two points, the "moral hazard" to women and their biological inferiority. It is a philosophy which would penalize all women because some women are morally frail and physically weak. It asks women to set their pace with the weakest member of their sex. All men are not strong. Happily it has

not occurred to society to limit the development of all men because some are weak. Would these protectionists be willing to
say that because some men-members of the Cabinet had been
suspected of moral frailty, no men should henceforth serve as
Cabinet Ministers? This principle of penalizing the strong because some are weak, which has been abandoned by enlightened educationalists, now awaits rejection in the industrial field.
Natural fitness, not "protection," will determine the extent of
competition.

Dock work, dray work, and coal-heaving are occupations
open to all men, and yet no one has ever seen the weakest members of the species rush into these occupations. Women will
be quite as sensible and adroit at avoiding work beyond their
strength as men have been, once they have a free choice. What
reason is there to believe that if tomorrow the whole industrial
field were opened to women on the same terms as men, women
would insist on doing the most menial tasks in the world, the
most difficult, the tasks for which they are the least fitted? May
it not rather be that men know the reverse will be true, which
has led some labor leaders to rush to the banner of "protection
for women only"? Furthermore, if this argument were sound,
then obviously women ought to have all the delightful office
jobs, ought to be relieved of such tasks as scrubbing floors
in office buildings, and ought to turn over this work to the
stronger male members of the species. If it is only their physical
strength that stands in their way, they should abandon drudgery by day and baby-tending by night, and, with the greatest
possible speed, become railroad presidents, bank presidents,
and other executive officers, whose weekly golf game is the
chief physical tax.

No one really believes today that the morals of an adult
grow stronger in the ratio that he is protected. Women as well
as men become more responsible in the realm of morals only
when all are free to behave according to the dictates of social
conscience. And obviously, if the streets are unsafe at night
for those women whose needs oblige them to work at night,
the answer is most emphatically not to prevent women from
earning their livelihood, but to make the streets safe for their
coming and going.

But, it is argued, women are more easily exploited in industry than men. There are reasons for this outside of sex, not the least of which is the shocking neglect by men's labor organizations to organize women in their trades. When women first went from the home into industry, they carried with them, among other things, the psychology of unpaid workers. For as workers in the home they had always done the unpaid work of the world. They had their keep, but neither wages nor partnership profits. And so they shrank from asking adequate pay. They thought they should be grateful for being permitted to play in the big game at all. They were docile. They were exploited. Gradually they became bolder. Gradually they entered the better-paid trades and professions. Gradually they asked higher remuneration. It is only now that they are well on the road to matching their wits and their intelligences with men, that women are told they must be "protected." Protection is a delusion. Protection, no matter how benevolent in motive, unless applied alike to both sexes, amounts to actual penalization.

The Woman's Party is not an industrial organization and therefore does not presume to say whether workers shall work eight or four hours a day, or what wages shall be paid for such work; whether more leisure for the masses shall be got by legislation or unionism. In the best interests of women, it stands against restrictions which are not alike for both sexes, and which, therefore, constantly limit the scope of women's entry into the field of more desirable and better paid work. It believes that no human being, man or woman, should be exploited by industry. As firmly it believes that just so long as sex is made the artificial barrier to labor-selling, merit can never become the criterion of an applicant for a job.

Woman's emancipation was delayed once upon a time while theologians debated the nature of her soul. Emancipation is still being delayed while good people debate with tender concern the strength of her body. There is nothing new in the biological argument. It has been brought forward, simultaneously with the moral argument, every time women have moved a step forward. Its ghost walked abroad when women asked to be permitted to speak in public; later, when they asked for an education; again when they asked to be allowed to enter the professions; and still more recently when they asked for the vote. The belief in woman's frailty, in spite of all the gray, spirit-breaking drudgery she has performed, is so profoundly woven into the fabric of a people's thought that it has to be challenged over and over again. It will be routed in the present controversy.

With each new gain, women become stronger, more robust, more competent and more useful members of society, and these ghosts vanish. Freer opportunities of self-expression have never damaged any group of human beings. No group of men or women was ever enlightened enough to tell any other group of men and women,—much less an entire sex,—what was best for them.

The National Woman's Party conceives women to be important, continuing, self-governing units of society. It conceives them to be possessed of talents and intelligences, of beauties and creative possibilities heretofore unfathomed. It proposes to do its uttermost to lift women from their present position of subjection and to put no human limits on the possibilities of their development.

To this end it seeks, as the next step, the equality of women in the law.

II—PROTECTION FOR WOMEN WORKERS

ALICE HAMILTON

There is a difference of opinion between two groups of women in this country with regard to the best way to secure for women freedom from discriminatory laws which hamper them as women and which survive as anachronisms in a modern society. The goal of all feminists is the same, the securing for women of as great a degree of self-determination as can be enjoyed in complex community life without detriment to others, and freedom from handicaps in the industrial struggle. The method whereby this is to be secured is the point of controversy. I belong to the group which holds that the right method is to repeal or alter one by one the laws that now hamper women or work injustice to them, and which opposes the constitutional amendment sponsored by the Woman's Party on the ground that it is too dangerously sweeping and all-inclusive. If no legislation is to be permitted except it apply to both sexes, we shall find it impossible to regulate by law the hours or wages or conditions of work of women and that would be, in my opinion, a harm far greater than the good that might be accomplished by removing certain antiquated abuses and injustices, which, bad as they are, do not injure nearly so many women as would be affected if all protective laws for working women were rendered unconstitutional.

It is a pity that words of general significance are used to describe this measure, for the result is a confusion which might be avoided by more precise terms. For instance, it is not really accurate to call this an amendment for "equal rights" for both sexes, when practically it forbids one sex to proceed along lines already tried and approved unless the other sex will come too. Organized working men in the United States long since adopted the policy of seeking improvement in hours, wages, and conditions of work through their unions and not by legislation. Women, whose labor organizations are young and feeble, have sought to secure reforms through legislation. This amendment would make it impossible for them to do so. The usual retort to that assertion is, that then the women must organize strongly, as men have done, but why? Trade unionism is a valuable weapon for the workers but it is not the only one. Women have never been strong in the trade union movement, not even in those industries which are overwhelmingly feminine, such, for instance, as the textile. Whatever be the reason for this, it is an indisputable fact, and it seems strange that women of the professional and leisure classes should wish to make it impossible for wage-earning women to use any method of procedure for their own betterment except one which they have shown themselves unable to use with any real power.

The advocates of the amendment quote in its favor working women who have lost their jobs because of laws prohibiting night work or overtime, and of course such cases do occur. Unfortunately there are always some individuals who lose out in any group action. The bitterest opponent of trade unionism is the highly skilled, exceptionally capable workman with an individualistic outlook on life, who resents any control from the group and wants to be let alone to work when and how he pleases. That his grievances are often real, nobody can deny, but if we are to live in a community, the greatest good to the greatest number must outweigh the rights of the individual.

For every woman linotypist who wishes to take night work on a newspaper, there must be hundreds of textile mill operatives who suffer from the compulsion to work on the night shift. For one supervisor or forewoman who wishes to work overtime, there must be hundreds of saleswomen and telephone girls who long to be freed from the necessity of so doing. It would seem that the safer, if slower, way would be to work out exemptions, so far as possible, in such legislation, to provide for those women who really do wish for entire freedom in making their bargains and are entitled to it.

We are told by members of the Woman's Party that if we "free" the working woman, allow her to "compete on equal terms with men," her industrial status will at once be raised. She is supposed now to be suffering from the handicap of laws regulating her working conditions and hours of labor and longing to be rid of them. But such a statement could never be made by anyone familiar with labor. It assumes that the present protective laws have always been in force and that the passage of the blanket amendment would usher in a new era of freedom and equality. Of course the reverse is true. Laws protecting women workers are of comparatively recent origin and are still far from universal throughout the country. It is not necessary to try the experiment of identical laws for the two sexes; we have been watching that experiment for decades and we can still observe it in many States. Compare for instance three pairs of States lying side by side. Will anyone say that it is better to be a woman wage earner in Indiana where hours are practically unrestricted than in Ohio where a woman is sure of a nine-hour day and a six-day week? Is the textile worker in Rhode Island freer and happier than her sister in Massachusetts because she is not handicapped by legal restrictions, except a ten-hour day, while the Massachusetts woman may work only nine hours, and that not without a break, must have time for her noon-day meal, one day of rest in seven, no night work, and is not allowed to sell her work for less than a minimum living wage? What of Missouri and Kansas? I should like to ask Kansas women if they envy the freedom of the women of Missouri and if they are ready to give up the laws which provide for an eight-hour day and a six-day week and a minimum wage and no night work. Any one who knows conditions in those States will say without hesitation that the so-called liberty of the women of Indiana, Missouri, and Rhode Island is a mockery and that, far from benefiting the woman wage earner, it simply hands her over to the exploiting employer.

One great source of weakness in the women's labor movement is the fact that so many of them are very young. Working men are scattered through the different age groups much as are the men in the population in general, except of course in the groups over fifty years, for their duration of life is shorter. But women wage earners are massed in the early age groups. Let me give the figures from a fairly typical manufacturing establishment, employing 3,326 men and 1,031 women. They are divided in the different groups as follows:

	Women	*Men*
15 to 20 years	33.5 per cent	14.2 per cent
21 to 25 "	29.5 " "	20.9 " "
26 to 30 "	16.0 " "	18.4 " "
31 to 40 "	14.2 " "	21.9 " "
41 to 50 "	5.6 " "	13.2 " "
51 to 60 "	0.9 " "	7.7 " "
Over 60 "	0 " "	3.4 " "

Of the women, only 11.3 per cent are over 35 years of age; of the men, 34.5 per cent. This means that a far larger proportion of women than of men go into this plant for a short period only, that most of them are at a time of life which is not characterized by prudence, foresight, and self-denial for the common good. They are not looking forward to a life of industrial employment, they hope to marry out of it as quickly as possible, and although many of them must return to it after marriage, that does not enter into their outlook before marriage. They are young, reckless of health and strength, individualistic, lacking the desire to organize, and quite powerless, without organization, to control in any way the conditions of their work.

On the other hand, the older women are as a rule even harder to bring together and more devoid of courage. They are usually mothers of families, widows, or deserted, or with sick or incompetent husbands; they carry the double burden of housework and factory work and they are recognized by all who know the

labor world as the most hopeless material for the union organizer, incapable of rebellion, capable of endless submission. It
is for these women that the laws prohibiting night work are
most needed. The father of a family, if he works at night, can
get his sleep during the day and yet have his meals served and
his children cared for; the mother of a family cannot, even if her
husband is there. It may be that some day the race will reach
such a point of development that the man will feel the pull of
responsibility toward the daily needs of his babies as keenly as
the woman does, but nobody could venture to say that we have
reached that stage as yet. The working mother is handicapped
by her own nature, she cannot take the sleep she needs till the
demands of her children have been satisfied; the father can and
does.

But there is more than this to be considered in the discussion
of special protection for working women. There is evidence
that they stand the strains of industry less well than men. In the
sickness insurance statistics of European countries women have
more days of absence on account of sickness than men do. We
have no such data in this country, but we have statistics which
show that the industrial disease par excellence, tuberculosis,
takes a heavier toll of working women than of working men.
The Federal Bureau of Labor tabulated the death records of
a textile city, Fall River, Massachusetts and published them as
part of the *Report on the Condition of Woman and Child Wage
Earners in the United States.* (Washington, 1912, Vol. XIV).
The following two tables give the general death rate per thousand inhabitants and the tuberculosis death rate, for men and
women mill operatives and for men and women outside the
mills:

ALL CAUSES OF DEATH PER 1,000 POPULATION

AGES	Men outside mills	Men in mills	Women outside mills	Women in mills
15 to 19 yrs.	4.64	2.48	2.85	4.91
20 to 24 "	5.22	4.41	3.07	5.68
25 to 29 "	4.13	4.47	5.04	7.66
30 to 34 "	8.7	8.46	7.09	11.3
35 to 39 "	5.67	11.69	5.9	11.57
40 to 44 "	9.99	7.2	7.69	14.57

The mill men have, on the whole, a death rate not strikingly different from that of the general population, better in some age groups, worse in others, but the women in the mills have in every group a death rate higher than the women outside the mills, and in most groups the contrast is very striking. The tuberculosis rates bring this out even more clearly:

DEATHS FROM TUBERCULOSIS PER 1,000 POPULATION

AGES	Men outside mills	Men in mills	Women outside mills	Women in mills
15 to 19 yrs.	0.93	1.6	1.10	2.23
20 to 24 "	1.39	2.61	0.99	2.51
25 to 29 "	1.45	1.57	1.71	4.53
30 to 34 "	3.36	4.46	2.19	4.91
35 to 39 "	3.99	3.05	1.00	3.86
40 to 44 "	1.52	3.02	0.23	2.35

The mill women have an excess death rate, compared to the women non-operatives, of 42 per cent to 96 per cent, and an excess tuberculosis death rate from 103 per cent to almost one thousand—922 per cent. We must remember also that the mill women are massed in the early age groups, where normally the death rate is low. If we compare the two sexes in the population outside the mill we see that the women have in most age groups a lower death rate from all diseases than the men. This is true in all communities. But the women in the mills have in every age group but one a much higher death rate than the men, and in that one the numbers are about equal. The greatest contrast is in the 25–29 age group, influenced doubtless by the deaths from child birth.

The total death rates from 15 to 44 years are as follows: Men outside mills, 2.04; women, 1.23. Men in mills, 2.63; women, 3.20.

The greater hazard of industrial work for young women is indicated by recent statistics published by the Metropolitan Life Company for the years 1911 to 1920. Up to ten years of age the tuberculosis death rate is about the same for both sexes, but then for the following twenty years the rate for women rises till it is considerably in excess of the men's rate, and it reaches its greatest height at about 27 years, while the men's rate is highest at 42 years. Drolet's figures for New York City show that the peak for women has in recent years fallen from the 25–29 age group to the 20–24 year group, and he attributes this change to the increased entrance of young women into industry.

When it comes to the poisonous trades, the care for special protection of women against the dangers of industry is even clearer. During the war in Europe it was necessary to employ in munition work women and such men as were incapacitated for military service by age or physical defect. The women represented an average group, the men an inferior, selected group, yet there was more sickness from poisonous explosives among the former than among the latter. In Germany the explosive chiefly used was dinitrobenzene, which is very poisonous. The proportion of cases of poisoning among the men in 1916 was 56.7 per hundred employed, among the women 66, while in 1918 when all were suffering from malnutrition, the cases rose to 100.5 per hundred men employed, but to 119 per hundred women.

Most of the data regarding the part played by sex in susceptibility to trade poisons have been gathered in the lead trades. In England, in those trades in which both men and women have been employed in contact with soluble lead compounds, such as pottery glazing and decorating and the production of white lead, it has been shown by abundant statistical evidence that women are at once more susceptible to lead poisoning and suffer more severely when they are poisoned. Recently the United States Public Health Service published a report of the potteries in New Jersey, Pennsylvania, Ohio, and West Virginia in which the same over-susceptibility of women is shown. They examined 1,809 men and women employed in work which brought them in contact with soluble lead and found that the average period of exposure to lead of the men who developed lead poisoning was 17 years, but the average period of exposure of the women was only 9.3 years. "It should also be mentioned that in most plants the length of day for the female worker is from one-half hour to one hour shorter than that of the male worker. It would seem, therefore, that the female reaches these stages of lead poisoning in about half the time required for the male to reach them."

The Germans do not find a greater susceptibility to lead among women nor did I find it in my investigation of American potteries, which was far less thorough than that of the Public Health Service. It is, however, admitted by every student that lead poisoning takes a more serious form in women than in men. Thus I found that only one in 17 of the men potters who had plumbism had the severe form, with involvement of the brain, while among the women one in four and a half of the cases of plumbism was of this kind. Prendergast, of the Staffordshire pottery towns, found that 34.9 per cent of the women with lead poisoning suffered from convulsions, delirium, or coma, while among the men only 15 per cent had this form. Blindness, partial or total, was present in 17.9 per cent of the women; in only 5.8 per cent of the men.

The advocates of the blanket amendment say that they do not oppose laws designed to protect the child, that they are ready to favor protection of "pregnant persons" and "nursing persons." This is, of course, an important concession. But the damage done by an industrial poison may antedate pregnancy. Women who have worked in a lead trade before marriage and still more women who work in lead after marriage are more likely to be sterile than women who have worked in other trades; if they conceive they are less likely to carry the child to term; and if they do they are less likely to bear a living child and their living children are less able to survive the first weeks of life. There are many proofs of this in the literature and I have selected from them a table compiled from Home Office records by Thomas Oliver, England's most noted specialist on industrial plumbism:

> To 100 mothers employed in housework, there were 43.2 miscarriages and stillbirths.
> To 100 mothers employed in mill work, there were 47.6 miscarriages and stillbirths.
> To 100 mothers employed in lead work before marriage, there were 86.0 miscarriages and stillbirths.
> To 100 mothers employed in lead work after marriage, there were 133.5 miscarriages and stillbirths,—an average of almost 1½ apiece.

There are statistics from French sources which show that lead poisoning in the father also has an effect on the offspring and this is confirmed by experiments on animals and birds, but it is, of course, obvious that a poison circulating in the blood of the mother can affect not only the germ cell but the child throughout its intra-uterine life, while poisoning of the father can affect only the germ cell. As a matter of fact lead has been isolated from the blood and organs of stillborn children of leaded mothers.

The belief in the "equality of the sexes," interpreted to mean their essential identity, is very attractive to many people. When I first entered the labor field my inclination was in that direction, for I come of a family of suffragists; my grandmother was a close friend of Susan B. Anthony, and I had certainly never wished for any sort of privilege or special protection during my own career as a professional woman. During the first years of my study of the poisonous trades I was filled with impatience because I could get no hearing when I urged the necessity of safeguarding the ignorant, unorganized, foreign laborers in our dangerous lead trades, while at the same time I saw protective laws passed for women who were employed in far less dangerous work. But experience is a thorough if hard teacher, and I have learned now to take what I can get and be thankful. The American legislator cannot be aroused to much indignation over descriptions of poisonous, dusty, heavy, hot, and filthy work if it is done by men. The pioneer spirit which scorns "paternalism," the Nordic spirit which holds southern European labor in contempt, stand in the way and are hard obstacles to overcome. But this same hard-boiled legislator has a soft side when it comes to women workers. I remember an absurd instance of this during the war. I was up in the mountains of Pennsylvania inspecting a dynamite plant. There were a few girls employed there, handling nothing worse than paraffined paper, but they had a nice washroom with running water, soap, and towels. The large number of men who were in contact with really dangerous poisons, such as nitroglycerine and dinitrotoluene, had only the mountain brook. The law of Pennsylvania was apparently responsible for this perfectly silly discrimination between the sexes, but it would never occur to me to even up matters by taking away from the women decent provisions for cleanliness till such time as the company could be forced to provide them for the men too.

In Holland, I am told, the two sexes have recently been put on an equality in industry, not by taking privileges away from the women, but by extending them to the men. Holland is an old country, which has long been used to labor legislation. I cannot believe that we in the United States are nearing that point very fast, though I should like to think so. Meantime, until we reach it, I must, as a practical person, familiar with the great, inarticulate body of working women, reiterate my belief that they are largely helpless, that they have very special needs which unaided they cannot attain, and that it would be a crime for the country to pass legislation which would not only make it impossible to better their lot in the near future but would even deprive them of the small measure of protection they now enjoy.

IDA M. TARBELL

Is Woman's Suffrage a Failure?
OCTOBER 1924

Ida M. Tarbell (1857–1944) was one of the most famous muckraking journalists, male or female, of the early twentieth century, known especially for her exposé of the Standard Oil Company published in *McClure's* magazine in 1902. She was also one of the most prominent women to speak out in opposition to women's suffrage. In some ways her close association with the antisuffrage cause made her an unlikely choice for a commission from *Good Housekeeping* to reflect on the impact of the Nineteenth Amendment as the 1924 election approached. Or maybe what was so unlikely was how positive Tarbell's assessment was. Now that women had the vote, she concluded, it was their duty to use it widely. And from the evidence she saw while crisscrossing the country, women were doing precisely that. Rather than simply declare women's suffrage a success or a failure, she took the long view, arguing that political experiments should be judged "not by decades, but rather by centuries."

One of several dismal refrains, more or less popular at the moment, celebrates the failure of woman's suffrage. Four years and the world is no better—possibly even worse. There is often a note of real despair in the chorus, for those who chant it staked large hopes of speedy social betterment on the giving of suffrage to women, and these hopes are unfilled. Their disappointment is as deep as their expectations were high.

The lament is more serious in its effects than many realize. It is probably the strongest of present deterrents to women's voting—lethargy aside. It chills the ardor of that group which acts vigorously only when stimulated by a new panacea; it gives a welcome excuse to women who are so busy with their personal affairs that they find it difficult to inform themselves about issues and candidates—"Why should I vote? A man who *knows* says suffrage is a failure." It is used, too, by not a few women who opposed suffrage and who still are glad to find proofs that they were right.

594

Now anything that hinders the general exercise of the franchise by women deserves attention. The vote is an obligation—a duty the state asks of us. To plead that we are "not interested," "did not believe in suffrage," are "too busy," is skulking. It is our business to vote as wisely and unselfishly as we are able— if only to counteract the mass of feminine unintelligence and selfishness certain to be mobilized by the always active forces of self-interest.

But has the conclusion that woman's suffrage is a failure any sounder base than the early hope that it would cure all our ills? That certainly was delusive. "The world do move," but it "do move" with exceeding deliberation and always according to laws. Votes never yet have stirred its pace to one faster than the laws laid down, and the claim that in woman's hand they would was always a cheat; but it is equally a cheat to declare that because woman's suffrage has not proved itself in four years the miracle-worker certain of its advocates fooled themselves into thinking it would be, it is therefore a flat failure. Both are jumped-at conclusions, ignoring the most important element in human enterprises—time—something that hasty-wits delight in scorning. "Do this and we will fly" they tell us. We do it and crash to the ground. Therefore all is lost. But is it? On the ground we can do what wisdom tells us we are, after all, condemned to do—crawl.

But is woman's suffrage even crawling? We find those who contend it is not—"Nothing has happened." And they despair— or exult—according to temperament or their historic attitude toward suffrage. Are they right? Has nothing happened? As one who has ever been lukewarm toward suffrage and who regarded the argument that quick and drastic remedial results were sure to come from it as mischievous and dishonest, I want to say that I believe something has happened—something rather more in the time than I at least thought probable—and that something is spreading. I base this judgment entirely on observation of things heard and seen.

Early in the present year I spent upwards of three months zig-zagging from Massachusetts to Texas, across twelve or fifteen states, and everywhere I halted, listening to more or less querulous discussion by women of what women are doing in the realm of public affairs. My eyes as well as my ears were open on this journey looking over exhibits the women were showing of their four years' experience with the ballot.

How about it? What conclusions can one draw from such a set of observations, bolstered as they are by similar experiences running back for several consecutive years? Is woman's interest in public matters more general and natural than before suffrage? Is she studying political measures more seriously? Has her faith in suffrage held out? Have the "antis" undergone a change of mind? What actual betterment of local affairs is due to woman's initiative and activity? What fresh vigor and illumination has she brought into state and national affairs?

Both my observations and my conclusions on these points are at variance with those of some of our most thoughtful women, women always to be listened to. There is George Madden Martin, who recently set down in print, after fourteen months journeying about the country, that she had made up her mind that American women in general lacked interest in public affairs, and what they had was rather in issues than in principles. I would not be justified in such a conclusion from what I heard and saw in the three months of which I am talking here, for in that time I was not in a single town in which I did not have ample evidence of lively concern in public questions. Everywhere the women I met as individuals and as groups—many of them formerly anti-suffragist—invariably soon turned the conversation to law enforcement, the oil scandal, the regulation of industry, the League of Nations, Coolidge, Smith, McAdoo, and there was always more or less appeal to principle—quite as much as in a similar group of men—and less acrimony—which surprised me.

Of course there have always been in every community women who followed political questions eagerly and who knew what they were talking about. Are there *more* of these now? That is the point. I think so. This shows in the immediateness with which political questions come up and in the attention all in a group give even if they can not contribute to the talk. It concerns them. They may be bored by the fact, but they feel the pull and obligation.

Law enforcement seemed to exercise the women I talked with more than any other matter. They are everywhere concerned about the boys and girls of college age whom they believe to be drinking as they never did before in our time—if at any time. I failed to find a woman—though I did more than one man—who was willing to run the danger of despoiling at least a slice of the rising generation by defying the Eighteenth Amendment and the Volstead Act on the ground that they violate personal liberty. Every woman with whom I talked on the matter was rigidly of Lincoln's mind:

"Bad laws if they exist should be repealed as soon as possible. Still, while they continue in force, for the sake of example, they should be religiously observed. Otherwise, you are bound sooner or later to come to mob rule."

I will not say that there are no women who dispute this view—I know that there are—only that in these three months I did not meet one of them.

After law enforcement the greatest number seemed to be concerned over the Tea Pot Dome affair, obviously because of its bearing on their party candidates. Women, as a rule, are very personal in their partisanship, and it hurts them to have those who represent them splashed as badly as many have been in this scandal. Nevertheless, while I frequently met a man who would say: "Why fuss? These leases you scold about will make money for the Government"—which is still to be proved—women invariably countered with, "That's not the question." And it is something to be glad of that many see that it is a question of the integrity of officials and the upholding of honorable and fair dealing.

One heartening exhibit, from my point of view, was the almost universal conviction that the legislation which has been built up in the last twenty years or so for guarding women and children in industry must not be endangered by the proposed blanket equal rights amendment to the Constitution. That amendment sounds well, and I had been under the impression that, reactionary as it is bound to be in its effects on industry, it would catch the ear and the support of large numbers of women. I was amazed by finding practically no backing for it, although I frequently heard it discussed. The truth is that serious women everywhere are deeply interested and fairly well informed on industrial conditions and are thoroughly committed to the idea of improving them and particularly of protecting women and children.

Now, certainly all of this argues interest of a healthy kind. It is not proof that one hundred percent or even fifty percent of our women think on these things, but it is proof that many are of a kind and in a position to spread their views, and in most places they are mighty busy doing that.

And they are taking to office holding. "Meet Mrs. A.—— member of our State Legislature"—"Meet Miss B.—— candidate for Congress."

For one born and reared as this writer was in hide-bound Pennsylvania, it is startling to find eight women in the legislature of that state. Moreover, to learn from their men fellow-members of the natural way they take their place and do their work. Alice Bentley, a representative from the northwestern corner of the state, seems to have particularly impressed herself. "Always feel at home with Alice," a member of the legislature of the opposite party told me. "She's educated, but that don't make any difference—not a bit stuck up. And practical! You can't fool her on graft, and she ain't afraid of her own side any more than of ours"—which is about as fine a tribute, politically speaking, as a woman could ask for or a constituency desire.

The lure of office is strengthening, spreading. We shall wake up one of these days to find that there is no legislative or executive department in state or nation that has not one or more women in it. They come, as they ought to, naturally, like men, through the automatic working of the machinery opened to them—not because they are women, but because they are human beings, following the instincts and opportunities of human beings. As a rule they settle down to business at once, working steadily and well. This is particularly true in clerical offices. In the last three years I have spent many hours in court houses in different states, and I can bear testimony, based on experience, to the superiority of women over men as guardians of public records. Too often the men about court houses are cheap politicians. They neglect their work, are often disorderly, and usually much more interested in gossip than in service. Not so, women. They are diligent, neat, exact. They respect their records, take pride in knowing them and in guarding them— and they banish the spittoon!

One of the anomalies of this situation is that there are women who do not take this result as a matter of course! Not a few old-style professional suffrage agitators seem actually to resent women coming noiselessly into public office and going about their business as other public servants do and not as women politicians vindicating their sex!

At a recent state convention of one of the great parties this attitude showed itself in a bitter attack on a woman for years an active worker for suffrage, who was filling a minor office in the state and filling it well. Her devotion to business, her determination to prove women fit for office by being herself fit, angered the women politicians. They insisted that she was betraying her sex because she would not use her office for feminine political purposes—a variation of the spoils system women were to uproot!

THE WOMAN REPRESENTATIVE

The clash with those who have not yet been able to lay aside the old struggle, now won, and accept their privileges and responsibilities in a logical and practical fashion, has led to an effort to define the model woman representative. What should she be? The few experiences with congresswomen to date have made dents, and one frequently hears Jeannette Rankin's inexperience, emotionalism, and spirit of innovation contrasted with Alice Robertson's experience, cool-headedness, and conservatism—generally to Miss Rankin's advantage. She was more understandable and sympathetic to women generally, I gather; nevertheless there is a growing and sensible conclusion forming that women should not try to go into office from the top, that they should begin at the bottom in local affairs and grow into the service as in other professions, and as all our most useful men officials do.

But how high can they hope to rise? A group of college girls put the question to me, "If we go in for public life, can we expect ever to reach the presidency?" It was a poser. But, after all, isn't the presidency the logic of what women have undertaken? It worked out so under the old régime—queens galore—and the public was as well off, sometimes better off, under them as under many men. A list of queens presents much ability, and no more craftiness, selfishness, cruelty, extravagance, unreason than men. Consider Catherine of Russia, Louise of Prussia, Maria Theresa of Austria, Elizabeth of England, Catherine di

Medici of France. And it was of Marie Antoinette that Mira-beau said she was the only man the king had about him. Down in Pennsylvania they are saying not exactly that, but a variation of it, about the Governor's lady. "As good as any man next to Pinchot," I heard a Democratic politician declare, "and away ahead of him as a politician!"—which is, I take it, close to the impression the onlooker is getting!

Training and experience ought to fit women in time for as sound statesmanship as the old régime did. Moreover, I am free to say that I know a half-dozen women in these United States that I believe would do better in the presidency than at least three or four incumbents since Lincoln, and nothing would be better for the country at this moment than to substitute this same half dozen for a half dozen senators I could name!

It is still too early to appraise the contributions of our women legislators, to say whether we shall get anything from them that we would not from men, to decide whether their methods will be more direct, frank, less devious and intriguing than those of men have proved. Are they going to see that regeneration does not lie in the making of many laws? Are they going to insist on loosening up the legal jam which holds up the free action of the country? Their value in legislative bodies is going to depend largely upon the common sense and straightforwardness with which they view the passing of new statutes.

ONE THING ACCOMPLISHED

I have had but one experience which showed that possibly we might expect something from them in this direction. This was in a Northwestern state where women have been holding office for a good many years. To a member of the assembly, a sensible, thoughtful, humorous person, I dared to put the question: "Have you and your colleague"—there were two of them at the moment in that body—"been able to do anything that men would not have done? That is, have you contributed something of your own?" She was quite honest in her reply: "We have done one thing that would not have been done, and I think only one. I had not been long in office before I was amazed to discover the faith men have in the making of many laws. Every man seemed to feel that his value as a legislator depended upon the number of bills that he introduced and put through. Moreover, I found these bills were often carelessly drawn—some of them defeated their own purpose—others were already on the statute books, others contradicted something we were committed to. So my colleague and I made up our minds that we would examine quietly every bill proposed, and if we found good reason for objections, we would make them—to the proposer. We found plenty of work, and it has turned out that there are few men in the assembly today, who when they have a bill to propose, do not first submit it to us, to see if there is anything the matter with it. We really have done a good deal of cleaning up in this way."

And then she chuckled. "After all, you know, all that it amounts to is that we are picking up after the men, just as women have always done."

But is not that the essence of what woman promised to do—prevent men making many of the mistakes which she thought they were making as legislators?

The most disappointing feature in a rapid survey of the field such as that on which I am basing these comments, is that one almost never comes on fresh, stirring thought, free and independent actions, illumination from the women who have gone into public life. Generally speaking, it is the same old thing—activity in party organization, fine party loyalty, faith in politics, and politics alone; and this is serious.

Men and women who supported suffrage ardently believed and promised that a wave of regeneration would follow its coming, that we would see vice in hiding, graft shamed out of court, chicanery in office and in administration rebuked; but none of these things seems to have happened. As a matter of fact, the only case that I have come across where women have broken openly with the old way of doing things, used their wits and their power to overthrow a local institution they considered bad, and have carried on for upwards of two years now, was in a Western town where there was a particularly sordid and partisan administration of town affairs. The women saw that they were not getting what they wanted in sanitation, in schools, in suppression of vice. They saw that as much of their money was going to support the party machine as to support the town, and they decided, regardless of party, on a commission form of government. There were men to back them up, and when they felt they were strong enough they went to the leaders, who met them with familiar enough counsel:

"Very fine, delighted that you are so interested in public affairs, that is as it should be; but you are, of course, inexperienced; you should know more about these things before you undertake anything so revolutionary as this. You do not see what we know so well, that the managerial form of government takes the personal touch out of the running of the town."

The women intimated that one of their ideas had been that they would save money by abolishing this "personal touch."

When they found that nothing was to be done with the political leaders on either side, they resolved to make it a woman's affair, and to the amazement of both party machines they succeeded. For two years now they have been, they claim, getting what they were after—their money's worth in increased order, cleanliness, and decency, as well as in improvement of schools.

Perhaps they do not realize that not the least of their achievement is pulling a brick from that tremendous foundation on which parties in this country build their power. Nowhere is partisanship stronger, more unenlightened, more sordid than in the machines which run our towns and cities. State and national politics have not the least justifiable relation to the streets of New York, the railways of Cleveland, the sanitation of Chicago, the regulation of vice everywhere. These are affairs personal to the municipality, and yet municipalities all over this country must see schools, streets, water, light, vice manipulated to strengthen Republican and Democratic party machinery.

THE SOCIAL MENACE

If there is a ray of hope in the little story above, it is only one ray in a great darkness. Practically everywhere, so far as my observation goes, it is as yet impossible to get the women of the towns to act outside of their parties, no matter how flagrant the abuse with which they are confronted. Not far from New York there is an historic town, delightful physically and socially, numbering among its women two or three former suffrage leaders of ability, cultivation, and experience in public affairs. The man who has been mayor of the town for several years is a member of the local aristocracy, an educated, cultivated gentleman. He belongs to the ruling state party and is an aspirant for a higher office. He is also the hope of county and district leaders. They expect him to deliver his town, and he has always done it. One of the ways in which he has kept himself strong since the passage of the Eighteenth Amendment has been to close his eyes to bootlegging and drinking. The town has become a safe refuge for bootleggers and a rendezvous for drinking parties from the whole country round. Most tragic has been the effect upon the working classes, of whom there is a large settlement, colored and white.

All this finally aroused the serious people of the community to active revolt, and a few months ago a candidate ran in opposition to the mayor on a platform of law enforcement. He was overwhelmingly defeated—defeated by the women of the town, who put their social and political relationships higher than they did law enforcement. To have voted against the lawless mayor might have injured the political prospects of themselves and their husbands and sons; it might have disturbed social ambitions and relations. The mother of the mayor, a distinguished lady of social power, let it be known that she would never speak again to anybody who voted against her son. And this is the way we are being "saved" by women!

LEADERS ARE NEEDED

It is not only that there is an absence of any free action by women in local or national affairs, but there seems to be no stirring new cry coming from the numberless conventions and assemblies that are crowding one another so fast. We have a great body of professional women convention followers in this country; they rush from state to state, from East to West, from North to South, thousands of them, almost feverishly active, determined and serious; but we are yet to hear from any one of these gatherings any call that catches the imagination, wrings the heart, arouses to righteous indignation. They are busy—oh, yes! The conventions are great successes, oh, yes! They go home to tell everybody how fine the meeting was, how much they got out of it! But somehow they do not succeed in stirring those of us who stay at home. I have a suspicion that these busy ladies are deceiving themselves about the real value of their excessive activity. It is not by conventions that the resolutions they pass—and let us call them always good—are to be made realities. If they are to amount to anything the great body of us who never or rarely go to conventions, hardly know that they are held, must seize them, carry them on. And if we are to do that it will be only because those who aspire to be our leaders shall put a glow in our eyes, arouse our intellects, stir our hearts to consecration—and so far they have not done anything of that kind.

It is one of the tragic features of the case that women have got their hands on political machinery and formulas when a good part of the world is realizing that they are not the fundamentals of salvation. There has been a notable loss of faith in recent years in politicians and their methods and ends, a growing sense they can not save the world. The Great War and the awful chaos it brought about has demonstrated the inadequacy of political devices. There has even come something like contempt for them, and you see the thoughtful and the masses—where the soundest instincts always are to be found—falling back on old things, on education, discipline, character, hard thinking, hard labor. There lies the regeneration of things; not in conferences, elections, resolutions, legislation. These latter are useful only as secondary tools and then only in proportion to the genuineness of the fundamentals to which men now turn.

But put the suffrage down as a secondary tool, it is still a powerful one—for evil as well as good. It takes time and experience to use it effectively—to use it so as to frustrate the harm the selfish plan always to do with it. Constant exercise of the voting power as intelligently and disinterestedly as we are able, with thoughtful study of the effects, the mistakes made, is a part of a woman's business. The only real failure at present in woman's suffrage is the failure to exercise it. To denounce it because we do not yet see anything particularly helpful or illuminating coming from its exercise is foolish and unjust.

One handles a new subject shyly and awkwardly. One does not know the vocabulary, etiquette, principles. Watch a grown man or woman tackling a new science, learning to drive a car, setting up a radio equipment; there is fumbling, error, confusion of meanings. The majority of women are probably still booth-shy, still a little awed by their responsibility, often a little afraid to talk politics because conscious that they are amateurs.

Perfectly true that we have increasing numbers that do not

suffer from the limitations of shyness, of humility—numbers who are glib, often to their own undoing in the hands of experienced politicians. But this is not the majority. The majority are not yet at home in the new harness. Moreover, can we expect anything else than that they should be slow in accepting the harness, learning how to wear it, absorbed, as the great majority of them are, with their daily occupations, domestic, economic, social?

No, the hasty-wits are wrong. It is too early to cry "Failure!" in this matter. All things considered, as much has been done as could be expected. Nature in a thousand ways calls to us that growth, even if unceasing, takes time. Men and women accept this for everything outside of themselves, and yet they are just as much under these laws of nature as the tree. It has always taken time to change a habit, to reform a settled attitude toward life, to grow a political mind. Political experiments must be judged not by decades, but rather by centuries. In fifty years from now we may be able to appraise woman's suffrage fairly—we certainly can not now.

DORIS STEVENS

Address to the Sixth Pan American Conference, Havana, Cuba

FEBRUARY 7, 1928

The National Woman's Party made the passage of international laws and treaties guaranteeing equal rights a high priority in the post-suffrage era. In early 1928 Doris Stevens laid out the case for an international equal rights treaty to the Sixth Pan American Conference, held in Havana, Cuba. She did not prevail, but her efforts along with those of feminists from various Latin American countries led to the establishment of the Inter-American Commission of Women (IACW), with Stevens as its first chair. At the Seventh International Conference of American States held in Montevideo, Uruguay, in 1933, delegates approved an Equal Nationality Treaty, a significant victory. While most Latin American feminists saw no dichotomy between agitating for equal rights and preserving their benefits and privileges as women, American feminists continued to be deeply divided on this issue.

Honorable Delegates:—

We are met together on a great historic occasion. This is the first time in the history of the world that women are come before an international body to plead for treaty action on their rights.

We are met in this beautiful hall already consecrated to new ideals of Panamericanism. I ask you to look well at the moving tapestries which hang on these walls. Twenty-one medallions represent the 21 Republics assembled here today. What is the artist's conception of each republic? It is a very simple concept. The splendid figures of two human beings: Man and Woman. The artist is right. That, in the last analysis, is all there is to a State: Man and Woman!

Behind us is another moving concept of the artist. Where a crown once symbolised autocratic authority, you now have substituted a golden Western Hemisphere ablaze with light. The torch of Freedom lights the golden replica of this hemisphere.

We could not, if we had searched far and wide, have found

more beautiful and appropriate symbols to the subject matter on which we address you today. These are the symbols of a new world, of a new hemisphere—with new ideals as to that most important of all human relationships; the relationship between man and woman. Humanly stated, our thesis today is Man and Woman; the ultimate power in the world.

You have it in your power to make these symbols come alive. You can, here and now, if you will, take decisive action toward making men and women equal before the law in this hemisphere. We are in the hands of a friendly body. You have already declared unanimously your belief that men and women should be equal before the law. Today we propose a method of obtaining that equality.

Great laws are born of deep convictions. They are not made by technicians.

It is our deep convictions that we bring you today. But that is not all we bring you. We stand ready to work with you, as eminent jurists, through your appointed commission, to hasten the procedure of our proposal. For we do not come before you unprepared. We have studied carefully the merits of our proposal. And since with rare exception men cannot feel as we do, the sting of belonging to a group which is classed as inferior, we ask to be allowed authoritative power—not as auxiliaries but as colleagues—to consult between this Conference and the next with the sub-commission assigned to study the abolition of the present discriminations against women or until that legal subjection of women is abolished in the Americas. We shall not fold our standards until this subjection is removed. You might better act wisely and justly immediately on what you will only have eventually to do.

Since the beginning of time, men with the best of intentions, no doubt, have been writing laws for our good. Since the beginning of time, brave and valiant women have been abolishing these same laws written for our good.

There is no limit to what man wishes to do for our good. Last week press despatches from the United States carried the news that a husband and father had killed his wife, the mother of his children, and the children. When questioned as to his motives, he replied that he did it for their good!

The Associated Press despatch reported from a seaport in

Algeria last week also, another example of man's desire to protect woman for her good. For the Mahommedan Women's good, custom does not permit them to bathe at the same time as men. Five women were drowned when the bath-house collapsed, while men were getting up their courage to break the man-made custom and enter the building reserved that day for women-bathers.

This, in the realm of custom, is the logical if absurd outcome of the iniquity of one code of conduct for women and another for men.

Is it any wonder that enlightened women are in revolt today against acts done for their good? We want no more laws written for our good and without our consent. We must have the right to direct our own destiny jointly with you.

For, you see, no man, no group of men, no government, no nation, no group of nations—ever had the right to withhold from us the rights we ask today. We ask to have restored, rights which have been usurped. These are our human rights.

From the year 1846, when the code of Estevan de Ferrater of Barcelona was proposed, to the year 1928—eminent men from all corners of the earth have drafted and proposed codes of international law embracing among many subjects, articles relating to the status of women. They have however been pre-eminently codes for men. A study of these codes shows at first a few articles concerning the status of women appearing. Each proposed article on the status of women reflects the then existing backward social position she held. More and more points on the status of women, it is true, have been included in these codes through the intervening years, although no code has been proposed giving women equality with men. Are we to permit to grow this vast network of one code for men with special articles inserted for women? If there were no free choice, it is conceivable that in two hundred years we might see our book-shelves staggering under the weight of a double stock of law books, heavy with special codes for women and special codes for men. It is even conceivable that in two hundred years a point would be reached where the codes for men and the codes for women might become identical. But we are not condemned to take any risk. We can exercise free choice. We can stop this method of codification and begin to write now international law for all human beings irrespective of sex.

Another danger which attends waiting upon evolution, lies in the fact that there is no marked tendency to take the most advanced law regarding women on each point. Though eminent jurists advocate and propose what they call "progressive codification", it is not found to be so for women. The most distinguished jurists agree that codification should be a rehabilitation of law, and even a creation of new laws when public opinion demands it.

Furthermore, when public opinion demands it, newer and speedier methods are taken to reach a goal.

We have chosen the road we propose to travel. That right at least cannot be denied us today.

It is fitting that the American Continent should be the first union of republics to be asked for an equal rights treaty. The demand for women's rights was born on this continent. Abigail Adams was, so far as we know, the first woman in modern history to write to her husband, John Adams, when the United States constitution was being formed after our war of independence: "While you are writing this new constitution, I pray you, do not forget the ladies. If you do, we shall foment a hot rebellion". Again, it was in 1848 in the United States of America that our great pioneers called a congress and wrote a stirring declaration of our rights. This agitation continued until our civil war in 1861. Again, the women demanded their rights at the same time that they demanded freedom for the black slaves. The slaves were freed. The women were not. It was not until 1919 that the political rights of women were written into our constitution.

It is not in our traditions to be content with what we have gained. It is not in our traditions to be laggards of liberty. The impulse to gather together our power and push on more rapidly, is strong in us.

We have chosen the treaty method because it is the most dignified. It is the easiest. It is the most permanent. It will not only abolish existing national and international inequalities. It will prevent new ones from being written. And lastly it obviates a cruel waste of energy. For we ought never be compelled to appeal for our rights to the most backward opinion in any State. Our appeal to the most select, the most cultivated, the most imaginative men in the world, should be welcomed, approved and answered in this most dignified method.

Some will tell us that rights of women lie exclusively in the domain of domestic law. This is purely a matter of opinion.

The extension of what was formerly considered purely domestic law into the domain of international law has been the most distinctive feature of legal history in the last quarter of a century. There is every reason to believe that international action will expand to embrace more and more all the acts of humankind. Global action may come in the future. Our proposal lies in the current of our time. You may delay it. You cannot stop it. We want to accelerate it.

Timid souls may say this has never been done. That answer does not move us. All compelling history of the world has been made by those who dared to establish great precedents, who adventured in unknown paths, who led the way. The men who follow are never remembered—it is those who lead, who direct the current of civilization.

There will be those who say: "Woman's rights are not a fit subject for treaty action". To this we answer: "Discriminations against women have already been made the subject of action by convention by certain of the Americas and amongst European nations through the League of Nations. If discriminations against us as women on the sole ground of sex can be made the subject of international conventions, so can our rights."

Let us examine the treaty-making power of my own country. The treaty-making power of the United States is granted in the constitution without any express limitation as to the subject matter of the treaty. Limitations on the subject matter are only implied. They are undefined and not judicially determined. Since no treaty has ever been held unconstitutional by any court in the United States—federal or state—it cannot be given as more than a matter of opinion (not law) that the subject matter of our treaty would be so held. Everything written on the point of what is and what is not fit subject for treaty action—and there has been a mass of opinion—is purely academic. It is *obiter dicta*. The best thought is that restraints on the treaty-making power ought to exist only in the concrete—not in the abstract.

Charles Henry Butler goes so far as to say that "it is still an undecided question whether the judicial department of the court has the power either to declare void a treaty made and ratified according to constitutional method, or to declare that the executive and legislative departments of the government exceeded the power vested in them by the people". (See Charles Henry Butler "The Treaty-Making Power of the United States", Vol. II, pp. 351–363. Also Woolsey "International Law" item 103, p. 160, 6 ed; also Ware v. Hylton—U.S. Sup. Court 1796—3 Dall. 199.)

Regarding the supremacy of a treaty over a conflicting state law, eminent jurists disagree. Time permitting, we could cite you opinions on each side of this controversy with the balance of modern opinion, perhaps, on the side of the supremacy of the national government. "The very words of our constitution imply that some treaties will be made in contravention of the laws of the State, whether the legislative authority under which they are passed is concurrent with that of Congress, or exclusive of that of Congress", says that eminent jurist Elihu Root (address made by Elihu Root at first annual meeting of the American Society of International Law . . . American Journal International Law, Vol. I, pp. 278–283, April 1907).

Finally, your distinguished member, His Excellency Orestes Ferrara, said in his report on "Treaties" to the Commission on Public International Law last week—in reference to the code of Public International Law, drawn up by the Conference of Jurists at Rio de Janeiro, April 1927:

"In not a single clause has limitation as to the content of treaties been defined. . . . The will of contracting parties (to a treaty) has been left in complete and absolute liberty".

We therefore offer you a treaty which we believe the United States Government and other governments of Panamerica are fully empowered to enter into. Legal interpretations may offer barriers. The U. S. constitution states none.

Men may differ as to their willingness to accept the rights of women as proper subject matter for treaty action. To persuade them to our point of view is the task we have undertaken.

We can only touch upon these points here.

We shall hope to discuss them exhaustively with the commission appointed to study equal rights for women.

Our proposed method of establishing equal rights is not as revolutionary as you might think—revolutionary in thought perhaps, but not in international procedure.

At the first conference of the International Labor Office of the League of Nations, (Washington 1919) three out of seven conventions were written for women-workers on the ground of sex. The second conference (Genoa 1920) wrote conventions applying to both sexes (adults and children). At the Third Conference (Geneva 1921) more conventions were written for both sexes among adults and children. In 1927 (Geneva) the same office wrote conventions on sickness insurance for workers of both sexes.

These are but a few of many examples which prove two things. Jurists have written conventions making women unequal before international law. Jurists have written conventions making men and women equal before international law. There is no fixed policy—except as there is the general evasion of accepting the idea of laws for human beings. Some of the conventions are for women and children of one sex. Some are for women and children of both sexes. Some are for men and women. The result is not only an appalling hodgepodge. It is manifestly stupid and unfair to both adults and children.

How much simpler it would be to take our clear and decisive method! The result would be one body of conventions for adult men and women, and another for children of both sexes. There could then be a housecleaning of all the useless conventions based on the arbitrary factor of sex.

Conventions have been proposed and ratified regulating the hours of work of women, regulating the time of day when women shall work—as was done by the convention of the International Conference at Berne in 1906—as was done by the Convention for the Unification of Protective Laws for Workmen and Laborers, signed February 7th, 1923 by Guatemala, El Salvador, Honduras, Nicaragua, Costa Rica. For example, Article I of this convention signed by the five central American countries, stipulates the time of day wherein women shall be permitted to work. Will you tell us this can be done and at the same time tell us that a treaty shall not be negotiated enabling adult women to choose their own times of work and their own occupations, which our treaty would enable them to do?

Again, will you tell us that the League of Nations (1921 Convention for Prevention of Traffic in Women and Children) can propose a convention for the suppression of the traffic in women, which convention is to date signed by more than thirty-five countries in the world—and in the same breath tell us that a treaty cannot be negotiated for other women? Must we become sex-slaves before we can be judged fit subjects for action by convention? International action was not taken on this shameful traffic primarily because women are sold and transported from one country to another. You know as well as we do that that international convention was written because the moral conscience of the world demanded it.

May I say in passing that it is our firm belief that if women were not held in contempt before the law, were not held socially inferior and cheap in the eyes of society, this traffic would never exist. Unconventionality yes, but not traffic in women. It is our firm belief that so swiftly as you make us your equals, so swiftly will your international conventions written on this subject fall into disuse because they will not be necessary.

We find, then, that international conventions are in operation affecting the following groups of women:

1) Women who work by day.
2) Women who work by night.
3) Women who are trafficked in.
4) Women before and after childbirth.
5) Women who are ill.
   and proposed for
6) Women who marry aliens.

Is it not folly to continue on this piece-meal path? Leave aside for a moment the justice of our claim. Leave aside all legal procedure, which is not always synonymous with common sense. Does not plain, homely common-sense compel you to embrace by treaty action now, the rights of all women and scrap all this idiotic segregation of women in conventions? Does not wisdom call to you to save yourselves and ourselves from further bulky, cumbersome, unjust international action? We hope they do.

Some of the delegates have advised us not to propose an equal rights treaty at this time. "This treaty will call up legal and juridical difficulties, and you will be defeated". Our answer to this is, gentlemen, that if you find our proposal difficult, that is your misfortune. If statesmen avoid all questions because they are difficult, nothing vital will ever be accomplished. The first requisite is to agree on the broad, general principle of equality between men and women set forth in the proposed treaty, and if your heart is in that agreement, your intelligence will settle the technical difficulties. On the point of defeat, this must be said: a defeat of the treaty will be your defeat—not ours.

There is another point we would like to call to your attention. Since working with this Conference, we have heard the opinion expressed—I regret to say—by one of our compatriots, that equal rights may be all right for the women of North America, but that the women of Latin America are not yet ready for them. We women resent and disbelieve in any hint of sectional superiority. It may be that there is a hope implied that, although we women of North America may be out of hand, the women of Latin America may still be kept under legal subjection. We do not believe that the men of North America are called upon to be tender protectors of the women of Latin America.

We do not look with approval upon this attempt to divide women. Our subjection is world-wide. The abolition of our subjection will be accomplished by world-wide solidarity of women. Furthermore, we have not noticed that the men of the northern and the southern Americas are reluctant to unite in Panamericanism because there may exist different customs, differing attitudes of mind toward your mutual problems. The unwarranted presumption is again: one code of conduct for women, another for men.

We bear witness today before you to the growing solidarity among the women of the Americas.

This Conference will long be remembered by what it does here for the women of the Americas. Nothing you gentlemen will do during this conference will be of such far-reaching importance as the action you will take toward the liberty of women. Nothing will so distinguish you for all time as to abandon at once all separate codes of law for men and women and to substitute in their place the great principle making women equal with men before the law.

We want to be your peers, your comrades, your helpmates,

your partners in the great adventure of life. These we shall be in a properly civilized society. You can hasten that day.

So long as inequality before the law exists between men and women, less is expected of women by men. Less is expected by women of themselves. This in turn affects our whole body of opinion, our whole culture. Less courage, less balance in judgment, a lower standard of public spirit, an indifference in international cooperation. This is the reward of inequality. This is a menace to men as well as to women. To expect less is to receive less. We stand ready to give all of our abilities to society, not our limited, restricted abilities. Do you want less?

Will you welcome the opportunity, or will you hesitate? Will you condemn us further to the ignoble, unworthy, unlovely procedure of begging every laggard in our hemisphere to concur before action is taken, or will you men whom we choose to call our intellectual equals release us by your acts?

We ask for immediate recommendation by the Conference of the proposed Equal Rights treaty, a tentative draft of which we now present to you. This treaty was drawn up by Alice Paul, of the U. S., beloved feminist leader and distinguished scholar of international law.

We have told you what we want. The rest is up to you. Who will be the first country to dare to trust its women with that degree of equality which will come through the negotiation of the treaty? Which country among you will claim this honor?

Panamericanism will move a swifter, lovelier, more rhythmic pace, if men and women run together.

DR. MARTA ROBERT

Statement on Woman Suffrage in Porto Rico
APRIL 25, 1928

Just as American Indians found themselves in a liminal position on citizenship and voting, so too did the female residents of Puerto Rico. When Congress passed the Jones Act in 1917 granting U.S. citizenship to residents of the island, it did not specifically address the question of women's suffrage, leaving it to the Puerto Rican legislature to set voting qualifications, which were quickly defined as for men only. When the Nineteenth Amendment was ratified in 1920, some Puerto Rican women claimed they now had the right to vote, but the courts rebuffed them, drawing on the precedent of *Minor v. Happersett* (1875, see pages 163–176 in this volume), which drew a distinction between citizenship and voting. In the 1920s Puerto Rican activists joined with American feminists from the National Woman's Party to challenge women's voteless status. When the Puerto Rican legislature repeatedly dragged its feet on the issue, activists exploited Puerto Rico's anomalous status as a territorial possession to ask the U.S. Congress to amend the Jones Act to include women's suffrage. On April 25, 1928, Dr. Marta Robert (1890–1986), the secretary of the Liga Social Sufragista of Porto Rico and the director of the San Juan Maternity Hospital, testified before the Committee on Territories and Insular Possessions in support of S. 753, which would have extended the franchise to Puerto Rican women. Rather than cede the issue to congressional oversight, the Puerto Rican legislature enfranchised literate women on April 16, 1929, almost a decade after the passage of the Nineteenth Amendment. Not until 1935 did all Puerto Rican women receive the right to vote.

We American citizens, natives of Porto Rico and members of the Liga Social Sufragista of Porto Rico, request from you gentlemen of the American Congress a favorable recommendation on the bill, S. 753, introduced by Senator Bingham, in order to amend the organic act of Porto Rico by giving Porto Rican women the right to vote in their own country.

Porto Rico, as a possession of the United States, is ruled under a special organic act that was enacted by this same

Congress in 1917. There is a paragraph or an article in this organic act, the Jones Act, as it is called, which says:

> Voters shall be citizens of the United States, 21 years of age or over, and have such educational qualification as may be prescribed by the legislature of Porto Rico, provided that no property qualification shall ever be imposed upon or required of anyone.

This article does not say anything about women and men; but, of course, by this same article of this organic law the legislature of Porto Rico was given the right to make any discriminations they wanted, except those relating to property. So, when they made their law, they limited the voting privilege in Porto Rico to the men. They did not include women.

We feel very sure that if this law had been enacted after the amendment to the Constitution of the United States it would have been unconstitutional.

The women of Porto Rico, long before the amendment to the Constitution was introduced, were struggling and working hard to get their political rights. In 1919 we were successful in getting the first bill for woman suffrage introduced in our legislature, but, of course, it was just introduced, and we did not progress at all. In 1923 we had another bill; and in 1925 we had still another, but they were all introduced in different legislatures, and none of them progressed at all.

So, in 1925, when we came to Washington and got acquainted with some prominent members of the National Woman's Party, they advised us to get some action from Congress. So, we went back with that idea in our mind, and it was very favorable for us that in the last session of Congress Senator Bingham introduced the first bill for woman suffrage in the American Senate.

In those days Mr. Kiess, a Representative from Pennsylvania, was in Porto Rico visiting the island, so we talked things over with him and he showed very great interest in women's rights in Porto Rico. But he advised us to wait for another chance with the legislature for action on woman suffrage.

We waited, but we wasted time. During those days we were waiting for our legislature to act in favor of us, Senator Bingham introduced the same bill again, in December, 1927. Mr. Kiess introduced the same bill, so we really thought that we were getting more attention in the American Congress than we were getting in our own legislature. We waited to see if our legislature was going to act. This time Mr. Barcelo, the president of the senate, introduced a bill. The governor, in his message to the legislature, recommended appropriate legislation for woman suffrage. So, you see, the governor was in favor of woman suffrage. That was something for Porto Rican women.

The president of the senate was for it, because he had introduced a bill for woman suffrage. Of course, the bill that Mr. Barcelo introduced was based on literacy, and it was a very conservative one indeed, but we thought it was just a step in our progress. We accepted it. Of course, we would like to have equal rights, but we could not go against the bill. We had to accept it because it was a part of what we were asking for. The Porto Rican senate approved the bill this time, but the house of representatives did not even want to introduce it. So we decided to come and ask you ourselves; having the hope that you gentlemen of the American Congress would take a little more interest in seeing justice done to Porto Rican women.

Taking into consideration our biological and physiological nature, our Porto Rican men can not argue that we are not fitted to act in political affairs and have our political rights. You know, there are more than 30 countries now that have admitted woman suffrage, and we Porto Rican women are the same as all the rest of the women in the world, from the standpoint of biology.

There is a feeling among our men that if we obtained our political franchise our maternal duties and our domestic duties would be the first to suffer. But I do not think so, because there are a lot of women in Porto Rico who have been working for a long time. They go every day and spend long hours working outside. They leave their children and they leave their homes, and yet their children and their homes are well taken care of. So, if we go to work and leave our children and our homes, why can we not go for a little while every four years and vote for the sake of our country? There is not any logical argument against it.

We Porto Rican women think that we are already prepared for it. Since the time of the Spanish dominion, we have been educated and taught and cultured. Before the Americans went to Porto Rico, of course, we were not allowed in professional affairs, but we had great women in literature and art, and after the Americans came there we were admitted to all the professions. We have doctors, dentists, lawyers, pharmacists, and a lot of women in industries. There are a great many women in commerce and in public offices. We have women everywhere. They have shown their efficiency. We really think that men need us in our country in all lines of activity. They need us because we have a higher understanding of the necessities of life. We bring up children. We educate them. We know what they need. If we know what our children need, if we know what our homes need, I think that we can find out better than men what our country needs. [Applause.]

They say that if we get the right to vote we will be influenced by our husbands or by our brothers or by any male relatives in our political feelings. Suppose we are influenced by them. I think there ought to be an intellectual balance. If the influence is a good one, well and good; and if it is not, we ought to be in a position where we can do something about it.

In democracies sovereignty is made by the feelings of all human persons. We feel more than justified in coming to you, because you gave us our American citizenship by an organic law. Why should we not ask you to give us complete citizenship in our country? By our organic act, and by the nineteenth amendment to the Constitution, we are allowed to come here to the United States, in any part of the United States, and after six months' residence we have the right to vote, as any of our sisters in the United States. But the only thing that prohibits us from going to Porto Rico and voting and exercising our electoral right is just a little injustice from our men when they make the electoral law in Porto Rico.

They say it is not a very prudent thing to give woman suffrage to all women; that they ought to give it, but under a literacy test. We might accept that, but if you make this organic law in favor of women in Porto Rico, they have a perfect right to set up any qualifications whatsoever, and provide a standard of literacy, but they have to do it for both men and women. I do not think they could do it just for women. They would have to do it for men and women.

They want us to let them act on the right of Porto Rican

women to vote, but they got their citizenship from an organic act of Congress, and they obtained their political rights from an organic act of Congress. This organic act covers all persons— men and women. The women should obtain the same right as all our citizens.

I am pretty sure that whatever arguments they bring forward against suffrage for women in Porto Rico are going to be very, very poor. They have no argument. They may say that we have come from a Latin people and that we ought not to have that change so suddenly. We have had the same education for the last 30 years as they have had. We come here to American colleges. We go back with an American education, and we exercise all our American rights in Porto Rico. Why should we not have the right to vote? It is not going to have any bad effect whatsoever on the Porto Rican government, but it will improve it.

So, gentlemen, you whose duty it is to see that Porto Rico progresses, as all the States of the United States progress, should give us the same rights as the American women of the United States, because we are a part of the United States. You should give us the same right to exercise this privilege in our country as we have to exercise it in any part of the United States.

That is all I have to say. [Applause.]

EL CONGRESO DE PUEBLO DE HABLA ESPAÑOLA

Resolutions Adopted by the Second Convention

DECEMBER 9–10, 1939

When El Congreso de Pueblo de Habla Española convened the first national civil rights conference for Spanish-speaking peoples in Los Angeles in April 1939, women comprised almost a third of its core activists. As part of its broad vision of Latinx unity and solidarity, extending not just to Americanized citizens but also to immigrant noncitizens, activists such as Luisa Moreno (1907–1992) and Josefina Fierro de Bright (1914–1998) made sure that the double discrimination that Mexican American women faced was addressed alongside other pressing questions such as labor organizing, civil liberties, health and housing, and immigration. At the second convention of El Congreso, held eight months later in Los Angeles, the delegates passed a resolution specifically devoted to women, which called for equal wages and rights with men, better conditions in the home, and the creation of women's committees to represent and address the concerns of Mexican American women. This commitment to women's rights was part of a larger agenda of social, economic, and political justice for Spanish-speaking people and other minorities that was grounded in grassroots activism and strong community engagement, areas where *Latinx* women traditionally excelled. As Luisa Moreno said forcefully, "One person can't do anything; it's only with others that things are accomplished."

YOUTH

WHEREAS: There exists at the present time a great need of organizing the Spanish-speaking youth to better its conditions and secure a life of peace, security, recreation, and culture,

BE IT RESOLVED: That the Youth Councils and Committees do everything possible to organize the Spanish-speaking youth of the State for peace and the betterment of their economic situation, their recreational and educational facilities, and their life in all its aspects.

That in every community possible there be organized a Youth Council composed of a minimum of two delegates for every thirty-five members or fraction thereof, to solve the problems of the community which most affect the young people. Each Council shall have its Executive Committee of a President, Educational Director, a Secretary, and a Treasurer, as a minimum.

That the Councils of the various localities shall meet periodically; that delegates shall be sent monthly from such Councils and youth clubs where no Council yet exists, to the meetings of the Regional Council.

That in order to coordinate the state work, a State Organizer and Educational Director be elected, who will have the aid and co-operation of the Los Angeles' Youth Council.

That in every locality Youth Clubs be organized, affiliated directly to the State Youth Committee. They shall maintain their delegates in the Youth Councils of their respective districts. Where no Youth Council exists, the youth delegations locally shall form part of the Local (adult) Council of the Congress; and where neither Council exists of either youth or adults, the Youth Clubs will have the important task of creating one in their own community.

That to formalize and facilitate the youth work, Charters shall be granted to the various Councils and Youth Clubs affiliated to the Congress, and that membership books, educational bulletins, and other technical materials be made for the purpose. And

BE IT FURTHER RESOLVED: That the Congress grant autonomy to the Youth when it organizes a Youth Congress of the State of California, the same close and friendly relationships which have existed up to the present, being maintained.

EDUCATION

WHEREAS: Discrimination exists in many schools of the state, and in the majority of cases the instruction is not adapted to the background, psychology, and the social, cultural, and economic situation of the Mexican child, resulting in a marked deficiency in the achievement of the pupil,

BE IT RESOLVED: That the Congress' fight against discrimination and segregation in the schools, and in favor of the establishment of bi-lingual classes for children up to the eighth year, in order that they may acquire a background in both languages; for the employment of Mexican teachers in the schools where there is a large percentage of Mexican children; for standardized schools for migratory workers; for the education of the adults, under Mexican or Spanish-speaking instructors; and that the Congress establish within its organization an educational department under an educational director who shall be educated as a member of the Executive Committee, for the purpose of educating the membership and the organizations affiliated to or identified with the program and problems of the Congress.

LABOR SUB-SESSION

Since the Spanish-Speaking People's Congress is an organization which, by its program and activities, bases itself upon the organization of workers, who constitute the immense majority of the Mexican and Hispanish American people, and consequently protects the rights of the people to organize, in the Second Convention of the State Congress the various delegations there assembled agreed upon the best method of improving the activities of the Congress, resolving:

1. That the Congress, through organized groups, undertake a program of extensive education among the Spanish-speaking people to bring to them the program of the organized workers.
2. That in this program be included clear explanations of the workers' right to organize for mutual aid, bargain collectively, to strike, picket, and protect themselves from vigilantes, to free speech, and to all the guarantees included in the Bill of Rights.
3. That this Convention declare itself officially in favor of all legislation favorable to organized labor.
4. That this Convention back the extension of social security benefits to include unemployment during strikes and lockouts.
5. That this Convention officially favor the abolition of special police squads for workers.
6. That this Convention go on record officially in favor of the liberalization of the wages and hours law, of Social

Security, of more adequate protection for the unemployed by means of constructive work projects, and the preservation of the Wagner Act in the spirit in which this law was written and enforced in the first three years of its life; and be it finally resolved that these resolutions be given all the publicity possible and be sent to all the organizations and groups affiliated to the Congress.

———•———

In view of the problems which the Spanish-speaking racial groups have in the State of California, and taking into consideration that the agencies of organized labor offer the best means of reaching them with an educational program,

BE IT RESOLVED: That the Congress make a definite effort to guide the people into the labor unions through the following methods:

1. Education of the trade unions; direct information to the locals concerning the problems which affect the Spanish-speaking people through
   a. Pamphlets
   b. Dramatic presentations and visual education
   c. A bureau of official speakers
   d. A constant exchange of correspondence between the organizations and their locals informing them of all the problems of the Spanish-speaking people.
2. Furnishing the International Unions directly with information on our problems;
3. Sending communications to all labor unions;
4. Direct education of the members so that the matters affecting them may be classified;
5. Conducting deliberations in meetings in both Spanish and English where a large number of Spanish-speaking members exists.
6. The taking of measures to educate their members in both languages, the Spanish-speaking members educating themselves by associating with other racial minority groups so as thus to share and participate in social matters.

7. Furnishing information in Spanish in the following forms to the people in general:
   a. By radio
   b. Public or Mass meetings
   c. Among religious groups
   d. Through the press
8. Education of our people to know the value of the Union Label on all products.
9. Better living conditions for the people, through legislation.
10. The inclusion of agricultural workers in all state and federal labor legislation.
11. The legislation of anti-child labor laws and the enforcement of compulsory education.
12. The urging of the Spanish-speaking people to realize the necessity of using their right to vote as citizens.
13. The informing of the Spanish-speaking people concerning all labor legislation.
14. The enforcement of pure food laws, and the doing of everything possible to prevent the organization of gambling.
15. Finally, be it resolved that the Congress take a very active part among the organizations affiliated, that these comply with the monthly organizational fees of $1.00, and that all organizations be invited to affiliate to the Congress, regardless of belief or creed.

CIVIL LIBERTIES, IMMIGRATION AND CITIZENSHIP

Since the European war has as its aim the redivision of the colonial countries and the conquest and reconquest of the markets and the resources of the world, motives which resemble in more than one aspect the fundamental conditions which impelled the same nations toward the great disaster of 1914 to 1918; considering that the peoples of the United States, Mexico and all Latin America desire peace and complete neutrality; realizing that certain forces dominated by the manufacturers of munitions, war tanks, submarines, trucks, and the bank financiers desire war, because of the great profit that would result from the demands for their merchandise of death, and consequently force the country step by step towards disaster; and in view of the fact that a war situation would give these elements the opportunity to restrict the civil rights guaranteed to the people by the American Constitution's Bill of Rights, concessions obtained through many years of struggle, and would result in a campaign of deportations of the Mexican parents through anti-alien laws while sending the Mexican-American youth to the battle fronts,

BE IT RESOLVED: That President Roosevelt, in a goodwill gesture convoke all nations in the name of democracy, in an international congress to stop the war before it spreads to the Americas; that Congress do everything possible to unify the people for peace and neutrality; that the Pro-Congress Clubs discuss the possibilities for peace, hold conferences on the subject; that the Congress make a renewed effort for the maintenance of the Bill of Rights of the Constitution, an energetic struggle against the deportations and anti-alien laws enacted in Washington and Sacramento; that it support a bill to facilitate the acquiring of citizenship; that the Mexican people be educated concerning the requirements exacted of the non-citizen resident in this country, as well as concerning the process of becoming a citizen; that a movement be initiated to amend the City Charter of Los Angeles, to place the Police Department under the control of the people, and to break the grasp of the politicians and racketeers; and that a campaign against police brutality be carried out.

BE IT FURTHER RESOLVED: That this Congress protests, condemns and will take the action which lies within its power, concerning the boards of education which refuse to provide free transportation for the Mexican children who reside in places remote from the schools; this refers especially to the Fillmore Board of Education which denies said service to the children of the "Rancho Sespe".

BE IT FURTHER RESOLVED: That this Congress condemns the brutal action of the police upon making arrests, in using violence while conducting prisoners to jail, and every case of refusal to allow the prisoner access to legal counsel, or the interviewing of his lawyer or group to obtain legal aid.

BE IT ALSO RESOLVED: That a special Secretariat of foreign relations be set up to have relations with the organizations of Mexico and Central and South America.

RELIEF AND RELATED PROBLEMS

WHEREAS: A large number of our population lacks employment and must maintain a constant struggle against the reactionary forces that are attempting to deprive the Mexican people of all aid,

BE IT RESOLVED: That the Congress fight against any reactionary or "anti-alien" measure harmful to our people; against the so-called "decentralization" of relief; for more adequate aid, and more work projects, whether of W.P.A., S.R.A. or of the county, without discrimination by reason of race, color, creed or nationality.

WHEREAS: Colonel Harrington, W.P.A. Administrator, has announced that he will not ask for an emergency appropriation for the W.P.A. program this year, and since President Roosevelt announces a three billion dollar appropriation for national defense, it is evident that the administration is seeking a way to carry out the defense program at the expense of the misery and hunger of 11 million unemployed; therefore

BE IT RESOLVED: That Congress launch an energetic campaign of telegrams and letters to President Roosevelt protesting and demanding that the unemployed relief program be continued and expanded.

BE IT ALSO RESOLVED: That the federal stamp system be established in the State of California, because this plan increases or will cause to increase the purchasing power of the needy. It is recommended that copies of this resolution be sent to the administrative bodies of the relief agencies.

WHEREAS: The B.I.R. relief budget is a miserable one, and that many of the clients are ill and need special diets to regain their health,

BE IT RESOLVED: That the Congress launch a campaign to

have the budgets raised by 27%, in accord with the studies made by the Heller Institute, a budget that would allow a decent standard of living.

BE IT FURTHER RESOLVED: That all possible aid be given to the Government plan of giving a $60.00 pension to those persons more than 60 years of age who are not able to support themselves.

WOMEN

WHEREAS: The Mexican woman, who for centuries has suffered oppression, has the responsibility of raising her children and of caring for the home, and even that of earning a livelihood for herself and her family, and since in this country she suffers double discrimination, as a woman and as a Mexican,

BE IT RESOLVED: That the Congress carry out a program of organization and education of the Mexican women, concerning home problems; that every Pro-Congress Club establish a Women's Committee as soon as possible; that it support and work for woman's equality, so that she may receive equal wages, enjoy the same rights as men in social, economic, and civil liberties, and use her vote for the defense of the Mexican and Spanish American people, and of American democracy.

BE IT FURTHER RESOLVED: That the feminine sex be represented on the State Executive Committee and on the other executive committees of Congress' groups.

CULTURE

WHEREAS: Enormous possibilities exist for the development of Mexican culture, our people's offering to the culture of the United States as a whole, and despite its present negative aspect, and considering the people who through force of circumstances have not been able to continue in this country their work as artist or artisan,

BE IT RESOLVED: That the Congress encourage the establishment of cooperatives for Mexican and Spanish American artists and artisans, and of cultural centers; that a series of programs, expositions, contests, and lectures for Mexicans and Spanish Americans be developed; and that the aid of all groups sympathetic to this movement be sought.

HEALTH AND HOUSING

WHEREAS: Deplorable unsanitary conditions exist in the Mexican districts, caused by the run-down and overcrowded state of a great number of the houses, the lack of adequate facilities, and the high percentage of persons afflicted with all kinds of diseases,

BE IT RESOLVED: That the Congress support the Housing Program of the Federal Government, in cooperation with the Government of the State of California, to construct new houses and to better the existing ones, protecting the rights of the small property owners and of the persons who may be or may have been on relief.

We manifest our desire for the peace and neutrality of the United States, asking that such national funds be used for constructive projects rather than for war materials. We ask that the Mexican workers be employed in the construction of the houses, and that there be no race discrimination against the renters when said houses are completed; and a more equitable apportioning of public funds is asked, to improve the drainage, paving, and lighting of the poor districts which lack those facilities.

BE IT RESOLVED: That the Congress support a health program by which the Federal Government may cooperate with the government of the State of California for the betterment of health conditions and the establishment of clinics in all needy districts, and particularly in the Mexican ones, both urban and rural where the greatest sickness occurs, employing Mexican doctors and personnel: and that the Congress aid in educating the Mexican and Spanish American people, particularly the Mexican mothers, in hygiene and home problems, by means of conferences, movies, etc. presented in the various districts, by the Women's Council, Pro Congress Clubs, and other organizations.

ENGLISH-SPEAKING PANEL

WHEREAS: We as an organization, believe that the present war in Europe has its basis in the division of the colonial countries and the conquest and reconquest of the trade and resources of the world, resembling in many aspects the conditions which caused the World War of 1914–1918; that it is essentially imperialistic in nature and can produce as its fruit, only suffering, poverty, and economic and political instability for the peoples of the world; and

WHEREAS: The interests which profit through war in the United States are already encouraging a false patriotism to be utilized against national minorities and progressive groups in the United States and against the progressive governments of the Latin American countries, as is evidenced by the recent demands for armed intervention of Mexico to return the Mexican oil resources to the American super-corporations, in an effort to transform the Good Neighbor Policy into a Monroe Doctrine of force and intervention, and

WHEREAS: The Mexicans and Spanish Americans have contributed to the culture and economic life of this country, being rooted in the soil of California and the Southwest since the days of the exploration and settlement of this territory by the Spaniards and Mexicans, and in the course of history have become an integral part of the American Nation, as well as link of culture and of friendly relations between the people of the United States and those of Latin America a link which is now menaced here and abroad by war, and

WHEREAS: The present status of the Hispanic American peoples native to and resident in this country constitutes a general denial of full rights and democratic liberties guaranteed by the Constitution and by the principles of democracy itself,

BE IT RESOLVED: That the American people represented here in this conference oppose every proposal that may be made to carry the United States towards war, to intervene in any way in the affairs of the Latin American nations; support the principles of the Good Neighbor policy as based on respect for the complete sovereignty of the Latin American peoples; oppose the limitation of civil liberties, guaranteed by the American Constitution and by the principles of democracy; condemn the practice of discrimination, intimidation, and deportation as a means of solving the economic, social, and cultural problems of the Spanish speaking and other minority peoples; and applaud the purposes and principles of the Spanish Speaking

People's Congress as a means of stimulating healthy growth and activity in democratic channels and of furthering the cause of economic, social, and civil liberty; and

BE IT FURTHER RESOLVED: That the American people here present voluntarily constitute themselves a Committee to help organize an English-speaking group, for the purpose of furthering a better understanding and closer and more friendly relations between the Anglo American and the Spanish American peoples, whether in the United States or in Latin America.

ELEANOR ROOSEVELT

Women in Politics
JANUARY 1940

Sixteen years after Ida Tarbell argued in *Good Housekeeping* that women's suffrage had not been a failure, First Lady Eleanor Roosevelt (1884–1962) returned to the same theme for the same magazine. While she concluded that women had voted more as individuals than as a group and had used suffrage approximately the same way men had, one thing stood out for her: "namely, that on the whole, during the last twenty years, government has been taking increasing cognizance of humanitarian questions, things that deal with the happiness of human beings, such as health, education, security." She continued, "There is nothing, of course, to prove that this is entirely because of the women's interest, and yet I think it is significant that this change has come about during the period when women have been exercising their franchise." In this excerpt, the first of a three-part series, she catalogued the myriad contributions that women were making to politics and public life in both elected and appointed positions, the sheer volume of the list confirming that politics and government were no longer reserved for men only. What she was too modest to mention was the role that she had played as the wife of President Franklin D. Roosevelt (1882–1945) in opening many of these opportunities for women in the New Deal.

We are about to have a collective coming of age! The women in the United States have been participants in government for nearly twenty years. I think it behooves us to look back on this period in which we have been serving our apprenticeship and decide what our accomplishments have been, how much good our education has done us, and whether we really are able to consider ourselves full-fledged citizens.

Where did we start and how far have we come?

Twenty years ago, when we were granted the right of suffrage, some people thought that women were going to revolutionize the conduct of government. Yet all we were given was the right to vote. Men had had the vote on a fairly universal basis ever since the country was established—without achieving Utopia. Everyone knew that corruption still existed, and that the gentlemen did not always devote themselves to their civic duties in the unselfish and ardent manner that might be expected in a democracy. In 1919, however, this fact did not seem to prevent the belief that all desirable reforms would come about by the granting of suffrage to women. Alas and alas, the reforms just did not happen!

Perhaps it would be as well to mention also that some of the dire results prophesied if women were given the vote haven't come about, either.

Let us see what women have actually done in public life thus far.

It is fair, I think, to speak first of some of the women who were leaders in the fight for suffrage because of their influence on the thought of the men and women of the period, even though they may not actually have held public office. By studying them, I think we can get a very good idea of the qualities women must bring to public life. Dr. Anna Howard Shaw is dead; but Mrs. Carrie Chapman Catt is still alive, and I have had the privilege of knowing her for many years. Both seem to have certain qualities in common: a deep belief in the justice of a cause; the power to organize and inspire other women; the ability to speak fluently, and to be both humorous and dramatic. Add good physical health—not a quality, perhaps, but an essential—and you have a picture of these two suffrage leaders.

Certain other suffrage leaders I know only from hearsay. Inez Milholland, for instance, was probably very able, and she certainly used her personal attractions to drive home her point! There is no question about it, both charm and good looks are useful weapons, which ladies can always use to good advantage when they have them, no matter what offices they hold.

Available facts about women who have actually occupied political office during the past twenty years are incomplete, and it is extremely difficult to get accurate information. We can get figures for certain years and nothing for other years. Fortunately, the League of Women Voters will shortly publish its 1939 compilation on women in public office, which will supplement our information.

There are certain trends, however, that even incomplete figures seem to show. In the past ten years fewer women have been elected to Congress and to state legislatures. The peak was reached in 1929, when thirty-eight states could boast of one hundred and forty-nine women in state legislatures. In 1939 there were only twenty-eight states having women representatives, and the total was only one hundred and twenty-nine women.

However, the change is so very slight that I think we may consider it a temporary fluctuation, indicating nothing more than that women haven't yet gained real confidence in themselves in that type of competition. Besides, as we shall see, the number of women in appointive positions is steadily increasing.

In the United States Senate, Gladys Pyle, Republican of South Dakota, was elected in November 1938 for an unexpired term, which ended January 3, 1939. And three other women Senators were appointed to finish out unexpired terms and then retired. Mrs. Hattie Caraway, Democrat of Arkansas, is the one woman who has really served as a United States Senator. She was first appointed to succeed her husband in 1931, and then elected in 1932 and reelected in 1938. She has, I think, gained confidence in her ability and is respected by men in political life. At first one heard that she was under this or that influence; that she was a rubber stamp; that she did little thinking for herself; but of late one hears a great deal more about her being a useful member of the Senate and having a mind of her own. There is no doubt that she has grown and that her record can bear comparison with that of any of her colleagues.

In the House of Representatives, we have had twenty-one women members. Jeannette Rankin served before the adoption of the federal suffrage amendment. Her state of Montana had passed a suffrage act of its own. She will always be remembered for her inability to vote for war. One of the dramatic incidents reported in the newspapers of the day was how she burst into tears and refused to cast her vote in favor of war. I was not present, but I have always had a certain sympathy with the gesture even though it was futile.

Of these twenty-one members, eleven have been Republicans and ten Democrats. In the short session of the 71st Congress, nine women's names were carried on the rolls of the House of Representatives. This is the largest number carried at any one time. Since then the number has been steadily decreasing, till today there are only four women members of the House: Mary

Norton of New Jersey, Caroline O'Day of New York, Edith Nourse Rogers of Massachusetts, and Jessie Sumner of Illinois. Three of these women I know well; all are good, hard-working members and on a par with the men who have served with them.

I always think of Mary Norton as being primarily interested in welfare work, though she has grown far beyond those first interests. Caroline O'Day has fixed ideas on the subject of war, which nothing could change. Anyone who has seen her signature would know that she can wield the artist's brush, so it is no surprise to find that she was for many years a painter and illustrator, working here and in Paris. Edith Nourse Rogers still has her interest in World War soldiers, and she still looks charming in her old Red Cross uniform.

I remember also Ruth Hanna McCormick Simms, who, as a member of the House of Representatives, did credit to a family that has often served the public. And Mrs. Florence Kahn of California was an able and witty member, who would be welcomed back by the House with open arms. The picture is much the same in state legislatures.

We have had only two women state governors, both Democrats—Mrs. Nellie Tayloe Ross of Wyoming and Mrs. Miriam A. Ferguson of Texas. I met Mrs. Ferguson once and then only for a few minutes; but it is generally conceded that her job was that of being her husband's mouthpiece. This is pardonable in private life, but extremely unwise in public life, where every individual should stand on his or her own feet.

Mrs. Ross went into politics through the urging of her husband's friends, notably the present Senator, Joseph O'Mahoney of Wyoming. As far as I know, she filled her office creditably, had good advisors, knew her own limitations, and was on the whole an average good governor, though not a great one. She was elected for one term only, and that does not permit a man or a woman to accomplish much.

We will find on the rolls of both the elective and appointive officials, according to the laws of their respective states, a number of women as secretaries of state, state treasurers, state auditors—which looks as though women are better mathematicians than they are credited with being!

In the appointive positions, the trend shows an upward

curve in both state and federal governments. This would seem to prove me correct in my surmise that women are not yet prepared to go out and stand up under the average political campaign. In addition men rarely are inclined to give them nominations for elective positions if there is a chance to elect a man; so, frequently, a woman is beaten for an elective office before she starts to run.

In the old days men always said that politics was too rough-and-tumble a business for women; but that idea is gradually wearing away. There is more truth in the statement that men have a different attitude toward politics than women. They play politics a little more like a game. With the men, it becomes a serious occupation for a few weeks before election; whereas women look upon it as a serious matter year in and year out. It is associated with their patriotism and their duty to their country.

There are moments when I think that women's fervor to work continuously does not make them very popular with the gentlemen!

Mrs. Mabel Walker Willebrandt won my admiration long before I actually met her, while she was making a name for herself in President Hoover's administration. She helped to attain a model federal prison for women. This institution, headed by Dr. Mary Harris, does great credit to the vision of the women who fought so hard to obtain a new type of prison for women offenders. The head of the Department of Home Economics in the Department of Agriculture is Dr. Louise Stanley. She has been working there for a great many years, just as has Mary Anderson, the head of the Women's Bureau in the Department of Labor. Both of them have built up able staffs and are considered to be very useful government employees.

Katharine Lenroot, for instance, now chief of the Children's Bureau in the Department of Labor, followed Grace Abbott, with whom she had worked for many years. Both women have done a social-service job; but at the same time they have had to be good politicians, for their job could be carried on only if the men in Congress were convinced that it was being well done and that the people at home were receiving a service which they desired and in which they believed.

In 1933 about thirty-five women came into important

positions in Washington, and in the last six or seven years there has been an increase in the number of women appointed to more important offices. Strange as it may seem, I think this is due to the work of a woman who never held any office, except that of Vice-Chairman of the Democratic National Committee in charge of the Women's Division—Miss Mary W. Dewson.

Miss Dewson was interested in politics because of what she thought women could achieve through political organizations. She began her career in Boston, at the age of twenty-three, as a supervisor of the Girls' Parole Department of Massachusetts. She made her contact with state legislatures while she worked for the Consumers' League. She came into partisan political work during a national campaign. When that was over, she stayed on in the National Democratic Committee, and I think virtually all the men, from the President and Postmaster General Farley to most of the other heads of Departments, will concede that there has rarely been a woman more active in getting women into political positions! She was almost uncomfortably honest, at times somewhat brusque; but she had a sense of humor and a loyalty and devotion that made many people admire her and grieve when she was transferred from political work to the Social Security Board and when, finally, because of illness, she had to retire from active work.

Many women in Washington today hold positions because of ability and preparation that has little or no connection with political work. They have been distinguished along some special line, and frequently they came in long before the present administration. But those who came in during this administration owe a great deal to Molly Dewson, and women as a whole should be grateful for the fact that she never backed a woman whom she did not think capable of holding the job she was trying to get. The record of women in office during the past few years shows that her judgment was, on the whole, good.

We have, for instance, the first woman member of a President's Cabinet—the Secretary of Labor, Miss Frances Perkins. Most of us find it difficult to recall the names of former Secretaries of Labor. I happen to remember one or two; but I find, when I ask my friends about them, that the only Secretary of Labor whom they know much about is Frances Perkins, the present encumbent. They do not always sing her praises; but they do know that she exists—first, because she had a career before she held her present office; next, because she has held an extremely difficult position in a most trying period and, on the whole, has acquitted herself well. She has never really learned to handle the press, so her newspaper contacts are bad. This is partly because she is suspicious of reporters, and those around her, trying to protect her, accentuate this suspicion. I cannot say that this attitude is never justified; but with her keen intuition and her wide experience and contact with human nature, she should be able to distinguish between the fine and trustworthy correspondents and those who cannot be trusted. Newspaper correspondents are no different from other human beings—they are good and bad. Years ago Louis Howe told me that no group of people has a higher standard of ethics, and I still believe that to be true.

This inability to deal with the press is, I think, Frances Perkins' greatest weakness. I think she has been the best Secretary of Labor this country has had.

Mrs. Nellie Tayloe Ross, whom I have already mentioned as a former Governor of Wyoming, was Vice-Chairman of the Democratic National Committee in 1928 and was appointed Director of the Mint in the Treasury Department in 1933. There is nothing spectacular about her job; but it requires steady work. I think she has always performed her duties conscientiously.

The first woman Assistant Secretary of the Treasury was appointed in 1934: Miss Josephine Roche of Colorado. She has long been interested in social questions, and she transformed her coal mines in Colorado, when she inherited them from her father, to meet the standards she felt should exist in that industry. She came to Washington a proved executive. She retired of her own volition, feeling that her business required her attention; but she has retained the position of Chairman of the Committee to study medical service in this country. This Committee is doing an excellent piece of work.

In one other important branch of the government, the diplomatic service, we have had our first woman minister to a foreign country—Ruth Bryan Rohde, who was appointed our Minister to Denmark in 1933. She identified herself to such an extent with the interests of the country to which she was accredited that she returned to us married to a Dane. She resigned in 1936. Mrs. J. Borden Harriman was appointed Minister to Norway in 1937. From all accounts, she has taken a great interest in the conditions of the people there and has been able to give to our country a very much better understanding of the Norwegian people.

Two women held major judicial posts in 1930. Florence Allen, a judge on the Supreme Court Bench in Ohio, and Genevieve R. Cline, who had been appointed to the United States Customs Court in New York City, which is a life commission. In 1939 Florence Allen was appointed by President Roosevelt to the United States Circuit Court of Appeals, 6th District. Miss Cline remained on the bench in New York. Miss Garrick H. Buck was made judge of the 5th District of the Supreme Court in Hawaii.

In the Labor Department we find Miss Mary La Dame, special assistant to the Secretary of Labor. Everyone knows the name of Mrs. Lucille Foster McMillin, on the Civil Service Commission. She, like Mrs. Ellen Woodward, formerly head of the women's and professional projects under the Works Progress Administration, and now on the Social Security Board, would impress you first as a very feminine woman with charm and social distinction; but both of them know how to be good executives and work hard. They may carry their sympathetic understanding of human problems with them in their working hours, but they also carry level heads and a keen intelligence, which makes them acceptable members of any men's conference. Mrs. Florence Kerr, who is now in the Works Progress Administration, is proving herself to be a good executive, also.

Miss Katherine Blackburn is head of one of the most interesting bureaus in Washington, the Bureau of Press Intelligence, which will get for any member of the government information on any subject! To be sure, the Library of Congress will do this, too, but not quite in the up-to-date, last-minute manner that Katherine Blackburn has evolved.

Over in the Printing Office is a woman who won her knowledge in the printing rooms of a number of newspapers. Miss Jo Coffin comes from the ranks of labor, just as does Miss Rose Schneiderman, who was a valuable member of the Advisory

Committee of the National Recovery Administration while it functioned, and who today is in the New York State Department of Labor as Secretary to the Commissioner. Both of them are interesting women, capable of firing the imagination of young people, resourceful, tactful, patient, and therefore valuable in their contacts with their superiors and their fellow workers.

Marian Bannister, the sister of Senator Carter Glass of Virginia, reminds me of the old French nobility. I am sure she could walk to the guillotine with absolute dignity and calm! She signs the President's pay check and all the mail that goes out of the office of the Treasurer.

Mrs. Jewell W. Swofford is chairman of the United States Employment Compensation Commission. And Laura S. Brown and Lucy Howorth are doing good work in the Veterans' Administration. For the first time there is a woman, Marion J. Harron, on the Board of Tax Appeals.

In 1939 there were approximately fifty-five women in major positions throughout the federal government. The number of women in clerical, fiscal, and professional positions has grown to 162,518.

Many other women I have not mentioned are competently filling important positions; but my list is already too long. I do not wish to close, however, without mentioning three women. Mrs. Mary Harriman Rumsey, who headed the Consumers' Division in the old NRA days, had a thankless job. She devoted herself to it nevertheless, and had she lived, would, I think, have helped in a field not as yet sufficiently developed in this country.

Two other women, while not actually holding public office, have done so much to affect the thinking of both men and women on political questions that I feel they should not be forgotten. One is Anne O'Hare McCormick, who was chosen last year as the woman of distinction for 1939. She has established a record in her interviews with important people who make world policies today. Her fairness, her ability to understand varying points of view and to report the essence of a conversation have won her distinction and a following among thinking people everywhere. Her analysis and presentation of world situations has helped clarify many difficult and universally interesting points.

The other woman is Dorothy Thompson, also a political writer of distinction, swayed perhaps by her own emotions, personal interests, and past experience, but still with such a gift of expression that she has a great following.

All these women are blazing trails for women in the future, and by the success or failure of their work they will either increase the possibility of women's participation in government or make the public less anxious to place women in positions of responsibility.

To me it seems that those who have borne the brunt of the fight thus far are rather shining examples of what women can do in the political arena if they really work, and I think it will be interesting to watch not individual women, but the accomplishment of women as a whole in the field of public affairs.

JOHN F. KENNEDY

President's Commission on the Status of Women

DECEMBER 14, 1961

Under criticism for his poor record on women's issues, President John F. Kennedy (1917–1963) asked Eleanor Roosevelt to serve as chair of a presidential commission to survey the status of American women. Overseen by Esther Peterson (1906–1997), the head of the Women's Bureau, the President's Commission on the Status of Women (PCSW) documented a range of barriers that limited women's full participation in American life, with special focus on education and employment. One of the most contentious issues it dealt with was protective labor legislation for women workers, the same issue that had roiled the post-suffrage women's movement in the 1920s. The American labor movement in general and labor feminists like Peterson adamantly opposed the Equal Rights Amendment, which they claimed would rob women workers of hard-won wage and hours protection. The final commission report, issued on what would have been Eleanor Roosevelt's seventy-ninth birthday on October 11, 1963 (she had died the year before), endorsed the principle of women's legal equality but did not anticipate the need for a constitutional amendment "now," a compromise designed to assuage ERA supporters. The PCSW's largest impact was the establishment of state commissions on the status of women. The networks of activist women they brought together played an important role in the revival of feminism, including the establishment of the National Organization for Women (NOW) in 1966.

EXECUTIVE ORDER 10980

WHEREAS prejudices and outmoded customs act as barriers to the full realization of women's basic rights which should be respected and fostered as part of our Nation's commitment to human dignity, freedom, and democracy; and

WHEREAS measures that contribute to family security and strengthen home life will advance the general welfare; and

WHEREAS it is in the national interest to promote the economy, security, and national defense through the most efficient and effective utilization of the skills of all persons; and

WHEREAS in every period of national emergency women have served with distinction in widely varied capacities but thereafter have been subject to treatment as a marginal group whose skills have been inadequately utilized; and

WHEREAS women should be assured the opportunity to develop their capacities and fulfill their aspirations on a continuing basis irrespective of national exigencies; and

WHEREAS a Governmental Commission should be charged with the responsibility for developing recommendations for overcoming discriminations in government and private employment on the basis of sex and for developing recommendations for services which will enable women to continue their role as wives and mothers while making a maximum contribution to the world around them:

NOW, THEREFORE, by virtue of the authority vested in me as President of the United States by the Constitution and statutes of the United States, it is ordered as follows:

PART I—ESTABLISHMENT OF THE PRESIDENT'S COMMISSION ON THE STATUS OF WOMEN

Sec. 101. There is hereby established the President's Commission on the Status of Women, referred to herein as the "Commission". The Commission shall terminate not later than October 1, 1963.

Sec. 102. The Commission shall be composed of twenty members appointed by the President from among persons with a competency in the area of public affairs and women's activities. In addition, the Secretary of Labor, the Attorney General, the Secretary of Health, Education and Welfare, the Secretary of Commerce, the Secretary of Agriculture and the Chairman of the Civil Service Commission shall also serve as members of the Commission. The President shall designate from among the membership a Chairman, a Vice-Chairman, and an Executive Vice-Chairman.

Sec. 103. In conformity with the Act of May 3, 1945 (59 Stat. 134, 31 U.S.C. 691), necessary facilitating assistance, including the provision of suitable office space by the Department of Labor, shall be furnished the Commission by the Federal agencies whose chief officials are members thereof. An Executive Secretary shall be detailed by the Secretary of Labor to serve the Commission.

Sec. 104. The Commission shall meet at the call of the Chairman.

Sec. 105. The Commission is authorized to use the services of consultants and experts as may be found necessary and as may be otherwise authorized by law.

PART II—DUTIES OF THE PRESIDENT'S COMMISSION
ON THE STATUS OF WOMEN

Sec. 201. The Commission shall review progress and make recommendations as needed for constructive action in the following areas:

(a) Employment policies and practices, including those on wages, under Federal contracts.

(b) Federal social insurance and tax laws as they affect the net earnings and other income of women.

(c) Federal and State labor laws dealing with such matters as hours, night work, and wages, to determine whether they are accomplishing the purposes for which they were established and whether they should be adapted to changing technological, economic, and social conditions.

(d) Differences in legal treatment of men and women in regard to political and civil rights, property rights, and family relations.

(e) New and expanded services that may be required for women as wives, mothers, and workers, including education, counseling, training, home services, and arrangements for care of children during the working day.

(f) The employment policies and practices of the Government of the United States, with reference to additional affirmative steps which should be taken through legislation, executive or administrative action to assure non-discrimination on the basis of sex and to enhance constructive employment opportunities for women.

Sec. 202. The Commission shall submit a final report of its recommendations to the President by October 1, 1963.

Sec. 203. All executive departments and agencies of the Federal Government are directed to cooperate with the Commission in the performance of its duties.

PART III—REMUNERATION AND EXPENSES

Sec. 301. Members of the Commission, except those receiving other compensation from the United States, shall receive such compensation as the President shall hereafter fix in a manner to be hereafter determined.

JOHN F. KENNEDY

THE WHITE HOUSE
December 14, 1961

FANNIE LOU HAMER

Testimony to the Credentials Committee, Democratic National Convention

AUGUST 22, 1964

On August 22, 1964, Fannie Lou Hamer (1917–1977) testified before the credentials committee at the Democratic National Convention in Atlantic City on behalf of the Mississippi Freedom Democratic Party (MFDP), a grassroots organization challenging the all-white convention delegation selected by the regular Democratic Party in that state. In riveting testimony, Hamer told the committee how when she tried to register to vote in 1962, the owner of the plantation where she worked as a sharecropper and timekeeper fired her and evicted her family. She became a field secretary for the Student Nonviolent Coordinating Committee (SNCC) and took an active role in voter registration drives, where she was subjected to the brutal beating in jail she described in this testimony, which was broadcast live by the major networks. President Lyndon Johnson, deeply concerned about losing support from southern white voters, hastily called a press conference to preempt Hamer's powerful presentation. The credentials committee refused to accept the MFDP's challenge. When party leaders brokered a deal that allowed the MFDP delegation two at-large seats with no voting rights, they were angrily rebuffed. However, four years later Hamer would serve as a delegate to the Democratic National Convention in Chicago.

Mr. Chairman, and to the Credentials Committee, my name is Mrs. Fannie Lou Hamer, and I live at 626 East Lafayette Street, Ruleville, Mississippi, Sunflower County, the home of Senator James O. Eastland and Senator Stennis.

It was the thirty-first of August in 1962, that eighteen of us traveled twenty-six miles to the county courthouse in Indianola to try to register to become first-class citizens. We was met in Indianola by policemen, highway patrolmen, and they only allowed two of us in to take the literacy test at the time. After we had taken this test and started back to Ruleville, we was held up by the city police and the state highway patrolmen and carried back to Indianola where the bus driver was charged that day with driving a bus the wrong color.

After we paid the fine among us, we continued on to Ruleville, and Reverend Jeff Sunny carried me four miles in the rural area where I had worked as a timekeeper and sharecropper for eighteen years. I was met there by my children, who told me that the plantation owner was angry because I had gone down, tried to register. After they told me, my husband came, and said the plantation owner was raising Cain because I had tried to register. And before he quit talking the plantation owner came and said, "Fannie Lou, do you know—did Pap tell you what I said?"

And I said, "Yes, sir."

He said, "Well, I mean that." Said, "If you don't go down and withdraw your registration, you will have to leave." Said, "Then if you go down and withdraw, then you still might have to go because we are not ready for that in Mississippi."

And I addressed him and told him and said, "I didn't try to register for you. I tried to register for myself." I had to leave that same night.

On the tenth of September 1962, sixteen bullets was fired into the home of Mr. and Mrs. Robert Tucker for me. That same night two girls was shot in Ruleville, Mississippi. Also, Mr. Joe McDonald's house was shot in.

And June the ninth, 1963, I had attended a voter registration workshop—was returning back to Mississippi. Ten of us was traveling by the Continental Trailways bus. When we got to Winona, Mississippi, which is in Montgomery County, four of the people got off to use the washroom, and two of the people—to use the restaurant—two of the people wanted to use the washroom. The four people that had gone in to use the restaurant was ordered out. During this time I was on the bus. But when I looked through the window and saw they had rushed out, I got off of the bus to see what had happened. And one of the ladies said, "It was a state highway patrolman and a chief of police ordered us out."

I got back on the bus and one of the persons had used the washroom got back on the bus, too. As soon as I was seated on the bus, I saw when they began to get the five people in a highway patrolman's car. I stepped off of the bus to see what was happening and somebody screamed from the car that the five workers was in and said, "Get that one there." And when

I went to get in the car, when the man told me I was under arrest, he kicked me.

I was carried to the county jail and put in the booking room. They left some of the people in the booking room and began to place us in cells. I was placed in a cell with a young woman called Miss Euvester Simpson. After I was placed in the cell, I began to hear sounds of licks and screams. I could hear the sounds of licks and horrible screams. And I could hear somebody say, "Can you say, 'yes, sir,' nigger? Can you say 'yes, sir'?" And they would say other horrible names.

She would say, "Yes, I can say 'yes, sir.'"

"So, well, say it."

She said, "I don't know you well enough." They beat her, I don't know how long. And after a while she began to pray, and asked God to have mercy on those people.

And it wasn't too long before three white men came to my cell. One of these men was a state highway patrolman and he asked me where I was from. And I told him Ruleville and he said, "We are going to check this." And they left my cell and it wasn't too long before they came back. He said, "You's from Ruleville all right," and he used a curse word. And he said, "We are going to make you wish you was dead."

I was carried out of that cell into another cell where they had two Negro prisoners. The state highway patrolmen ordered the first Negro to take the blackjack. The first Negro prisoner ordered me, by orders from the state highway patrolman, for me to lay down on a bunk bed on my face.

And I laid on my face and the first Negro began to beat. And I was beat by the first Negro until he was exhausted. I was holding my hands behind me at that time on my left side, because I suffered from polio when I was six years old. After the first Negro had beat until he was exhausted, the state highway patrolman ordered the second Negro to take the blackjack. The second Negro began to beat and I began to work my feet, and the state highway patrolman ordered the first Negro had beat me to sit on my feet—to keep me from working my feet. I began to scream and one white man got up and began to beat me in my head and tell me to hush. One white man—my dress had worked up high—he walked over and pulled my dress, I pulled my dress down and he pulled my dress back up.

I was in jail when Medgar Evers was murdered.

All of this is on account of we want to register, to become first-class citizens. And if the Freedom Democratic Party is not seated now, I question America. Is this America, the land of the free and the home of the brave, where we have to sleep with our telephones off of the hooks because our lives be threatened daily, because we want to live as decent human beings, in America? Thank you.

CONSTANCE BAKER MOTLEY

Speech to the Southern Christian Leadership Conference
AUGUST 9, 1965

For African American women, indeed for most minority women, the
Civil Rights Act of 1964 and the Voting Rights Act of 1965 had a far
greater impact on their political and legal status than the Nineteenth
Amendment. The cornerstone of the Civil Rights Act of 1964 was
Title VII, which outlawed discrimination in employment on the basis
of race, religion, sex, or national origin. Another section barred discrimination in public accommodations, which resulted in the desegregation of public facilities throughout the South, although obstacles to
black voting rights remained. In response, Congress passed the Voting
Rights Act of 1965, which suspended literacy tests and other measures
designed to keep African Americans from registering to vote, and authorized federal registrars to intervene whenever less than 50 percent
of the voting-age population was registered. The passage of that pathbreaking legislation was the backdrop for this speech by Constance
Baker Motley (1921–2005) to the Southern Christian Leadership
Conference in Birmingham, Alabama, on August 9, 1965. Motley had
worked closely with Thurgood Marshall (1908–1993) at the NAACP
on *Brown v. Board of Education* and later became a federal judge. Her
prediction that the Voting Rights Act would "rewrite the history of the
Southern states" was quickly confirmed: in 1971, 62 percent of eligible
blacks were registered, compared to only 20 percent in 1960. While
her speech focuses more on race than on gender, Motley's salute to
Rosa Parks (1913–2005) demonstrates her awareness of the key role
that African American women played in the larger freedom struggle.

First, I want to say how pleased I am to have this opportunity
to address the Southern Christian Leadership Conference on its
return to desegregated Birmingham. Your coveted invitation to
be the guest speaker at this opening night banquet is, indeed,
a high compliment.

No city in America owes more to the SCLC than Birmingham. Your crusade for freedom put Birmingham on the civil
rights map and has assured it a place in the history of our fight
for freedom.

I am especially proud to be here to honor the movement's most celebrated daughter, Rosa Parks.

We do honor tonight Mrs. Parks, the freedom fighter whose proud refusal to move to the back of the bus in Montgomery, Alabama, ten years ago was an act of courage comparable in importance to that of the Yankee Militiaman at Concord, who "fired the shot heard 'round the world." No Emerson has yet given Mrs. Park's historic act the poetic commemoration which it deserves, but when the history of the second half of the twentieth century is written there is no doubt in my mind that Montgomery, 1955, will rank with Fort Sumter, 1861, and Concord, Massachusetts, 1775, as a turning point in our nation's history.

It is, of course, always a great pleasure to see Martin King, but especially on a memorable occasion such as this. The record Dr. King has compiled in the last ten years has established him not only as America's most widely acclaimed freedom fighter but as spokesman for the entire country. He is an American hero of authentic distinction who has achieved an unprecedented position of respect and prestige throughout the world. His inspiring oratory, his doctrine of aggressive restraint, his sweeping influence for good over the entire American scene, have made him a leader of unique importance—every great cause requires great leadership. We are fortunate indeed that, at this time in history, Dr. King came to us to serve and to lead.

The Civil Rights Act of 1964, that historic declaration of human equality, would have been thought impossible ten years ago at the time Mrs. Parks refused to obey the order to move to the back of the bus. Yet, today, we find that momentous act significantly strengthened and implemented by the Voting Rights Act of 1965. The Voting Rights Act will rewrite the history of the southern United States in the next few decades. Nevertheless, its passage through congress was relatively tranquil. It is a measure of the strength of the civil rights forces that such a significant legislation—this pioneer involvement by the federal government in an area previously left to state misrule—was passed with such near unanimity.

Notably, most of the opposition to the new voting rights act came from states where people are denied the right to vote. That opposition, we hope, has been now put down for all time by the passage of this new act. Consequently, we can all well understand the new-found fear and trembling on the part of the Jim Crow governors and legislators as they contemplate the future expansion of their constituencies. Let the new voters of the 1960s remember at the polls officials whose racist appeals kept them in political bondage. But let them never forget those civil rights martyrs who laid down their lives for this new day.

The importance of the Voting Rights Act was illustrated by the historic manner in which it was signed last Friday by President Johnson. The president and the entire cabinet assembled and went to the rotunda of the Capitol. There the president spoke on this second great landmark in civil rights legislation passed during the Johnson administration. With unprecedented speed, the Justice Department has moved toward implementation of the Voting Rights Bill by the filing of a suit in Mississippi to bar enforcement of that state's poll tax law.

I believe that wise exercise of the right to vote is now the keystone to actual equality, legal equality having been won. It is through the ballot that the great social changes which transformed America in the past have been authorized. The voting strength of Negroes does not mean only civil rights legislation and the complete destruction of state-supported segregation and discrimination. It means an equal share in the state's revenues for all communities and individuals, regardless of race. It means paved streets in the Negro community as well as in the white community. And it means the harnessing of the power and resources of the state to provide the economic changes required for the elimination of poverty and illiteracy. The gains achieved in the civil rights area thus provide hope for gains in other areas. All this will be part of the impact of the Voting Rights Act of 1965.

Another important gain which has been won in recent years is the ruling of the United States Supreme Court in support of that honored but often ignored principle known as "one man, one vote." The elimination of malapportionment and rural domination of state legislatures has enfranchised city voters and brought legislators closer to the realities of the twentieth century.

In this connection we should be thankful for the recent defeat in the United States Senate of the Dirksen Amendment which would have overruled the Supreme Court's "one man, one vote" decision. Yet, we must remember that this amendment, which would have allowed for the reapportionment of one house of the state legislature, on a basis other than population, actually received a majority of votes in the Senate. It received fifty-seven votes while only thirty-nine were cast against it. Needless to say, every senator from the states where Negroes are denied the right to vote supported this amendment. It was only defeated because a two-thirds vote is required for a constitutional amendment. We cannot be secure when, in the most heavily democratic and liberal senate of this century, such a proposal could come within seven voters of adoption.

Another result of the "one man, one vote" decision has been the end of the state of Georgia's county unit system, under which a candidate who received a majority of votes could actually be defeated by overweighted rural ballots in a statewide primary. As if it were not bad enough that Negroes were not allowed to vote in Georgia, when they did vote, their votes were not counted equally. But the fact that such an utter perversion of majority rule could have persisted for so long, and the fact that it took federal intervention to destroy it, shows how fragile our liberties are.

Today, 1965, ten Negroes sit in the Georgia Legislature, two senators and eight representatives. Some day the legislatures of all southern states will contain Negroes in substantial numbers. That day cannot come too soon.

I should say at this time that as many of you know I hold the office of president of the Borough of Manhattan. In this an elective office I represent 1,700,000 residents in the heart of New York City. My jurisdiction includes Black Harlem and Park Avenue, Wall Street, and Chinatown. Manhattan's newly created Puerto Rican ghettoes and the famous Lower East Side. I am the twentieth person to hold the office of borough president since the position was established with the consolidation of five boroughs (counties) into New York City on January 1, 1898. In the beginning, most of the borough presidents were Irish-Americans. In the 1930s and '40s there was a string of Jewish borough presidents. In November 1953, a Negro was elected to hold this position for the first time.

When the borough presidency was held by a member of a

white minority group, one did not hear racist charges or complaints. Historically in New York as in many areas candidates had been nominated for office for many different reasons one of which is their ethnic appeal. The tradition of the balanced ticket in a melting pot society is an old custom that has been adhered to by reformers and traditionalists alike. Yet, when this rotation of office brings a succession of Negroes into a high position there is an undercurrent of dissatisfaction. The quality of the candidate is ignored and the feeling is piously expressed that race should not be a factor in the selection of candidates. Where were all these critics when Negroes were excluded from candidacy or public office because of their race? I believe that full equality demands treatment of the Negro community the same way that our society treats its other communities and that includes the political recognition of the Negro.

I believe in electing people without regard to their race, and I am aware that those who cry "race"—on both sides—are often those who have no more worthy arguments to present. But I do not believe that all the merit and all the fitness to govern can be found in people of one color. I look forward to the day when race will be relegated to obscurity as a criterion in the selection of candidates for high office. But until that happy day we must all remain aware of our longstanding struggle to prevent discrimination and to gain first-class citizenship for the Negro. And I know as you know that first-class citizenship means not only the right to vote but the right to run for office and the right to hold public office. In order to do this, it will be necessary for Negroes by the hundreds of thousands to take advantage of the new federal laws and to register and vote.

A Negro who does not vote is just plain ungrateful to those who already have died in the fight for freedom. A Negro who does not vote is not helping to make a better world for his or her children. A Negro who does not vote is lending aid and support to the racists who argue that Negroes will not assume the responsibilities of citizenship. Any person who does not vote is failing to serve the cause of freedom, his own freedom, his people's freedom, and his country's freedom.

The theme of this convention is the "Grand Alliance." This term is used to denote the alliance of organized labor, the church liberals, and intellectuals along with the civil rights movement. This is the confederation which has provided the momentum for much of America's social progress. The Grand Alliance is the backbone of the fight for freedom. The partners of the alliance believe in human rights not merely in the exaltation of property rights and state's rights.

Under the leadership of Dr. Martin Luther King the alliance has strengthened and taken shape. Now, more than ever, all its components are becoming involved in the full struggle for equality. That means not only political and social equality, but economic equality which makes possible the full enjoyment of legal equality.

The alliance currently exists in a relatively informal sense depending on relations between individuals. It is underfinanced and overextended. Although noble in purpose, it is a fledgling in operation. It is in need of substantial assistance from all the allies if it is to take its rightful place as the people's lobby.

The alliance should support the reformation of American society in a great many areas. It should seek massive federal assistance for employment and training of the unemployed adult male population especially among Negroes. It must seek such assistance to teach children to read, to integrate our schools, to build decent homes, and to provide adequate health care for all Americans.

In its struggle for the achievement of these social goals the alliance should use all the time-honored methods which Americans have used to seek freedom. I am reminded of a statement made just six days ago by President Johnson, at the White House. The president said: "So free speech, free press, free religion, the right of assembly, yes, the right of petition, the right to buy ads, and to have teach-ins and sit ins, and parade and march and demonstrate, well they are all still radical ideas, and so are secret ballots and so is the principle of equal dignity and so is the principle of equal rights for all the sons and daughters of man. But all of these things are what America stands for and all of these things are what you and all other Americans need to stand up for today."

President Johnson thus encouraged the fullest range of expression for Americans anxious to improve social conditions and to implement court decisions already won. I think we should consider his remarks carefully and be guided by his words. We should not be weary. We must move toward full equality for our children's sake. Let's not forget them.

In pursuit of this goal, now is the time to finish the task of integrating our schools. In this struggle we have a strong new ally in the Department of Health, Education, and Welfare, which now has the responsibility for withholding federal funds from school districts which refuse to desegregate. Tonight we are dining in a white hotel in Birmingham, several hundred of us. But how many Negroes will go to school with whites in Birmingham come September 1965? How many Negro teachers will teach white children who are now teaching Negro children? The Department of Health, Education, and Welfare has its responsibility but we also have ours. Our responsibility is to secure for our children all of the rights for which the civil rights revolution of the last decade was fought. There are today no more Jim Crow buses—there are only Negroes who are afraid to ride up front. There are no more segregated public recreational facilities—only Negroes who are afraid to take advantage of their rights. There are no more legally segregated schools—only Negro parents en masse to take their children by the hand to a white school in September 1965. I predict that such a demonstration by Negro parents coupled with the new federal determination to require compliance with the school desegregation decision as a condition of federal financial assistance will bring a swift end to segregated school systems in the south. Just as Rosa Parks's courageous refusal to be segregated brought about the end of Jim Crow travel in this nation so every Negro mother has it within her power to end school segregation.

Rosa Parks we honor you tonight because yours is the kind of courage and determination and nonviolent spirit we all need for the future. Your name will be remembered as long as freedom is abroad in this land. My prayer in Birmingham tonight is that Negro women everywhere will follow your example and hasten the day when all of our hard won legal rights are secure in practice here and throughout the land.

CHRONOLOGY

NOTE ON THE TEXTS

NOTE ON THE ILLUSTRATIONS

NOTES

INDEX

Chronology

1776   The Declaration of Independence, adopted by the Continental Congress on July 4, declares that "all men are created equal" but does not grant political or legal equality to either women or enslaved African Americans. Several months earlier Abigail Adams had chided her husband John to "remember the ladies" when framing the legal basis of the new government.

1787   The U.S. Constitution, ratified on June 21, puts voting qualifications in the hands of individual states, which limit the franchise to men and often include property requirements. New Jersey is the exception, offering the vote to property-owning "inhabitants" regardless of sex.

1807   Propertied women lose the right to vote in New Jersey when the state legislature passes a law that defines voters as adult white taxpaying men.

1832   A freeborn black essayist and reformer, Maria W. Stewart becomes the first lecturer, black or white, to address the topic of women's rights before a mixed audience including men and women. Her speech forthrightly confronts the oppression of African Americans and calls on them to determine their own futures. Stewart gives three additional lectures over the next year before withdrawing from public life in 1833.

1837   Abolitionist Sarah Moore Grimké publishes *Letters on the Equality of the Sexes*, fifteen letters nominally addressed to Mary S. Parker, the president of the Boston Female Anti-Slavery Society, but intended for a popular audience. The letters range widely over religion, culture, and politics and promote Grimké's radical view that women should be able to participate in those realms on equal terms with men.

1838   Angelina Grimké, Sarah Moore Grimké's older sister, addresses the Massachusetts legislature in February about slavery, the first woman to do so. The careers of both Grimké sisters demonstrate the close links between the abolitionist cause and the emerging women's rights movement in the 1830s and 1840s.

1840   Lucretia Mott and Elizabeth Cady Stanton meet at the World Anti-Slavery Convention in London in June, where they are relegated to sit in a separate section from the main gathering because of their sex. In response, they discuss holding a women's rights convention in the United States when they return home.

1845   Margaret Fuller publishes her seminal work *Woman in the Nineteenth Century*, an expanded version of her essay "The Great Lawsuit. Man versus Men. Woman versus Women," which appeared in *The Dial* in 1843. A journalist and editor, Fuller is a leading intellectual of her time and a bold thinker on the role of women in public and private spheres.

1846   Six women from Jefferson County, New York, petition the state legislature for suffrage.

1848   The New York Married Women's Property Act, enacted on April 7, allows women to own and control their own property and becomes a model for other states. The Seneca Falls Convention, held in Seneca Falls, New York, in July, adopts a "Declaration of Sentiments" and eleven resolutions, including a demand for the "elective franchise" for women.

1850   The First National Woman's Rights Convention is held in Worcester, Massachusetts. Featured speakers include Paulina Wright Davis, Abby Kelley Foster, Harriot Kezia Hunt, William Lloyd Garrison, Ernestine Rose, Lucretia Mott, Frederick Douglass, and Lucy Stone.

1851   Sojourner Truth addresses the Ohio Woman's Rights Convention in Akron, Ohio. Born into slavery and achieving freedom around 1827, Truth becomes one of the most widely known African American women of the nineteenth century, rivalled only by Harriet Tubman, who is twenty years her junior. Throughout her life, Truth consistently refuses to separate race from sex, insisting that black women's voices be heard in both freedom movements.

1852   The Third National Woman's Rights Convention is held in Syracuse, New York. Lucretia Mott serves as president and Susan B. Anthony makes her first women's rights speech.

1855   Lucy Stone and Henry Browne Blackwell issue a public protest against the institution of marriage when they marry on May 1; Stone refuses to take her husband's name. Stone and Blackwell, both antislavery and women's rights advocates, had met through the antislavery movement.

1860 New York State passes a law in March allowing married women to control their wages and earnings. This bill continues the trend begun by the 1848 Married Women's Property Act to expand the legal rights of women, especially married women.

1863 The Woman's Loyal National League is founded to support the war effort in the North during the Civil War and to press for a constitutional amendment to abolish slavery. It presents Congress with petitions containing over 400,000 signatures calling for the end of slavery and is a major factor in the passage of the Thirteenth Amendment in 1865.

1866 At the first women's rights convention held after the Civil War, the American Equal Rights Association is formed to work for universal suffrage. Its constitution defines its purpose as "to secure Equal Rights for all American citizens, especially the right of suffrage, irrespective of race, color or sex."

1867 Kansas defeats referenda on women's suffrage and black suffrage, despite the efforts of Elizabeth Cady Stanton, Susan B. Anthony, Lucy Stone, and Henry Blackwell, all of whom campaign in the state.

1868 The Fourteenth Amendment, extending citizenship to "all persons born or naturalized in the United States," is ratified on July 9, and introduces the word "male" into the Constitution. One hundred seventy-two women in Vineland, New Jersey, attempt to vote in the presidential election in November. The first edition of *The Revolution*, a women's rights newspaper started by Susan B. Anthony and Elizabeth Cady Stanton, is published; it folds two years later.

1869 Disputes over the Fifteenth Amendment enfranchising black men split the women's rights movement into the American Woman Suffrage Association (AWSA), headed by Lucy Stone, Julia Ward Howe, and Henry Blackwell, and the National Woman Suffrage Association (NWSA), led by Elizabeth Cady Stanton and Susan B. Anthony. Wyoming Territory is the first to pass a bill giving full voting rights to women.

1870 Ratified on February 3, the Fifteenth Amendment grants suffrage without regard to "race, color, or previous condition of servitude" but fails to include the category of sex. Utah Territory passes a bill giving voting rights to women, the second territory to do so. The *Woman's Journal*, a women's rights weekly newspaper, is founded in Boston by Lucy Stone and Henry Browne Blackwell. It will later be edited by their daughter, Alice Stone Blackwell.

1871 Victoria Woodhull argues in an address to the House Judiciary Committee that women already have the right to vote because they are "persons" as defined by the Fourteenth Amendment. Woodhull, a flamboyant personality who will run for president in 1872 (even though at age thirty-four she is constitutionally ineligible), will become a liability to the suffrage movement when she exposes a major scandal involving widely respected clergyman Henry Ward Beecher and a female parishioner in 1875.

1872 Susan B. Anthony casts her vote in Rochester, New York, for the presidential election. Two weeks later she and fourteen other women are arrested and charged with voting illegally. She is found guilty but refuses to pay the fine and does not go to jail.

1874 The Woman's Christian Temperance Union (WCTU) is formed, which will campaign not only for prohibition but also for suffrage and other reforms under its "Do Everything" motto.

1875 Michigan and Minnesota grant women the right to vote for local school boards. *Minor v. Happersett* rules that the Fourteenth Amendment does not grant women the right to vote, conclusively ending NWSA's "New Departure" legal strategy, under which women had attempted to register to vote with the argument that they were citizens.

1876 Susan B. Anthony, Matilda Joslyn Gage, and three other suffragists disrupt the proceedings celebrating the nation's centennial in Philadelphia on July 4 by handing out a "Declaration of Rights for Women" to the assembled crowd. The manifesto seeks equal rights for women, including the right to vote.

1878 The federal women's suffrage amendment, popularly known as the Susan B. Anthony Amendment, is introduced in Congress for the first time by Senator Aaron A. Sargent of California. Its language—"the right of citizens to vote shall not be denied or abridged by the United States or by any State on account of sex"—will remain unchanged through its passage as the Nineteenth Amendment in 1920.

1880   Mary Ann Shadd Cary, a journalist and lawyer, organizes the Colored Women's Progressive Franchise Association in Washington, D.C., an auxiliary of the NWSA. New York grants school suffrage to women.

1881   The first volume of the *History of Woman Suffrage*, edited by Elizabeth Cady Stanton, Susan B. Anthony, and Matilda Joslyn Gage, is published; volumes II and III will be published in 1882 and 1886.

1882   The Chinese Restriction Act prohibits all immigration from China for ten years and bars Chinese men from citizenship. In 1888 Congress will make the act permanent, a policy that lasts until 1943.

1883   Washington Territory passes a bill giving full voting rights to women, becoming the third territory to allow its women to vote.

1884   The WCTU under its second president, Frances Willard, formally endorses women's suffrage. Willard will remain the dynamic leader of the WCTU until her death in 1898.

1885   Mary Tape protests the exclusion of Chinese American students from local schools to the San Francisco Board of Education. Her court challenge is victorious but Chinese American students are segregated in separate schools going forward.

1886   Mormon women hold a mass meeting in May in Salt Lake City to protest the federal government's campaign to outlaw polygamy.

1887   The Edmunds-Tucker Act, passed by Congress in January, rescinds women's suffrage in Utah. Women in Kansas gain municipal suffrage. The Dawes General Allotment Act distributes shared tribal holdings as individual allotments of 160 acres and opens up the remaining land, about one hundred million acres, for white settlers.

1888   The Washington State Supreme Court rescinds women's suffrage. The International Council for Women, representing fifty-three women's organizations from nine countries, is founded and holds its first meeting in Washington, D.C. Rachel Foster Avery takes the lead in planning the convention and Susan B. Anthony presides over many of the sessions.

1890   The rival suffrage organizations NWSA and AWSA reunite as the National American Woman Suffrage Association (NAWSA). Wyoming is the first state to enter the Union with full suffrage rights for women. New Zealand becomes the first country to enfranchise women.

1892   Anna J. Cooper publishes *A Voice from the South, By a Black Woman of the South*. An Oberlin graduate as well as an educator and writer, Cooper has an expansive agenda that includes not only larger roles for women but also general uplift for her race.

1893   Colorado becomes the first state to enfranchise women by popular referendum. The World's Congress of Representative Women is held as part of the World's Columbian Exhibition in Chicago in May; it is attended by Jane Addams, Susan B. Anthony, Frances Ellen Watkins Harper, Lucy Stone, and others. Lucy Stone dies in October.

1894   The New York State Constitutional Convention refuses to remove the word "male" from the description of eligible voters. Josephine St. Pierre Ruffin begins publishing *The Woman's Era*, the first national newspaper for African American women, in Boston.

1895   The Massachusetts Association Opposed to the Further Extension of Suffrage to Women and the New York State Association Opposed to Woman Suffrage are founded. Elizabeth Cady Stanton publishes the first volume of her controversial *Woman's Bible*, which aims to disprove that the Bible taught that women should be subservient to men, earning a rebuke from NAWSA.

1896   Women win full voting rights in Idaho and the new state of Utah. A California referendum on women's suffrage is soundly defeated. The National Federation of Afro-American Women and the National League of Colored Women merge to form the National Association of Colored Women; Mary Church Terrell serves as its first president.

1900   Carrie Chapman Catt, a graduate of Iowa State University and former school superintendent who has been active in the suffrage movement since the 1880s, becomes president of NAWSA, succeeding Susan B. Anthony in a symbolic generational passing of the leadership torch. She will serve until 1904, when she will step down to take care of her ailing husband.

1902   Elizabeth Cady Stanton dies in October, four years after
        publishing her autobiography, *Eighty Years and More*. The
        fourth volume of the *History of Woman Suffrage*, edited by
        Susan B. Anthony and Ida Husted Harper, is published.
        Women in Australia are enfranchised.

1903   The NAWSA convention in New Orleans passes a states'
        rights resolution allowing southern suffrage groups to ex-
        clude African American women from membership, an ex-
        plicitly racist strategy in pursuit of the vote. The convention
        also gives states free rein to decide how to pitch arguments
        for suffrage, a clear opening for southerners to argue that
        enfranchising white women will offset what was referred to
        as "the Negro problem."

1904   Anna Howard Shaw, an ordained Methodist minister and
        forceful orator, takes over from Carrie Chapman Catt as
        president of NAWSA. The International Woman Suffrage
        Alliance, which will work to promote votes for women
        around the world as part of its commitment to women's
        rights, is formed at the International Council of Women
        convention in Berlin; Carrie Chapman Catt serves as its
        president from 1904 to 1923.

1906   Susan B. Anthony dies in March, aged eighty-six, after de-
        voting more than sixty years of her life to the cause of wom-
        en's rights. She becomes the most widely known "founding
        mother" of suffrage history, far eclipsing Elizabeth Cady
        Stanton and Lucy Stone.

1907   Harriot Stanton Blatch, Elizabeth Cady Stanton's daughter,
        founds the Equality League of Self-Supporting Women,
        an independent organization in New York City to attract
        working-class women to the movement. It will be renamed
        the Women's Political Union in 1910.

1908   The National College Equal Suffrage League, which aims
        to attract younger, college-educated women to the suffrage
        movement, is established with M. Carey Thomas as presi-
        dent after Maud Wood Park, Radcliffe class of 1898, orga-
        nizes the first College Equal Suffrage League in Boston in
        1900.

1909   Suffragists start holding open-air meetings and parades. The
        Men's League for Woman Suffrage is founded in New York
        "to give moral support to men and to give political sup-
        port to women." The radical British suffragette Emmeline

Pankhurst comes to America on a fundraising tour for the British suffrage movement.

1910   Washington State approves full voting rights for women. The first suffrage parade organized by the Women's Political Union takes place in New York City in May, despite objections of some supporters that such a public demonstration will hurt rather than help the cause.

1911   A California women's suffrage referendum passes by a slim majority, an important state victory with national implications because of the large number of newly enfranchised women. The National Association Opposed to Woman Suffrage (NAOWS) is established in New York by Josephine Jewell Dodge. The Triangle Shirtwaist Fire kills 146 workers, mainly young immigrant women, in New York City in March.

1912   The Progressive Party includes a women's suffrage plank in its platform; Jane Addams seconds the nomination of Theodore Roosevelt as the Progressive Party candidate for president. Oregon, Kansas, and Arizona give full voting rights to women. Guandong Province in China briefly enfranchises women.

1913   Ida B. Wells-Barnett founds the Alpha Suffrage Club in Chicago, the first African American women's suffrage group in the city. Under the auspices of the Congressional Committee of NAWSA, Alice Paul organizes a suffrage parade in Washington, D.C., timed to coincide with Woodrow Wilson's inauguration in March. Illinois grants presidential and municipal suffrage to women. The Southern States Woman Suffrage Conference is formed to lobby state legislatures in a region where women's suffrage struggles to gain traction.

1914   At odds with NAWSA, Alice Paul's Congressional Committee reorganizes as the Congressional Union. Montana and Nevada approve full voting rights for women. The National Federation of Women's Clubs endorses women's suffrage.

1915   Referenda on women's suffrage are soundly defeated in New York, Massachusetts, New Jersey, and Pennsylvania. W.E.B. Du Bois organizes a symposium on "Votes for Women" for *The Crisis*, the official magazine of the National Association for the Advancement of Colored People. Alice Duer Miller publishes *Are Women People?: A Book of Rhymes for Suffrage Times*.

1916   Alice Paul forms the National Woman's Party (NWP). Jeannette Rankin of Montana is the first woman elected to Congress. NAWSA president Carrie Chapman Catt introduces her "Winning Plan," a campaign to work for state suffrage laws while primarily focusing on the passage of a federal amendment.

1917   NWP "Silent Sentinels" begin picketing the White House in January. The United States enters World War I in April but the NWP pickets continue their protests. In June the pickets are arrested for disorderly conduct and are sent to prison, where they undertake hunger strikes and are force-fed. New York State offers full voting rights to women after a successful referendum, a huge breakthrough in a key eastern state.

1918   Michigan, South Dakota, and Oklahoma referenda give full voting rights to women. President Woodrow Wilson formally endorses the federal women's suffrage amendment. The House of Representatives passes the women's suffrage amendment but it fails in the Senate.

1919   NWP protestors light "watchfires for freedom" in Lafayette Park, across from the White House. The Senate passes the suffrage amendment in June and sends it to the states for ratification. The Southern Women's League for the Rejection of the Proposed Susan B. Anthony Amendment is formed in Alabama.

1920   The League of Women Voters is founded in Chicago at the final NAWSA convention. Tennessee becomes the thirty-sixth state to ratify the Nineteenth Amendment on August 18 and it becomes part of the U.S. Constitution on August 26 in time for women to vote in the 1920 presidential election.

1922   *Fairchild v. Hughes* and *Leser v. Garnett* uphold the Nineteenth Amendment. The fifth and sixth volumes of the *History of Woman Suffrage,* edited by Ida Husted Harper, are published.

1923   Alice Paul proposes an Equal Rights Amendment to the U.S. Constitution on the seventy-fifth anniversary of the Seneca Falls Convention. Its text reads: "Men and women shall have equal rights throughout the United States and every place subject to its jurisdiction. Congress shall have power to enforce this article by appropriate legislation." It has still not been passed.

1924   The Indian Citizenship Act grants U.S. citizenship to American Indians but many states, especially in the West, continue to bar them from voting.

1928   The Inter-American Commission on Women is formed at the Sixth Pan-American Conference in Havana, Cuba, to promote women's rights and encourage collaboration on women's issues in the Americas. Doris Stevens serves as its first chair.

1935   All Puerto Rican women, who became U.S. citizens under the Jones Act of 1917, become eligible to vote, significantly extending the franchise beyond literate Puerto Rican women, who had received the right to vote in 1929.

1939   El Congreso de Pueblo de Habla Española, the first national civil rights gathering for Spanish-speaking people, calls for the creation of women's committees to represent the interests of Mexican American women as part of its broader commitment to improve labor conditions and promote civil rights for Latinos living in the United States.

1943   The repeal of the Chinese Exclusion Act makes Chinese Americans eligible for citizenship, allowing them to vote after decades of being excluded from the polls.

1952   The Walter-McCarran Act extends the right to become citizens to all immigrants of Asian ancestry.

1961   President John F. Kennedy establishes the President's Commission on the Status of Women with Eleanor Roosevelt as chair. Its 1963 report, *American Women*, is an important factor in the revival of feminism, especially through its encouragement of the creation of state and local commissions on the status of women.

1962   Fannie Lou Hamer and seventeen other African Americans unsuccessfully attempt to register to vote in Indianola, Mississippi, as part of a voting rights drive organized by the Student Non-Violent Coordinating Committee (SNCC).

1964   The Twenty-Fourth Amendment abolishes poll taxes and literacy tests. The Civil Rights Act prohibits job discrimination on the basis of race or sex and establishes the Equal Employment Opportunity Commission.

1965   The Voting Rights Act forbids states from imposing discriminatory restrictions on voters, significantly expanding the registration of African Americans and other minorities.

Note on the Texts

This volume collects ninety selections of suffrage and antisuffrage writing, composed or delivered from 1776 to 1965, including fiction and poetry, essays and personal memoirs, pamphlets, speeches, plays, and legal documents. They are presented roughly in chronological order. In cases where there is only one printed or manuscript source for a document, the text offered here comes from that source. Where there is more than one printed source for a document, the text printed in this volume is taken from the first published source, or else the source that appears to contain the fewest editorial alterations in the spelling, capitalization, paragraphing, and punctuation of the original.

Many of the texts chosen for inclusion in this volume were first collected by Elizabeth Cady Stanton and Susan B. Anthony, with their co-editor Matilda Joslyn Gage and, for the last three volumes, Ida Husted Harper, in their monumental six-volume *History of Woman Suffrage*, which combined primary documents (from the beginning of the suffrage movement to the ratification of the Nineteenth Amendment in 1920) with long essays on the history of the movement and the historical condition of women, as well as reminiscences of movement leaders. It was published from 1881 to 1922, with the final two volumes appearing after Anthony's death. In the introduction to the first volume, Stanton and Anthony wrote, "We hope the contribution we have made may enable some other hand in the future to write a more complete history of 'the most momentous reform that has yet been launched on the world—the first organized protest against the injustice which has brooded over the character and destiny of one-half the human race.'"

Anthony had for years saved letters, newspaper clippings, and other texts of historical value to the suffrage movement, which formed the nucleus of the rich collection of primary documents she and Stanton published. As historian Ellen Carol DuBois has written, "There is nothing in the annals of American reform quite like *History of Woman Suffrage*, a prolonged, deliberate effort on the part of activists to ensure their place in the historical record." It also set the narrative for the women's suffrage movement for decades, making the march toward the fulfillment of women's rights seem inevitable. Nevertheless, the *History of Woman Suffrage* neglected certain parts of the history of the suffrage movement, including the role of Lucy Stone and her American Woman Suffrage Association (AWSA), which was a rival to the National Woman Suffrage Association led by Stanton and Anthony, as well as the National Woman's Party founded in 1913 by Alice Paul. It also paid scant attention to the work and the struggle of minority women.

There are also some textual problems posed by the texts printed in *History of Woman Suffrage*. A comparison of the texts as edited by Stanton and Anthony with their original publications reveals frequent changes in spelling, punctuation, and paragraphing. In addition, selections from the original texts are frequently printed without indicating that omissions had been made. For example, to cite an extreme case, the record of the debates at the third American Equal Rights Association Meeting in 1869, which resulted in the formation of the rival American Woman Suffrage Association of Lucy Stone and Frederick Douglass as well as Stanton and Anthony's National Woman Suffrage Association, was first published in Stanton and Anthony's newspaper, *The Revolution*, in the May 20, May 27, and July 8 issues. The text printed in *History of Woman Suffrage* contains some material from all three issues, though not in chronological order, and deletes lengthy passages of the debates and resolutions that were brought forward but not approved. It removes Stephen Foster's accusation that Susan B. Anthony had misappropriated funds, as well as part of the debate between Anthony and Frederick Douglass. It also contains a passage about Free Love for which Library of America cannot find an original source, in *The Revolution* or elsewhere. For these reasons, the texts chosen for inclusion in this volume do not use *History of Woman Suffrage* as their source.

The following is a list of the pieces included in this volume, in the order of their appearance, giving the source of each text.

Abigail Adams and John Adams, "Letters." Abigail Adams, "Letter to John Adams, March 31–April 5, 1776"; John Adams, "Letter to Abigail Adams, April 14, 1776"; and Abigail Adams, "Letter to John Adams, May 7–9, 1776." *The Adams Family Correspondence*, volume I, L. H. Butterfield, ed. (Cambridge: The Belknap Press of Harvard University Press, 1963), pp. 369–71, 381–83, and 401–403. Copyright © 1963 by the Massachusetts Historical Society. Reprinted by permission.

"Article IV (Voter Qualifications), New Jersey State Constitution." *Acts of the Council and General Assembly of the State of New-Jersey, from the Establishment of the present Government, and Declaration of Independence, to the End of the first Sitting of the eighth Session, on the 24th Day of December, 1783; with the Constitution Prefixed. To which is annexed, An Appendix containing the Articles of*

Confederation of the United States, &c. With Two Alphabetical Tables and an Index, Peter Wilson, ed. (Trenton: Isaac Collins, 1784), p. v.

Maria W. Miller Stewart, "Lecture, Delivered at the Franklin Hall." *Productions of Mrs. Maria W. Stewart, Presented to the First African Baptist Church and Society, of the City of Boston* (Boston: Friends of Freedom and Virtue, 1835), pp. 51–56.

Sarah Moore Grimké, "Letter XII. Legal Disabilities of Women, from *Letters on the Equality of the Sexes*." *Letters on the Equality of the Sexes, and the Condition of Women Addressed to Mary S. Parker* (Boston: Isaac Knapp, 1838), pp. 74–83.

Angelina Grimké, "Address to the Massachusetts Legislature." *The Liberator*, Vol. 8, no. 9 (March 2, 1838), p. 35.

Margaret Fuller, from "The Great Lawsuit." *The Dial: A Magazine for Literature, Philosophy, and Religion*, July 1843, pp. 11–14.

Eleanor Vincent, Lydia A. Williams, Lydia Osborn, Susan Ormsby, Amy Ormsby, and Anna Bishop, "Petition to the Constitutional Convention of the State of New York, August 8, 1846." William G. Bishop and William H. Attree, eds., *Report of the Debates and Proceedings of the Convention for the Revision of the Constitution of the State of New-York, 1846* (Albany: Evening Atlas, 1846), p. 646.

Seneca Falls Convention, "Declaration of Sentiments and Resolutions." *Report of the Woman's Rights Convention. Held at Seneca Falls, N. Y., July 19th and 20th, 1848* (Rochester, NY: John Dick at the North Star Office, 1848), pp. 4–12.

Sojourner Truth, "Speech to Ohio Woman's Rights Convention." *Anti-Slavery Bugle*, June 21, 1851.

Ernestine L. Rose, "Speech to the Second National Woman's Rights Convention." *The Proceedings of the Woman's Rights Convention, held at Worcester, October 15th and 16th, 1851* (New York: Fowlers and Wells, No. 131 Nassau Street, 1852), pp. 36–47.

New York Herald, "The Woman's Rights Convention—The Last Act of the Drama." *New York Herald*, September 14, 1852.

Harriot K. Hunt, "Tax Protest." *Glances and Glimpses; or Fifty Years Social, Including Twenty Years Professional Life* (Boston: John P. Jewett and Company, 1856), pp. 294–95.

Elizabeth Cady Stanton, "Address to the Legislature of New-York." *Address to the Legislature of New-York, adopted by the State Woman's Rights Convention, Held at Albany, Tuesday and Wednesday, February 14 & 15, 1854* (Albany: Weed, Parsons & Company, 1854).

Lucy Stone and Henry Browne Blackwell, "Marriage Protest." *The Liberator* Vol. 25, no. 18 (May 4, 1855), p. 71.

Lucy Stone, "Address to Seventh National Woman's Rights Convention, New York City." *Proceedings of the Seventh National Woman's*

Rights Convention, Held in New York City, at the Broadway Tabernacle, on Tuesday and Wednesday, Nov. 25th and 26th, 1856 (New York: Edward O. Jenkins, 1856), pp. 4–6.

"Call to the Woman's Loyal National League Meeting of May 14, 1863" and "Resolutions and Debate." *Proceedings of the Meeting of the Loyal Women of the Republic, Held in New York, May 14, 1863* (New York: Phair & Co., Printers, 1863), pp. 3–4, 15–31.

Frances Ellen Watkins Harper, "Speech at the Eleventh National Woman's Rights Convention." *Proceedings of the Eleventh National Woman's Rights Convention, held at the Church of the Puritans, New York, May 10, 1866* (New York: Robert J. Johnston, 1866), pp. 45–48.

Sojourner Truth, "Address to the First Annual Meeting of the American Equal Rights Association, New York City." *Proceedings of the First Anniversary of the American Equal Rights Association, held at the Church of the Puritans, New York, May 9 and 10, 1867* (New York: Robert J. Johnston, 1867), pp. 20–21.

"Debates at the American Equal Rights Association Meeting, New York City." *The Revolution*, Vol. 3, no. 20 (May 20, 1869), pp. 305–8 and Vol. 3, no. 21 (May 27, 1869), pp. 321–22.

Frederick Douglass, "Woman and the Ballot." *The New National Era*, October 27, 1870.

Victoria Woodhull, "Address to the House Judiciary Committee." *The Origin, Tendencies and Principles of Government: or, A Review of the Rise and Fall of Nations from Early Historic Time to the Present* (New York: Woodhull, Claflin & Co., 1871), pp. 40B–40F.

"*Minor v. Happersett.*" Waite, Morrison Remick, and Supreme Court Of The United States. *U.S. Reports: Minor v. Happersett, 88 U.S. 21 Wall. 162.* (1875), pp. 162–78.

National Woman Suffrage Association, "Declaration of Rights of the Women of the United States." *Declaration of rights of the women of the United States by the National Woman Suffrage Association* (1876).

Susan B. Anthony, "Woman Wants Bread, Not the Ballot!" Ida Husted Harper, *The Life and Work of Susan B. Anthony Including Public Addresses, Her Own Letters and Many from Her Contemporaries During Fifty Years*, Vol. 2 (Indianapolis: The Hollenbeck Press, 1898), pp. 996–1003.

Matilda Joslyn Gage, "Indian Citizenship." *National Citizen and Ballot Box* (May 1878), p. 2.

Mary Tape, "Letter to the San Francisco Board of Education." *Daily Alta California*, April 16, 1885, p. 1.

Mormon Women of Utah, *"Mormon" Women's Protest: An Appeal for*

Freedom, Justice and Equal Rights (Salt Lake City, Utah, 1886), pp. 17–19.

The New York Times, "They Enter a Protest." *The New York Times*, October 29, 1886.

George Vest, "Remarks of Senator Vest of Missouri on the joint resolution proposing an amendment to the Constitution to extend suffrage to women." *Congressional Record*, January 25, 1887, p. 986.

Alice C. Fletcher, "The Legal Conditions of Indian Women." National Woman Suffrage Association, *Report of the International Council of Women, March 25–April 1, 1888* (Washington, D.C., 1888), pp. 237–41.

Anna J. Cooper, from "*A Voice from the South, by a Black Woman of the South.*" *A Voice from the South, by a Black Woman of the South* (Xenia, Ohio: The Aldine Printing House, 1892), pp. 134–37, 142–45.

Colorado Equal Suffrage Association, *To the Women of Colorado.* Colorado Suffrage Referendum Leaflet 3 (Denver, Colorado, 1893). Western History Collection, Denver Public Library.

Committee on Protest against Woman Suffrage, "To the Constitutional Convention of New York State." (Brooklyn, NY: Committee on Protest against Woman Suffrage, 1894).

Fannie Barrier Williams, "Women in Politics." *The Woman's Era*, Vol. I, no. 8 (November 1894), pp. 12–13.

Josephine St. Pierre Ruffin, "Address at the First National Conference of Black Women's Clubs." *The Woman's Era*, Vol. 2, no. 5 (August 1895), pp. 13–15.

Elizabeth Cady Stanton, "Significance and History of the Ballot." *Report of Hearing before the Committee on Woman Suffrage, February 15, 1898* (Washington, D.C.: Government Printing Office, 1898), pp. 21–24.

Frances E. Willard, "The Ballot for the Home." *The Woman's Journal*, Equal Suffrage leaflet, Vol. 7, no. 2 (March 1898), pp. 1–2.

National American Woman Suffrage Association, "On Behalf of Hawaiian Women." *Woman's Journal* (February 11, 1899), p. 42.

Abigail Scott Duniway, "How to Win the Ballot." *Path Breaking: An Autobiographical History of the Equal Suffrage Movement in Pacific Coast States* (Portland, Oregon: James, Kerns & Abbott Co., 1914), pp. 150–62.

Belle Kearney, "The South and Woman Suffrage." *Woman's Journal*, Vol. 34, no. 14 (April 4, 1903), pp. 106–7.

Annie Nathan Meyer, "Woman's Assumption of Sex Superiority." *The North American Review*, Vol 178, no. 1 (January 1904), pp. 103–9.

Mary Church Terrell, "The Progress of Colored Women." Mary Church Terrell papers, Reel 21, Manuscript Division, Library of Congress.

Grover Cleveland, "Would Woman Suffrage be Unwise?" *Ladies' Home Journal*, Vol. 22, no. 11 (October 1905), pp. 7–8.

Finley Peter Dunne, "Mr. Dooley on Woman's Suffrage." *The American Magazine*, Vol. 67 (June 1909), pp. 198–200.

Alice Hill Chittenden, "The Counter Influence to Woman Suffrage." *The Independent*, Vol. 67 (July 29, 1909), pp. 246–49.

Florence H. Luscomb, "Our Open-Air Campaign." Unpublished speech, 1909. Woman's Rights Collection, Schlesinger Library.

Jane Addams, "Why Women Should Vote." *Ladies' Home Journal*, Vol. 27, no. 2 (January 1910), pp. 21–22.

Harriot Stanton Blatch, from "The Women's Political Union." *Challenging Years: The Memoirs of Harriot Stanton Blatch* (New York: G. P. Putnam's Sons, 1940), pp. 129–34. Reprinted by permission of Coline Jenkins on behalf of the Cady Stanton family.

Charlotte Perkins Gilman, "Something to Vote For." *The Forerunner*, Vol. 2, no. 6 (June 1911), pp. 143–53.

Alice Stone Blackwell, "Militant Methods." NAWSA pamphlet, MC 399 (Suffrage/US/Pamphlets), Schlesinger Library.

Leonora O'Reilly, "Statement before Joint Congressional Session of Congress, March 13, 1912." *Woman Suffrage: Hearings Before a Joint Committee of the Committee on the Judiciary and the Committee on Woman Suffrage, United States Senate, Sixty-Second Congress, Second Session*, Senate Document 601 (Washington, D.C.: Government Printing House, 1912), pp. 22–24.

Max Eastman, "Values of the Vote." *Values of the Vote: Address before the Men's League for Woman Suffrage of New York, March 21, 1912*, pamphlet (New York: The Men's League for Woman Suffrage).

Josephine Jewell Dodge, "The Lesson That Came from the Sea—What it Means to the Suffrage Cause." *Woman's Protest*, Vol. 1, no. 1 (April/May 1912), pp. 8–9.

Marie Jenney Howe, "An Anti-Suffrage Monologue." *An Anti-Suffrage Monologue* (New York: National Woman Suffrage Publishing Co., 1912), pp. 3–8.

Los Angeles Times, "Squaws Beat Militants to Right of Franchise." *Los Angeles Times* (January 31, 1913), p. 11.

Alice Paul, "Testimony at Suffrage Parade Hearings." *Suffrage Parade: Hearings Before a Subcommittee of the Committee on the District of Columbia, United States Senate* (1913), pp. 131–35.

Helen Hamilton Gardener, "Woman Suffrage, Which Way?" *Woman Suffrage, Which Way?* (National Woman Suffrage Publishing Co., 1915).

Mary Johnston, "A Difference of Opinion." *Hagar* (Boston: Houghton Mifflin Company, 1913), pp. 313–22.

Mabel Lee, "The Meaning of Woman Suffrage." *The Chinese Students' Monthly* (May 12, 1914), pp. 526–31.

Mary Roberts Coolidge, "Raising the Level of Suffrage in California, Or What Have They Done With It?" *Out West* (August 1914), pp. 72–73.

Hazel MacKaye, "Pageants as a Means of Suffrage Propaganda." *The Suffragist*, Vol. 2, no. 48 (November 28, 1914), pp. 6–7.

Ida B. Wells, "Seeking the Negro Vote." *Crusade for Justice: The Autobiography of Ida B. Wells*, ed. Alfreda M. Duster (Chicago: University of Chicago Press, 1970), pp. 345–53. Copyright © 1970 by The University of Chicago Press. Reprinted by permission.

The Crisis, "Votes for Women: A Symposium by Leading Thinkers of Colored America." *The Crisis* (August 1915), pp. 178–92.

Oreola Williams Haskell, "The Greatest Thing." *Banner Bearers: Tales from the Suffrage Campaign* (Geneva, NY: W. F. Humphrey, 1920), pp. 238–47.

Arthur Raymond Brown, "How It Feels to be the Husband of a Suffragette." *How It Feels to be the Husband of a Suffragette* (New York: George H. Doran Company, 1915), pp. 19–42.

Alice Duer Miller, from *Are Women People?* "Why We Oppose Pockets for Women," "Why We Oppose Votes for Men," and "Feminism." *Are Women People?: A Book of Rhymes for Suffrage Times* (New York: George H. Doran Company, 1915), pp. 44, 50, 64.

Abby Scott Baker, "Letter to the Editor of *The Outlook*." *The Outlook* (August 23, 1916), pp. 1002–4.

Carrie Chapman Catt, "The Crisis." *The Woman's Journal and Suffrage News* (September 16, 1916), pp. 299, 301–3.

Boston Equal Suffrage Association for Good Government, "Industrial Department Letter Series No. 1–10." Folder 140, Florence Luscomb Papers, Woman's Rights Collection, Schlesinger Library.

Maud Wood Park, "To NAWSA Congressional Chairmen, March 21, 1917." *Front Door Lobby* (Boston: Beacon Press, 1960), pp. 65–68.

The New York Times, "Silent, Silly and Offensive" and "Militants Get 3 Days; Lack Time to Starve." *The New York Times*, January 11, 1917, June 28, 1917.

Alice Hill Chittenden, "Woman's Service or Woman Suffrage." *Woman's Protest*, Vol. 11, no. 1 (May 1917), p. 5.

Lavinia Dock, "The Young Are at the Gates." *The Suffragist*, Vol. 5, no. 75 (June 30, 1917), p. 5.

Caroline Katzenstein, "Prison Experiences with Emphasis on the Night of Terror." *Lifting the Curtain: The State and National*

Woman Suffrage Campaigns in Pennsylvania as I Saw Them (Philadelphia: Dorrance & Company, 1955), pp. 244–55.

Woodrow Wilson, "Address to the Senate on the Nineteenth Amendment." *The Papers of Woodrow Wilson*, Vol. 51, September 14–November 8, 1918 (Princeton, New Jersey: Princeton University Press, 1985), pp. 158–61. Copyright © 1985 by Princeton University Press. Reprinted by permission.

The Suffragist, "Reminding the President When He Landed in Boston." *The Suffragist*, Vol. 7, no. 9 (March 1, 1919), pp. 6–9.

Southern Women's League for the Rejection of the Proposed Susan B. Anthony Amendment to the Constitution of the United States, "Declaration of Principles" (Pamphlet, 1919). Josephine Pearson Papers, Tennessee State Library and Archives. Courtesy of Tennessee Historical Society.

Maud Wood Park, "A Perfect Moment." *Front Door Lobby* (Boston: Beacon Press, 1960), pp. 272–77.

Gertrude Foster Brown, from *Your Vote and How to Use It. Your Vote and How to Use It* (New York: Harper and Brothers, 1918), pp. 1–7.

"Fairchild v. Hughes." Brandeis, Louis Dembitz, and Supreme Court Of The United States. *U.S. Reports: Fairchild v. Hughes,* 258 U.S. 126 (October term, 1921), pp. 127–30. "Leser v. Garnett." Brandeis, Louis Dembitz, and Supreme Court Of The United States. *U.S. Reports: Leser v. Garnett,* 258 U.S. 130. (October term, 1921), pp. 135–37.

"Indian Citizenship Act." United States Statutes at Large 43:253.

Doris Stevens and Dr. Alice Hamilton, "The 'Blanket' Amendment: A Debate." *Forum* LXXII, no. 2 (August 1924), pp. 145–60.

Ida M. Tarbell, "Is Woman's Suffrage a Failure?" *Good Housekeeping* (October 1924), pp. 18–19, 237–40, 242.

Doris Stevens, "Address In Behalf of the Equal Rights Treaty, Havana, Cuba." Doris Stevens Papers, Schlesinger Library.

Dr. Marta Robert, "Statement on Woman Suffrage in Porto Rico." *Woman Suffrage in Porto Rico: Hearing before the Committee on Territories and Insular Possessions, United States Senate, Seventieth Congress, First Session, on S. 753* (Washington, D.C.: Government Printing Office, 1928), pp. 2–4.

El Congreso de Pueblo de Habla Española, "Resolutions Adopted by the Second Convention of the Spanish Speaking People's Congress of California, Dec. 9 and 10, 1939." Ernest Galarza Collection, Stanford Special Collections, pp. 1–6.

Eleanor Roosevelt, "Women in Politics." *Good Housekeeping* (January 1940), pp. 18–19, 150.

John F. Kennedy, "Executive Order 10980 Establishing the

President's Commission on the Status of Women." December 14, 1961. Papers of John F. Kennedy. Presidential Papers. White House Central Files. Chronological File. President's Outgoing Executive Correspondence. December 1961 (2 of 3 folders). John F. Kennedy Presidential Library and Museum.

Fannie Lou Hamer, "Testimony to the Credentials Committee, Democratic National Convention." *The Speeches of Fannie Lou Hamer: To Tell It Like It Is*, Maegan Parker Brooks and David W. Houck, eds. (Jackson: University Press of Mississippi, 2011), pp. 43–45.

Constance Baker Motley, "Speech to the Southern Christian Leadership Conference, Birmingham, Alabama, August 9, 1965." *Women and the Civil Rights Movement, 1954–1965*, Davis W. Houck and David E. Dixon, eds. (Jackson: University Press of Mississippi, 2009), pp. 308–13. Reprinted by permission of Joel Motley.

This volume presents the texts of the printings chosen as sources here but does not attempt to reproduce nontextual features of their typographic design or physical layout. The texts are printed without alteration except for the correction of typographical errors and the modernization of eighteenth-century typography, such as the long "s" and the placement of a quotation mark at the beginning of every line of a quoted passage. Single quotation marks have been changed to double quotation marks in Sarah Moore Grimké's *Letters on the Equality of the Sexes*. Spelling, punctuation, and capitalization are often expressive features, and they are not otherwise altered, even when inconsistent or irregular. The following is a list of typographical errors corrected, cited by page and line number: 18.36, rigths; 29.8, shame? Let; 35.3, commumity; 39.22, w. M Clintock; 39.25, Mary S. Mirror; 39.28, Woodard; 39.38, M Clintock; 40.2, Sophrone; 40.5, R. A. Culvert; 40.16, M Clintock; 40.22, Salding; 40.30, Matthews,; 54.37, Wolstonecrafts; 62.12, Swishelm,; 69.5, Hurlburt; 69.34, Westminister; 78.22, chidren; 100.5 and *passim*, Halleck:; 100.25 and .26, Angeline; 103.12 and 13, Coleman; 119.31, anniversaay; 122.3, distinguishedm; 122.4, importanc; 124.22, Amenia; 126.20, committtee; 130.33, objects; 133.5, fastenad; 135.20, women."; 136.24, feet heaved; 139.7, Stewart; 139.27, applaus.); 144.6, came; 145.35, women; 162.17–18, "ad inconvenienti,"; 162.19, theConstitution.; 190.32, 1867,; 193.17, estops; 224.9, comtemplation; 228.31–32, principal; 230.14, Itwould; 234.10–11, backwoods for; 235.11, aleniating; 248.3, Australian women,; 254.5, Herbert,; 275.35, beneficent would; 276.18, customes; 277.8, great pros; 277.18, Bourgereau; 278.4, practicle; 278.40, comparitively; 279.1, they women are; 279.25, they call they call; 279.28, maids equally; 279.30, coral; 280.4, aimiable; 280.13, lain wake; 280.19, discussion servant; 308.25, perseverence; 312.18, black; 313.38, so so."; 328.16, Lees; 330.25, Earnest; 336.19, silent.; 338.28, *Platform*,; 339.15, "no" Much; 343.28, Mrs. Billings; 347.12, distributer; 348.7, 'o; 349.18, primative; 371.20, *constitutents*.; 379.3, show that couldn't; 389.33, make, it but; 397.33, Swathmore; 398.18, question State; 399.1, beern eported; 401.35, Englantine; 409.25, Kirchway; 479.15, The Fifteenth; 494.31, call you; 495.18, member every; 517.28, 1251; 527.18, Miss Mabel Dock; 527.19, Jamieson; 532.20, loosing; 535.22, sometimes negligent afflicted; 550.11, hitsoric; 554.2, evey; 554.4, BOLESHVISM,; 595.4, did no; 596.7–8, suffrage.; 598.13, Bently; 599.20, Jeanette; 610.27, rights.; 623.1, eight; 628.19, social economic; 634.27, Janet; 636.31, employes.

Note on the Illustrations

1. Sarah M. Grimké, *Letters on the Equality of the Sexes and the Condition of Woman* (Boston: Isaac Knapp, 1838). First edition cover, The Gilder Lehrman Institute of American History, GLC06552.
2. "Am I not a woman and a sister?", after medallion created by Elizabeth Margaret Chandler. *The Liberator* (March 17, 1832), p. 42.
3. James S. Baillie, "Leaders of the Woman's Rights Convention Taking an Airing" (1848). Schlesinger Library, Radcliffe Institute, Harvard University.
4. "Women's Emancipation," *Harper's New Monthly Magazine*, (August 1851), p. 424.
5. "Woman suffrage in Wyoming Territory.—Scene at the polls in Cheyenne / from a photo. By Kirkland," *Frank Leslie's Illustrated Newspaper* (November 24, 1888). Library of Congress.
6. Sallie E. Garrity, photograph of Ida B. Wells-Barnett (c. 1893). National Portrait Gallery, Smithsonian Institution.
7. *Woman's Journal* button with portrait of Lucy Stone (n.d.). Schlesinger Library, Radcliffe Institute, Harvard University.
8. Edmonston, Washington, D.C., "Susan B. Anthony and Elizabeth Cady Stanton. Two great pioneers in the Equal Rights cause. Without them, American women would not have progressed as far as they have in their fight for freedom" (c. 1891). Library of Congress.
9. Henrietta Briggs-Wall, "American Woman and Her Political Peers" (c. 1893). Library of Congress.
10. Boston Women's Anti-Suffrage Association, "The Anti-Suffrage Rose: Song," words and music by Phil Hanna (1915). Library of Congress.
11. Chicago Women's Suffrage Ballot Box (April 9, 1912). Chicago History Museum.
12. Benjamin Moran Dale, "Official program—Woman suffrage procession, Washington, D.C. March 3, 1913."
13. Woman Suffrage button (1914). National Museum of American History, 1980.0606.189.
14. Suffrage valentine "Since, in this progressive age" (after 1869?). S.l: s.n. Library Company of Philadelphia.
15. National Woman Suffrage Company, "Give mother the vote, we need it" (n.d.). Schlesinger Library, Radcliffe Institute, Harvard University.

16. National American Woman Suffrage Association, "Votes for Women—The Woman's Reason," translations in Polish, French, German, English. Florence Luscomb Papers in the Woman's Rights Collection. Suffrage flyers in various languages from several states, 1904–19. WRC, folder 640. Schlesinger Library, Radcliffe Institute, Harvard University.

17. W. F. Winter, "Votes for Workers" (Carl Hentschel, c. 1907–18). Schlesinger Library, Radcliffe Institute, Harvard University.

18. *The Crisis* (August 1915), cover from a composite photograph by Hinton Gilmore.

19. "Nine African-American women posed, standing, full length, with Nannie Burroughs holding banner reading 'Banner State Woman's National Baptist Convention'" (1905–15). Library of Congress.

20. "Woman to the Rescue!" *The Crisis* (May 1916), p. 43.

21. Henry Mayer, "The Awakening." *Puck* (February 20, 1915), centerfold. Library of Congress.

22. Harris & Ewing, photograph of "Prison Pin" (c. 1917–19). Schlesinger Library, Radcliffe Institute, Harvard University.

23. Clifford Norton Studio, photograph of Carrie Chapman Catt (1920). Library of Congress.

24. Nina E. Allender, "Any good Suffragist the morning after." *Suffragist* (February 1920), p. 222.

25. Warren K. Leffler, photograph of Fannie Lou Hamer at the Democratic National Convention, Atlantic City, New Jersey (August 1964). Library of Congress.

26. John T. McCutcheon, "How high will she go?" (1937). Chicago History Museum.

Notes

In the notes below, the reference numbers denote page and line of this volume (the line count includes headings, but not rule lines). No note is made for material included in the eleventh edition of Merriam-Webster's Collegiate Dictionary, except for certain cases where common words and terms have specific historical meanings or inflections. Biblical quotations and allusions are keyed to the King James Version; references to Shakespeare to *The Riverside Shakespeare*, ed. G. Blakemore Evans (Boston: Houghton Mifflin, 1974). For further biographical background, references to other studies, and more detailed notes, see Ellen Carol DuBois, *Suffrage: Women's Long Battle for the Vote* (New York: Simon and Schuster, 2020); Eleanor Flexner (and Ellen Fitzpatrick), *Century of Struggle: The Woman's Rights Movement in the United States* (Cambridge, MA: The Belknap Press [enlarged edition], 1996); Lisa Tetrault, *The Myth of Seneca Falls: Memory and the Women's Suffrage Movement, 1848–1898* (Chapel Hill: The University of North Carolina Press, 2014); Susan Ware, *Why They Marched: Untold Stories of the Women Who Fought for the Right to Vote* (Cambridge, MA: The Belknap Press, 2019); and Rosalyn Terborg-Penn, *African American Women in the Struggle for the Vote, 1850–1920* (Bloomington: Indiana University Press, 1998).

10.9 Ochlocracy.] Mob rule.

11.29–30 "Charm . . . we obey."] Adams slightly misquotes lines from a poem by Alexander Pope (1688–1744), "Of the Characters of Women: An Epistle to a Lady": "Please by receiving, by submitting sway / Yet have your humour most, when you obey."

12.4–5 "engaged in . . . vice and faction."] From *Cato: A Tragedy*, play written by British dramatist Joseph Addison (1672–1719).

12.10 fyall] Fayal or Faial Island, in the Azores.

14.24–28 Why sit ye . . . we shall but die.] 2 Kings 7:3–4.

15.1–2 servant . . . drawers of water!] Joshua 9:23.

15.26–27 "Tell it not . . . of Askelon!"] 2 Samuel 1:20.

16.11 the Liberator] The *Liberator* was an abolitionist newspaper founded by William Lloyd Garrison and Isaac Knapp in 1831.

16.12 colonizationists] Colonizationists encouraged the resettlement of North American free blacks in West Africa, the Caribbean, or Canada.

16.31   thorns and thistles.] Cf. Genesis 3:18.

17.4   Ethiopia . . . unto God] Cf. Psalm 68:31.

17.29–31   Have pity . . . touched us.] Cf. Job 19:21.

17.34–35   "——born to bloom . . . desert air."] Thomas Gray, "Elegy Written in a Country Churchyard" (1751).

18.5   made myself . . . among the people] Cf. Jeremiah 19:18.

20.11–12   Prof. Follen . . . our Country,'] Dr. Charles Follen, "The Cause of Freedom in Our Country," *Quarterly Anti-Slavery Magazine* (October 1836).

20.17–30   Blackstone, in . . . her love.'] Sir William Blackstone (1723–1780), *Commentaries on the Laws of England* (1765–1770).

20.33   a mere nullity.] A law or treaty that has not been repealed but has lost force or authority.

25.17–18   Harriet Martineau's Society in America] British social and economic writer Harriet Martineau recorded her observations of her travels in New England, the Midwest, and the South in *Society in America* (1837).

25.38–39   a help meet . . . unto himself,'] Genesis 2:18.

26.20   Ecclesiastical bodies] Ecclesiastical courts exercising jurisdiction over religious or spiritual matters.

27.29–30   eastern monarch . . . the sword.] In the Bible, Esther, the Jewish queen of the Persian king Ahasuerus (Xerxes), foils a plot to have all the Jews in the kingdom killed.

28.5–7   'What wilt . . . the kingdom'] Esther 5:3.

28.14–16   'If *I* have . . . my request.'] Esther 7:3.

30.24   the Anti-Slavery party] The American Anti-Slavery Society was founded in 1833 by William Lloyd Garrison and Arthur Tappan. Slavery became a presidential campaign issue starting in 1848 through the Free Soil Party and later the Republican Party.

31.37–38   favorites of Louis the Fourteenth . . . journeys] Louis XIV of France (1638–1715), also known as the Sun King, had at least eight mistresses.

32.9   Quaker preachers] Quakers believed that men and women were equal in spiritual matters, including in the "ministry," or the prerogative to speak during a Quaker meeting.

32.19   Washingtonian societies] The Washingtonian Movement was a Temperance fellowship founded in 1840.

34.33–35   "from the great body . . . the inhabitants,"] Cf. James Madison, "The Federalist No. 39": "It is *essential* to such a government, that it be derived from the great body of the society, not from an inconsiderable proportion, or a favored class of it; otherwise a handful of tyrannical nobles, exercising their oppressions by a delegation of their powers, might aspire to the rank of republicans, and claim for their government the honorable title of republic."

38.26   Apostolic authority] I.e., the twelve apostles of Jesus, who were all men.

39.17–40.16   Lucretia Mott . . . Thomas M'Clintock] Lucretia Mott (1793–1880), Thomas McClintock (1792–1876), Mary Ann McClintock (1800–1884), Amy Post (1802–1889), and Catharine A. F. Stebbins (1823–1904) were all Quaker abolitionists and reformers who became active in women's rights.

40.32–41.2   "that man shall pursue . . . obligation to any other."] William Blackstone, *Commentaries on the Laws of England in Four Books* (1765–70), Vol. 3, p. 2.

44.2   Eve caused man to sin.] Cf. Genesis 3.

44.5–7   When Lazarus . . . came forth.] Cf. John 11:1–44.

45.30   Revolution of 1848] The 1848 Revolution in France overthrew King Louis Philippe I and led to the creation of the French Second Republic under Napoleon III.

49.22   the Fugitive Slave Law.] The Fugitive Slave Act of 1850 required that all escaped slaves be returned to their masters, even if they were apprehended in nonslave states.

49.28   self-styled Union Safety Committee] The Union Safety Committee, made up of northern businessmen with financial ties to the South, supported the Fugitive Slave Law and raised thousands of dollars in its support.

54.36–38   De Staëls, . . . Jagellos] Anne-Louise-Germaine de Staël (1766–1817), a French writer and intellectual; Marie-Jeanne "Manon" Roland de La Platière (1754–1793), the wife of the leader of the Girondists during the French Revolution; Mary Somerville (1780–1872), Scottish scientific writer; Mary Wollstonecraft (1759–1797), English writer and women's rights activist; Lydia Howard Sigourney (1791–1865), American poet; Frances Wright (1795–1852), Scottish-American feminist and abolitionist; Harriet Martineau (1802–1876), British social theorist; Felicia Dorothea Hemans (1793–1835), English writer; Margaret Fuller (1810–1850), American writer and Transcendentalist; Jagello, possibly referring to Jadwiga (c. 1373–1399), the first female monarch of Poland, who married Jogaila, Grand Duke of Lithuania, and with him founded the Jagello dynasty.

56.21–22   Rev. Mr. Bellows] Henry Whitney Bellows (1814–1882) was an American clergyman who edited the *Christian Inquirer*, a Unitarian newspaper, starting in 1846.

57.36–37   That worse than Egyptian darkness] Cf. Exodus 10:21–22.

58.26–27   what will Mrs. Grundy say?] Mrs. Grundy, a character in English playwright Thomas Morton's comedy *Speed the Plough* (1798), refers to a narrow-minded or prudish person.

59.30 Rev. Mr. Hatch] Reverend Junius Lorrin Hatch (1825–1902) was minister of the Evangelical Congregational Church of Gloucester, Massachusetts, 1853–55, and the Unitarian Universalist Church of Concord, New Hampshire, 1864–66.

60.40–61.1 "be clothed . . . every day,"] Luke 16:19.

61.14–15 Mrs. Oakes Smith, Mrs. Paulina Davis] Elizabeth Oakes Smith (1806–1893), writer and lecturer; Paulina Wright Davis (1813–1876), abolitionist, suffragist, and educator.

61.15 Mrs. Rose] See Ernestine L. Rose, "Speech to the Second National Woman's Rights Convention," pages 45–58 in this volume.

61.18 Mrs. Oakes Smith's book] Elizabeth Oakes Smith, *Woman and Her Needs* (1851).

62.12 Mrs. Swishelm] Jane Grey Cannon Swisshelm (1815–1884), journalist and women's rights activist.

63.11 Dr. Harriot K. Hunt] Dr. Harriot Kezia Hunt (1805–1875), Boston physician. See also Dr. Hunt's tax protest, pages 64–66 in this volume.

63.28 Rev. Mr. May] Reverend Samuel J. May (1797–1871), minister, abolitionist, and reformer; he was the uncle of Louisa May Alcott.

67.25–27 "The thinking minds . . . the Old."] Thomas Carlyle, "Signs of the Times," *Edinburgh Review* (1829).

69.5–8 Judge Hurlbut . . . work on human rights] Elisha Powell Hurlbut (1807–1889) published *Essays on Human Rights and Their Political Guaranties* in 1845.

69.20 Minerva-like] Minerva was the Roman god of wisdom who, according to Roman myth, was born when she sprang fully armed out of her father Jupiter's head.

69.25 The Countess of Pembroke] Lady Anne Clifford, 14th Baroness de Clifford (1590–1676), held and exercised the office of high sheriff of Westmoreland from 1653 to 1676.

70.28–29 Charles the First refused . . . tribunal] Charles I of England (1600–1649) refused to accept demands for a constitutional monarchy and was executed for high treason.

73.28–35 "Nay, look not big . . . in Padua."] *The Taming of the Shrew*, III.ii.228–35.

75.8 the new law in this state] New York Married Women's Property Act, 1848, which allowed women to own and control their own property.

75.13   "femme covert"] A married woman.

87.24–25   Our first effort . . . Boston] This meeting occurred after the New England Anti-Slavery Convention on May 30, 1850; it led to the call for the convention held in Worcester on October 16–17, 1850.

88.31   Senator Sholes] Charles Sholes (1816–1867), senator from Wisconsin, 1866–67.

89.1–2   Mrs. Bloomer] Amelia Jenks Bloomer (1818–1894), dress reformer and women's rights advocate.

89.29   The Howitts] English writers William Howitt (1792–1879) and Mary Howitt (1799–1888).

89.30   Mrs. Jameson] Anne Brownell Jameson (1794–1860), Anglo-Irish writer and historian.

94.18–22   Instead of President Lincoln's . . . sent forth.] The Emancipation Proclamation, which went into effect on January 1, 1863, two years after the beginning of the Civil War, freed enslaved African Americans in the states then in rebellion.

94.24   Moloch of war] Moloch is the biblical name of a Canaanite deity associated with child sacrifice.

97.11   Mrs. Hoyt of Wisconsin] Mrs. Elizabeth Orpha Sampson Hoyt (1828–1912), poet and teacher.

99.27   Sarah Hallock] Sarah Hull Hallock (d. 1884), women's rights activist from Milton, New York.

101.30–31   "Governments derive . . . the governed."] From the Declaration of Independence.

103.12   Speech of Lucy N. Colman.] Lucy N. Colman (1817–1906), abolitionist and Freethinker.

104.15–16   that an Anti-Slavery Convention broke up] The split was caused in the American Anti-Slavery Society by the appointment of Abby Kelley (1811–1887), a Massachusetts abolitionist, to the business committee in 1839.

105.35   Lady's Union League] Union Leagues were men's clubs established during the Civil War to promote loyalty to the Union cause.

107.7–8   those who are called copperheads] A faction of northern Democrats who wanted to make a peace settlement with the Confederacy.

114.14–15   situation of Ishmael . . . against me] Cf. Genesis 16:11–12.

115.3–4   the Dred Scott decision] *Dred Scott v. Sanford* (1857) ruled that a slave who resided in a free state or territory was not entitled to his freedom and that African Americans were not citizens of the United States.

115.10 Judge Taney] Roger Brooke Taney (1777–1864), the chief justice of the U.S. Supreme Court, wrote the *Dred Scott* decision.

115.14 Louisiana Second] Two regiments of the black Louisiana Native Guards, the 1st and the 3rd, took part in the unsuccessful Union assault on the Confederate lines at Port Hudson, Louisiana, on May 27, 1863. Contemporary press accounts in the North incorrectly reported that the 2nd Louisiana Native Guards had participated in the attack and lost 600 men.

115.16 Olustee] The Battle of Olustee was fought in Baker County, Florida, on February 20, 1864; soldiers from the black 54th Massachusetts Volunteer Infantry Regiment under the command of Colonel Edward N. Hallowell (1837–1871) helped cover the Union retreat after the Confederate victory.

115.21–22 a woman . . . "Moses,"] Harriet Tubman (c. 1820–1913), a former slave who helped other slaves escape to freedom on the Underground Railroad, was called "Moses" by abolitionist William Lloyd Garrison, a reference to the biblical figure who led the Israelites to freedom from Egyptian slavery.

115.26–27 one of Montgomery's most successful expeditions] Colonel James Montgomery (1814–1871) led the black 2nd South Carolina Volunteers on a raid in June 1863 that freed more than 700 slaves. Tubman is credited with gathering intelligence for the raid and served on the expedition.

115.29 conflict with a brutal conductor] Tubman suffered a serious injury to her left arm while traveling through New Jersey on the Camden and South Amboy Railroad in October 1865 when a conductor and two other men dragged her from a regular car into the smoking car.

121.35 Rev. Mr. Frothingham] Octavius Frothingham (1822–1895), clergyman and author who spoke at the convention.

125.28 Educated Suffrage] Limiting the vote to those who could pass a literacy test or meet a similar educational standard.

125.36 George Francis Train] Train (1829–1904) was a wealthy merchant who provided the initial funding for the newspaper *The Revolution*. His opposition to enfranchising black men made him a controversial figure in the women's suffrage movement.

126.22–23 Parker Pillsbury . . . Charles K. Whipple] Members of the Trust Fund for the AERA: Pillsbury (1809–1898), minister and abolitionist. Abby Kelley Foster (1811–1887), abolitionist and reformer who married Reverend Stephen Foster. Charles K. Whipple (1808–1900), author of *The Family Relation, as affected by Slavery* (1858).

130.25 Working Women's Association] The Working Women's Association was formed in New York in 1868 at the offices of *The Revolution* to create "an association of working-women which might act for the interests of its members"; Susan B. Anthony was active in the group.

131.34   Ku-Kluxes] The Ku Klux Klan was founded in 1865 by former officers of the Confederate Army; its vigilante groups promoted white supremacy and harassed African Americans.

133.5   *a la Eugenie*] Probably the à l'impératrice hairstyle, named after Empress Eugénie de Montijo, the wife of Napoleon III of France, in which the hair is smoothed back behind the temples and then worn in long ringlets behind.

139.13   like Banquo's ghost, it will not down] A murdered character in *Macbeth* whose ghost haunts the Scottish king.

139.28–30   Dr. Watts's hymn . . . Lord."] Isaac Watts and James Manning Winchell, Hymn #98, from Psalm 119, in *An Arrangement of the Psalms, Hymns and Spiritual Songs of Isaac Watts* (1820).

141.4   Mr. Beecher] Henry Ward Beecher (1813–1887), American clergyman.

141.19   Mrs. Gage, of Onondaga, New York] Matilda Joslyn Gage (1826–1898), suffragist and author. See also pages 196–98 in this volume.

145.19   Mrs. Harper (colored)] Frances Ellen Watkins Harper; see also pages 112–15 in this volume.

145.39   Mr. C. C. Burleigh] Charles C. Burleigh (1810–1878), a prominent lecturer, author, and abolitionist.

146.34–35   Madame Anneke, . . . d'Hericourt] Mathilde Franziska Anneke (1817–1884), a German-American socialist. Jenny d'Héricourt (1809–1875), a French feminist writer.

147.5   the Hutchinsons] The Hutchinson Family Singers, founded in 1840, were a popular singing group that toured widely.

151.12–13   France and Prussia . . . warm blood.] The Franco-Prussian War broke out on July 19, 1870.

151.13–14   NAPOLEON told us the "Empire means peace,"] Napoleon III, in a speech at Bordeaux, October 9, 1852.

160.40–161.3   "The night is far . . . the day."] Romans 13:12.

161.8   *ita lex Scripta est*] Latin: so the law is written.

162.17–18   "ab incovenienti"] Latin: from hardship or inconvenience.

168.13   the pre-emption laws] Preemption holds that if Congress has enacted legislation it will supersede state laws on the same subject.

168.17   the homestead law.] The Homestead Act of 1862 provided settlers with 160 acres of public land if they lived on it continuously for five years; women as well as men could stake claims.

173.11   a bill of attainder] An act of the legislature singling out for punishment an individual or group of individuals without a trial.

178.32   WRIT OF HABEAS CORPUS] A court order demanding that a public official bring an imprisoned individual to court to show a valid reason for detention.

178.33   *lettres de cachet*] Orders authorizing imprisonment without trial.

180.2–4   Lord Coke's assertion . . . civil right."] Sir Edward Coke (1552–1634), an English jurist who defended English common law against royal interference. The quotation, however, comes from James Otis, *The Rights of the British Colonies Asserted and Proved* (Boston, 1764), one of the most influential pamphlets from the beginning of the American Revolution: "The very act of taxing, exercised over those who are not represented, appears to me to be depriving them of one of their most essential rights, as freemen; and if continued, seems to be in effect an entire disfranchisement of every civil right." Otis frequently paraphrased Lord Coke.

180.20–21   forbidding the importation of Chinese women] In 1870 the California legislature passed "An Act to Prevent the Kidnapping and Importation of Mongolian, Chinese and Japanese Females, for Criminal or Demoralizing Purposes."

181.7–8   A bill . . . disfranchise the women of Utah] Women voted in the territory of Utah from 1870 until 1887, when Congress passed the Edmunds-Tucker Act, disenfranchising them. When Utah became a state in 1896, women regained the vote.

181.39   a black man was not a citizen] *Dred Scott v. Sanford* (1857).

182.2   a woman, though a citizen, had not the right to vote] *Minor v. Happersett* (1875); see also pages 163–76 in this volume.

182.11–13   Abigail Adams . . . representation."] See pages 5–12 in this volume.

186.5   "new thing under the sun"] Cf. Ecclesiastes 1:19.

186.14–15   "monster bread meetings," . . . John Bright] Bright (1811–1889) was a British politician who supported free trade and helped repeal the Corn Laws in 1846; "monster bread meetings" were convened by workingmen to protest their economic condition.

186.23   George Thompson] George Donisthorpe Thompson (1804–1878), British antislavery activist.

186.28–29   "The Glory and Shame of England."] C. Edwards Lester, *The Glory and Shame of England* (1841).

186.35   "Put Yourself in his Place"] A novel (1870) about the abuses of trade unions by British novelist Charles Reade (1814–1884).

187.5   "household suffrage" bill of 1867] The Representation of the People Act of 1867 extended the vote to male heads of household, significantly expanding the working-class vote in England.

187.15   Robert Lowe] Robert Lowe, 1st Viscount Sherbrooke (1811–1892), a British statesman known for his opposition to electoral reform.

189.21   a one-term Whig administration] The Whig Party was active from the 1830s to the 1850s; it elected William Henry Harrison and Zachary Taylor to the presidency in 1840 and 1848, respectively.

190.38   the president of this union] Kate Mullany (1845–1906) founded the all-female Collar Laundry Union in Troy, New York, in 1864 and led her workers out on strike that year.

192.14–15   "No man is good enough . . . consent;"] From Lincoln's speech in Peoria on October 16, 1854, explaining his opposition to the Kansas-Nebraska Act, which allowed those territories to decide for themselves whether to allow slavery.

196.30   Iroquois, or "Six Nations"] The Iroquois or Haudenosaunee Confederacy was made up of the Mohawk, Onondaga, Oneida, Cayuga, Seneca, and Tuscarora peoples.

197.30–31   Green Corn Dance . . . White Dog.] Respectively, an annual ceremony practiced by American Indians associated with the beginning of the corn harvest, and a rite in which one or two white dogs were strangled and burned as a sacrifice.

198.34   jewel . . . toad's head] Cf. *As You Like It*, II.i.13–14: "the toad, ugly and venomous, / wears yet a precious jewel in his head."

203.6–7   Senators Call, Morgan, Teller, Brown] Wilkinson Call (1834–1910), Democratic senator from Florida, 1879–97. John Tyler Morgan (1824–1907), Democratic senator from Alabama, 1877–1907. Henry Moore Teller (1830–1914), Democratic senator from Colorado, 1876–82 and 1885–1909. Joseph Brown (1821–1894), Democratic senator from Georgia, 1880–91.

203.7   Belva H. Lockwood] Belva Lockwood (1830–1917), a pioneering lawyer, ran for president in 1884 and 1888 and spoke out in favor of Mormons.

204.35–205.1   Caroline Gilkey Rogers . . . Harriet R. Shattuck] Caroline Gilkey Rogers (c. 1837–1899), a suffragist from Lansingburgh, New York. Mary Seymour Howell (1844–1931), a lecturer and suffragist. Marguerite Moore (1849–?), an Irish-Catholic activist. Harriette Robinson Shattuck (1850–1937), a Massachusetts suffragist.

207.15–16   The Senator from New Hampshire] Henry W. Blair (1834–1920) served as the Republican senator from New Hampshire from 1879 to 1891. He chaired the Committee on Education and Labor.

211.39   Sun Dance] An important healing ceremony practiced by the Lakota (Sioux) and other Plains Indians.

213.11   *impedimenta*] Latin: things that impede.

213.18   Chief Cornplanter] Cornplanter (c. 1750–1836) was a leading Sioux warrior active in the Iroquois or Haudenosaunee Confederacy.

218.9   *mauvais succes*] French: poor or bad success.

222.28–29   New Mexico and Arizona are trembling in the balance.] Arizona gave women the vote in 1912, but women in New Mexico did not receive it until the Nineteenth Amendment passed in 1920.

222.31–32   victory in Kansas is assured in 1894] Kansas defeated a suffrage referendum in 1894 but passed one in 1912.

229.32–33   a recent act . . . permitted to vote] In 1891, Illinois passed a bill that allowed women to vote for the University of Illinois board of trustees. In 1894, four women were among the thirteen candidates who ran for the board, and Republican candidate Lucy Flower (1837–1921) won a place, aided by the votes of African American women.

234.16–17   "mete, right and our bounden duty"] From the preface to the Eucharistic Prayer in the Anglican *Book of Common Prayer*.

236.23   Senator Lodge . . . Senator Kyle] Henry Cabot Lodge (1850–1924), a historian and senator from Massachusetts, 1893–1924; and James H. Kyle (1854–1901), a Populist senator from South Dakota, 1891–1901.

237.6   Francis Joseph] Franz Joseph I (1830–1916), Emperor of Austria, 1848–1916, and King of Hungary, 1867–1916.

240.40   statue in the square Chateau d'Eau] The Place du Château d'Eau was renamed the Place de la République in 1879. The statue features the figure of Marianne, the symbol of the French Republic. She is surrounded by statues personifying liberty, equality, and fraternity, as well as the lion guarding the ballot box.

243.27   women of Washington Territory] Women in Washington Territory were given the right to vote by the legislature in 1883, but that right was repealed on a technicality by the Territorial Supreme Court in 1888.

243.39–244.3   Chief Justice Groesbeck . . . gambling and immorality."] Herman V. S. Groesbeck (1849–1928) served on the Wyoming State Supreme Court from 1890 to 1897.

244.15–18   Judge W. A. Johnston . . . city governments."] William A. Johnston (1848–1937) served as a justice of the Kansas Supreme Court from 1880 to 1935.

244.19–20   Kansas submitted to the voters . . . an amendment] Kansas women won municipal suffrage in 1887, but male voters defeated a full women's suffrage referendum in 1894, just as they had in 1867.

245.17–18   Even at the antipodes . . . New Zealand] New Zealand granted women the right to vote in parliamentary elections in 1893, the first country in the world to do so. Antipodes refers to both New Zealand and Australia, being diametrically opposed on the globe to the Western Hemisphere.

248.11 Hon. John D. Long] John Davis Long (1838–1915), a former Republican governor of Massachusetts, served as secretary of the navy from 1897 to 1902.

248.23–27 RACHEL FOSTER AVERY . . . CATHARINE WAUGH MCCULLOUGH] Rachel Foster Avery (1858–1919), a Pennsylvania suffragist who worked closely with Susan B. Anthony. Alice Stone Blackwell (1857–1950), editor of the *Woman's Journal* and the daughter of Lucy Stone and Henry Blackwell; see also pages 353–60 in this volume. Laura Clay (1849–1941), a Kentucky suffragist. Catharine Waugh McCullough (1862–1945), a lawyer and Illinois suffragist.

251.3 "over every living thing upon the earth"] Genesis 1:28.

253.27–30 Mary A. Livermore . . . National White Cross Association] Mary Livermore (1820–1905), journalist and suffragist, was a member of the U.S. Sanitary Commission during the Civil War. Clara Barton (1821–1912), was a nurse who founded the American Red Cross. Jane Creighton lived in Portland, Oregon. The National White Cross Association was founded by doctors "to obtain through common study and experiment, the best practical scientific aids for us in their practice."

253.40 Bok's latest fad in "Battenburg"] Edward W. Bok (1863–1930) served as editor of the *Ladies' Home Journal* from 1889 to 1919; the magazine did not support women's suffrage. Battenburg is a light checkered sponge cake covered in jam and marzipan.

254.3–5 Emily B. Ketchum . . . Elizabeth Boynton Harbert] Emily B. Ketchum (1838–1907), Michigan suffragist. Elizabeth Boynton Harbert (1819–1890), abolitionist and author.

255.1–2 "The bravest battles . . . mothers of men."] "The Bravest Battle that was ever Fought" (1898) by Joaquin Miller (1837–1913), who was often called the "Poet of the Sierras" or the "Byron of the Rockies."

255.20–21 as many little children as poor John Rogers of historical memory] A Bible translator (c. 1505–1555) who became the first Protestant martyr under Mary I of England; he left behind ten children.

257.9 Dr. Annice F. Jeffreys] Annice Florence Jeffreys (1862–1911), a Portland, Oregon, physician.

257.13 Gail Hamilton] The pseudonym of American writer and essayist Mary Abigail Dodge (1833–1896).

262.33–34 Tuskegee] The Tuskegee Institute, a historically black university founded in 1881, is most closely associated with Booker T. Washington (1856–1915).

264.25–27 Margaret Brent . . . wife of John Adams] Margaret Brent (c. 1601–c. 1671) petitioned for the right to vote in Maryland's general assembly after she was named the lord proprietor's attorney. For the appeal of Abigail Adams to her husband John, see pages 5–12 in this volume.

267.26   Fusion party, and to the tiger of Tammany] The Fusion Party was a municipal organization in New York City; fusion voting means that more than one political party supports a common candidate. Tammany Hall was a New York City political organization that epitomized the power of political machines; cartoonist Thomas Nast (1840–1902) popularized the tiger as a symbol of Tammany Hall.

273.7–8   Fielding . . . "Pamela"] Samuel Richardson (1689–1761) published the epistolary novel *Pamela; Or, Virtue Rewarded* in 1740; a parody by Henry Fielding (1707–1754), *Shamela,* was published in 1741.

278.8   National Association of Colored Women] The National Association of Colored Women was formed in Washington, D.C., in 1896. When it incorporated in 1904, it became known as the National Association of Colored Women's Clubs.

278.36–38   May Wright Sewall . . . Ida Husted Harper] May Wright Sewall (1844–1920), reformer and peace activist. Hannah G. Solomon (1858–1942), social reformer and founder of the National Council of Jewish Women. Mary Wood Swift (1841–1927), president of the National Council of Women and the California Woman Suffrage Association. Ida Husted Harper (1851–1931), journalist and author.

285.16–18   publish some views . . . woman's clubs and their tendencies] Grover Cleveland, "Women's Mission and Women's Clubs," *Ladies' Home Journal* 22 (May 1905), pp. 3–4.

288.13–14   A woman speaking in opposition] Emily Perkins Bissell (1861–1948) testified before the Senate Committee on Woman Suffrage in 1900.

288.20–23   A distinguished writer . . . figuratively."] Mrs. C. F. Corbin, "Letters from a Chimney Corner," quoted in Senate Report No. 70, Part 2, Forty-ninth Congress, first session.

290.21–22   a member of the House of Representatives] John Calhoun Bell (1851–1933) represented Colorado's 2nd District as a Populist from 1893 to 1903.

292.11–12   a book . . . by a very painstaking and conscientious woman] Elizabeth McCracken, *The Women of America* (New York: The Macmillan Company, 1904).

296.33–34   Cobden Republican Marchin' Club] The Cobden Club was a men's club founded in London in 1866 for supporters of Free Trade.

296.35   Sam'l J. Tilden] Samuel J. Tilden (1814–1886) lost to Rutherford B. Hayes in the disputed presidential election of 1876.

296.39   James G. Blaine] Blaine (1830–1893) was a Republican politician from Maine who served as Speaker of the U.S. House of Representatives, 1869–75, before serving in the Senate from 1876 to 1881.

297.4–5 Lookout Mountain . . . Anteetam] Civil War battles: The Battle of Lookout Mountain was fought in Chattanooga, Tennessee, on November 23, 1863; the Battle of Antietam was fought in Sharpsburg, Maryland, on September 17, 1862.

297.30 Phlippeens an' th' Sandwich Islands] Spain ceded the Philippines to the U.S. in 1898. The Sandwich Islands (Hawaii) were annexed by the United States in 1898 and became a territory in 1900.

300.4 Mrs. Humphry Ward] Mary Augusta Ward (1851–1920) was a British novelist and founder of the Women's National Anti-Suffrage League in London; she visited the United States in 1908. Ward's article appeared in *The Times* on September 1, 1908.

300.10–11 English suffragette methods] The term "suffragette" referred to the British movement; American suffragists avoided the term, because they wanted to distance themselves from the British movement's deployment of violence against property.

302.4–5 Mr. Brigham H. Roberts, a Mormon with three wives] Brigham Henry Roberts (1857–1933) was elected to the U.S. House of Representatives in 1898, but the House refused to seat him because he had practiced plural marriage.

304.36–39 "Either sex is an appalling blunder . . . intellectual world."] "Women at Oxford and Cambridge," *The Living Age*, vol. 216 (January–March 1898), p. 228.

305.18–21 "The women who bring . . . the home."] See the petition of the Committee on Protest against Woman Suffrage to the Constitutional Convention of New York State, pp. 223–27 in this volume.

308.13–14 Equal Suffrage Association] The Boston Equal Suffrage Association for Good Government (BESAGG) was founded in 1901; see also pages 508–19 in this volume.

308.38 Mrs. Fitzgerald] Susan Walker Fitzgerald (1871–1943) was the executive secretary of BESAGG.

310.7 Mrs. Dennett (Mary Ware Dennett)] Mary Ware Dennett (1872–1943), suffragist and birth control activist.

311.38 Salvation Army] Founded in London in 1865 as a Protestant Christian organization, the Salvation Army started work in the United States in 1880.

318.5–6 Chicago campaign . . . Charter Convention] In 1907 voters defeated a proposed new charter for the city of Chicago because it had been heavily influenced by the state legislature at the expense of Chicago home rule.

319.29–30 mothers' school clubs and mothers' congresses] The National Congress of Mothers was founded in 1897; it later became the National Parent-Teacher Association.

321.17–18 Juvenile Court movement] Responding to the argument that youths should not be treated as adults in the courts, Chicago created the first Juvenile Court in 1899.

323.36 ardent advocate of free silver] Republican William J. McKinley defeated Democrat William Jennings Bryan in 1896. Bryan strongly supported Free Silver, a monetary policy that favored unlimited coinage of silver rather than strict reliance on the gold standard.

326.34–35 Equality League of Self-Supporting Women] Founded by Harriot Stanton Blatch in 1907, it was renamed the Women's Political Union in 1910.

327.17 Equal Franchise Society] The Equal Franchise Society was founded in New York City in 1908 by Katherine Duer Mackay (1878–1930); Elizabeth Callender (Mrs. Richard) Stevens (c. 1870–c. 1963) resigned in 1910.

328.2 Collegiate Equal Suffrage League] Founded in 1900 by Maud Wood Park (1871–1955) and Inez Haynes Irwin (1873–1970). In 1908 the various state and local chapters formed the National College Equal Suffrage League.

328.16–17 Mrs. James Lee Laidlaw] Harriet Burton (Mrs. James Lee) Laidlaw (1873–1949) was a prominent New York City suffragist.

328.20–22 Jessica Finch . . . Assemblyman Toombs] Jessica Garretson Finch (1871–1949), educator and suffragist. Jessie Ashley (1861–1919), lawyer and socialist. Elizabeth Ellsworth Cook (1884–1981), pacifist and suffragist. Frederick R. Toombs, Republican assemblyman from Nassau County, New York.

330.13 Elsa Gregori] An American-born Italian (1876–?) singer and composer; the march she wrote for the parade began: "Come ev'ry matron ev'ry maid / That in this fair land of ours doth dwell, / Hear the clarion call bidding us one & all / Tarry no more but haste the rank to swell."

330.13–14 Inez Milholland and Sarah McPike] Milholland (1886–1916) was a lawyer who often led suffrage parades on horseback. Sarah McPike (1870–1943) belonged to the Women's Trade Union League and in 1911 founded the St. Catherine's Welfare Association, which was affiliated with NAWSA. From 1923 to 1930 she would serve as the first female secretary of the New York State Labor Department.

330.16–19 "Forward out of error, . . . forward into light."] These stanzas were adapted from the hymn "Forward! Be Our Watchword" by English hymnodist Henry Alford (1810–1871) and became an anthem for the suffrage movement.

330.25–27 Mrs. Earnest Seton Thompson . . . Beatrice Forbes-Robertson] Grace Gallatin Seton Thompson (1872–1952), author and suffragist. Flora Dodge (Fola) La Follette (1882–1970), suffragist and labor activist. Beatrice Forbes-Robertson (1883–1967), English actress.

330.28 Men's League for Woman Suffrage] The Men's League for Woman Suffrage was founded in 1909 and included a number of prominent New Yorkers: James Lee Laidlaw (d. 1932), broker; Witter Bynner (1881–1968), poet; George Foster Peabody (1852–1938), banker and philanthropist; Colonel George Harvey (1864–1928), publisher of the *North American Review* and *Harper's Weekly*; Frederick Rowland Hazard (1858–1917), civic and industrial leader; Hamilton Holt (1872–1951), editor and publisher; and Oswald Garrison Villard (1872–1949), journalist and editor.

330.35   Mayor Gaynor] William Jay Gaynor (1849–1913) served as mayor of New York City from 1910 to 1913.

354.34   Mrs. Pankhurst and her daughter, Christabel] Emmeline Pankhurst (1858–1928) was a leading British suffragette who founded the Women's Social and Political Union in 1903. Her daughters Christabel (1880–1958) and Sylvia (1882–1960) also participated in the movement.

357.36   Israel Zangwill] Zangwill (1864–1921), a British author best known for his support of Zionism, a movement for the establishment of a Jewish state.

358.4–7   Lady Constance Lytton . . . Carrie Nation] Lytton (1869–1923) campaigned for prison reform and birth control in addition to women's suffrage. Carrie Nation (1846–1911) was an American Temperance activist.

358.21   Mrs. H. M. Brailsford] Jane Esdon Brailsford (1874–1937), a Scottish suffragist who was married to a prominent journalist, Henry Brailsford, a founding member of the Men's League for Women's Suffrage in 1907.

359.21   Olive Schreiner] Schreiner (1855–1920) was a South African writer best known for *The Story of an African Farm* (1883). *Women and Labour* was published in 1911.

361.34–35   "the easy way"] I.e., prostitution. Female prostitutes risked arrest and imprisonment while their male clients were rarely prosecuted.

364.3   piled it onto Eve's back.] Cf. Genesis 2; Eve is often blamed for this "original sin."

366.1   this proposal at it appeared in the *Outlook*] Lyman Abbott, "Women's Rights," *The Outlook*, vol. 100 (February 10, 1912), p. 302.

366.26   keynote of his recent editorial] Theodore Roosevelt, "Women's Rights and the Duties of Both Men and Women," *The Outlook* (February 3, 1912), pp. 262–66.

367.30   Emma Goldman] Goldman (1869–1940), an anarchist, labor activist, and writer, published *Anarchism and Other Essays* in 1911.

367.32   Miss Ida Tarbell] Tarbell (1857–1944), the muckraking author of an exposé of Standard Oil, was a prominent antisuffragist; the quote comes from her introduction to *The Book of Woman's Power* (New York: The Macmillan Company, 1911).

373.4   Rev. Dr. Leighton Parks] Parks (1852–1938), an Episcopal clergyman who was rector of St. Bartholomew's Church in New York City. His remarks appeared in "Religious Views of the 'Titanic'," *The Literary Digest* (May 4, 1912), p. 938.

373.16   Dr. Charles H. Parkhurst] Parkhurst (1842–1933), a clergyman and social reformer who led the Madison Square Presbyterian Church in New York City from 1880 to 1918.

380.7   Nurses' Settlement] Lillian Wald founded the Nurses' Settlement on New York City's Lower East Side in 1893 as a nursing service for immigrants; because of its location, it became known as the Henry Street Settlement.

380.21–22   "Seek and ye shall find."] Matthew 7:7.

381.10   "Let the women keep silent in the churches."] 1 Corinthians 14:34.

381.11–12   Paul says, . . . fear of the angels."] Cf. 1 Corinthians 11:10.

381.16   Emperor Kaiser Wilhelm] Wilhelm II (1859–1941) reigned as German emperor and king of Prussia from 1888 until his abdication in November 1918.

381.17–18   Elijah, Elisha, . . . Jeremiah] Hebrew prophets.

383.25   The CHAIRMAN.] The hearing was held before a subcommittee of the Senate Committee on the District of Columbia; Senator Wesley Livsey Jones of Washington most likely served as its chair.

384.1–2   President Taft] William Howard Taft lost the 1912 election to Woodrow Wilson but was still in office at the time the parade was being planned.

384.16   Maj. Sylvester] Major Richard Sylvester (1859–1930) was the chief of the Washington, D.C., police force.

386.19–20   Secretary Stimson . . . Gen. Johnston] Henry L. Stimson (1867–1950) served as Taft's secretary of war from 1911 to 1912; Brigadier General John A. Johnston (1858–1940), retired, was one of three commissioners of the District of Columbia who had oversight of the police.

387.22   Rosalie Jones] "General" Rosalie Gardiner Jones (1883–1978) led a band of supporters (also known as Pilgrims) on a march by foot from New York to Washington, D.C., in February 1913.

391.28   the South has had some rather trying experiences] I.e., the Fourteenth and Fifteenth Amendments.

394.7   "Feminist movement"] The term "feminism" derived from the French *féminisme* but was not widely used in the U.S. until the second decade of the twentieth century.

395.13–14   article written . . . William Randolph Hearst] Editorial, "The Americanism of Thomas Jefferson is Best Democracy; Let the Democratic Party Follow It for its own Benefit and for the Benefit of the Nation," *Chicago Examiner*, April 14, 1913.

395.27–34   Hon. William Jennings Bryan . . . face of anyone."] Address found in *Proceedings of the Continental Congress of the National Society of the Daughters of the American Revolution* (1913), pp. 19–21.

397.35   In a recent book Senator John Sharp Williams] Williams (1854–1932) was a Democrat from Mississippi who served in the House of Representatives from 1903 to 1909 and the Senate from 1911 to 1923. *Thomas Jefferson: His Permanent Influence on American Institutions* was published by Columbia University Press in 1913.

401.23   Gilead Balm] A variation on "There is a Balm in Gilead," a traditional African American spiritual; cf. Jeremiah 8:22.

401.26   Hagar] The protagonist shares a name with a biblical character long associated with the suffering of enslaved women. Hagar is the Egyptian slave of Sarah in the book of Genesis, who offers her as a concubine to her husband Abraham. Later Hagar and her son Ishmael are cast out into the wilderness, where they are rescued by God.

409.25   Professor Kirchwey] George Washington Kirchwey (1855–1942), an American legal scholar who taught at Columbia University.

410.34–35   "Just government depends on the consent of the governed."] The Declaration of Independence. The concept of consent of the governed was originally proposed by philosopher John Locke (1632–1704).

411.16–21   Sermon on the Mount . . . Marx] Jesus's Sermon on the Mount (Matthew 5–7) includes the Beatitudes and the Lord's Prayer. Jean-Jacques Rousseau (1712–1778) was a French philosopher; Karl Marx (1818–1883) and Friedrich Engels (1820–1895) published *The Communist Manifesto* in 1848.

413.23   President Jordan] David Starr Jordan (1851–1931), the first president of Stanford University.

415.20–21   China in this her period of reconstruction] After the collapse of the Qing dynasty, China declared itself a republic in 1912 under Sun Yat-sen (1866–1925), the first leader of the Nationalist Party of China.

417.27–29   The W.C.T.U. . . . Juvenile Protective Association] The Woman's Christian Temperance Union (WCTU) was founded in 1873–74; the General Federation of Women's Clubs was founded in 1890; the National Civil League was founded in 1894 to promote civic engagement; the Juvenile Protective Association was formed in 1907 to address juvenile delinquency.

417.40–418.2   Equal Guardianship . . . Red Light Abatement Law] Equal guardianship laws guaranteed that mothers would have rights over their children, instead of automatically granting those rights to fathers. Separate detention homes for girls was a key Progressive demand. "Red Light" districts referred to areas where prostitution and other illegal activities thrived; Red Light Abatement Laws attempted to curtail or eliminate prostitution.

420.19   Metropolitan Pageant] "A Dream of Freedom," a pageant by Margaret Tuttle, was sponsored by the New York Woman Suffrage Party.

421.1 a "hikers" campaign] A reference to "General" Rosalie Gardiner Jones's Pilgrims March in 1913 (see also note 387.22).

421.7–9 Nordica . . . Sarah Truax] Lillian Nordica (1857–1914), an American opera singer. Mary G. Shaw (1854–1929), an actress and playwright involved with the Professional Women's League. Hedwig Reicher (1884–1971), German actress. Sarah Truax (1872–1958), American actress and stage director.

423.19 the Equal Franchise Society] The Equal Franchise Society was founded in New York City in 1908 by Katherine Duer Mackay (1878–1930).

426.23 Oscar DePriest] Oscar Stanton DePriest (1871–1951), a Republican politician and successful real estate contractor, was elected to the Chicago City Council (which consists of aldermen from local wards) in 1914. In 1929 he became the first African American elected to Congress in the twentieth century.

428.5 Mr. Barnett] Ida B. Wells married Ferdinand L. Barnett (1852–1936), an attorney and civil rights activist, in 1895.

428.13 Mr. William Hale Thompson] William ("Big Bill") Hale Thompson (1869–1944) was a Republican politician who served as mayor of Chicago, 1915–23 and 1927–31.

430.21 Chief Justice Olson] Judge Harry Olson had secured Ida Wells-Barnett a patronage appointment as an adult probation officer in the Municipal Court in 1913.

434.11 the social evil] Prostitution.

435.30 "A Doll's House:"] Henrik Ibsen's 1879 play *A Doll's House* tells the story of Nora, a married woman with three children, who at the end of the play walks out on her husband and family.

437.5–7 "There is neither Jew nor Greek . . . Christ Jesus"] Galatians 3:28.

438.20–21 Benjamin Wade] Benjamin "Bluff" Wade (1880–1878) served as Republican senator from Ohio from 1851 to 1869.

439.22 Hector and Andromache] In Homer's *Iliad*, Andromache foresees the death of her husband Hector and goes to meet him with their infant son Astyanax in order to plead that he withdraw from the battle.

439.33–440.2 "At no time of her life. . . actions at law."] Thomas George Tucker, *Life in Ancient Athens* (1906), p. 83.

442.9 The recent decision of the Supreme Court] *Guinn v. U.S.* (1915) ruled unconstitutional certain exemptions to literacy tests that were designed to protect the voting rights of illiterate whites while disenfranchising African Americans.

443.9 MRS. PAUL LAURENCE DUNBAR] Alice Moore (1875–1935), a teacher and poet, married Paul Laurence Dunbar (1872–1906), an African American writer and playwright, in 1898.

443.10 Matthew Arnold . . . "criticism of life"] Matthew Arnold (1822–1888), a Victorian poet and literary critic. See "The Study of Poetry" in T. H. Ward, ed., *The English Poets* (1880).

444.15–16 Miss Nannie H. Burroughs . . . Mrs. Mary McLeod Bethune] Nannie H. Burroughs (1879–1961), Charlotte Hawkins Brown (1883–1961), and Mary McLeod Bethune (1875–1955) were all African American educators.

445.18 Bone of my bone, flesh of my flesh] Cf. Genesis 2:23.

446.17–18 movement for the City Beautiful] The City Beautiful Movement of the 1880s and 1890s was dedicated to the beautification of American cities.

448.15–16 Mr. Witter Bynner's recently published poem "The New World:"] Witter Bynner (1881–1968) was an American poet also known by the pen name Emanuel Morgan; "The New World" was published in 1915.

451.10–11 Ednah Cheney, Abby Morton Diaz] Ednah Dow Littlehale Cheney (1824–1904) and Abby Morton Diaz (1821–1904) were women's rights activists and reformers in Massachusetts.

451.32–33 Young Women's Christian Association] The Young Women's Christian Association (YWCA) originally helped young women moving to cities from rural areas but expanded to serve the needs of working women. Its branches, while segregated, were vital to African American communities.

455.3 Miss Zona Gale] Zona Gale (1874–1938), American novelist and playwright.

470.23–24 Schopenhauer . . . has a fit every time he sees a skirt] Arthur Schopenhauer (1788–1860), German philosopher who was a noted misogynist.

472.18 Gutenberg liquor law] Possibly the Raines Law, passed by the New York State legislature in 1896, which prohibited the sale of alcoholic beverages on Sunday—the only day off for many workingmen—with the exception of guests in hotels. Saloons quickly added furnished rooms so they could apply for hotel licenses.

472.38 "her price is above rubies."] Proverbs 31:10.

476.22–24 Senator Newlands . . . Senator Pittman] Francis G. Newlands (1846–1917), Democratic senator from Nevada, 1903–17; Key Pittman (1872–1940), Democratic senator from Nevada, 1913–40.

476.34 the Progressive Party] Formed in 1912 after Theodore Roosevelt lost the Republican nomination to William Howard Taft. The Progressive Party did not put forward a candidate in the 1916 election.

477.4 Miss Anne Martin] Anne Martin (1875–1951), a Nevada suffragist.

477.13 Suffrage Special] In 1914 the Congressional Union organized a whistle-stop tour of the West to campaign against Democratic candidates (even those who supported women's suffrage) because of the party's lackluster support for the cause.

479.8   Mason and Dixon's line] The boundary between Maryland and Pennsylvania, the northern limit of slaveowning states; more broadly, the symbolic
divide between North and South.

479.16   Senators should be elected by the people.] The Seventeenth Amendment, adopted in 1913, mandated the popular election of U.S. senators, super-
seding the earlier practice of their election by state legislatures.

480.10   Governor Glynn] Martin H. Glynn (1871–1924), governor of New
York from 1913 to 1914.

480.14–15   Colonel Roosevelt weeping for his stolen issue] Ex-President and
Republican Theodore Roosevelt led the Preparedness Movement after the
outbreak of World War I, arguing that the U.S. military should be strengthened for defensive purposes; President Woodrow Wilson, a Democrat, initially
opposed it, preferring to maintain strict neutrality.

484.16   Lord Derby] Edward Stanley, 17th Earl of Derby (1865–1948), British secretary of state for war in 1916–18 and 1922–24.

484.21   Lord Sydenham] George Clarke, 1st Baron Sydenham of Combe
(1848–1933), a retired British army officer.

487.12   political liberty, similar to that of 1848] The Revolutions of 1848 were
a series of political upheavals against the monarchies in Sicily, France, Germany, Italy, and the Austrian Empire. All ended in failure.

487.30   Mrs. Henry Fawcett] Dame Millicent Fawcett (1847–1929), a prominent British suffragette.

491.30   Eufame McIlyane] In 1591, Eufame Maclayne or MacCalzean was
burned at the stake during the North Berick Witch Trials in Scotland for using
pain relief to relieve women's pain during childbirth; she was also accused of
attempting to murder members of her family as well as James VI.

492.11–14   Hon. Champ Clark said . . . . . . are against it."] James Beauchamp
(Champ) Clark (1850–1921) of Kentucky served as Speaker of the House from
1911 to 1919.

493.19–20   Mother Grundy] See note 58.26–27.

494.20   Hon. John Finlay] John Finlay (1837–1910), Canadian member of
parliament, 1904–8.

496.32   "The Remonstrance,"] *The Remonstrance* was the official publication
of the Massachusetts Association Opposed to the Further Extension of Suffrage to Women.

499.21   inroads of the prohibition movement] The Prohibition Movement,
led by the Anti-Saloon League, spearheaded the drive to pass the Eighteenth
Amendment, which banned the production, importation, and sale of alcoholic
beverages and was ratified in 1919. The country went dry on January 17, 1920.

500.9–10   A French philosopher said . . . its principles."] Charles-Louis de

Secondat, Baron de La Brède et de Montesquieu, *The Spirit of the Laws*, part 1, book 8, chapter 1 (1748).

504.15   Naturalization laws] The Naturalization Act of 1790 offered citizenship to any alien, "being a free white person," who had been in the country for two years; the Naturalization Act of 1870 extended this to "aliens of African nativity and to persons of African descent."

504.16   enfranchised the Indians] The Dawes Act of 1887 offered a limited path to citizenship for Native Americans. Full U.S. citizenship was not granted until 1924. See also the Indian Citizenship Act, pp. 575–76 in this volume.

504.37   uprising of the Sioux Indians] The Dakota War of 1862, also known as the Sioux uprising, was a conflict over land in southwest Minnesota between American Indian tribes and encroaching white settlers backed by U.S. military troops.

510.19–20   Strike of the textile workers of Lawrence] In 1912, 20,000 immigrant workers led by the Industrial Workers of the World (IWW, or Wobblies) staged a two-month strike to protest pay cuts linked to shorter hours in the Lawrence, Massachusetts, textile mills.

518.31–33   "*That all governments . . . is tyranny,*"] The first phrase comes from the Declaration of Independence; the second is generally attributed to James Otis, a Massachusetts patriot, in 1761.

520.25   the extra session] On April 2, 1917, Woodrow Wilson asked a special joint session of Congress to declare war against Germany; it would do so on April 6.

522.19   Mrs. Catt] Carrie Chapman Catt (1859–1947), president of the National American Woman Suffrage Association.

525.35–36   EUGENE V. DEBS . . . BOUCK WHITE] Eugene V. Debs (1855–1926) was a founding member of the Industrial Workers of the World, a militant international labor union formed in 1905, and a five-time candidate of the Socialist Party for president; Bouck White (1874–1951) was a Congregational minister and socialist.

527.16–19   Mabel Vernon . . . Maud Jamison] Mabel Vernon (1883–1975), Katherine Morey, and Virginia Arnold (b. 1880) were National Woman's Party organizers; Lavinia Dock (1858–1956) was an NWP advisor; Maud Jamison was a state officer; and Annie Arniel had just joined the NWP.

528.28–29   "Once to every man . . . evil side."] From "Verses Suggested by the Present Crisis" (1845), poem by James Russell Lowell (1819–1891) published in the *Boston Courier* in response to the debate over slavery and the impending war with Mexico.

534.15–16   Julia Emory] A Maryland-born suffragist (1885–1979).

536.20–21   Katherine Rolston Fisher] National Woman's Party picketer (1871–1950).

537.9 Mrs. Kendall] Ada Davenport Kendall (1867–1950), New York journalist.

537.18–19 Dr. Harvey W. Wiley.] Wiley (1844–1930), a chemist, was instrumental in the passage of the Pure Food and Drug Act of 1906.

537.20–21 Diet of Worms] The council convened in 1521 by the Holy Roman Emperor to decide the fate of Martin Luther, the central figure of the Protestant Revolution, and which declared Luther an "obstinate heretic."

537.35–36 Mrs. Lawrence Lewis] Dora Lewis (1862–1928), early National Woman's Party supporter.

538.17–18 Mary A. Nolan] Florida suffragist and picketer (d. 1925).

538.38 Mrs. Cosu] Alice Mary Clarisse Cosu (b. 1868), Louisiana suffragist.

540.14 Paula Jakobi] Suffragist and playwright (1870–1960).

541.9 forcibly fed] Force-feeding involves feeding people against their will, usually by a plastic feeding tube inserted through the nose or mouth into the stomach, a dangerous and very painful procedure.

541.31 Dudley Field Malone] Attorney and politician (1882–1950).

542.2–3 Elsie Hill] Connecticut suffragist (1883–1970) and daughter of Congressman Ebenezer J. Hill.

542.13 Maud Younger] California suffragist (1870–1936) and labor activist.

542.14 Mrs. Thomas Hepburn] Katharine Houghton Hepburn (1878–1951), Connecticut suffragist and birth control activist.

542.14 Mrs. William Kent] Elizabeth Thatcher Kent (1868–1952), wife of California congressman William Kent.

542.20–21 Mrs. John Rogers, Jr.] Elizabeth Selden White Rogers (1868–1950), New York suffragist and civic leader.

548.27 Boston, the "cradle of liberty"] Faneuil Hall in Boston was the site of speeches encouraging independence from Britain during the American Revolution.

548.37 Czarist Russia of three years ago] The Russian Revolution of 1917 ended the rule of the Romanov dynasty and put Vladimir Lenin and the Bolshevik Party in power.

549.35 Mrs. Samuel Warren] Mabel Bayard Warren (1861–1924), Massachusetts suffragist.

549.35–36 Lois Warren Shaw] New Hampshire suffragist (1884–1964).

550.9 Katherine Morey] See also note 527.16–19.

551.6 Louise Sykes] Louise Ryckman Sykes (b. 1868), Cambridge suffragist.

551.8 Elsie Hill] See note 542.2–3.

551.14 Mrs. Robert Treat Whitehouse] Florence Brooks Whitehouse (1869–1945), Maine suffragist.

551.15 Agnes H. Morey] Massachusetts suffragist and mother of Katherine Morey (see note 527.16–19).

558.15 Helen Gardener] Helen Hamilton Gardener (1853–1925) was an author and lecturer who played a key role as NAWSA's liaison to Woodrow Wilson.

559.32 Harriet Taylor Upton] Ohio suffrage leader (1853–1945).

560.16–17 Charl Ormond Williams] Tennessee suffragist (1885–1969).

566.1 recent granting of suffrage . . . New York State] New York State granted women full suffrage in a referendum approved by voters on November 6, 1917.

568.6–8 Plato said, . . . constitute it."] Winthrop Talbot attributes this quote to Plato's *Republic* in "The Imperial Plan in German Schooling," *Century Illustrated Monthly Magazine*, Vol. 95, no. 2 (December 1917).

570.3 interlocutory injunction] A legal process in which a party to a contract institutes an action asking for equitable relief.

579.3–4 old English Common Law or the Napoleonic Code] Common Law is the body of law based on custom and precedent developed in Britain; it forms the basis for much of the U.S. legal system. The Napoleonic Code is the French civil code established under Napoleon in 1804.

589.33–34 the Metropolitan Life Company] Founded in 1868 to provide insurance, annuities, and health benefits to policyholders.

589.39 Drolet's figures for New York City] Godias J. Drolet (1888–1968) worked for the Statistical and Research Service of the New York Tuberculosis and Health Association.

591.5 plumbism] The technical term for lead poisoning.

591.7 Prendergast] Dr. Dowling Prendergast, *The Potter and Lead Poisoning* (1898). Dowling was the senior physician at the North Staffordshire Infirmary in Britain.

591.25–26 records by Thomas Oliver] See "A Lecture on Lead Poisoning and the Race," *British Medical Journal*, Vol. 1, no. 2628 (May 13, 1911), pp. 1096–98.

596.15–16 George Madden Martin] Martin (1866–1946) was a novelist best known for *Emmy Lou, Her Book and Heart* (1902). Her "American Women and Public Affairs" was published in the *Atlantic Monthly* (February 1924).

596.26–27 The League of Nations . . . McAdoo] The League of Nations was founded in 1920 to maintain world peace after World War I; Calvin Coolidge (1872–1933) was the thirtieth U.S. president, 1923–29; Alfred E. Smith (1873–

1933) was a four-term governor of New York who ran for president in 1928; William Gibbs McAdoo (1863–1941) unsuccessfully ran for the Democratic nomination for president in 1920 and 1924.

597.4–5   Eighteenth Amendment and the Volstead Act] The Volstead Act, also known as the National Prohibition Act, provided enforcement procedures to carry out the Eighteenth Amendment, which prohibited the manufacture and sale of alcoholic beverages.

597.7–11   Lincoln's mind: . . . mob rule."] Abraham Lincoln expressed these views in his 1838 Lyceum Address.

597.16   Tea Pot Dome affair] The Teapot Dome Scandal involved the leasing of petroleum reserves in 1922 by Secretary of the Interior Albert Fall, who was later convicted of accepting bribes from oil companies.

598.12–13   Alice Bentley] Alice M. Bentley (1859–1949) served as a Republican member of the Pennsylvania House of Representatives from 1923 to 1928.

599.20   Jeannette Rankin's] Rankin (1880–1973) was elected to the U.S. House of Representatives in 1916 from Montana, becoming the first woman to serve in Congress.

599.22   Alice Robertson's] Robertson (1854–1931) was the second woman elected to Congress, winning election in 1920 as a Republican from Oklahoma but failing to win reelection in 1922.

600.1–2   Mirabeau . . . only man the king had about him.] Honoré-Gabriel Riqueti, comte de Mirabeau (1749–1791), a president of the National Assembly during the French Revolution; the quote comes from a letter Mirabeau wrote on June 14, 1790.

600.4–5   next to Pinchot] Cornelia Bryce Pinchot (1881–1960) was a Progressive reformer married to Gifford Pinchot (1865–1946), who served as governor of Pennsylvania in 1922–26 and 1930–34.

606.25   ideals of Panamericanism] Pan-Americanism seeks to encourage diplomatic, political, economic, and social ties among the nations of North, Central, and South America.

608.19   code of Estevan de Ferrater] See Esteban de Ferrater, *Codigo de Derecho International* (Barcelona, 1846), one of the earliest collections and codifications of international treaties and law.

609.6–7   what they call "progressive codification"] In 1924 the League of Nations created the Committee of Experts for the Progressive Codification of International Law to codify and develop new fields of law "ripe for international agreement," including laws concerning nationality and territorial waters.

609.17–23   Abigail Adams . . . hot rebellion"] See Abigail Adams, letter to John Adams of March 31, 1776, pp. 5–12 in this volume.

609.23–25   in 1848 . . . declaration of our rights.] See Seneca Falls Convention, "Declaration of Sentiments and Resolutions," pp. 36–42 in this volume.

610.38–39   It is *obiter dicta.*] Latin: by the way. The phrase is often applied to an expression of opinion by a judge "said in passing."

611.1   Charles Henry Butler] Butler (1859–1940) was an American lawyer who advised the National Woman's Party.

611.19   jurist Elihu Root] Root (1845–1937) was a lawyer who served as secretary of state under Theodore Roosevelt.

611.23–24   Orestes Ferrara] Ferrara (1876–1972) was an Italian who fought for Cuban independence and served in Cuba's House of Representatives.

612.4–5   International Labor office of the League of Nations] The International Labor Organization (ILO), an agency established by the Treaty of Versailles in 1919 to promote international labor standards.

613.1–2   (1921 Convention for . . . Women and Children)] The International Convention for the Suppression of the Traffic in Women and Children was a 1921 multilateral treaty of the League of Nations dealing with sexual exploitation and human trafficking at the international level.

615.19–21   Alice Paul . . . scholar of international law.] Paul (1885–1977) received an LLB from Washington College of Law in 1922 and earned a doctorate in civil law from American University in 1928. The Equal Rights Treaty was modeled on the Equal Rights Amendment, first introduced in the United States by the National Woman's Party in 1923.

616.32   Senator Bingham] Hiram Bingham (1875–1956) served as the Republican senator from Connecticut from 1925 to 1933.

617.30   Mr. Kiess] Edgar Raymond Kiess (1875–1930) served as a Republican member of the House of Representatives from Pennsylvania from 1923 to 1930.

623.38–624.7   That this Convention go on record . . . Congress.] The Fair Labor Standards Act of 1938 set a minimum wage, guaranteed overtime pay, and prohibited child labor. The Social Security Act of 1935 established a system of old-age benefits, unemployment insurance, and aid to dependent mothers and children. The National Labor Relations Act of 1935, also known as the Wagner Act, protected the rights of workers to form and join labor unions.

626.17   deportations and anti-alien laws] During the Great Depression in the 1930s, perhaps a third of the Mexican American population, primarily immigrants, returned to Mexico. A formal deportation policy by the U.S. Government was partly responsible, but many Mexicans "voluntarily" left when work ran out and they were denied relief.

627.12   W.P.A.] The Works Progress Administration (WPA) was established in 1935 to provide jobs and carry out public works projects; the California State Relief Administration (SRA), created in 1935, was the successor to the State Emergency Relief Administration created in 1933.

630.12   Good Neighbor policy] Franklin Roosevelt's Good Neighbor Policy promoted non-intervention in the domestic affairs of Latin American countries in the 1930s. It renounced Theodore Roosevelt's 1904 corollary to the Monroe Doctrine, which allowed the U.S. to use military force to intervene in the affairs of Latin American countries.

633.18   Carrie Chapman Catt] See note 522.19.

633.25–26   Inez Milholland] See note 330.13–14.

633.35   the League of Women Voters] A nonpartisan organization founded in 1920 to prepare women for their new roles as voters and citizens.

634.11   Gladys Pyle] Pyle (1890–1989), a South Dakota Republican long active in politics, served only two months.

634.27   Jeannette Rankin] See note 599.20.

634.40–635.1   Mary Norton] Mary Teresa Norton (1875–1959), a Democrat, represented a New Jersey district in the House of Representatives from 1925 to 1951.

635.1   Caroline O'Day] Caroline Love Goodwin O'Day (1869–1943), a Democrat, served as New York State's at-large representative in Congress from 1935 to 1943.

635.2   Jessie Sumner] Sumner (1898–1994), a Republican, represented a district in Illinois in the House of Representatives from 1939 to 1947.

635.15   Ruth Hanna McCormick Simms] Simms (1880–1944) served as the at-large representative from Illinois from 1929 to 1931.

635.17   Florence Kahn] Florence Prag Kahn (1866–1948) served as a Republican member of Congress from California from 1925 to 1937, succeeding her husband who died in office.

635.22–23   Miriam A. Ferguson] Miriam "Ma" Ferguson (1875–1961) twice served as governor of Texas, 1925–27 and 1933–35.

636.20   Mabel Walker Willebrandt] Willebrandt (1889–1963) was the U.S. assistant district attorney in charge of handling cases related to Prohibition and the Volstead Act from 1921 to 1929.

636.24   Dr. Mary Harris] Harris was the warden of the minimum-security facility for female inmates in Alderson, West Virginia, which opened in 1927.

636.27   Dr. Louise Stanley] Stanley (1883–1954) served as head of the Bureau of Home Economics in the Department of Agriculture from 1923 to 1943.

636.28–29   Mary Anderson] Anderson (1872–1964) was a labor activist who headed the Women's Bureau from 1920 to 1944.

636.32   Katharine Lenroot] Lenroot (1891–1982) was a Wisconsin child welfare leader who served as chief of the Children's Bureau from 1934 to 1951.

636.33   Grace Abbott] Abbott (1878–1939) was a social worker who served as chief of the Children's Bureau from 1921 to 1934.

637.6   Miss Mary W. Dewson] Mary ("Molly") Williams Dewson (1874–1962) headed the Women's Division of the Democratic National Committee and served on the Social Security Board from 1937 to 1938.

637.15–16   Postmaster General Farley] James Farley (1888–1972) was chair of the Democratic National Committee and postmaster general under Franklin Delano Roosevelt.

638.14   Louis Howe] Louis McHenry Howe (1871–1936) was a political advisor to Franklin Roosevelt.

638.27   Josephine Roche] Josephine Aspinwall Roche (1886–1976) served as assistant secretary of the treasury from 1934 to 1937.

639.3   Mrs. J. Borden Harriman] Florence "Daisy" Jaffray Harriman (1870–1967) served as U.S. minister to Norway from 1937 to 1941.

639.8–9   Florence Allen] Florence Ellinwood Allen (1884–1966) was an associate justice of the Ohio Supreme Court from 1923 to 1934 before Franklin Roosevelt elevated her to the U.S. Court of Appeals for the Sixth Circuit, where she served until 1959.

639.9–10   Genevieve R. Cline] Cline (1877–1959) was a judge of the U.S. Customs Court from 1928 to 1953.

639.17   Mary La Dame] La Dame (1884–1972) was associate director of the U.S. Employment Service from 1934 to 1938 before becoming a special assistant to Frances Perkins.

639.19   Lucille Foster McMillin] McMillin (1879–1949) served on the U.S. Civil Service Commission from 1933 to 1949.

639.20   Ellen Woodward] Ellen Sullivan Woodward (1887–1971) was director of the Women's Division at the Federal Emergency Relief Administration from 1933 to 1935, director of Women's and Professional Projects for the Works Progress Administration from 1935 to 1938, and a member of the Social Security Board from 1938 to 1946.

639.29   Florence Kerr] Kerr (1890–1974) was a regional director of the WPA's Women's and Professional Projects Division and then its head from 1938 to 1943.

639.31   Katherine Blackburn] Blackburn (1892–1972) became director of the Division of Press Intelligence in 1933 and became special assistant for Press Dissemination in the State Department in 1936.

639.38–39   Jo Coffin] Coffin (1880–1943) was assistant to the public printer in the Government Printing Office from 1934 to 1941.

639.39–40   Rose Schneiderman] Schneiderman (1882–1972) was a labor activist who served on the Labor Advisory Board of the National Recovery Administration and as New York secretary of labor from 1937 to 1943.

640.8   Marian Bannister] Marian Glass Bannister (1875–1951) was the assistant treasurer of the U.S. from 1933 to 1951.

640.13   Jewell W. Swofford] Swofford was the first woman member of the U.S. Employees' Compensation Committee.

640.14   Laura S. Brown] A lawyer (1870–?) and member of the Board of Appeals of the Veterans Administration from 1934 until at least 1943.

640.15   Lucy Howorth] Lucy Somerville Howorth (1895–1997) was a member of the Board of Appeals of the Veterans Administration from 1934 to 1950.

640.16–17   Marion J. Harron] Harron (1903–1972) was a U.S. Tax Court judge from 1936 to 1960.

640.25   Mary Harriman Rumsey] Rumsey (1881–1934), chair of the Consumers' Advisory Board of the National Recovery Administration, died after a riding accident in December 1934.

646.27–28   Senator James O. Eastland and Senator Stennis.] Senator James Eastland (1904–1984) served from 1943 to 1978; Senator John Stennis (1901–1995) served from 1947 to 1989. Both were Democrats.

649.1   Medgar Evers] Evers (1925–1963) was a civil rights activist who was murdered outside his home in Jackson, Mississippi, by Byron De La Beckwith, a member of the White Citizens' Council. His death occurred just hours after President John F. Kennedy delivered a major civil rights address; both his murder and the resulting trials received national attention and spurred civil rights protests.

650.30   the Southern Christian Leadership Conference] The SCLC is a civil rights organization founded in 1957 in the wake of the Montgomery Bus Boycott.

651.7   the shot heard 'round the world.] I.e., the first skirmish in the American Revolution, at the Old North Bridge in Concord, Massachusetts, on April 19, 1775. The phrase comes from the opening stanza of Ralph Waldo Emerson's "Concord Hymn" (1837).

651.14   Martin King] Reverend Martin Luther King, Jr. (1929–1968), the national civil rights leader, was the first president of the SCLC.

652.33–35   The ruling . . . "one man, one vote."] *Reynold v. Sims* (1964).

652.40   Dirksen Amendment] Everett Dirksen, Republican senator from Illinois from 1951 to 1969, supported a constitutional amendment that would allow legislative districts of unequal population.

655.28–36   The president said: "So free speech . . . for today."] Lyndon Baines Johnson, "Remarks to the International Platform Association upon receiving the Association's Annual Award," August 3, 1965.

Index

Abbott, Abby Frances Hamlin, 226
Abbott, Grace, 636
Aberdeen, S.D., 497
Abolition, xxi–xxii, 19, 27, 43, 45, 61, 63, 84, 91, 97, 102–6, 108, 112, 119, 123, 125, 127–29, 149, 438, 451. *See also* Slavery
Adam and Eve, 52, 364
Adams, Abigail, xviii, xxi, 5–8, 10–12, 182, 264, 609
Adams, John, 5, 8–10, 182, 264, 609
Adams, John Quincy, 182
Adams, Samuel, 77
Addams, Jane: "Why Women Should Vote," 315–25
Addison, Joseph: *Cato*, 12
Adkins v. Children's Hospital of the District of Columbia, 569
Adler, Felix, 374–75
Africa, 95
African Americans, xvii–xxi, xxiv, xxvi, 5, 9–10, 91, 158–59, 185, 192, 198–99, 242, 361, 410, 479, 503, 527; address by Josephine St. Pierre Ruffin, 232–35; Anna J. Cooper on the South, 216–20; and Chicago politics, 425–32; citizenship for, xxii, 157, 163–64, 169, 172–73, 181–82, 236, 569, 655; Constance Baker Motley on voting rights, 650–57; described as inferior, 59, 62; education of, 84, 262, 276–77, 656; equal rights for freed slaves tied to equal rights for women, 91, 93–106, 108–9; Fannie Barrier Williams on women in politics, 228–31; Fannie Lou Hamer on black voter registration in the South, 646–49; Frederick Douglass on black suffrage, 149–53; Ida B. Wells on black women voting in Chicago, 425–32; lecture by Maria Stewart, 14–18; male voters, 13, 68, 70; Mary Church Terrell on progress of black women, 275–81; and political parties, 189, 207; in the South,
216–20, 261–65, 553, 646–54; speech by Frances Ellen Watkins Harper, 112–18; speech by Sojourner Truth, 43–44; suffrage for black men versus suffrage for women, 119, 126–31, 143–45, 147, 149, 151–53, 236, 438; in suffrage parades, 382; symposium on black women's suffrage, 433–58; working women, 145, 278–80. *See also* Slavery
African Methodist Episcopal Church, 436
Agassiz Public School, 452
Agitator, 138, 147
Agriculture Department, U.S., 636
Ahasuerus, 27–28
Akron, Ohio, 43
Alabama, 175, 277, 553, 650–51
Albany, N.Y., 67, 227, 365, 489
Alberta, 487
Alford, Henry, 330
Algeria, 608
Allen, Florence E., 639
Alpha Suffrage Club, 425–27, 430
American Antislavery Society, 27
American Constitutional League, 570
American Equal Rights Association, xx, 112, 116–19, 147, 149
American Indians, xxi, xxvii, 9–10, 496–97, 616; citizenship for, 196–98, 575–76; Dakota War, 504–5; Dawes Act, 210, 504; full suffrage for women, xix; gender roles, 31, 210–15; Indian Citizenship Act, 575–76; in suffrage parades, 382
Americanism, 480, 504
American Magazine, 293
American Suffragettes, 326
American Woman Suffrage Association, xvii, xxii, 119, 201
Anderson, C. W., 458
Anderson, Mary, 636
Anglo-Saxonism, 262–66
Anneke, Mathilde F., 120–21, 124, 146, 183

Anthony, Susan B., xxii, 87, 116, 163, 223, 275, 278, 419, 438, 489, 491, 496, 592; and American Equal Rights Association, 119–21, 126–30, 134–35, 137, 140–46; *The History of Woman Suffrage*, xvii, xxi, 91, 196; and National American Woman Suffrage Association, 248; and National Woman Suffrage Association, 177, 183–84, 256–57; Seneca Falls Convention, 36; and Woman's Loyal National League, 91–97, 101–2, 108–11; "Woman Wants Bread, Not the Ballot!", 185–95

Antioch College, 89, 100

Anti-Slavery Bugle, 43

Antislavery movement. *See* Abolition

Antisuffrage movement, xix–xxi, xxiv–xxvi, 104, 122, 473, 508, 543, 594; allies of, 502, 505; on assumption of women's sex superiority, 267–74; need to overcome, 491–92; petition to New York constitutional convention, 223–27; and ratification of Nineteenth Amendment, 556–59; in the South, 553–54; and *Titanic* sinking, 372–75; on violation of women's essential nature, 376–81; on women's suffrage as not beneficial, 299–306; and World War I, 5 28–30

Apaches, 497

Arapahos, 210

Arizona, 513, 556–57

Arizona Territory, 124, 222, 247, 299

Arkansas, 175, 244–45, 553, 556, 634

Army, black troops in, 115

Arneil, Anne, 527

Arnold, Matthew, 443

Arnold, Virginia, 527

Articles of Confederation, 165

Asberry, N.J., 458

Ashley, James H., 124

Ashley, Jessie, 328

Asquith, Herbert H., 354–57, 471, 487

Associated Press, 607

Atlanta, Ga., 435, 439

Atlantic City, N.J., 481, 646

Austin, Mary, 330

Australia, 248, 264, 318, 378

Austria, 46, 237, 483, 599

Avery, Rachel Foster, 248

Bachelder, Mrs. L. S., 120, 142

Baker, Abby Scott: Letter to Editor of *The Outlook*, 475–80

Baker, Jean H., xxviii

Balderston, William, 245

Baldwin, Maria L., 382; "Votes for Teachers," 452–53

Baltimore, Md., 114, 454, 572

Bannister, Marian G., 640

Barcelo, Antonio, 618

Barcelona, Spain, 608

Barker, Caroline, 40

Barker, Eunice, 39

Barker, William G., 40

Barnard College, 267, 409

Barnett, Ferdinand L., 428–29

Barney, Nora Stanton Blatch, 330

Barnstable, Mass., 309, 313

Barton, Clara, 253

Bedford, Mass., 308

Beecher, Henry Ward, 124, 141, 157

Beecher, Mrs. William C., 227

Beiderhasse, Josephine, 329

Bell, John Calhoun, 290

Bellows, Henry Whitney, 56

Belmont, Alva Vanderbilt, 327, 330, 542

Bentley, Alice M., 598

Bergen, Mrs. Tunis G., 227

Berlin, Germany, 275–76, 280, 486

Bethune, Mary McLeod, 444

Bible, 14–18, 23, 25, 42, 59–62, 114, 131, 142, 160–61, 186, 251, 380–81, 437, 445, 472

Bill of Rights, U.S., 68, 160–61, 179, 411, 626

Bills of attainder, 173–74, 178

Bingham, Hiram, 616–17

Birmingham, Ala., 650, 656

Birrell, Augustine, 359

Bishop, Anna, 34–35

Bishop, Harriet, 124

Bissell, Emily Perkins, 288

Blackburn, Katherine, 639

Blackstone, William, 19–20, 40–41

Blackwell, Alice Stone, 84, 248, 489–90; "Militant Methods," 353–60

Blackwell, Antoinette Brown, 63, 120, 124–25, 132, 143, 489

Blackwell, Elizabeth, 489
Blackwell, Henry Browne, 84–86, 119, 121, 125, 127, 132, 145–47
Blaine, James G., 296
Blair, Henry W., 207
Blake, Lillie Devereux, 177, 183, 204–5, 254
"Blanket" amendment. See Equal Rights Amendment
Blatch, Harriot Stanton, 67, 531; "The Women's Political Union," 326–31
Bloomer, Amelia Jenks, 89, 120
Boise, Idaho, 245
Bok, Edward W., 253, 282
Bolsheviks, 549
Bonnel, Rachel D., 39
Bonnin, Gertrude Simmons (Zitkála-Šá), 575
Booth, Edwin, 134
Boston, Mass., xviii, 14, 25, 30, 87, 126, 129, 136, 142, 145, 203, 232, 277, 303, 438, 454, 496, 637; letter series on conditions for working women, 508–19; open-air meetings in, 308–9, 313; protests surrounding President Wilson's visit, 548–52; during Revolutionary War, 6, 9, 11; tax protest in, 64–66
Boston & Maine Railroad, 498
Boston Equal Suffrage Association for Good Government, 308, 508–19
Boston Female Anti-Slavery Society, 19
Boston League of Women Voters, 508
Boston Working Women's Association, 142
Bouguereau, William-Adolphe, 277
Bovee, Virginia, 535–36
Boynton, Lizzie, 120
Brailsford, Jane E., 358–59
Braintree, Mass., 5. 10
Braithewaite, William Stanley: "Democracy and Art," 447–48
Brandeis, Louis, 569, 572
Brawley, Benjamin: "Politics and Womanliness," 435–36
Brazil, 177
Brent, Margaret, 264
Bribery, 501–2
Bridgeport Farmer, 303
Bright, John, 186
Bristol, England, 357

Britain, 45, 120, 157, 170, 289, 375, 411, 475, 517; and American Revolution, 5, 13, 165, 179; full suffrage in, 487–89, 505; labor in, 185–88, 484–85, 590–91; legal status of women in, 48, 72, 74, 579; militant methods of suffragettes, xxiii, 300, 307, 353–60, 412, 469, 471; municipal suffrage in, 247–48, 318; open-air meetings in, 326; Parliament, 70, 89, 186–88, 237, 353–57, 487; women holding office in, 69–70; women's rights movement in, 87, 89, 410, 415; women's suffrage on Isle of Man, 264; working women in, 484–85, 590–91; and World War I, 483–85, 545
Brockport Normal School, 228
Brooklyn, N.Y., 223, 305–6, 459
Brougham, Henry, 89
Brown, Arthur Raymond, 565; How It Feels to Be the Husband of a Suffragette, 468–72
Brown, Charlotte Hawkins, 444
Brown, Gertrude Foster, 468; Your Vote and How to Use It, 565–68
Brown, Joseph, 203
Brown, Laura S., 640
Brown, Olympia, 183
Browning, Elizabeth Barrett, 89
Browning, Robert, 89
Brownlow, Louis, 535
Brown v. Board of Education, 650
Bruce, B. K.: "Colored Women's Clubs," 454–55
Bruno, Giordano, 491
Bryan, William Jennings, 323–24, 395–96
Buck, Garrick H., 639
Buffalo, N.Y., 189, 489
Bunker, Edwin S., 121, 125
Bunker, Joel, 40
Bureau of Indian Affairs, 382, 575
Bureau of Labor, 580
Bureau of Press Intelligence, 639
Burleigh, Charles C., 121, 140, 145–46
Burns, Lucy, 533–35, 539, 541
Burroughs, Nannie H., 444; "Black Women and Reform," 448–49
Burroughs, William, 40
Butler, Charles Henry, 611

Butterworth, Emily Dee, 540
Bynner, Witter, 330; "The New World," 448
Byron, Lord (George Gordon), 54

Calder, William M., 560
California, 97–98, 124, 391, 399, 635; Chinese Americans in 199–200; constitution, 302; eight-hour workday for women, 513; legislature, 626; Mexican Americans in, 622, 624, 626–27, 629–30; ratification of Nineteenth Amendment, 557; suffrage referendum in, 299, 302, 416–18; voting in presidential elections, 476
California Civic League, 417
California Equal Suffrage Association, 416–18
California Federation of Women's Clubs, 417
California State Relief Administration, 627
Call, Wilkinson, 203
Calnan, Eleanor, 550
Cambridge, Mass., 452
Canada, 198, 245, 247, 277, 318, 477, 487, 505, 521
Capitalism, 187, 190–94, 365
Capron, E. W., 40
Caraway, Hattie, 634
Carlyle, Thomas: "Signs of the Times," 67
Catherine de' Medici, 599–600
Catherine II, 599
Catholics, xxv, 256
Catt, Carrie Chapman, xxii–xxiii, xxvii, 248, 275, 328, 522, 528, 553, 555–61, 633; "The Crisis," 481–507; *Woman Suffrage and Politics*, 556
Centennial Commission, 177
Chalkstone, Mrs., 97–98
Chamberlain, Jacob, 40
Channing, W. H., 63
Charles I, 70
Charleston, S.C., 19, 399
Chase, Elizabeth, 124
Cheever, George B., 92
Cheney, Ednah D. L., 451
Chesnutt, Charles W.: "Women's Rights," 440–41

Cheyennes, 210
Chicago, Ill., 138–39, 146, 148, 228, 293, 399, 444, 602, 646; African American women as voters, 425–32; education in, 316, 319–21; Jane Addams on, 315–23; municipal suffrage in, 318, 435; registered women voters in, 287; Woman's Party launched in, 475–76; women in politics, 229
Chicago Board of Education, 319
Chickasaws, 196
Child custody, 38, 50–51, 78–79, 85, 88, 131–32, 180–81, 412, 417, 447, 579
Child welfare, xxv, 444–46, 453–54, 506, 514, 516–17, 581
China, 150, 409, 415
Chinese Americans, xxi, 145, 180–81, 185, 187, 193, 199–200, 409
Chinese Exclusion Act, 409
Chinese Students' Association, 409
Chinese Students' Monthly, 409
Chippewas, 382
Chittenden, Alice Hill, xxv; "The Counter Influence to Woman Suffrage," 299–306; "Woman's Service or Woman Suffrage," 528–30
Chittenden, Mrs. S. B., 227
Chivalry, 160, 391–92
Choctaws, 196
Christian Endeavor, 490
Christian Inquirer, 56
Christianity, 18, 59, 96, 122, 142, 196–97, 199, 214–15, 242, 410–12, 436–37, 448
Churchill, Winston S., 356
Church of the Pilgrims, 92
Cincinnati, Ohio, 87
Citizenship, 29, 180, 264, 398, 400, 418, 425, 440, 477, 519, 567–68, 632; for African Americans, xxii, 157, 163–64, 169, 172–73, 181–82, 236, 569, 655; for American Indians, 196–98, 210, 575–76; for Chinese Americans, 409, 415; for Hawaiian Islanders, 246; for Mexican Americans, 626; and naturalization, 65, 159, 164–67, 196, 479, 504, 565; for Puerto Ricans, 616–17, 619–20; Supreme Court rules voting not as right of, 163–76; voting as right

of, xxv, xxvii, 37, 68, 157–61, 178, 229–30, 238, 365, 368–70, 448, 456, 569, 654
City Beautiful Movement, 446
Civil disobedience, 353, 651
Civil rights, 35, 91, 93, 101, 177, 183, 439–40, 621, 625–26, 628, 631, 644, 652
Civil Rights Act, 650–51
Civil rights movement, xviii, xxi, 650–51
Civil Service Commission, 639
Civil War, xx, xxii, 27, 45, 91–96, 98, 104, 106, 112, 115–16, 138, 172, 179, 187, 236, 253, 262, 275, 297, 438–39, 470, 482, 504, 609, 651
Claflin, Tennessee, 157
Clark, Champ, 492
Clark University, 439
Clay, Laura, 248, 553
Clement, Percival W., 557
Cleveland, Grover, 203; "Would Woman Suffrage Be Unwise?" 282–92
Cleveland, Ohio, 60, 287, 303, 420, 602
Clifford, Carrie W.: "'Votes for Children,'" 445–46
Cline, Genevieve R., 639
Cobden Club, 296
Coffin, Jo, 639
Coke, Edward, 180
Colman, Lucy N., 103–5
Colleges/universities, 38, 65, 89, 100–101, 139, 180–81, 216, 233, 270, 275–77, 490
Collegiate Equal Suffrage League, 328
Collins, Josephine, 550
Colonization movement, 16
Colorado, 399, 638; constitution, 181, 221; effect of full suffrage, 253, 290, 292, 300, 305, 378, 392–93; eight-hour workday for women, 513; pensions for women, 581; ratification of Nineteenth Amendment, 557; school suffrage in, 247; suffrage referendum in , 221–22, 244, 247, 302, 498; voting in presidential elections, 476
Colorado Non-Partisan Equal Suffrage Association, 221–22
Colorado Springs, Colo., 477
Colorado Territory, 264
Colored Women's League, 232
Columbia River, 258
Columbia University, 365, 409
Columbus, Christopher, 196
Common law, 70, 72, 74, 158, 166, 202, 579
Communist Manifesto, 411
Concord, Mass., 19, 30, 147, 651
Confederacy, 94
Conger, Sarah Pike, 330
Congreso de Pueblo de Habla Española, 621–31
Congress, U.S., 63, 94–95, 169, 175, 193, 246, 288, 290, 302, 424, 438, 475, 504, 506–7, 573, 611; addresses/ statements/testimony by women before, 157–62, 361–64, 383–90; and American Indian citizenship, 196–97, 575–76; and disenfranchisement of Mormon women, 181, 201, 203; and disenfranchisement of Washington (D.C.) voters, 442–43; lobbying, xxvi, 307, 365, 481, 520–24, 531, 543; and naturalization, 166–67, 479; petitions to, 39, 91; President Wilson's address on Nineteenth Amendment, 543–48; and proposed Equal Rights Amendment, 580; and Puerto Rican citizenship, 616–18, 620; women in, 598–99, 633–36, 653; women's suffrage amendment in, 119, 206–9, 236–37, 398–400, 555. See also specific legislation
Congressional Record, 206
Congressional Union for Woman Suffrage, 383, 419, 477
Conklin, Elizabeth, 39
Conklin, Mary, 39
Connecticut, 124, 170, 247, 287, 303, 330, 557, 573
Connecticut College for Women, 551
Connelly, Betty, 550
Conservative Party (Britain), 188, 355–56
Constitution, California, 302
Constitution, Colorado, 181, 221
Constitution, Connecticut, 170
Constitution, Delaware, 171
Constitution, Georgia, 171

Constitution, Hawaii Territory, 246
Constitution, Indiana, 478
Constitution, Maryland, 171, 572
Constitution, Massachusetts, 170, 519
Constitution, Michigan, 302
Constitution, Missouri, 164, 168
Constitution, New Hampshire, 170,
    478, 498
Constitution, New Jersey, 14, 170
Constitution, New York, 34–35, 68, 70,
    170, 223–27, 305
Constitution, North Carolina, 171
Constitution, Oklahoma, 302
Constitution, Pennsylvania, 170–71
Constitution, Rhode Island, 170
Constitution, South Carolina, 171
Constitution, U.S., 92, 195, 241, 395,
    441, 626; and citizenship, 157–61,
    163–73, 181–82; and equal rights,
    140; and right to protest, 383;
    and slavery, 95, 181. See also Bill of
    Rights *and specific constitutional
    amendments*
Constitution, Virginia, 171
Constitution, Washington, 256
Constitution, Wisconsin, 88
Constitutions, state, xxvii, 121, 163,
    170–71, 174–75, 178, 237, 265, 399,
    478, 495, 502–4, 569
Consumers' League, 637
Continental Congress, 5, 13
Contracts, 72–73
Cook, Coralie Franklin: "'Votes for
    Mothers,'" 444–45
Cook, Elizabeth Ellsworth, 328
Coolidge, Calvin, 575–76, 596
Coolidge, Mary Roberts: "Raising
    the Level of Suffrage in California,"
    416–18
Cooper, Anna J., xxi; *A Voice from the
    South, by a Black Woman of the South,*
    216–20
Cooper Union, 92, 146
Copernicus, Nicolaus, 491
Corbin, Mrs. C. F., 288
Cornplanter, Chief, 213
Corruption, 500–504, 575
Costa Rica, 612
Cosu, Alice, 538–39
Couzins, Phoebe W., 120, 138, 177, 183
Cowan, W. R., 426–27

Crary, B. F., 243
Creeks, 196
Creighton, Jane, 253
Crisis, The, 433–58
Croaker, Deacon, 136
Crogman, W. H.: "Woman in the
    Ancient State," 439–40
Cromwell, Edward, 125
Crusades, 58
Cuba, 198
Culver, M. A., 40
Cummins, Albert B., 576

Dakota War, 504–5
Daniels, Lou, 550
Daughters of the American Revolution,
    396
Davis, Andrew Jackson, 120
Davis, Cynthia, 40
Davis, Elizabeth Lindsay: "Votes for
    Philanthropy," 455–56
Davis, Katherine B., 444
Davis, Mary A., 125
Davis, Mary F., 120, 143–44
Davis, Paulina Wright, 61, 119–20,
    143–44, 183
Dawes Act, 210, 504
Day, Dorothy, 538
Debs, Eugene V., 525
Declaration of Independence, 5, 36,
    101, 108–9, 142, 165, 264, 395,
    410–11, 434, 518
Declaration of Rights of the Women of
    the United States, 177–84, 241
Declaration of Sentiments and
    Resolutions, xxi, 36–42, 609
De Héricourt, Jeanne, 120–21, 146–47
Delaware, 124, 171, 302, 557–58
Dell, Thomas, 40
Dell, William S., 40
Democracy, xxiv, xxvii, 101, 111, 366,
    368, 370, 391–92, 397, 400, 410–12,
    415, 434, 447–48, 487, 504, 545,
    548–49, 551, 568, 626, 628, 630–31,
    633
Democratic Party, 189, 206–7, 229,
    256, 282, 385, 395, 398, 426, 475,
    480–81, 499, 503, 543, 548, 553, 556,
    600, 602, 634–35, 637–38, 646–49
Democratic-Republican Party, 189,
    191, 395

Deneen, Charles S., 431
Denmark, 505, 638–39
Dennett, Mary Ware, 310
Denver, Colo., 297, 399, 498
Denver Brewers' Association, 221
De Priest, Oscar, 426–28; "Chicago and Woman's Suffrage," 435
Derby, Earl of (Edward Stanley), 484
De Silver, Mary Block, 227
Detention Home for Girls, 417–18
Dewey, John, 331, 365
Dewson, Mary W., 637
Dial, The, 30
Diaz, Abby Morton, 451
Dickinson, Anna, 137
Diet of Worms, 537
Dillingham, William P., 389
Dirksen Amendment, 653
Diseases, industrial, 515–16, 588–92
Disraeli, Benjamin, 188
District of Columbia. *See* Washington, D.C.
Divorce, 38, 412, 415
Dock, Lavinia, 527; "The Young Are at the Gates," 531–32
Dodge, Josephine Jewell: "The Lesson That Came from the Sea," 372–75
Doggett, Kate, 120
Doty, Elias J., 40
Doty, Susan R., 40
Douglass, Frederick, 40, 119–20, 124, 127–32, 139–40, 144–46, 276, 438; "Woman and the Ballot," 149–53
Drake, Julia Ann, 39
Dred Scott v. Sandford, 115
Drolet, Godias J., 589
Du Bois, W.E.B., 433
Dunbar, Alice: "Votes and Literature," 443
Duniway, Abigail Scott: "How to Win the Ballot," 249–58
Dunmore, Earl of (John Murray), 5
Dunne, Finley Peter: "Mr. Dooley on Woman's Suffrage," 293–98
Dunniway, A. Jane, 183

Eastland, James O., 646
Eastman, Crystal, 365
Eastman, Ida Rauh, 365
Eastman, Max: "Values of the Vote," 365–71

Eaton, Harriet Cady, 39
Education, xxii, 67, 394, 415, 446; of African Americans, 84, 262, 276–77, 656; in Britain, 187–88, 237; of Chinese Americans, 199–200; higher, 38, 65, 89, 100–101, 139, 180–81, 216, 233, 270, 275–77, 490; of Mexican Americans, 624–26; need for better access by women, 55, 65, 130, 229, 237; professional, 64–65, 180; school suffrage, xxiv, 221, 247, 286–87, 302–3, 321, 451; in the South, 262–63; and suffrage, 130, 237–40, 270; teachers, 193, 452–53; vocational, 142, 262; voter, 565–68; women on boards of education, 319–20, 444–45
1876 Centennial, 177–84, 204
Eighteenth Amendment, 571, 597, 603
Eight-hour day, 513, 586
Elder, Robert, 328
Election of 1856, 89
Election of 1872, 132, 157, 179
Election of 1896, 476
Election of 1900, 476
Election of 1904, 265, 476
Election of 1908, 476
Election of 1912, 476
Election of 1916, 475–81, 490
Election of 1920, xxvii, 555, 558
Election of 1924, 594
Eleventh National Woman's Rights Convention, 112–16
Eliot, George (Mary Ann Evans), 443
Elizabeth I, 599
El Salvador, 612
Emancipation Proclamation, 93–94, 98
Emerson, Ralph Waldo, 30; "Concord Hymn," 651
Emory, Julia, 534
Employment Compensation Commission, 640
Encyclopedia Britannica, 437–38
Engels, Friedrich, 411
Equal Franchise Society, 328, 331, 423
Equal Guardianship of Children, 417
Equality, argument for, xxv, xxviii, 5, 16, 19, 35, 37, 41–42, 45–46, 48–49, 53, 55, 61, 80, 85, 91, 98, 101, 109, 118, 120, 128, 134, 140, 146, 149–50,

178, 180, 183, 194–95, 215, 238, 264, 372, 374–75, 409–12, 415, 440, 447, 567, 577–86, 592, 606, 613–15, 621, 628, 642, 652, 655–56
Equality League of Self-Supporting Women, 326, 328–29, 531
Equal Nationality Treaty, 606, 613–15
Equal Rights Amendment, xix, 577–93, 597, 642
Equal Rights Party, 157
Esther, 27–28
Ettelson, Samuel, 426
Eugenics, 413
Evers, Medgar, 649
Everybody's Magazine, 468
Expediency, argument for, xxv–xxvi, 53, 285–87

Fairchild, Charles S., 569
Fairchild, Lucius, 124
Fairchild v. Hughes, 569–72
Fair Labor Standards Act, 623
Fall River, Mass., 310, 312, 588–89
Farley, James A., 637
Farmers' Association, 499
Farmington, Conn., 299
Favre, Jules, 146
Fawcett, Millicent, 487
Federalist, The, 34
Femininity, xxv, 56, 59, 61, 134, 208–9, 250, 282, 358, 373, 376, 416, 443
Feminism, 14, 376, 394, 409–15, 473–74, 584, 606, 616, 642
Femme couvert, 75, 81
Ferguson, Miriam A., 635
Ferrara, Orestes, 611
Ferrater, Esteban de, 608
Feudalism, 81, 158
Field, Anna C., 121, 125
Field, Mrs. George White, 226
Fielding, Henry: *Pamela*, 273
Fierro de Bright, Josefina, 621
Fifteenth Amendment, xxii, 119, 125, 127, 132, 140, 144, 146, 149, 172, 189, 206, 230, 236, 442, 456, 573
15th Street Presbyterian Church, 433
Fifth Amendment, 179
Fillmore Board of Education, 626
Finch, Jessica G., 328
Finlay, John, 494
Fire protection, 511

First National Conference of Representatives of Black Women's Clubs, 232–35
First National Woman's Rights Convention, 45, 56, 64
Fisher, Katherine Rolston, 536–37
Fitzgerald, Susan Walker, 308, 310, 313
Fletcher, Alice C.: "The Legal Conditions of Indian Women," 210–15
Florida, 124
Foley, Maud, 509–13, 515–19
Follen, Charles, 20
Foltz, Clara Shortridge, 416
Foote, Elisha, 40
Foote, Eunice Newton, 39
Forbes-Robertson, Beatrice, 330
Forerunner, The, 332
Fort Sumter, 651
Forum, The, 577
Foster, Abby Kelly, 126
Foster, Stephen S., 121, 125–27
Fourteenth Amendment, xxii, 157, 163–64, 169, 172–73, 181–82, 236, 569
Fowler, Frances, 550
France, 45–46, 98, 146, 204, 240–41, 411, 483, 591, 600
Franco-Prussian War, 151
Franklin Hall, 14
Franz Josef, 237
Freedom Fighters, 651
Free love, 157
French Revolution, 328
Frink, Mary Ann, 39
Frothingham, Octavius, 121–24, 128
Fugitive slaves, 49, 131
Fuller, Cynthia, 40
Fuller, Margaret, 54; "The Great Lawsuit," 30–33; *Woman in the Nineteenth Century*, 30
Fusion Party, 267–68

Gage, Frances Dana, 43
Gage, Mary A., 120–21
Gage, Mary E., 125
Gage, Matilda Joslyn, 120, 141, 177, 183, 204–5; *The History of Woman Suffrage*, xvii, xxi, 91, 196; "Indian Citizenship," 196–98; *Women, Church, and State*, 196

Gage, Portia, 124
Gale, Zona, 455
Galileo Galilei, 491
Gandhi, Mohandas K., 533
Gannon, Dr., 541
Gardener, Helen Hamilton, 558–59; "Woman Suffrage, Which Way?" 391–400
Garment workers, 512
Garrett, Thomas, 124
Garrison, William Lloyd, 63, 124, 139, 438, 491
Gaskell, Elizabeth, 89
Gaynor, William J., 330
George III, 488, 549
Georgia, 171, 175, 499, 653
German Americans, 117
Germany, 98, 146, 151, 410–11, 483, 486, 500, 528, 590, 599
Gibbons, Abby H., 121
Gibbs, Experience, 40
Gilbert, Mary, 40
Gild, Lydia, 39
Gillespie, Mabel, 509–14, 516–19
Gillett, Frederick H., 576
Gilman, Charlotte Perkins, 330; "Something to Vote For," 332–52
Gladstone, William, 188
Glass, Carter, 640
Glynn, Martin H., 480
Goldman, Emma, 366–68
Good Housekeeping, 594, 632
Good Neighbor Policy, 630
Gordon, Jane Zane, 575
Gordon, Jean, 261
Gordon, Kate M., 261, 553
Gordon, Laura De Force, 183
Government, voter education about, 565–68
Gram, Betty, 550
Grand Rapids, Mich., 249
Grant, Ulysses S., 131
Gray, Thomas: "Elegy in a Country Churchyard," 17
Greece, ancient, 32, 436–37, 439–40
Greeley, Horace, 63, 189
Greenwich Village, 365, 376
Gregori, Elsa, 330
Griffing, Josephine, 120–21, 124
Grimké, Angelina. *See* Weld, Angelina Grimké

Grimké, Francis J.: "The Logic of Woman Suffrage," 433–34
Grimké, Sarah Moore, 27; *Letters on the Equality of the Sexes*, 19–26
Groesbeck, Herman V. S., 243–44
Gross, Mrs. Irving, 550
Guatemala, 612
Guinn v. United States, 442

Habeas corpus, 178
Haines, Lilian M., 227
Halifax, N.S., 277
Hall, Jeanie Stewart Boyd, 227
Hall, Ray, 205
Hallock, Sarah Hull, 99–100, 103–4
Hallowell, Edward N., 115
Hallowell, Mary H., 39
Hallowell, Sarah, 39
Hamer, Fannie Lou, xxi; Testimony to Credentials Committee, Democratic National Convention, 646–49
Hamilton, Alice, 577; "Protection for Women Workers," 584–93
Hamilton, Gail (Mary Abigail Dodge), 257
Hanaford, Phoebe Ann Coffin, 120–21
Hancock, John, 77
Happersett, Reese, 163
Harbert, Elizabeth Boynton, 254
Harding, George, 426–27
Harper, Frances Ellen Watkins, xx, 116, 145; Speech at Eleventh National Woman's Rights Convention, 112–15
Harper, Ida Husted, 278
Harper's Weekly, 331
Harriman, Florence J., 639
Harrington, Francis C., 627
Harris, Ellen M., 124
Harris, Mary, 636
Harron, Marion J., 640
Harvard Medical College, 64–65
Harvard University, 89, 210, 577
Harvey, George, 330
Haskell, Oreola Williams: *Banner Bearers*, 459; "The Greatest Thing," 459–67
Hatch, Junius L., 59–60, 63
Hatley, Henry, 40
Havana, Cuba, 606
Haven, Gilbert, 124, 140–42
Hawaii, Territory of, 246–48, 297, 639

Hawkes, Dr. Mrs., 124
Hawkins, Alfred, 360
Haynes, Edith, 310
Hazard, Frederick, 330
Health, Education, and Welfare
    Department, U.S., 656
Health laws, 514–16
Hearst, William Randolph, 395
Heath, Mrs., 120
Hemans, Felicia Dorothea, 54
Henderson, Jessica, 550
Henderson, Wilma, 550
Henry Street Settlement House, 531
Hepburn, Katharine Houghton, 542
Herndon, Minnie, 537–38
Hershaw, L. M.: "Disfranchisement
    in the District of Columbia,"
    442–43
Heterodoxy, 376
Higginson, Thomas Wentworth,
    84–86, 125
Hill, Elsie, 542, 551
Hindus, 77, 150
History of Woman Suffrage, The
    (Stanton, Anthony, and Gage), xvii,
    xxi, 91, 196
Hoffman, Sarah, 39
Holmes, Mrs., 120
Holt, Hamilton, 330
Homer: *Iliad*, 439
Homestead Act, 168
Honduras, 612
Hooker, Isabella B., 124
Hoover, Herbert, 636
Hope, John, 458
Hopkins, Monroe, 387
Hoskins, Charles L., 40
House Judiciary Committee, 157–62,
    398
Howard, Pamela Hermance, 227
Howe, Julia Ward, 119, 124, 129, 254,
    367, 438, 451
Howe, Louis M., 638
Howell, Mary Seymour, 204–5
Howitt, Anna Mary, 89
Howorth, Lucy S., 640
Hoyt, Elizabeth Orpha Sampson,
    97–99, 102, 105–6, 108–9
Hulit, Mr., 428
Hull House, 315, 317–18
Human rights, 87, 90, 98, 100, 103,

107, 143, 178, 182–83, 396, 398, 442,
    608
Hunger strikes, xxiii, 352, 355, 358, 525,
    527, 533
Hunt, Harriot K., 63–66
Hunt, Jane C., 39
Hunt, Richard, 40
Hunton, A. W.: "Y.W.C.A.," 451–52
Hurlbut, Elisha P., 69
Hurst, John: "Christianity and
    Woman," 436–37
Husband's name, taken by wife, 84,
    459
Hutchinson, James, Jr., 124
Hutchinson Family Singers, 147–48

Ibsen, Henrik: *A Doll's House*, 435–36
Iceland, 505
Idaho, 245, 248, 253, 290, 300, 302,
    476, 556–57
Idaho Territory, 264
Ide, Fannie Ogden, 227
Illinois, 124, 305, 392, 399, 635;
    legislature, 555–56; pensions for
    women, 477; property rights
    for women, 88; ratification of
    Nineteenth Amendment, 555–56;
    school suffrage in, 247; suffrage for
    African American women, 425–32;
    voting in presidential elections, 476
Illinois Woman's Suffrage Association,
    425
Illiteracy, 207
Immigrants, xviii, xx–xxi, 65, 190,
    236–37, 239, 400, 409, 503–4, 592,
    621, 626
Indiana, 88, 175, 478, 499, 521, 557,
    586–87
Indian Citizenship Act, 575–76
Indianola, Miss., 646
Indians. *See* American Indians
Industrialism, 185, 187–88, 411, 413,
    508–9, 517–18
Industrial Workers of the World, 526
Inter-American Commission of
    Women, 606
Interior Department, U.S., 575
International Convention for the
    Suppression of the Traffic in Women
    and Children, 613
International Convention for the

Unification of Protective Laws for Workmen and Laborers, 612
International Council of Women, 210, 275–76
International Labor Organization, 612
International law, 610–15
International Woman Suffrage Association, 275
Iowa, 124, 248, 418, 502, 556
Ireland, 132, 248
Irish Americans, 361, 654
Iroquois, 196, 198
Isle of Man, 264
Israel, ancient, 29
Italian Americans, 317–18, 320
Italy, 483

Jack, Mrs. C. C., 551
Jackson, M. E.: "The Self-Supporting Woman and the Ballot," 450
Jackson, Mercy B., 139
Jagiello, Appolonia, 54
Jakobi, Paula, 540–41
Jameson, Anna Brownell, 89
Jamison, Maud, 527
Japan, 500
Japanese Americans, 181
Jefferson, Thomas, 128, 189, 397–98, 410
Jefferson County, N.Y., 34, 36
Jeffreys, Annice F., 257
Jenkins, Margaret, 40
Jenness Miller, Annie, 386
Jesus, 81, 255, 410, 437, 491
Jews, 45, 98, 319, 436–37, 491, 654
Jim Crow laws, xix–xx, 425, 652, 656
Joan of Arc, 491
John, King, 517
Johnson, Andrew, 113
Johnson, James Weldon: "'About Aunties,'" 437–38
Johnson, Lyndon B., 646, 652, 655–56
Johnson, Oliver, 125
Johnson, Samuel, 139
Johnston, John A., 386–87
Johnston, Mary, xix; Hagar, 401–8
Johnston, Robert J., 121, 125
Johnston, William A., 244
Johnstown Academy, 67
Jones, Anna H.: "Woman Suffrage and Social Reform," 453–54

Jones, Jane Graham, 183
Jones, John, 40
Jones, Lucy, 39
Jones, Rosalie G., 387
Jones, Wesley L., 383–90
Jones Act, 616–17
Jordan, David Starr, 413
Julian, George W., 124
Justice, argument for, xxv–xxvi, 25, 56, 64, 71–72, 76–77, 80, 83, 86, 89, 106–7, 109, 129, 160, 191, 194–95, 215, 238, 398, 409–10, 415, 456, 545, 567
Justice Department, U.S., 558, 652
Juvenile Protective League, 321, 417

Kahn, Florence P., 635
Kansas, 124, 132, 175, 222, 244, 247, 299, 303–4, 476, 556, 586
Katzenstein, Caroline: Lifting the Curtain, 533; "Prison Experiences with Emphasis on the Night of Terror," 533–42
Kean, Edmund, 134
Kearney, Belle, xix; "The South and Woman Suffrage," 261–66
Kelley, Abbie, 489, 491
Kendall, Ada D., 537
Kennedy, John F.: President's Commission on the Status of Women, 642–45
Kent, Elizabeth Thacher, 542
Kentucky, 174, 247, 264, 553, 557
Kernan, Francis, 196
Kerr, Florence, 639
Ketchum, Emily B., 254
Kiess, Edgar R., 617
King, Martin Luther, Jr., 651, 655
King, Phebe, 39
Kings County Political Equality League, 459
Kirchwey, George W., 409
Kirk, Eleanor, 120, 143
Knights of Labor, 361
Ku Klux Klan, 131
Kyle, James H., 236

Labor Department, U.S., 636–39, 643–44
Labour Party (Britain), 356–57
La Dame, Mary, 639

Ladies' Home Journal, 253, 282, 285–86, 315
La Follette, Fola, 330
Laidlaw, Harriet Burton, 328
Laidlaw, James Lee, 330
Land Office, U.S., 442
Latham, Hannah J., 40
Latham, Lavinia, 40
Lathrop, Julia C., 444
Latin America, 606–15, 625, 627, 630–31
Law enforcement, 596–97
Lawrence, Mass., 510
Lead poisoning, 590–92
League of Nations, 548, 596, 610, 612–13
League of Women Voters, xix, 416, 565, 633
Lee, Mabel: "The Meaning of Woman Suffrage," 409–15
Lee, Richard Henry, 264
Leech, Mrs. John E., 227
Legal rights, 19–29, 31, 41, 45, 48–50, 52, 68, 85, 87–88, 412, 440, 533, 656
Legislature, California, 626
Legislature, Colorado, 290
Legislature, Delaware, 558
Legislature, Georgia, 653
Legislature, Idaho, 245
Legislature, Illinois, 555–56
Legislature, Maine, 88
Legislature, Maryland, 572
Legislature, Massachusetts, 27–28, 67, 303, 512–14
Legislature, Nebraska, 89
Legislature, New Jersey, 13
Legislature, New York, 67–83, 88, 129, 143, 328
Legislature, Oregon, 256–58, 300
Legislature, Puerto Rico Territory, 616–18
Legislature, Rhode Island, 139
Legislature, South Dakota, 248
Legislature, Tennessee, 558–59, 574
Legislature, Utah, 290
Legislature, Vermont, 557
Legislature, Washington, 248
Legislature, Washington Territory, 255–56
Legislature, West Virginia, 574
Legislature, Wisconsin, 555

Legislatures, state, xxvii, 39, 121, 140, 169, 265, 303, 363, 370, 478, 501–2, 504–6, 522, 555–59, 569, 633–34, 637, 652–53
Lenroot, Katharine, 636
Leser, Oscar, 572
Leser v. Garnett, 569, 572–74
Leslie, Elizabeth, 39
Lester, Edwards: *The Glory and Shame of England*, 186
Lewis, Dora Kelly, 537–39, 541
Lewis, Rose, 550
Lewis, W. H., 458
Liberal Party (Britain), 188, 354–57
Liberator, The, 16, 84
Liga Social Sufragista de Porto Rico, 616
Lincoln, Abraham, 93–95, 98, 192, 278, 597, 600
Lindsley, A. L., 124
Literacy tests, 650
Livermore, Mary A., 119–21, 124–25, 138–39, 141, 146–48, 253–54
Liverpool, England, 359
Lobbying, xxvi, 307, 365, 481, 520–24, 531, 543
Lockwood, Belva A., 183, 203
Lodge, Henry Cabot, 236
Logan, Olive, 120, 133–38
London, England, 89, 177, 353–60, 489
Long, John D., 248
Long Island, 198
Longley, Mrs., 120
Los Angeles, Calif., 369, 416, 621–22, 626
Los Angeles Times, 382
Loughridge, Mr., 124
Louis XIV, 31
Louise of Mecklenburg-Strelitz, 599
Louisiana, 24–26, 248, 261, 264, 302, 399
Louisiana 2nd Regiment, 115
Louisville, Ky., 207
Lovey, J. F., 147
Lowden, Frank O., 556
Lowe, Robert, 187
Lowell, James Russell: "Verses Suggested by the Present Crisis," 528
Lozier, Clemence S., 183
Lundin, Fred, 430–31

Luscomb, Florence H., 508; "Our Open-Air Campaign," 307–14
Lutherans, 318
Lynch, John R.: "States' Rights and the Suffrage," 441–42
Lynching, 425
Lynn, Mass., 139
Lytton, Constance, 358–59

Macdonald, Mary, 120
Mackay, Katherine Duer, 327, 330
MacKaye, Hazel: *Allegory*, 419; *Equal Rights Pageant*, 419; "Pageants as a Means of Suffrage Propaganda," 419–24; *Six Periods of American Life*, 419
Maclayne, Eufame, 491
Macready, George, 134
Madison, James, 34
Madison, Wis., 105–6
Magna Carta, 410–11, 517
Maine, 88, 124, 557
Malone, Dudley Field, 541–42
Manchester, England, 186
Manitoba, 487
Mansel, Edith, 375
Marie Antoinette, 600
Marriage, 130; ceremony of, 84–86; women's rights in, 20–26, 30–31, 36–38, 45, 47–51, 72–75, 85–86, 88, 178, 180, 192, 202–3, 265, 412–14, 579
Marshall, Thurgood, 650
Marshfield, Mass., 309, 312
Martin, Anne, 477
Martin, Eliza, 40
Martin, George Madden, 596
Martin, Mary, 40
Martineau, Harriet, 54, 89; *Society in America*, 25
Marx, Karl, 411
Mary, Virgin, 73
Maryland, 112, 124, 171, 264, 572
Massachusetts, 124, 127, 131, 142–43, 305, 330, 366, 451, 549, 635, 637; child labor in, 516; constitution, 170, 519; eight-hour workday for women, 513, 586; legislature, 27–28, 67, 303, 512–14; municipal suffrage in, 286, 303; open-air meetings in, 307–14; petitions by women, 27–29; property rights for women, 25, 88; ratification of Nineteenth Amendment, 556; school suffrage in, 247, 286–87, 303; suffrage referendum in, 502; working women in, 508–19
Massachusetts Institute of Technology, 307
Massachusetts Woman's Suffrage Association, 451
Mass demonstrations, 353, 525–28, 531–33, 548–52
Masses, The, 365
Mathews, Delia, 39
Mathews, Dorothy, 39
Mathews, Jacob, 40
May, Samuel J., 63
Mayflower, 81
Mayo-Smith, Mabel Ford, 227
McAdoo, William G., 596
McClintock, Elizabeth, W., 39
McClintock, Mary, 39
McClintock, Mary Ann, 39, 183
McClintock, Thomas, 40
McClure, Alfretta, 310
McClure's, 594
McCormick, Anne O'Hare, 640
McCracken, Elizabeth, 292
McCulloch, Catharine Waugh, 248
McDonald, Joe, 647
McKeen, Mrs. James, 227
McKinley, William, 323–24
McMillin, Lucille Foster, 639
Men's League for Woman Suffrage, 330, 365, 419, 468
Merritt, John J., 125
Metcalf, Jonathan, 40
Methodists, 133, 490
Metropolitan Life Insurance Company, 589
Metropolitan Pageant, 420
Mexican Americans, xix, 621–31
Mexico, 198, 261, 477, 500, 625–27, 630
Meyer, Annie Nathan, xxv; "Woman's Assumption of Sex Superiority," 267–74
Michigan, 88, 124, 247, 302, 498, 501, 556
Milholland, Inez, 330, 365, 633
Militant methods, xxiii, 300, 307, 353–

60, 412, 469, 471, 525–27, 531–32,
    548–52
Mill, John Stuart, 139, 187
Miller, Alice Duer: *Are Women People?*,
    473–74
Miller, Elizabeth Smith, 125
Miller, J. K., 124
Miller, Joaquin, 255
Milliken, Nathan J., 40
Mills, Anson, 386
Milton, N.Y., 52
Milwaukee, Wis., 142, 146
Minimum wage, 569, 586
Minnesota, 124, 175, 247, 556
Minnesota Association of Colored
    Women's Clubs, 457
Minor, Francis, 163
Minor, Mary L., 39
Minor, Virginia L., 124, 163, 168,
    183
Minor v. Happersett, 163–76, 182, 616
Mirabeau, comte de (Honoré-Gabriel
    Riqueti), 600
Mississippi, 261, 265, 646–49, 652
Mississippi Freedom Democratic Party,
    646, 649
Mississippi Institute and College for
    Girls, 265
Missouri, 25, 124, 163–64, 168, 175,
    499, 556, 586–87
Mitchell, S.D., 496
Moller, Mrs., 387
Monroe Doctrine, 630
Montana, 247, 299, 476, 556, 634
Montana Territory, 124
Montesquieu, baron de (Charles-Louis
    de Secondat), 500
Montevideo, Uruguay, 606
Montgomery, Ala., 651
Montgomery, James, 115
Moore, Joseph H., 124
Moore, Marguerite, 204–5
Moore, Mrs. Thomas S., 226
Morality, 26, 38, 41–42, 74, 107–8, 152,
    160, 195, 277, 284
Morehouse College, 435
Moreno, Luisa, 621
Morey, Agnes H., 551–52
Morey, Katherine, 527, 550
Morgan, G. W., 458
Morgan, John Tyler, 203

Mormons, 88, 201–3, 302, 312
Morrison, Mrs. David M., 227
Morton, Eleanor, 533
Moses, 491
Mosher, Phebe, 39
Mosher, Sarah A., 40
Motherhood, 78–81, 367–68, 414,
    444–45, 514, 581
Motley, Constance Baker, xxi; Speech
    to Southern Christian Leadership
    Conference, 650–57
Mott, James, 40
Mott, Lucretia, 36, 39, 61, 63, 119, 122,
    124, 143, 183, 254, 489
Mott, Lydia, 121
Moulder, Andrew Jackson, 200
Mount, Lydia, 39
Mullany, Kate, 190–91
Mullowney, Alexander, 527
Municipal suffrage, xxiv, 247–48, 267,
    286, 302–4, 318, 357, 425, 435
Murray, Mrs. Lindley, Jr., 227
Muslims, 197, 608

Napoléon Bonaparte, 151
Napoleonic Code, 579
Nast, Thomas, 267
Nathan, Maud, 267
Nation, Carrie, 358
National American Woman Suffrage
    Association, xxii–xxiii, 201, 246–49,
    256, 261, 315, 327, 353, 365, 376, 383,
    391, 409, 481, 520–24, 528–29, 531,
    543, 555, 560, 565
National Association for the
    Advancement of Colored People,
    315, 433, 650
National Association of Colored
    Women, 232, 278, 433, 443–44,
    446, 453–54
National Association Opposed to
    Woman Suffrage, 299
National Child Labor Committee, 315
National Civil League, 417
National Conference of Representatives
    of Black Women's Clubs, 232–35
National Council of Women, 149
National Federation of Afro-American
    Women, 232
National Labor Relations Act (Wagner
    Act), 624

National League of Colored Women, 454

National Organization for Women, 642

National Recovery Administration, 640

National Red Cross Society, 253

National Union of Women's Suffrage Societies, 375

National White Cross Association, 253

National Woman's Party, xvii, xxiii–xxiv, xxvi, 353, 383, 391, 419, 525, 527–28, 531, 534, 539, 541, 543, 548–51, 577–78, 580, 583–84, 586, 606, 616–17

National Woman Suffrage Association, xvii, xxii, 119, 147, 157, 177–84, 201, 203, 206

Native Americans. *See* American Indians

Naturalization, 65, 159, 164–67, 196, 479, 504, 565

Nebraska, 89, 247, 498, 556

Netherlands, 592–93

Nevada, 121, 124, 299, 476, 556–57

New Bedford, Mass., 310–12

New Brunswick, 247

New Deal, 627, 632, 639–40

New Departure, 163

New England, 24, 27

New England Working Women's Convention, 142

New Era Club, 232

New Hampshire, 88, 124, 170, 247, 302, 478, 498, 556

New Jersey, 27, 124, 330, 543, 635; child custody in, 131–32; constitution, 14, 170; early women's suffrage in, xviii, 13, 173, 175, 264; legislature, 13; ratification of Nineteenth Amendment, 557; school suffrage in, 247; suffrage referendum in, 499; working women in, 590

Newlands, Francis G., 476

Newman, Mrs., 120

New Mexico, 556–57

New Mexico Territory, 222

New Northwest, 249

New Orleans, La., 129, 149, 261, 391, 399

Newton, Isaac, 54

New York, 27, 43, 49, 124, 143, 305, 326, 330, 459, 489, 569, 571, 635, 640; American Indians in, 196–98; antisuffrage movement in, 223–27, 528–30; child custody in, 132, 579; constitution, 34–35, 68, 70, 170, 223–27, 305; legislature, 67–83, 88, 129, 143, 328; petitions by women, 34–35, 129, 143, 223–27; property rights for women, 70, 75, 88, 189; ratification of Nineteenth Amendment, 556, 560; school suffrage in, 247, 287, 302–3; suffrage pageants in, 423; suffrage referendum in, 499–500, 502, 565–66; working women in, 190

New York American, 328

New York City, 14, 60, 114, 139, 143, 162, 258, 290, 293, 361, 421, 531, 602, 639; abolition conventions in, 104; ethnic/racial groups in, 653–54; intellectual establishment of, 365, 376; municipal elections in, 267, 459–68; protests in, 548; and ratification of Nineteenth Amendment, 560; Statue of Liberty unveiling, 204–5; suffrage conventions in, 87, 91–92, 102, 116, 119, 141; suffrage fiction set in, 459–67; suffrage pageants in, 420, 423; suffrage parades in, 326–31, 409, 468; treatment of African American women, 129, 149; working women in, 363, 378, 380, 589–90

New York City Woman Suffrage Party, 459, 560

New York Evening Post, 375

New York Evening Telegram, 327

New York Herald, 59–63, 374

New York Journal, 373

New York State Association Opposed to Woman Suffrage, 223, 528–29

New York State Constitutional Convention, 223–27

New York State Woman Suffrage Association, 468, 565

New York Sun, 327

New York Times, 204–5, 330–31, 525–27

New York Tribune, 30, 189, 474

New York Woman's Rights Convention, 67

New York Woman Suffrage Association, 204, 327
New York Woman Suffrage Party, 376
New York Working Women's Association, 120, 130, 143
New York World, 143
New Zealand, 245, 247, 264
Nicaragua, 612
Nichols, Clarinda I. H., 183
Nineteenth Amendment, xvii, xxiii, xxvii–xxviii, 361, 409, 580, 594, 609, 634; and American Indian women, 575; congressional action on, xxvi, 206–9, 521–22, 548; first introduced in Congress, 119, 206; legal challenges to, 569–74; "long," xviii; and Mexican American women, 630; need for, 238, 257, 475–79; and need for Equal Rights Amendment, 580; President Wilson's speech on, 543–47, 550; and Puerto Rican women, 616–19; ratification of, xxiv, xxvi, 481, 548, 553, 555–61, 565, 569, 573; southern opposition to, 553–54; versus state suffrage, xxii, 265, 391–92, 398, 495, 501, 503, 505–7, 553–54; and Voting Rights Acts, xix, 575, 650–53
Nolan, Mary A., 538–39
Nordica, Lillian, 421
Norris, Hugh, 426
North Carolina, 124, 171
North Dakota, 247, 502, 521, 556–57
Norton, Mary T., 634–35
Norton, Sarah F., 120, 130–31, 143
Norway, 639
Norwich, Conn., 135
Nurses' Settlement, 380
Nye, E., 124

Oberlin College, 84, 89, 100, 216, 275
O'Brien, Matthew, 539–40
Occoquan Workhouse, 533–42
O'Connell, Daniel, 132
O'Day, Caroline, 635
Ohio, 88–89, 113, 124, 247, 303, 501, 521, 556, 586, 590, 639
Ohio Federation of Colored Women's Clubs, 445
Ohio Woman's Rights Convention, 43
Oklahoma, 302, 556–57

Oliver, Thomas, 591
Olson, Harry, 430–32
Olustee, battle of, 115
Omahas, 210
O'Mahoney, Joseph, 635
Oneidas, 197
Onondaga, N.Y., 141, 196–97
Ontario, 247
Open-air meetings, xxiii, 307–14, 326
Oregon, 124, 252–53, 255; eight-hour workday for women, 513; legislature, 256–58, 300; ratification of Nineteenth Amendment, 556–57; school suffrage in, 247; suffrage referendum in, 249, 258, 299–302, 498; voting in presidential elections, 476
Oregon Congress of Women, 256
Oregon Equal Suffrage Association, 258
O'Reilly, Leonora: Statement before Joint Congressional Committee, 361–64
Ormsby, Amy, 34–35
Ormsby, Susan, 34–35
Osborn, Lydia, 34–35
Ossoli, Giovanni Angelo, 30
Otis, James, 518
Outlook, The, 366, 371, 475–80
Owen, Robert, 45

Page, Mary Hutcheson, 508, 520
Pageants, 419–24
Paine, Catharine C., 39
Painter, Nell Irvin, 43
Palestine, 58
Palmer, Rhoda, 40
Pan-Americanism, 606, 614–15
Pankhurst, Christabel, 354
Pankhurst, Emmeline, 353–55
Pankhurst, Sylvia, 375
Parades, xxiii, 326–31, 365, 382–90, 409, 419, 425, 468
Paris, France, 177, 240–41, 277, 635
Park, Maud Wood, 481, 508, 543; Letter to NAWSA Congressional Chairmen, 520–24; "A Perfect Moment," 555–61
Parker, Margaret A., 205
Parker, Mary S., 19
Parker, Theodore, 30

Parkhurst, Charles H., 373
Parks, Leighton, 373
Parks, Rosa, 650–51, 656
Parliament, British, 70, 89, 186–88, 237, 353–57, 487
Pasadena, Calif., 416
Patton, Alice Hutchinson, 120, 125
Paul (apostle), 381
Paul, Alice, xvii, xxiii, 353, 382, 391, 419, 476, 525, 528–29, 531, 533, 577; Testimony before Senate Committee about Suffrage Parade, 383–90
Pawnees, 210
Peabody, George Foster, 330, 365
Peabody Museum, 210
Peckham, Elizabeth, 120–21, 142
Pedro II, 177
Pembroke, Countess of (Anne Clifford), 69
Pennsylvania, 124, 170, 330, 499, 502, 556, 590, 592, 598, 600
Pensions, 477, 581
Pericles, 436
Perkins, Frances, 637–38
Persia, ancient, 27–28
Peterson, Esther, 642
Phelps, Mrs., 120
Philadelphia, Pa., 5, 13, 19, 114, 177, 183–84
Philippines, 297
Phillips, Saron, 40
Phillips, Wendell, 119, 122, 126, 132, 438
Pilgrims, 70, 81
Pillsbury, Mrs., 124
Pillsbury, Parker, 126
Pinchot, Cornelia B., 600
Pinchot, Gifford, 600
Pitcher, Sally, 39
Pittman, Key, 476
Pittsburgh, Pa., 499
Plant, Hannah, 39
Plato, 568
Plymouth Colony, 81
Poland, 45, 319, 489
Police reprisals, 353–54, 626
Political Equality League, 330, 416, 427
Political rights, 20, 34–35, 61, 65, 91, 93, 101, 122, 144, 177, 183, 185, 204–5, 285, 490, 569, 617, 620, 644

Politicians, women, 63, 69, 226, 229, 271, 598–602, 632–41
Politics, voter education about, 565–68
Poll taxes, 65, 652
Polygamy, 201–2, 302
Pomeroy, Samuel C., 120
Pope, Alexander: "Of the Characters of Women," 11
Populist Party, 221
Porter, Ann, 40
Post, Amy, 39, 183
Pottery industry, 590–91
Pottier, Berry, 550
Prendergast, W. Dowling, 591
Prentice, Mrs. W. S. P., 227
Presbyterians, 256, 433
President's Commission on the Status of Women, 642–45
Prison sentences, xxiii, 353–54, 358–59, 525, 527, 531–42, 552, 626
Progressive Party, 398
Prohibition, xxv, 256, 477, 499, 506, 526, 571, 597, 603
Property rights, xxii, 21, 23–25, 30, 36–38, 49–51, 70, 75, 88, 112–13, 143, 159, 180, 263, 289, 302, 489–90, 644
Prostitution, 130, 180, 361, 418, 434, 445
Protestants, 256
Prussia, 151, 599
Pryor, George W., 40
Pryor, Margaret, 39
Public Health Service, 591
Puerto Rico, Territory of, xix, 616–20
Pugh, Sarah, 183
Purvis, Harriet, 125
Purvis, Robert, 124, 438
Putnam, Carolyn Rosalie Richard Haines, 226
Pyle, Gladys, 634

Quakers, xxiii, 19, 32, 39
Quebec, 247
Quinn, Susan, 39

Race, Rebecca, 40
Racism, xix–xx, 196, 200, 261, 382, 425, 652, 654
Raines Act, 472
Randolph, Mary D., 572

Rankin, Jeannette, 599, 634

Ratification, xxvi, 481, 548, 553, 555–61, 565, 569, 573

Reade, Charles: *Put Yourself in His Place*, 186

Reconstruction, xviii, 236

Red Light Abatement Act, 418

Reforms, 123, 229, 242, 446, 453–55, 491, 508–19, 585, 633

Reicher, Hedwig, 421

Religious freedom, 38, 42, 490

Remonstrance, The, 496

Report on the Condition of Woman and Child Wage Earners in the United States, 588–89

Republicanism, 49, 80, 91, 101, 111, 120, 160, 164, 173, 185, 197, 207, 237, 239, 241, 391, 441, 568

Republican Party, 87, 189, 191, 206, 221, 228–29, 256, 323–24, 398, 430, 480–81, 496, 503, 505, 548, 556, 560, 602, 634

Revolution, The, 119–20, 125–28, 135, 138

Revolutionary War, 5–12, 24, 64, 68, 92–93, 102–3, 108, 179, 188, 412, 470, 518, 549, 609, 651

Revolutions of 1848, 45, 487

Reynolds v. Sims, 651

Rhode Island, 88, 124, 139, 170, 557, 586–87

Rhode Island Association of Colored Women's Clubs, 450

Richmond, Va., 115

Ridley, Martha, 39

Ripley, Mrs. George H., 227

Ristori, Adelaide, 134

Robert, Marta: Statement on Woman Suffrage in Puerto Rico, 616–20

Roberts, Albert H., 558–59

Roberts, Brigham H., 302

Robertson, Alice, 599

Robinson, Charles, 124

Robinson, Marius, 43

Roche, Josephine A., 638

Rochester, N.Y., 163

Roewer, Rosa Heinzen, 550

Rogers, Caroline Gilkey, 204–5

Rogers, Edith Nourse, 635

Rogers, Elizabeth Selden White, 542

Rogers, John, 255

Rohde, Ruth Bryan, 638–39

Roland de La Platière, Marie-Jeanne, 54

Rome, ancient, 79, 436, 440

Roosevelt, Eleanor, xix, 642; "Women in Politics," 632–41

Roosevelt, Franklin D., 626–27, 632, 639

Roosevelt, Theodore, 281, 365–68, 371, 480; "Women's Rights and the Duties of Both Men and Women," 366

Root, Elihu, 611

Rose, Ernestine L., 59, 61, 91, 97–100, 106–7, 119–21, 124, 139, 142–43, 147, 183, 489; Speech to Second National Woman's Rights Convention, 45–58

Ross, Nellie Tayloe, 635, 638

Rousseau, Jean-Jacques, 411

Rudolph, Commissioner, 388

Ruffin, Josephine St. Pierre, xxi, 454; Address at First National Conference of Representatives of Black Women's Clubs, 232–35; "'Trust the Women!,'" 451

Ruleville, Miss., 646–48

Rumsey, Mary Harriman, 640

Russia, 46, 185, 319, 483, 491, 599

Russian, Mrs. H. D., 550

Russian Americans, 497

Russian Revolution, 549

Sacramento, Calif., 626

Safford, A. P. K., 124

St. Louis, Mo., 138, 163, 499

Salem, Ohio, 43

Salt Lake City, Utah, 201

Salvation Army, 311

Sand, George (Amantine-Lucile-Aurore Dupin), 443

San Francisco, Calif., 399, 416

San Francisco Board of Education, 199–200

Sargent, Aaron A., 206

Sargent, Ellen C., 183

Saskatchewan, 487

Savonarola, Girolamo, 491

Schienhoeff, Mr., 141

Schneiderman, Rose, 639–40

Schopenhauer, Arthur, 470

Schooley, Azaliah, 40

Schooley, Margaret, 40
School suffrage, xxiv, 221, 247, 286–87, 302–3, 321, 451
Schreiner, Olive: *Woman and Labor*, 359
Scott, Anne Firor, xxviii
Scott, Deborah, 39
Second National Woman's Rights Convention, 45, 59
Segur, Antoinette, 40
Seminoles, 196
Senate Committee on Privileges and Elections, 206
Senate Committee on Territories and Insular Possessions, 616
Senate Select Committee on Woman Suffrage, 236
Seneca Falls, N.Y., 36, 67, 419
Seneca Falls Convention, xvii–xviii, xxi, xxviii, 34, 36–43, 87, 143, 149, 609
Sermon on the Mount, 411
Seton Thompson, Grace Gallatin, 330
Seventeenth Amendment, 479
Seventh National Woman's Rights Convention, 87–90
Sewall, Mary Wright, 278
Sex slaves, 613
Seymour, Henry, 40
Seymour, Henry W., 40
Seymour, Malvina, 39
Shakespeare, William, 54; *As You Like It*, 198; *Macbeth*, 139; *The Taming of the Shrew*, 73
Shanghai, China, 199
Shattuck, Harriet R., 205
Shaw, Anna Howard, xxiii, 248, 275, 278, 327–28, 330, 409, 481, 489, 496, 633
Shaw, Catharine, 39
Shaw, Lois Warren, 549–50
Shaw, Mary G., 421
Shaw, Pauline Agassiz, 508
Shear, Stephen, 40
Sholes, Charles, 88
Shuler, Nettie Rogers, xxvii; *Woman Suffrage and Politics*, 556
Sigourney, Lydia Howard, 54
Simms, Ruth Hanna McCormick, 635
Simpson, Euvester, 648
Sioux, 210, 496, 504–5, 575
Sisson, Sarah, 40

Sixth Amendment, 179
Sixth National Woman's Rights Convention, 87
Sixth Pan American Conference, 606–15
Skenandoah, Chief, 197
Slave insurrections, 95
Slavery, 19, 21, 28–29, 71, 108, 112–13, 116–17, 119, 151, 228, 261–62; of American Indian women, 210, 215; *Dred Scott* decision, 115; Emancipation Proclamation, 93–94, 98; female slaves, 14–18, 20, 43, 216, 275, 277; fugitive slaves, 49, 131; laws concerning, 24; pro-slavery arguments, 437; Thirteenth Amendment, 91, 123, 236, 609; treatment of women compared with, 26, 31, 33, 73, 80, 96, 100–101, 109, 152–53, 159, 193; in West Indies, 186. *See also* Abolition; African Americans
Slave trade, 95
Small, Ruth, 549–50
Smalldridge, Robert, 40
Smith, Alfred E., 560, 596
Smith, Elizabeth D., 40
Smith, Elizabeth Oakes, 61–62; *Woman and Her Needs*, 61
Smith, Gerrit, 63
Smith, Sarah, 40
Socialism, 45, 63, 365, 411, 554
Socialist Party, 256, 525–26
Social Security, 623–24, 637, 639
Socrates, 73, 491
Solomon, Hannah G., 278
Somerville, Mary, 54
South, women's suffrage in, xix–xx, 216–20, 261–66, 391–92, 399–401, 543, 553–54
Southard, Mrs. George H., 227
South Australia, 248
South Carolina, 124, 171, 399
South Dakota, 247–48, 302, 495–98, 504–5, 557, 634
Southern Christian Leadership Conference, 650–57
Southern States Suffrage Conference, 391
Southern Women's League, 553–54
Spain, 618, 630
Spalding, David, 40

Spalding, Lucy, 40
Spanish-American War, xx, 246, 297
Spence, Mrs., 107–8
Spencer, Sara Andrews, 177, 183
Staël, Anne-Louise-Germaine de, 54
Standard Oil Company, 594
Stanford University, 413
Stanton, Elizabeth Cady, xxii, xxviii, 87, 112, 149, 157, 254, 326, 438, 489; Address to New York Legislature, 67–83; and American Equal Rights Association, 119–20, 124–31, 134–35, 137–41, 143, 145, 147; *The History of Woman Suffrage*, xvii, xxi, 91, 196; and National Woman Suffrage Association, 183; Seneca Falls Convention, 36, 39; "Significance and History of the Ballot," 236–41; *Woman's Bible*, 196; and Woman's Loyal National League, 91–92
State Department, U.S., 559–60, 573
States' rights, xx, 163, 261, 266, 441–42, 506, 553
State suffrage, xix, xxii–xxiii, xxvi, 13, 237, 247, 286–87, 290, 302, 391, 398, 425, 441–42, 475–80, 500–501, 543, 556
Statue of Liberty, 204–5
Stebbins, Catharine A. F., 39
Steinway Hall, 119
Stennis, John C., 646
Stevens, Doris, 543, 577; Address to Sixth Pan American Conference, 606–15; "Suffrage Does Not Give Equality," 577–84
Stevens, Elizabeth Callender, 327
Stewart, Maria W., xviii, xx, xxii, 27; Lecture at Franklin Hall, 14–18
Stillman, James W., 139
Stillman, Mrs. Thomas E., 227
Stimson, Henry L., 386–90
Stone, Lucy, xvii, xxii, 61, 63, 119–21, 131–32, 139, 143, 146–47, 254, 451, 489, 491; Address to Seventh National Woman's Rights Convention, 87–90; Marriage Protest, 84–86
Stowe, Harriet Beecher, 254, 443
Strikes, 185–86, 190–91, 510

Student Nonviolent Coordinating Committee, 646
Studwell, Edwin A., 121, 124
Suffrage House, 520
Suffragette, use of term, xxiii, 300, 353, 468
Suffragist, The, 419, 531, 548–52
Sullivan, Rose, 509–13, 515–19
Sulzer, William, 388
Sumner, Jessie, 635
Sunny, Jeff, 647
Supreme Court, Arkansas, 244–45
Supreme Court, California, 199
Supreme Court, Kansas, 244
Supreme Court, New York, 69
Supreme Court, Ohio, 639
Supreme Court, U.S., 161–62, 302, 442, 558, 652–53; *Adkins v. Children's Hospital of the District of Columbia*, 569; *Brown v. Board of Education*, 650; *Dred Scott v. Sandford*, 115, 181; *Fairchild v. Hughes*, 569–72; *Leser v. Garnett*, 569, 572–74; *Minor v. Happersett*, 163–76, 182, 616; *Reynolds v. Sims*, 651
Supreme Court, Washington Territory, 243
Supreme Court, Wyoming, 243–44
"Susan B. Anthony" amendment. *See* Nineteenth Amendment
Swift, Mary Wood, 278
Swisshelm, Jane, 62
Swofford, Jewell W., 640
Sydenham, Baron (George Clarke), 484
Sykes, Louise R., 551
Sylvester, Richard H., 384–88, 390
Syracuse, N.Y., 59–60, 196

Taft, William Howard, 384–85
Talbert, Mary B.: "Women and Colored Women," 443–44
Tammany Hall, 267–68
Taney, Roger B., 115
Tape, Joseph, 199
Tape, Mamie, 199–200
Tape, Mary: Letter to San Francisco Board of Education, 199–200
Tape v. Hurley, 199
Tarbell, Ida, 367, 632; "Is Woman Suffrage a Failure?", 594–605

Taxation, xxv, 35, 38, 47, 64–66, 70, 75, 77, 82, 149, 159–60, 179–80, 198, 247–48, 264, 289, 302, 440, 518–19, 644
Taylor, Sophronia, 40
Teachers, women as, 193, 452–53
Teapot Dome scandal, 596–97
Teller, Henry M., 203
Temperance movement, xxii, 32, 102, 106, 123, 179, 195, 229, 233, 242–45, 417, 434, 446, 471, 489, 497–500
Tennessee, xxvi, 124, 174, 553, 555, 558–60, 573–74
Terrell, Mary Church, xxi, 433; "The Progress of Colored Women," 275–81; "Woman Suffrage and the 15th Amendment," 456–57
Terrell, Robert H.: "Our Debt to Suffragists," 438–39
Tewksbury, Betsey, 39
Texas, 124, 175, 499, 516, 553, 556, 635
Textile industry, 509–10, 515, 586, 588–89
Third National Woman's Rights Convention, 59–63, 196
Third National Woman Suffrage Association Convention, 157
Thirteenth Amendment, 91, 123, 236, 609
Thompson, Belle, 205
Thompson, Dorothy, 641
Thompson, George D., 186
Thompson, William Hale, 428–32
Thomson, Adelaide, 183
Thoreau, Henry David, 30
Tilden, Samuel J., 296
Tillman, Samuel D., 40
Tilton, Elizabeth R., 124, 157
Times (London), 484
Titanic, R.M.S., 372–75
Toombs, Frederick R., 328
Tracy, Frederick U., 64
Trade unions. See Unions
Train, George Francis, 125–26
Transcendentalists, 30
Treasury Department, U.S., 638
Treaties, 606, 610–15
Trial by jury, 70–72, 139, 179, 208, 255
Troy, N.Y., 190–91
Troy Female Seminary, 67
Truax, Sarah, 421

Truth, Sojourner, xx–xxii; Address to First Meeting of American Equal Rights Association, 116–18; Speech to Ohio Woman's Rights Convention, 43–44
Tuberculosis, 588–89
Tubman, Harriet, 115
Tucker, Robert, 647
Tucker, Thomas George: Life in Ancient Athens, 439
Turner, Lillian D.: "Votes for Housewives," 457
Turner, Mrs. H. L., 550
Tuskegee Institute, 262
Tuttle, Margaret, 420
Tyng, Katherine, 310

Underhill, Edward F., 40
Underhill, Martha, 39
Underwood, John C., 124
Unions, 185–86, 190–91, 271, 279, 361, 499, 585
Union Safety Committee, 49
Unitarians, 56, 376
United States Sanitary Commission, 253
Universal suffrage, xxiv, xxviii, 49, 112, 125, 150, 181, 206, 231, 238–39, 437, 443, 487, 580
University of Chicago, 277
Upton, Harriet Taylor, 248, 559
Utah, 248, 253, 290, 300, 476, 556
Utah Territory, 181, 201–3, 221, 264, 302

Vail, Mary E., 40
Van Buren, Martin, 189
Van Tassel, Isaac, 40
Vermont, 88, 124, 174, 247, 557, 573
Vernon, Mabel, 527
Vest, George: Remarks on Amendment to Extend Suffrage to Women, 206–9
Victoria, Queen, 289
Vienna, Austria, 177
Villard, Oswald Garrison, 330
Vincent, Eleanor, 34–35
Virginia, 95, 124, 171, 264, 401
Vocational education, 142, 262
Volstead Act, 597
Voter education, 565–68

Votes for Women, xxviii
Votes for Women Club, 416
Voting Rights Act (1965), xix, 575,
    650–53
Voting Rights Act (1975), 575

Waddill, Edmund, 540
Wade, Benjamin F., 124, 438
Wagner Act (National Labor Relations
    Act), 624
Waite, Morrison, 163
Walker, Judge, 88
Wallace, William J., 197
Ward, Mary Augusta, 300–301, 304
War Department, U.S., 386–89
Warfare, 47, 150–51, 253–54, 413, 487
Waring, Mary Fitzbutler: "Training
    and the Ballot," 446–47
Warren, Mabel B., 549
Warren, Mercy, 264
Warren, Pascia P., 551
Washington, 247–48, 256, 299, 302,
    476–77, 513, 556–57
Washington (D.C.) Board of
    Education, 444
Washington, D.C., 14, 114, 117, 124,
    138, 149, 157, 180, 216, 241, 391,
    433, 480, 575, 617, 626; arrested
    protestors on Occoquan Workhouse,
    533–42; disenfranchisement in,
    442–43; lobbying in, xxvi, 307, 365,
    481, 520–42, 531, 543; protests in,
    525–27, 532–33, 550; and ratification
    of Nineteenth Amendment, 555,
    559–60; suffrage conventions in,
    197, 210, 395, 454; suffrage pageants
    in, 421; suffrage parades in, xxiii,
    382–90, 419, 425; women in politics
    and government service, 632–41
Washington, George, 5, 10, 128, 381
Washingtonian Movement, 32
Washington Post, 397
Washington Territory, 207, 243, 255–56
Waters, Cecilia Streett, 572
Watts, Isaac, 139
Weld, Angelina Grimké, 19, 67, 91,
    100–101; Address to Massachusetts
    Legislature, 27–29; *Appeal to the
    Christian Women of the South*, 27
Weld, Theodore, 27
Wells, Emmeline, 201

Wells, Ida B., xxi; *Crusade for Justice*,
    425; "Seeking the Negro Vote,"
    425–32
Wendt, Mathilde F., 120, 183
West, women's suffrage in, xviii–xix,
    xxiii, xxvi, 105, 207, 221, 243–44,
    247, 249, 255–58, 264, 299, 391–92,
    399–400, 475–80, 556
West Indies, 186
Westminster Review, 61
West Virginia, 483, 557, 573–74, 590
Wheatley, John, 277
Wheatley, Phyllis, 277
Wheeler, Marjorie Spruill, 261
Whipple, Charles K., 126
Whitcomb, Camilla, 550
White, Armenia, 124
White, Bouck, 526
White, Ruth, 524
Whitehouse, Florence Brooks, 551
Whitney, Sarah, 39
Whittaker, W. H., 537–38, 540
Widows, 50, 75–78, 81–82, 85, 136–37,
    168, 247, 477, 510, 581
Wilberforce, Ohio, 454
Wiley, Harvey W., 537
Wilhelm II, 381
Willard, Emma, 67
Willard, Frances E.: "The Ballot for the
    Home," 242–45
Willebrandt, Mabel Walker, 636
Williams, Charl Ormond, 560
Williams, Fannie Barrier, xxi; "Women
    in Politics," 228–31
Williams, John Sharp, 397–98
Williams, Justin, 40
Williams, Lydia A., 34–35
Wilson, Henry, 142–43
Wilson, Woodrow, xxiii, xxvi, 382–83,
    391, 396–97, 421, 425, 475, 480, 518,
    525–26, 528, 534, 548–52, 558, 560;
    Address to Senate on Nineteenth
    Amendment, 543–47
Winchester, Margaret E., 125
Wines, Guy, 124
Winona, Miss., 647
Wisconsin, 97–99, 105, 124;
    constitution, 88; legislature,
    555; property rights for women,
    88; ratification of Nineteenth

Amendment, 555–56; school suffrage in, 247; suffrage referendum in, 501–2

Wisconsin Soldiers' Aid Society, 106

Wollstonecraft, Mary, 54

Woman's Christian Temperance Union, 242, 245, 417, 471

Woman's Era, The, 232

Woman's Exponent, 201

Woman's Journal, 353, 489

Woman's Loyal National League, 91–111

Woman's Party, 475–76, 479

Woman's Suffrage League of New York City, 327, 329

Women's Bureau, 642

Women's clubs, xxiv, 230, 232–35, 282, 285–88, 332, 417, 425–27, 433, 445, 450, 454–55, 457

Women's Equality Day, 555

Women's Political Union, 326, 329–30

Women's rights movement, xviii, xxi, xxiv, 14, 19, 36, 45, 59, 84, 91, 99, 102–9, 112, 120, 128, 135, 142, 149, 196, 235, 273, 304, 394, 409–15, 438

Women's Social and Political Union, 353

Women's Trade Union League, 361

Wood, William, 328

Woodhull, Victoria Claflin, 163; Address to House Judiciary Committee, 157–62

Woods, Katherine, 388

Woods, Sarah R., 39

Woodward, Charlotte, 39

Woodward, Ellen S., 639

Woodworth, S. E., 40

Worcester, Mass., 45, 59, 64, 112

Worcester Spy, 84

Workers, 185–95

Working women, xxvi, 89, 117, 130, 134, 136–37, 193–94, 322–23, 411–14, 450; African American, 145, 278–80; eight-hour workday for, 513, 586; international conventions, 612–13; labor conditions, 508–19; in Massachusetts, 508–19; minimum wage for 569, 586; need for congressional action, 361–64; in New York City, 363, 378, 380, 589–90; organized into trade unions, 185–86, 190–91, 279, 361, 585; and President's Commission on the Status of Women, 642–45; professional, 64–65, 180, 326, 619; protective legislation versus equal rights, xix, 577–93; Puerto Rican, 619; strikes by, 185–86, 190–91; vocational training for, 142; wages of, 305–6; wives as, 37–38, 82, 490; during World War I, 483–86

Works Progress Administration, 627, 639

World's Columbian Exposition, 228

World's Congress of Representative Women, 228

World's Temperance Convention, 489

World War I, xxvi, 477, 482–88, 500, 528–30, 545–46, 548, 590, 592, 604, 630

World War II, 625, 629–30, 635

Wright, Edward H., 427, 431

Wright, Elizabeth, 124

Wright, Frances, 54

Wright, Martha Coffin, 36, 39, 124

Wyandottes, 575

Wyoming, 240, 243–44, 253, 290, 300, 476, 556–57, 635, 638

Wyoming Territory, 207, 221, 247, 264, 302

Yale University, 89

Yankton Sioux, 575

Young, Brigham, 88

Young, Ella Flagg, 444

Younger, Maud, 542

Young Women's Christian Association, 451–52

Zangwill, Israel, 357–58

Zion's Herald, 140

Zitkála-Šá (Gertrude Simmons Bonnin), 575

This book is set in 10 point ITC Galliard Pro, a face designed for digital composition by Matthew Carter and based on the sixteenth-century face Granjon. The paper is acid-free lightweight opaque that will not turn yellow or brittle with age. The binding is sewn, which allows the book to open easily and lie flat. The binding board is covered in Brillianta, a woven rayon cloth made by Van Heek–Scholco Textielfabrieken, Holland. Composition by Gopa & Ted2, Inc. Printing by Sheridan Grand Rapids, Grand Rapids MI. Binding by Dekker Bookbinding, Wyoming MI. Designed by Bruce Campbell.

THE LIBRARY OF AMERICA SERIES

Library of America fosters appreciation of America's literary heritage by publishing, and keeping permanently in print, authoritative editions of America's best and most significant writing. An independent nonprofit organization, it was founded in 1979 with seed funding from the National Endowment for the Humanities and the Ford Foundation.

1. Herman Melville: Typee, Omoo, Mardi
2. Nathaniel Hawthorne: Tales & Sketches
3. Walt Whitman: Poetry & Prose
4. Harriet Beecher Stowe: Three Novels
5. Mark Twain: Mississippi Writings
6. Jack London: Novels & Stories
7. Jack London: Novels & Social Writings
8. William Dean Howells: Novels 1875–1886
9. Herman Melville: Redburn, White-Jacket, Moby-Dick
10. Nathaniel Hawthorne: Collected Novels
11 & 12. Francis Parkman: France and England in North America
13. Henry James: Novels 1871–1880
14. Henry Adams: Novels, Mont Saint Michel, The Education
15. Ralph Waldo Emerson: Essays & Lectures
16. Washington Irving: History, Tales & Sketches
17. Thomas Jefferson: Writings
18. Stephen Crane: Prose & Poetry
19. Edgar Allan Poe: Poetry & Tales
20. Edgar Allan Poe: Essays & Reviews
21. Mark Twain: The Innocents Abroad, Roughing It
22 & 23. Henry James: Literary Criticism
24. Herman Melville: Pierre, Israel Potter, The Confidence-Man, Tales & Billy Budd
25. William Faulkner: Novels 1930–1935
26 & 27. James Fenimore Cooper: The Leatherstocking Tales
28. Henry David Thoreau: A Week, Walden, The Maine Woods, Cape Cod
29. Henry James: Novels 1881–1886
30. Edith Wharton: Novels
31 & 32. Henry Adams: History of the U.S. during the Administrations of Jefferson & Madison
33. Frank Norris: Novels & Essays
34. W.E.B. Du Bois: Writings
35. Willa Cather: Early Novels & Stories
36. Theodore Dreiser: Sister Carrie, Jennie Gerhardt, Twelve Men
37. Benjamin Franklin: Writings (2 vols.)
38. William James: Writings 1902–1910
39. Flannery O'Connor: Collected Works
40, 41, & 42. Eugene O'Neill: Complete Plays
43. Henry James: Novels 1886–1890
44. William Dean Howells: Novels 1886–1888
45 & 46. Abraham Lincoln: Speeches & Writings
47. Edith Wharton: Novellas & Other Writings
48. William Faulkner: Novels 1936–1940
49. Willa Cather: Later Novels
50. Ulysses S. Grant: Memoirs & Selected Letters
51. William Tecumseh Sherman: Memoirs
52. Washington Irving: Bracebridge Hall, Tales of a Traveller, The Alhambra
53. Francis Parkman: The Oregon Trail, The Conspiracy of Pontiac
54. James Fenimore Cooper: Sea Tales
55 & 56. Richard Wright: Works
57. Willa Cather: Stories, Poems, & Other Writings
58. William James: Writings 1878–1899
59. Sinclair Lewis: Main Street & Babbitt
60 & 61. Mark Twain: Collected Tales, Sketches, Speeches, & Essays
62 & 63. The Debate on the Constitution
64 & 65. Henry James: Collected Travel Writings
66 & 67. American Poetry: The Nineteenth Century
68. Frederick Douglass: Autobiographies
69. Sarah Orne Jewett: Novels & Stories
70. Ralph Waldo Emerson: Collected Poems & Translations
71. Mark Twain: Historical Romances
72. John Steinbeck: Novels & Stories 1932–1937
73. William Faulkner: Novels 1942–1954
74 & 75. Zora Neale Hurston: Novels, Stories, & Other Writings
76. Thomas Paine: Collected Writings
77 & 78. Reporting World War II: American Journalism
79 & 80. Raymond Chandler: Novels, Stories, & Other Writings

81. Robert Frost: Collected Poems, Prose, & Plays
82 & 83. Henry James: Complete Stories 1892–1910
84. William Bartram: Travels & Other Writings
85. John Dos Passos: U.S.A.
86. John Steinbeck: The Grapes of Wrath & Other Writings 1936–1941
87, 88, & 89. Vladimir Nabokov: Novels & Other Writings
90. James Thurber: Writings & Drawings
91. George Washington: Writings
92. John Muir: Nature Writings
93. Nathanael West: Novels & Other Writings
94 & 95. Crime Novels: American Noir of the 1930s, 40s, & 50s
96. Wallace Stevens: Collected Poetry & Prose
97. James Baldwin: Early Novels & Stories
98. James Baldwin: Collected Essays
99 & 100. Gertrude Stein: Writings
101 & 102. Eudora Welty: Novels, Stories, & Other Writings
103. Charles Brockden Brown: Three Gothic Novels
104 & 105. Reporting Vietnam: American Journalism
106 & 107. Henry James: Complete Stories 1874–1891
108. American Sermons
109. James Madison: Writings
110. Dashiell Hammett: Complete Novels
111. Henry James: Complete Stories 1864–1874
112. William Faulkner: Novels 1957–1962
113. John James Audubon: Writings & Drawings
114. Slave Narratives
115 & 116. American Poetry: The Twentieth Century
117. F. Scott Fitzgerald: Novels & Stories 1920–1922
118. Henry Wadsworth Longfellow: Poems & Other Writings
119 & 120. Tennessee Williams: Collected Plays
121 & 122. Edith Wharton: Collected Stories
123. The American Revolution: Writings from the War of Independence
124. Henry David Thoreau: Collected Essays & Poems
125. Dashiell Hammett: Crime Stories & Other Writings
126 & 127. Dawn Powell: Novels
128. Carson McCullers: Complete Novels
129. Alexander Hamilton: Writings
130. Mark Twain: The Gilded Age & Later Novels
131. Charles W. Chesnutt: Stories, Novels, & Essays
132. John Steinbeck: Novels 1942–1952
133. Sinclair Lewis: Arrowsmith, Elmer Gantry, Dodsworth
134 & 135. Paul Bowles: Novels, Stories, & Other Writings
136. Kate Chopin: Complete Novels & Stories
137 & 138. Reporting Civil Rights: American Journalism
139. Henry James: Novels 1896–1899
140. Theodore Dreiser: An American Tragedy
141. Saul Bellow: Novels 1944–1953
142. John Dos Passos: Novels 1920–1925
143. John Dos Passos: Travel Books & Other Writings
144. Ezra Pound: Poems & Translations
145. James Weldon Johnson: Writings
146. Washington Irving: Three Western Narratives
147. Alexis de Tocqueville: Democracy in America
148. James T. Farrell: Studs Lonigan Trilogy
149, 150, & 151. Isaac Bashevis Singer: Collected Stories
152. Kaufman & Co.: Broadway Comedies
153. Theodore Roosevelt: Rough Riders, An Autobiography
154. Theodore Roosevelt: Letters & Speeches
155. H. P. Lovecraft: Tales
156. Louisa May Alcott: Little Women, Little Men, Jo's Boys
157. Philip Roth: Novels & Stories 1959–1962
158. Philip Roth: Novels 1967–1972
159. James Agee: Let Us Now Praise Famous Men, A Death in the Family, Shorter Fiction
160. James Agee: Film Writing & Selected Journalism
161. Richard Henry Dana Jr.: Two Years Before the Mast & Other Voyages
162. Henry James: Novels 1901–1902
163. Arthur Miller: Plays 1944–1961
164. William Faulkner: Novels 1926–1929
165. Philip Roth: Novels 1973–1977
166 & 167. American Speeches: Political Oratory
168. Hart Crane: Complete Poems & Selected Letters

169. Saul Bellow: Novels 1956–1964
170. John Steinbeck: Travels with Charley & Later Novels
171. Capt. John Smith: Writings with Other Narratives
172. Thornton Wilder: Collected Plays & Writings on Theater
173. Philip K. Dick: Four Novels of the 1960s
174. Jack Kerouac: Road Novels 1957–1960
175. Philip Roth: Zuckerman Bound
176 & 177. Edmund Wilson: Literary Essays & Reviews
178. American Poetry: The 17th & 18th Centuries
179. William Maxwell: Early Novels & Stories
180. Elizabeth Bishop: Poems, Prose, & Letters
181. A. J. Liebling: World War II Writings
182. American Earth: Environmental Writing Since Thoreau
183. Philip K. Dick: Five Novels of the 1960s & 70s
184. William Maxwell: Later Novels & Stories
185. Philip Roth: Novels & Other Narratives 1986–1991
186. Katherine Anne Porter: Collected Stories & Other Writings
187. John Ashbery: Collected Poems 1956–1987
188 & 189. John Cheever: Complete Novels & Collected Stories
190. Lafcadio Hearn: American Writings
191. A. J. Liebling: The Sweet Science & Other Writings
192. The Lincoln Anthology
193. Philip K. Dick: VALIS & Later Novels
194. Thornton Wilder: The Bridge of San Luis Rey & Other Novels 1926–1948
195. Raymond Carver: Collected Stories
196 & 197. American Fantastic Tales
198. John Marshall: Writings
199. The Mark Twain Anthology
200. Mark Twain: A Tramp Abroad, Following the Equator, Other Travels
201 & 202. Ralph Waldo Emerson: Selected Journals
203. The American Stage: Writing on Theater
204. Shirley Jackson: Novels & Stories
205. Philip Roth: Novels 1993–1995
206 & 207. H. L. Mencken: Prejudices
208. John Kenneth Galbraith: The Affluent Society & Other Writings 1952–1967
209. Saul Bellow: Novels 1970–1982
210 & 211. Lynd Ward: Six Novels in Woodcuts
212. The Civil War: The First Year
213 & 214. John Adams: Revolutionary Writings
215. Henry James: Novels 1903–1911
216. Kurt Vonnegut: Novels & Stories 1963–1973
217 & 218. Harlem Renaissance Novels
219. Ambrose Bierce: The Devil's Dictionary, Tales, & Memoirs
220. Philip Roth: The American Trilogy 1997–2000
221. The Civil War: The Second Year
222. Barbara W. Tuchman: The Guns of August, The Proud Tower
223. Arthur Miller: Plays 1964–1982
224. Thornton Wilder: The Eighth Day, Theophilus North, Autobiographical Writings
225. David Goodis: Five Noir Novels of the 1940s & 50s
226. Kurt Vonnegut: Novels & Stories 1950–1962
227 & 228. American Science Fiction: Nine Novels of the 1950s
229 & 230. Laura Ingalls Wilder: The Little House Books
231. Jack Kerouac: Collected Poems
232. The War of 1812
233. American Antislavery Writings
234. The Civil War: The Third Year
235. Sherwood Anderson: Collected Stories
236. Philip Roth: Novels 2001–2007
237. Philip Roth: Nemeses
238. Aldo Leopold: A Sand County Almanac & Other Writings
239. May Swenson: Collected Poems
240 & 241. W. S. Merwin: Collected Poems
242 & 243. John Updike: Collected Stories
244. Ring Lardner: Stories & Other Writings
245. Jonathan Edwards: Writings from the Great Awakening
246. Susan Sontag: Essays of the 1960s & 70s
247. William Wells Brown: Clotel & Other Writings
248 & 249. Bernard Malamud: Novels & Stories of the 1940s, 50s, & 60s
250. The Civil War: The Final Year
251. Shakespeare in America

252. Kurt Vonnegut: Novels 1976–1985
253 & 254. American Musicals 1927–1969
255. Elmore Leonard: Four Novels of the 1970s
256. Louisa May Alcott: Work, Eight Cousins, Rose in Bloom, Stories & Other Writings
257. H. L. Mencken: The Days Trilogy
258. Virgil Thomson: Music Chronicles 1940–1954
259. Art in America 1945–1970
260. Saul Bellow: Novels 1984–2000
261. Arthur Miller: Plays 1987–2004
262. Jack Kerouac: Visions of Cody, Visions of Gerard, Big Sur
263. Reinhold Niebuhr: Major Works on Religion & Politics
264. Ross Macdonald: Four Novels of the 1950s
265 & 266. The American Revolution: Writings from the Pamphlet Debate
267. Elmore Leonard: Four Novels of the 1980s
268 & 269. Women Crime Writers: Suspense Novels of the 1940s & 50s
270. Frederick Law Olmsted: Writings on Landscape, Culture, & Society
271. Edith Wharton: Four Novels of the 1920s
272. James Baldwin: Later Novels
273. Kurt Vonnegut: Novels 1987–1997
274. Henry James: Autobiographies
275. Abigail Adams: Letters
276. John Adams: Writings from the New Nation 1784–1826
277. Virgil Thomson: The State of Music & Other Writings
278. War No More: American Antiwar & Peace Writing
279. Ross Macdonald: Three Novels of the Early 1960s
280. Elmore Leonard: Four Later Novels
281. Ursula K. Le Guin: The Complete Orsinia
282. John O'Hara: Stories
283. The Unknown Kerouac: Rare, Unpublished & Newly Translated Writings
284. Albert Murray: Collected Essays & Memoirs
285 & 286. Loren Eiseley: Collected Essays on Evolution, Nature, & the Cosmos
287. Carson McCullers: Stories, Plays & Other Writings
288. Jane Bowles: Collected Writings
289. World War I and America: Told by the Americans Who Lived It
290 & 291. Mary McCarthy: The Complete Fiction
292. Susan Sontag: Later Essays
293 & 294. John Quincy Adams: Diaries
295. Ross Macdonald: Four Later Novels
296 & 297. Ursula K. Le Guin: The Hainish Novels & Stories
298 & 299. Peter Taylor: The Complete Stories
300. Philip Roth: Why Write? Collected Nonfiction 1960–2014
301. John Ashbery: Collected Poems 1991–2000
302. Wendell Berry: Port William Novels & Stories: The Civil War to World War II
303. Reconstruction: Voices from America's First Great Struggle for Racial Equality
304. Albert Murray: Collected Novels & Poems
305 & 306. Norman Mailer: The Sixties
307. Rachel Carson: Silent Spring & Other Writings on the Environment
308. Elmore Leonard: Westerns
309 & 310. Madeleine L'Engle: The Kairos Novels
311. John Updike: Novels 1959–1965
312. James Fenimore Cooper: Two Novels of the American Revolution
313. John O'Hara: Four Novels of the 1930s
314. Ann Petry: The Street, The Narrows
315. Ursula K. Le Guin: Always Coming Home
316 & 317. Wendell Berry: Collected Essays
318. Cornelius Ryan: The Longest Day, A Bridge Too Far
319. Booth Tarkington: Novels & Stories
320. Herman Melville: Complete Poems
321 & 322. American Science Fiction: Eight Classic Novels of the 1960s
323. Frances Hodgson Burnett: The Secret Garden, A Little Princess, Little Lord Fauntleroy
324. Jean Stafford: Complete Novels
325. Joan Didion: The 1960s & 70s
326. John Updike: Novels 1968–1975
327. Constance Fenimore Woolson: Collected Stories
328. Robert Stone: Dog Soldiers, Flag for Sunrise, Outerbridge Reach
329. Jonathan Schell: The Fate of the Earth, The Abolition, The Unconquerable World
330. Richard Hofstadter: Anti-Intellectualism in American Life, The Paranoid Style in American Politics, Uncollected Essays 1956–1965

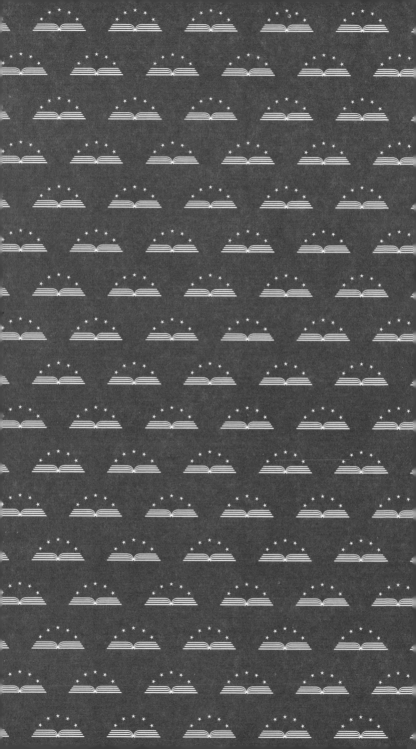